# THE SALT MERCHANTS
## OF TIANJIN

# THE
# SALT MERCHANTS
# OF TIANJIN

*State-Making and Civil Society
in Late Imperial China*

Kwan Man Bun

University of Hawai'i Press
Honolulu

01   02   03   04   05   06      6   5   4   3   2   1

**Library of Congress Cataloging-in-Publication Data**

Kwan, Man Bun.
The salt merchants of Tianjin : state-making and civil society in late Imperial China /
Kwan Man Bun.
p.   cm.
Includes bibliographical references and index.
ISBN 0–8248–2275–7 (cloth : alk. paper)
1. Salt industry and trade—Political aspects—China—Tianjin—History.   2.
Merchants—China—Tianjin—Political activity—History.   3. Government
monopolies—China—Tianjin—History.   4. Salt—Taxation—China—Tianjin—
History.   5. Taxes, Farming of—China—Tianjin—History.   6. China—History—
1861–1912.   I. Title: State-making and civil society in late Imperial
China.   II. Title.

HD9213.C43   T525   2001
381'.456644'095115409034—dc21                 00–060760

This book has been published with the help of the
Charles Phelps Taft Memorial Fund, University of Cincinnati.

Designed by Kenneth Miyamoto
Printed by The Maple-Vail Book Manufacturing Group

# Contents

# Acknowledgments

Whenever doubt surfaced—and such moments have been numerous so long has this book been in the making—the opportunity of expressing my gratitude kept me going.

Among the many who have shaped my work, Philip Huang and David Farquhar taught me, first, that a dialogue must be maintained between fact and theory and, second, the imperative of rewriting. Hal Kahn, G. W. Skinner, and Lyman P. Van Slyke provoked me to think about history and anthropology while tolerating my pedantry and pleas for incomplete grades. Mary Rankin commented extensively on an earlier version of the manuscript and suggested many ways to improve it. M. K. Chan, Wellington Chan, Parks Coble, Bob Gardella, Bill Kirby, Lillian Li, Susan Mann, Andrea McElderry, Jonathan Ocko, Ben Schwartz, Matti Zelin, and David Zweig offered cherished words of encouragement. Linda Grove generously fulfilled my appetite for Japanese-language material and scholarship. Roger Daniels, Wayne Durrill, Bruce Levine, Zane Miller, Barbara Ramusack, and Ann Twinam read and commented on all or parts of the manuscript, offering their vast learning and steadfast support as only dedicated teachers and colleagues could do.

I am forever indebted to my friends in Tianjin. Hu Rong and Zhou Xingwei introduced me to Nankai and helped make it my second home. Feng Chengbai, Liu Zehua, Teng Waizhao, Wei Hongyun, Xiong Xingmei, and Yan Tiezheng took me under their wings during my three years of teaching and research. Liu Haiyan, Yu Ke, and Zhang Limin cheerfully tolerated the intrusion of this southern barbarian and shared everything they know about the city and its people. By their example, they have taught me how to persevere.

The generous support of the Fairbank Center and the Charles Phelps Taft Memorial Fund has made the research, revision, and publication of this book possible. Judith Daniels and Don Yoder salvaged the manuscript from my ungrammatical prose. Patricia Crosby and Masako Ikeda of the University of Hawai'i Press handled the manuscript with great efficiency and understanding.

Last but not least, my family has unfailingly tolerated my irresponsibility as a son and brother. As the youngest, I could always count on its support without even asking. My wife, Elizabeth, and son, Timothy, have shared my frustration and excitement. At last I have something to show for my long disappearance into the basement. To my mother, I dedicate this book. After our father's premature passage, she single-handedly nurtured us. Any errors, of course, are mine.

# INTRODUCTION

On an early June afternoon of 1911, over a hundred leading citizens, representatives of various trades, managers of local charities, and village heads from the suburbs, all clad in their official-buttoned caps and gowns, marched on Tianjin's many yamen. With the city's economy in turmoil, they insisted on voicing their concerns. As a reluctant governor-general and other officials listened, the citizens pleaded for the immediate release of Wang Xianbin (1856–1939).[1] Wang—the city's "single indispensable person"—a head merchant of the Changlu Salt Division, chairman of the Chamber of Commerce, owner of industrial enterprises, benefactor of local charities and schools, and a calligrapher, had been declared bankrupt by the state and imprisoned for failing to repay his bank loans. Ten other salt merchants had also had their properties, including salt monopolies, real estate, and shares of industrial enterprises, expropriated.

The fall of Wang and his colleagues might seem unremarkable. As operators of the state salt monopolies, the merchants had long been a despised lot:

> They purchased official titles, became head merchants,
> Celebrated for their opulence.
> But riches and status never lasted three generations in our city.
> Be patient and see the ephemeral fate awaiting them.[2]

Squandering their wealth in conspicuous consumption, they abused the state's trust with their shady business practices. Never strong enough to convert their wealth to political power, their bankruptcy

1

and expropriation were common, if not routine, under the regulation of an efficient and flexible bureaucracy.[3] In short, the salt merchants appeared to deserve their "inconstant" fortune.

Yet the significance of what according to the *Dagongbao (L'Impartial)* was an unusual display of unity for the city's often feuding citizenry can only be appreciated in the context of Tianjin's *longue durée* of social, political, and economic change. Beginning as an isolated garrison post in the tenth century, Tianjin had evolved into an administrative center for the district, prefecture, province, and the Changlu Salt Division by late imperial times. But state power did not permeate every aspect of Tianjin, nor did the city exist only to serve the capital. This book explores the many ways that Tianjin's economy, households, customs, and culture negotiated with the state in late imperial China.

The book is also about the challenges of state-making. The voluminous theoretical literature on the subject has largely used Europe as a benchmark against which other societies are measured. Modern state building meant direct control of societal resources by a strong, centralized, and professional bureaucracy.[4] Beginning in the fifteenth century, European rulers appropriated to themselves the forces of coercion and violence. By the nineteenth century, European states had internalized coercive/extractive functions and reduced their dependence on tax farmers and other middlemen. Revenue farming became a symbol of nonrationality and an obstacle to the expansion of state power.[5] The role of cities and urbanites was similarly transformed in this process of "modern" political and social development. What had once been relatively autonomous cities began to lose their hard-won independence as states "claimed functions that had traditionally been the local and territorial prerogatives of the major cities."[6]

What the urban bourgeoisie lost, however, was regained through representative institutions. Commercial expansion in England—an allegedly peaceful pursuit that produced "a certain sense of exact justice . . . which forbid our always adhering rigidly to the rules of private interest"—contributed to the rise of an urban bourgeoisie characterized by "agreeable manners."[7] Philosophers from Thomas Hobbes to John Locke, followed by Bernard Mandeville and Adam Smith, advocated the unfettered pursuit of individual private self-interest so that free competition could promote economic efficiency, growth, and a harmonious public order.[8] As social equals, intellectuals, professionals, and merchants participated in friendly debate and conversation that fostered tolerance, detachment, and a respect for consensus while helping to shape public opinion. Rational discourse thus furnished the foundation of a civil society that would in turn challenge, redefine, and limit the power of the state.

It was a controversial ideal contested not merely by kings but also philosophers.[9] Unimpressed by this enthusiastic liberal-democratic vision, Hegel viewed civil society, or *bürgerliche Öffentlichkeit,* not as a natural condition for freedom but as an aspect of ethical life that he divided into family, society, and state. In the family, an individual's responsibilities toward other members transcend his or her personal needs. Once outside the family, however, this ethic disintegrates as people strive to satisfy their needs by producing and exchanging the product of their labor in the marketplace. Profoundly skeptical of this restless battlefield where private interest meets private interest, Hegel considered civil society an arena of dissoluteness, misery, and ethical corruption that must be regulated and dominated by the superior capacity of the state.[10]

Despite their many disagreements, Marx shared with Hegel a distrust of private interest and the bourgeois state: civil society is a fraud, an ex post facto justification of the seizure of power from weak monarchs by a rising bourgeoisie, a masking of institutionalized greed. Promising an illusory political equality while perpetuating economic inequality—such was the modern state, which was little more than "a committee for managing the common affairs of the whole bourgeoisie."[11]

Recent attempts to revitalize the concept of civil society preserve these theoretical tensions. Emphasizing the role of intellectuals and rational discourse rather than the economy, Jürgen Habermas traces the creation of a politically active and informed public with the potential of social integration in eighteenth-century England, France, and Germany—only to be usurped by the "staging agencies" of commercialized mass media. American liberals and conservatives alike, by contrast, in addition to activists in Eastern Europe, Latin America, and lately China, are attracted to a concept of civil society that promises opposition to an all-powerful state and reconciliation of the public and private "good."[12]

As appealing as these promises may be, in practice the concept raises as many questions as it answers. The critical role played by the state and the bureaucracy remains ambiguous: simultaneously the nemesis and protector of civil society. In the Lockean version, civil society expresses the market-oriented interaction of private economic subjects struggling to free themselves from estate hierarchy and state paternalism. Paradoxically, the bourgeoisie also requires the state to legislate, enforce, and defend a system of private law, property, contract, employment, inheritance, and, last but not least, a hands-off economic policy. Other formulations have sidestepped this contradiction by emphasizing the nonantagonistic relationship between civil society and the state.[13]

If civil society thus loses some of its appeal as a concept capable of mobilizing society against an autocratic state today, its historical praxis too needs reassessing. The modern European division between society and state did not arise ex nihilo.[14] In England, where the liberal-democratic tradition of civil society supposedly first evolved, Mervyn James has found that Durham, despite the establishment of a new industrial elite and the integration of the city's economy into the national market, was unable to influence national policy or resist the increasing breach of its autonomy by policies and tensions having their roots in London and beyond. As the British Empire expanded, the merchant princes and bankers of London intermarried and supported each other, forming networks that influenced Parliament, national policy, the country, and the colonies. This was a far cry from the free-entry-and-exit civil society envisioned by their Scottish countrymen.[15] Similarly, the element of "rationality" in public opinion, even when conducted in public, might be exaggerated.[16] For all its democratic pretensions, this hierarchical civil society, whether constituted as members-only club, drawing-room bourgeoisie, or salon-bound intellectuals, did not operate on the basis of free and equal association any more than the birth-based society it partially replaced. Rather, exclusivity, education, property, connections, and patronage constituted the historical and economic reality.[17]

If theory diverged from practice even in the prototypical civil society of England, attempts to impose this ideal type on China not surprisingly fell short. Scholars have found that "never did the Chinese merchants attain autonomy."[18] Prone to compromise and Janus-faced politically, Chinese urban leaders reinforce Max Weber's influential view of Chinese cities as administrative centers lacking autonomy from the state.[19] The allegiance of itinerant merchants to their native place and the tight control that the state exercised over cities as administrative centers meant that merchants were never able to develop an urban identity or use the cities as a haven in which to pursue their economic and political interests.[20] Fettered property rights compromised by an immature (if not irrational) legal system and dependence on the state through networks of patronage rules out the possibility of a true civil society.[21]

Recent scholarship has revisited many of these issues. If Weber and other scholars pointed to urban failures, William Rowe found in China developments that might be analogous to the emergence of a bourgeois public sphere in early modern Europe. His seminal work on Hankou and his other essays depict a bustling commercial metropolis with an extensive hinterland even before the arrival of foreign traders. Its sophisticated merchants, active in a wide variety of nonstate-related civic causes, laid the foundation for the development of a civil society as a counterbalance, if not a challenge, to the Qing state.[22]

Likewise Mary Rankin observes that state dominance of Zhejiang province was neither complete nor inevitable. By distinguishing various categories of activity—*guan* (official or state), *gong* (public, shared, or just), and *si* (private or selfish)—she traces the growing involvement since the late Ming dynasty of nonofficial scholar-gentry elites (although merchants might participate) in public affairs at the local and rural level. By the end of the nineteenth century, a civil society influencing official policy had finally emerged in China.[23]

Rowe and Rankin's conclusions have provoked much interest and debate. That a civil society or public spheres once existed in China might have removed some of the stigma of backwardness (if not stagnation) implicit in this comparative exercise, but the utility of an ideal type as yet unrealized anywhere in the world remains open to question.[24] Just as Habermas has warned against applying his formulation to "any number of historical situations that represent formally similar constellations," imposing concepts such as civil society or public sphere on Chinese history risks charges of orientalism.[25]

Applying the myriad definitions for civil society to China, moreover, produced contradictory results. Following Marx's law of inverse relationship between the development of commercial and industrial capital, a "true" bourgeoisie can only be based on industrial development; a "bourgeoisie"—and their resulting civil society—founded on commercial capital is thus an anomaly.[26] Yu Yingshi divorces civil society from its bourgeois economic foundation, however, emphasizing instead the critical role of intellectuals. Inspired by Confucianism and the moral imperative of serving the public good, they led a loyal opposition whether as officials or as critics.[27] Other historians detect little state presence in local administration—given the state's logistical and organizational problems. Local control was thus frequently exercised through "informal governance" by the gentry—variously defined as ex-officials, degree holders, or scholar-literati and the lineage organizations they controlled—resulting in a variety of regional patterns.[28] Tracing the rise of public charities since the Song dynasty, other historians argue that the nineteenth-century transition from informal governance by local elites to their formal participation in local government merely institutionalized a fait accompli, reflecting minute changes within an otherwise stagnant tradition.[29] In short, the existence of a Chinese "civil society," whether defined as "urban" *(shimin shehui)* or "citizenry" *(gongmin shehui),* is fraught with theoretical and empirical problems.[30]

These theoretical variations on the civil society theme cannot be reconciled easily, for they involve different historical and state-building traditions, great geographical distances, and the complex interplay of urbanization and economic, social, and political changes. Without imposing an idealized European model on China, this book continues the dialogue between theory and history in full recognition of the possibility of "multiple modernities."[31] Employing such terms as "public sphere" or "civil society" as points of reference rather than a universal model, late imperial China is seen as a field of action where state and society negotiate, cooperate, and contest in various interlocked public spheres.[32] An analysis of Tianjin's urbanization process, salt business, household strategy, customs (both civil and business), development of an urban identity and culture, social services, and late Qing political and economic reforms yields equivocal, contradictory, and shifting results. Instead of casting state and society as mutually exclusive entities, this version of a Chinese "civil society" accommodates the expansive role of local mercantile elites in nonstate urban public services—reinforcing the state's authority while destabilizing it as they learned to cooperate and operate local networks of wealth and influence. Patronage and working with the state, in this view, could be a useful compromise compatible with emerging or mature civil societies.[33] This local approach also facilitates a critical reconstruction of the state/society relationship that explores its local meanings, not in order to serve certain teleological hierarchies (and perpetuate ethnocentric judgments), but to compare the alternatives and possibilities in late imperial urban China. A study of Tianjin reveals the internal dynamics and changes in their own terms: novel institutions built on "old" Janus-faced elite/ state relationships.[34]

Tianjin began as a humble frontier military settlement in the tenth century and remained an isolated coastal fort for much of its history. After the establishment of Beijing as the national capital by the Mongols in 1272, the city's location at the confluence of the Grand Canal and the Haihe made it useful for the capital but proved a mixed blessing for Tianjin. While the city benefited from the commercial traffic on the canal, the strategic need to supply and protect Beijing came with a price. Maintenance of the Grand Canal took precedence over attempts at reclamation and development of the city's agricultural potential and economic base while exposing the city to the perennial threat of flooding.

What sustained Tianjin was trade—especially the salt of Changlu. The salt merchants, who also served as tax farmers, were a small yet important group of citizens who have received little attention from historians.[35] Although revenue farming integrated this wealthy segment of the population into public finance, it has often been castigated as a temporary expedience, if not an "oriental" detour, from the true path to modern statehood.[36] Yet for much of Chinese history, the salt tax was an integral part of public finance with a history that reversed the European sequence: from direct state control during the Han dynasty to indirect revenue farming. For various reasons, including revenue stability and cost effectiveness, the Ming and the Qing dynasties both granted private merchants the exclusive privilege of transporting and selling salt in exchange for guaranteed fulfillment of the salt tax, or gabelle.

If revenue farming is a reasonable (if not quite "rational") response to the problem of raising revenue without a bloated bureaucracy consuming much of what it collects, the relegation of what had once been an official function to quasi-official *(guan)* if not totally private *(si)* enterprise was disturbing to many critics.[37] The blurring of these categories led to abuses—as Pu Songling has captured so succinctly in his story lamenting the plight of salt smugglers: "What the state defines as illegal is that which does not follow its rule, while officials and merchants label as smuggling that which they did not smuggle themselves."[38] Heuristic categories of "state," "public," and "private" were subject to constant negotiation and compromise.

Revenue farming had other costs as well. While some of their Yangzhou counterparts even styled themselves as official-merchants *(guanshang)*, salt merchants in Tianjin referred to themselves simply as merchants, or occasionally as merchants with a responsibility *(zhishang)*. Aside from their individual and collective responsibility for the salt taxes, the salt merchants paid interest *(bili)* on deposits made by the Imperial Household Department and other state agencies, a practice condemned by some historians as usury.[39] With every phase of the salt trade subject to strict official supervision and, at times, unrealistic policies, the power of silver was often used to circumvent state regulations. For all the moral indignation and censure it bred, corruption—"organized slander" by the state and the officials and literati who benefited from it—was also an "emollient, a solvent, or a lubricant," a reaction to complex structural conflicts and the need for political compromise.[40] Indeed, while the salt merchants' assumed loyalty to the state might be based on the millions of taels of silver in capital involved, their interests, economic or otherwise, did not always coincide with those of the state.

The salt merchants' family, business, and family business too were all part of the negotiation between the state, the public, and the private. To understand this merchants' milieu, we need to examine the process of its formation, its economic foundation, and the lives of its members. Individuals were by no means free from the constraints of the market or the state even in the privacy of their "castles." Bound by emotional ties of intimacy, they remained subject to the laws of patriarchy (or matriarchy) and property necessary to sustain the household as the essential institution for social and economic reproduction. The household head *(jiazhang)* was recognized and his or her authority was reinforced by the state and stood as the interface between the state, public, and domestic spheres. The household head controlled the deployment of the household's capital, human as well as financial, for its common good, although this authority might be delegated to household managers *(dangjia)*.

This is not to argue that the criticisms of the family system—lack of equality and freedom, gerontocracy, patriarchy—raised by the May Fourth generation are groundless. But the voluminous archives on domestic disputes over rights, specifically individual and corporate property rights, suggest that household members customarily sought redress in the courts when they thought their rights had been violated.[41] Cases involving combinations of kin as litigants—grandmother against grandson, father against son, brother against brother, branch against branch—illuminate the complex interaction between state order, local customs, and legal culture.[42] Unlike women from scholar-literati elite households who might be confined to the inner (*nei*, as opposed to the outer, *wai*) domain in a gender-based division of labor, women in these salt merchant households had important roles to play in the household's business.[43] As the household experienced the family cycle, local magistrates and salt commissioners struggled to maintain harmony among their litigious charges, routinely relying on the expert mediation and arbitration of the head merchants. In cases where formal legal principles were at odds with local custom, resolution was often negotiated between the merchants and the state.[44]

If the family history of these merchant princes is often messy, the same is true for that of the state. Far from constituting a monolithic entity, the court in Beijing, ministers of the central government, and local officials might have separate, though often converging, interests as each tried to appropriate to itself greater authority and dominate. The interstitial niches provided the arena in which a variety of local elites—from the respected scholar-gentry to the ill-reputed salt merchants and even more unconventional "elites" such as Tianjin's famed ruffians, the *hunhunr*—could participate, compete, and cooperate in public affairs.[45] It was their activities that gave Tianjin a distinctive urban culture and identity, pulling the city through times good and bad.

The salt merchants' carefully nurtured system of networks and cultural entrepreneurship contributed to that distinctive urban culture and identity. While not defenseless against the state and the bureaucracy, the merchants nevertheless needed access to the world of officials—and, through it, the imperial court—to help preserve their privileges and wealth. A reconstruction of the family history of two leading eighteenth-century Changlu merchant households reveals a networking culture that gave them access to high places and influenced state decisions. The salt merchants' expensive garden parties, poetry clubs, and opera performances, in addition to their art, antiques, book collections, and other scholarly affectations, easily condemned as pretentious and wasteful, could also be sound investments.[46]

As the salt merchants settled in Tianjin, buried their dead, and intermarried, they wove closely linked local networks allowing them to take root and become leading citizens. Whether as an expression of their Confucian public-mindedness or as a public relations exercise, or simply at the instigation of local officials, salt merchants became active in a broad range of social services beginning in the seventeenth century. In a city with few "natives," their wealth more than made up for the disadvantage, if any, of being recent arrivals. Receiving sobriquets befitting their status and fortune, they became the pride of the city and made up a majority of its "Big Eight" families *(badajia)*.[47] Drawing upon locality, occupation, fellowship, and common cause, as well as kinship networks, they wove a web of social activities ranging from road construction, disaster relief, and charities to firefighting.[48]

Tianjin's urban milieu also paved the way for the salt merchants' participation and expansion into other local activities. As the Qing state and local government strained to meet the challenges of the Taiping Movement and successive foreign invasions, the city's merchant community became increasingly active in initiating, funding, and institutionalizing such services as orphanages and soup kitchens, often without official instigation and recognition. With their expansion into hitherto inaccessible territories such as local militia and education, providing not only financial support but also active management and curriculum design, the merchants eclipsed the literati-official gentry as leading citizens of the city. Thus was born the term "merchant-gentry" *(shenshang)*.[49]

While unsettling to some scholar-gentry, this shift of social status and boundaries was reinforced by a rising tide of nationalism and reforms of late Qing. Tianjin's merchant community, led by activist salt merchants, invested in new industries and modern joint-stock enterprises in an effort to strengthen the country through industrial development. As a strategy to incorporate and mobilize these newcomers, the provincial and subsequently the central government institutionalized local self-government councils and organizations to support the implementation of legal, economic, and political reforms. The salt merchants and other commercial interests were well represented in these new local bodies—unlike the provincial and national assemblies where scholar-officials and gentry with advanced civil service examination degrees still dominated.[50] While dismissed by some historians as "reformist and tame," conservative, and essentially part of the Qing bureaucracy, these new local institutions, including the Chamber of Commerce, quickly outgrew their officially designated role. They provided legitimate venues for merchants to articulate their concern over such issues as currency reform, taxation, and gov-

ernment expenditure.[51] Transcending both guild and local limits,
the chamber represented citywide commercial interests and coordinated the obstruction of, if not opposition to, state policies at the
national level. A few salt merchants even played a leading role in the
constitutional and the revolutionary movements. In the process, the
relationship between the Qing state and Tianjin's merchant community became seriously strained.

The expropriation of Wang Xianbin and his colleagues brought
this strain to a breaking point. Their indebtedness was not unprecedented in size. Nor did the foreign banks demand immediate repayment of all their loans, much less the assumption of direct operation
of the monopolies. But as the merchants scrambled and haggled,
what had been a business dispute between foreign banks and private
Chinese citizens assumed crisis proportions for Tianjin and the state.
Pursuing a state-building strategy of centralized control, the court in
Beijing imposed a settlement contrary to the spirit, if not the letter,
of the reforms and laws it had promulgated for the avowed purpose
of protecting merchants. Abrogating centuries of "useful compromises" that had once integrated state and local society seemed a
small price to pay for China to become "modern" and withstand the
threat of foreign imperialism.

# 1.
# THE CITY

Tianjin is a young city by Chinese standards. When Neolithic cities first appeared on the North China plain, the land on which Tianjin now stands was just being formed. By the Northern Song dynasty (960–1126), sedimentary action of the Yellow River, the Yongdinghe, and other rivers had created a marshy lowland ideal for defense against invading horsemen. The Haihe, then known as the Jiehe, or Boundary River, formed part of the border with the Khitans, and outposts dotted its west bank. One of these, Zhiguzhai (see Maps 1 and 2), has been identified as Tianjin's earliest settlement, although Neolithic artifacts in the area make that claim somewhat moot.[1] How did Tianjin grow from the seven surname groups who called Haijin-zhen (the administrative name for Zhigu) their home in 1316 to become North China's main entrepôt and economic center with a population of over 100,000 by 1840? What roles did the state play in this process? Did the city exist only to serve Beijing?[2]

The military function of these tenth-century stockades *(zhai)*—and the presence of many yamen ranging from the lowly magistrate to the commissioner of the northern ports by late Qing—suggest the overwhelming role of the state in the making of Tianjin, allowing little, if any, autonomy for its residents. As a city of recent settlers and sojourning merchants who owe their loyalties to their native places elsewhere, an indigenous community spirit would presumably have been lacking.

But by mid-Qing, if not earlier, the city's population, a majority of whom engaged in commerce, was larger than its functions as a military outpost, a transshipment terminal on the Grand Canal system,

and an administrative center would explain. Indeed, the state's shifting priorities and the need to supply Beijing through the Grand
Canal enjoyed a higher priority than the growth of Tianjin. Combined
with technological and environmental constraints, the state's equivocal position toward reclamation frustrated attempts to exploit the
region's agricultural potential. To the extent that the state and Beijing's presence stimulated the city's urbanization, its effect was limited and limiting. It was commerce that gave the city's enterprising
population great mobility and an economic hinterland far beyond its
administrative boundary. In overcoming all these adversities, human

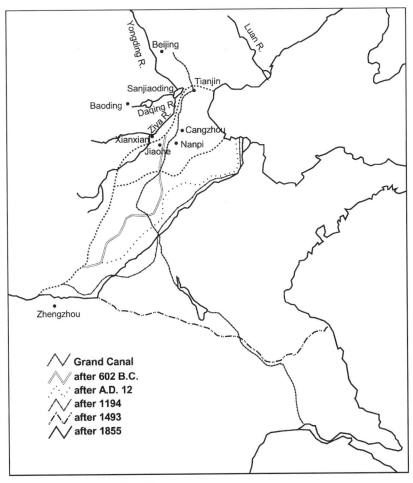

Map 1. Shifts of the Yellow River

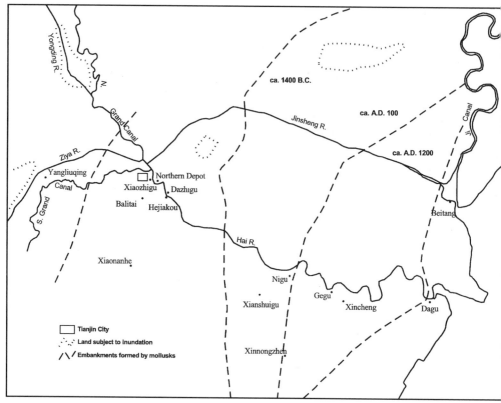

Map 2. Tianjin and Vicinity

or natural, the fast talkers of Tianjin *(weizuizi)* took their place of pride among the urbanites of Zhili province, joining the oily-mouths of Beijing *(jingyouzi)* and the government runners of Baoding *(goutuizi)*.[3]

## From Military Settlement to Administrative Center

In 1400, the Ming Prince of Yan, Zhu Di, forded the rivers here on his way to dethrone his nephew. To commemorate this auspicious event, the new emperor created the Guard Station at the Ford of Heaven (Tianjinwei) in 1404 and the Left Guard Station in 1405.[4] Another contingent, the Tianjin Guard, was added in 1406 because "Zhigu was important for the busy oceangoing traffic and the abundance of fertile land for military colonization," giving the city a military population of 16,800.[5] More men were stationed here when pirates, both Chinese and Japanese, threatened the coast.

Just as pirates came and went, so too did strategic needs. With the empire at peace, the Yongle Emperor (r. 1403–1424) decreed in 1415 that soldiers stationed at Tianjin should serve part of their tour in public construction projects in Beijing. To earn their keep, the remaining men were scattered to agricultural colonies in Cangzhou and Nanpi, leaving a garrison of only 763 men.[6] Peace bred complacency. The modest stamped-earth city walls built in 1404 were allowed to fall into disrepair. Passing by one night, Li Dongyang (1447–1516) was startled to see soldiers strolling the merlons and crenelles "as if they were flat." By 1622, Bi Zhiyan (1569–1638), recently appointed commissioner of Tianjin, complained of a city with breached walls and a silted moat.[7]

Even more limiting to Tianjin's growth, its jurisdiction as a guard station was confined to the walled area. The commissioner of Tianjin should oversee military affairs, the appointment read, not tax collection or administration of justice. Barracks could not be built across the river from the city because that land fell under the control of the provincial governor. Li Banghua (1574–1644), Bi's successor, likened himself to a "new daughter-in-law" struggling against an unsympathetic mother-in-law. To his superiors in Beijing, apparently, Tianjin did not exist. Order was difficult to maintain, especially with the rowdy soldiers recruited from Henan. In short, Tianjin's military function contributed little to further the city's urbanization.[8]

If Beijing's strategic considerations proved to be shifting, the necessity to support the empire and feed the emperor, his household, relatives, bureaucracy, and guards was perennial. The Jurchen, Mongol, Chinese, and Manchu rulers who made Beijing their capital solved the problem by shipping grain from provinces in the south and taxing salt. For better or for worse, Tianjin's growth as a city was inextricably entwined with these two pillars of public finance.

The transport of tribute grain, whether by the coastal route or the Grand Canal, was a costly system: a picul (1 picul = 133.33 pounds) of tribute grain was transported at the cost of several piculs, and Zhang Han (1512–1595), who once served as a commissioner of tribute grain transport, described the system as a "drain as deep as the heavenly chasm."[9] Yet with so many mouths to feed in the capital, there was little alternative.

The journey, moreover, was perilous. Even after the completion of the Grand Canal, the Mongols continued to use the faster, though dangerous, coastal route:

> Those seafarers who ventured east,
> How many returned?
> The people of Jiangsu who sailed north last year,
> Braving the northern wind and
> Waves pounding like rocks.
> Once the grain was delivered,
> They celebrated their successful return,
> Giving feasts for the neighborhood.
> He who sought promotion this year
> Offered prayers to the Heavenly Consort—
> But to no avail. He was blown overboard,
> Into the water of Dark Ocean.
> Now we know the seas are tombs.
> Mark my words,
> By land forget not the trail of Laizhou,
> By sea remember Shamen Island.[10]

Dazhigu, the area lining both sides of the Haihe south of Sanchakou where the Haihe and the northern Grand Canal met, became a key transshipment terminal (see Map 4 on p. 27). From a modest 46,050 piculs shipped in 1283, shipments of tribute grain grew to more than 3 million piculs annually. The Commander of Ten Thousand stationed at Linqing (Linqing Wanhufu) was transferred to Dazhigu in 1290 to perform escort duties, and a shipping bureau was created. Between 1435 and 1656, an official from the Board of Revenue oversaw the unloading and storage of shipments.[11]

Officials also made Tianjin their home to administer the salt tax. Salt production in the vicinity of Tianjin had a long history, predating even the founding of the city. As early as the Spring and Autumn period (770–476 B.C.), *Guanzi* mentioned Bohai Gulf as an area of salt production.[12] The inundation of Western Han, however, disrupted the development of the industry until the Song dynasty, although for security reasons both public and private trade of salt and other commodities across the borders with the Khitans and then the Jurchens were forbidden.[13] Under the Mongols, salt production in the vicinity of Tianjin flourished; salt superintendents began to supervise production fields at Sanchagu and Dazhigu in 1236.[14]

The tribute-grain system and the administration of the gabelle thus differentiated Zhigu from other settlements in North China. With the declaration of Beijing again as the national capital in 1403, the region's development took a new turn. In 1411 repairs to a critical stretch of the Grand Canal between Jining and Linqing were completed, and Song Li recommended diverting at least part of the tribute-grain transport to the canal. With four times the capacity, twenty canal boats could be built for the cost of one oceangoing junk.[15] Despite his staunch support of Zheng He's seafaring expeditions, the Yongle Emperor stopped sea shipments altogether in 1415, and the route itself was soon forgotten. Junks from the south sailed only as far north as Jiaozhou, while junks from Tianjin traveled as far as Yongping to the north and Haicang in Shandong to the south. Traffic round the horn of the Shandong peninsula, however, was only sporadic.[16] Dazhigu was hard hit as tribute grain and goods no longer came up the Haihe.

With this policy change, the locus of Tianjin's development shifted north from Dazhigu to Xiaozhigu—a wedge of land between the city and the confluence of the northern and southern Grand Canal. Over ten thousand tribute-grain boats may well have brought Tianjin a transient population of at least 120,000 each year.[17] The city could boast of some 208 granaries, supplemented later with another 1,400 storage silos north of Tianjin.[18] Xiaozhigu soon became Tianjin's downtown district with a concentration of businesses, temples, and wealth.

During the Ming dynasty, Tianjin continued to play a key role in the administration of public finance. With commerce flourishing, the state began to tap into this revenue source with tax stations and offices. Tianjin's commercial tax helped finance the Wanli Emperor's (r. 1573–1620) reconstruction of the imperial palace.[19] Ma Tong, his trusted eunuch, supervised the collection of the city's brokerage fees. Reflecting the rising importance of the city in the administration of the salt tax, the branch office of the Changlu commissioner stationed at Qingzhou, Shandong (Qingzhou Fensi), the Zhigu Salt Monitor Station (Zhigu Piyansuo), and the vice-commander for salt transport (yanyun dusi) were all reassigned to Tianjin in 1612.[20]

Into the Qing dynasty, the administrative centrality of Tianjin continued to wax. In 1665, the customs station (chaoguan) at Hexiwu, responsible for the collection of transit duties on all shipping under the Board of Revenue, was transferred to Tianjin, followed three years later by the Changlu supervisor.[21] In 1677, they were joined by the Changlu commissioner from Cangzhou together with most of his supporting bureaucracy: registrar (jinglisi), administrative clerk *(zhishi)*, and treasurer *(kudashi)*.[22] Recognizing Tianjin's importance, the Yongzheng Emperor completed the city's evolution from a military outpost to an administrative center in 1725 by promoting it to a department *(zhou)*, an autonomous department *(zhilizhou)*, and a prefectural seat with seven districts under its jurisdiction six years later.[23]

## Shifting State Policies and Their Impact

The concentration of these state offices, complete with their bureaucracies, undoubtedly contributed to the growth of the city's population, although it is difficult to gauge their impact without census data. The commercial growth of the city, however, was frustrated by the Qing state's policies toward trade along the coast and the Grand Canal.

While Tianjin was spared much of the bloodshed of Ming-Qing transition, the fallout from the Manchu campaign against remnants of Ming resistance did affect the city when the court imposed a series of prohibitions on coastal traffic to contain Zheng Chenggong's forays from Taiwan. Residents on the coast were relocated 30 *li* inland. At a time when a fishing net was considered evidence of treason, the harsh treatment of two Tianjin seafarers *(chuanhu)* is not surprising. Sailing before the ban with the proper permits for Shandong, they were caught in a storm and beached near Yangzhou. By the time their junks were repaired it was too late in the season for the trip home. When they finally returned to Tianjin the next year, their long absence and the incriminating cargo of goods and merchants from Huizhou, Zhejiang, Shanxi, Henan, and Shaanxi aroused suspicion and they were prosecuted as spies.[24]

After the conquest of Taiwan in 1684, coastal trade developed quickly, although restrictions on the size of seafaring junks remained.[25] Tianjin's own junks, the so-called boats of the guard station *(weichuan)*, smaller and less sturdy, could be found venturing beyond Shandong to call at Shanghai.[26] Junk ownership *(yangchuan* or *haihu)* became highly profitable as the Gao and the Han families took their place as two of Tianjin's "Big Eight" households.[27] By the early nineteenth century, at least nine thousand junks plied the coast.[28] In the north three ports—Tianjin, Niuzhuang in the northeast, and Dengzhou in Shandong—formed a triangular trade. Shanghai, the major interchange between north and south, had at least three thousand craft and its own guild, insurance, and broker services.[29] Junks as far away as Fujian, Taiwan, Guangdong, and even Siam, using a direct route away from the coast, were also active in the coastal trade, arriving in Tianjin in June and leaving in October.[30]

The lifting of the coastal trade ban, however, was partial: Tianjin's trade with the Northeast remained vulnerable to the state's shifting policies. To preserve the wealth of the Manchu homeland, grain from Fengtian was prohibited from entering China proper. Shortages in Hebei, Shandong, and Henan eventually forced a temporary suspension of the ban, but it was reimposed whenever Fengtian reported poor harvests.[31] Traffic inside the Bohai Gulf between Tianjin, Shandong, and Fengtian was thus frequently disrupted, putting "thousands" of sailors out of work.[32]

What was good for Beijing and the empire therefore might be detrimental to Tianjin. North China's hydrology, combined with the state's water conservation policies, also constrained the city's commercial and agricultural development.[33] Traffic on the Grand Canal was restricted, and the water that could be used for irrigation and land reclamation was diverted to ensure timely delivery of tribute grain.

Part of Tianjin's hydrological problem flowed from the Yongdinghe, or Ever Stable River. Wishfully renamed by the Kangxi Emperor from its previous name, Wudinghe (Unstable River), it was anything but stable, breaking or shifting its channel 794 times between 1736 and 1911. During the Yuan dynasty, attempts were made to harness this silt-laden miniature Yellow River.[34] After several failed attempts, dikes were built to prevent it from flooding Beijing. This turned the low-lying areas as far south as Tianjin into a holding reservoir before the Haihe discharged the water. The silt had to be dredged periodically, and the frequent failure to do so meant persistent waterlogging and uprooting of nearby residents.[35] (See Map 2 for some of the flooded areas.)

The Grand Canal presented another set of problems. Water could not be diverted for irrigation when it started to thaw in February, since the flow must be conserved to ensure passage of Henan and Shandong's tribute-grain boats due at Tongzhou in the third month each year. When summer rain did arrive, the excess water discharged from the canal inundated the fields nearby. The officials' predicament and the peasants' woe were captured in a doleful regional litany: "Reports of flooding would be entertained for districts west of the canal, but permission to improve the drainage would not be granted."

A long list of statesmen—beginning with Yu Ji (1272–1348) and reiterated by Xu Jingming (d. 1590), Xu Guangqi (1562–1633), Zuo Guangdou (1575–1625), and Lin Zexu (1785–1850), among others —all thought they had an elegant solution to the people's woe.[36] By draining off the excess water for irrigation and reclaiming flooded land through paddy rice cultivation, dependence upon the costly tribute-grain system would be reduced and the region's agrarian economy improved.

Balancing the conflicting goals of tribute-grain transport, flood prevention, and land reclamation as well as political interests, however, proved almost impossible. Promising schemes would ignite political firestorms pitting northerners against southerners and factional struggles.[37] To safeguard Beijing's security and supplies, the Kangxi Emperor forbade the opening of dikes and riverbanks around the capital for irrigation. Twice the emperor rejected reclamation proposals, taking special care to explain that while he was fully aware of the potential benefits, such enterprises would not succeed without a comprehensive system of water control.[38]

Subsequent attempts at water control and reclamation suggest that the emperor might have been too optimistic. Quite apart from the technological limitations, conditions for paddy rice cultivation in Tianjin were marginal.[39] During the "Little Ice Age" from 1550 to 1850, the region had 150 to 180 frost-free days a year; paddy rice, depending on the strain, needed 160 to 190 days. Climatic conditions required for the cultivation of paddy rice were met for only two months in a year.[40] To overcome these limitations, timely irrigation and massive manpower were required, a lesson eventually learned by Li Hongzhang (1823–1901).[41] In 1890, when a censor again extolled the benefits of land reclamation in Zhili, Li the governor-general dismissed the proposal as archaic hearsay. His costly attempt, carried out by Zhou Shengchuan's 60,000-man Sheng Battalion, took over six years to complete.[42] Shen Baozhen (1820–1879) summarized six centuries of futility succinctly: "Agriculture and the Grand Canal were incompatible with each other."[43]

Beijing's decision in favor of the tribute-grain transport system meant that some three hundred rivers on the North China plain flowed into the Haihe, that stretch of river between Tianjin and the Bohai Gulf. Notwithstanding a legendary water-parting arrow buried beneath Sanchakou, the Haihe was not the ideal channel for so much water. The river, with banks of clay and sand, was a labyrinth of twists and turns. From Tianjin to Dagu where it reached the sea, a distance of some 25 miles by land, the river meandered over 65 miles. The city and the country surrounding it, a dry brown steppe stretching to the horizon, were often flooded, creating the seventy-two lakes *(gu)* so admired by local literati in their poems. Villages with the characters "terrace" *(tai)* or "swamp" *(wa)* or "encirclement" *(quan)* in their names dotted the suburbs. As local folklore would have it, Liu Bowen, Merlin of the Hongwu Emperor, had foretold Tianjin's fate: Water and fire, not war, would make the city suffer.[44]

Environmental conditions, technological limitations, and Beijing's dependence on the Grand Canal thus combined to defeat efforts to promote Tianjin's agriculture. The city could boast of famous agricultural products bearing its name—cabbage, leeks, onions, and turnips—but its agricultural development had to wait until the twentieth century.[45] Apart from vegetable gardening, a result rather than a cause of Tianjin's growth, the city's residents had little to do with the agriculture of its immediate environs except as a source of night-soil.[46] The enterprising residents of Tianjin would have to find other ways to survive and prosper.

## Trade with the Interior

Tianjin's location on the north–south traffic routes—whether by the Grand Canal or the coast—made it the equivalent of Shanghai for North China. Long before the town became famous for its fiery brew, its residents enjoyed fine wine from as far away as Dongyang in Zhejiang. Although evidence of the variety and quantity of imports from the south is lacking, a Yuan-dynasty poet described the bustling scene: "Pots and porcelain from Jiangsu and cloth from Zhejiang filled the streets."[47] Beginning in 1423, the Ming state permitted sailors serving on board the tribute-grain junks to carry 10 piculs of local produce or goods—later increased to 60 but reduced again in 1522 to 10—for their journey north. This privilege must have been abused, however, for a later decree made the tribute-grain boats off-limits to wine, glutinous rice, flowers, bamboo, lumber, utensils, and goods consigned by merchants and "influential" people. Effective or not, such a ban suggests the variety of articles being shipped. While Tianjin was not the only place where cargoes were unloaded and transshipped, and thus not the sole benefactor of the sailors' private trade, the city served as the northern terminus of the grain boats.

Despite the image of a commercial backwater, North China contained plenty of opportunities for inter- and intraregional commerce.[48] From the coastal area came supplies of salt and fishing products as well as imports from the south. Low-lying districts inside the triangular area of Beijing, Tianjin, and Baoding supplied the region with mats and baskets woven from fibrous plants and other freshwater products. On the North China plain, wheat, raw cotton, and sweet potatoes had become commodities by mid-Qing, supplemented by products of the peasant household economy such as cotton yarn and cloth. From the mountains bordering the North China plain came fruits, building materials, coal, lumber, and other "mountain goods" (shanhuo).[49] Beyond the mountain ranges was the Mongolian steppe with its bountiful supply of herbs, felts, wool, skins, and other products of animal husbandry.

A transport network of rivers and overland routes made possible the distribution of imports and collection of exports from the interior of North China. Tianjin's effective distance for overland transport by horse-drawn cart was approximately 300 li.[50] Over short distances, market boats (jichuan) ferried passengers and goods back and forth between Tianjin and its neighboring districts.[51] For intra- and interprovincial long-distance trade in the nineteenth century, thanks to foreign traders intent on gaining access into North China, the routes into the interior from Tianjin are well documented (see Map 3).[52]

The first leg of the journey followed closely the waterborne transport network developed and maintained for the Changlu salt trade. Each spring and fall, more than three thousand junks of various sizes plied the waterways.[53] To the north, the northern Grand Canal afforded passage from Tianjin to Beijing via Zhangjiawan, site of a salt depot, and smaller boats traveled as far as Shunyi. For northeastern Hebei, the Beihe and other rivers feeding into the Ji Canal, connecting Jixian and Beitang, permitted waterborne transport for Sanhe, Pinggu, Yutian, and Fengrun districts. Northeast of this area was the Luanhe, navigable as far as Chengde for smaller boats and utilized by coastal trade junks transporting grain from the Northeast to Luanxian since the reign of Emperor Daoguang (r. 1821–1850).[54] Further northeast, Liaohe and its tributaries had been accessible since 1683 to Tianjin's lumber merchants.[55] Traffic on other rivers such as the Yongding was limited and local.[56]

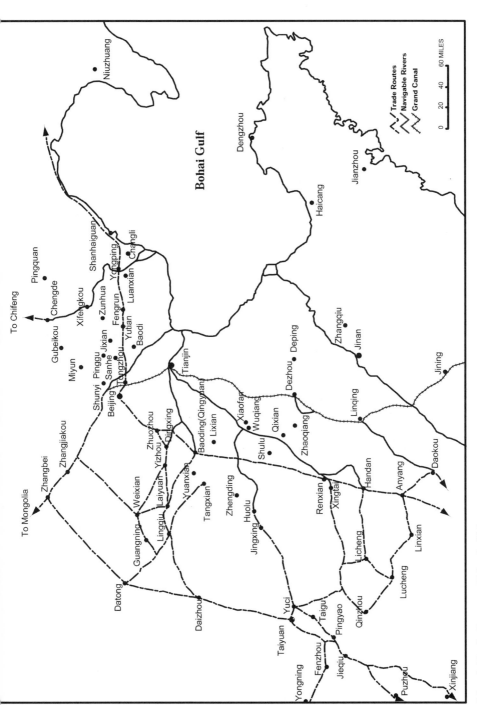

Map 3. Trade Routes of North China

Traffic to central Hebei and beyond, besides the Grand Canal, was served by the Daqinghe, navigable from Tianjin to Baoding since 1485. To serve this major salt distribution center, the route was maintained often at the salt merchants' expense.[57] Merchants, salt, and other goods could also travel south by boat on the Ziyahe to Wuqiang where the river was joined by the Hutou, Fuyang, and Jiang-shui rivers. Each was navigable as far as Zhengding (Shijiazhuang), Handan, and Qixian respectively.[58] Xiaofan (Wuqiang district), Lige-zhuang (Jixian), and Xingjiawan (Renxian) on the Ziyahe served as distribution centers. Boats headed toward Henan continued on the Grand Canal until they turned west on the Wei River (Weishui). Dao-kou, a market town in Junxian in Zhangde prefecture, was the major depot for salt, although during the high-water season boats could reach as far as Huaiqing prefecture on the northern bank of the Yellow River.[59]

This river-borne transport network emanating from Tianjin, with more than fifty thousand junk trips each year by the early twentieth century, also served North China's long-distance trade.[60] Various termini upstream connected the traffic with caravans that carried goods to and from the interior.[61] Goods destined for the Northwest, Mongolia, and Siberia traveled north to Tongzhou (near Zhang-jiawan) where camel caravans took over for the journey to Zhangjia-kou (Kalgan) and thence to Zhangbei where they could follow any one of the five routes into Inner Asia.[62]

Shanxi and Henan were similarly served by seven routes over the Taihang Mountains. From Zhangjiakou, a cart road ran southwest to Datong. A mule track between Daizhou (Weixian) and Zhuozhou also served northern Shanxi and Hebei. Qingyuan, connected to Tianjin by the Daqinghe, was the terminal of another cart route, via Yuanxian and Laiyuan (Guangchang in the Qing dynasty), to Shanxi by way of Lingqiu. To the south, the traffic was channeled through Fallen Horse Pass (Daoma Pass) in Tangxian. For southern Shanxi, a mule and camel track connected Xingtai and Qinzhou. From Handan in Hebei, too, a road led through the Taihang Mountains into south-eastern Shanxi via Licheng.

A trunk route served central Shanxi and Hebei.[63] Goods from Tianjin traveled southwest on the Ziya River and then on the Hutuo until they were unloaded at Xiaofan of Wuqiang district onto carts. Continuing on to Huolu, the goods were repacked onto mules or camels for the trip over the Taihang Mountains on a path cleared for caravan traffic during the reign of the Kangxi Emperor. The destinations could be Taigu, Pingyao, or Jieqiu, home of the Shanxi merchants, or Taiyuan, the provincial capital. From there caravans could head north into Mongolia via Datong or, via Fenzhou and Yongning, to northern Shaanxi and thence to Gansu. Another route out of Taiyuan ran southwest, via Puzhou, to Xi'an and then into Xinjiang province.

For the market northeast of Tianjin, besides the coastal sea route, goods were transported on small junks to Beitang on the Jinzhonghe and thence by land to Shanhaiguan and beyond via Luanxian and Changli. The northern Grand Canal could also be utilized as far as Tongzhou where a provincial road led northeast to Miyun through the Gubeikou Pass to Jehol (Chengde). From Tongzhou, too, a road ran east to Zunhua via Sanhe and Jixian. At Zunhua, merchants could head north to Pingquan and Chifeng via Xifengkou or south again to join the coastal road to Shanhaiguan. As a result of Baodi's development into a native cloth trade center, a road also led from it, via Yutian, to Xifengkou and thence to Eastern Mongolia.

By the mid-eighteenth century, if not earlier, trade of salt, cotton, grains, and other imports from South and Central China via Tianjin had blossomed. Merchants from Shanxi, Guangdong, Jiangsu, and Jiangxi, among others, maintained their guilds in the city. Enterprising Tianjin merchants, too, ranged far and wide to seek their fortunes —including those from Yangliuqing who pioneered the business of "chasing the main camp" (*gandaying*) with the northwestern interior and came to dominate the economy in Xinjiang.[64] On market days from January to April, wagon trains loaded with goods accompanied by dozens of pole-carriers departed for Xinjiang. It was a dangerous journey. With bandits, mountains, and deserts to conquer, the anguish of the poor and the landless males who plied it is captured succinctly in a local proverb: "A new brood each year, Yangliuqing is a cuckolds' nest."[65]

However costly in human and economic terms, it was this transport network that propelled Tianjin's growth into the major commercial center of North China. By the late nineteenth century, the city's commercial hinterland not only covered the North China plain north of the Yellow River but extended beyond the Taihang Mountains into the steppes of Mongolia and the deserts of Gansu and Ningxia and the southern part of the Liaodong peninsula. In terms of provincial boundaries, this functional region covered Hebei, Shanxi,

Mongolia, Gansu, Xinjiang, that part of Shandong north of the Yellow River, the northeastern half of Shaanxi, one-fifth of Henan, and one-tenth of Liaodong. Overcoming the mountains and the deserts, trade linked the household economies of urban merchants, rural peasants, and pastoral nomads together through a far-flung network of markets, towns, and cities, engulfing them in a process of commercialization and urbanization.[66] Serving a hinterland much larger than its administrative boundary, Tianjin did not exist for Beijing alone.

## A City of Newcomers

Trade thus became the lifeline of the city that, according to Charles Gutzlaff, reminded him of Liverpool:

> The scene, as we approached Teen-tsin [Tianjin], became very lively. Great numbers of boats and junks, almost blocking up the passage, and crowds of people on shore, bespoke a place of considerable trade ... [and] quite extensive. More than five hundred junks arrive annually from the southern ports of China, and from Cochin-China and Siam. . . . In no other part of China is trade so lucrative as in this.[67]

In 1845, systematic data on the occupational structure of the district's residents became available for the first time. There was a total of 32,761 households in the city and the surrounding built-up area; of these, 11,626 were registered as business households (*puhu*), 5,711 as peddlers, and 372 as salt merchants. Thus over 54 percent of the city's households depended on commerce, while only 7.1 percent, 2,338 households, were registered as in the service of the state (*yingyi*).[68]

Beyond sheer numbers, however, not much is known about Tianjin's citizens. Gao Ningwen, the local gazetteer, observed that Tianjin simply did not have natives.[69] A handful might trace their ancestry to Shanxi as a result of the resettlement policy in early Ming; others claimed descent from among the 309 hereditary garrison commanders and soldiers stationed at the city. Whatever the population growth during the Ming dynasty, however, the warfare of late Ming negated much of the gain.[70] By early Qing, local gazetteers recorded a dwindling native population easily outnumbered by settlers from all parts of the empire, especially Jiangsu and Anhui, who had been attracted to Tianjin by its salt trade and other commercial opportunities.

In this city of settlers, there was no particular disadvantage attached to being a newcomer: the distinction between "native" (longtime residents) and "sojourners" *(qiaoyu)*, who might have lived in Tianjin for generations, had become blurred.[71] Both displayed a feisty pride of their city—celebrating victories over rowdy sailors from Henan and Ningbo or giving Anhui soldiers lessons on proper behavior, as we shall see in Chapter 4.[72] While there was no legal requirement for sojourners to change their domicile, or *yizhi*, many Changlu salt merchants took that step to qualify their offspring for the civil service examination slots specifically created for them in Tianjin. As they settled in the city beginning in early Qing, intermarried, and buried their dead locally, they became very much part of local society. Their residential pattern is captured in the local adage: "East is rich, west is lowly, north for nobles, south occupied by the poor."[73] (See Map 4.)

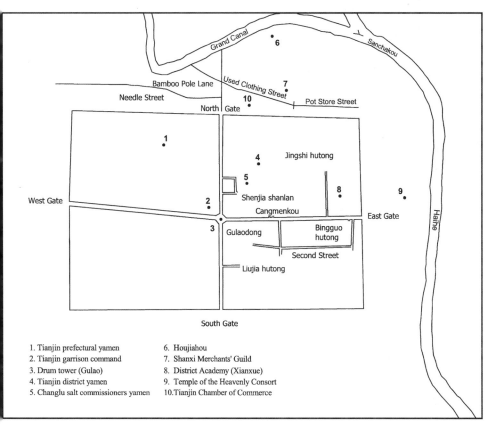

1. Tianjin prefectural yamen
2. Tianjin garrison command
3. Drum tower (Gulao)
4. Tianjin district yamen
5. Changlu salt commissioners yamen
6. Houjiahou
7. Shanxi Merchants' Guild
8. District Academy (Xianxue)
9. Temple of the Heavenly Consort
10. Tianjin Chamber of Commerce

Map 4. Street Map of Tianjin City

The urbanization of Tianjin thus took the city away from its origin as a military base. By virtue of its location on the Grand Canal, the river systems of the North China plain, and various overland routes, the city served an economic hinterland far beyond its administrative boundaries. The many functions it assumed—as a transshipment point of tribute grain for Beijing, for example, and a terminal for goods imported from South and Central China—gave it a far more diversified economy than a collection of barracks and government offices could have provided. Despite periodic flooding and limited agricultural resources, the city had become the economic center for North China by the nineteenth century, if not earlier. Led by the salt merchants of Changlu, the "fast talkers" of this humble guard station had come a long way.

# 2.

# THE GABELLE AND BUSINESS

The salt tax, or gabelle, had a long history in China as a stable source of revenue from a broad population base even at a low rate. To ensure its collection, a full spectrum of state institutions had evolved since 114 B.C. for salt production, transportation, and distribution. By the mid-seventeenth century, the Ming state derived almost half its annual income from salt. It financed production by hereditary saltern households and granted the exclusive privilege of transport and sale of the salt to merchants who had prepaid in kind or with silver.[1]

Pressed for revenue to finance their conquest, the Manchu conquerors had two simple objectives: an uninterrupted salt supply and revenue from it. Realizing these twin goals, however, proved nearly impossible. Demand for salt, a daily necessity, was certain; but utilizing it as a source of revenue was problematic. With much of the land still beyond Manchu control, designing and implementing a state-operated system was time-consuming and uncertain in returns.[2] By necessity, if not by choice, the Qing state farmed out the salt tax, making it as much a banking as well as a tax system. Tendering a substantial security deposit referred to as the nest price *(wojia)*—an advance to secure salt monopolies—the successful bidders were enrolled in the Changlu Syndicate register *(gangce)* as hereditary dealers with the right to harvest salt from their own pans (or purchase it from saltern households) and to transport and sell it in designated districts *(bao'e renban)*.[3] Henceforth these capitalists would advance the tax—secured on the proceeds they were then authorized to collect from consumers as part of the price of salt. For the first year of the new dynasty's reign, they subscribed 719,550 *yin,* meeting Changlu's quota exactly.[4]

Despite the young dynasty's success in attracting investment from its newly conquered subjects, this aspect of the Manchu's state building has received mixed reviews. From an institutional perspective, the Qing inherited an elaborate monitoring system.[5] Yet high-minded statesmen and scholars had long faulted the system for its deviation from the Confucian principles of proper governance, low taxes, and a direct relationship between rulers and ruled. Skeptical of private interests, they pointed to the merchants' corrupting influence and the many problems that beset the trade: an unreliable salt supply to outlying areas with long turnaround times and high transport costs; smuggling from producing areas where the salt tax far exceeded the cost and price of salt; and the jumble of tax rates among the divisions and within each division. (For the boundary of the Changlu Division see Map 5.)[6] Close supervision of this complex system was required, yet the requisite bureaucracy should not be allowed to consume too much of the revenue; thus the bureaucrats, too, must be checked.

Why did the Qing state, given its organizational ability, not replace dishonest merchants with a bureaucracy? Why did the merchants persevere in a business that made so many demands on them? Baffled contemporaries and historians offer a variety of explanations. To some historians, the state's strong presence meant it exploited the salt merchants through squeezes and donations; others see the state and the merchants colluding to cheat the public they served.[7] Max Weber, in his pioneering study on the sociology of taxation, depicted revenue farming as nonrational and predatory—an institution tolerated only by a state too weak to collect its revenue directly.[8] Yet this early Qing attempt at privatization could also be considered a laudable shrinking of an intrusive state. Wealthy citizens shared their fortunes with the state, facilitating a critical integration of society, economy, and political order.[9]

Each of these competing perspectives captures different phases and aspects of the Qing gabelle administration. Focusing on the state's shifting priorities and capabilities, this chapter analyzes how the Changlu Division, while generating a steady flow of revenue much of the time, engendered contradictions often difficult to resolve. The state and the bureaucracy, as both enforcers and beneficiaries of the system, created conflicts of interest. Flexible and creative, the Qing state met its inflexible revenue goals by coercing, compromising, and

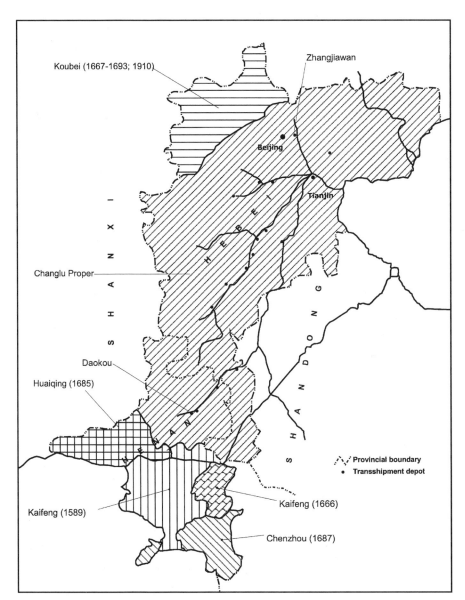

Map 5. Changlu Salt Division

negotiating with the salt merchants as the empire went through a predatory phase in early Qing to a nurturing phase (mid-Kangxi to the end of Qianlong) and back to a predatory phase (post-Qianlong to 1911). With all the elaborate procedures and codes, Qing salt tax farming was not a system adopted by a weak state incapable of extracting revenue from the economy. The merchants paid dearly for their privileges, though this business expense was offset to some extent by their successful lobbying for deferments and installment payments. In pursuit of profit, they circumvented state regulations by sharing their gains with rent-seeking emperors and officials. Thus the salt merchants' relationship with the state cannot be accurately characterized as collusion nor can it be called exploitation by a flexible and efficient bureaucracy.[10]

## Changlu Administration by Design

In learning the art of ruling, the Manchu conquerors initially preserved much of the Ming salt administration structure, including the eleven major salt divisions and boundaries. Encompassing as many as six provinces in the case of Lianghuai, each division was served by a producing area and a navigable river system providing cheap and efficient water transport while the mountain ranges forming the water divides provided a measure of boundary security.[11] The annual district quotas of salt consumption—and hence the amount of the salt tax—set in *yin* under the Ming were preserved.

Although no single official or office of the central government was responsible for the planning, regulation, and implementation of the salt tax and industry, the Board of Revenue, specifically the Shandong Bureau of Pure Functionaries (Shandong Qinglisi), administered the gabelle. Headed by three directors (rank 5A) and a supporting staff of six secretaries, it conducted annual audits (*zouxiao*) of the salt tax remitted to the capital and transfer payments due various agencies.[12] Primarily a transmission center of documents and repository for ledgers, the Board of Revenue rarely initiated policy. Instead a variety of agencies, including the Grand Secretariat, the Censorate, and provincial governors, identified problems and proposed solutions. This diffuse authority continued at the divisional level. The Censorate appointed salt supervisors (*yanzheng*) to oversee the divisions, although many of those in Changlu were deputed from the Imperial Household Department with routine endorsement by the Censorate. While appointments could be renewed, most supervisors served for only one year, leading to a lack of continuity and expertise. In fact, after 1860 the position was absorbed by the office of the Zhili governor-general.[13]

The day-to-day administration of the divisions fell to the salt commissioners (yanyunshi) supported by a small specialized staff as well as provincial and local officials. Each division had its own mix of institutional arrangements based on historical precedent and local conditions. In the more inaccessible areas of each division where transport costs, taxes, fees, and profits for merchants combined to make salt too expensive for residents, local magistrates often assumed responsibility for securing salt supplies by incorporating the salt tax into the land tax—as in Changlu's five districts of Xunhua prefecture. Districts contiguous to or encompassing major salt fields with an abundant and cheap supply, such as the seven districts of Yongping prefecture, alternated between using local salt peddlers and government supplies.[14]

Such institutional flexibility, however, did not apply to the divisional cores where the population's ability to evade the salt tax was limited. That control began with the Board of Revenue where, for a brief period in early Qing, Changlu salt merchants applied directly for yin certificates and paid the tax and fees.[15] After 1665, the certificates were delivered to Tianjin where the commissioner would issue them with a notification slip (zhidan) specifying the merchant, the salt yard he should use, the deadline for the transaction, and the number of bales, or yin, needed. The merchant or his agent then registered the slip with the respective inspectorates and applied for a shipping permit (chuanpiao) to move the salt to either one of the two salt depots located in Tianjin (Northern Depot) and Cangzhou (Southern Depot).

The Northern Depot on the eastern bank of the Haihe opposite Tianjin held a two-year supply for the division. After checking that the merchants had the specified amount of salt in storage, the inspector would clip the lower right corner of the certificates and return them to the commissioner's office for verification. The commissioner's seal was then affixed and the upper right corner clipped. With the mutilated certificates, the merchants could then proceed to the inspectorate for release of the salt from the depot within a set deadline.[16]

An elaborate procedure governed the release. First, the bales of "raw" salt, piled six or nine high in stacks over 200 feet long at the outer (older) mound of the depot, were checked for proper weight.[17] The commissioner himself would check the bales at random with weights issued by the Board of Revenue. Weighed, sealed, stamped, and removed to the inner or new mound, the salt was then declared "ripe" and ready for release. But before that could happen, the merchants had to apply for shipping notices and notify, with the appropriate fees, six different offices: the circuit intendant of Tianjin, the commander of the local garrison, the northern subsupervisorate, the inspectorate, the commissioner, and the Changlu supervisor whose presence was required for the occasion.

Supervision beyond the depot became the charge of local officials. While the salt merchants arranged the transportation, the journey was closely monitored to ensure prompt arrival and sale within the designated districts and not en route. Each bale of salt in transit had to be accompanied at all times by its *yin* certificate, a shipping passport *(yanchuan hupiao),* and a waterway schedule *(shuicheng)* for officials along the specified route.[18] Retail outlets were periodically inspected by the state for weight and price. Denominated in copper cash per *jin,* any price adjustment required special approval from the throne.[19]

To ensure that the salt merchants and the supervising bureaucracy performed their duties faithfully, a review system *(kaocheng)* was instituted in 1650. Punishment, graded in severity and calibrated to the size of the arrears, awaited district magistrates who failed to make the consumption quota: forfeiture of salary, suspension, demotion, reassignment, and dismissal. Merchants too were disciplined: twenty bamboo strokes and wearing the cangue for one month was mandated for missing one-tenth of the salt tax due; total failure meant a hundred strokes and banishment for three years.[20]

The Changlu Division, with its codes and regulations, was thus a "minimalist" bureaucratic machine. To keep the administrative cost in check, only a handful of specialists were used and local officials monitored the salt merchants and their business. Under this system, the state might not have maximized its revenue but the consumption quota and the revenue farming system shielded it from market fluctuations and the expenses needed to operate an extensive transport and distribution network. Merchants as private citizens assumed these risks and advanced the salt tax in exchange for the exclusive and hereditary privilege to deal in salt. At the same time, the people were protected by retail prices set by the state.

## The Changlu Division in Action

The young dynasty's pressing revenue needs, however, soon generated dysfunctional pressure for the Changlu Division.[21] Rulers rule, and this task includes using whatever means available to extract the necessary economic resources for their survival. Like their counterparts elsewhere, the Manchus soon learned that an old tax is a good tax; nor could it be considered onerous if it was paid, if only in part.[22] Resurrection of tributes and levies, followed by tax increases in early Qing, soon became a nightmare for merchants.

The authority to impose tributes is the sine qua non of state power. In 1644, Changlu, the closest salt-producing division to the capital, became the only division required to deliver 900,000 *jin* of salt annually as tribute for the emperor, his household, and the officials at the Board of Revenue and the Censorate. In 1654, imperial princes and a select group of high officials were granted one *jin* of salt for every tael of their salary. When the emperor and high officials found their entitlements far exceeded their dietary needs, the surplus was commuted to silver.[23]

The mounting need for revenue, however, proved far more exacting than tribute. In 1648, the Board of Revenue demanded that the merchants take up all the accumulated *yin* certificates—abrogating the regent Dorgon's promise of allowing merchants to subscribe for only the *yin* certificates needed for the season.[24] Beginning in 1655, levies that Dorgon had abolished in 1644 (and fees that bureaucrats had forgotten) were resurrected.[25] Meticulous research through the archives has further uncovered the Ming practice of printing an extra 15,000 *yin* certificates as reserve each year—to be sold when additional revenue was needed for such urgent tasks as the campaign against the Manchus. With revenue needs mounting, the reserve was incorporated into the regular *yin* quota, which meant an increase of 45,000 *yin* to the Changlu Division, one Ming *yin* having been split into three in 1644.[26]

The regime's pressing need for revenue did not stop there. In the following year, another 120,000 *yin* was added to the Changlu quota, accompanied by a general rate increase of 0.0478 tael per *yin*. When the merchants complained that they could not possibly sell so much salt, the quota increase was rescinded but not the additional tax—resulting in yet another increase of 0.071 tael per *yin*.[27] All these adjustments meant that by 1658 the rate per *yin* for the Changlu salt merchants stood at 0.3855 tael: a 45 percent increase since 1644.

Whether the rising salt tax was an onerous burden on the salt merchants is not clear. But even officials acknowledged that with Zhili's population scattered by Manchu noblemen's expropriation of land *(quandi)*, sales of salt had suffered.[28] Citing as precedent the practice adopted by the Lianghuai Division, in 1661 the Changlu supervisor won a reprieve: tax in arrears would be paid in monthly installments over four years, a practice referred to as *fennian daizheng*.[29] As for the backlog of more than 200,000 *yin*, merchants would pay 3 *yin* of tax on every two sold—in effect another rate increase—but the merchants were at least spared paying for salt they could not sell.[30]

The Qing state's ability to improve the salt business was limited, but the rebellion of the Three Feudatories (1673–1681) necessitated more, not less, revenue. In 1675, every *yin* in the empire was assessed an additional levy of 0.05 tael; Changlu's share came to 38,664 taels. The search for revenue uncovered another loophole in 1678: salt consumed during the extra month in leap years. The Board of Revenue calculated that the Changlu consumption quota should be increased by 64,441 *yin* and the merchants' due adjusted accordingly.

The same year also saw the only general adjustment during the Qing period of the consumption quota inherited from the high point of Ming population. While officials conceded that the population had yet to recover from the ravages of dynastic change, increases were inferred from the estimated number of excess fiscal adult male units *(yuding)* at ratios of one *yin* to 7, 10, or 13 *ding*. Changlu's quota increased to 924,695 *yin* carrying a tax of 452,545 taels.[31]

A rising salt tax was merely part of the merchants' woes: their plight was worsened by large-scale salt smuggling by Manchu nobles, soldiers, and strongmen in an unpacified North China.[32] Some merchants fled their substantial "nest price" to avoid certain expropriation. Others survived by selling their properties and daughters.[33] To provide what relief it could for the merchants, the state belatedly standardized its collection procedure for Changlu. Between 1664 and 1760, the Changlu merchants came to enjoy the same treatment afforded their Lianghuai and Zhejiang counterparts. They would receive their *yin* certificates upon payment of 30 percent of the quota; the balance was to be paid before the fifth month of the following year, a practice known as *xianyin houke*. In effect, the salt merchants came to enjoy a grace period for their tax payment.[34]

The Manchus thus began by adopting Ming institutions and procedures. But the young dynasty was creative enough to move quickly beyond them. Inflexible in revenue needs but flexible in its methods, the Qing state began extracting what it could from the economy. With the dynasty's survival at stake, the financial viability of the salt merchants—or, for that matter, the welfare of its subjects—mattered little. The salt merchants, their stereotypical image of great wealth and collusion with officials notwithstanding, fell victim to a predatory state.

## Nurturing Phase

Predatory, however, is not the same as exploitative. Raising revenue to ensure survival was a policy decision; exploitation implies malice.[35] After the suppression of the Three Feudatories in 1681, the Qing state inaugurated a nurturing relationship with the salt merchants. The Kangxi, Yongzheng, and Qianlong Emperors repealed the tax increases, reduced consumption quotas, adjusted prices in response to fluctuations in the exchange rate between copper cash and silver, redrew divisional boundaries, and reformed the accounting procedures. These and other policies such as accommodations *(tongrong)* —as well as frequent if not routine extensions of tax payment by annual installments from three to twelve years *(fennian daizheng)*— allowed salt merchants to make a profit. At the same time, various state agencies, including the Imperial Household Department, found a safe haven for their deposits and loans with the salt merchants. All these measures combined to usher in a period of prosperity for the Changlu Division.

The process began with a more realistic assessment of salt consumption and, consequently, the salt tax. The leap-year addition of 1678, the surcharge of 1675, and, despite the objection of the Board of Revenue, the consumption quota increase of 1678—all were repealed.[36] Other reforms allowed the merchants to respond with greater flexibility to an ever-changing market. As in other divisions, the Changlu gabelle was calculated and tendered in silver. Changlu was unique, however, in that the state set the retail price of salt in copper cash, making the merchants vulnerable to fluctuations in the exchange rate between copper cash and silver from the official rate of 1,000 copper cash to one tael of silver.[37] In 1688, when the rate reached 1,400 cash to one tael, the price was adjusted to sixteen copper cash per *jin*.[38] Subsequent attempts to raise prices to reflect the falling value of copper cash were opposed by local gentry and ruffians, as well as by emperors concerned with social stability and the welfare of the people.[39] In 1732, when the exchange rate climbed to 2,000 cash for one tael, the Yongzheng Emperor finally added one copper cash to the price of salt.[40] In 1764, the price of salt was again adjusted upward—followed by additional raises in 1770, 1771, 1782, and 1788.[41] All the additional copper cash collected went to the salt merchants to compensate for their exchange rate losses.

Redrawing divisional boundaries to deter smuggling enhanced the merchants' hold on their monopolies as well, and hence their profits. With the different rates between divisions and the varying rates and prices within divisions, maintenance of franchise and divisional boundaries was crucial to both profit and, by extension, the state's revenue. But while the divisional boundaries were shaped by physical barriers, antismuggling measures were based on administrative boundaries. To the extent that these territorial systems did not coincide, antismuggling efforts were hampered by difficulties in coordination across jurisdictional boundaries. The Qing state did what it could—as in the case of the five districts of Yifeng, Taikang, Tongxu, Lanyang, and Jixian. In 1666, these were finally rejoined with the rest of Kaifeng prefecture for Changlu, ending a tug-of-war since 1589 among the Hedong, Shandong, and Changlu Divisions. The transfer yielded a net increase of 1,640 taels in tax for the state.[42]

Yet the merchants and the people might get more than they bargained for. In 1687, the emperor transferred the five districts of Chenzhou, together with Wuyang district, to Changlu after merchants and residents argued that they might benefit from lower transport costs and better quality. The districts' consumption quota of 9,100 *yin* (3,312,400 *jin* of salt at 364 *jin* and 1.04 taels per *yin* in tax) was deducted from the Lianghuai Division, creating an accounting problem for the Board of Revenue. Lianghuai's salt tax rate was more than twice that of Changlu. To maintain revenue neutrality, the consumption quota of these six districts was increased to 20,419 *yin* (5,104,790 *jin* at 250 *jin* and 0.46 tael per *yin* in tax). The populace of the districts, observed the supervisor, would enjoy the extra 2 million *jin* of salt.[43]

While divisional boundaries were sometimes redrawn, the state did not make changes that might jeopardize its paramount interest: revenue stability. The fourteen districts of Shangcai prefecture, Henan, were assigned to the Lianghuai Division—which had the highest salt tax rate in the empire—although the districts could easily have been served by Changlu with cheaper and better salt. Officials repeatedly denied the petitions of local residents to switch on the grounds that doing so would threaten the core of Lianghuai's market.[44]

Without jeopardizing the state's revenue, the Changlu merchants succeeded in modifying the regulations that governed them. First applied in the Lianghuai Division in 1662, the controversial practice of *yin* quota accommodation *(tongrong)* permitted salt merchants to transfer among themselves *yin* quota from underperforming "tired" districts *(pi'an)* to prosperous ones *(chang'an)* that had already exceeded their quota. While critics complained that the practice indulged indolent merchants and made their supervision difficult, it offered overstocked merchants a respite—and, moreover, the state benefited from revenue that might otherwise have fallen in arrears. Beginning in 1690, operators of Changlu monopolies designated as "tired" were allowed to transfer up to 40 percent of their *yin* quota.[45]

The salt merchants further benefited from changes in the Board of Revenue's accounting procedures. In 1760, using the rationale that the salt merchants had just shipped their salt for the spring season and their cash flow was low, the annual audit was postponed from the fifth to the tenth month. Six years later, on the occasion of a visit to Tianjin, the emperor expressed his approval of the salt merchants' hospitality by extending the deadline another month. Somewhat belatedly, the tenth month was recognized as yet another inconvenient time for the salt merchants because the proceeds from the sales of the fall season could not be delivered to Tianjin in time for their tax payment.[46] During this nurturing phase, the three emperors granted a total of twenty-three deferments—as opposed to only once earlier and five times thereafter. Overruling the Board of Revenue's routine denial of deferments and extensions, the emperors noted that the Changlu salt merchants, hit by floods and rain and short of capital as always, merited special consideration.

The salt merchants' prosperity was fed also by deposits and loans from the emperor's private purse dispensed through the Imperial

Household Department. As manager of his vast portfolio of manors, pawnshops, salt monopolies, and cash—and bursar for his myriad expenses including the maintenance of temples and imperial tombs and bonuses and welfare payments for Manchu soldiers—the department had to invest carefully to make ends meet.[47] But in a preindustrial economy, there were few financial instruments and investment opportunities capable of absorbing hundreds of thousands of taels with minimal management. Land might be indestructible, the Imperial Household Department argued, but it was vulnerable to floods and drought, the rental return was low, and the management of tenants was laborious.[48] Loans to salt merchants—the first made to Changlu merchants in 1704—promised better returns, although they blurred the distinction between public finance, the emperor's private purse, and "private" enterprise. Loans from the three emperors totaled at least 3.2 million taels.[49] Of this amount, at least 1.5 million taels went to salt merchants serving concurrently as royal importers of Japanese copper.[50] In part to ensure the safety of the emperor's "investments," officials deputed from the Imperial Household Department began to serve as supervisors of the major salt divisions.[51]

In addition to direct loans, the Imperial Household Department also deposited state funds with Changlu merchants at interest rates from 10 to 20 percent per annum. With no repayment schedule specified, the deposits generated annual interest payments to meet the budgetary needs of various state agencies, including the imperial observatory.[52] Deposits of 133,000 taels and 17,000 taels came from Wancheng and Enfeng, both part of the emperor's pawnshop chain in Beijing. The annual interest of 18,360 taels, originally earmarked for expenses and salary augmentation for officials at the Imperial Household Department, then as supplemental salary (*yanglianyin* or literally "integrity-nourishing silver") for the minister in charge of the department *(neidachen)*, eventually was returned to the emperor's private coffers.[53]

For charging interest and making loans to the salt merchants, the emperors have been characterized by historians as usurers.[54] From a business perspective, however, these loans and the deposits made sense for both the state and the merchants who took them.[55] Usually carrying a nominal interest rate of 12 percent a year, they were a relatively cheap source of capital for the salt merchants; the annual interest rate for commercial loans then hovered above 20 percent.[56] Despite his reservations about the propriety of these loans, the Qianlong Emperor defended the practice. Where, he asked, could the merchants find a cheaper source of long-term credit?[57] Collected by the Board of Revenue, the interest went toward expenses the state would otherwise have had to fund from its current cash flow. To this extent, the loans from the emperors' private purse and deposits from the state might be considered part of the nurturing policy benefiting both the salt merchants and the state, although when total interest payments exceeded the principal, the emperors might also be violating the Qing Code on loans.[58]

For the time being, however, all the *yin* reductions, deferments, accommodations, loans, and deposits, together with a fast-growing population, helped usher in a period of prosperity for the Changlu salt merchants. In 1730, Changlu merchants who had exhausted their annual quotas applied for extra *yin* certificates *(yuyin)*; by 1843, the last documented case in the archives, the Changlu supervisor had applied for extra certificates fifty-five times, with amounts ranging from 30,000 to 150,000 *yin*.[59] Although not all the extra certificates were sold, the salt merchants' willingness to pay for them suggests that they were doing a brisk business.


## The Price of Prosperity

Prosperity, however, did not come cheap for either the merchants or the state. While merchants who took in loans and deposits may have benefited from increased liquidity—and the state received a steady flow of revenue—their economic history (and accounting) remains unwritten. Not only did the state lose interest on deferred salt tax and waivers, but the revenue farming system was increasingly compromised by a courtship among emperors, officials, and the salt merchants through an array of lobbying devices: donations, customary fees, and bribery.

The controversial practice of reciprocating donations *(baoxiao)* is a matter of public record.[60] For Changlu, they began in 1721 with Wang Tingyang's contribution of 200,000 taels toward the campaign in the Northwest, followed a year later by another 180,000 taels for famine relief in Shanxi. The Yongzheng Emperor was troubled by the appearance of impropriety, feeling perhaps that acceptance of the donation might diminish the state's dignity. In his rescript on the donation to renovate the Temple of the Sea God in 1725, however,

Yongzheng approved not merely the offer but also the merchant: "He [Wang] is a good merchant and an interesting man."[61] He re-affirmed his goodwill toward the Changlu salt merchants in 1732 by a price increase of one copper cash per *jin*. Later that year, the salt merchants donated 100,000 taels to help defray military expenses. The emperor accepted the donation but decreed that it should be applied toward the year's due. One year later, the weight for a bale of salt was increased ten *jin*, tax free, to compensate the merchants for tret *(luhao)*.[62] The cause and effect of these exchanges is difficult to establish, but the pattern of give and take is consistent. During the Qianlong Emperor's reign, the Changlu merchants received defer-ments, waivers, price increases, deposits, and loans. They reciprocated with donations to their well-liked emperor, including an elaborately carved bed, renovation of his palaces, travel lodges, and roads, as well as a drydock for his barges and operas for his grand tours.

Even with his disdain for accounting accuracy, the astute Qianlong Emperor could not have missed the paradox of over 2.5 million taels in contributions from merchants whose dire circumstances justified tax deferments and waivers.[63] Both the emperor and the merchants rationalized their actions in rhetorical proclamations. In granting deferments and waivers, the emperor justified their decision in such terms as strengthening the salt merchants *(yu shangli)* and accom-modating the demand of the masses *(zi minshi)*. The wisdom of the *Yijing* (Book of Changes)—advising that wealth should be distrib-uted below rather than concentrated in the hands of those above—had been taken to heart.[64]

For their part, the merchants pleaded for the emperor's conde-scending acceptance *(shangshou)* of their donations. "We who have the good fortune to be born in this glorious age with eternal peace assured by the august emperor's virtue hereby willingly contribute two hundred thousand taels of silver for the expense of settling the frontiers"—thus read a 1759 petition. For this modest contribution, the salt merchants declared that they expected no guerdon. The emperor responded with a lengthy honor list.[65]

Appearance of impropriety, however, haunted both the emperors and the merchants. In playing their part as virtuous rulers, the em-perors risked the appearance of being bought. In an age ever con-cerned with proper governance *(zhengti)*, the line between donations and bribery was thin indeed. At times the emperors broke the pattern of exchange, making both merchants and officials uncertain, a decision that echoed Han Fei's advice two millennia earlier: the way of the ruler requires that his desires not be revealed, or the door would be open to those below for pandering.[66]

## The State's Shifting Needs

By the turn of the nineteenth century, the emperors' nurturing policies had left a mixed legacy. All the salt tax deferments, loans, and deposits meant that annual dues became larger and larger. And while the emperors might be well intentioned, their loans and deposits could become onerous not merely because of the "discounts" from 5 to 20 percent charged by officials handling the loans. Taking for granted the merchants' ability to pay, the emperors and the Imperial Household Department were loath to suffer any loss on their "investments." Successors to bankrupt merchants were held liable for the principal and the interest accrued. When they, too, eventually failed under the mounting debt, these loans became the collective responsibility of the Changlu Syndicate to be repaid in annual installments through a special levy of 0.2 tael per *yin* beginning in 1782. A special levy of 0.442 tael per *yin* was instituted the following year on all salt merchants in order to repay accumulated gabelle and interest on loans and deposits in arrears.[67]

The salt merchants' dependence on the emperor's good grace also meant that, with a new emperor ascending the throne, they would have to start anew to cultivate him. In 1800, when the merchants applied for a price increase, the Jiaqing Emperor rejected the application, citing his father on the undesirability of concentrating wealth in the imperial coffers. His priorities seemed clear: the welfare of the people came before the liquidity of the merchants and salt tax shortfalls. But the last reason in his edict revealed his anger: the merchants were not contributing, or at least not adequately, to his military campaigns. No one, of course, dared to contradict the emperor's short memory: the Changlu salt merchants did volunteer a donation of 1 million taels two months after the Qianlong Emperor's death in 1799 for the campaign against the White Lotus, of which the Jiaqing Emperor graciously accepted only 396,000 taels.[68]

An empire torn by successive rebellions and foreign invasions in the late nineteenth century did not leave the salt business unaffected. To replenish a depleted treasury, the state unilaterally imposed a series of price increases beginning with 2 *wen* added to finance repairs of the Grand Canal when the Yellow River broke its dikes. Officials expected no effect on sales from the approximately 600,000 strings of copper cash raised for the state.[69] Three years later, the emperor finally recognized the salt merchants' difficulties. Instead of a price reduction to discourage smuggling, he approved another increase of 1 *wen* per *jin:* half the additional revenue was to compensate the merchants; the remainder was earmarked for payment of salt tax in arrears. In 1825, 1838, and 1842 prices were again increased to help pay for repairs of the Grand Canal and construction of coastal defenses at Dagu.[70]

These price increases for the benefit of the state treasury led to a period of declining sales. As the price of legal salt climbed, smuggling did also. The state attempted to help the legal trade by a combination of weight increases, deferments, suspensions, and, as a last resort, *yin* quota reductions. Between 1807 and 1846, more than 100 *jin* of salt was added to a *yin* of salt, tax free, on various pretexts.[71] Deferments were granted in 1801, 1803, 1804, and periodically thereafter; 10 percent of Changlu's consumption quota, or 96,650 *yin,* was suspended beginning in 1820. The tax due on the suspended *yin,* however, was added to the remaining *yin* taken out by the salt merchants.[72] As gabelle in arrears and unclaimed *yin* certificates accumulated, the annual consumption quota of the Changlu Division was finally reduced by 100,000 *yin* and the 63,383 taels of salt tax was waived in 1843.[73]

What the state gave away, however, it took back in the form of donations. Between 1799 and 1841, at least 2,422,520 taels was donated for various causes.[74] When the salt merchants failed to fulfill even their gabelle obligations, the donations were added to their total debt. By 1846, that debt had ballooned to 23,431,402 taels comprising principal and interest on loans and deposits, installment payments on donations, and current salt tax and deferments.[75]

The reemergence of the copper cash/silver exchange rate problem further hampered the salt merchants' struggle to survive this cycle of the state's predatory policy. A growing population, hoarding, and foreign trade deficits meant an appreciation of silver vis-à-vis copper cash. In 1812, the same year they received a belated price increase of

1 *wen* per *jin*, the salt merchants pleaded, without success, to have the exchange rate between copper cash and silver adjusted from 1,000 to 1,100 *wen* to 1 tael. Citing losses of over 700,000 taels a year because of the sagging price of copper cash, the salt merchants again applied for a price increase of 2 *wen* per *jin* in 1824. The proposal was rejected, however, on the grounds that the 1 *wen* increase of 1812 was still in effect.[76]

Both the salt merchants and officials wanted a more flexible pricing system. In 1827, Changlu Supervisor Ayanga appealed to the throne for a floating exchange rate (*yinzhuang*, literally "silver pile") based on the market price of silver. Despite an after-tax gross profit of 3 million taels, the salt merchants were losing more than 1 million taels a year. Salt production cost them 600,000 taels, transportation 1.9 million taels, marketing expenses 1.2 million taels, and 700,000 taels in fees to local officials. In return for the proposed change, they volunteered a discount of 3 *wen* per *jin* to cushion the shock.[77]

The Daoguang Emperor, however, had more than the solvency of the salt merchants in mind; a price increase might aggravate popular unrest. With any shortfall already the merchants' collective responsibility, he was skeptical that the salt merchants would be able to fulfill all their tax obligations with the price increase. Their record, he noted, had not been persuasive.[78]

Indeed, dynastic decline and foreign encroachment increased the need for more revenue and limited the state's options in reforming the system. Tried and true measures such as adding more than 200 *jin* of tax-free salt to each *yin*, combined with deferments and waivers, brought little relief. At the same time, the state took more than 700,000 taels in donations and an unprecedented 300,000-tael loan in 1894 from the salt merchants to finance the first Sino-Japanese War.[79] To ensure that foreign indemnities and other expenses were paid on time, the state rescinded in 1903 its policy of "salt first, tax later." Henceforth there would be no grace period of salt tax. All the gabelle (0.685 tael per *yin*), interest payments on loans and deposits (0.0420 tael per *yin*), and other surcharges must now be paid in full before *yin* certificates were released.[80] By 1911 *lijin*—price increases to pay for railroad and coastal defense construction, foreign indemnities, political reforms, and Yuan Shikai's new army—had added 6.51 taels to each *yin* of salt: an amount far exceeding the 1.88 taels of gabelle, interest payments, and miscellaneous fees.[81]

## Smuggling, Corruption, and Profits

While the salt merchants' fortunes waxed and waned with the dynasty's cycle of prosperity and decline, three features seemed to be constant for the salt trade: smuggling, corruption, and profits.

Large-scale smuggling began with a flawed weighing procedure. One *jin* of salt at the depot was actually 17.3 instead of the nominal 16 *liang* (ounces)—thanks to a set of adulterated weights issued by the Board of Revenue—so that merchants could "legally" pack more salt into their bales. Even officials acknowledged that it was common practice to pack an extra 100 *jin* of salt, crushing overworked scales at the depot.[82] Tianjin became the main distribution center of this tax-free salt, a fact known to emperors since early Qing. Sailors on tribute-grain boats would purchase the salt and unload it on their return trip along the Grand Canal, or Changlu merchants would send their salt to neighboring Hedong and Lianghuai Divisions where higher tax rates ruled.[83]

Such flagrant violation of the law would not have been possible without the benign neglect, if not tacit cooperation, of officials from the highest rank to lowly yamen runners. Numerous edicts, the earliest dated 1651, decried official corruption. Routine bans issued against "squeezing" the salt merchants betrayed their ineffectiveness —a fact of life compounded by a grossly underpaid bureaucracy.[84] The Changlu salt merchants paid 0.15 tael of silver per *yin* beginning in 1651 to cover all the commissioner's administrative costs, secretaries, accountants, and runners.[85] Until 1663, when the merchants donated a mansion for his use, the Changlu supervisor did not even command his own yamen in Tianjin or in Beijing; the Changlu commissioner, for all his responsibilities and hundreds of thousands of taels in revenue, received an annual salary of only 130 taels.[86] A forgiving Kangxi Emperor certainly knew of the kickbacks imposed by his ministers, warning the salt supervisor not to pursue the matter.[87] According to the Yongzheng Emperor, who enjoyed embarrassing his brothers and contenders to the throne, it was public knowledge that they had accepted 110,000 taels of silver from the Changlu salt merchants to facilitate an application for deferment.[88] The crimes perpetrated by the salt merchants, he declared, were minor compared to the abuse of authority by officials.[89] Finally acknowledging the unrealistically low salaries, he legalized, institutionalized, and negotiated "subsidies" to officials by using the *yin* registration fees from Changlu salt merchants to "nourish their integrity."[90]

These, however, were the payments known to the Changlu commissioner. Unknown to him, much less the Board of Revenue, were the "contributions" the salt merchants negotiated with local officials. According to an investigation in 1849, these varied with the profitability of the district, ranging from several hundred to thousands of taels. There were quarterly contributions to the district magistrate, the yamen runners, and the garrison commander; mandatory too were birthday gifts in cash for the magistrate and his wife; gratuities were expected for each of the major festivals. The goodwill of magistrates assuming their posts in midyear would be secured by "welcoming subsidies."[91] Sixty-two years later, officials reported no fewer than eleven categories of customary "contributions" from salt merchants.[92] In addition, the so-called up-front fees *(menmian laofei)* and other gratuities were also due the subdistrict bureaucracy. For the fifth month, when demand for salt was usually weak, such fees amounted to 15 percent of the local retail operating expenses.[93]

Whether or not these levies and contributions proved onerous to the salt merchants, they had to be paid. In the aftermath of the Boxer Uprising, when a salt merchant petitioned for relief from such levies amounting to over a thousand strings per quarter, an unsympathetic commissioner ruled that such fees had been collected for so long that a sudden stop to the practice would be unacceptable.[94]

Indeed, a case might even be made that the more "fees" proffered to officials, the more profitable the business became.[95] The candid memoir of a one-time salt clerk sheds light on this issue. In 1881, after his father's death, Wang Xitong joined a salt-retailing outlet in the Xiuwu district of Henan as an apprentice with the nominal salary of 1,000 *wen* a month. This naive sixteen-year-old observed with disgust and amazement price manipulation and product adulteration. The salt price for the district was officially 29 copper cash per *jin*—or 1.8125 copper cash per *liang* at 16 *liang* to a *jin*—but the outlet could not turn a tidy profit unless the selling price was 32. Facilitated by the gifts and fees, the salt merchants reached an understanding with local officials: customers would receive 14.5 *liang* for every *jin* of salt they bought, or 2 copper cash per *liang*. On top of this "illegal" price increase, the counter clerk was trained to manipulate the scales, a technique referred to in salt merchants' parlance as "a dead price balanced by a dynamic steelyard" *(sijia huocheng)*. Potential troublemakers such as local stipend students, yamen runners, and ruffians got 16 *liang* or more for their *jin* of salt to buy their silence, but children, women, peasants, the weak, and the meek might receive only 10.[96]

Regardless of the weight standard used, the merchants further enhanced their profits by adulterating their merchandise. Adding dirt, deliberately or not, increased the weight of the salt sold. Slightly better would be the use of water. The less scrupulous added gypsum and alum. Participating employees received as a monthly bonus a portion of the extra income—an amount reportedly exceeding their nominal salaries.[97]

The merchants' complaints of loss, therefore, must be taken with a grain of salt. With profits determined in part by the ability to circumvent state regulations—extra or manipulated weight, adulteration, exploitation of exchange rates, smuggling—it is difficult to determine their profitability. Even amidst the turmoil of late Qing, some Changlu salt merchants could still turn a profit. Yan Xiu's diary provides a rare account: a gross profit of 3.2 taels per *yin* in 1904 for the household's monopoly of Sanhe.[98] For the division—assuming an average *wojia* of 8 taels per *yin*, or 7 million taels, and 2 million taels in operating capital—the gross rate of return to capital would be at least 20 percent on profits of 2 to 3 million taels.[99] Wooden chests of silver delivered from the monopolies to the merchants' mansions remained a regular scene in the city.[100]

The paradox of profits against claims of loss—and an efficient revenue extraction system amidst charges of corruption—remind us of Wang Shouji's comments on the Changlu Division. After twenty years at the Shandong bureau of the Board of Revenue, Wang still found his colleagues and the salt merchants unfathomable.[101] To the extent that this chapter has unraveled the "morass" of salt *(yanhutu)*, it also illustrates the complex negotiation between the state and the salt merchants. In peacetime, the state nurtured the salt trade. But it enforced a confiscatory policy, resurrecting old taxes or raising new ones according to its needs, when under pressure. Although the merchants were protected by a legal system that promised justice, they were also in a monopolistic business because of the emperor's grace. Such privilege had its price, and the trade was regulated by an elaborate array of controls that, at least on paper, left little room for maneuver: market, price, and exchange rate were all fixed. They also wrestled with a rent-seeking bureaucracy that demanded a share of the profit.

The ability of the merchants to defend themselves was limited, but donations, bribery, and even smuggling were weapons with which they could ameliorate, if not counter, the state's intrusion into their economy. If the relationship between the state, personified by the emperor and the bureaucracy, and the salt merchants was one of negotiated reciprocity, albeit an unequal and inconsistent one, it was not quite the feudal collusion once perceived. For better or for worse, Tianjin's economy and society were founded on this relationship.

# 3.

# THE HOUSEHOLD
# AND THE LAW

The state left its imprint on the salt merchants' household economy as well. As household and business expanded and contracted through successive cycles, frequent quarrels broke out over entitlements (if not rights), management of household properties, and contractual obligations. These litigious subjects taxed the expertise and resources of the local magistrate. As judge, prosecutor, jury, and investigator, this figure had to abide by established legal principles and procedures to the satisfaction of his superiors. But overwhelmed as he and his secretaries often were with homicide, theft, and other crimes, disputes between private parties over property and rights—what European legal tradition would classify as civil cases—received only as much attention as officials could afford for such minor matters (xishi).[1]

This seemingly halfhearted concern for civil cases contributed to the controversies surrounding China's legal system. On the one hand, an autocratic state presumably left little room for local autonomy, especially for city dwellers who lived under the yamen's shadow. On the other hand, a cursory glance of the Qing Code (Da Qing lüli) confirms that it dealt mostly with penal cases, and extensive use of mediators suggests that the state remained aloof from civil cases.[2] Indeed, the absence of a separate civil or commercial code has led some scholars to conclude that China had little civil law.[3] Instead, irrational patrimonial factors compromised private personal property rights.[4] Bankruptcy and contractual disputes were usually arbitrated by guilds "which have never been within the law."[5] China was portrayed as a land where "local customs prevailed," uncodified and varying from locale to locale.[6] Even when officials adjudicated, they practiced *cadi* justice, not "according . . . to formal rules and without regard to persons."[7] Imbued with humanistic values, they were inferior as technical administrators to the jurists of the Western world trained under a "formally organized legal system."[8]

Recent studies have revised this anarchic picture. The legal system of late imperial China concerned itself with protecting individuals and their property. It prohibited killing, bodily injury, damage of property, or refusing to pay debts.[9] While a separate civil code was not drafted until 1911, statutes pertaining to civil matters *(minshi)* scattered in the Qing Code had long been enforced.[10] Studies on rural Tainan, Baxian, and Baodi reveal that local officials routinely intervened in disputes among nonelites over marriage, succession, property, loans, and contracts. Far from being arbitrary or irrational, court documents portray officials consistently applying the code, or the implicit principles which flowed from it, with carefully crafted legal rulings that detailed the discovered facts, points of contention, and reasons for the decision.[11] To the extent that customary practices internalized the implicit principles of the code, they coexisted in relative harmony and were just as effective, if not more so, in promoting order.[12]

This chapter extends these findings to an urban and commercial environment. With thousands of taels at stake in many of these cases, how did local officials overcome their lack of expertise in commercial practices? What happened if formal law conflicted with informal custom? How and when, if ever, did custom become law? What if social desiderata—the authority of household head over juniors, household harmony, the exalted status of widows—clashed with the Qing Code on property rights? How did officials, infused with Confucian normative ideals, reconcile these insoluble tangles? Did officials administer the law consistently when the state's interests clashed with those of the salt merchants? The cases examined in this chapter reveal a hierarchy of "laws": from local customary practice (including mediation) to social desiderata, the Qing Code, and the state's sovereign interests. How officials decided which mode of conflict resolution to apply in civil cases demonstrates further complex interplay between the state, the public, and the private realm in Tianjin.[13]

## Household Strategy, Household Head, and the Law

Although their incidence cannot be determined, extended households were probably the major form of domestic organization among
Tianjin's wealthy.[14] Inspired by the ideal of coresidence and sharing
of wealth *(tongju gongcai)*, household members would pool their
income, meet their expenses from a common budget, and take their
meals together. Elaborate rules were devised and transmitted in
the form of household instructions infused with the Confucian
ideals of filial piety and domestic harmony. Accumulation of personal property by sons and daughters-in-law was repeatedly forbidden in the Classics: since sons had no authority, even over their
own bodies, worldly possessions were superfluous.[15] A harmonious
household according to the Confucian ideal was one in which each
member internalized his or her respect and responsibility toward
other members without concern for personal interests.

Many salt merchants found this cultural ideal appealing. To them
the household was not merely a vehicle for the transmission of values
but also a unit of production, consumption, and investment—as well
as an institution through which they reproduced themselves. Under
the direction of a forceful and shrewd merchant who doubled as
father and household head *(jiazhang)*, his nuclear family would evolve
in time into an extended household with several generations living
under one roof. After his death, his sons and grandsons might divide
and form stem families. Or they might continue as a joint family with
a member from the most senior generation serving as head. Income
from their salt monopolies, urban real estate, businesses, native banks,
and pawnshops would be pooled and shared. Decisions on education
and the marriage alliances of household members would fall under
the head's authority. More than two hundred mouths of the "Bei"
Huas thus lived under one roof for eight generations, their livelihood
sustained by the Tongzhou monopoly, reportedly the most lucrative
in the Changlu Division.[16]

Harmony of the household meant order, a vital concern shared
by the state and the household head. He or she was legitimized as
the legal representative with authority over the management of household affairs; under the Tang dynasty, any male heir agitating for
household division *(fenjia)* against the will of grandparents or parents
was deemed unfilial, one of the ten abominations *(shi'e)* carrying three
years of banishment or sixty lashes.[17] The household head's authority

reached a new height in A.D. 968 when the death penalty was imposed on wayward sons setting up separate households and finances.[18] In 1009, the state decreed that anyone convicted of instigating a male heir to agitate for household division, or lending him money against his inheritance, would be banished.[19] Another loophole was closed in 1316: it became a crime for a son to obtain loans from outside the household against his father's wish.[20] The Qing Code preserved the household head's powers to educate and nurture, manage household finances, engage in matchmaking, and choose an heir for those juniors without male issue. In return, he or she must be fair and accept responsibility for high crimes committed by household members under their charge.[21]

While the Qing Code and substatutes delineated the household head's extensive, if not absolute, authority and provided a legal framework within which the household economy was to operate, local custom and evolving household arrangements also shaped actual practice. In North China, for instance, the household head could register with the local magistrate *(li'an)* a public disavowal of any unauthorized debts incurred by a junior member and, as a last resort, disinherit him.[22] The head might exercise his or her authority personally or delegate the management of the household's corporate property—a good way to prepare the younger generation for household management and, by extension, public service.

A picture of the salt merchant's household organization emerges from Yan Xiu's (1860–1929) correspondence and memoir. The Yans' apical ancestor, Yingqiao, migrated from Zhejiang and sojourned in Tianjin as a merchant in early Qing. Although his body was returned to Cixi for burial, his son settled in Tianjin.[23] A fifth-generation descendant, Daoheng (1805–1872), pursued a career in the salt trade as a manager and acquired the Sanhe monopoly in 1852 under the corporate name of Yuanchang. His only son, Kekuan (1829–1880), abandoned his scholarly aspirations and became a Changlu head merchant in 1870.

As the oldest son, Yan Zhen followed his father as a salt merchant.[24] This local custom allowed his brothers to study for the civil service examinations—a strategy that paid off when Yan Xiu achieved the *jinshi* degree in 1883. Despite this coveted achievement, Yan Xiu maintained his concern with the ephemerality of household wealth and its proper management.[25] His career might take him far from home, but he continued to participate in management decisions about personnel appointments and pay.[26] And for good reason: the household financed his bureaucratic career as he went heavily into debt while serving in Guizhou (1894–1897) and Beijing (1886–1894 and 1905–1909). In a letter in 1896, he confided his financial woes to his elder brother: he could hardly break even on his official income. Yan Xiu's familiarity with household affairs prepared him well. In 1898, his official career faltering after he petitioned for a drastic overhaul of the civil service examination system, he retired to Tianjin and, after his brother's death, succeeded him as household head. In this capacity he regularly solicited the opinions of junior and senior, including his brother's widow, on major issues such as whether to offer the Sanhe monopoly for lease.[27] Routine matters were handled by his nephew and two sons who formed a management team (dangjia) responsible for budgeting, determining the proper amount for gifts, allowances for household members, food, and periodic audits of the household bursar (zhangfang).

Day-to-day operation of the monopoly was entrusted to two professional managers: one headed the main office in Tianjin (neidian), the other Sanhe (waidian, or outer office). Each had a staff of accountants, assistant managers (fushou), and clerks (siyou) at the outlets. The household management team audited the ledgers periodically, but it was the managers who made policy decisions on personnel, salary, bonus, leave, and benefits in circulars (gongxin) following extensive consultation with the dangjia team and Yan Xiu.[28]

For the good of the household, Yan Xiu also arranged marriages for his sons and daughters, nephew and nieces, with an assortment of "Big Eight" Huas, Bians, Lis, and Hans; he himself referred to the Shis and the Huangs as relatives by marriage.[29] Such kinship ties, as part of the household strategy, facilitated mutual support among these merchant princes. When Yan found himself stretched in financing local educational programs, the Huas lent a helping hand in the form of 1,000 taels.[30]

The salt merchants' success, then, might be attributed in part to their household strategy. At its best, the extended household enhanced capital accumulation, if not solidarity, while extending its reach beyond the commercial sphere into networks of local, regional, and national elites.[31] The overarching concept of the household as a hierarchical group—bound at its core by kinship, reciprocity, and intimacy and reinforced by local custom and state code—had as its aim survival and, beyond that, the freedom of household members, in both leisure and other pursuits, made possible only with wealth. As economic units, salt merchant households diversified their investments to take advantage of the many opportunities available in a commercial city such as Tianjin. Assisted by capable household managers and professional staff, supported by rituals and a value system that emphasized obedience and the common good, a strong head might unify the household toward the creation and preservation of its wealth, influence, and status, with his or her authority sanctioned by the state.

## Business Customs and Contracts

The salt merchants did not survive and prosper, however, merely because of their household strategy. In their business dealings with each other, they followed local commercial practices and written contracts —all part of a legal framework enforced through the Changlu Syndicate (Lugang Gongsuo). To the extent that they were accepted by the state and the courts, these customs constituted a firm basis for their business dealings.

Officially registered Changlu merchants fell into three main categories: the owner *(yeshang)*, the lessee *(zushang)*, and the sublessee *(daishang)*. Most of the merchants were owners who acquired the right to sell salt in a designated district or districts from their predecessor or the state through the payment of the "nest price." Unlike other revenue-farming systems in which franchises were subject to periodic public bidding, the Changlu salt merchants bought and sold monopolies as private property, setting the price among themselves without any state involvement.[32]

The contracts for these transactions were detailed but straightforward and contained all the essential elements of a contract: competent parties, warranty by the selling party, offer, acceptance, consideration, and mutuality of agreement without coercion. Neither kin nor neighbors (in this case, holders of contiguous monopolies) enjoyed the first right of refusal frequently encountered in rural land transactions and deeds.[33] The five-year statute of limitations governing land transfer was equally applicable in the sale of a monopoly.[34] Beyond the usual seller's guarantee that the monopoly was free of encumbrance, a valid sales contract (signed in duplicate) required witnesses, four registered Changlu salt merchants as guarantors, and endorsement by the head merchants. The new owner would then effect a change of name and register with the commissioner *(geng-ming renban)* to assume full responsibility for all taxes, levies, and fees due and for dealing in salt for the designated monopoly.

As an alternative to outright sale, leasing allowed salt merchants to retain ownership of their monopolies and yet be assured of a steady income. Citing an inability to operate the monopoly (despite the elaborate investigation and guarantee process designed to establish that ability), an owner might lease the right to a lessee for a specified period ranging from four to twenty years; the usual term was ten years. Obligations consistent with the customary business practices of Tianjin were clearly defined for both parties. Most leases involved interest-free security deposits *(yazu)* and loans (interest-bearing, non-interest-bearing, or both) from the lessee to the owner. Sometimes, the rent (*xianzu*, literally "current rent") was payable in one lump sum up front; in other cases by the month, quarter, or as specified. If the deposits and loans were substantial, a lower rent might be negotiated—reflecting an understanding, if only implicitly, of opportunity cost and discount on present value. As a gesture of goodwill to cement their long-term relationship, the lessee's obligations, in addition to security deposit and rent, included occasional advances (repayable) or subsidies (nonrepayable) for funerals or marriages as well as loans, with or without interest, to the owner.

For this investment, the lessee obtained the right to operate the monopoly and the responsibility for all losses, taxes, and levies. He or she also enjoyed by custom a first right of refusal for renewal—but see Cao (née Li) vs. Sun—and a year's advance notice before termination of the lease. In rare instances, a sublessee might assume the rights and responsibilities of the lessee for the remainder of a lease, subject to the owner's approval. Custom prohibited repossession of the monopoly before the expiration of the lease, and a lease could be broken only with the owner's consent.[35] By custom, too, an existing lease would not preclude the sale of a monopoly *(zu bu ya mai)*, unlike rural land transactions in Taiwan.[36]

The contracts also addressed issues specific to the salt business: the concerns for reciprocity, customary obligations, and economic calculation. The frequency and amount of loans, interest or non-interest-bearing, and occasional advances or subsidies for funerals or marriages that could be demanded of the lessee were explicitly stipulated in many cases. The use of the formulary phrase *(fayan)* "no document, no interest" *(wuxi bu cheng piao)* indicated that a loan would not incur any interest. Other clauses detailed the maximum amount of salt inventory permitted upon lease expiration with the formulaic phrase "so delivered, thus returned" *(yuanzhuang yuanxie)* to prevent a deliberate overstock. Conditions governing repossession and penalties for contract violations were also stipulated. All loans, security deposits, and taxes advanced by the lessee had to be repaid—as well as compensation if the owner wanted to repossess before the lease expired.

Consistent usage of contracts—together with a specialized vocabulary and formulary phrases embodying fairness, honesty, and reciprocity between the contracting parties—thus constituted an integral part of the Changlu salt merchants' private and public economy. Compared to rural land transactions, ownership rights of these commercial properties seemed less fettered by claims of kith and kin. Recognized by the state, understood and entered into willingly, these contracts gave private citizens a measure of certainty and, in the process, promoted economic efficiency, if not "rationality," defined in terms of maximization—whether of profits or goodwill, or both, for these urban merchants.[37]

## Roles of the Head Merchants

Once the elaborate regulations governing aspects of the salt trade, fees, and gabelle collection were met—and so long as the merchants' disputes did not disrupt the flow of taxes or threaten the supply of salt to consumers—the Qing state mostly left the salt merchants to themselves. When contractual disputes arose, relatives and household friends might attempt mediation. If they failed, fellow salt merchants would join the discussion. And if this application of "public opinion" failed and both sides remained obdurate, the matter finally became a suit for the courts to decide. Even then, the commissioner routinely requested the assistance of the head merchants to mediate and arbitrate the dispute with their expertise and institutional memory.

Elected by the salt merchants from among themselves and confirmed by the state, the four head merchants played a crucial, if ambiguous, role in the operation of the Changlu Division. Straddling the official and the private, they referred to themselves as merchants with a duty *(zhishang)* in their communications to the state but were not officials as such—even though most of them held official titles purchased or won through civil service examinations. Their duties, as listed in their appointment letter, included investigation of salt smuggling and other "hidden" irregularities. They were expected to set an example by paying their tax obligations promptly.[38] More important, the head merchants' authority and reputation were based on their service record and guardianship of the merchants' customary practices *(tonggang dali)*. To ensure the supply of salt to consumers, for instance, the head merchants enforced the syndicate's rule that holders of an expired lease should continue operating the monopoly but not pay any rent if the owner failed to repossess the monopoly.[39]

Although their authority remained largely unwritten, the head merchants thus played an important role in resolving complicated civil and commercial cases with their intimate knowledge of customary practice and institutional memory. In 1896, Wang Yasun, the owner of Mixian, resumed operation of the monopoly through a partnership with six shares of 10,000 taels each, his monopoly counting as three. A Ms. Ning subscribed a share under the hall name of "Xiu'ai Tang," raising the capital by selling a shop, pieces of commercial property, and boats.[40] Eight years later, Ning filed suit for breach of contract. In a court hearing on October 17, 1904, she presented a partnership contract that named her son-in-law Zhang Chengben as her nominee. Wang denied that she had ever been a partner, however, because Zhang had died before putting up the money. On November 11, the head merchants filed a brief in favor of the plaintiff. Without accusing Wang of fraud, they noted that by custom a partner would receive a copy of the signed and witnessed contract only after his or her share had been subscribed in full. Since the authenticity of the signatures was not contested, and Wang could not explain how the document came into Ning's possession, the contract should be upheld. Wang finally conceded that he might have been negligent in his business conduct. As the monopoly had been faring poorly, the head merchants proposed a refund of 6,000 taels and dissolution of the partnership, a settlement that both sides accepted.[41]

This settlement highlights several salient features of the Changlu Division—aside from the fact that women could be silent business partners. (As we shall see, salt merchants' widows, too, enjoyed special status.) It illustrates why officials, instead of insisting on exercising their authority, relied on mediation and arbitration by the head merchants in resolving complex civil and commercial cases. Nominated by merchants and appointed by the state without term limit, they outlasted the yearlong tenure of most supervisors and commissioners, providing the necessary continuity and institutional memory for the operation of the Changlu Division. While they were not legally trained, they were not arbitrary in their mediation and arbitrations: the tests of evidence and "public opinion" still applied. As keepers of local customary business practices, they commanded a respect for their expertise that might not be claimed by officials. Instances of head merchants abusing their influence are not unknown, but their authority allowed the salt merchants a limited juridical sphere of their own.

## Customary Practices and the Law

This is not to argue, however, that the merchants either enjoyed legal autonomy or were above the law as their contemporaries and historians often charged. (See Chapter 2.) At best the salt merchants' donations, lobbying, household economy, and reliance on customary practices and institutions afforded them limited protection in their private domain and business from the state. Custom could not replace law, however, nor did officials accept merchant practices as coequal to their rulings. Not unlike the experience of English common law, practice might be continuous, ancient, and certain, but the test of "reasonableness" and the quo warranto assault remained—as the "Highsteps" (Gaotaijie) Huas learned from their brush with the law.[42]

One of the city's Big Eight families, the Huas exploited to their advantage the ambivalence of collective and individual ownership in their business dealings.[43] Under the corporate name of Hua Jicheng, the household owned and operated the monopolies of Anzhou, Rongcheng, Tianjin, and Wuqing. In 1912, a widow Hua (née Zhang) sued the household for repayment of her loan of 3,000 strings of cash, outstanding since 1877. Hua Chengyan, in his capacity as household head, defended the household with the argument that the loan, taken out under the name of Houdefu with the signature of Hua Chengyun, should be treated as a personal rather than a household debt.

The magistrate took a different view, however, and decided in favor of the plaintiff. Sidestepping the thorny issue of determining what was personal and what was collective, he argued that if the court found the distinction less than clear, the plaintiff could not reasonably be expected to make that distinction. If Hua Chengyun conducted his business under the name of Houdefu and represented it falsely as the corporate property of the Hua household, the magistrate reasoned, Chengyan as the household head should have knowledge about it. That he did not object or stop Chengyun suggested either negligence or condoning of his brother's activities. The court ruled that the household should produce Chengyun, a stipend student and expectant prefect, for interrogation within one month or, failing that, assume responsibility for the loan.

The magistrate's ruling did not impress the Huas. While Chengyun continued his absence, protected by his status as a civil service examination degree holder, Chengyan appealed on the grounds that the household had filed a petition in 1879 with the local magistrate absolving itself of any responsibility for personal debts incurred by its individual members unauthorized by the household head. Invoking this local custom, he insisted that the household could not be held liable.[44] But the Provincial Court of Zhili disagreed. The court reasoned that even if the loan had been a personal loan, the fact that Chengyan and his brothers had yet to undergo household division meant that they should share responsibility. Overruling the local custom, the court decided that the right of the creditor could not be abrogated by the household's unilateral declaration. The Huas were ordered to pay, in addition to the principal, half of the accumulated interest, an amount equal to the principal as required under the Qing Code.[45] Neither status nor custom, however ancient, certain, and continuous, could replace law—specifically the rights of creditors.

## Gerontocracy and the Law

If conflicts between business customs and the Qing Code could be resolved by reasoning—legal or simple "common sense"—disputes involving implicit principles in the code—household harmony and rights vested with property ownership—presented a more difficult problem for officials. As the households of these merchant princes underwent cycles of development and division, corporate property and the privileged position of the household head generated strains common to Chinese households elsewhere.[46] Not only did parental authority decline as offspring reached adulthood, but the advantages of wealth sharing were also challenged constantly by individual interests. As jural equals, fathers and sons wrangled in court over the appropriation of household properties. Household heads found their authority usurped by junior members of the household. Branches sued each other over rights and responsibilities. Brothers fought over deployment, management, and sharing of household resources.

Acrimony was bred, in part, by the very success of the pooled-income and shared-expense household strategy. The members' ability to contribute to the household income varied, and the resourceful sometimes resented the "free riders." Li Shutong's alienation from his family—the "Philanthropist" Lis of Liangdian Houjie—began with his expensive tastes and the slight he felt as a concubine's son. His strained relationship with his elder brother led him into a self-imposed exile in Shanghai, leaving a young wife and sons to fend for themselves. His son, Li Duan, recalled bitterly how his cousins lived on the household's corporate income from salt monopolies, a native bank, and real estate but kept their salaries to themselves—and when the household finally underwent division, seized more than their share in violation of the principle of equality on a per stirps basis.[47]

Another source of friction came from the fact that while the household head and seniors often enjoyed a bigger share of the household budget, some wanted still more. Thus Hua Fengqi, household manager of the "Bei" Huas, found himself harassed by his uncle's widow. Employing a tactic that the household used against its business opponents, she traveled to Tongzhou and caused a rumpus at the head office of the household's salt monopoly, refusing to return to Tianjin without 3,000 strings of copper cash and an increased monthly stipend. Another widow of the household soon joined her, forcing an exasperated Fengqi to petition for their removal under court order.[48]

Even more damaging to the household economy were impatient male heirs. By law, all eligible male heirs were entitled to an equal share of inheritance. Unauthorized use of household property that could be theirs in due course—a constant temptation for impatient juniors—was thus distinguished from theft of other people's property, which carried the penalty of strangulation for amounts over 120 taels. The most the hasty son could get was a hundred lashes with light bamboo.[49]

For the Changlu salt merchants, the archives were littered with cases involving wayward sons and grandsons. In 1886, Li Enpei, operator of the Jiyuan monopoly, leased the monopoly of Mengxian from

Zheng Zuolin for eight years. After Zheng died, his brother Zuoji renewed the lease in 1894. Four years into the lease, Zuoji's son Linsun took it upon himself to lease the monopoly to Zeng Wenguang for ten years. When Li filed suit in 1899, he was joined by Zeng who accused the Zhengs of leasing the monopoly to two parties. The son's day in court was averted when Zeng decided to assume his posting as a magistrate in Henan province. Li repaid on behalf of Linsun an 800-tael loan from Zeng and extended the lease for ten more years.[50]

## Household Division and the Law

However appalling by Confucian standards, then, domestic strife over property was a fact of life often involving the state. Household division with the blessing of the grandparents or parents became legal under the Mongols in 1271.[51] By the Ming period, household division against the wishes of the grandparents or parents was a crime only if they pressed the charge in person—which would expose the seniors to humiliation in open court as failures in parenting. Even then, the penalty awaiting the unfilial offspring was reduced to one hundred heavy bamboo strokes.[52] Many a father or household head thus wisely forestalled acrimony by effecting a timely division. Even under the best of circumstances, however, the process was painful and difficult to execute: every item in the household had to be assessed and accounted for. When disputes within households resisted all the well-developed procedures of local custom and head merchants and mediators also failed, local officials intervened as a last resort with solutions ranging from separate residence but continued coparcenership *(fenju bu xichan)* to total division.

The case of Feng vs. Feng illustrates how, even when the Qing Code clearly allowed for household division, officials decided not to pursue that course of action. Feng Enshou (1775–1844), one of the leading salt merchants of his time, leased or owned more than twenty monopolies at the height of his career. After the household's expropriation by the state in 1846, it was left with only four: Zhuozhou, Qingyuan, Fuping, and Quyang. These were subsequently leased out on the authority of the household matriarch. Soon after her death in 1907, the brothers Xuebin (1854–1907) and Xuezhang (b. 1862) agreed to renew the lease, but Xueyan (1856–1923) blocked the proposal by accusing the lessee of fraudulent accounting and delinquent rent payments. Unable to effect a resolution acceptable to both his brother and the lessee, Xuebin returned to Zhuozhou and died later that year.[53]

Xueyan now considered himself the household head and acted accordingly to negotiate a preliminary contract *(caohetong)* to lease the monopolies to He Fuxian. Enraged by this blatant disregard of their rights, Xuezhang and Xuebin's widow joined forces. After friends and relatives failed to resolve the differences, both sides gathered fellow salt merchants *(gangyou,* literally "syndicate friends") for support. In 1910, the widow as a *zhiguafu* filed for household division, asserting her right as custodian of her deceased husband's estate.

Xueyan opposed this challenge to his authority as household head. In his brief, he argued that the division meant a forced sale of the monopolies at an unfavorable price. Instructed by the Changlu commissioner to investigate and mediate, the head merchant Li Shiyu of the "Philanthropist" Lis brokered a compromise. The contract with He was voided and a new lessee located, notwithstanding Xuezhang's contractual responsibility to settle any disputes with household members. Henceforth the three branches would maintain separate residences, but there would be no formal division of the household's corporate property: income was to be shared without a formal document specifying how it was to be divided.[54]

The Fengs' dispute illustrates the sequence of attempts undertaken to resolve household quarrels. Relatives and friends would attempt mediation. If their efforts failed, fellow merchants of the Changlu Syndicate might be mobilized, taking sides as they got involved. If this application of "public opinion" also failed, the matter became a suit for the court to decide. In this instance, the commissioner requested the head merchants' mediation without fear that his authority might be compromised.[55] Although the plaintiffs were within their right to request a formal division, mediation preserved some semblance of a household economy, a result endorsed by officials.

Indeed, it remained the official's (and the state's) prerogative to persuade the litigants to accept what was in their best interest. In such civil cases, the magistrate enjoyed considerable latitude so long as his decision did not jeopardize the state's revenue flow—as in the case of Liu vs. Liu. Liu Yuye, the founder of the household's fortune, had bequeathed the monopoly of Luancheng to his two sons, Xiangting and Jingting. During the reign of the Qianlong Emperor, the monopolies of Huolu and Jingxing were added as corporate household property under the capable management of Shoucheng, Jingting's son. By the early twentieth century ownership was divided into 30.5 shares held by four branches of the household; each share was entitled to a dividend of 300 taels each year from the salt business's annual net profit of 20,000 to 30,000 taels, in addition to earnings from a native bank at Luancheng. Liu Youlan appeared as the registered owner and operator of the monopolies *(chuming de dongjia)*, and his branch controlled five shares out of the total.

In 1904, Liu Enze filed suit against his uncle Youlan and his nephew Youzhi accusing them of mismanagement and misappropriation of household corporate property. According to Enze and his son Zigong, their branch, which held one share of Luancheng and three shares of the monopolies of Jingxing and Huolu, was denied not only its portion of the dividends but also the right to participate in the management of the monopolies. As the owners on record, Youlan and his son Youzhi monopolized the household's extensive interests in salt monopolies and native banks, appropriating for themselves at least 270,000 taels in profits. When Enze tried to join the management in Tianjin and force an audit, Youzhi ordered his eviction from the premises.

In both cases, the commissioner's Solomonic ruling balanced the formal rights of ownership against the substantive claims of kinship. Even after Enshao, Enze's brother, testified in court that his branch had cashed in its share of the monopolies in 1880, thus clearing Youzhi of any fiduciary duty toward a former shareholder, the commissioner decided not to apply the Qing Code to the fullest extent. Instead of prosecuting Enze for filing a meritless plaint, he suggested that Youzhi might placate his less fortunate kin with 2,000 taels (and an additional 200 taels to help defray Enze's expenses).[56]

One can only speculate why the commissioner ruled so generously, if not particularly "rationally," in Enze's favor. By paying, perhaps Youzhi hoped that he would be spared more frivolous and embarrassing lawsuits. The settlement might even reaffirm or restore family values for the Lius and enhance Youzhi and Younan's reputation as caring benefactors of their kin. In addition, this affirmation of mutual support for kin did not cost the state a grain of silver. And the litigants both gained something—arguably a better outcome than a winner-take-all decision in favor of the defendants alone as mandated by the code.

With revenue and the supply of salt at risk, however, officials would protect the state's interests even if this meant a formal household division by court order—as in the case of *Wang* vs. *Wang*. The household's fortune was based on the Wandu monopoly held under the corporate name Fuchengyu. Ownership was divided among three branches. In his capacity as household manager, Wang Yu had leased the monopoly to Qunyi in 1894 and then to Jinyiheng in 1898 for ten years with an annual rent of 3,000 strings of copper cash.[57]

With the lease renewal pending in 1907, Wang Yu tried unsuccessfully to sell the monopoly, touching off a series of legal battles. The other two branches filed suit on October 28, 1907, accusing Yu of misappropriating household funds; Zhang Lipu, manager of the firm Deyuan, also filed suit. According to Zhang, he had lent the wheeling and dealing household manager 3,000 taels at a monthly interest of 4 percent to be repaid upon expiration of the current lease. In the event that Wang Yu could not repay the loan, Zhang would lease or purchase the monopoly at a price not to exceed 80,000 taels. Wang Yu countered by accusing the other branches of conspiring to divide household corporate property and challenge his authority as household manager.

To break the deadlock, the Changlu commissioner suggested that the two other branches buy out Wang Yu's branch. Failing that, he proposed that the monopoly be leased to a third party. When no lessee met the Wangs' many demands, the commissioner awarded operation of the monopoly to Wang Yu—with the provision that he pay the other branches annual rent and a security deposit as required in a lease. The household remained hopelessly divided, however, and the commissioner threatened to put the monopoly into official receivership to ensure the district's salt supply. To avoid losing the monopoly altogether, the other two branches buried their differences and allowed Wang Yu and his partner to lease the monopoly at an annual rent of 4,000 strings of copper cash. To remove any ambiguity, Wandu was subdivided into three equal market sectors—each of the three branches selecting one by lot under the commissioner's supervision—and Wang Yu and his partner signed three copies of the lease, one for each of the branches.[58] The transformation of the Wangs from kin into formal contracting parties completed the household cycle, favoring in the process the implicit rights that came with ownership over the privileged position of the household head.[59]

Taken together, these changes suggest that the more wealth and male heirs that the salt merchants' household strategy produced, the less likely were voluntary compliance and successful mediation. The flexibility of local custom and mediation by the public and the state could sometimes effect a settlement that allowed the household to continue as an economic unit while preserving as much as possible the social desiderata of reciprocity and mutual responsibility. If, however, the state's interests in revenue stability and salt supply were threatened, officials would act according to the Qing Code—Weber's dictum that "nothing can be more rigidly prescribed than the clan economy of China" notwithstanding.[60]

## Corporate and Individual Property Rights

State involvement in the salt merchants' private household economy did not always stop at mediation, therefore, nor was kinship the only consideration in settling household disputes. Household harmony, however laudable and desirable, had to be weighed against other concerns—including the rights of ownership that came with personal private property, whether it be the individual entrepreneur, his widows, or his heirs, without which economic and social stability would be undermined.

Much of the confusion over fettered property rights in China stems from the two different categories of property recognized by the state and local custom: the collective property of the household and that which was acquired by members of the household through their own efforts.[61] Collective property was held corporately, in perpetuity, to be transmitted to the next generation intact. There was no individual owner, therefore, nor anyone invested with the sole authority to dispose of it. Individuals could own property, by contrast, complete with the rights vested therein.

Different local customs applied to these categories. Changlu salt merchants followed a simple test: the source of financing. When a monopoly was acquired with capital from a household's corporate coffers, it became corporate property—as in the case of the Zhangs who bought the monopoly of Shenze by selling 400 *mu* of the household's land.[62] Property held corporately was usually inalienable, and elaborate measures were adopted to prevent its sale.[63] Contracts involving salt monopolies held as corporate property were signed by both fathers (or mothers) and sons, suggesting that they held the monopoly in common.[64] As such, the parents (or the household head) were mere custodians.

A father, however, could do as he wished with the properties he acquired by his own effort, except that he was required by law to be equitable when settling his estate. Sons who contributed to building up the household's holdings under their father might, depending on local custom, claim a proportionately larger share of their father's estate. In parts of rural North China, households seem to have emphasized equality regardless of individual contribution.[65]

The court thus upheld, if only implicitly, an individual's right of ownership and, by extension, his legal heir or custodian's entitlement to such rights. But the task of distinguishing between what was corporate and what was personal could be daunting—made so deliberately by the salt merchants in order to escape liability, as illustrated by the case of *Huang* vs. *Huang*. The household's founder Huang Futing acquired the Xianxian monopoly in 1840 and added Neihuang in 1853. His son Xiao'en inherited the operation of the monopolies and, in turn, passed them on to his son Diansun who died without an heir. In 1908, Huang Baochen, son of Futing's brother Xin'en, filed suit against the widows of Xiao'en and Diansun for appropriating the two monopolies. He established that his father Xin'en had been the registered *yeshang* of Xianxian, under the corporate name Yongcheng, and claimed that although Futing might have been the operator of the monopolies, he was merely managing the corporate property of the household.[66]

In the first ruling, the prefect of Tianjin rejected Baochen's claim. As it was a recognized practice for one person to register under aliases in the operation of different monopolies, the registration of Xin'en as the owner of Xianxian could not be admitted as evidence of actual ownership. (But see the discussion later on *Zheng* vs. *Zheng*.) The prefect relied instead on the head merchant Yang Junyuan, who testified that Huang Futing was the sole founder *(yiren shouchuang)* of the two monopolies in question. In other words, the widows were legal custodians of their deceased husband's estate and therefore not subject to Baochen's authority.[67]

An unhappy Baochen immediately appealed to the Superior Court of Tianjin. As the surviving male of the senior generation—and therefore the household head by custom—he argued that the monopolies should be his to manage as well. Since his father had been the registered owner, he pointedly asked whether one could be held liable for taxes and levies of a monopoly one did not "own." Once again the court found against him, reasoning that Xiao'en and Diansun had been the owner-operators of the monopolies for so long that if Baochen had a claim, it should have been filed long ago. (Nor had he disputed the widows' status as legal custodians earlier.)

## Widows and the Law

Admired and exalted for their chastity, widows occupied a unique position in Chinese society, the salt business, and Tianjin. Unlike women from scholar-literati households cast stereotypically as exploited and cloistered, salt merchant wives and widows seemed less encumbered by that rigid inner *(nei)* and outer *(wai)* gender division of labor. Some became accomplished poets—in part because of their household's ability to afford publication of their works. Others performed critical tasks for their household in public—perhaps deployed as shock troops in business disputes or as legal representatives of the household.[68]

Women also played a role in Tianjin's economy. Contracts and land deeds from Tianjin bear signatures of women, indicating that they could, in their own right, buy and sell property.[69] But they still seem to have been hidden from view in the salt trade: no female can be identified under her own name *(benming)* in Changlu Syndicate registers. Tianjin's male-dominated business world, however, did not prevent women from participating in the salt trade as partners or through the household corporation *(tanghao)*. No law prohibited women as peddlers or shopkeepers or investors in the salt business (as the widow Ning was). Indeed, an imperial decree issued in 1488 authorized widows of salt merchants to represent and operate monopolies on behalf of their deceased husbands.[70]

A widow's privileges, of course, were contingent upon her remaining true to her dead husband rather than her gender.[71] Nevertheless widows were not shy in exploiting their privileges to the fullest—as did the widow of Zhang Mao. In 1908, she filed suit against Zhou Tonghui for kidnaping and forcing her son to sign a backdated contract leasing the monopoly to Zhou for a security deposit of 11,000 taels and an annual rent of 1,300 taels. She did not, however, dwell on these heinous allegations but went on to complain that she had received only 1,000 taels of the security deposit, the balance being withheld to settle her son's debts. An astute commissioner recognized this underhanded attempt for more rent: by admitting that she had accepted a portion of the security deposit, she must have known about, if not approved, the lease. Ignoring her allegations (or the crime of false accusation), he suggested a compromise that both sides accepted: an increase of 170 taels in the annual rent.[72]

Compassion for widows, however, had its limits. When pitted against the profit motive and property rights, the customary practice of first right of refusal and the moral imperative to treat widows with respect mattered little—as discovered by the widow of Cao Rongxuan (née Li). Her husband had successfully operated several monopolies, including the lease on two-thirds of Sun Tinglin's Wuyi monopoly, for over twenty years.[73] Soon after her husband's death, however, she felt that her contractual and customary rights to first refusal as the existing lessee were abrogated when Sun leased the monopoly to Li Baoheng (1861–1920) of "Philanthropist" Li fame. She sued. In the court hearing, Li Ziming, a fellow salt merchant (unrelated to Baoheng), testified that Baoheng, as one of the head merchants, should not have competed against her if only on the moral ground that widows be treated with compassion. The commissioner, however, caught in yet another conflict among customary practice, morality, and property rights, ruled that he could not compromise Sun's ownership by compelling him to renew Ms. Cao's lease. After all, Sun had been offered slightly better terms.[74]

Widows of salt merchants were not the only casualties in this decision. However well intentioned, customary practice and the Qing Code were limited in their power to effect desirable social behavior. The Confucian ideal of social harmony and compassion—values endorsed by the state and embodied in contractual provisions—proved inadequate when confronted by property rights and an equally potent economic rationality (profit motive).

## Supremacy of State Interest

If property owners were within their rights in pursuing profit maximization (or minimizing loss) through their customary practices, what about the state's concern for revenue stability? An answer might be gleaned from another case involving the litigious Zhengs. In 1900, the Zhengs were embroiled in a bitter court fight when Zheng Zuoji sued his nephew Zheng Tang for leasing the monopoly of Jixian to Guo Jin'qing without his approval. The elder Zuoji testified that the monopolies of Jixian and Mengxian had been acquired by his older brother Zuolin with capital derived from sale of household property left by their father, Yueshan.[75] Upon Zuolin's death in 1892, Zuoji assumed the mantle as household head with authority over the household's corporate properties and contracted for the leasing of the Mengxian monopoly. That authority, he argued, should hold for Jixian as well. Defending himself, Zheng Tang countered that Zuoji and his son Linsun had appropriated to themselves all the proceeds from the Mengxian lease, forcing him to protect his interest.

Rendering a decision on this seemingly open-and-shut case of an impatient junior challenging the household head turned out to be a difficult process. The case hinged on whether there had been a household division and, if so, who owned which monopoly. Although Linsun testified in court that the household had yet to be divided, his father admitted three days later that indeed there had been a division, at least in appearance. As a legal maneuver to limit liability should either monopoly fail, the Zheng family had filed a petition at Wenxian, Henan, in 1886 stipulating that Mengxian would henceforth be operated by Zuoji. In practice, however, the income from the monopolies, Zuoji insisted, was still shared by the entire household.

The magistrate of Wenxian added another twist to this legal tangle. He confirmed that the Zhengs had indeed filed a petition in 1886—but, for reasons unknown, it lacked an official endorsement, which implied that the household division, if there had been one, was null and void. Yulu, then governor-general of Zhili, referred the case to the commissioner with the opinion that there had been no household division and hence the Jixian monopoly was still household corporate property.

Yang Zonglian, the commissioner, disagreed with his superior. He dismissed the suit because, by Zuoji's own admission, a household division had in fact taken place, even though the Zhengs intended it as a maneuver to limit liability. Reversing the courts' acceptance of this customary practice, the commissioner declared that it was a legal fraud to evade full liability to the state, and thus an abuse of the law (wanfa), if not actually a crime.

A disappointed Zuoji, who undoubtedly still believed that he had local custom on his side, quickly appealed the decision. He reiterated that the registration of monopolies under different names to limit the household's liability should not be construed as a household division. Furthermore, he argued, the commissioner's ruling should be overturned because the Wenxian yamen did not have a legally valid record of that division. As a compromise he volunteered to operate the monopolies as household head until his nephew came of age. The offer, however, came too late; Yang had already submitted his decision on May 17, 1900, to the governor-general for approval. On May 23, Yulu concurred with Yang's interpretation that a household division had taken place. Zuoji's claim was denied.[76]

Such cases reveal the state's priorities. The salt merchants were left largely alone to their customary practices in their business dealings. But when social desiderata such as the authority of the household head or compassion for widows clashed with ownership rights, the state protected the latter. Ultimately, customary practices and rights of ownership—however ancient, certain, continuous, and reasonable —were subject to the state's quo warranto assault.

## Corruption and the Rule of Law

If the salt merchants' civil cases were decided by officials as prescribed by the Qing Code, including the implicit principles and the state's priority, there remains the question of corruption. With more than three thousand official and unofficial runners serving the district magistracy, strict supervision was nearly impossible.[77] Officials, of course, rarely left incriminating evidence in their files. All too often, therefore, court papers depict an orderly, legally "rational" world. Even when their decisions seemed consistent with the code, the procedure and execution of their rulings might still be tainted by irregularities if not influence and corruption. In other words, court documents alone may not allow a full appreciation of the legal system in late Qing—as illustrated by yet another encounter with the law involving the Feng household.

In 1898, the firm Yutong filed suit against the Fengs seeking repayment of a debt and accumulated interest. Unaware that a warrant had been issued against him, Xuezhang was hauled off the street and thrown into a holding cell at the magistrate's yamen. Unlike other salt merchants who managed to tie up the court for years, Feng received an expedited hearing by the magistrate later that afternoon and was given one month to repay. That evening the grace period was reduced in half by a vermilion slip (*zhupi*) issued by the magistrate's office.

After regaining his freedom the next day, Feng traced the cause of these rapid proceedings to the plaintiff's considerable facility (*shou-yan*, literally "hands and eyes") at the yamen.[78]

Taken together, these cases involving the salt merchants offer us a glimpse into the complex interaction between the private domain of household, the public, the economy, and the state in late imperial China. These urban merchant princes generated plenty of disputes among themselves, frequently necessitating the mediation of friends and colleagues. Persuasion by "public opinion" and "fairness" frequently achieved an equitable settlement that kept the state and officials at bay.[79] Even when such disputes became lawsuits, the head merchants played a prominent role in investigating and offering their expertise in local business practices. To this extent, the salt merchants enjoyed a juridical sphere, however limited, of their own.

Not all disputes could be mediated or arbitrated successfully, however, especially those involving ownership and the rights vested with it. When all mediation failed, officials had to intervene. With few provisions in the Qing Code to guide them, they followed Tianjin's local customs, which differed from those applicable to rural property transfers and leases. Neither kin nor neighbors, for instance, could claim the first right of refusal. If the state's interest was not at risk, ownership rights could be compromised when pitted against the ideal of domestic harmony and mutual responsibility among kin. When the litigants were not related by blood, the rights of ownership were affirmed to maintain the social and economic order at large. But when the state's interests were at risk, officials could overturn a long-accepted custom such as registering under different names to limit liability. Certainly the complex negotiation between state, society, economy, and private interests provided fertile ground for corruption in its many forms. Even when rulings appear to be legally sound, corruption or influence peddling may still have played a part. Custom and the Qing Code thus coexisted in relative harmony and tension as civil cases were decided by the code and, ultimately, the sovereign interests of the state as interpreted by local officials.

# 4.
# MERCHANT CULTURE

Tianjin's urban culture offered another field of negotiation between state and society. For much of China's history, the scholar-official was the career of choice. Whether in or out of office, scholar-officials considered righting public morals and customs *(yifeng yixu)* part of their social responsibility. In this process, Confucianism as a moral philosophy and state orthodoxy became a form of cultural capital.[1] Conferring on themselves the privilege of deciding a hierarchy of culture from "high" to "low," literati-officials deemed poetry, collections of paintings, books, and antiques as respectable, but gaily colored clothing, "lewd" customs, and extravagant spending were lowly forms to be tolerated or even banned if necessary. In this cultural and social order, "rural" and "urban" lost their analytical value (for those who subscribe to the state orthodoxy at least).[2] Merchants ranked lowest behind literati-scholars *(shi)*, farmers *(nong)*, and artisans *(gong)*, and their literati affectations were considered pretentious if not a threat to high culture.[3]

Such was the power of this cultural hegemony that while a few intellectuals of late imperial China far ahead of their times advocated the pursuit of profit as a worthy and morally fulfilling goal, the gap between intellectual history and social history lingered until the late nineteenth century (if not beyond).[4] Just as successful British industrial entrepreneurs found the appeal of country-house living, or "falling into the establishment," irresistible, their Chinese contemporaries too succumbed to the pressure of social conformity. This orthodoxy explains why Yangzhou's salt merchants failed to develop into a full-fledged capitalist system: they squandered their wealth in a vainglorious attempt to acquire books, art, and other affectations of the truly cultured.[5] Recent scholarship, however, would argue that commercial capitalism prospered to the extent it did with the internalization of Confucianism, leading to the emergence of the Confucian merchant *(rushang)* or the way of the merchant *(gudao)*.[6] Either way, "Confucianism" played a crucial role.

This chapter examines the sybaritic culture spawned by the salt merchants of Tianjin: a social reality and self-fashioning at odds with the dominant Confucian paradigm of self-cultivation.[7] A reconstruction of the family history of the Zhangs and the Zhas, two leading eighteenth-century Changlu salt merchant households, reveals a two-pronged strategy: political networking and cultural entrepreneurship. If the salt merchants' garden parties, poetry clubs, and cultivation of the realm's leading literati seemed extravagant, such activities might also be sound investments. Their selected guests gave them access to high places, the latest policy changes, and the emperor's intentions —all of which might affect their fortunes. To be sure, the strategy carried considerable risks if they became entangled in the factional struggles among these powerful people or suffered condemnation by self-righteous guardians of the Confucian orthodoxy. But the promise of returns was huge.

As part of their cultural entrepreneurship, the salt merchants' sponsorship of parades (see Chapter 5), operatic performances, cricket fights, and other fashion-setting activities also shaped Tianjin's vibrant urban culture and identity. Merchants and commoners alike evolved their orthopraxy from the stories they encountered on widely circulated woodblock prints from Yangliuqing (or heard in opera and drama banned elsewhere).[8] Percussion music such as *yangge, lianhuale,* and clapper-accompanied opera *(bangzi),* as well as current tunes *(shidiao)* performed by professional male and female artists, found a receptive audience. Much to the chagrin of the proper and the official, such performances reveal that these lowly urban residents, including the salt merchants, were actively constructing their culture. "High" and "low" negotiated over a lingering gulf of status and attitude.

## Lifestyle of the Rich and Notorious

The Changlu salt merchants were certainly guilty of hedonism and extravagance. Their flaunting of wealth, haughty daily routines, religious practices, and sponsorship of popular performances of lewd songs and operas fueled the growth of an urban sybaritic culture.[9] Like their Yangzhou counterparts, they compensated for their social humiliation with conspicuous consumption on a grand scale.[10] In 1737, Zha Li and his entourage thoroughly enjoyed their excursion to the Haiguangsi (Temple of the Oceanic Influence) about a mile south of the city. From the temple's tower, he admired a flooded Tianjin and enlivened at nightfall the dreary scene for its embattled residents by releasing thousands of floating lanterns (shuideng).[11] Such spectacles, however, paled when compared to those of his distant relative Youqi who, according to one source, was once fined 800,000 taels for bribing the guards of Zhengyangmen, the main southern gate of Beijing, to overlook his curfew violation. Equally notorious were the thousands of taels he lavished on twelve maids for the exclusive purpose of serving his meals. Immortalized in a Beijing opera, his extravagant displays captured the popular imagination.[12]

The salt merchants' block-sized mansions are neglected today, but signs of their former grandeur survive. Surrounded by high walls of elaborately hand-carved bricks, a mansion's front compound housed accounting offices, servants' quarters, and kitchens. Beyond was a maze of interconnected compounds, one for each of the married male offspring.[13] Separate quarters housed maids, chefs, and other servants, in addition to musicians, gardeners, and handlers of opium pipes, crickets, goldfish, birds, and other exotic pets for the masters' entertainment. In season, family and friends frequently staged cricket fights and their wagers were publicized throughout the city.[14] Tea salons, theaters, bath houses, restaurants, and expensive brothels were all concentrated conveniently at Houjiahou where merchants held court.[15]

From their opulent daily life to annual festivities, many salt merchants pursued extravagance with a vengeance. Breakfast was served at two in the afternoon, a schedule befitting a grand household (dajiafan). Birthdays, marriages, and funerals were sumptuous affairs that created traffic jams and kept the city abuzz. The sixtieth birthday celebration of the Feng family's matriarch in 1890 took months of preparation and lasted for days with porcelain commissioned from the kilns of Jingdezhen; opera troupes, acrobats, singers, and magicians from Beijing entertained the guests.[16] To serve their demand, Tianjin developed a whole line of service industries from catering to furniture rental.[17] Dowry and bridal gifts were paraded around the city by porters wearing uniforms borrowed from the Imperial

Procession Guards—inviting in one case sarcastic comment from the crowd that the newlyweds had everything they needed except a pair of coffins.[18]

In death, too, the salt merchants entertained their fellow citizens.[19] Professional funeral managers served both the dead and the living with an eye toward enhancing the household's stature within the community.[20] Well-heeled relatives and associates engaged Buddhist monks, nuns, Taoist priests, and lamas (a must for the really rich) from Beijing to perform daily services, sometimes lasting for weeks, to ensure safe passage for the departed. Mile-long funeral processions provided pomp rivaling that of the Heavenly Consort's annual parade. The coffin, however, might remain unburied for years and be set afloat every time the city was flooded, much to the horror of public health advocates and those beholden to filial piety as a cardinal virtue.[21]

From the Confucian perspective, the salt merchants' religious practices, too, were decidedly wanting: an eclectic and practical potpourri of Buddhism, Taoism, local deities, and folk wisdom. Many of the rituals were performed by the women of the household, with regular offerings to popular deities such as the god of wealth, the Eight Immortals, and, leaving no stone unturned, obscure icons such as Mister Zhang or the household spirit (jiaxian).[22] To secure specific blessings, offerings were made to the Heavenly Consort, who performed double duty as the patron saint of sailors and sponsor of marital fertility. Not to be overlooked was her lady-in-waiting, Songzi Niangniang, who specialized in the delivery of male heirs. These religious practices suggest an overwhelming pragmatism not to be confused with an agnostic Confucianism.

Growing up amidst abundant wealth and distractions, sons of salt merchants not surprisingly found studying a chore. They would much rather spend time practicing with their neighborhood yangge troupe. In their memoirs, two generations of the Fengs recalled bitterly rote memorization of the Confucian Classics. Even when they expressed an interest in a practical business skill, such as the use of abacus, their learned teachers rebuffed them in no uncertain terms. An aspiring Confucian gentleman should not waste time on such a vulgar skill.[23]

## The Zhangs and the Zhas

To the highbrow, the salt merchants' petty-mindedness was only to be expected. What was unconscionable was their assault on the literati-official's prerogative as arbiters of culture and taste. The audacious among them even aspired to join the exalted ranks of scholar-officials. For such impertinence, they would pay dearly—as can be seen from the Zhangs and the Zhas.

## The Zhangs

The apical ancestor of the Zhangs migrated from Fengyang prefecture in Anhui to Hebei in 1371, settling first at Hejian and then Linyu. Early in the reign of the Shunzhi Emperor, Zhang Xiyin began the family's long social climb. His discreet biography portrays him as a resourceful farmer who brought peace to the community by cooperating with the Manchu garrison. Such skills made him a valued adviser to officials in Beijing. In 1661 he became the operator of the monopolies of Jizhou, Zunhua, Fengrun, Yutian, Sanhe, Xianghe, Baodi, and Pinggu in the Changlu Division. Two years later, he passed away leaving a seven-year old son, Zhang Lin, and a brother, Zhang Xishi, who continued the salt operation.[24]

Under Zhang Lin, a resourceful and capable stipend student according to a local gazetteer, the household continued its upwardly mobile journey. He entrusted the business to a manager and embarked upon a bureaucratic career as a secretary with the Board of Public Works. His years in the capital were notable not only for the steady promotions he received but also for his association with some of the realm's leading literati. His residence in Beijing, referred to variously as the "single-acre abode" (Yimuju) or "single-acre mound and pond" (Yimu shanchi), was the site of many garden parties attended by literary luminaries such as Jiang Chenying (1628–1699), whose erudition earned the Kangxi Emperor's admiration as one of the four learned commoners *(buyi)* of the realm.[25] By 1693, Zhang was a senior secretary at the Board of War. A string of provincial appointments followed. Despite a demotion in 1700 for mishandling famine relief in Shaanxi and negligence in supervising his subordinates in Anhui, he was appointed financial commissioner of Yunnan.[26]

Zhang Lin's dual career as an official and a salt merchant, however, finally caught up with him. In 1700, Mu Shen of the Office of Scrutiny impeached Zhang on the grounds of unfavorable public opinion *(yulun);* his sideline business as a salt merchant was unbecoming for an official. Details of the charges do not survive, but apparently they were severe enough for the Board of Personnel to recommend his dismissal.[27] Zhang retired to Tianjin as a salt merchant and a generous host. His many villas scattered about the city became renowned for their well-attended garden parties as well as their art and antique collections. Eminent literati paid him homage and served as his poet in residence, including Jiang Chenying, Wu Wen (1644–1704), and Zhao Zhishen (1662–1744).[28] His guest list contained other familiar literati of High Qing who also served at the Southern Study at one time or another: Zha Xiazhong (1650–1727) who also taught Zhang's sons (and Mingju's too), Mei Wending (1633–1721) the mathematician, and Fang Bao (1668–1749) the classical essayist.[29]

Service at the Southern Study, of course, was the dream of every aspiring literatus in the realm. As conceived by the Kangxi Emperor, it was to be his literary advisorate, far removed from the formal political process at the Grand Secretariat.[30] In daily contact with the emperor, however, the select few who served in the Southern Study acquired enormous influence. While not all the emperor's decrees were drafted there, secret memorials from trusted aides would be filed and read. As reported in the secret memorials of Wang Hongxu (1645–1723), any matter deemed important enough for the emperor's attention could be pursued: from the latest rumors in the capital to cases pending at the Censorate. Bypassing the usual bureaucratic channels, the sealed memorials, filed directly at the study, influenced the emperor without much public debate.[31] Members of the study became privy to the emperor's latest concerns and interests not to mention his dislikes—all invaluable intelligence to officials. Even high officials such as Mingju (1635–1708) received "debriefings" when Gao Shiqi (1645–1704), a charter member of the Southern Study, came off duty, while other seekers of information lined the alley outside.[32] Packing the study became a vital matter to rival court factions. In the words of Fang Bao, a veteran of its politics, the place was a war zone *(zengdi)*.[33]

Zhang Lin no doubt appreciated the importance of networking for his business. Mingju, a central figure in the political factionalism that plagued much of the Kangxi Emperor's reign, provided capital for the operation of the Chenzhou monopolies.[34] From the Imperial Household Department came 370,000 taels to operate the eight-district monopoly of Jizhou. (On the role of these loans in raising capital for the salt merchants, see Chapter 2.) He also led another syndicate, including his brother and Zha Richang (corporate name: Zha Tianxing, 1667–1741), for another 419,000-tael loan from the same source in 1704, allegedly facilitated by a 20,000-tael fee to Zha

Sheng (1650–1707), nephew of Xiazhong and yet another veteran of the Southern Study.[35]

Information, too, was crucial. Zhang Lin found out about his impending trouble when his sources at the Southern Study alerted him to the emperor's curiosity regarding a hoodlum named Li Xiu. Inspired by the Kangxi Emperor's query at the study, Wang Hongxu decided to investigate. He reported Li as the manager of Zhang Lin's salt operation, a vile character who frequented various government offices.[36] When he learned that the subjects of his investigation had become alarmed, a horrified Wang Hongxu begged the emperor to tighten security in the study to protect his intelligence operation.

Zhang Lin's strategy thus gave him access, but it also exposed him to the transitive law of the network: a friend of a friend warranted a warm reception; a foe's friend was fair game. His association with Mingju and the surrounding cast of literati made him a convenient target. Even after Mingju was dismissed as grand secretary in 1689, his rivalry with Songgotu's faction continued unabated in the race for succession among the imperial princes.[37] Li Guangdi (1642–1718), Songgotu's protégé, minced no words in expressing how he detested Mingju and his associates.[38]

It was also Li who, as governor-general of Zhili, impeached Zhang in 1705 on a charge of salt smuggling.[39] When local officials questioned Zhang Lin's salt operation, they allegedly were told to mind their own business. The capital for his operation, Zhang Lin admonished them, came from the Imperial Household Department. Although technically true—it was legally a loan, though his default might result in a loss for the emperor's personal purse, a responsibility no official would take—the claim nonetheless was an act of lèse-majesté. For these crimes Zhang Lin and his associates were sentenced to death and his properties, valued at close to 1 million taels, were confiscated.[40] But the emperor also overruled the recommendation of the Board of Punishment and ordered an indefinite stay of execution. He was even prepared to pardon them if they paid their debt in full within the year.[41]

What accounted for Kangxi's mercy toward Zhang Lin is not clear, although Zhang's investment in political networking might have borne fruit. Zha Tianxing, Zhang's business associate and codefendant, allegedly approached Zha Sheng for his intercession. Several days later, Sheng sent word that it was done and clemency was assured.[42] While local officials scrambled to locate more of Zhang

Lin's elusive assets, loyal visitors continued to visit him with dedicated poems: the last extant poem, dated 1709, was in honor of his pot of plum blossoms.[43]

## The Zhas

Cultural entrepreneurship in the form of art collections, garden parties, and poetry clubs thus doubled as a cover for political networking. The Zhas carried this two-pronged strategy to a new height by combining it with strategically selected marriages.

Zha Tianxing, whose father died when he was three, grew up poor.[44] Brought up by his brother-in-law, he found employment as a clerk at the Tianjin Customs Office, a highly lucrative hereditary post that resembled a partnership with seats readily bought and sold.[45] But Tianxing was not content with his lowly status as a member of the subbureaucracy. Before long he found himself implicated as one of Zhang Lin's associates in making illegal profits from salt smuggling and receiving improper loans from the Imperial Household Department. Owing some 210,000 taels against a net worth of 125,081 taels, he was jailed, convicted, and sentenced to death. Unlike Zhang Lin, however, he managed to repay all his loans. A fair-minded Kangxi even refunded a portion of the interest paid, reasoning that his ministers had unfairly collected interest for the entire eight-year term of a loan that had been repaid in full after only one year. Tianxing received a pardon and regained his freedom in 1709.[46]

If this brush with the law moderated Tianxing's ambition, it was not apparent in his subsequent behavior. Three years later he was again imprisoned on a charge of tampering with the civil service examination. According to the indictment, Zha engaged Shao Bo, already a *juren,* to take the Shuntian provincial examination in 1711 for Zha's eldest son, Weiren (1694–1749). The scheme was uncovered, not because the hired brush failed, but because of his startling success. "Zha Weiren" placed first in the examination—a surprise for someone rumored to be illiterate. Faced with the prospect of an investigation, father and son fled south to Shaoxing, Zhejiang, but were caught, tried, and sentenced to death in 1713. Unlike other salt merchants who were promptly executed for similar crimes in Jiangnan and Fujian in 1711, however, the Zhas were eventually pardoned.[47]

Again, how and why the course of justice was derailed in this case is unclear. Zhang Zhao's (1691–1745) preface to Weiren's poetry collection, "Poems from the Hut in the Shadow of Flowers" *(Huaying'an ji)*, offered a clue. A fellow *jinshi* named Zhao Houchi told Zhang that the chief censor, Zhao Shenqiao (1644–1720), felt responsible for Zha's predicament since he was the chief examiner for the class of 1711.[48] The case had allegedly been orchestrated by Tao the Affable, commander of the Imperial Guard, who spread rumors of bribery and influence peddling in the examination in order to punish Zhao for his reform of the copper procurement system and dismissal of two Changlu salt merchants.[49] If Zhao did help, it was eased by 20,000 taels of silver offered by Tianxing's wife to redeem her husband's crime.[50] The father was freed in 1718, and the son received a pardon in 1720.

Returning to Tianjin to pursue a strategy of cultural entrepreneurship and networking, father and son bought 100 *mu* of land 3 *li* west of the city and created the "Manor West of the River" (Shuixizhuang) with pavilions and buildings well stocked with antiques, paintings, and an impressive library.[51] A familiar cast of literati made up the Zhas' guest list. Zha Xiazhong considered Weiren his son and taught him the art of poetry. Xiazhong's younger brother Pu called Tianxing his brother and Shuixizhuang his "cozy nest" for two years after achieving a *jinshi* degree.[52] Leading poets such as Li E (1692–1752), Hang Shijun (1696–1772), Wan Guangtai (1712–1750), Wang Kang (b. 1704), and Fu Zeng all felt at home.[53] The manor's poem collection, printed under the title *Gushang tijinji* by Weiren, enjoyed brisk sales in South China. Weiren's reputation as a poet and scholar received another boost when Li E compared their notes on the "Masterpieces of Poems with Irregular Meter" *(Juemiao haoci)* and decided that Zha's annotation was superior; the work was eventually published as a joint effort.[54]

Celebrated as one of the three renowned gardens of the realm where the learned and scholarly converged, the manor became the focal point of the Zha network. Chen Yuanlong (1652–1736) dedicated an essay to it and composed poems admiring the exquisite gardens. After a distinguished career—which included service at the Southern Study with Zha Sheng, various boards, and the Grand Secretariat—Chen stopped at the manor to share fond reminiscences of childhood with Tianxing.[55] Chen's nephew, Chen Shiguan (1680–1757), then a vice-minister at the Board of Revenue, saluted Tianxing as an uncle and contributed an essay in honor of his seventieth birthday.[56]

Local officials, too, found the manor hospitable. Song Jing, the first magistrate of the Tianjin autonomous department *(zhilizhou)* when it was created in 1725, and Zhang Can, Changlu commissioner the same year, spent time at the manor exchanging poems.[57] Zhang's successor, Chen Shixia (d. 1738), honored Tianxing's second wife (née Wang) in an essay claiming almost two decades of friendship.[58] Another provincial official, Chen Pengnian (1663–1723) of Hunan, introduced to the family by Zha Xiazhong and Zha Pu, contributed a preface to Weiren's poetry collection.[59] During his tenure as a sub-prefectural magistrate of Tianjin in charge of river conservation, Yinglian (1707–1783), the future grand secretary and grandfather of Heshen (1750–1799), frequently called on the many poets in residence and exchanged poems with the hosts.[60] Chen Yi, the hydraulic engineer in charge of Tianjin's reclamation, proclaimed proudly that he knew Tianxing better than anyone.[61]

All these literary luminaries, however, lost their lustre when the realm's chief patron of the arts, the Qianlong Emperor himself, visited the manor in 1748 and found it an agreeable place. Such an extraordinary honor, of course, carried a price: the Zhas felt obliged to relinquish part of the manor to the throne. Renamed the Mustard Garden by Qianlong in 1771, it became a shrine to his presence, not to be used by other men, however rich and powerful.

In return, the Zhas attained what they wanted: a measure of immortality, if not respectability. Their name became a synonym for wealth in the local dialect, as in Kuo ("Wide") Zha.[62] Degrees in the civil service examination followed, with the Zhas claiming the city as their domicile.[63] Weiren's younger brother Weiyi (1700–1763) served as a subprefectural prefect in South China but soon retired to Tianjin as a salt merchant, poet, amateur painter, and activist in local public affairs.[64] The youngest brother, Zha Li (1715–1782), became a senior secretary in the Board of Revenue in 1748, received commendations for his role in the campaign against the Great and Small Jinchuan rebels, and capped his career as governor of Hunan in 1782.[65] His son Chun was a judiciary commissioner of Hubei. Each of the four generations after Tianxing produced at least one *jinshi* or *juren*.[66] The family's long-standing tie with the Haining Chens was reinforced when Weiren's son Shanhe married a daughter of Chen Bangxian, a *jinshi*, a renowned calligrapher, and a veteran of the Southern Study who served the Qianlong Emperor as a vice-minister of the Board of Rites.[67] The household's fortune was safe at last.

## Risks and Benefits

Successful as the Zhangs and the Zhas were, their strategy, whether articulated as literati affectations or networking, certainly risked ridicule and resentment from proper society. Zhu Tongyi's claim to fame among his fellow literati came at the expense of Zhang Lin: rejection of Zhang's invitations, contempt for Zhang's poetry, and his own abject poverty.[68]

If local literati found the salt merchants' "copper stench" and literary affectations offensive, the highborn disapproved of their networking culture as corrupting cultivation (zuanying). Prince Li chided officials and fellow aristocrats for associating with the Zhas.[69] Time and again high officials blemished their careers as a result of their ties to the salt merchants. After years on the waiting list, the appointment of Zha Youqi (Zha Sheng's great-grandson and one of the biggest Changlu merchants of the time under the corporate name of Jianggongyuan) as a secretary at the Board of Revenue in 1807 prompted a bureaucratic battle and policy review. The rule of avoidance—long enforced in the provinces to avoid potential conflict of interest among officials related to each other through kinship—had hitherto been waived for officials serving in the capital, but Dai Quheng (1755–1811), then minister of the board, was Zha's relative by marriage. The Board of Personnel proposed that the rule should also apply in the capital, and new regulations were promulgated accordingly to distinguish among various kinds and degrees of relationship. The emperor concurred. And finding the kinship ties generated by marriage (ernu yinqin) potentially compromising, he decreed that Zha should be reassigned to the Board of Punishment to await an appropriate vacancy.[70]

The censor Hua Jie, however, thought that the ties between Zha and Dai were not merely compromising but criminal. In 1809, he charged that Youqi, protected by Dai, conspired to withhold the required security deposit to the Imperial Household Department. In his arrogance, Zha had also demeaned the dignity of state office by having three grand secretaries serve as receptionists during his mother's funeral. The charges against Dai were even more serious: conspiracy to manipulate the results of the metropolitan examination, abuse of his authority at the Board of Revenue, and attempting to pack the Southern Study with his students and associates. When the emperor's own investigation yielded little evidence of wrongdoing,

Hua Jie was demoted for filing groundless charges. But the exposure of Dai's myriad ties had derailed his career. To avoid a conflict of interest with his uncle Dai Junyuan, then serving as director-general of the Capital Granaries, he was demoted to the Board of Public Works.[71]

Zha Youqi escaped this investigation relatively unscathed. But as someone deeply entangled in bureaucratic politics, he remained a vulnerable target. In 1812 Li Zongchao, another censor rumored to bear a grudge against Zha for having been denied a substantial bribe, indicted him on a charge of tampering with the weights issued by the Board of Revenue. Even though there was no evidence of Zha's direct involvement in this conspiracy, investigators concluded that, as the biggest operator in the division, he stood to benefit most from the tampering. For his negligence he was fined 455,652 taels—five times the profit he made from the extra salt packed. With his deep pockets, however, Zha paid in full the penalty two months ahead of schedule and escaped banishment. Seven years later, he even recovered the title of rank 6 official by donating 30,000 taels of silver toward emergency flood relief and continued as a Changlu salt merchant.[72]

The salt merchants' experience demonstrated that their riches made them tempting targets. Being wealthy and well connected, however, helped them to manage those risks and facilitated their recovery from temporary setbacks. The Zhangs capitalized on Zhang Lin's network when his great-grandson, Yingtou, called on Fang Bao the classical essayist at Tongcheng. Fang, whose distinguished career at the Southern Study and civil service had come to an abrupt end when his letters requesting favors on behalf of others became public, obliged the nineteen-year-old with an introduction: "Presenting herewith the grandson of Zhang Lin."[73] Although brief, it was adequate. Yingtou continued his journey, visiting relatives and his grandfather's old acquaintances, and collected enough support to rebuild the household's fortune. Under the able management of his salt merchant brother, Yingchen, the household prospered. Yingtou's son Hubai brought honor to himself and the household as a *juren* in 1768, a *jinshi* in 1769, and a commissioner of education in Henan.[74]

To dismiss the salt merchants' literary affectations as mere replication of the "high culture" practiced by literati-officials is to miss not only the complex phenomenon of networking but also the broad social and political implications of their cultural entrepreneurship. The costly garden parties, poetry clubs, and expensive art collections could be sound investments. Leading literati of the realm on their way to and from Beijing for the civil service examinations, or seeking the patronage of the emperor and high officials, were received with great honor and hospitality by the salt merchants. When men like Zha Xiazhong entered government service, these investments would be repaid many times over. Approachable as old acquaintances, they became an invaluable source of information placed at the highest level. While extending the salt merchants' reach beyond the city, the presence of these nationally renowned literati also broke the hegemonic hold of Tianjin's scholar-officials on the local cultural scene and added another dimension to the negotiation between culture and class.

## Urban Culture and Identity

In entertaining themselves and their fellow citizens, the salt merchants' patronage of popular opera and tunes that formed the core of Tianjin's urban culture confirms what their critics had long been saying: despite all the affectations, the impression of Confucianism on the salt merchants was only skin deep.[75] Of the 622 such compositions collected by a mid-eighteenth-century Tianjin artist, twenty-five celebrated dynastic peace and prosperity and three promoted filial piety —themes the high-minded would approve. Another fifty-eight were drawn from poetic dramas and short stories *(chuanqi)*, such as "West-Wing Romance" ("Xixiangji") and the "Water Margins" ("Shuihuizhuan"), which were banned elsewhere in the empire.[76] The remaining two-thirds of the collection dealt with puerile themes: fantasizing an affair, a female yearning for the return of her beloved merchant, and other explicit expressions of passion.[77] The five titles describing the loneliness of a supposedly celibate nun were probably even more offensive to keepers of public morals.[78] When female singers began to appear on stage in the late nineteenth century, their performances were repeatedly banned.[79]

The songs also exhibited a hedonistic, commercial, and urban bias at odds with a Confucianism that recognized no distinction between rural and urban. In "A Chaste Yellow Basket Keeping Me Company," a girl laments being born into a poor rural family. Selling her embroidery in the city, she longs for a marriage that will allow her to enjoy all the pleasures of urban life as befits her beauty.[80] An ill-prepared daughter-in-law from the countryside who knows little beyond tending the fields finds her mother-in-law condescending.[81] Songs advocating "nothing is better than a cup of wine in my hand" or "seek great fortunes" offered audiences alternatives to the exacting demands for moral self-cultivation.[82]

The salt merchants' sponsorship of festivals that drew crowds from the surrounding districts to celebrate the birthday of the Heavenly Consort in the third month, or the city god's annual inspection tour in the fourth month, espoused similar themes as well as enhancing the city's identity.[83] No silver was spared in their quest for public recognition. One salt merchant acquired the finest silk from Nanjing's imperial mill, dyed blood red with *honghua (Carthamus tinctorius)* from Xinjiang, for bier pole covers and a parasol, so that no one could miss the priceless green jade ring on his thumb as he paraded through the city with the Heavenly Consort. Others financed their neighborhood's entry in the parades or vied for the honor of contributing the tallest incense tower.[84]

The Changlu merchants' collective contribution of eight richly decorated floats (*taige,* or "pavilion borne on poles") through the Changlu Syndicate was a fixture of the parade. Each float depicted a theme in popular folk drama: the first float, as befitted the occasion, portrayed the Eight Immortals presenting birthday gifts. Following were scenes from stories such as "Water Margins," "Journey to the West," "Legend of the White Serpent," or "Zhongkuai Marrying Off His Sister"—all questioning the nature of justice and morality of the existing order and for those reasons banned elsewhere.[85] "Legend of the White Serpent," for instance, began during the Tang dynasty as a love story between Bei Niangzi, a serpent assuming human form, and Xu Xian. As literati added embellishments, weaving in Fa Hai the monk, it evolved into a tragedy pitting morality against love. Fa Hai persuades Xu to leave, has Bei imprisoned under the Luifeng pagoda, and morality triumphs at the expense of love and the audience's sympathy.[86] While the salt merchants might not be consciously challenging the cultural hegemony and moral positions of the scholar-official elite, their sponsorship of such performances promoted social criticism through a culture of laughter à la Bakhtin. Just as a stunning "Green Serpent," female companion to the White Serpent in the legend, makes an enchanted literatus a laughingstock of the witnessing crowd ("she" turns out to be an old man), beauty, indeed, depends on the beholder.[87]

Other participants in the parade made their discontent explicit:

> Between heaven and earth, the human world is
> Replete with imperfection.
> While the poor suffer
> The rich hoard their gold. . . .
> The learned fail their civil service examination
> Yet the incompetent become high officials. . . .
> How could this be so?[88]

Instead of accepting things as they were, these urban dwellers asked what should be and established, however fleetingly, an altered social structure.

Under the cover of the festivities, the "Sincere Carry-On Official Society" (Chengyi Kangxiang Guanshenghui) inside the South Gate went even further in mocking official pomposity with placards announcing the approach of "officials": "Acting Magistrate of Meigui [Rose] District" and "Magistrate of Tianjiang [Sweet Paste] Department," followed by a buffoon, dressed in official garb, administering justice atop a camel.[89] The citizens of Tianjin might not be highly educated, but they had something to say about the world around them. Where Confucianism did not provide an answer, or at least a satisfactory answer, these otherwise inarticulate urbanites communicated in their own language and sought approval from their fellow citizens through the parades. In short, this aspect of urban popular culture took on a life of its own.

Both the dazzling high society of poetry clubs, garden parties, art collections, and associations with literati and officials, as well as the "low culture" public spectacles they mounted, were the salt merchants' response to the forces that shaped their outlook, business, and world. In the attempt to gain respectability and ensure their continued prosperity, the salt merchants' networking and cultural entrepreneurship brought together the bureaucracy, economy, and society. Though their villas might be under the shadow of state offices, the salt merchants created in their banquets and poetry parties access to the powerful. The investment was costly, the risks were great, but the return could be spectacular.

Besides flaunting their wealth, the salt merchants' cultural entrepreneurship had implications beyond entertaining their fellow citizens and visitors. Their festivals, cutting across class and space, mobilized urban and suburban neighborhoods alike. Their participation and support in parades encouraged the citizens to work together, contributing to the growth of Tianjin's community spirit. Under the cover of the festive mood, some delivered their critique of society inviting the audience's comments and participation. Far from being mere passive receivers of "high culture," these urbanites were negotiating, transacting, and constructing their own culture and identity.

# 5.
# SOCIAL SERVICES

Beginning in the seventeenth century, Tianjin's salt merchants became increasingly active in a broad range of urban social services. Not only did they fund road construction, city wall maintenance, soup kitchens, orphanages, and fire brigades, but they eventually operated the city's academies and militias. Interpreting this development has stirred considerable debate. Some scholars see a "Confucian public-mindedness" at work.[1] The weakness of this argument is that while Confucianism has indeed been influential in Chinese history since the Han dynasty, if not earlier, organized private philanthropy of the type discussed here dates from the Song dynasty. While the salt merchants' ethical standards were undoubtedly informed by Confucianism (or at least a vulgar version of it), Buddhism and Taoism were also important influences.

A more mundane, if not cynical, explanation might focus on the love/hate relationship between the salt merchants and their fellow citizens. As noted in the previous chapter, the salt merchants often invested in an extravagant lifestyle. Indeed, their pretensions to poetry, learning, and the arts intruded upon the scholars' domain and the local literati establishment loved to scorn them. In the eyes of the poor and the needy, it was tainted profits that built their opulent mansions. Generous donations and an active interest in local public charities and services, in this view, might be the means to acquire respectability and social acceptance.

Habermasian concepts of the public sphere and civil society enrich as well as complicate our effort to understand the salt merchants'

public life. While not mutually exclusive of the perspectives just outlined, this approach emphasizes the resemblance of late imperial
China to the early modern European experience of an increasingly
active urban bourgeoisie fighting for autonomy from the state. Pressed
by domestic rebellion, foreign invasion, and financial crisis, Tianjin's
local elites who had been involved in informal governance expanded
the range of their services. Although more of the same may not con-
stitute a fundamental change in the nature of Chinese society, a weak-
ened Qing state does suggest a replication of the idealized European
model of a zero-sum game, if not confrontation, between state and
society.[2]

Tianjin's experience, however, suggests yet another social process
at work: the emergence of merchant-gentry as a social category. To
be sure, the state's official presence remained in this region without
rich and responsible elites, especially in administering large-scale
disaster relief, but the merchants' passive participation in early and
high Qing gave way to more voluntary activism when the Qing state
was rocked by internal rebellion and foreign threats in the nineteenth
century. In a city of immigrants with many of the scholar-gentry themselves recent settlers, the merchants' domicile status was not an issue.[3]
The Changlu salt merchants supplemented many of the services performed by the state—disaster relief, social services, and urban infra-
structure (roads, firefighting, city wall maintenance) especially during
and after the Taiping Rebellion—and expanded into new territories
such as militias and local education.

This is not to argue, however, that the salt merchants were pitted
against the state at the local level, much less at a national level. While
their activism may have eclipsed local scholar-gentry who lacked the
necessary economic resources, the salt merchants' activities and extensive networks reinforced the dynasty by stabilizing local society in
a turbulent time. The relationship between state and salt merchants
remained symbiotic; nor was the merchants' expanding influence
achieved without guidance or control from above. As subjects, the
merchants continued to observe the law and proper procedures by
registering (li'an or zhai'an) their organizations. While this coexpan-
sion of state and society may not be a distinctively Chinese phenomenon, it did lay the foundation for a network of local commercial
elites engaged in social activities traditional and new—an activism that
the state, local officials, and scholar-gentry might find destabilizing,
if not an actual threat, to their authority and hegemony.[4]

## Disaster Relief

Disaster relief for Tianjin had long been part of the state's responsibility.[5] The city, as discussed in Chapter 1, was particularly vulnerable to floods, but they were not the only ills to affect it. The district reported calamities in at least 150 of the Qing dynasty's reign of 267 years: floods (114), droughts (20), locusts, and ravages of war, not to mention the periodic fires that swept the city. According to the severity of the disaster, the state provided assistance in the form of land tax deferments (forty-six times); a combination of deferment and waiver, waiver only, deferment and relief (fifty-one times); and efforts involving substantial outlays of cash, grain, and, by special decree, padded jackets (forty-nine times).[6]

This state activism is all the more impressive in the context of a much criticized bureaucracy. Although Tianjin's proximity to the capital and the large number of officials traveling through it on the way to or from Beijing made disaster reports difficult to suppress, a stringent bureaucratic procedure did not help: reports of disaster had to be on record by the sixth month in the summer and the ninth month in the fall. Operating under tight deadlines, with meager resources and strict requirements for surveying and verification, officials reported natural calamities with great reluctance.[7] The burden was so severe, indeed, that some risked their careers by not reporting marginal, or even verifiable, cases.[8]

State disaster relief was further marred by corruption and ineptitude. Throughout the Qing period, high officials and scholars steeped in the so-called statecraft tradition warned that local subbureaucracies must be excluded from relief operations. Relying on yamen runners and village headmen who received little or no remuneration from the state made matters worse.[9] Indeed, even when relief or tax deferments had been granted, unscrupulous officials and runners might continue collecting taxes—or neglect to apply taxes already collected toward future dues—all to line their own pockets.[10] Embezzling disaster relief funds was not unheard of, and criticisms were frequent.[11] An indignant Mei Chengdong left a poem dated 1820 condemning callous officials who kept a crowd waiting for padded jackets until thirteen people were crushed to death. In 1877, more than a thousand refugees were injured and a hundred died when a government-operated gruel kitchen caught fire and officials fled the scene leaving the gates locked.[12]

Privatization of relief efforts was thus deemed an acceptable, if not necessary, solution. Interference by officials was explicitly forbidden, and state policy encouraged the wealthy to donate by granting plaques in their honor and, on occasion, titles. Provincial governors became involved officially only when they audited the ledgers to confirm the donor's eligibility for guerdon.[13] The state did not, however, remove itself from the field entirely. Even in the late nineteenth century, when it was in dire financial straits, the state remained the only agency capable of organizing and providing sustained relief for large-scale natural calamities like the great North China drought of 1876–1879.[14] In the provision of emergency and disaster relief, private citizens and the state cooperated in a division of labor.

## Urban Social Services

The division of labor between state and local society was institutionalized along rural and urban lines. State relief operations excluded residents of market towns and cities unless specifically authorized by imperial decree.[15] Urban areas, with their economies based on commerce, presumably would be able to recover from drought or floods on their own. When the state did fund and operate urban welfare institutions—orphanages and homes for the old and widowed—such services were limited in scale. Homes for the sick and needy of Tianjin prefecture and district could offer assistance to only sixty and forty-four persons respectively.[16] Even then local officials might not make good use of the meager resources available to them. During his four-year tenure as circuit intendant from 1862 to 1865, Li Tongwen ignored his relatives' raid on the orphanage (Yuyingtang) endowment every year but one.[17]

Following its policy in the countryside, the state accommodated, if not encouraged, privatization to remedy this neglect of urban social services: soup kitchens; free burials; orphanages; homes for the old, infirm, and widowed.[18] Table 1 summarizes the data by periods coinciding with the dynasty's rise, heyday, and decline and by categories of initiative. In the absence of ledgers and other records, it is impossible to measure and compare relative contributions and the number of people served. But one thing is undeniable: while the involvement of the state, officials, and scholar-gentry continued, merchants, especially the Changlu merchants, became increasingly active in initiating, financing, and operating such services.

Table 1. Urban Service Initiatives by State and Society

| Period | State | Scholar-Gentry | Merchant |
|--------|-------|----------------|----------|
| 1644–1684 | 2 | 4 | 3 |
| 1685–1797 | 17 | 6 | 24 |
| 1798–1911 | 16 | 5 | 43 |
| Total | 35 | 15 | 70 |

Source: Kwan (1999: 271–286)

There were many reasons for the merchants' public service, beginning with their business interest. In 1736, as a form of social welfare, the Qianlong Emperor offered some of Tianjin's poor the privilege of peddling tax-free salt.[19] Those eligible had to be local residents, over sixty or under fifteen years of age, disabled, or elderly women without family support. Duly verified by neighbors and registered with the local government, they would be issued a waist tag (yaopai)—hence the term "tag salt" (paiyan)—entitling them to buy up to 40 jin of salt at the yard each day. To prevent abuse of this privilege, they had to carry the salt on foot. In practice, however, this well-intentioned "workfare" was compromised by enforcement problems. Updating the roster as the old passed away and the young came of age required constant vigilance by local officials. And the tags could be misused: carrying several days worth of accumulated salt by wheelbarrow, for example, or letting a family member or friend use the tag on behalf of the old, infirm, or otherwise disabled rightful holder. Fewer than seven hundred tags were issued for Tianjin, but the peddlers purchased over 31,000 yin each year—an amount far surpassing the statutory quota of 700 yin for the district. Alarmed by the great number of smuggling cases pending—Tianjin alone had more cases than Zhili and Henan provinces combined—the Changlu commissioner petitioned in 1752 to end the practice. In return, the salt merchants volunteered to subsidize each tag holder 24 copper cash per day.[20]

The substitution of private charity for the tag privilege did not merely improve the salt merchants' hold on the market: it also enhanced their reputation as compassionate and caring citizens, a bargain not lost to these astute businessmen. Thus merchant princes such as the Lis acquired the sobriquet "Philanthropist" as befitting their generosity and wealth.[21] It was also sound public relations for them to perform public services in their monopoly districts. Feng Xuezhang, part owner of the salt monopoly at Zhuozhou, not only endowed a mutual aid society (Tongji Shantang) but was elected its general manager. Overcoming a hostile local magistrate who denied even requests for office space, Feng raised 600 yuan from fellow salt merchants in Tianjin to assist flood victims ignored by the official.[22]

## Firefighting

Such activism was also born of necessity. Although firefighting was the duty of local government, since the Song dynasty private citizens had increasingly defended their own properties.[23] In Tianjin, this tradition began with Wu Tingyu, a salt merchant who donated fire engines and organized the Tongshan brigade *(shuihui)* early in the reign of the Kangxi Emperor. Following his example, Meng Gouli, the Changlu supervisor, donated four fire engines and laid the foundation for a citywide network of fire brigades, including Zha Tianxing's (see Chapter 4) Shangshan brigade.[24]

By the late nineteenth century, Tianjin's voluntary fire companies were lauded as among the best-organized in the realm.[25] Alarms were relayed by gongs *(chuanluo,* "stringing the gongs"); the companies and separate crews responsible for clearing fire lanes and hauling water mobilized along the gong route *(luodao).* The social composition of the firefighters *(wushan,* or "martial crew," who trained together regularly) and supporting crews *(wenshan)* is not clear, but the ranks were mostly ruffians *(hunhunr)* and transport workers under their control.[26]

Receiving little support from the state, accepting only snacks for their services, the fire companies cooperated to raise funds from the public, especially the salt merchants. Each spring and autumn, the public Bureau for Fire Companies (Shuihui Gongsuo) and the chiefs of the fire companies, some hailing from the ranks of the so-called gowned ruffians *(paodai hunhunr,* or *hunhunr* who had accumulated enough wealth or influence to become neighborhood leaders), would lead a citywide donation drive through a banquet with opera performances for the firefighters and donors. Any surplus would go toward new equipment as well as maintenance of the stations and the public bureau. The Changlu salt merchants collectively contributed at least 1,000 taels each year in addition to sponsoring their neighborhood company.[27]

While complaints of extortionary demands by these "volunteers" are not unknown, Tianjin's residents did not question their loyalty to their turf and, by extension, the city. Stories of their valor fed local pride: how firefighters chased away "barbaric" Ningbo sailors in 1850 and 1853, for example, and taught good manners to unruly Anhui soldiers.[28]

By the late nineteenth century, then, the city was served by privately organized and funded charitable institutions so extensive that a local paper boasted that Tianjin was second to none in the realm.[29] Minimally supervised and regulated by the state, these private agencies—whether a result of state-sanctioned privatization, the salt merchants' desire for respectability and good public relations, or an impulse of urban self-help—brought Tianjin's residents together to overcome calamities and contributed to the city's viability as a community.

## The City's Militia

This community spirit furnished the foundation for merchant activism in September 1853, when the Northern Expeditionary Force of the Taipings advanced toward Tianjin.[30] Manchu forces were in disarray, the treasury was empty, and the city's garrison could muster only eight hundred men, the bulk having been transferred south to Jiangnan.[31] In desperation the emperor entrusted the task of organizing the city's militia defense to the highest-ranking (and presumably most loyal) local scholar-gentry: Liang Baochang, a retired governor-general of Guangdong and Guangxi. He and his associates began to help themselves to the funding, however, and posters soon appeared to denounce them for embezzlement.[32]

Without the scholar-gentry initiatives and leadership found elsewhere, Tianjin residents had to fend for themselves. The salt merchants of Changlu, led by Zhang Jinwen (1795–1875), quickly recruited whatever manpower was available. Firefighters and prisoners, many of them *hunhunr*, were mobilized.[33] At his own expense, Zhang recruited a thousand workers to construct barricades and put his son in command of a reserve of 180 men. From snacks to hot peppers (vital in bolstering the morale of the garrison from Sichuan), Zhang managed the campaign's logistics. He was credited with supplying the Manchu relief force with ammunition, firearms, binoculars, and rotating cannon mounts more mobile than those issued by the

Board of War. In preparation for the city's defense, no silver was spared, no details missed—including two piculs of garlic to protect against Taiping witchcraft.[34]

The motives behind Zhang's exemplary voluntarism remain murky.[35] He began as a a kitchen helper for Linqing (1791–1846). Recognizing his many talents, Linqing entrusted Zhang with the wealth he had amassed in his long bureaucratic career—a career that included the commissionership of the Grand Canal, reportedly one of the most lucrative in the realm.[36] With Linqing's backing, Zhang, under the corporate name of "Yizhaolin," had acquired the monopolies of Anyang, Linxian, Tangyin, Qixian, Fangshan, Liang-xiang, and Linzhang and, under the corporate name "Qingdefeng," the monopolies of Wen'an and Baoding by 1865.[37] When the Tai-pings threatened Tianjin, Wenqian, Linqing's son-in-law, was the Changlu commissioner. By the time the Taiping withdrew, Zhang (or Linqing) had contributed 39,000 strings of copper cash for the cause. This generosity earned Chonghou (1826–1893), Linqing's son, the right to wear a peacock feather on his official's cap.[38]

Perhaps it was his close relationship with officials that made Zhang such a loyal and generous subject. In any case, the fact that it was the salt merchants, not the scholar-gentry, who came through with finan-cial and material support at this critical moment for the dynasty sug-gests that, for better or for worse, this was a society in flux. Which-ever version of his background we accept, the resourceful Zhang became indispensable to the city's officials during the crisis of the Second Opium War. By his own account, he was in Wen'an district tending to his business when a letter from the circuit intendant, the prefect, and the magistrate of Tianjin urged his immediate return. News had come from Shanghai that an Anglo-French expeditionary force had set sail for Tianjin to open negotiations. Mindful, perhaps, of Canton's success in rebuffing foreign demands by a demonstration of popular sentiment, the court directed Zhang Hua Shu and Bei Yin-zhang, a circuit intendant on home leave, to organize a militia. In a dispute over who should be in charge, however, Zhang organized his own Merchants and Shopkeepers Militia on April 19, 1858. To over-come apathy and fear, he had his militia officially designated for Tianjin's defense alone and declared it would not be deployed else-where. At the beating of a drum, 2,400 of his men from sixty-four wards of the city and suburbs would assemble to defend the city.[39]

The sudden collapse of the Qing forces, however, kept the militia

from ever being tested in battle. Described by the invaders as "orna-
mented pastry," the Dagu forts—toward the reinforcement of which
Zhang had contributed 14,000 strings of copper cash—fell after two
hours of heavy fighting on May 20. Leaving behind a poem dedicated
to his wife (and leaving Tianjin to its own resources), the governor-
general fled. As the invaders cautiously made their way up the
Haihe, Zhang and his associates kept order in the panic-stricken city.
When eight foreign gunboats finally arrived on May 25, Zhang sent
his associates, gifts and supplies in tow, to plead for the city and
resumption of trade.

During the monthlong negotiations for the Treaty of Tianjin,
Zhang's militia bureau saw to all the daily needs of the foreigners—
from arranging lodging and beds to supplying straw hats and sedan
chairs complete with bearers. Even though he held no official position, Zhang again discharged his responsibilities admirably, receiving
compliments from the invaders.[40] Spurning other salt merchants'
offers of help and halfhearted offers of reimbursement, Zhang spent
more than 35,000 taels of silver by the time the foreigners departed.[41]
Already entitled to the regalia of a rank 2 official—the highest available for purchase—Zhang did not seek promotion nor was he interested in an official appointment. Instead, he impertinently asked for
a piece of calligraphy by the imperial hand, a request that was un-
gratefully ignored. Zhang had to settle for a votive tablet sent by the
governor-general of Zhili.[42]

Late Qing international diplomacy, however, provided ample opportunities for Zhang to prove his indispensability. The foreign
powers were due back for the ratification of the treaty in 1859, but a
determined Xianfeng Emperor directed the Mongolian general Senggerinchin to prepare for war. On the second day of the Chinese New
Year, anxious local officials again asked Zhang to mobilize his militia.
Now 2,700 strong, it maintained order in the city. Anyone who looked
suspicious was arrested and interrogated. The Dagu forts were rebuilt
and the Haihe closed to traffic. Later in the year, the Anglo-French
delegation returned as promised and, although offered an alternate
route to Beijing via Beitang, insisted on the route they had taken the
year before. This time, however, their cannons proved inadequate
and they were forced to retreat. The Changlu salt merchants contributed 2,000 taels for Senggerinchin's troops. Zhang himself donated
10,000 taels, 5,000 catties of explosives, and uniforms for the soldiers.[43]

War was now inevitable. Construction of an outer wall, "Senggerinchin's Folly," was proposed, and the state made it clear who should pay: "Gentry members and the rich must give all they can. . . . Anyone who ignores the call, or dares to defy repeated official orders, or fails to make payment, will be charged with deliberate obstruction of defenses, for which no leniency will be granted."[44] Senggerinchin was even more explicit in his order to local officials: "Discard all sentiments and impress upon the gentry, the rich, merchants and commoners alike, the urgency of this matter. . . . If any of them dares procrastinate, they will be arrested and impeached. Make this clear so that they cannot claim they have not been warned."[45]

These threats produced the desired result. The total subscription came to 31,980 taels and 4,400 strings of copper cash; Zhang alone contributed 1,000 taels.[46] The Mongolian general was even more impressed by Zhang's idea for the construction of makeshift batteries: filling with sand the straw-mat sacks used to transport salt. Once again Zhang proved resourceful, earning himself immortality in the form of a Tianjin proverb: "Hai Zhangwu building batteries—no big deal" ("Hai Zhangwu xiu paotai—xiaoshi yiduan").

The euphoria of victory, however, was short-lived. The 30,000-strong Anglo-French Expeditionary Force returned, overcame the coastal defenses, stormed the city, and marched on to Beijing, forcing the emperor to flee.[47] Once again Zhang helped maintain law and order in the city as well as provisioning the foreigners. When a desperate court in Beijing ordered Zhang's militia to attack the 10,000-man foreign garrison left behind to secure Dagu, he advised local officials to ignore the decree. To attack such a superior force with his men would be suicidal, and a violation of the promise that his militia was strictly for the city's defense.[48] Despite this willful disobedience, Zhang was not charged for treason but was summoned instead for an audience with Prince Gong in the capital.

Zhang again proved his worth. On several occasions he served as an intermediary between the Qing state and the foreign diplomats. Resourceful and daring, he even tried his hand at policymaking, suggesting the use of foreign mercenaries to fight the Taipings, an idea that bore fruit in the formation of the "Ever Victorious Army."[49] This time Zhang was showered with rewards for his distinguished services. He was granted the extraordinary honor of wearing the regalia of a rank 1 official with a peacock feather on his cap; his son received the honorary title of a salt commissioner; his grandson was awarded an honorary *juren*.[50]

Despite all these official endorsements, local literati continued to spurn Zhang. Votive tablets might hang in his mansion for his many donations to endow permanent places in the local civil service examination, but a proposal to induct him into the Hall of Distinguished Natives (Xiangyanci) after his death was soundly rejected. He did not possess the requisite qualities of unimpeachable character and distinguished scholarship.[51]

## Local Education

The tension between copper cash and ink brush continued as salt merchants steadily expanded their role in local society in the aftermath of the Taiping Movement. (See also Chapter 8.) Education had long been the domain of officials and scholar-gentry, beginning with the construction and repair of the guard station's academy *(weixue)* during the Ming period. Although the salt merchants operated their private household schools *(jiashu)* or free schools *(yishu)* for the poor, their role in local public education was confined to donations of land and endowments until the late nineteenth century when education was increasingly viewed as a means of rescuing China from foreign encroachment. Educational reforms in Tianjin, summarized in Table 2, were facilitated by Yan Xiu and his network of merchant relatives, friends, and colleagues discussed earlier.[52]

Yan was an enigmatic character: a rare successful combination, at least for Tianjin, of gentry and merchant occupation. (See Chapter 3 on the Yan household.) A *jinshi*, he belonged to the ranks of scholar-gentry. But he was also a controversial figure, an outcast from Beijing politics and scorned by fellow scholar-officials for his reformist ideas. As Guizhou education commissioner, he had proposed a special examination, the *jingji teke*, as an alternative to the civil service exam-

Table 2. Urban Educational Initiatives by State and Society

| Period | State | Scholar-Gentry | Merchant |
|---|---|---|---|
| 1644–1684 | 2 | 0 | 2 |
| 1685–1797 | 10 | 1 | 4 |
| 1798–1911 | 26 | 11 | 30 |
| Total | 38 | 12 | 36 |

*Source:* Kwan (1999: 262–270)

ination based on eight-part essays.[53] Ostracized for this heresy, he retired to Tianjin in 1898 to head the Yan extended household and its monopoly of Sanhe district. Supported by the household's wealth, he established a household school, the Mengyang Xueshu. Supervised by Zhang Boling (1876–1951), a graduate of Li Hongzhang's naval academy in Tianjin, the school offered a novel curriculum of English, mathematics, geography, and chemistry.[54] Witnessing firsthand the ravages of the Boxer campaign, Yan reaffirmed his commitment to the importance of education and traveled to Japan in 1902 at his own expense to observe its educational system.[55]

In addition to using his household resources for education, Yan Xiu mobilized other salt merchants in this enterprise. Soon after the Boxer Movement, the "Yide" Wangs and the Yans merged their household schools. From this small beginning, the school grew into the private Nankai Primary and Middle Schools and, eventually, Nankai University.[56] In the spring of 1902, Wang Xianbin and Li Baoheng (1861–1920) of the "Philanthropist" Lis approached Lin Zhaohan (1862–1933), Yan's business manager and an activist in educational reforms, for advice on the establishment of primary schools for Tianjin. They then endowed two schools with a curriculum patterned after Yan's Mengyang Xueshu.[57] Later in the year, the two schools were combined with one endowed by Wang Wenyu, head merchant of Changlu. Occupying the former campus of Huiwen Shuyuan, this school eventually developed into the First Private Primary School (Minli Diyi Xiaoxue). Encouraged by Yan Xiu, the Zhangs and the Bians together endowed a second primary school using the campus of Wenjin Shuyuan.[58]

When the Allied Provisional Government returned the city to Chinese jurisdiction in August 1902, Yuan Shikai, the new governor-general, found not only these willing local merchant activists but also the rudiments of a reformed local education system. As part of his strategy to incorporate and mobilize local elites, Yuan, through his aide Xu Shichang, recruited Yan Xiu as director of the Department of Schools (Zhili Xuexiaosi) in 1904. Coming from a fellow native *(tongxiang)* and classmate *(tongnian)* such as Xu, it was an offer that Yan could not refuse. Before assuming office, Yan and Zhang Boling toured Japan again, this time focusing on its primary education. Upon his return, Yan embarked on an ambitious overhaul of the province's educational institutions. In each district of Zhili, academies were replaced by schools supervised by a bureau of educational affairs and supported by an educational promotion office *(chuanxue suo)* headed by local elites. The directors of the Tianjin office included Yan's business associates and relatives-by-marriage Lin Zhaohan, Hua Zeyuan (b. 1876), and Bian Yuchang (1863–1908).[59] Under Yan's direction, educational institutions in the province multiplied rapidly and were declared a national model by the central government. By 1911, Zhili was served by one of the most extensive school systems in the country; Tianjin alone had 156 educational institutions ranging from kindergartens for boys and girls to a university.[60]

Such rapid expansion required financial support beyond the already strained means of the central and provincial governments. Left to its own resources, each district raised the additional revenue from a variety of sources: broker licenses, new fees for the registration of land deeds, rents from state land, confiscation of temple properties, and levies on junks and specific goods.[61] Abused by embezzlers, these additional levies were met by resistance and sometimes riots, both rural and urban.[62]

Although Tianjin's experience became a model for the nation and delegations from other provinces studied its program, Tianjin experienced its share of difficulties in financing these expensive programs. Conservative and reform-minded gentry members clashed in the suburb town of Yixingbu, and controversy erupted in villages such as Caijiatai where villagers converted temples into schools and raised revenue for their maintenance by renting or selling temple properties.[63] Beginning in 1902, successive local magistrates imposed brokers' licensing fees on more and more trades. Not surprisingly, merchants soon complained of arbitrary and inflated fees. By 1911, a total of 27,000 strings of copper cash and 300 silver dollars was being collected annually—enough to support, however, only the Educational Promotion Office, an agricultural secondary school, and the Industrial Arts Bureau (Gongyiju).[64]

Even when available, state funds had to be used carefully. Yan Xiu had to be circumspect to avoid ensnaring his associates in political controversy. Thus he instructed his son to decline further subsidy for his kindergarten or the middle school from Lu Muzhai (1856–1948), Yan's replacement as provincial education commissioner. Lu, Yan wrote his nephews, was being criticized, not so much because he awarded public funds to these private organizations, but because of an appearance of favoritism to his relative by marriage.[65]

Despite such interference, the bulk of the funding needed for the new schools in Tianjin came from the salt merchants and their networks. Yan Xiu prevailed upon Xu Shichang, then governor-general of the newly created northeastern provinces, for a 1,200-tael donation to the private middle school.[66] To prevent a government takeover of the school they had endowed and the resulting loss of face *(timen)*, the salt merchants Wang Xianbin, Li Baoheng, Wang Xiaolin, and Zhang Bing insisted that they would finance the institution.[67] Through surcharges or donations, the Changlu salt merchants collectively raised 10,000 taels each year to cover the operating expenses of the Changlu Middle School (Changlu Zhongxuetang), which was intended to serve their sons.[68] In 1905 alone, 69,400 taels was solicited to start seven primary schools for boys, six for girls, and another 20,000 taels to finance the provincial bureau of educational affairs.[69] In 1908 the salt merchants contributed 0.15 tael of silver per *yin* to finance the Beiyang Normal College (Beiyang Shifan Xuetang) and an attached primary school.[70]

By late imperial times, then, the salt merchants of Changlu had become indispensable residents of Tianjin. Officials relied on them to raise, voluntarily or otherwise, donations and revenue for various purposes—filling a void that a ponderous bureaucracy would not, or could not, fill. Such prominence had its price, however. Given the broad range of expensive social activities they undertook, the salt merchants' accumulation of wealth may have been slowed.

The reasons for the salt merchants' social activism were complex. Confucian public-mindedness might have been one impulse, just as honorary plaques and official titles were good public relations. A certain degree of coercion, while not explicitly applied, was constant —as in the case of Wang Yisun's (1876–1930) donation to Beijing's Beiyang Xiaoxue (Beiyang Primary School) instead of his private middle school in Tianjin.[71] We have also seen how the salt merchants curried favor by voluntarily donating the yamen for the Changlu supervisor and commissioner in Tianjin or obediently following officials' lead in contributing to worthy causes such as the local academies.

Whether this "public spirit" represented a gradual emergence of urban autonomy, then, is equivocal. Although the salt merchants were increasingly active in local affairs—an activism sanctioned by the state and for which they were suitably rewarded—they still needed the endorsement of local officials. As a strategy to gain support for their reforms, officials such as Yuan Shikai did not hesitate to incorporate local elite networks. The relationship between officials and merchants was one of symbiosis: their wide range of activities and services supplemented the state in stabilizing local society when it was threatened by internal rebellion and foreign invasion. In this way, the reach of both the merchants and the state expanded together. The merchants made little attempt to confront the state, much less overthrow it.

This is not to say, however, that the relationship between state and local society remained unaffected. Just as Zhang Jinwen willfully disobeyed imperial decrees that deployed his militia beyond Tianjin, just as other salt merchants insisted on the independence of privately endowed schools, the rise of a well-connected local elite with control of its militia and other resources indicated a society undergoing change and a shifting balance between state and society. Rather than dictating state policy, officials now found themselves negotiating with citizens under their charge—in the process creating new possibilities, as we shall see in the next two chapters.

# 6.
# CHANGING TIMES

Whatever their motivations, the salt merchants' activism prepared them well for the tumultuous times of late Qing. Amidst domestic rebellions, foreign invasions, and economic crises, they countered by expanding their market at home and abroad. Diversifying from their traditional businesses, they began to invest in new industries that made up the bulk of Tianjin's "modern" sector before 1911 and, as part of the late Qing state-sponsored reforms, helped establish the Tianjin Chamber of Commerce in 1904. Under its leader, the Changlu head merchant Wang Xianbin, the chamber stabilized Tianjin's market and integrated it as part of the national financial market. In addition to managing successive financial crises—cash shortage in 1902, silver debasement, the import crisis of 1908—the chamber performed a variety of public services and defended the city's mercantile interests.[1] When officials tried to impose new taxes and a stamp duty, they encountered a vocal organization that resisted their policies.[2]

Tianjin's record of merchant activism thus differs from Shanghai and Canton. Instead of a Shanghai chamber ignoring the central government or the central government bypassing provincial and local governments in asserting its direct control over local chambers—or violent confrontations between the state and its subjects—Tianjin's experience points to yet another possibility.[3] As officials in the central, provincial, and local governments debated how much authority they might concede, merchants found a legitimate role to play in local society. Tianjin's chamber soon grew in influence beyond the subsidiary, or even intermediary, role conceived by officials.[4] In the process, it transcended local horizons to join forces with merchants in other parts of the country to protect their interests. Contemporary critics might castigate these merchant activists as "bandits who abused the state's trust, interfered with proper local governance, and preyed on their fellow defenseless citizens," just as historians have dismissed them as "reformist and tame," part of the Qing bureaucracy, or a politically Janus-faced national bourgeoisie dependent upon a corrupt state.[5] There is, however, a more charitable interpretation: state and society were learning to work together to survive difficult economic times.

## Improvements and Investments

In view of the tight regulation of the salt trade (see Chapter 2), the salt merchants continued to lobby officials and the state for policy changes that could improve their business, including rail transport and market expansion. North China's new railroads offered speed, less wastage, and year-round operation. (Rivers in Hebei were frozen in the winter months, and the trip from Tianjin to Henan took at least a month.) Beginning in 1903, Beijing's salt supply went by rail. By 1911, the salt merchants had finally obtained permission to switch to rail transport throughout the Changlu Division. In vain local officials argued that the policy shift complicated their duty of monitoring salt movements.[6]

With the prospect of raising additional revenue softening the state's resolve, more reforms followed. Over the opposition of the commander of the Chahar garrison, Yuan Shikai (1859–1916) obtained the court's approval to reunite the ten districts of Xuanhua and the three subprefectures of Zhangjiakou, Dushikou, and Dolon with Changlu.[7] In 1910, the Lianghuai Division lost the fourteen districts of Yuning prefecture and Guangzhou autonomous department in Henan province to Changlu. In support of the reform, the Henan Provincial Consultative Assembly asked pointedly: Why should the people of Henan pay more if Changlu can supply cheaper salt of better quality?[8] Not only was the price of Changlu salt half that of Lianghuai salt because of lower transport costs, but the Lianghuai Division had purchased 1.2 million *yin* of salt from Shandong and Changlu between 1906 and 1910 to make up for its declining production. Utilizing their excess production capacity, Tianjin's salt merchants also discovered for the first time markets in Japan, Korea, Russia, and Hong Kong, exporting some 58,000 tons of Changlu salt between 1905 and 1908.[9] It might not be the best of times, but these salt merchants were not frozen in tradition.

The Changlu salt merchants' continued commitment to their traditional salt business (and their pawnshops, native banks, and real estate) did not mean they were not interested in modern enterprises. In their quest for profits, these astute businessmen took note of Tianjin's bountiful supply of raw materials and the 75 million consumers in its vast hinterland.[10] Wang Xianbin, Li Baoheng, and members from the Hua, Wang, and Bian households were founding shareholders of the Tianjin Huasheng Machine-Made Candle and Soap Company, Ltd. (Tianjin Huasheng Jiqi Zhuzao Youxian Gongsi), capitalized at 94,000 taels.[11] They were also shareholders in the Linji Cigarette Company (Linji Juanyan Gongsi), the Beiyang Insurance Company (Beiyang Baoxian Gongsi), the Beiyang Match Company (Beiyang Huochai Gongshi), and the Tianjin-Pukou Bank, Ltd. (Jin-Pu Zhiye Yinhang Youxian Gongshi).[12] Mu Yunxiang, a member of the "Big Eight" Zhengxingde Mu family, himself a salt merchant operating the monopolies of Zhengding and Lingshou, founded Tianjin's electric light company.[13] In 1905, Yan Xiu's son Zhiyi (1882–1935) and Song Zejiu (1867–1956) launched the Tianjin Soap Manufacturing Company, Ltd. (Tianjin Zaoyi Youxian Gongsi).[14] Wang Yisun was reportedly the principal behind a magnet factory.[15]

Setting their sights beyond Tianjin, Wang Xianbin, Wang Tongxian, and Li Baoheng cooperated to raise 150,000 taels in capital for Beijing's Harmony Accordion Manufacturing Company, Ltd. (Zhonghe Fengqinchang Youxian Gongsi), while Yan Xiu invested 500 yuan of his household's capital in a glass factory (Yiming Boli Gongsi) established by his relative Hua Xuesu (1872–1927) in Beijing.[16] He also joined other Changlu salt merchants in supporting his friend Zhou Xuexi's (1865–1947) enterprises in North China. Despite a preference for associates with a scholar-official background, Zhou solicited financial support from the merchants for his industrial conglomerate: the Luanzhou Colliery, the Chee Hsin Cement Company (Qixin Yanghui Gongsi), the Yao Hua Mechanical Glass Company, Ltd. (Yaohua Boli Youxian Gongsi), and the Huaxin Spinning Mills. The cousins Li Baoxian (1875–1958) and Baoqian (1887–1976) from the "Philanthropist" Lis were major shareholders of Zhou's Chee Hsin Cement Company, which dominated the trade in China.[17] Yet another cousin, Shijian (1870–1932), managed the company and later served on the board of directors.[18] The Li household became one of the largest shareholders of the Luanzhou Colliery, which later merged with the Kaiping Colliery to form the Kailan Mining Administration.[19]

Indeed, this group of salt merchants did not confine their investments within the country. Li Shizeng, a son of Grand Secretary Li Hongcao and a vegetarian, envisioned a European market for tofu while studying in France. He patented the manufacturing process and, with soybeans and workers imported from North China, established a processing plant, the Usine Caseo Sojaine, at Colombes in Paris. To finance this enterprise, he persuaded his father-in-law, Yao Xueyuan (1843–1914), head merchant of the Changlu Division, to mobilize other salt merchants.[20] The company's sponsors came from all over the country, including Yan Xiu, Wang Xianbin, and the "Philanthropist" Lis of Tianjin. Li Shizhen (1853–1928) reportedly committed 300,000 taels on behalf of the Tianjin-Pukou Railroad Repurchase Fund.[21]

Perhaps the largest industrial investment by Changlu salt merchants, however, was in the Cableway Company, Ltd. (Gaoxian Tielu Gongsi), founded in 1906 by a group headed by Wang Xianbin and Li Baoheng to ship coal from Fangshan district to Beijing.[22] Until the development of the Kailan mines, the district supplied much of Beijing and Tianjin's energy needs, but its rugged terrain forced miners and shippers to depend on camels and draft animals.[23] For an expected annual net profit of over 300,000 taels, the group invested 2 million taels on a Dutch-designed cableway system to bring coal from the mines to the market.[24]

Taken together, these enterprises constituted a sizable portion of industrial investment in Tianjin and North China at the time. They also represented a departure from the city's pattern of industrialization before 1900, when most of the enterprises were state-owned and operated or closely connected with compradors and reform-minded bureaucrats.[25] It also meant, for some salt merchants at least, an expanding economic interest beyond their traditional businesses and state-imposed boundaries.

## The Cash Shortage Crisis

These investments were all the more remarkable in the context of an unsettled economy. The Tianjin of late Qing was buffeted by a succession of financial crises brought on by foreign invasion, infrastructural problems, and a government straining to meet its needs. The merchant community of Tianjin, led by the salt merchants, became increasingly active in promoting and protecting their interests. Learning to work with officials through their own institutions, they dealt effectively with the successive economic crises that rocked the city. The first was the cash crunch of 1902 to 1907.

In the aftermath of the Boxer Movement all cash—whether silver or copper—disappeared into the ground or the hands of invaders. Prudent Shanghai native bankers withheld credit for Tianjin, while Shanxi banks withdrew their loans of 15 million taels.[26] After the Allied Provisional Government relinquished control of the city in 1902, local officials, against the advice of the city's merchant community, tried to conserve the local money supply by banning all outward movement of silver and copper cash.[27] Trade between Tianjin and its hinterland faltered: merchants in the interior feared they would not receive cash for their shipments, nor could they settle their debts in Tianjin. Discount and interest rates soared in the cash-starved city. At its peak, cashing a 1,000-tael draft commanded a premium of 350 taels.[28]

Unsuccessful in his efforts to obtain relief from the central government, Yuan Shikai turned to the merchant community of Tianjin.[29] Through the compradors Wu Maoding and Wang Zongtang, he approached the city's foreign banks for a 1.5-million-tael loan for the Tianjin Developmental Bank (Tianjin Kaitong Yinhang). This attempt, too, proved fruitless. As further security for their money, the foreign banks demanded Yuan's guarantee, in his capacity as governor-general, of the loans made by the proposed bank to native banks.[30] Unwilling to sign this blank check, Yuan then approached Tianjin's own substantial households. Five of the city's Big Eight—the Yangs, the Shis, the Bians, the Lis, and the Wangs—responded by forming the Tianjin Zhicheng Yinhang (Tianjin Zhicheng Bank). Backed by a pledge of support from the provincial government and the 500,000 taels capital they raised, the bank issued fully convertible notes to ease the cash shortage and provided much needed credit to grain dealers to ensure the city's food supply.[31]

Soon, however, the merchants began to complain of official inflexibility if not interference. The financial problems could not be legislated away by restricting sycee movement or by outlawing discount rates. The merchants, including Wang Xianbin and Dou Rongguang, petitioned for more freedom and a more efficient organization.[32] In this public disagreement with the state, the merchants emerged victorious. The ineffective Bureau of Commercial Affairs (Tianjin Shangwuju) was replaced by the Public Forum for Commercial Affairs (Tianjin Shangwu Gongsuo) on May 13, 1903.[33] Yuan Shikai's appointees to the bureau, Wu Maoding and Wang Zongtang, were replaced by Bian Yuguang, Ning Xingpu, Yao Lianyuan, and Wang Xianbin.[34]

State supervision, however, remained strong in the new organization. Ning Fupeng (b. 1859), prefect of Tianjin, prepared the charter of the Public Forum for Commercial Affairs, charging it with the responsibility for resolving the cash-shortage crisis.[35] Toward this goal, the forum set the exchange rate of silver with other currencies and exhibited it daily on a placard next to its entrance.[36] It selected forty native banks to underwrite the sale of copper coins produced by the Beiyang Mint and presented a five-point proposal to Yuan Shikai to resolve the problems of money supply and financial instability. All debts were to be deferred and repaid by installment. To boost the local money supply, copper cash was to be imported from other provinces; the forum would issue and guarantee notes. Trade would be stimulated by reducing the number of branch stations for the native customs and by waiver of additional *lijin*. By year's end, however, apart from the notes issued by the forum and debt deferment, none of the promised reforms had been carried out. Frustrated by what they considered official procrastination, the four directors threatened to resign.[37]

The merchants' newfound strength, if not independence, was to some extent the result of their personal initiative. The forum received a monthly government subsidy of 100 taels drawn from brokers' licensing fees, but this sum met only a fraction of its expenditures. The directors, all substantial merchants, drew only a transportation subsidy of 10 taels each month and donated their time as well as more than 3,000 taels of the forum's annual expenses. In addition, Bian Yuguang provided office space after it moved from its temporary quarters at the porcelain dealers' guild.[38] With the city's merchant community behind them, their voice carried more weight with local officials.[39]

Coaxed by Yuan Shikai's placating words, the merchant directors continued with their effort in stabilizing Tianjin's financial market. They persuaded the local magistrate to act on their recommendations: banning the export of copper cash and coins by arbitragers to Shandong; declaring a moratorium on debts including those due the local government; and lifting the ban on sycee export to attract silver from other parts of China. Finally, the forum established a commercial native bank (Shangwu Qianzhuang) with 200,000 taels in capital subscribed by merchant-gentry to issue fully convertible notes denominated in copper cash. Thirty merchants and firms were chosen to promote these notes as a substitute for cash. By 1905, the cash crisis was over: native banks could now ship large quantities of silver. The forum, now renamed the Chamber of Commerce, possessed enough authority to instruct local officials not to interfere with these shipments.[40]

## The Chamber of Commerce

The merchants' effective self-help justified the need for a chamber of commerce. In 1904, when the Qing court approved the formation of chambers of commerce on the recommendation of the newly established Ministry of Commerce, sixty-one of Tianjin's leading native banks, grain dealers, sight-draft banks (piaohao), and merchants jointly petitioned for the creation of the Tianjin General Chamber of Commerce on the basis of the Public Forum. They recommended that Ning Xingpu be appointed chairman, Wang Xianbin vice-chairman, and Yao Lianyuan and Bian Yuguang executive directors.[41]

*Formation*

In making these recommendations, the merchants were not usurping the state's prerogative. The principle of public nomination, as defined in clause four of the Concise Charter promulgated by the ministry, directed that representatives of various trades should nominate candidates to lead the chamber. The authority to appoint, however, remained with the ministry, and this it exercised by naming Wang Xianbin as chairman, Ning as vice-chairman, and Hua Shiming (1851–1907) as the organization's representative in Beijing.[42] Nevertheless, this was a departure from the state's unilateral decision to appoint Wu Maoding and Wang Zongtang to the Bureau of Commercial Affairs in 1903.

With the Concise Charter, the state also redefined and enhanced the authority of the new chambers. While the forum's charter gave the merchant organization authority to adjudicate commercial disputes, the new chambers were charged with the additional responsibilities of promoting and protecting local commercial interests. Clause seven of the Concise Charter empowered the chairman to investigate all matters affecting merchants and to appeal to the ministry if grievances were not addressed adequately or exceeded the authority of local officials. The principle of openness was imposed: meetings must be conducted and decisions made in public; expenses were subject to annual audit. The Concise Charter also recognized the diversity of local conditions, however, and permitted chambers to promulgate discretionary charters *(bianyi zhangcheng)* subject to the ministry's approval (clause fourteen). The nominees must be men of integrity and considerable wealth, who commanded the confidence of their peers, and have the status of at least five years of local residence. Under the ministry's direct authority, the chambers enjoyed some latitude in defining their local role and selecting their officers.

Whether or not the ministry intended to reassert its authority as part of its state-building effort (see Chapter 8), its declaration led to a bureaucratic turf battle between Beijing and provincial officials. Invoking the authority granted by the Concise Charter, the merchants found a novel and legal platform from which to promote their interests. The first task of the Tianjin General Chamber of Commerce was to draft its discretionary charter. If its predecessor, the forum, was constrained by a charter decreed by local officials, this time the chamber and its directors consulted fellow merchants to prepare their own. Instead of merchants being summoned to the yamen for instructions, Ning Fupeng made the trip to confer with the directors.[43]

The thirty-clause provisional charter produced by the merchants elaborated on the authority granted by the ministry. Most of the clauses dealt with daily administration and meeting procedures, but the merchants added the appointment of vice-chairman and, given Tianjin's status as a treaty port, an attorney and interpreters to facilitate negotiations with foreign merchants. Their version also provided for the nomination of candidates to the board of directors, and from this pool of nominees two auditors and two executive directors would be selected.

Determined not to be bypassed, Yuan Shikai insisted on putting his stamp on the chamber by faulting the merchants' charter. His reading of the Concise Charter found no mention of an attorney and an executive director. Accordingly, he ruled that these proposed positions, as well as a full-time executive director, should be eliminated.

He also faulted the merchants' power to solicit *(yue)* the nomination of directors. This, Yuan felt, would make the chamber's officers too powerful and indeed might even violate the principle of public nomination *(gongju)*.

Zaizhen (1876–1947), however, found the merchants' discretionary charter acceptable. Son of Grand Minister of State Yi-kuang, Yuan's key ally in the capital, the Beile Prince and the director of the new ministry had the political muscle to overrule provincial opposition, including Yuan. While agreeing with Yuan that clause four of the discretionary charter might contradict the principle of public nomination, the minister was satisfied with the merchants' draft, which specified that each trade should nominate its own representatives as directors. He concurred that the Concise Charter did not provide for the appointment of executive directors, but overworked chairmen and other officers needed all the assistance they could get, he ruled, and the foreign presence in Tianjin did necessitate frequent legal representation. To make these new institutions effective, the ministry was prepared to be flexible. Accordingly, Yuan's objections were overruled and the discretionary charter was approved with minor stylistic changes.[44] In this skirmish between the central government and provincial officials, the merchants had snatched a victory.

With the arrival of its official seal from Beijing, Tianjin's Chamber of Commerce was formally established on January 13, 1905, although it had been serving the city since late 1904.[45] A secretariat, supported by accounting, services, arbitration, and research departments, each with a full-time director, performed the chamber's daily operations. Policymaking and supervision came from the twelve-member board of directors elected from among the seventy-one candidates nominated by the forty major trades in the city. Consistently represented on the board were salt, grain, and silk merchants as well as native banks. Reflecting the importance of foreign trade for the city, compradors and foreign goods importers were also represented from 1905 to 1911.[46] Unlike Shanghai's elitism, membership in Tianjin was open to all who could afford the annual dues of 4 to 20 yuan. By June 1905, the chamber could boast of 581 members.[47]

*Activities*

Continuing the work of the Public Forum in regulating Tianjin's chaotic currency market by setting exchange rates, the chamber began to perform a wide range of services for local residents and officials. It assumed duties designated by the state such as litigation involving commercial and contractual disputes. As its authority became accepted, the chamber acted as an intermediary between the local government and merchants in matters ranging from municipal administration to urban land use. As a conduit for the views of local citizens, the chamber received petitions from both members and nonmembers: shopkeepers, merchants, transport workers, even rickshaw pullers protesting the construction of tramways by the Compagnie de Tramways et d'Eclariage Electriques de Tientsin.[48]

Promoting industrial and commercial development, the chamber also sponsored study societies. The Zhili Society for Commercial Studies (Zhili Shangye Yanjiu Zongsuo), established under its auspices, met weekly to study various trade issues.[49] During the last years of the Qing dynasty, Tianjin merchants founded a host of organizations, independently or as chamber affiliates, including the North China Mercantile Society (Beiyang Shangtuan Gonghui) in 1909, the North China Society for Commercial Studies (Beiyang Shangxue Gonghui) by sojourning merchants from South China, and the Tianjin Society for the Study of Commerce and Industry (Tianjin Gongshang Yanjiu Zonghui), also known as Gongwu Fanhui (Branch Society on Industrial Affairs) in 1911. Reports on the activities of trade and industry societies, including shoes, silk, cotton cloth, copper cash, grain, and metallurgy, filled the pages of the *Dagongbao*. A foundation was laid in vocational training with the establishment of elementary and secondary commercial schools in 1906 enrolling a total of one hundred students; Wang Xianbin provided more than 20,000 yuan in funding.[50]

As an organization of merchants, the chamber spared no effort promoting the city's trade, both national and international. In 1905 it launched its own newspaper, the *Tianjin shangbao* (Tianjin Commercial Gazette), to articulate the merchants' perspective in the mass media.[51] When a U.S. trade delegation touring China visited Tianjin in 1910, Wang Xianbin orchestrated the local arrangements and paid for a reception.[52] He was also instrumental in Tianjin's participation at a national fair held at Nanjing (Nanyang Quanyehui) the same year. Wang himself attended with products chosen for exhibition after an extensive provincial survey. For the first time, merchants from all over the country not merely promoted their goods but also worked together to enhance their status and business.[53]

## Copper Coin Crisis

Above all, the Chamber of Commerce was kept busy protecting mercantile interests in a series of economic crises created, at least in part, by official policies. The first to hit was the copper coin *(tongyuan)* crisis, followed by the silver debasement and the looming bankruptcy of importers of foreign goods. In their attempt to address these financial problems, the merchants encountered their share of failure and success.

As part of the post-Boxer reforms, the central government finally authorized the long-awaited production of standardized copper coins by the provincial mints to ease the shortage of officially minted copper cash.[54] With great efficiency, a new Beiyang Mint was built in 1902 in seventy days; by year's end it was producing 300,000 copper coins a day. In great demand, the copper coins commanded an agio—that is, the exchange rate between copper coins and silver dollars fell below the official rate of one hundred copper coins to one silver dollar. In addition, as the token value exceeded the intrinsic value of the metals in these coins, the mints reaped a seignorage windfall. Officials at the Board of Revenue and in the provinces were elated: in one masterly stroke they had solved the problems of silver depreciation, the shortage of copper cash, and the financing of reforms.

An astute Yuan Shikai, with his ambitious programs to fund, immediately expanded the mint's production to capture as much as possible the "modest" agio and seignorage profits of 600,000 taels each year.[55] Production of copper coins should be stepped up, he urged; the demand in Hebei alone would take at least three years to satisfy. Millions of copper coins of various denominations flowed from the Beiyang Mint to supply Shandong, Henan, Shanxi, and the Northeast.[56] By 1907, it had produced a total of 682 million copper coins of various denominations. As other provincial mints joined the race, each with different copper content, the chaos was compounded by an influx of even more copper coins smuggled into the country from Korea, Japan, and Vietnam and sold by the barrel.[57]

This rapid expansion in money supply predictably caused inflation in Tianjin and the region. The price of water in the city, for instance, jumped from 6 *wen* to 8 *wen* per bucket.[58] For the salt merchants, however, raising their price was not an option: this required an imperial decree. In better times, they might have been able to absorb the loss or send more payoffs to secure the cooperation of local officials. When they tried to pass some of the loss onto the consumers, as the firm

Dexingyi did in the district of Quyang, they were inundated with law-suits charging violation of the official price.[59] While their customers insisted on the local exchange rate and cash standard, the salt merchants saw their profits disappear when they converted their cash income into silver. The Tianjin salt merchants also claimed losses stemming from unscrupulous exchange dealers who manipulated the rate or from silver assayers who minted substandard silver sycee to take advantage of the demand.[60]

To address the erosion of their profits, the salt merchants repeat-edly petitioned the government for reforms, including the intro-duction of a flexible exchange rate between copper coins and silver. The Changlu commissioner, however, dismissed these proposals as attempts to reduce the merchants' obligations to the state and raise the price of salt.[61] The merchants then applied for a dual pricing system: one for customers using copper cash and another for those using copper coins. Even officials operating the monopolies taken over by the state joined in the petition.[62] Zhou Xuexi, the Changlu commissioner, however, would not tolerate this veiled criticism of his accomplishments. For he was the director of the Beiyang Mint and one of the masterminds behind the tidal flood of copper coins.[63]

As operators of the state monopoly system, the salt merchants could do little against the state. As a representative of Tianjin's mer-chant community, however, Wang Xianbin, supported by other mer-chants, could propose various solutions to the problem. As early as 1904, the Public Forum had warned of the importation of coins from other provinces and abroad—all with different copper content.[64] In 1907, Wang presented a three-point proposal to Yang Shixiang (1860–1909), Yuan Shikai's successor, to bring order to the volatile exchange market. To prevent further decline in the value of the copper coins vis-à-vis silver and other currencies, production at the Beiyang Mint had to be suspended. In addition, vigilant antismuggling efforts were needed and ways would have to be found to suppress dealers in the foreign concessions from importing and selling copper coins of even lower copper content. A special official provincial currency bureau (Beiyang Guanqianju) should be established to purchase excess copper coins with fully convertible banknotes or silver to stabilize the exchange rate.[65]

Officials in Beijing and the provinces, however, could not afford to stop the flow of profits into their coffers. Because of overminting, copper coins no longer commanded an agio—but it was easy to stamp ever larger denominations on the coins. To protect their profits, officials erected barriers against copper coins from other mints and, to ward off arbitragers, severely restricted the amount of copper coins carried by travelers. Visitors to Beijing could enter the city with no more than two thousand (later reduced to five hundred) copper coins; travelers to Tianjin were initially allowed two thousand then five hundred, and ultimately only one hundred copper coins.[66]

The effect of this last measure was disastrous for commerce—in particular, the salt merchants, who were not permitted to ship their copper cash or coins across provincial boundaries in exchange for silver to pay their taxes. Even such influential merchants as the Zhangs of "Hai" Zhangwu fame (see Chapter 5) had a copper cash shipment of 18,140 strings to Shanxi seized by the goods tax station *(huojuanju)* at Shijiazhuang. The Zhangs contended that the copper cash was still within the province, that as legal tender it was not a merchandise (hence beyond the tax station's jurisdiction), that its movement by train had not been publicly banned, and that they had a contract with a native bank to exchange the copper cash for silver to meet its tax obligations. Officials, however, were not impressed. The case finally reached the governor-general, who conceded that while the shipment might not have been illegal, the Zhangs had failed to notify the government properly. He therefore confiscated 10 percent of the copper cash as a reward for the officials who made the seizure.[67]

What began as a promising reform thus created more problems for the merchants. Recognizing that its efforts were largely futile—and that Beijing's support of the exchange rate of copper coins with a token fund of 1 million taels was far from adequate—the Chamber of Commerce petitioned the state to explore other sources of revenue before the flood of copper coins caused the economy irreparable damage. The merchants proposed the withdrawal of copper coins as legal tender and their replacement by silver coins of various denominations—hence the establishment of a true silver standard. In 1910, Wang Xianbin was appointed an adviser on currency reform to the Ministry of General Accounts (Duzhi Bu), a small recognition of his expertise and concern for the public good.[68]

## Silver Debasement and Foreign Import Crisis

Even if the state had the resolve and resources to adopt silver as the sole legal tender, problems continued to plague the monetary system. Apart from the myriad local standards, Tianjin's self-regulating silver smelters *(lufang)* had been looted by the Allied Expeditionary Force during the Boxer Movement and never reopened. Their successors were not as scrupulous in maintaining the city's standard *(hangcheng)* of 99.2 percent. Tempted by the appreciation of silver as copper coins flooded the market, they smelted and put into circulation substandard sycee.[69] Sensing a potential problem, the Chamber of Commerce petitioned Yuan Shikai for the establishment of a public assaying bureau (Gongguju) to enforce the city's silver standard as early as 1905. Yuan, however, rejected the proposal on the grounds that merchants from other parts of the country might be forced to pay an additional assay charge.[70]

Although Yuan's concern was valid, the problem of debasement remained; the silver content of sycee minted in Tianjin declined even further. In 1908, Cai Shaoji (1859–1933), circuit intendant of the Tianjin Maritime Customs, issued a simple order. Henceforth all customs duties must be tendered in sycee of standard touch. Cai, of course, was merely acting in the interests of the state. He had little idea of the ramifications of his proclamation or the diplomatic and economic crises he would precipitate. Chinese merchants and foreign banks alike protested that they should not have to bear the cost of assaying, resmelting, and adding silver to bring the sycee to standard touch.[71] Until they were compensated or assured of a resolution on who should bear the costs, the foreign banks in Tianjin would not release over 1 million taels of substandard silver in their vaults.

Withdrawing so much silver from circulation predictably caused a liquidity crunch with disastrous effects. Chinese dealers, with their credit cut off, could not take delivery of orders made the previous year —a situation aggravated by foreign importers' excessive trading.[72] Imports began to accumulate at Tianjin's godowns until foreign importers filed claims with their consuls totaling 14 million taels for the goods and interest charges. The Chinese court enforced the code of unlimited liability with predictable results: a wave of bankruptcies and suicides of Chinese merchants followed.

What had been a civil matter between private merchants now became a public and diplomatic affair. In late 1908, the British Consul in Tianjin proposed in a confidential memo that the matter be taken up in Beijing.[73] Under heavy diplomatic pressure from the British, Japanese, French, and German consuls, the Chinese government intervened. In a meeting with Yang Shixiang, the governor-general, a delegation of foreign consuls demanded that foreign bank loans to these importers be secured by a state guarantee. Rejecting the demand, a harassed Yang gave the chamber three days to find a solution to the problem. He saw no reason why the state should be involved in such a civil matter. Adhering to a strict interpretation of the law, Yang argued that the current treaty system did not require the Chinese government to assume liabilities incurred by its citizens in private commercial transactions. It would offer assistance in collection of debts, but no more.[74]

To overcome Yang's reluctance, more diplomatic pressure was needed—and this the ambassadors of Japan, France, and Germany applied in Beijing. Prodded into action, the Foreign Ministry requested further information from Yang Shixiang on March 6, 1909, forcing an overworked Yang (he died three months later) to meet again with the foreign consuls in Tianjin. During this meeting it was agreed that a Chinese and foreign joint commission, composed of officials and merchant representatives, would be established to explore solutions to the problem.[75]

Chinese representatives to the Joint Commission, including the chairman of the Chamber of Commerce, Wang Xianbin, fought hard: Chinese merchants should be protected from unfair trading practices; the ledgers should be audited; the exorbitant interest charges should be reduced.[76] Foreign representatives, however, were equally determined to recover their losses by ascertaining "a true statement of Chinese assets" including goods in hand, cash, accounts receivable, as well as shares, title deeds, and other securities held by all partners —past or current—jointly and separately liable for all debts incurred by their partnerships.[77] Grueling negotiations drawn out over sixty meetings finally reduced the amount of indebtedness to 5 million taels.

Wang Xianbin and his associates played a crucial role in exploring ways of raising this amount. The Chamber of Commerce proposed holding lottery raffles.[78] Chen Kuilong (1857–1949), the new governor-general, explored the idea with officials in Beijing.[79] The Foreign Ministry's initial response was noncommittal. If lottery was the only alternative, the ministry would not stand in the way, although the use of such a gambit risked the appearance of impropriety for the state. Running the game as a merchant organization, the chamber's dignity would not be compromised.[80] Officials at the Finance Ministry, however, found such a measure unlikely to survive a ministry review.

Citing criticisms of excessive generosity toward the merchants by the Provincial Consultative Assembly, the Finance Ministry vetoed the idea.[81]

The Chamber of Commerce finally came forth with a solution. To settle all outstanding claims of foreign creditors, a new bank, the Commercial Guarantee Bank of Zhili (Beiyang Baoshang Yinhang), would issue approximately 5 million taels of twenty-five-year bonds with yields between 4 and 5 percent a year. Repayment of principal would commence in the sixth year, the amount to be determined at such time by the bank's six-member board, three Chinese and three foreigners. The bank's 4 million taels of capital would come from foreign and Chinese banks without state guarantee and merchant assets.[82] In turn, the bank would take over all the stockpiled imports and finance its disposal. Profits from this and other banking operations would service the outstanding bonds. With an initial infusion of 150,000 taels, the bank opened for business.[83] As a cosigner for the bank loans, the Chamber of Commerce appointed Liu Yue-chen, an executive director of the chamber, as the bank's first manager. The Public Assaying Bureau was finally established under the supervision of the chamber, and the smelters eventually absorbed the loss stemming from reminting and wastage. To increase the local supply of silver, a system of discount rates and daily telegraph communication was instituted to facilitate movement of silver from Shanghai.[84]

## Stalemate over Stamp Duty

Collaboration between officials and merchants, however, was only one dimension of a society in flux. They could also stand in opposition—as illustrated by the state's repeated attempts to impose a stamp duty. First proposed in 1896 by Chen Bi, then with the Censorate, the idea had not attracted much interest. Twelve years later, negotiations to end the opium trade and the anticipated decline in revenue that would result from the ban necessitated an alternative source for the state's depleted treasury. On December 30, 1902, Yuan Shikai submitted a detailed plan for the collection of a stamp duty in the coastal provinces and received a quick approval.[85] Wasting no time, Yuan imposed the duty on all ledgers, contracts, tickets, bills of lading, land tenancy deeds, leases, bank drafts, household division documents, pawnshop receipts, and company stock certificates. Without the stamps, all such documents were declared null and void. The resulting uproar forced Beijing to reconsider, however, and the program was suspended in 1903.[86]

Four years later, a financially strapped Qing Court ordered the program resurrected. Zaize, the recently appointed minister of finance, assisted by Chen Bi, targeted Zhili as the test province. Zhang Zhenfang (1863–1933), brother-in-law to Yuan Shikai's half-brother Shidong, was put in charge, assisted by Ning Fupeng, the former prefect of Tianjin who had suffered the indignity of having to pay homage to the Tianjin General Chamber of Commerce instead of dictating his terms.[87]

The Tianjin Chamber of Commerce led the opposition to the new levy, beginning with a series of petitions, the first one signed by 796 local merchants. When the petition was rejected by Beijing and Yang Shixiang, the governor-general, Wang Xianbin countered with one signed by 1,877 merchants. Invoking such authorities as Confucius and Mencius, the merchants' arguments were pointed and concise. Merely because foreign countries had stamp duties did not mean that China should follow suit. The state and officials must heed what the Classics advised so long ago: "If the people enjoy plenty, with whom will the prince share want? But if the people are in want, with whom will the prince share plenty?"[88] As loyal and public-minded subjects, the merchants promised willing compliance if the funds from the stamp duty were indeed spent on programs to stop opium smoking. But without any guarantee or indication that the revenue would finance such programs, they insisted that they should not be burdened by more taxes without representation.[89] Chambers of commerce all over the country demonstrated their support by waging a telegram campaign. Despite Zhang Zhenfang's determination to make Tianjin an example, Yang Shixiang wavered in the face of the merchants' adamant refusal to comply. A stalemate resulted.[90]

State and society thus negotiated their way through the difficult times of late Qing. There is no question of the merchants' subordination to the state: its charters, appointment of personnel, seal, and authority were all derived from state mandate. From Beijing's perspective, these organizations were part of its state-building effort to reintegrate the empire vertically, unite and mobilize its subjects (if not quite citizens), and strengthen the central government. The merchants proved useful as they learned to work with officials in Tianjin and Beijing. Unlike lofty scholar-officials, they could perform undignified tasks—holding a lottery, for example, or haggling with foreigners—as in the foreign import crisis.

Nevertheless, the merchants' efforts of self-help slowly but surely moved their organizations beyond the subordinate or even intermediary role originally conceived by officials and the state. Bureaucratic politics between central and provincial government gave the merchants a space to protect their interests. Transcending guild limits, the Chamber of Commerce enjoyed a territorial jurisdiction, represented and protected the city's mercantile community, and took on causes with regional and national ramifications. Shanghai's experience might therefore not be unique; nor was such activism primarily local and rural. Wang Xianbin, in his multiple capacities as salt merchant, chairman of the Chamber of Commerce, and adviser to the Ministry of Finance, cooperated with officials to stabilize the city's economy and protected mercantile interests against both the state and foreign diplomats. Defining civil society as a confrontation between state and society, therefore, would miss the complexity of late imperial China when state and society expanded together, negotiating, confronting, yet learning to work with each other.

# 7.
# SHIFTING POLITICS

The rise of Tianjin's Chamber of Commerce, then, does not mean that an idealized "civil society" distilled from the experience of Europe had been realized in the city. Yet Tianjin's version of "civil society," like its counterparts in London and elsewhere, did not arise ex nihilo. These merchant princes relied on formal and open institutions as well as informal and exclusive networks to conduct their business and pursue their interests. Figures such as Wang Xianbin were enmeshed in the matrix of an evolving Chinese social and political culture despite the novelty of the institutions through which they worked.

As self-conscious merchants flexed their strength in promoting their interests and stabilized the city's economy, they also opened fissures in local society. To late Qing rulers and reformers, the creation of an informed and responsible citizenry was among their cherished, yet equivocal, goals.[1] Promotion of local self-government, as well as legal, educational, economic, social, and constitutional reforms, together seemed to point to the construction of a new citizenry, but contemporary critics castigated the students returned from abroad (especially those from Japan) who masterminded many of these reforms. Naive and self-serving, these students had neither the political experience nor the support of the local society they planned to remake.[2] Sponsors of the reforms in Beijing, local officials, local scholar-gentry, merchant activists—each promoted and participated in the new institutions from their own perspective. The rhetoric and vocabulary—"feudal" *(fengjian)*, for instance—might be familiar, but their meanings had had to be negotiated, contested, and constructed.

The Qing state's objectives varied. They were defined in part by rivalries within the imperial family for influence and the succession: Zaifeng the regent, representing the Daoguang Emperor's branch, versus candidates of various collateral lines, including Zaizhen, whose father Yikuang inherited the title of Prince Qing, and an ambitious Zaize, husband of the empress dowager's niece.[3] Moreover, Beijing's shifting relationship with powerful Han Chinese provincial governors complicates the politics of reform. In 1900, when the capital was under attack by the Allies during the Boxer Movement, provincial governors in South and Central China had declared neutrality. After the dust had settled, the dynasty labored to restore its credibility if not legitimacy. In his confidential memorials to the throne, Zaize championed the reforms as a means to reassert Manchu control of the empire. As minister for drafting the constitution and eventually finance minister and controller-general of the Salt Administration, he pursued a policy of centralization through nationalization.[4]

An ambitious Yuan Shikai certainly knew how precarious his position was. Despite the empress dowager's confidence in him, Yuan Shikai knew that leading Manchu noblemen harbored deep suspicion of him as commander of a newly created army. Nor could Zaifeng, the regent for the young Xuantong Emperor, forget Yuan's betrayal of his brother the Guangxu Emperor in 1898. But as an astute politician, he also appreciated the opportunities. His secretary, Zhang Yilin (1867–1943), recounted how Yuan once opposed self-government and constitutional monarchy. In Yuan's view, the populace was simply not ready. But he soon told Zhang to prepare a memorial urging the throne to adopt a constitution.[5]

What caused this change of heart is not clear. Perhaps Yuan, knowing his many enemies, would feel more secure if the theoretically absolute emperor were circumscribed by a constitution. Perhaps he wanted to preempt the central government. As his rival Zaize argued, the avowed goals for local self-government—to facilitate communication between the state and its subjects, to prepare them as citizens, and to assist the state's rule of local society—might at the same time make life difficult for local officials.[6] Legitimate self-government councils and assemblies might support their paternalistic magistrate (*fumuguan*). But they might just as easily challenge him, or pursue their case with his superiors, or, even worse, take it all the way to the capital. By presenting his own design, Yuan could define the agenda, preserve his power, and enhance his reputation as an efficient administrator and reformer.[7]

Whatever the motivations of the parties concerned, the decision to create local councils, as well as provincial and national assemblies, unleashed a contentious process exposing the society's fault lines. Scholar-gentry, merchants, and activists used these legitimate forums to articulate their interests publicly. The result was not what the returned students expected—a corporatist citizenry unified by the complementary functions each party performed in local society—but, instead, a fractious society.

## Merchant Politics

Tianjin's salt merchants, as we have seen, were no strangers to politics and the art of networking, although their tactics might seem amateurish. In his quest for wealth and influence, Wang Xianbin encountered his share of troubles. In 1907, a censor implicated him in a scandal involving Prince Zaizhen. On a mission to the Northeast, the Beile Prince was lavishly entertained by Duan Zhigui (1869–1925) and presented with a much acclaimed opera singer, Yang Cuixi. Cementing the goodwill, Duan allegedly raised from Wang a 100,000-tael birthday gift for Prince Qing—an investment that yielded Duan the governorship of Heilongjiang. Subsequent investigation cleared Wang of any role in the affair. The censor was dismissed for filing this malicious charge; Zaizhen resigned to avoid embarrassing his father.[8]

While Wang Xianbin's political skills might be wanting, as chairman of the Chamber of Commerce he had become indispensable in Tianjin. The wide variety of activities sponsored or performed by the chamber gave it great influence. Officially inspired and organized to assist the state in local matters, it had evolved into an institution active, not merely in local economic interests, but also national politics.

This activism began in 1905 following a proposal by the United States government to impose further restrictions on Chinese immigrants. In May, the Shanghai General Chamber of Commerce solicited the help of other chambers in organizing a national boycott of American goods.[9] Tianjin's merchant community reacted enthusiastically: Wang advocated that a boycott of American imports was the most effective way to fight the injustice, a patriotic stance applauded by the *Dagongbao*. More than two hundred chamber members voted to participate in the boycott, and a fine of 5,000 yuan would be imposed on any offenders caught selling American-made goods.[10] Students from the schools that the merchants funded gave stirring speeches to mobilize their fellow citizens.[11]

Popular opinion, however, was no match for a determined Yuan Shikai and the Qing state. Unwilling to risk antagonizing the United States at a critical juncture in the peace settlement of the Russo-Japanese War, Yuan opposed the boycott. The chamber's directors were summoned to his yamen and ordered to desist. The Police Bureau then outlawed any assembly of more than twenty persons without prior approval.[12] Undaunted, the merchants petitioned for Yuan's support to open negotiations with the United States—unaware that the governor-general had already cabled the Foreign Ministry urging the throne to suppress the boycott. On August 18, 1905, the *Dagongbao* was banned for its continued agitation. Finally, an imperial edict from Beijing forbade any further discussion of the subject.[13]

While official pressure prevented the Chamber of Commerce from pursuing the national boycott further, the merchants of Tianjin, individually or organized, soon found other legitimate venues to express their political views. Yuan Shikai, as part of his reform program in local self-government, had launched community compacts *(baoyue)* with elections of headmen by villagers. In his memorial to the throne, Yuan (or his secretaries) couched the experiment in traditional terms. According to the *Book of Rites,* the ancients had created an orderly and harmonious society with more than two-thirds of the bureaucracy devoted to local administration. Proper governance was facilitated by these officials who were on intimate terms with the governed. It was only after the Sui dynasty, when overworked magistrates assumed sole responsibility for the districts under their charge, that corrupt runners and other unsavory characters were able to abuse the system. Yuan argued that local self-government by elected representatives would reintroduce grassroots support for the empire's unity and strength.

Turning his attention to Tianjin, now the provincial capital, Yuan established the municipal administration conference (Shizheng Yihui) to facilitate communication between the local government and gentry members, including merchants, in 1906.[14] With funding from fines and a contribution of 90,000 taels from the salt merchant "Zhende" Huangs, one of the Big Eight, Yuan Shikai created a bureau (Tianjinfu Zizhiju) and an institute (Tianjin Zizhi Yanjiusuo) for the study of self-government to train the province's gentry.[15]

Later in the year, a forum made up of representatives of local institutions to promote self-government (Zizhi Qicheng Yanjiuhui) was commissioned to draft a self-government charter. Yuan's new bureau nominated twelve members including the salt merchants Wang Xianbin, Yang Junyuan, Li Shiming, Hua Chenghan (1836–1908), and Lin Zhaohan. These merchants were joined by other Big Eight members with a merchant background: Shi Yuanshi (1849–1919), Bian Baolian (1841–1916), and Bian Yuchang. The self-government institute sent its representatives, too, including Hua Zehao (b. 1874) and Sun Hongyi (1872–1935), both from salt merchant families.[16] Ten other merchants and native bankers were nominated by the Chamber of Commerce to ensure a broad-based support. The bureau published a vernacular paper and engaged speakers to publicize the benefits of self-government, and the chamber organized meetings for its members.[17]

After nineteen meetings, the self-government forum adopted a charter modeled on the Japanese bicameral system—anticipating Beijing's official promulgation by almost two years.[18] The charter called for the creation of deliberative assemblies *(yishihui)* and executive councils *(dongshihui),* with the local magistrate as ex-officio chairman, for the district and municipality of Tianjin. Elected delegates would serve two-year terms. Any male resident over the age of twenty-five *sui* (twenty-four years) not dependent on public welfare and able to write his own name, age, address, and occupation was eligible to vote.[19] The qualifications for candidates standing for election, however, favored the educated (graduates of primary school or above, ex-officials, degree holders, stipend students, or those with publications certified by officials), the well-off (a minimum of 2,000 yuan in assets or managing enterprises worth over 5,000 yuan), and gentry with a record of public service. Mobilizing a skeptical populace for Tianjin's first public election, Yuan Shikai's impatience notwithstanding, was a difficult task. Surveys to determine eligibility were met with apathy and suspicion: a government survey might be a ploy to identify the wealthy for more taxes. Some 800,000 residents of Tianjin yielded an electorate of only 12,461. Only 2,572 were qualified as candidates to stand for election.[20]

The apathy of the district's residents contributed to the dominance of the educated in the first district assembly. Of the twenty-five (out of a total of thirty) assemblymen whose occupations can be identified, seven were educators and eight came from the self-government bureau; two scholar-gentry, five representatives of rural areas, and three salt merchants accounted for the remainder.[21] In subsequent elections, educators and self-government activists continued to predominate, although rural areas contributed an increasing number of representatives, eventually accounting for more than half of the assembly.[22] While the wealthy merchants constituted a minority in the district assemblies, they did supply some of the leaders. Li Shiming (1851–1927) of the "Philanthropist" Lis was elected chairman of the 1907 assembly. In subsequent elections, his nephew Baoxiang (1885–1921) sat on the standing committee and Hua Xueqi served as vice-speaker of the 1911 assembly.[23]

The same pattern applies to the municipal assembly. Although outnumbered by the educated, salt merchants turned merchant-gentry were represented in the first class of assemblymen by Lin Zhaohan and Hua Guangli. In subsequent elections, at least two Lis from the "Philanthropist" Lis and an assortment of Zhous, Wangs, and Zhangs were elected to the body. The ubiquitous Wang Xianbin—or those with a salt merchant background such as Yan Zhixing (d. 1913), nephew of Yan Xiu—served as honorary advisers.[24] Wang Guanbao, one of the head merchants of the Changlu Division, was elected chairman of the municipal executive council (Tianjin Xiancheng Dongshihui) after a term as vice-speaker of the municipal assembly.[25]

Tianjin's salt merchants were also active in the 140-member Provincial Consultative Assembly (Zhili Ziyiju), which was financed by the Changlu gabelle. Representing the seven districts of Tianjin, an electorate of 7,132 elected a delegation of six including Li Shiming, who became chairman of the Committee on Internal Affairs and Member Qualification.[26] Other representatives included Sun Hongyi, son of a salt merchant from the Tianjin suburb of Beicang. A close friend of Yan Xiu, Sun had been active in the development of local education, including primary schools in Beicang, a telegraphy school, and a girl's school (Puyu Nüxue).[27] A third member, Hu Jiaqi (b. 1870), whose studies in Japan were financed by Yan Xiu, served as principal of Tianjin prefectural middle school before his election.[28]

By virtue of the considerable taxes they paid to the state, the salt merchants also dominated the seats reserved for the country's largest taxpayers in the National Consultative Assembly (Zizhengyuan). Of Zhili's twenty candidates, each paying a minimum of 20,000 taels in state taxes, all except one were salt merchants.[29] The two men eventually elected—Yang Xiceng and Li Shiyu (1855–1917)—were among the biggest Changlu salt merchants at the time.[30] Hu Jiaq represented the Provincial Consultative Assembly in the National Consultative Assembly; Sun Hongyi served as an alternate member.[31]

In addition to services in these local, provincial, and national assemblies, several salt merchants helped to organize groups promoting local self-government and constitutional monarchy. Wang Guanbao was elected chairman of the Society for the Study of Administrative Affairs of Tianjin Municipality (Tianjin Xiancheng Yanjiuhui), an organization coordinating the activities of local self-government bodies. Li Shiming founded the Society for the Promotion of Constitutional Monarchy (Xianzheng xieyihui) in 1910.[32] These well-heeled merchants could easily afford the expense of promoting such worthy causes, and their participation in the political process marked the rise of the merchant-gentry—to be distinguished from the scholar-gentry.

## Growing Conflicts with the State

The court and officials, charting a careful course of reform, viewed these developments with increasing weariness if not alarm. On the one hand, the court, increasingly swayed by young imperial princes such as Zaize, saw political reform and the creation of new institutions as a means to recentralize authority in Manchu hands. Undeterred by an assassination attempt, Zaize led a mission to Europe, Japan, and the United States in 1905–1906 to study constitutional government in operation. Upon his return, he was appointed minister for drafting a new constitution. His commitment to expanded participation in government was equivocal, however, and his understanding of the meaning and implications of constitutional monarchy uncertain.[33] In a confidential memorial to the throne, he outlined the advantages of constitutional monarchy: the preservation of Manchu rule, a bulwark against foreign threats, and a means to quell internal rebellion. Following the Japanese model, the emperor would retain much of his authority—and indeed might even regain some of the power lost to provincial officials since the Taiping Rebellion. With sound political instinct, Zaize predicted that provincial officials, already threatened by the newly created assemblies, would oppose his scheme. As for the citizenry, they would patiently wait until they completed their training.[34]

On the other hand, neither the court nor the provincial bureaucracy could afford to concede too much power to these local self-government bodies. Once appetites had been whetted, these institutions might want more—as did Shanghai's General Works Board (Gongchengju) in assuming extensive de facto powers in finance, local education, administration of justice, and police.[35] Local officials urged the court to define clearly the extent of local self-government: the shifting boundaries between official and gentry-led self-government depended too much on ad hoc arrangements, giving rise to acrimony.

Even before the central government moved to limit the authority of these new self-governing bodies, Yuan Shikai and his associates jealously guarded their authority. The Chamber of Commerce received a sound rebuke from Yuan for the charter it drafted for the Tianjin Commercial Currency Company, Ltd. (Tianjin Shangwu Tongyu Youxian Gongsi). Running the company was the merchants' business, but using such phrases as "administration" *(xingzheng)* or "public affairs" *(gongshi)* must remain the officials' prerogative.[36]

Confronted by provincial and local officials who felt that their authority had been compromised by these self-government institutions, the constitutional drafting bureau under Zaize proposed to the throne in 1908 that all matters not expressly delegated would remain under official jurisdiction. Administration of justice and local police were too important to delegate to the self-government bodies, but education, public health, transportation, the local economy, charity, public utilities, and other activities that had been gentry-managed and gentry-financed without abuse or corruption would be appropriate.[37] As a safeguard against abuse, local officials reserved the authority to supervise and abolish these organizations.

If provincial officials and those in charge of drafting the self-government reforms thought the boundaries they had delimited would harness the new institutions, they were mistaken. The elected representatives and the assemblies they filled were not content with an advisory role or with observing the officially defined boundary between local government and local self-government. Wang Guanbao, the salt merchant speaker of the municipal assembly, insisted that he and his colleagues were no longer children living in fear of harsh schoolmasters. As elected representatives they should now command respect.[38]

But Wang and his colleagues soon proved to be difficult students. Invoking the authority of its charter, the district assembly notified

the magistrate that it meant to investigate Tianjin's Industrial Arts
Bureau (Gongyiju) for corruption and mismanagement. Another investigation mounted by Sun Hongyi and his associates ended with
the dismissal of the director of the Tianjin-Pukou Railroad for corruption and land speculation. On April 6, 1909, the assembly served
notice that it would audit the accounts of the district government's
donations and levies section (Juanwuke). Subsequent investigations
revealed that 90,000 strings of copper cash in brokers' licensing fees
and other contributions had been pocketed by the local magistrate.[39]
Such initiatives soon strained the relationship between the self-government bodies and various levels of the bureaucracy as officials
found their decisions and authority challenged from below.[40]

The vigilance of the self-government bodies was not merely a
result of irritation with brokers' fees or contributions exacted by officials, which were perfectly legal and customary. At stake was their
attempt to carve out a source of revenue for themselves. From the
beginning, when the district assembly complained about the delayed
election for Tianjin's municipal executive council, it faulted the local
magistrate who had appropriated all the local revenue and would
not yield a copper cash. The paltry 500 taels per month from the
state was far from adequate for the assembly's needs. In an effort to
garner a source of revenue for itself, the assembly argued that it was
only reasonable for the land tax collected from the district to be
used for local purposes—an argument that went nowhere with officials. Several attempts to allocate broker fees in order to finance
local self-government failed. Stonewalled by local officials, the assembly threatened in vain to take the matter to the Censorate in Beijing.[41]

The Provincial Consultative Assembly was similarly frustrated in
this struggle with the bureaucracy over power and money. Even
before his election to the assembly, Sun Hongyi had urged Wang
Xianbin to protect Tianjin's interests by publicizing and preparing
for the coming election. Since every detail pertaining to the administration of the province would fall under the assembly's purview, including taxation and levies vital to its residents, Sun argued that
Tianjin could be protected only if it were represented by the largest
possible number of delegates.

Under the leadership of activists such as Sun, the assembly
launched a series of inquiries on provincial officials. During its first
meeting, twenty-eight resolutions, the bulk of which involved the
raising and appropriation of local revenues, were passed and sent to

the governor-general for immediate action. One resolution asked that the 50,000 taels contributed by the syndicate of salt merchants operating the Tianjin and Wuqing salt monopolies be returned to the districts for local use.[42] Once again officials refused; neither Zhang Zhenfang the commissioner nor Zaize the controller-general would yield a grain. The officials insisted that the salt merchants' contributions to secure the right to the monopolies should, as part of the state's regular income, be distinguished from donations.[43]

Apart from their claims on revenue, the self-government bodies also wanted to share decision making with officials as equal partners instead of ad hoc informal mediation behind the scene. A tentative step was made in this direction when, at the governor-general's request, the Provincial Consultative Assembly nominated candidates for his advisory board. Chen Kuilong chose eight leading citizens of the province, including Yan Xiu, from the list. These board members, however, soon complained of being outvoted by sixteen officials. Denied equal representation, they resigned and the experiment died a quick death.[44]

The accomplishments of these self-government institutions should not be exaggerated. Guarding its domain zealously, the bureaucracy deflected questions from the assemblies with avalanches of documents that satisfied no one except paper suppliers and printers.[45] What was novel, however, was that local officials and residents could no longer rely exclusively on informal mediation to resolve disputes —or, failing that, violent confrontations.[46] An alternative was now available: legitimate and formal institutions affording a dialogue between officials and elected representatives.

## The Constitutional Movement

Effective or not, the political discourse nurtured by these local self-government bodies gave expression to a growing desire for constitutional monarchy. As elected representatives of the people, they saw themselves as the foundation of the country's political future. In his inaugural speech to the district executive council, Xu Wei, an honorary member of the Tianjin district council, observed that, without local self-government, any future parliament would be ineffective. Members of the council must fulfill their duties as citizens and not remain passive subjects.[47]

The creation of these self-government bodies unleashed waves of rising expectations. Although the Qing court tried to delay establishment of a constitutional monarchy as long as possible, members of these bodies agitated for a parliament as soon as possible. After the elections for the Provincial Consultative Assemblies, the Federation of Provincial Consultative Assemblies (Ziyiju Lianhehui) was established—ostensibly to coordinate the activities of the various assemblies.[48] Under the leadership of Zhang Jian and Sun Hongyi, it became a national lobby group when Sun and other representatives traveled to Shanghai for consultations with fellow assemblymen from sixteen provinces. In January 1910 the assemblymen, under Sun's leadership, submitted a petition drafted by Zhang Jian urging the throne to convene a parliament in one year.[49] When the petition was promptly rejected, the undaunted assemblymen, led again by Sun, continued filing petitions much to the displeasure of the court. Sun was also instrumental in the organization of one of the earliest national political parties in China: the Friends of the Constitution (Xianyouhui), made up of radical members of the provincial and national assemblies.[50]

The inaugural meeting of the National Consultative Assembly in October 1910 presented another occasion for the constitutionalists to press their demands. A delegation of members from various provincial assemblies, led by Sun Hongyi and supported financially by the salt merchant Wang Guanbao, submitted yet another petition to the throne.[51] The court bowed to this pressure, however, finally agreeing to convene a parliament in 1917—a shrewd move that split the petitioners. The moderates, led by Zhang Jian, declared victory and returned home; the conservative members of the assembly, including Li Shiyu, formed the Imperial Society for the Solid Progress of Constitutional Monarchy (Diguo Xianzheng Shijinhui) to promote an orderly transition to constitutional monarchy and competed against Sun's party for members in Tianjin.[52]

Sun, Wang, and the Lis were not the only Tianjin salt merchants active in the constitutional movement. As chairman of the Chamber of Commerce, Wang Xianbin coordinated a national campaign to solicit support from other provincial chambers and those in Zhili. Representatives of Shanghai's merchant community journeyed to Tianjin to discuss a joint effort.[53] In a speech to his wealthy brethren standing for election to the National Consultative Assembly, Wang reiterated his support for constitutional monarchy. Recounting the difficulties he had encountered in the survey for qualified candidates, he reminded them that responsibility accompanied privilege. The assembly, the equivalent of Japan's upper house, should play an important role in preparing China's transition to constitutional monarchy—a goal that should be realized as soon as possible. As representatives of the wealthy, their charge was to promote economic development to ensure China's survival.[54]

In addition to invoking the concept of commercial warfare *(shangzhan)* to justify the rising status of merchants, Wang defended their right to the reserved seats for big taxpayers in the National Consultative Assembly.[55] It might seem one-sided, as some landlord-cum-degree-holders alleged, to have nineteen Tianjin salt merchants on the final list as opposed to only one landlord-cum-degree-holder. But it would be unfair to these big taxpayers if their numbers were limited to make room for candidates paying paltry sums elsewhere in the province.

Implicit in Wang's argument, of course, was the power of money and the principle of representation with taxation. As a founding member of the Society for Repayment of the National Debt (Chouhuan Guozhaihui), Wang had been coordinating a national effort to raise donations to repay the 115 million pounds sterling in indemnities and interest incurred as a result of the Sino-Japanese War and the Boxer Movement.[56] Buried under this mountain of debt and threatened by an imminent loss of national sovereignty, he argued, China would be unable to undertake any meaningful reforms. No sacrifice was too big to achieve repayment—provided the court acceded to popular demand. Supporting his words with action, Wang financed meetings of the society in Beijing to raise donations and mobilize support in the country.[57] His feelings were shared by members of the Provincial Consultative Assembly who linked the repayment campaign to the movement for constitutional monarchy. Without a parliament to monitor the state's decisions, the people should not be responsible for the repayment of foreign debt, nor should any new debt be incurred.[58] Wang Guanbao the salt merchant financed the lobbying effort in Beijing.[59]

Emboldened by the support, the radical wing of the constitutional movement, led by Sun Hongyi, pressed on for the convocation of a parliament in 1911.[60] When the Provincial Consultative Assembly delegation from the Northeast was expelled from Beijing for its continued agitation, students from the many schools in Tianjin founded or funded by the salt merchants were outraged—a future leader of the Chinese Communist Party, Li Dazhao (1889–1927), among them. The students held rallies and wrote posters in blood to demonstrate their determination. Many cut off their queues, as did merchants, in protest.[61] Wen Shilin (1870–1935), a close associate of Sun Hongyi, was elected chairman of the National Association of Student Petitioners (Quanguo Xuesheng Qingyuan Tongzhihui).[62] On December 20, 1910, more than three thousand students demonstrated in Tianjin and were joined on their march to the governor-general's yamen by Wang Xianbin and other local leaders. Wen, Wang, and Yan Fengge (b. 1857), representing respectively the students, merchants, and the Provincial Consultative Assembly, presented a petition. After heated debate, the governor-general reluctantly agreed to forward it to Beijing.

The Qing court reacted quickly and decisively to this direct challenge to its authority. Wen was arrested and exiled to Xinjiang—despite a rescue effort mounted by Zhang Boling with the support of members of the district assembly and the Provincial Consultative Assembly.[63] Advocates of constitutionalism, including Li Dazhao, were thoroughly disillusioned. They began to see revolution as the only path to national salvation.[64]

## Enemies and Friends

All politics, of course, is local. Although the activists among the salt merchants joined the pursuit of constitutional monarchy, merchant-gentry and scholar-gentry differed in their interests and priorities. With the abolition of the civil service examination in 1906, competition for status intensified as many aspiring bureaucrats turned to education, combined with public service, for an equally promising career as members of local assemblies and councils. In many districts, they clashed repeatedly—particularly over who should lead the local self-government bodies.[65]

Tianjin's experience was no exception. In early 1911, Wang Guanbao found himself under fire as his scholar-gentry colleagues complained repeatedly about the arbitrary way he ran the municipal assembly. They also accused him of violating the self-government charter by accepting compensation from the syndicate of salt merchants operating the Beijing monopoly, not to mention his huge monthly salary of 150 yuan and transportation subsidy of 30 yuan. Charging Wang with altering his attendance record, the members attempted unsuccessfully to have him recalled.[66]

At the provincial level, the scholar-gentry who dominated the Provincial Consultative Assembly were deeply suspicious of what they perceived as collusion between officials and merchants. They criticized the establishment of the Commercial Guarantee Bank of Zhili (discussed in the previous chapter) as a dangerous precedent—arguing that the populace should not be responsible for debts incurred by private merchants—and questioned the governor-general's authority over the bank.[67] The salt merchants, in particular, presented yet another convenient target for criticism and attack in the assembly. They were charged with many questionable practices ranging from salt adulteration to the disruptions caused by their antismuggling forces. In turn, the salt merchants complained of added expenses to comply with the changes and, as a result, dwindling profits.[68]

The hostility between the salt merchants and the assembly was heightened by the distribution of the shares of the Tianjin-Pukou Railroad Company financed by the price increase of 4 *wen* per *jin* in 1910. Much to the glee of officials—and over the opposition of salt merchants—the Provincial Consultative Assembly pushed through a program under the guise of developing the provincial economy to divert part of the railroad fund to establish a spinning mill.[69] The Li brothers from the "Philanthropist" Lis, however, whose native bank served as the depository for the railroad fund, refused to comply. Their strategic positions in the assembly and the Changlu Syndicate enabled them to thwart repeated attempts to remove the fund from the household's control.

Unable to accomplish its goal, the assembly proposed a compromise: additional revenue would be used to purchase railroad stock that the salt merchants and the assembly would then divide equally. Some members of the Provincial Consultative Assembly went even further by arguing that it was the people of Zhili who, as consumers, had paid for the price increase. As elected representatives of the province, the assembly should therefore control all the stock purchased. It passed a resolution demanding 90 percent of the stock, leaving only 10 percent to the salt merchants. In turn, the salt merchants fought back by arguing that the stock was fair compensation for their loss in sales. Both the price increase as well as the increased smuggling it caused had cut deep into their profits.[70]

As part of the state-building reforms in late Qing to create a new unity, the creation of multiple levels of self-government bodies thus proved as divisive as they were unifying. Between the state (as personified in the Manchu imperial princes) and provincial officials, different expectations and motivations created a space for local societies and interests to gain a legitimate toehold in public affairs. Increasingly, government became a challenge for officials.

The reforms also fostered a fractious local society. Rather than taking to heart the interests of the common good, the active participants—established scholar-gentry with high civil service examination degrees or bureaucratic experience, local educators and self-government activists holding lower degrees, and merchants—often competed for resources, positions, and status in local society. Now that their path to glory, the civil service examination, was closed, the scholars and aspiring officials had to compete for leadership in local, provincial, and national affairs.[71]

With their expanding role in late Qing society, the Changlu salt merchants participated in this process as arrivistes. Time and again they had proved their worth in resolving local problems and, bolstered by this experience, were now demanding linkage of representation to taxation. Local councils and provincial assemblies afforded them even more opportunities to articulate their interests. They cooperated with other elites and helped, directly and indirectly, to limit the power of the state. They also contributed to the drive for constitutional monarchy. For such rebellious behavior and other excesses, as we shall see, Wang Xianbin and his colleagues would pay dearly.

# 8.
# THE CRASH

Early on the morning of July 17, 1911, Wang Xianbin's family was evicted from its eighty-eight-room mansion on Second Street (Er-du-jie). Nine other salt merchants, including Li Baoheng, suffered a similar fate. Later that morning, Zhang Zhenfang the Changlu commissioner inspected Wang and Li's vacated mansions and their furnishings with satisfaction. Sealed and inventoried, the mansions and all its contents were auctioned off.[1]

Explanations of this episode vary in their persuasiveness. According to some contemporaries, the crash was orchestrated by Zhang Zhenfang who wanted to apply pressure for the rehabilitation of his relative Yuan Shikai.[2] If true, Zhang would have been taking a great risk, considering Yuan's many powerful adversaries, such as Grand Secretary Natong (1856–1925) who reportedly was deeply dissatisfied with the handling of the "crisis."[3] The *Dagongbao* attributed the haste to Zhang's impatience. He could not wait to assume his new office as judicial commissioner of Henan (rank 3a), a promotion from Changlu commissioner (rank 3b). But an astute governor-general such as Chen Kuilong, steeped in the art of bureaucratic warfare, could easily, and actually did, delay Zhang's departure. To settle a personal grudge, Zhang's action in forcing Wang Xianbin and others into bankruptcy would kill two birds with one stone: clearing the Provincial Consultative Assembly's charge of his corruption and incompetence and avenging Wang's obstruction of his stamp duty initiative (see Chapter 6).

If the personal motives of the Chinese officials remain murky, what the foreign consuls and banks wanted—besides repayment of the bank loans—is also difficult to reconstruct. Some historians suggest that the foreign banks wanted direct control of the salt monopolies.[4] Foreign consuls insisted that the Qing government assume full responsibility for the loans because the salt merchants, as operators of the monopoly system, were agents of the state.[5] There is no question that Wang Xianbin, Li Baoheng, and their colleagues borrowed from the foreign banks and diverted at least a portion of the loans to finance their own investments. Even though their total debts, both foreign and domestic, amounted to almost 10 million taels, this was not exceptional compared to the magnitude of other financial crises that had plagued the coastal economy of China or the foreign import crisis discussed in Chapter 6. Although the ten bankrupt salt merchants could not repay all their debts in cash immediately, they still had more than 3 million taels of salt inventory—in addition to real estate, shares in industrial enterprises, and other assets including the Cableway Company with a book value of over 2 million taels and their share of 1 million taels in railroad stocks. Why did the state resort to such drastic measures? To understand this episode, we need to place it in the shifting zone between state and society in late Qing. Expropriation was just one of the most visible results of a financial crisis that gripped the city. Intense negotiations, debates, and politics engulfed the merchants, their organizations, local government, provincial officials, ministers in Beijing, the banks, and the foreign consuls representing their national interests.

## Borrowing Time

The crash had long been in the making. After the Boxer Movement, the salt merchants found their city and businesses devastated. Scores of native banks, which had financed the salt trade with more than 2 million taels, closed their doors after systematic looting by the Allied troops. Redemption of the salt inventory seized by the Allied Expeditionary Force cost over 1 million taels. Relocation of the depots condemned by the Italians and Austrians as their concessions cost a fortune in silver that the merchants did not have. With the state struggling to finance the Boxer Indemnity and other reforms, the salt merchants' frequent pleas for loans tried the patience of officials.[6]

In late 1901, Hua Xueqi obtained permission to borrow 34,900 taels from the Russo-Asiatic Bank to finance the purchase of salt seized by the Russian occupation force. On behalf of the Changlu Division, he also arranged a 200,000-tael revolving line of credit from the bank. All that was required was an official authorization letter (*yutie*, literally "instruction slip") from the commissioner and a collective guarantee by all the merchants of the Changlu Division.[7]

From this modest beginning, successive Changlu commissioners routinely granted the salt merchants permission to raise foreign bank loans. In 1903, Tang Shaoyi (1860–1938), then circuit intendant of the Tianjin Maritime Customs Service, even arranged and guaranteed the salt merchants' two-year loan of 400,000 taels at an annual interest rate of 8.5 percent from the Yokohama Specie Bank.[8] With these new sources of credit, merchants paid their taxes promptly and officials found relief from constant pleas for state loans.

One obstacle, however, remained. The foreign banks required collateral or, in lieu of it, a state guarantee for the loans. To satisfy them, Wang Xianbin and his colleagues improved on the authorization letter with two additional provisos. The named merchant—not the state or any of its agencies—would be responsible for repayment of the loan, a principle conveyed in the phrase "merchant loan, merchant repay" (*shangjie shanghuan*). Moreover, Wang Xianbin and other head merchants were authorized to place in receivership monopolies operated by any salt merchant behind in his repayment. Since repayment was explicitly the merchants' responsibility, some officials saw little need of their involvement but understood the provision as an additional guarantee of repayment by the merchants.[9] Essential to any loan package, authorization letters were issued by the commissioners, at times even retroactively.[10] Business between the salt merchants and the foreign banks blossomed.[11]

As a legal document, however, the authorization letter was flawed, perhaps deliberately so. Officials might feel comfortable with the document since the responsibility to repay the loans clearly rested with the salt merchants, not the state, as specified in the phrase "merchant loan, merchant repay." But the clause providing for the appointment of official receivers was rife with complications. Foreign banks interpreted the provision as an official guarantee of repayment—making collateral from the salt merchants unnecessary. By implication, it even gave them the right to seize and operate the monopolies until the loans were repaid. For the salt merchants, the letter of authorization was a convenient tool to secure loans without putting up the requisite collateral. (They certainly knew that to use their monopoly privilege as collateral was illegal.)

The key issue, however, was who would operate the affected monopoly in the event of receivership. The commissioner could appoint an official receiver, perhaps even foreign ones, as in the case of expatriates serving in the Imperial Maritime Customs Service or the Commercial Guarantee Bank of Zhili. In actual practice, however, Wang Xianbin and other head merchants enjoyed considerable latitude on the two occasions the provision was invoked. In one case, the owner of the monopoly sued unsuccessfully for illegal seizure, affirming the legality of the provision and the head merchants' authority.[12] In the other case, involving "Yuanfengrun," Wang Xianbin arranged for an acceptable manager to take over, allowing the bankrupted owner to retain control of the monopolies.[13]

Despite these ambiguities, the letter of authorization arrangement worked smoothly so long as the salt merchants were able to service the loans. Indeed, the ease with which credit could be obtained may have led them to borrow excessively. In 1909, Wang Xianbin and Li Baoheng petitioned Zhang Zhenfang for another letter of authorization. To ensure delivery of salt to the districts on time, the salt merchants needed a new 3-million-tael revolving line of credit from the Russo-Asiatic Bank. Wang and Li were granted power of attorney to act on behalf of their colleagues.[14] Such authority was not unprecedented: Zhou Xuexi had once authorized the head merchants to handle all matters related to the "sale" of the salt depot seized by the Austrian concession. The two head merchants discharged this additional responsibility efficiently—too well, perhaps, for their own good.

## Disaster

The beginning of the end for Wang Xianbin and his associates came in May 1910. The Deutsch-Asiatische Bank asked Chen Kuilong, governor-general of Zhili, to register (*li'an*, literally "establish a file") loans totaling 1,080,000 taels made to the Changlu salt merchants, noting that Wang and Li had diverted part of the loan to invest in the Cableway Company and the Usine Caseo Sojaine at Colombes.[15]

The governor-general resented this additional responsibility, although *li'an* was a routine administrative procedure, an official recognition that such loans existed.[16] Instructed to investigate, Zhang Zhenfang immediately ordered Wang Xianbin and Li Baoheng to report on all the loans the salt merchants had secured from foreign banks. On the following day, before any answer could be expected, however, Zhang reported to Chen that he could not fathom the request: loans obtained by the salt merchants were private arrangements between the merchants and the foreign banks, a private matter that did not concern the state.[17]

How the governor-general was soothed by maneuvers behind the scene is unclear. A local paper reported that Zhang, without his superiors' knowledge, had affixed his official seal and signature to guarantee the loans—thereby involving the state in what had thus far been a private matter.[18] If true, he must have known that if the foreign banks pressed their claim, the state would be responsible for the loan, the principle of "merchant loan, merchant repay" notwithstanding. Officially Zhang instructed the head merchants to repay the Deutsch-Asiatische Bank immediately and prohibited any new loans. This ban, if carried out, would have been disastrous for the bank, and Meng Qi, its comprador, notified the head merchants on July 26, 1910, that the entire matter was a clerical error. Not without a certain relish, the salt merchants reported to the commissioner that despite their repeated offers, the bank adamantly refused to accept repayment of the loan.

Although this "unfortunate misunderstanding" was rectified, the problem of the salt merchants' solvency persisted. In the spring of 1911, the Banque de L'Indo-Chine declined to extend any more credit. And when the salt merchants missed several payments, the German consul again requested the governor-general to register the loans from the Deutsch-Asiatische Bank. The Russo-Asiatic Bank and the Banque de L'Indo-Chine soon followed suit with requests totaling 4,910,720 taels.[19] They demanded that their liens be attached to all the salt merchants' monopolies, properties, and other investments.

An annoyed Chen Kuilong promptly passed the matter on to Zhang Zhenfang who, three days later, once again instructed Wang and Li to report on the extent of foreign bank loans. Criticizing them for misleading him and procrastination, he charged them with misusing the letters of authorization as collateral and diverting a sizable portion of the loan for their own use—charges he had earlier dis-

missed. Revealing his knowledge of the merchants' activities, he admitted that for nearly a year he had been urging the salt merchants
to repay all foreign bank loans. According to Wang Xianbin's 1910
report, these loans totaled only some 3.2 million taels. The latest communication from the foreign banks, however, listed loans of almost 6
million taels, with Wang and Li responsible for 3.28 million taels between them.[20] Under mounting pressure, Wang and Li finally divulged
that the Changlu Division owed 7 million taels in loans and interest
to various foreign and domestic banks.[21]

Identifying the debtors, however, was far easier than solving the
problem—a task that occupied Zhang Zhenfang for months in intense
negotiations among the parties concerned while creating an economic
crisis for Tianjin. Initially the commissioner sought quick individual
settlements with each of the banks. He proposed that 1 million taels
worth of stock in the Tianjin-Pukou and the Loyang-Tongguan
railroads held by the Changlu salt merchants be transferred to the
Deutsch-Asiatische Bank to settle its claim.[22] What he did not con-
sider, however, was how those merchants who did not borrow from
the foreign banks would be compensated for their railroad stock or
whether foreign ownership of the stocks would violate the railroad
companies' charters. Not unexpectedly, the salt merchants balked at
Zhang's decision, arguing that their property should not be used to
settle debts they had not incurred. The five-day deadline imposed by
Zhang expired without any action.

All the parties, however, continued their search for an acceptable
solution. Through the Chamber of Commerce, the salt merchants
submitted a proposal to reschedule the debts at a reduced interest
rate. For nearly a decade, the salt merchants argued, the revolving loan arrangement had functioned smoothly. They pleaded for
state assistance as dealers of foreign imports had received in the
1908 crisis. With more assets and less foreign debt than the importers,
they were better able to meet their obligations. If the loan payments
could be rescheduled and the interest charges reduced, all their debts
would be repaid—and, more-over, there would be no mass bankruptcy
to disrupt Tianjin and the region's economy.[23] Zhang endorsed the
chamber's plan two days later, ordering it to open negotiations with
representatives of the foreign banks. The Deutsch-Asiatische Bank
agreed to extend the deadline for overdue payments by forty-five days
—half of the three-month grace period the chamber requested, but
a respite nonetheless.

On the same day that Zhang authorized the chamber to negotiate, Wang Xianbin and Li Baoheng submitted their own settlement plan. After consulting with their colleagues, they proposed the consolidation of all the salt merchants' foreign debts to be repaid by installments over eighteen years. The monopolies of the affected merchants would be operated collectively by a trusted manager; the profits would go toward repayment of foreign debts. Wang and Li pledged the projected 300,000 taels of annual profit from the Cableway Company to repay what they owed.

Following a meeting at the Chamber of Commerce, the Changlu salt merchants improved upon Wang and Li's plan.[24] An eighteen-year extension became twenty-four years with the interest rate reduced to 4 percent in the merchants' revised offer. They also proposed the formation of a company (Changlu Baoshang Gongsi) to operate the monopolies owned by Wang and Li and, as well, replacement of the copper-cash and coin-based pricing system in the Changlu Division with one based on silver. With credit tightening, they also wanted government loans in order to avoid delays in salt shipments.

The Changlu salt merchants were burying their differences. Just as a solution seemed within sight, however, the foreign banks began breaking ranks. The Banque de L'Indo-Chine, supported by the French consul, refused to accept the chamber's mediation because it would make this international dispute a civil matter among merchants. All negotiations, the consul insisted, must be between the foreign creditors and the commissioner or his official delegate.

With the ball back in his court, Zhang made another attempt at a quick settlement. This time he expanded on the idea of a company to take over the insolvent salt merchants' monopolies to include the Cableway Company; profits of both would be applied to the debt. The bankrupt salt merchants would pay a surcharge of 1 tael per *yin* (totaling 300,000 taels)—which, together with 90,000 taels contributed by solvent salt merchants (calculated at 0.3 tael per *yin*) and 140,000 taels from the merchants' share in the recent price increases, would repay the foreign banks by installment.[25] The Tianjin-Pukou Railroad stock due the insolvent salt merchants would be transferred to the solvent salt merchants to compensate them for their contribution. If the salt merchants rejected this settlement, some "shortsighted and shallow official" such as himself would put all the affected monopolies in official receivership. Carrying out his threat that the remaining salt merchants would not remain solvent for long, he ordered salt merchants contiguous to state-operated monopolies to move all their retail outlets three Chinese miles *(li)* from their respective district borders to protect state sales.[26]

If Zhang Zhenfang hoped that the salt merchants would heed his threats, he was mistaken. They remained deeply divided over who should pay and how, while Zhang's position became precarious as "rumors" circulated about his corruption.[27] He instructed the prefect and magistrate to arrest the ten defaulting merchants and seize their property. When the Chamber of Commerce protested, Zhang cabled from Beijing a stay of his order.[28]

On the last day of the temporary stay, a majority of salt merchants submitted yet another proposal: annual installments of 500,000 taels from a surcharge of 1 tael per *yin* from bankrupt salt merchants and 0.3 tael per *yin* from solvent merchants, in addition to the 120,000 taels raised from the commissioner's treasury. Any shortfall would be met by the profits from the Cableway Company and, as a last resort, would be the collective responsibility of the salt merchants in the division.[29] The chamber, meanwhile, approached the Kailan Mining Administration and the Commercial Guarantee Bank of Zhili, both Sino-foreign enterprises, for a 2.2-million-tael loan, using the Cableway Company as collateral, to be guaranteed by the Changlu Division. Although the companies responded favorably, the governor-general and the commissioner forbade any more loans to the salt merchants.[30]

There is little evidence, at least to this point, of a conspiracy to ruin the salt merchants. Much like the foreign import crisis of 1908, the various parties involved—merchants (solvent or bankrupt), the chamber, local officials, foreign banks, and consuls—proposed a variety of solutions. Zhang Zhenfang blamed his predecessors (perhaps even Yuan Shikai, his relative), just as he was highly critical of Beijing's policy.[31] But pressure from the diplomatic corps transformed a private matter between salt merchants and foreign banks into an issue not only public but international. Intervention by the central government became inevitable.

## Solution

The events between late May and early June 1911 cannot be reconstructed in full, but the crisis had finally become a matter of concern for Beijing's statesmen. The 1911 trade report of the Imperial Maritime Customs noted: "After several months of correspondence and interviews, the foreign banks had gained their case: the minister of the Board of Finance instructed the provincial authorities to take over the gabelle's indebtedness and liquidate the claim with promptitude."[32] Zhang Zhenfang's audiences in Beijing suggests that powerful ministers in the capital were now involved.

As a leading advocate for the centralization of Manchu authority under a constitutional monarchy, Zaize might have taken this opportunity to seize for Beijing more power and revenue. Over the opposition of provincial governors, he had been appointed controller-general of the Salt Administration—a post created ostensibly to reform the system, resolve jurisdictional disputes between provinces over boundaries and smuggling, and centralize personnel appointments in his hands as well as all the gabelle due the central government. Zaize probably had calculated that a nationalization of the bankrupted salt merchants' monopolies would give the state control of yet more revenue resources and, at the same time, curtail the power of provincial governors who had taken control of salt administration and revenue after the Taiping Rebellion.[33]

The strategy was not his alone. His Manchu colleagues in the "Imperial" Cabinet shared the approach and had nationalized provincial railroads by borrowing 6 million pounds sterling from the Four-Power Consortium.[34] Serious disturbances in Sichuan and elsewhere were a small price to pay for reasserting Manchu authority. What began as a business dispute became a battle between the salt merchants and the Qing state—and between local officials and the central government—engulfing more and more groups and taking on regional and national ramifications.

Under pressure from Beijing and charges of corruption, Zhang Zhenfang confronted the salt merchants. On May 31, he again ordered the arrest of the ten salt merchants and the seizure of their property. Wang Xianbin and others presented themselves. But Liu Shiying, one of the bankrupt merchants, disappeared, and officials arrested Zhang Kangshu, his brother-in-law, instead. Officials also detained Hua Xueqi's son, Hua Yishu, in lieu of his father.[35]

Nor did Zhang stop there. On June 2, he ordered the Changlu salt merchants to pay a surcharge of 1.5 taels per *yin*. The 600,000 taels collected each year would go toward the repayment of all foreign bank loans. Any merchant who failed to pay might lose his monopoly. This time the salt merchants heeded the commissioner's one-day deadline under the impression that the monopolies would be spared an official takeover.[36] Their relief, however, was short-lived. On the following morning, the commissioner elaborated on his order: monopolies owned or operated by the bankrupt merchants would still be confiscated and operated by the state. The salt merchants were stunned. After all, the plan would not cost the state a grain of silver, while the onerous surcharge would have reduced their profits by as much as one-third. Somewhat belatedly, even Zhang recognized that the scheme was unfair to those salt merchants who had not taken out any foreign bank loans. He therefore allowed it a quiet death.[37]

But the problem remained, and Zhang formulated yet another scheme—one that eventually formed the basis of the settlement adopted by the state. Seven million taels were to be borrowed from the Da Qing Government Bank to repay all the bank loans and interest immediately.[38] Salt merchants who had taken out bank loans were divided into three groups. The ten worst offenders, including Wang Xianbin and Li Baoheng, whose gross indebtedness exceeded 6.5 million taels, would be declared bankrupt. The monopolies they owned or operated, some sixty-three in all, would be confiscated and operated by the state. In the second group were five salt merchants who owed a total of 250,000 taels. Although declared insolvent, these merchants possessed enough property to settle their debts. A third class of twenty-five salt merchants with some 1.4 million taels of bank loans were judged solvent but required to repay all their loans by the end of the fifth month—that is, by June 25, 1911.[39] This time the surcharge was set at 1.5 taels on each *yin* quota, or 900,000 taels each year. Thus with the merchants' share of the price increase, a total of 14,560,000 taels would be collected over fourteen years. After making interest payments, the remaining 3.8 million taels would reimburse those salt merchants who had not taken out any bank loans but were nevertheless required to pay the surcharge.

Against his critics, Zhang defended his plan as necessary to protect China's sovereignty and the state's authority over an important source of revenue—an argument he had dismissed when it was raised by the salt merchants and other petitioners.[40] To prevent any recurrence of the problem, Zhang further declared that the state would no longer recognize any loans, foreign or otherwise, to the salt merchants. Indeed, the use of any salt monopolies, inventory, contracts, and other non-salt-related properties owned by salt merchants, such as real estate and stocks, as loan collateral was explicitly forbidden, and all the native and foreign banks in Tianjin were so notified.[41]

Zhang's plan sent shock waves through the economy of Tianjin and beyond. As the price of silver soared and credit became impossible to obtain, the remaining salt merchants found themselves under siege.[42] Zhang Hongjun, manager of a salt firm, submitted three critical petitions against the commissioner's plan. It was unfair, not only to those salt merchants who did not borrow from the foreign banks, but also to Chinese creditors whose loans had not been addressed. In addition, with their current income seized and credit dried up, the salt merchants could not finance the season's shipments, thereby jeopardizing the supply of salt to consumers. The commissioner's charge was to protect the salt merchants, not ruin them. His actions would alienate a citizenry already unsettled by the state's railroad nationalization scheme. The humble manager implored the Chamber of Commerce to confront the commissioner.[43]

With its chairman jailed, the chamber mounted a rescue effort. Ning Xingpu, himself no stranger to the salt trade, organized the merchant community of the city in a media campaign. Mass meetings were held, and petitions urging the preservation of the monopoly system so that the salt merchants could repay all their foreign and domestic debts rained on the governor-general and the Provincial Consultative Assembly.[44] Wang Xianbin should be released so that he could dedicate himself, as he had so many times before, to resolving the crisis confronting the city.[45]

Aiming at the source of the crisis, the chamber sent a delegation to Beijing to plead for the bankrupted merchants. Zaize, however, rejected its plea as a blatant attempt to interfere with state affairs.[46] He accused the merchants of trying to frighten Tianjin's naive residents and instructed the governor-general to use the police to maintain public order. Fearing further aggravation of a tense situation, the prefect of Tianjin refused to allow the delegation to brief the chamber about its humiliating experience in Beijing.[47]

The chamber was not the only merchant organization that protested Zhang's settlement plan. Even the North China Society for Commercial Studies, an organization of sojourning merchants from South China long at odds with the chamber, filed a petition citing the many public services of the salt merchants, especially Wang and Li. Another petition submitted in the name of all the merchants and commercial establishments of the city made the same argument—

and was followed in short order by one from the importers of foreign goods and compradors. Song Zejiu (1867–1956), merchant activist and chairman of the Tianjin Society for the Study of Commerce and Industry, praised Wang as the single indispensable person in Tianjin.[48]

Educational institutions, public services, and charities in which the salt merchants or their donations played an instrumental role also joined the petition drive, with graduates and principals of the various schools pleading on behalf of Wang Xianbin.[49] Zhang Boling, chairman of the Zhili Provincial Society for the Banning of Opium, filed a separate petition citing Wang's major donations to the society.[50] In their petition to Zhang Zhenfang, the fire companies of Tianjin listed the services Wang had performed for the state during the Boxer Movement. The commissioner, however, remained unimpressed. Although the petitioners were acting within the law, he commented, their arguments were irrelevant.[51]

With their livelihood at stake, the citizens of Tianjin demonstrated unprecedented solidarity. They institutionalized that unity with the formation of the Society for the Preservation of Tianjin (Tianjin Weichihui) following a meeting of more than three hundred concerned citizens. Liu Mengyang, Wang Mengchen, and Li Zihe, representing a broad alliance of the city's mass media, educational institutions, and self-government bodies, were elected leaders.[52] On their own initiative, they explored various solutions to the crisis with the foreign banks, including the possibility of repaying the loans by installment. Armed with the bankers' favorable response, they sought unsuccessfully to meet with Zhang Zhenfang immediately. When they did meet in the afternoon of June 10, it was already too late: Zaize, the controller-general, was now in charge. Early that morning, the order had been issued for the expropriation of five more salt merchants.[53]

Determined to protect the economic viability of the city, the society kept trying. It sent a delegation to Beijing for an audience with Zaize and warned the Beile Prince that the state was jeopardizing the livelihood of hundreds of thousands of people as well as the stability of the realm.[54] Appealing to local sentiment, the delegation met with Assistant Grand Secretary Xu Shichang and other Tianjin natives serving as officials in the capital.[55] On June 6 these officials, concerned with the welfare of their city, met and considered whether to impeach Zhang or to solicit the assistance of the governor-general.[56]

Indeed, dissatisfaction with Zhang Zhenfang, now identified by the

*Dagongbao* as the enemy of the Changlu salt merchants, was widespread. The Society for the Promotion of Constitutional Monarchy, founded by head merchant Li Shiming, petitioned the governorgeneral and pointed out the flaws of Zhang's scheme. The profitability of the Cableway Company and its reliability as a source to help repay the debt were questionable. Moreover, the society believed that the state would not profit from the confiscated monopolies to the extent it expected, since it lacked the expertise to operate them. Reminding Zhang of his disastrous experience as the official operator of the Yongping monopolies before he became the Changlu commissioner, he of all people should have known better.[57] The society also noted that the confiscation of the railroad company shares was improper, if not illegal, since they were the collective property of all the salt merchants of the Changlu Division and not the personal property of the bankrupt ten. Furthermore, the merchants were the only buffer against assumption of direct control and operation of the salt trade by foreign interests.[58]

The many self-government assemblies, too, did not stand idle. After a series of well-attended meetings, the municipal assembly criticized Zhang's neglect of debts to Chinese merchants and disapproved of the provision requiring the twenty-five salt merchants who were deemed solvent to repay all their bank loans within the month. A strongly worded petition was delivered to the Provincial Consultative Assembly for transmission to the governor-general and the Salt Administration.[59] Aside from the devastating effects this would have on the local economy, the assembly questioned the ability of stateappointed receivers to operate the monopolies efficiently: a huge bureaucracy, the assembly pointed out, often meant corruption, disruption, and riots. Unaccustomed to such challenges to their authority and competence, Zhang Zhenfang dismissed the municipal assembly's petition as absurd and Zaize called it "inflammatory." When enraged assembly members threatened to resign, it took no less than the governor-general to coax them back to their posts.[60]

Equally strong antiofficial feelings found expression in the Provincial Consultative Assembly. Its members raised a series of pointed questions: Why did Zhang arrest Wang Xianbin and others when the foreign banks had yet to initiate proceedings against them?[61] Why did Zhang order the salt merchants to repay all bank loans—whether foreign or Chinese—by June 25? If most salt merchants were solvent, why must they repay all their loans? Had Zhang exceeded his authority in requiring the solvent merchants to pay the surcharge? Finally the assembly asked whether Zhang, or his predecessors, were not themselves at least partly responsible for failing to supervise the salt merchants. It then resolved to impeach Zhang Zhenfang for corruption and incompetence: since he became commissioner in 1909, the assembly alleged, his secretary Huang Cheng'an had accepted a fee of 10,000 taels for every authorization letter issued and Zhang himself had received a commission of 5 percent of the foreign bank loans.[62]

Brushing aside all these charges, Zhang Zhenfang and his superiors imposed their solution. The rescue plan for the Changlu Division submitted by the Salt Administration to the throne castigated irresponsible merchants for contracting loans and then defaulting on them. To avoid losing its credibility and protect its sovereignty over the salt monopolies, the state had no choice but to intervene. The state plan differed from Zhang's by calling for repayment of the loan in fourteen years from various sources: 500,000 taels from the profits of the monopolies confiscated and operated by the state; 180,000 taels from the salt merchants' share of four price increases; 40,000 taels from the profits of the Tianjin-Wuqing monopolies; and 30,000 taels from the antismuggling budget. In addition, some 300,000 taels of annual profit from the state operation of the Cableway Company that Wang and Li owned and the Yongping prefecture monopolies would provide secondary security. As a guarantee, the commissioner deposited twenty-eight forward-dated gabelle receipts with the bank. A satisfied court approved these provisions on July 3, 1911 —as well as Zaize's recommendation that the energetic Zhang Zhenfang, despite his negligent supervision of the salt merchants, be retained as Changlu commissioner to ensure smooth operation of the confiscated monopolies.[63]

## Aftermath

Wang Xianbin and his colleagues were released on August 13 to the custody of the Tianjin Chamber of Commerce, but the crisis lingered on.[64] Widespread disturbances and suits filed by Chinese creditors against the bankrupt salt merchants forced the state to intercede again. His dislike of the offending salt merchants notwithstanding, the commissioner finally offered to settle the claims of Chinese creditors at a steep discount of 16 cents on the yuan.[65] The chamber was put in charge: posting notices, placing advertisements in news-papers, requesting creditors to register their claims.[66]

One month later, besieged by hundreds of creditors, the chamber appealed to Zhang Zhenfang. The auction of the salt merchants' personal effects and real estate yielded only 320,000 taels, while their debts had climbed to almost 1.8 million taels.[67] Negotiations ensued, and finally an additional 600,000 taels was borrowed from the Da Qing Government Bank to be repaid by the expected profits of the Cableway Company. Together with 100,000 taels supplied by the Changlu commissioner and 110,000 taels in bonds secured by the bankrupt salt merchants' railroad stocks and bonds, the debts were settled at approximately 50 cents on the yuan—inequitable no doubt, compared with the settlement offered to the foreign banks, but a siz-able improvement over the commissioner's initial offer.[68]

Although the creditors were more or less placated, the contrac-tual obligations assumed by the state remained an issue. Particularly troubling were cases involving a bankrupt merchant who was a lessee. According to the repealed bankruptcy code of 1906, third-party prop-erty managed by a bankrupt merchant should be returned to the original owners.[69] Could the state unilaterally assume the remainder of the lease? Could the owners be compelled to allow state operation of their monopolies until the loans were repaid? If so, on what terms?[70] All these issues were eventually settled in the state's favor—although Zhang, almost as an afterthought, decided that since many of the monopolies were leased by the bankrupt salt merchants, rent should be paid to the lessors. He soon added the condition that the security deposits held by the lessors must be returned in full to the state before the rents could be paid. When this radical departure from the merchants' customary practice met with strenuous opposition, the commissioner argued that the owners were partially responsible for leasing the monopolies to such unworthy characters. As a concession, he ruled that owners would receive half the rent until the security deposit was fully repaid—yet another departure from the merchants' customary practice, if not a violation of the Qing Code.[71]

The crash of 1911 was the last in a series of financial crises to hit Tianjin before the fall of the dynasty. There is no question that some salt merchants overextended themselves, not merely in business, but also in their social services and political activities. But the forces that shaped their downfall were complex. The actions of Zhang and his superiors highlight the ambiguities and limitations of the salt monopoly system. Who actually "owned" the monopolies? What were the rights and responsibilities (both legal and fiduciary) of the salt merchants toward the state and other institutions with which they had business dealings? Foreign interests in late Qing were clearly more effective than Chinese organizations like the Zhili Provincial Consultative Assembly in achieving what they wanted. Yet it was the Qing state that, however weak and tottering in hindsight, had the legitimacy and authority to impose its will on its subjects.

While Zhang Zhenfang was acting within a tradition of statecraft that assumed the state's primacy, he was also operating outside the law and local custom. Several of his rulings were arbitrary: the requirement that all loans be repaid within the month, for example, and the ban on salt merchants' use of non-salt-related properties as collateral. If the vigorous political, legal, and economic reforms of the golden decade were designed to provide a foundation upon which the economy could develop, issues of enforcement remained—as well as the question how theory, practice, and rhetoric would interact.

However one assesses responsibility for the salt merchants' plight, their privileged world lay in shambles. While arches built in their honor stood proudly on the streets, these leading citizens were sent to prison.[72] Wang could no longer afford to support local, much less national, causes. Nor could his fellow salt merchants. After the Wuchang Rebellion broke out, a desperate Qing court approached the Changlu salt merchants for contributions and loans to help restore its mandate. But unlike their forebears under similar circumstances during the Taiping Rebellion, or their counterparts in the Lianghuai Division, the remaining Changlu salt merchants balked.[73] Others, such as Sun Hongyi, went even further and almost succeeded in persuading the Qing garrisons at Luanzhou and Shijiazhuang to declare independence and organize a provisional government in Tianjin.[74] For the moment at least, the tables had been turned.

# EPILOGUE

Tianjin of late imperial and modern times, beset by internal rebellion and by invasion from without, underwent significant changes in its relationship with the state. In this the dynamics were similar to, yet different from, the idealized Western European experience. Since the seventeenth century, the city's merchant princes had been constructing their society and identity through economic activities, local business and legal customs, culture, and social services. The Qing state made "useful compromises" with these merchants, securing social and revenue stability in the exchange. This interpretation of a Chinese "civil" society is not based on the assumptions that state and society must be mutually exclusive domains, forever locked in a zero-sum game over power, or that a state must centralize all the instruments of coercion as in the modern West.

As the foregoing chapters illustrate, the city's dynamics of change is different—not merely from its successful (and less successful) bourgeois European counterparts but also from other parts of rural and urban China. Compared to their counterparts in Furong, for example, Tianjin's merchant princes seem to have been a more consistent source of civic pride and local managerial effort.[1] Unlike Quanzhou where overseas Chinese returned to develop the city's public services, it was salt merchants who assumed these responsibilities in their adopted native place.[2] Although Tianjin evolved with merchant support a host of grassroots organizations such as the firefighting *shuihui*, it stopped short of neighborhood self-governments such as those found in Suzhou. Nor were they quite so bold as their Shanghai colleagues who argued that self-government institutions left no room for autocratic state power. Instead, Tianjin offered collaboration as well as challenges.[3] Its merchant princes had long learned how to work with the state and its local representatives, had accumulated political capital through cultural entrepreneurship to protect their interests (if not claims), and had exploited the gap between the local bureaucracy and the central government.

Mobilization of Tianjin's salt merchants in local public affairs reflected the particular history of the city. In participating in public life, they were motivated less by a desire to compete against the state than a complex of economic, cultural, social, and psychological reasons. Countering the scorn heaped upon them, they led an exclusive network of kin by marriage, wealth, business interests, and identity in funding local charities and urban services and providing both regular and emergency relief to their fellow citizens. By late Qing, the salt merchants supported local society by funding local militias, schools, and the Chamber of Commerce. They had appropriated the vocabulary of citizenship and nationalism and added their voice to the discourse on state building.[4]

In outgrowing the subsidiary or even intermediary role as conceived by officials, the merchants also added to the cacophony of late Qing reforms. For the Manchu statesmen in the capital, the reforms were but a means to recapture their authority thought to be lost to Han Chinese provincial governors. For provincial and local officials, the reforms promoted a new balance, not merely between the central and local government, but also between the rulers and the ruled. For students and intellectuals back from abroad, the panacea for China's woes—constitutionalism, national parliament, provincial assemblies, and local self-government bodies—would provide the institutional means to create a new citizenry and realize a corporatist vision of state and society.

Whatever their motives, promoters of late Qing reforms, in their optimism to concentrate power and resources while mobilizing and expanding social participation, overlooked the dangers, if not contradictions, in their programs.[5] Under the threat of foreign invasion and imminent colonialization, the center had to be strong enough to hold the country together. Condemned to modernize, predatory state-building strategies that violated centuries of useful compromises

—strategies such as the seizure of salt monopolies from bankrupted salt merchants or threatening the takeover of the remaining salt merchants—were but a small price to pay.

In practice, too, a state-imposed program to cultivate a new citizenry not only clashed with the imperative of a strong central government but served to divide local society. Indeed, the merchants' growing activism destabilized Tianjin's society—a development fed by scholar-gentry who were forced by the abolition of the civil service examination system in 1905 to find alternate careers to maintain their lofty social status. In urban as well as rural China, degree holders found themselves confronting not merely merchants but also unruly graduates of new education institutions and peasant activists.[6] The promulgation of local self-government through assemblies and councils further aggravated this conflict as the ink brush competed with silver for funding, status, resource, and influence. A state-building strategy thought to be the secret of the West or Japan might be transplanted to China. But for the new institutions to take root and acquire legitimacy, the time was much too short and the forces of division unleashed too great for the regime.

The end of the Qing dynasty thus began several months, if not years, before what happened in Wuchang and was set in motion as much by what some historians have called a golden decade of vigorous political, economic, and social reform as by rebel soldiers. With the fall of the dynasty, both state and society lost. In 1914, Yuan Shikai declared his experiment in local government dead. The republican state, denying local initiatives that had once been routine, asserted itself. All matters pertaining to governance were guarded jealously by the central and local governments.[7] China became locked in a vicious cycle of confrontation and revolution. While the country could ill afford more revolutions, warlordism feasted on what remained of the state and society.[8]

Tianjin, of course, survived. Not all was lost for the remaining merchants, but a new generation of the Chinese bourgeoisie would have to battle over the same terrain again.[9] Together with the city's capitalists, students, and intellectuals, they would find themselves under the guns of rampaging soldiers and demanding warlords. In the harsh times of modernity even Liu Bowen's prophecy—water and fire, not war, would ravage Tianjin—had lost its magic.

# Notes

ABBREVIATIONS

BZJ            Qian Yiji, comp. *Beizhuanji* (Anthology of tombstone biogra-
               phies). Reprinted Shanghai: Guji chubanshe, 1987.
CL             Changlu yanyunshishi dang (Archives of the Changlu Salt
               Commissioner). First National Archives, Beijing.
CLHB           Changlu yanyunshishi dang (Archives of the Changlu Salt
               Commissioner). Hebei Provincial Archives.
CLYFZJQ        Wang Zhanglun et al. *Changlu yanfazhi* (Codes of the Changlu
               Salt Division). 1805 ed.
CLYFZQL        Jing Rui et al. "Changlu yanfazhi" (Codes of the Changlu Salt
               Division). Manuscript ca. 1792. Special Collections, Nankai
               University Library.
CLYFZYZ        Duan Ruhui et al. *Changlu yanfazhi* (Codes of the Changlu
               Salt Division). 1727 ed. Reprinted Taipei: Xuesheng shudian,
               1966.
CLYWZY         *Changlu yanwu zouyi* (Memorials and petitions to the
               throne regarding the Changlu Salt Division). Rescripts.
               Institute of Economics, Chinese Academy of Social Sciences,
               Beijing.
CLYYGX         "Changlu yanyince" (Handbook of Changlu salt quotas).
               Manuscript ca. 1891. Special Collections, Nankai University
               Library.
DGB            *Dagongbao (L'Impartial)*. Tianjin.
FM             Qing Foreign Ministry Archives. Academia Sinica.
FO             Foreign Office Archives. Public Records Office, U.K.
GCXZ           Li Yuandu, comp. *Guochao xianzheng shilüe* (Brief biographies
               of the virtuous during the Qing dynasty). Reprinted Chang-
               sha: Yuelu shushe, 1991.

GGBWYYK    *Gugong bowuyuan yuankan* (Journal of the Imperial Palace
           Museum).
GGWX       *Gugong wenxian* (Historical materials from the National
           Palace Museum).
GXCDHL     *Guangxu chao Donghualu* (Historical record of the reign of
           Emperor Guangxu). 5 vols. 1909 ed. Reprinted Beijing:
           Zhonghua shuju, 1958.
GZDYZC     *Gongzhongdang Yongzheng chao* (Palace archives from the
           Yongzheng period).
HCZDLZ     Xi Yufu, comp. *Huangchao zhengdian leizuan* (Sources on the
           governmental institutions of the august dynasty arranged by
           categories). 1903 ed.
JAS        *Journal of Asian Studies.*
JDSYJ      *Jindaishi yanjiu* (Studies on modern Chinese history).
JJYJSJK    *Zhongguo shehui kexue yuan Jingji yanjiusuo jikan* (*Journal
           of the Institute of Economics,* Chinese Academy of Social
           Sciences).
JMBJTS     *Jinmen baojia tushuo* (Household register of Tianjin).
           1846 ed.
KXCZPHWYZ  Zhongguo diyi lishi dang'anguan, comp. *Kangxi chao zhupi
           hanwen yuzhi* (Vermilion brush endorsed memorials in
           Chinese from the reign of the Kangxi Emperor). 8 vols.
           Beijing: Dang'an chubanshe, 1984.
LSDA       *Lishi dang'an* (Historical archives).
LSDL       *Lishi dili* (Historical geography).
LSYJ       *Lishi yanjiu* (Historical studies).
MC         *Modern China.*
MQSL       *Ming-Qing shiliao* (Historical sources of the Ming and Qing
           dynasties).
MS         Zhang Tingyu et al. *Mingshi* (History of the Ming dynasty).
           Reprinted Beijing: Zhonghua shuju, 1974.
MTZSL      *Ming taizu shilu* (Veritable records of the Ming Taizu
           Emperor).
NW         *Neiwufu laiwen* (Communications from the Imperial
           Household Department). First National Archives,
           Beijing.
QDCD       *Qingdai chaodang* (Archival materials from the Qing dynasty).
           Institute of Economics, Chinese Academy of Social Sciences,
           Beijing.
QJZ        *Kangxi qijuzhu* (Daily record of the Kangxi Emperor). 3 vols.
           Beijing: Zhonghua shuju, 1984.
QSG        Zhao Erxun et al. *Qingshi gao* (Draft history of the Qing
           dynasty). Reprinted Beijing: Zhonghua shuju, 1977.
QSL        *Qingshi liechuan* (Biographies of the Qing dynasty). Reprinted
           Beijing: Zhonghua shuju, 1987.
QSLC       Zhongguo shehui kexueyuan Lishi yanjiusuo Qingshi
           yanjiushi, ed. *Qingshi luncong* (Articles on Qing history).

| | |
|---|---|
| QSLDGC | Qingshilu: Daoguangchao (Veritable records of the Daoguang Emperor). Reprinted Beijing: Zhonghua Honghua shuju, 1986. |
| QSLJQC | Qingshilu: Jiaqingchao (Jiaqing Emperor). |
| QSLKXC | Qingshilu: Kangxichao (Kangxi Emperor). |
| QSLQLC | Qingshilu: Qianlongchao (Qianlong Emperor). |
| QSLSZC | Qingshilu: Shunzhichao (Shunzhi Emperor). |
| QSLTZC | Qingshilu: Tongzhichao (Tongzhi Emperor). |
| QSLXFC | Qingshilu: Xianfengchao (Xianfeng Emperor). |
| QSLYZC | Qingshilu: Yongzhengchao (Yongzheng Emperor). |
| QYFZ | Zhang Moujiong, comp. Qing yanfazhi (Salt codes of the Qing dynasty). Beijing: Yanwuchu, 1920. |
| TJFZ | Wu Tinghua et al. Tianjin fuzhi (Gazetteer of Tianjin prefecture). 1739 ed. |
| TJFZX | Xu Zongliang et al. Tianjin fuzhi (Gazetteer of Tianjin prefecture). 1899 ed. |
| TJGSSLCK | Tianjin gongshang shiliao congkan (Historical materials on commerce and industries of Tianjin). |
| TJLSZL | Tianjin lishi ziliao (Sources on Tianjin history). |
| TJSHDAXB | Tianjinshi dang'anguan et al. Tianjin shanghui dang'an huibian (Selections from the Tianjin Chamber of Commerce archive). Tianjin: Renmin chubanshe. Vol. 1: 1989; vol. 2: 1991. |
| TJSHKX | Tianjin shehui kexue (Social sciences of Tianjin). |
| TJSYJ | Tianjinshi yanjiu (Studies of Tianjin history). |
| TJSZ | Tianjin shizhi (Historical chronicle of Tianjin). |
| TJWSCK | Tianjin wenshi congkan (Anthology of historical materials on Tianjin). |
| TJWSZL | Tianjin wenshi ziliao (Historical materials of Tianjin). |
| TJWZ | Xie Zhudou et al. Tianjin weizhi (Gazetteer of Tianjin Guard Station). 1674 ed. Reprinted 1982. |
| TJXXZ | Gao Ningwen et al. Tianjin xian xinzhi (New gazetteer of Tianjin district). 1931 ed. |
| TJXZ | Wu Tinghua et al. Tianjin xianzhi (Gazetteer of Tianjin district). 1739 ed. |
| TMA | Tianjin Chamber of Commerce Archive. Tianjin Municipal Archive, Tianjin. |
| WSZLXJ | Wenshi ziliao xuanji (Selected materials on history). Beijing: Zhongguo renmin zhengzi hieshang huiyi, 1960–. |
| XTJXZ | Jiang Yuhong et al. Xu Tianjin xianzhi (Gazetteer of Tianjin district). 1870 ed. |
| YSKZY | Yuan Shikai zouyi (Collected memorials of Yuan Shikai). 3 vols. Tianjin: Guji chubanshe, 1987. |
| ZB | Zhibao (Upright Daily). Tianjin. |
| ZGJJSYJ | Zhongguo jingjishi yanjiu (Chinese economic history). |
| ZGSHJJSYJ | Zhongguo shehui jingjishi yanjiu (Social and economic history of China). |

INTRODUCTION

1. *DGB*, 6/5/1911.

2. Zhou Chuliang, "Jinmen zhuzhici" (Rhymed poems of Tianjin), in Hao Fusen (n.d).

3. Thomas Metzger, "The Organizational Capabilities of the Ch'ing State in the Field of Commerce," in Willmott (1972:33–45); Metzger (1973); and Bergère (1989:16). On the politics of commercial capitalists in general see, for example, Fox-Genovese and Genovese (1983).

4. For various disciplinary approaches see Tilly (1975:601–638); Strauss (1998); and Wong (1997).

5. Weber (1968, 3:965) and (1982:334).

6. Tilly (1990); Wim P. Blockmans, "State Formation in Preindustrial Europe," in Tilly et al. (1994:242).

7. Montesquieu (1990: bk. XX, pp. 1–2).

8. See, for example, Locke (1965:368–369) and Ferguson (1966).

9. Keane (1998:6) and Ehrenberg (1999).

10. Hegel (1967).

11. Karl Marx, "Manifesto of the Communist Party," in Feuer (1959:9). On Marx's position toward civil society see, for example, Ehrenberg (1999:134–137).

12. For a survey of these theoretical developments and their political implications see Habermas (1989), Seligman (1992), Gellner (1994), Zhu Shiqun (1995), and He Baogang (1997).

13. Alfred Stepan, "State Power and the Strength of Civil Society in the Southern Cone of Latin America," in Skocpol et al. (1985:318).

14. For the French, Italian, and German traditions see Cohen and Arato (1992:78) and Keane (1988:15–16).

15. On Durham see James (1974:190). On London see Williams (1988) and Brenner (1992).

16. Even Habermas concedes this point. See Calhoun (1992:463).

17. Holub (1991:4); Eley in Calhoun (1992), 321; and Morris (1998).

18. Mandel (1968, 1:124); see also Balazs (1964:78).

19. Weber (1958) and Tang Lixing (1993:305–323). For a review of the Weberian literature on Chinese cities see Bernstein (1988:chap. 1).

20. Fu Zhufu, "Zhongguo gudai chengshi zai guomin jingji zhong de diwei he zuoyong" (The position and effects of cities in the national economy of ancient China), in Fu Zhufu (1980, 1:321–386) and Bergère (1989:7).

21. Chung (1998:15).

22. Habermas (1989) and Rowe (1984; 1989; 1990; 1993).

23. Rankin (1986; 1992).

24. Kuhn (1994:301–307); Brook and Frolic (1997:21); Keane (1998); Morris (1998:289).

25. Habermas (1989:xvii) and Zhu Ying (1997:120–122).

26. Ma Min (1995:5).

27. Yu Yingshi (1987a:99–106; 1994). On Confucian public-mindedness see Cheng I-fan, "Kung as an Ethos in Late Nineteenth-Century China," in Cohen and Schrecker (1976); and Chang Hao, "The Intellectual Heritage of the Confucian Ideal of *Ching-shih*," in Tu Wei-ming (1996:72–91).

28. Regional patterns of elite domination are identified in Esherick and Rankin (1990). On informal governance see Skinner (1977:336–339).

29. Fuma Susumu (1986); Liang Qizhi (1986; 1997); Wakeman (1993); Kuhn (1994); and He Yaofu (1994:141).

30. For problems in translating the term into Chinese see Wang Shaoguang (1991).

31. Eisenstadt and Schluchter (1998:1–18).

32. This China-centered approach draws heavily from the seminal works of Huang (1993), Cohen (1984), and Wong (1997).

33. Gellner (1994:91–92); Roniger and Guneş-Ayata (1994:3–10).

34. Zhu Ying (1991a; 1991b); Pearson (1997:52).

35. Ho Ping-ti (1954) remains the classic treatment of salt merchants as failures in commercial capitalism and social climbers. Merchants as members of the local gentry have received little attention as most studies have focused on the scholar-literati. See, for example, Brook (1993:12–29) and Chow Kai-wing (1994:2–14).

36. Ian Copland and Michael R. Godley, "Revenue Farming in Comparative Perspective," in Butcher and Dick (1993:47–48); Salzmann (1993). On China see the pioneering work of Mann (1987a).

37. I owe this "downsizing" insight to Salzmann (1991).

38. Pu Songling (1981, 4:2304).

39. Wei Qingyuan, "Kang, Yong, Qian shiqi gaolitai de ersheng fazhan" (The vicious development of usury during the Kangxi, Yongzheng, and Qianlong periods), in Wei Qingyuan (1984:27–31); Lin Yongkang (1984); and Liu Qiugen (1995:117).

40. Huntington (1968:59–61); Nathaniel H. Leff, "Economic Development Through Bureaucratic Corruption," in Heidenheimer (1970:510–520); and Sumner (1990:17).

41. See, for example, Jonathan Ocko, "Hierarchy and Harmony: Family Conflict as Seen in Ch'ing Legal Cases," in Liu Kwang-ching (1990:212–230).

42. On the household's quest for the good life as a universal theme see Booth (1993).

43. On the extensive role of women in merchant families see Shih (1995).

44. The case of Changlu salt merchants affirms and elaborates the findings of Hugh T. Scogin that the Qing legal system was actively engaged in civil cases. See Bernhardt and Huang (1994) and Zhou Guangyuan (1995).

45. On the hunhunr and construction of Tianjin's urban identity see Kwan (2000).

46. Bergère (1989:23).

47. Identified more by popular acclaim than scientific poll, membership of the Big Eight defies precise definition. Certainly it changed in time as families declined and were replaced. By the second half of the nineteenth century, acknowledged members included the Han (coastal shipping; corporate name: Tiancheng), the Shi (landholding), the Liu (landholding), the Mu (tea, salt, and grain trade), and the families of salt merchants: the Gao (corporate name: Yideyu), the Huang (corporate name: Zhende; sobriquet: King Huang III), the Yang (corporate name: Changyuan) who came to the city from Shaanxi, and the

Zhang (corporate name: Yizhaolin; sobriquet: Haizhangwu) from neighboring Jinghai district. By the turn of the century, accepted members included the Bian (cotton yarn and cloth; seafood; individual members engaged in the salt trade), who came from Wujin in 1715, and several families of salt merchants: the Hua, who settled in the city in 1663 (corporate name: Hua Jicheng; sobriquet: "Gao-taijie" or Highsteps, otherwise known as Southern "Nan" Huas to distinguish them from Northern "Bei" Huas under the corporate name of Changyu but whose apical ancestor, also from Wuxi, arrived in Tianjin in 1534); the Wang (corporate name: Yide; sobriquet: Hempsack King) from Shanxi; and the Li from Qunshan (corporate name: Ruichang; sobriquet: Philanthropist Lis). See Tianjinshi zheng-xie mishuchu (1974); Xin Chengzhang (1982); and interview with Wang Zhiquan, 8/7/1997.

48. Brook and Frolic (1997:25–29). I have added kinship networks as an organizational principle.

49. He Yaofu (1994:120).

50. These developments are explored primarily at national and provincial levels in Thompson (1995).

51. On various perspectives on late Qing reforms see MacKinnon (1980:163–179), Min Tu-ki (1989), and Chen Xiangyang (1998). For reviews of the historical role of the various chambers of commerce see Zhu Ying (1984), Xu Dingxin (1986), and Zhang Xiaobo (1995:25–26).

CHAPTER 1: THE CITY

1. On the archaeological history of Tianjin see Ao Chengnong (1976), Han Jiagu (1979), and Chen Kewei (1979). On the issue of earliest settlement see Hou Renzhi (1945).

2. See, for example, Chen Hua (1996:77).

3. Lin Xi (1997:1–6).

4. On the naming of Tianjin see Li Dongyang, "Xiuzuo weicheng jiuji" (Stele in memory of city wall construction), in *TJWZ, juan* 4, 10a–b.

5. *MTZSL, juan* 36, 5b. On the organization of the guard station see *MS, juan* 90, 2193. Each station had a nominal strength of 5,600 men.

6. Gao Xiang et al. (1964), *juan* 11, 7a.

7. Li Dongyang in *TJWZ, juan* 1, 2b; *juan* 4, 10a–b. See also Bi Zhiyan (1622), *juan* 1, 56a, memorial dated 8/2/1621.

8. Li Banghua (1842), *juan* 4, 53a; Bi Zhiyan (1622), *juan* 2, 3b, memorial dated 9/20/1621.

9. *MS, juan* 223, 5881–5882; Zhang Han (1985), *juan* 8, 158–161.

10. Zang Menglin, "Ode of Zhigu," in Zheng Shiwei et al. (1873), *juan* 8, 30a.

11. *TJWZ, juan* 2, 25a–26b; *juan* 4, 6a–8a.

12. *Guanzi* (1920), *juan* 22, 1a–2b.

13. Tuo Tuo et al. (1977), *juan* 273, 9329.

14. *TJWZ, juan* 4, 5b–6a; Tuo Tuo et al. (1977), *juan* 94, 2386–2387.

15. *MS, juan* 153, 4204–4205.

16. Subsequent advocates of sea transport had to rediscover the route. See, for example, *MS, juan* 225, 5915.

17. Changes in the Ming tribute-grain system are summarized in *MS, juan* 79, 1916–1921. The statutory number of tribute-grain boats was once 11,775 with a transport corps of 121,500. See Xi Shu et al. (n.d.), *juan* 3, 2b; Lu Yong (1982), *juan* 12, 150.

18. *TJWZ, juan* 1, 3a. Three granaries were built east of the Drum Tower; the name Cangmenkou (Granary Gate) is still in use.

19. *MS, juan* 81, 1976–1978.

20. *TJXZ, juan* 14, 29a; *CLYFZYZ, juan* 4, 4b–6b.

21. *TJWZ, juan* 2, 35b–36a; *TJXZ, juan* 14, 59b.

22. *CLYFZYZ, juan* 5, 1b–6a and 19a–19b.

23. *QSLYZC*, 4/19/1725; 11/4/1725; 11/13/1726; 3/30/1731.

24. *MQSL, ji*, 4:302b–303b, 337b–338b, and 343b–344a. The ban was first issued on August 6, 1656. See *QSLSZC*, 8/6/1656. For the extensive literature on this policy see Zhu Delan, "Qingchu qianjieling shi Zhongguochuan haishang maoyi zhi yanjiu" (The ban on coastal traffic and trade in early Qing), in Zhongguo haiyang fazhanshi lunwenji bianji weiyuanhui (1986:105–160).

25. For the lifting of the ban against Shandong and the coastal junk trade see *QSG, juan* 125, 3765. On "traditional" coastal trade see Xie Jianren in He Changning (1903), *juan* 48, 9b; Akira Matsura, "Shindai ni okeru genan bōeki ni tsuite" (On the coastal trade during the Qing period), in Ono Kazuko (1983: 595–650); Kōsaka Masanori (1971); Guo Songyi (1982); and Ng Chin-keong (1983).

26. *GZDYZC*, 5/18/1725. Junks from Tianjin ventured as far south as Changyi (Haicang of the Yuan dynasty) in Shandong by the reign of the Yongzheng Emperor but were not found in Shanghai until decades later. See Guo Songyi (1982:96); Fan Bochuan (1985:48); and *TJXZ, juan* 21, 49a–49b.

27. On the Gaos and the Hans see Tianjinshi zhengxie mishuchu (1974:4); Xin Chengzhang (1982:44–45); and Tianjinshi shanghui (1933:33).

28. By late nineteenth century, the total number of coastal junks was estimated at 5,700. See Tian Yukang (1987:43–44). This estimate does not include junks from the northern ports such as Tianjin, Jiaozhou, Niuzhuang, and others. Fan Bochuan (1985:71–78) thus put the number of coastal junks at close to 10,000 with a total capacity of 1.5 million tons.

29. Qian Yong (1979), I: *juan* 4, 108.

30. See Guo Songyi (1982:102); Ng Chin-keong (1983:app. C); and Matsura Akira (1988a; 1988b). On Taiwan see Yao Ying (1867), *juan* 12, 14a.

31. Official policy shifted many times. Kangxi approved the traffic from Tianjin to Fengtian by sea in 1694 (*QSLKXC*, 4/2/1694). But the ban was often reimposed thereafter due to bad harvests in Fengtian. See, for example, *QSLJQC*, 7/3/1812 and 4/27/1822.

32. *TJXZ, juan* 21, 49b. Ports in Shandong opened to facilitate the grain traffic were frequently closed for security reasons. See, for instance, *QSLQLC*, 9/26/1772.

33. On the formation of the Haihe River system see Tan Qixiang (1986) and Zhu Kezhen, "Zhili dili de huanjing he shuizai" (Geography and flooding in Zhili), in Zhu Kezhen (1979:108–116). On Tianjin's hydraulic problems see Qiao Hong (1960).

34. Shuili shuidian kexue yanjiuyuan (1981:12); Zhonghua dilizhi bianjibu (1957:50). See also Hitch (1935).

35. *HCZDLZ, juan* 38, 48.

36. For a discussion of Xu Jingming's work see Shimizu Taiji (1928) and Shen Defu (1980), *juan* 12, 320–332. On Xu Guangqi see *MS, juan* 251, 6493–6495; Hummel (1970, 2:316–318); and Liang Jiamian (1981). On his agricultural experiment in Tianjin see Xu Guangqi (1979), *juan* 12, *juan* 25. For Zuo see *Tianjin-wei tunken tiaokuan* (Regulations on the colonization and reclamation of Tianjin garrison command), dated 1624, Rare Books Collection, Beijing Library. For Lin Zexu and other reclamation attempts during the Qing period see *HCZDLZ, juan* 39.

37. Zheng Kecheng (1988:322–350); *MS, juan* 244, 6329; Goodrich and Fang (1976, 2:1305–1308).

38. *QSG, juan* 129, 3824.

39. On the constraints imposed by agricultural technology see Timothy Brook, "Ming-Qing liangdai Hebei diqu tuiguang zhongdao he zhongdao zishu de qing-kuang" (The promotion of paddy rice and technology in Hebei during the Ming and Qing), in Li Guohao et al. (1986:633–654).

40. Ping Buqing (1980), I, *juan* 1, 79–80; Tianjin diwei wadi gaizao bangong-shi (1958:19). See also Chen Cheng-siang, "The Length of the Growing Season: As Determined by the Effectiveness of the Rainfall," in Chen Cheng-siang (1984: 111); Tianjin shiyuan dilixi (1981:24). On climatic changes see Zhu Kezhen, "Zhongguo jin wuqian'nian lai qihou bianqian de chubu yanjiu" (Climatic change in China during the last five thousand years), in Zhu Kezhen (1979:475–498).

41. On Senggerinchin's 4,000-*mu* project and Chonghou's attempt at Xian-shuigu involving 3,540 *mu*, see *QSG, juan* 129, 3853; *QSLTZC,* 1/11/1866; and *TJFZ, juan* 28, 24a–26a.

42. For Li's reclamation project see Wu Bangxing (1842). Li's rejection was drafted by Zhou Fu. See Zhou Fu (1922), memorials, *juan* 5, 17a–22a.

43. *QSG, juan* 122, 3581; *juan* 127, 3791–3792.

44. *ZB,* 1/31/1901.

45. On Tianjin's agriculture see Wu Ou (1931) and "Tianjinxian shuli diao-cha baogaoshu" (Survey report on irrigation in Tianjin district), in *Zhili shiye congkan* (Zhili industrial gazette) 1(4) (April 1923):1–3 and 1(5) (May 1923):1–3.

46. Vegetable gardening along the Haihe developed after 1900. See *DGB,* 9/11/1930. The nightsoil trade was big business in Tianjin and gentry members made abortive attempts to corner the market. Exporting approximately 300,000 *shi* each year as far as Shandong, the city was carved up by collectors—mostly immigrants from Shandong—each jealously guarding his turf. See *ZB,* 4/24/1898; *DGB,* 7/27/1906, 11/7/1908, 5/17/1909, 7/8/1915; and Liu Yanchen (1943:94).

47. On wine import see "Jieyunhailiangguan Wanggong Donglugong jiuqu-shibei" (Stele in memory of tribute-grain transport commissioners of Wang and Donglu), in *TJWZ, juan* 4, 6a–7a. On imports from the south see Zhang Zhu (1934), *juan* 4, 23b.

48. See, for example, Loren Brandt's review of Philip C. C. Huang's *The Peasant Economy and Social Change in North China* in Brandt (1987:674).

49. Wang Kerun (1754). On the four production systems in North China—

coastal, lowlands, plains, and mountains—see Yang Zhongqi [Ji Jin] (1915). See also Jiang Shoupeng (1996) for a survey of commercialization in North China during the Ming and Qing periods.

50. For estimates on transport costs see Jernigan (1905:230–231) and Shina chūtongun (Rikugan) Shireibu Ōtsu shokutaku kōanhan (1937:784).

51. FO 674/36, British Consul Forest's report on "Charges for carriage of passengers upon Chinese rivers and canals in the neighborhood of Tianjin" dated 9/12/1879. See also DGB, 3/19/1907 (to Hejian), 10/15/1910 (to Yangliuqing), and 7/6/1913 (to Cangxian). The owners of these boats also traded on their own account. See ZB, 9/22/1898.

52. FO 674/13, J. Morgan to Rutherford Alcock dated 6/11/1868. See also Fan I-chun (1992) and Liu Xiusheng (1993).

53. ZB, 5/11/1895.

54. Yang Wending et al. (1896), juan 8, 18a. A shift in the river's channel rendered it unnavigable for coastal junks after 1910. Interview with Wu Chengming, Tianjin, May 28, 1988.

55. QSLKXC, 7/14/1683.

56. See Ijūin Hikokichi (1907, 1:93).

57. This section of the Daqinghe, also known as the Fuhe, was dredged to make it navigable for small boats in 1485 and then larger trade junks in 1491. See Zhao Ying, "Baodingfu xinjian Tianshuiqiao ji" (Essay commemorating construction of the Tianshui bridge), in Zhang Lü et al. (1494), juan 3, 9a; juan 24, 19b–21b. A thirty-mile stretch was silted up, requiring a loan of 50,000 taels from the treasury of the Changlu commissioner to clear. See CL 173.275 dated 2/1/1906.

58. The Fuyang was navigable as far as Cixian in 1482. See Wang Jiong et al. (1756), juan 2, 8a.

59. On the junk fleet from Henan, said to be making three thousand trips a year to Tianjin, see DGB, 11/27/1904.

60. See Shina chūtongun shireibu (1986:89 and 92–93).

61. The following discussion of overland trade routes, unless otherwise noted, is condensed from these sources: Zhilisheng shangpin chenlisuo (1917); local gazetteers; and Council of the China Branch of the Royal Asiatic Society (1878: 1–213).

62. DGB, 12/15/1911.

63. GXCDHL, 9/2/1881; FO 674/13, J. Morgan to Rutherford Alcock dated 6/11/1868.

64. On Yangliuqing's trade with the Northwest see Wang Xingang et al. (1983) and Wang Hongda (n.d.:16–18). For the wheeling and dealing of Tianjin merchants in Xinjiang see Li Fu (1983) and DGB, 8/24/1910.

65. DGB, 1/20/1931.

66. Shina chūtongun Shireibu Ōtsu shokutaku kōanhan (1937:127–128) and Jincheng yinhang zongjinglichu Tianjin diaocha fenbu (1927:table 3). On Tianjin's wheat supply from Hebei province see Mai Shudu (1930). Dwight Perkins thus errs when he argues that it was the rise of coastal steamship shipping that made possible the urbanization of Tianjin in the nineteenth and twentieth centuries. The evidence suggests that the city's population had long been depen-

dent on grain trade—wheat, sorghum, millet, and maize—from Shandong and Henan, as well as from the Northeast on coastal junks. See Perkins (1969:142 and 151).

67. Gutzlaff (1968:134–135). Comparing Tianjin with Xiamen, Hugh Lindsay was much less impressed with the northern port; see *FO* 17/12, Hugh Lindsay to Lord Amherst, 1832.

68. Retabulated from data in *JMBJTS*. Note that the survey did not include officials, a point also made by Momose Hiromu (1980:260).

69. *TJWZ, juan* 2, 2b; Gao Ningwen (1982), *juan* 2, 19b, and *juan* 4, 8b; Lo Shuwei (1993:96–97). *JMBJTS,* however, registered 746 natives *(tuzhu),* or less than 3 percent of the city's number of households.

70. *MTZSL, juan* 61, 1b; *TJWZ, juan* 2, 13a–15b; Bi Zhiyan (1622), *juan* 1, 56a, memorial dated 8/2/1621; and Xu Tongzi (1935).

71. Xu Shiluan (1986:173) and Gao Ningwen (1982), *juan* 3, 19a–19b.

72. Hao Jinrong, "Jinmen jishi shi" (Poems on events in Tianjin), in Hao Fusen (n.d.), *juan* 5.

73. *DGB,* 1/9/1931; Chen Yong (1995:52–53). Of the 391 salt merchants enumerated in the *JMBJTS,* 159 made their home within the city wall, especially along Second Street (Erdujie) running parallel to the main thoroughfare leading toward East Gate. The expensive and highly commercialized neighborhoods outside East and North Gates together claimed 162. Another 34 inhabited the wedge of land between the southern Grand Canal and the northwestern corner of the city wall where one could find the city's main entertainment district of Houjiahou.

## CHAPTER 2: THE GABELLE AND BUSINESS

1. On the evolution of the gabelle in world history see Multhauf (1978) and Adshead (1991).

2. Little is known of pre-1644 Manchu policy on salt tax. Scattered references suggest that the government produced, collected, and distributed salt. See Zhongguo diyi lishi dang'anguan et al. (1990, 1:161 and 544).

3. *CLYFZYZ, juan* 2, 22b; *QYFZ, juan* 17, 2a; *QSG, juan* 123, 3606; and Zuo Buqing (1986:52).

4. 158,973 taels of gabelle were collected. See *QSLSZC, juan* 12, 15b. On the Manchu conquest, see Wakeman (1985). The *yin* was a fiscal accounting and weight unit as well as an official permit for salt in transit.

5. Metzger in Willmott (1972:32–45) and Metzger (1973).

6. See, for example, Gu Yanwu (1990, 1:476–477).

7. See Wei Qingyuan (1984) on the former view; for the latter perspective see Xue Zongzheng (1982).

8. Weber (1968, 3:965; 1982:334).

9. Glade (1986) and Salzmann (1993).

10. On the realities of the battle against corruption see Park (1993).

11. Chiang Tao-chang (1983). There is considerable disagreement on how the divisional boundaries were drawn. To some extent it was a matter of historical precedent. Thus the extensive territory of the Lianghuai Division was a legacy of

the Southern Tang dynasty (937–975). See Tian Qiuye and Zhou Weiliang (1979: 21 and 183). Adshead (1970:10), however, argues that it was "a natural monopoly area before being made a legal one."

12. *Da Qing huidian* (1899), *juan* 20–23.

13. This conclusion was reached by the Board of Personnel as early as 1653, although the position was restored in 1655. See *CLYFZYZ, juan* 4, 2a.

14. *CLYFZYZ, juan* 7, 2a; *CLYFZJQ, juan* 7, 4a.

15. *CLYFZYZ, juan* 7, 45a; Yanwuchu (n.d.:36). Lin Yongkang is therefore inaccurate when he writes that "salt first, tax later" had been the procedure followed since early Qing until the reign of the Qianlong Emperor. See Lin Yongkang (1983:85).

16. This elaborate procedure is reconstructed from *QYFZ, juan* 19, 1a–b; *CLYFZYZ, juan* 2, 13b–14b, *juan* 7, 46b; and Yanwuchu (n.d.:37).

17. *CLYFZYZ, juan* 7, 47a–b.

18. All these documents required separate registration and a notification fee *(gao fei)* at 0.02663 tael per *yin*. See Yanwuchu (n.d.:37).

19. *QYFZ, juan* 17, 1b.

20. *QYFZ, juan* 3, 21–b, *juan* 6, 8a–13b; *CLYFZYZ, juan* 8, 3b–13b; and Chen Feng (1988:46). On the normative aspects of this system see Metzger (1973:235–417).

21. On the anomalies of the Ming system see Huang (1974:202–204 and 221–223).

22. Webber and Wildavsky (1986:552).

23. Wang Shouji (1873:1b) and *CLYFZYZ, juan* 6, 15a–19a. Nevertheless, the tribute was a fraction of Changlu's annual production capacity of over 3 million bales in late Qing. See *CLHB* 5646.

24. Wang Shouli's memorial to the throne dated 9/10/1647 reprinted in *LSDA* 1:9 (1988).

25. The commutation to silver of salt destined for Ming imperial princes (the so-called *jingshan yin*); the levy for the 1606 Ningxia military campaign; the reminting charge *(dizhuyin)* of 0.003 tael per *yin* to bring to standard touch the silver tendered for salt tax payment; and a penalty, imposed during the Ming on merchants found overpacking their bales, incorporated into the tax quota regardless of the salt merchants' innocence or guilt. See Wang Shouji (1873), *Changlu*, 2a.

26. Memorial of Wang Bingqian to the throne dated 3/30/1656 reprinted in *LSDA* 2:12–13 (1988).

27. *CLYFZYZ, juan* 7, 31b, *juan* 11, 13b–18b; *QYFZ, juan* 14, 2a; Yanwuchu (n.d.:31).

28. Changlu Supervisor Zhang Zhongyuan's memorial to the throne dated 7/1/1653 in *LSDA* 1:12 (1988).

29. Chen Feng (1988:4) and Zhang Zhongyi's memorial to the throne dated 1661 in *CLYFZYZ, juan* 11, 25b–26a, 28b, 31a–32a. Subsequently, the Board of Revenue overturned its own decision and insisted that the backlog be cleared in two years. See *CLYFZYZ, juan* 7, 5a–5b; *juan* 11, 30a–30b, 31b–32a.

30. *CLYFZYZ, juan* 7, 28b; *juan* 11, 5a–6a; 34b–35b; 38a.

31. Chen Feng (1988:14); *CLYFZYZ, juan* 7, 9b–22b.

32. Memorials complaining about these powerful smugglers were filed in 1646, 1647, 1648, 1653, and 1660. Subsequent complaints are too numerous to list here, which suggests that the problem was never solved even after the restoration of peace. See, for example, *CLYFZYZ, juan* 1, 4a, *juan* 11, 4b, 19a; and *CLYFZJQ, juan* 1, 2a.

33. Tian Liushan's memorial to the throne dated 3/9/1660 reprinted in *LSDA* 2:17–18 (1988).

34. Until then this procedure, long the rule for the Lianghuai and Zhejiang Divisions, had been applied to Changlu for only one year in 1659. See *CLYFZYZ, juan* 7, 45b.

35. I owe this formulation to Margaret Levi (1988).

36. See, respectively, *CLYFZYZ, juan* 7, 22b; 38b; 39a; 24b–25b.

37. The long-term movement of the exchange rate between copper cash and silver during the Qing is too complex an issue to deal with here. Depleted copper mines in China, imports from Japan, the silver influx in early Qing, the outflow in late Qing—all played a part. See Yang Duanliu (1962:192) and Sasaki Masaya (1954:95–101).

38. *CLYFZJQ, juan* 1, 19b–20a.

39. On the attempt of 1703 see *QYFZ, juan* 20, 1b; *CLYFZJQ, juan* 10, 6a.

40. *QYFZ, juan* 20, 1b.

41. *CLYFZJQ, juan* 10, 9b; *QYFZ, juan* 21, 4a.

42. *CLYFZYZ, juan* 11, 30b–31b.

43. *CLYFZYZ, juan* 7, 23b–24b. This was enough for 200,000 people a year at 8 *jin* per person.

44. Li Xu's memorial to the Kangxi Emperor in Gugong bowuyuan Ming-Qing dang'anbu (1976:46).

45. *CLYFZYZ, juan* 11, 40a–b; *CLYFZJQ, juan* 10, 12a–12b. Lin Zhenhan thus errs in stating that the practice began with Changlu; see Lin Zhenhan (1988:*you* 59).

46. *CLYFZJQ, juan* 5, 10a. Demand for Changlu salt was highest before winter when vegetables were pickled. See *CL* 173.178, petition of Changlu salt merchants dated 9/7/1903.

47. On the Imperial Household Department see Torbert (1977) and Qi Meiqin (1998).

48. Li Keyi (1989:20).

49. Lin Yongkang (1986) traces such loans to the reign of the Yongzheng Emperor; but see *KXCZPHWYZ*, memorial of Zhao Hongxie to the Kangxi Emperor dated 9/17/1705.

50. The story of "royal" merchants as managers for the investments of the Imperial Household Department is too complicated to treat adequately here. See, for example, Wei Qingyuan and Wu Qiyan (1981) and Qi Meiqin (1998).

51. These supervisors, many of them imperial bondservants *(baoyi)*, also collected intelligence for the emperor. See, for example, Gugong bowuyuan Ming-Qing dang'anbu (1976) and Qi Meiqin (1998).

52. Calling such interest payments a tax is thus technically inaccurate. See Adshead (1970:24).

53. *NW* 441.2748. For a history of the pawnshops see *LSDA* 4:16–20 (1985).

54. Wei Qingyuan and Wu Qiyan (1981); Lin Yongkang (1984); Wu Qiyan, "Cong dang'an kan Qing qianqi Changlu guanyanshang de ruogan wenti" (Issues on official Changlu salt merchants in early Qing as seen from archival materials), in Zhongguo diyi lishi dang'anguan (1988, 1:492–515); and Qi Meiqin (1998:141–145).

55. *QSLQLC,* 3/28/1759. In his rescript the Kangxi Emperor decided against granting any more loans to the salt merchants, although he did not elaborate on his reasons. Was it because he had suffered losses as in the case of Zhang Lin (see Chapter 4)? See Gugong bowuyuan Ming-Qing dang'anbu (1976:220).

56. Li Keyi (1989:21). By way of comparison, interest rates in Europe and England during the period were approximately the same: 10 to 15 percent a year. See Goldsmith (1987).

57. *QSLQLC,* 3/38/1759; *CLYFZJQ, juan* 2, 25a–25b.

58. See Wu Tan (1991:522). At 12 percent interest a year, it would take under nine years for total interest paid to exceed the principal.

59. *QYFZ, juan* 14, 12a. The tally is based on archives housed at the Academia Sinica of Taiwan and vermilion-brush endorsed memorials held by the First National Archives in Beijing.

60. Chen Feng (1988:216–234); *QSG, juan* 123, 3613; *CLYFZJQ, juan* 5, 2a; and Zeng Yangfeng (1915). On the concept of *bao* in Chinese culture see Yang Liensheng (1987).

61. Memorial of Meng Gaoli to the throne dated 9/28/1726 in *GGWX* 4.1: 132 (1971); *GZDYZC,* memorial dated 9/9/1727.

62. Memorial of E Li to the throne dated the tenth month of 1732 in *CLYFZJQ, juan* 5, 2a–2b; *CLYFZQL, juan* 6, 7a, 49b.

63. Accountants of the empire were scrupulous in keeping their books accurate down to one-trillionth part of a tael. An astute Qianlong pointed out that such precision was misplaced and spared latter-day historians by decreeing that henceforth all accounts should stop at one-thousandth part of a tael. See *CLYFZJQ, juan* 2, 12a, Qianlong's decree dated 11/25/1766.

64. *I-Ching* (1963:150).

65. *CLYFZJQ, juan* 5, 8a–9b.

66. *QSLQLC,* 3/25/1749.

67. *CLYFZJQ, juan* 16, 26a–26b.

68. *TJFZX, juan* 31, 37a; *HCZDLZ, juan* 81, 6b; and *CLYFZJQ, juan* 2, 35a–b. On the proposed price increase see *QSG, juan* 340, 11093.

69. *QYFZ, juan* 21, 4a–5b; Song Xiang et al. (1809), *juan* 5, 20a; and *QSLJQC,* 2/18/1809.

70. The price increases are documented in *QDCD* 145, memorial dated 2/24/1825; and *QYFZ, juan* 21, 5a–7b.

71. In 1807, some 13 *jin* was added to compensate the salt merchants for evaporation; see *QYFZ, juan* 19, 3b. Another 35 *jin* was added in 1820, 20 *jin* in 1828, and 38 *jin* in 1841, all tax free, to help the salt merchants. See Yang Shounan (1913:10b).

72. On the tax deferments see *CLYFZJQ, juan* 6, 11b, 12a, 13b, 14a respectively. Ten *yin* of salt was packed into nine bales of salt, thereby saving the salt merchants transport costs. See Wang Shouji (1873).

73. Originally intended for five years, the reduction was repeatedly extended until 1911. See *QYFZ, juan* 23, 20a.

74. Kwan (1999:259).

75. *CLYWZY,* memorial of Prince Ding to the throne in 1849.

76. *QDCD* 145, memorial of Censor Cai Xuecun and decree endorsing Cai's recommendation dated 11/18/1824. The exchange rate between copper cash and silver, according to the memorial, had been rising since 1810 and reached the rate of between 1,200 and 1,300 *wen* per tael.

77. *QDCD* 145, memorial dated 12/8/1827; *QYFZ, juan* 21, 6a–b.

78. *QYFZ, juan* 21, 6b–7a; "Daoguang nianjian Changlu canhuo ji bubo kuiqian shiliao" (Materials on expropriation and arrears of Changlu gabelle during the reign of the Daoguang Emperor), *LSDA* 2:15–26 (1985).

79. The original request was 500,000 taels. See *CL* 173.92, head merchants' report to the commissioner dated 12/15/1895.

80. Yanwuchu (n.d.:54).

81. *QYFZ, juan* 23, 48b–49a; *juan* 24, 1a–3a; *QDCD* 145, memorial of Zheng Yuanshan dated 9/27/1862.

82. *QYFZ, juan* 19, 5; *ZB,* 9/7/1896.

83. See, for example, *QSLSZC,* 7/18/1647; *QJZ,* 12/15/1681; *QSLQLC,* 5/29/1788; *QSLJQC,* 11/8/1817; *QSLDGC,* 5/16/1831; and *QSLTZC,* 12/5/1869.

84. See, for example, *CLYFZYZ, juan* 1, 3b.

85. *CLYFZYZ, juan* 11, 5a–6a.

86. *CLYFZYZ, juan* 4, 8b, *juan* 5, 1b–2a. The commissioner did not enjoy an official residence in Tianjin until 1688.

87. Gugong bowuyuan Ming-Qing dang'anbu (1975:26). See also the discussion in Chapter 5.

88. *CLYFZYZ, juan* 11, 86b–87a; *GGWX* 4.1:82 (1972).

89. *QSLYZC,* 2/25/1724.

90. *QYFZ, juan* 38, 2a; *CL* 173.225. On the "integrity-nourishing silver" see Saeki Tomi (1970–1972) and Zelin (1984:119–121).

91. *QYFZ, juan* 19, 3a.

92. Memorial of Prince Ding to the throne dated second month of 1849 in *CLYWZY; CL* 173.497, Chen Youzhang report to the Changlu commissioner dated 7/11/1911.

93. See memorial of Jiqing to the throne dated 7/7/1753. Documentation of such expenses is rare. The only Changlu evidence, which covered the fifth month of an unknown year, probably for Yongnian district, was recorded on a slip of paper included in *CLYYGX.*

94. Ruling on a petition from Xiangchengxin of Qizhou dated 1/5/1901 in *CL* 173.111.

95. Thomas Metzger suggests that because of their low profit rate, the salt merchants could not afford to offer "bribes." See Metzger in Willmott (1972:37).

96. Wang Xitong (1939), *juan* 1, 37a. Xiuwu district was a part of Huaiqing prefecture transferred to the Changlu Division in 1685.

97. Wang Xitong (n.d.), *juan* 1, 38a, *juan* 4, 8b.

98. Yan Xiu (n.d.), "Yan Fansun riji," note between diary entries 7/5/1905 and 7/6/1905. Salt, transport, and marketing constituted 12 percent of his cost, taxes and fees 55.8 percent, and price increases due the state the remainder.

99. The "nest price" for Changlu was cited at 7 million taels on 966,046 *yin,* or an average of 7.24 taels per *yin,* although private transactions among the merchants could fetch as high as 20 taels per *yin.* Three million taels in profit for the Changlu Division seemed to be the accepted figure. See *ZB,* 5/2/1896; *DGB,* 6/14/1903; *CL,* 173.178, petition of merchants for official loans dated 9/7/1903; and Jin Dayang (1980:77).

100. Li Duan (1983).

101. Wang Shouji (1873:11a).

CHAPTER 3: THE HOUSEHOLD AND THE LAW

1. Magistrates were required to compile routine reports on the number of such cases filed and expeditiously resolved. See Wu Tan (1991:880).

2. Rosser H. Brockman, "Commercial Contract Law in Late Nineteenth Century Taiwan," in Cohen et al. (1980:85).

3. Zhang Jinfan (1990:383) and Ye Xiaoxin (1993:2).

4. Weber (1966:237); Schurmann (1955); Kroker (1959:123–146); and Huang (1989).

5. Kotenev (1925:251).

6. Riasanovsky (1976:5).

7. Weber (1951:149). For a critique of Weber's sociology of law see Liang Zhiping (1996) and Kwan (1997).

8. Weber (1982:343).

9. Li Zhimin (1988:186–199) and MacCormack (1996:xiv).

10. Li Zhimin (1988:1–3) and Ye Xiaoxin (1993:605–607).

11. Bernhardt and Huang (1994); Huang (1996); Wang Shirong (1997a; 1997b). Ruling could also be brief, however. See Zheng Qin (1988:212–216) and Zhang Jinfan et al. (1994:565–566).

12. Wakefield (1998:127). The semiotic school questions the modern privileging of code over custom. See Bernard S. Jackson, "Code and Custom," in Kevelson (1994:119–138).

13. Koguchi Hikota (1988:35–49) cites three modes of conflict resolution practiced by local officials—according to the Qing Code, extension of the code, and "common sense"—but does not analyze the circumstances causing officials to switch from one mode to another. Zhang Jinfan lists the code, rites *(li),* common sense *(qingli),* and customs as the adjudication principles in civil cases but fails to address potential conflicts among them. See Zhang Jinfan et al. (1998: 293–298; 1999:206–215).

14. See "Tianjinshi zhi fengsu diaocha" (Survey of customs of Tianjin), *Hebei yuekan* 1(3) (March 1933):4. Given the various phases of the family cycle, attempts to calculate and interpret changes in Tianjin's mean household size suffer from a lack of properly segregated data. See, for example, Rozman (1982).

15. Among the guidelines to a daughter-in-law's proper behavior is the requirement that she should keep no private property, savings, or utensils. See *Liji, juan* 27, 1463. To demonstrate filial piety, a son should not hold his own property. See *Liji, juan* 1, 1235; *juan* 51, 1621. This argument is reinforced by Zhu Xi during the Confucian renewal of the Song dynasty. See Zhu Xi (n.d.), *juan* 99, 6a.

16. This branch of the Huas could be traced back to Wuxi; their apical ancestor Hua Jin settled in Tianjin during the reign of the Jiajing Emperor (r. 1522–1566). Under the corporate name of Changyu, the household also owned the monopoly of Xincheng. See *ZB*, 1/2/1896.

17. Nishida Taichirō (1974:169); Wang Fu (1968), *juan* 85, 1559.

18. Gu Yanwu (1990, 1:629–632). This decree, applicable to Sichuan and Shaanxi, was rescinded in 983.

19. Xu Song (1936:*juan* 13220, 44b); Zhu Xi (n.d.), *juan* 99, 6a–6b.

20. Yuan Cai (n.d.), *juan* 1, 8; Shen Jiaben (1985), *juan* 8, 1114.

21. Zhu Yong (1987:44 and 154–177); Zhang Jinfan et al. (1998:30–35).

22. The status of the household head varied from district to district in Hebei. See Sifa xingzhengbu (1969, 3:1295–1407). Disinheritance was also common in parts of North China. See, for instance, the discussion on Gaoyang cited in Sifa xingzhengbu (1969, 3:1300).

23. Yan Xiu (n.d.), "Yan Fansun riji," diary entry dated 12/23/1898.

24. The prerogatives of the eldest and firstborn also varied from place to place in China. See Fazheng xueshe (1962, 5.2, 13b–14b). The eldest or firstborn might be entitled to an extra share of the household property (as would his son if he had one). In North China, the eldest son was entitled to manage the household estate on the death of the father. See Sifa xingzhengbu (1969, 3:1373–1378).

25. Yan Xiu (n.d.), "Yan Fansun riji," diary entry dated 7/10/1880.

26. Yan Xiu (n.d.), "Yanshi jiashu," letters dated 3/14/1891, 5/8/1891, and 9/22/1896.

27. Ibid., letters dated 6/7/1906 and 6/6/1907.

28. Ibid., letters dated 7/27/1907, 5/3/1908, 7/7/1908, 11/11/1908, and 12/31/1908.

29. Yan Xiu (n.d.), "Yan Fansun riji," diary entries dated 5/17/1899, 7/27/1910, 8/14/1910, and 3/20/1911. Such alliances could be multigeneration affairs. Yan's sister was married to Hua Shiguan of the "Highsteps" Huas, while the eldest son of Hua Shikui, Shiguan's brother, married one of Yan's daughters.

30. Ibid., diary entry dated 2/28/1911.

31. This household network strategy has recently been reincarnated as "network capitalism" as part of the post-Confucian economic culture that contributed to the Asian economic miracle—begging the question of why an earlier generation of economists and social scientists dismissed such behavior as particularistic and an obstacle to "modernization." See Clegg and Redding (1990:38) and Tu Wei-ming (1996).

32. *QSG, juan* 123, 3606.

33. The first right of refusal for rural land property enjoyed by kin and neighbors had been outlawed in Henan province in 1725. See Tian Wenjing (1995:256). None of the available urban land deeds from Qing Tianjin contain the formulary phrase of preemptive rights of kin and neighbors. See Tianjinshi fangdichan chanquan shichang guanlichu (1995).

34. Wu Tan (1991:435). For an application of the statute of limitations see *CL* 173.105, *Wang Peizhi* vs. *Zheng Zizhou*, ruling dated 6/28/1899.

35. For a translation and analysis of these contracts see Kwan (1997).

36. *CL* 173.277, plaint filed by Fuchengyu dated the eighth month of 1906. On Taiwan see Liu Chang Bin (1983:197).

37. Chen and Myers (1976; 1978); Ramon Myers, "Customary Law, Markets, and Resource Transactions in Late Imperial China," in Ransom et al. (1982:273–298); and Zhang Jinfan et al. (1998:277–281). On the use of contracts in promoting economic efficiency see Posner (1977:chap. 4) and Kronman et al. (1979:5–7).

38. For the function of the syndicates and their leaders in Lianghuai see the report of the Board of Revenue to the throne on Wang Guozuo's ten suggestions dated the seventh month of 1644 in *CLYFZYZ, juan* 11, 4a.

39. *CL* 173.124.

40. *CL* 173.213, petition of Ms. Ning dated 7/11/1904. There were advantages, as we shall see, to using a family hall name.

41. *CL* 173.213, report of the head merchants dated 9/29/1904 after the commissioner repeated his request on 9/19/1904.

42. In English common law, the doctrine of custom applies the following test before a custom can be accepted as law: the practice must be ancient *(antiqua consuetudeo)*, continuous, certain, and reasonable. Even then the king or his representative could challenge a custom on the basis that it was not conferred by law (quo warranto). See Loux (1992:183–218).

43. This branch of the Huas migrated from Wuxi to Shaoxing during the reign of the Tianshun Emperor (r. 1457–1464) and then to Dong'an district. In 1663, Hua Wenbing from this branch settled in Tianjin as a salt merchant and became its apical ancestor. See Hua Changqing et al. (1909:preface).

44. Making such public declarations, in time appearing as advertisements in local newspapers, seems to have been the modus operandi for Tianjin's wealthy households; practitioners included other Big Eight families such as the "Zhende" Huangs in 1908, the Bians in 1909, and another branch of the Huas. See, respectively, *TJSHDAXB* I (1989), 1:897–898; II (1991), 2:2057; and *DGB*, 3/22/1907.

45. Ruling on Hua vs. Hua dated 8/8/1912 in Zhili gaodeng shanpanting (1914, II:63–65).

46. For a seminal treatment of the subject in general see Cohen (1976).

47. The colorful life of Li Shutong (1880–1942) is described in Feng Zikai and Song Yunbin (1963:100–115); Boorman and Howard (1968, II:323–328); and Li Duan (1983).

48. *CL* 173.210, petition filed by Hua Fengqi dated 9/17/1904 and court order executed 10/4/1904.

49. On the relevant provisions in the Qing Code see Bodde and Morris (1967:247–249).

50. *CL* 173.105; 173.292.

51. See *Yuan dianzhang* (1990:273).

52. *Da Ming lü* (1989), *juan* 4, 23a. Unless instructed by the deceased, household division during the three-year period was still a crime punishable by eighty strokes of heavy bamboo. See Ren Penglian (1871), *juan* 8, 45a; Li Wenzhi (1983:281).

53. *CL* 173.101, petition by Feng Xueyin dated 9/20/1907; petition by Feng Xuebin's widow dated 9/18/1907; Feng Xuezhang (1919).

54. Feng Xuezhang (1919).

55. Zhang Jinfan et al. (1994:568).

56. *CL* 173.218, plaint filed by Liu Enze on 5/22/1904, 5/27/1904, and settlement dated 12/24/1905. On the relevant code on filing meritless lawsuits and the statute of limitations governing property transfer see Wu Tan (1991:435, 887–888, 898–899).

57. *CL* 173.184, 173.277, and 173.317.

58. *CL* 173.277, suit filed 4/5/1908, petition filed 11/19/1909, and decision dated 12/11/1909.

59. The controversy over the household head's authority is summarized in Niida Noboru (1962, 3:329–364) and Shiga Shuzō, "Family Property and the Law of Inheritance in Traditional China," in Buxbaum (1978:109–150).

60. Weber (1982:313). The "clan" used by the translator here has also been rendered as "sib" association elsewhere. See Weber (1951:86–90).

61. Sung Lung-sheng, "Property and Family Division," in Ahern and Gates (1981:360–362).

62. *CL* 173.297, testimony of Ms. Zhang dated 7/6/1907.

63. *ZB*, 1/23/1901, advertisement by Wang Jingxuan.

64. See, for example, the contract signed by the Feng brothers and their sons leasing Zhuozhou to the Lius in *CL* 173.356; see also a sales contract between Guo Jing and Li Baoheng dated 1902 in *CL* 173.135.

65. Sung Lung-sheng in Ahern and Gates (1981:367); and Shiga (1978:113–114).

66. *CL* 173.359, contract between Zhang Jiren and Huang Futing dated 4/15/1853 and affidavit of Huang Baochen filed 7/14/1908.

67. *CL* 173.359, ruling of the prefect of Tianjin dated 7/14/1908 and report of head merchant Yang Junyuan dated 7/14/1908.

68. Gao Ningwen (1982), *juan* 2, 22a; *CL* 173.124, *Liu* vs. *Hua*.

69. Zhang Chuanxi (1995:1344) and deeds dated 1890, 1904, and 1913 in Tianjinshi fangdichan chanquan shichang guanlichu (1995:12–13, 18–19, 32–33). The stereotypical image of late imperial Chinese women has been demolished by Mann (1997).

70. *CLYFZYZ, juan* 1, 5b. In addressing the court, the widow Ning would refer to herself as a widow with an official duty *(zhiguafu)*. See also *CL* 173.326, Zhang (née Li) vs. Zhang Yitai dated 2/1/1907.

71. On the widow's "zone of interplay," if not empowerment, see Sommer (1996:77–130) and Bernhardt (1999:59–65).

72. Zhang had obtained the monopoly in 1896 by selling more than 400 *mu* of land owned by the household. See *CL* 173.297, testimony of Ms. Zhang (née Zhao) dated 7/6/1907.

73. *CL* 173.184, with a security deposit of 5,350 taels, a loan of 1,000 taels at an interest rate of 0.8 percent a month, and subsidies for no more than three funerals or marriages over the ten-year term of the contract.

74. *CL* 173.457; the terms remained the same except that Sun was entitled to one subsidy each year for a marriage or funeral should the occasion arise.

75. *CL* 173.107, suit filed 1/6/1900 and testimony of Zheng Zuoji dated 1/25/1900.

76. *CL* 173.107, petition by Zheng Zuoji dated 1/18/1900; report from Wen-xian magistrate to the Changlu commissioner dated 3/17/1900; Yulu's opinion issued 5/3/1900; the commissioner's ruling dated 5/6/1900; and Zheng Zuoji's petitions dated 5/19/1900 and 6/7/1900.

77. *GXCDHL,* 3/16/1903, Yuan Shikai's memorial to the throne.

78. Feng Xuezhang (1919).

79. This method of conflict resolution was frequently encountered in law-suits involving elite merchants and commoners alike. Indeed, bypassing media-tion might jeopardize a plaintiff's case. Yingyu, circuit intendant of Tianjin from 1855 to 1858, dismissed Wang Tianfu's plaint against his brother for depriving him of his rightful inheritance. The intendant justified his ruling by faulting Tianfu for not discussing the matter among themselves and enlisting mediation by relatives. The notice, complete with typographical errors, was posted outside the yamen as a matter of public record. See Feng Jicai (1995:26).

## CHAPTER 4: MERCHANT CULTURE

1. Zhang Hongyi (1989:40–41); Bergère (1989:23); Lufrano (1997:5 and 184). On the examination system, cultural hegemony, and social reproduction see Bourdieu and Passeron (1990:142).

2. F. W. Mote, "The Transformation of Nanking," in Skinner (1977); Bergère (1989:35–36); Liu and Faure (1996).

3. See, for example, Li Tou (1960); Ho Ping-ti (1954); and Xiao Guoliang, "Qingdai Lianghuai yanshang de shechixing xiaofei ji qi jingji yingxiang" (The extravagance of Qing Lianghuai salt merchants and its economic effects), re-printed in Chen Ran et al. (1987:452–468).

4. Yu Yingshi (1987a:104–110); Huang Zongxi (1955), public finance *(caiji)* 3, 41. But see Zhu Ying (1998) on the lingering gulf.

5. Peter Mathias, "Entrepreneurs, Managers, and Business Men in Eighteenth-Century Britain," in Mathias and Davis (1996:29).

6. Yu Yingshi (1987a:97–121); Ding Gang (1996); Lufrano (1997:42–50).

7. Mukerji and Schudson (1991:35) and Ginzburg (1982).

8. On "orthodoxy" versus "orthopraxy" see James Watson, "Rites or Beliefs? The Construction of a Unified Culture in Late Imperial China," in Dittmer and Kim (1993:84).

9. The social role of gardens for the literati is explored in Smith (1992).

10. Li Tou (1960), *juan* 6, 10a.

11. Zha Li (1770), *juan* 29, 1a.

12. Li Boyuan (1983), *juan* 3, 2a; Dai Yu'an (1986:14).

13. "Yi ge ye yi ge yuan" (a compound for each of the masters). Interview with Li Shiyu, July 6, 1986. The floor plan of "Changyuan" Yangs' mansion is re-produced in Gao Zhonglin et al. (1990:49, pl. 85).

14. Zhao Yuanli (1934:8b); Li Ranxi (1986:346).

15. Dai Yu'an (1986:103).

16. Feng Xuezhang (1919).

17. Interview with Xu Jingxing, July 6, 1986; Yang Shaozhou (1989).

18. Jin Dayang (1980:97); Li Ranxi (1986:231); Yang Shaozhou (1989:243–244).

19. For the social and economic functions of funeral rites in North China see Yang (1967:36–38) and Naquin, "Funerals in North China: Uniformity and Variation," in Watson and Rawski (1988). On Tianjin variations see Zhang Honglai (1928) and Chen Enrong (1918).

20. Laoxiang (1984).

21. *TJXXZ, juan* 18, 8b.

22. The salt merchants left few written records of their religious practices. Much of the information on this topic came from interviews with Li Shiyu, Huang Fuxian, and Zhao Ju, August 10, 1994. For the array of deities worshiped see "Tianjin shenma mulu" (Catalog of deities in Tianjin), *Hebei yuekan* 4(2) (1936):3.

23. Feng Xuezhang (1919) and Feng Wenqian (n.d.).

24. For a genealogy of the Zhang family see Yu Henian (1934:1–4) and Xu Tongzi (1935). Jiang Chenying composed Xinyin's tomb inscription at the request of Zhang Lin. See Jiang Chenying (1889), *juan* 10, 8a–10a. See *CLYFZYZ, juan* 7, 4a–b, for the monopolies operated by the family.

25. See Jiang Chenying (1889), *juan* 10, 8a; Wu Wen (n.d.), *juan* 6, 3b; and Zhao Zhishen (n.d.), *juan* 9, 1b.

26. *TJXXZ, juan* 21.1, 32a–32b; *QSLKXC,* 4/21/1700 and 9/9/1700.

27. *QSLKXC,* 12/17/1700 and 1/10/1701.

28. Chen Jingzhang (1992:18–26).

29. Wu Zhenyu (1983), *juan* 7, 340; *QSG, juan* 506, 13944–13951; and Hummel (1970, 2:570–571). For a biography of Zha see *QSG, juan* 484, 13366; *QSL, juan* 71, 236–246; and Hummel (1970, 1:21). For poems he dedicated to Mingju see Zha Xiazhong (n.d.), *juan* 8, 4b, 9a–9b; *juan* 17, 1a. Mei lived in Tianjin in 1691–1692 and served Zhang Lin during the latter's tenure in Fujian. See Li Yan (1925). On Fang see Jiang Chenying (1889), *juan* 18, 23a–b, *juan* 27, 18b; and Fang Bao (1991:350–351).

30. The Southern Study (Nanshufang) was established on November 14, 1677. See *QJZ,* I:331. Zhu Jinpu is quite accurate in placing the study within the institutional context of Qing central government, although he underestimated its ex officio role. On the controversy surrounding the study see Chen Jinning (1985); Silas Wu (1968); Liang Xijie and Meng Chaoxin (1991:438–459); and Zhu Jinpu (1990).

31. On the brilliant career of Wang see *QSG, juan* 270, 10003; *QSL, juan* 10, 13a–18a; Hummel (1970, 2:826); *GCXZ, juan* 10, 688–695; *QSL, juan* 10, 688–695; and *BZJ, juan* 21, 192–193. These confidential memorials were routinely burned after the emperors' perusal.

32. Zhao Yi (1982), *juan* 2, 42.

33. Fang Bao (1991), *juan* 12, 291.

34. *KXCZPHWYZ,* Zhao Hongxie's memorials to the throne dated 5/28/1709 and 5/3/1710.

35. *QSL, juan* 71, 5812; memorial from Tuoheqi dated 5/19/1705 in Zhongguo diyi lishi dang'anguan (1996:1646); and *KXCZPHWYZ,* Zhao Hongxie's memorial to the emperor dated 9/6/1706.

36. Gugong wenxianguan (1931, 12:11b).

37. Zhaolian (1980), *juan* 3, 448; Yan Chongnian (1989); Yang Zhen (1996: 112–128).

38. On Li's animosity see Li Guangdi (n.d.), *juan* 10, 14, 18, especially *juan* 13, 11b–12a.

39. *QSLKXC*, 7/22/1705.

40. *QSLKXC*, 11/28/1705.

41. *KXCZPHWYZ*, Zhao Hongxie's memorial to Kangxi dated 1/20/1707; and *QJZ*, 3:2034, 2036, entries dated 11/29/1706 and 1/1/1707, respectively.

42. Memorial from Tuoheqi dated 5/19/1705 in Zhongguo diyi lishi dang'anguan (1996:1646). Zha's name has been transcribed with homonyms.

43. Zha Xi, "Poem dedicated to Zhang Lin's pot of plum blossoms," cited in Gao Ningwen (1982), *juan* 3, 20a. Zhang languished in jail until at least 1713.

44. On Zha Xiu, Tianxing's apical ancestor, see Hang Shijun (1888) *juan* 43; Zha Lubai (1941:preface); and interview with Zha Lubai, 8/14/1994.

45. On the price for a seat in the Customs Office see *ZB*, 9/4/1896.

46. *QJZ*, III, entry dated 1/15/1707. The family's genealogy also noted that his mother (née Liu) traveled to Jehol three times to plead for clemency. See Zha Lubai (1941), *juan* 2, 16a.

47. Sources on the case are found in *KXCZPHWYZ*, Zhao Hongxie's memorial to the throne dated 5/10/1712; *QSLKXC*, 3/19/1713; and Jiang Liangqi (1980), *juan* 22, 361. For a biography of Zha Weiren see Hummel (1970, 1:20); Min Erchang (1987), *juan* 45, 1528; and Liu Shangheng (1990:48–54).

48. Zhang Zhao, preface to *Huaying'an ji*, in Zha Weiren (n.d.). Zhang and Zha shared a cell that Zha named the hut in the shadow of flowers. Subsequently Zhang also received a pardon and went on to serve the Qianlong Emperor in the Southern Study before his appointment as director of the Board of Punishment. See *QSG, juan* 304, 10493–10495; *QSL, juan* 19, 1450–1455. For a biography of Zhao see *QSG, juan* 263, 9912–9916; *QSL, juan* 12, 834–838; and Hummel (1970, 1:80).

49. Zhao's memorial to remove the Jins and the Wangs as purveyors of copper was cited in *QSLKXC*, 7/4/1715. See also Shen Zhaoyun (1924), *juan* 1, 39b.

50. Gao Ningwen (1982), *juan* 3, 29a.

51. On gardens and retreats built by Changlu salt merchants see Wang Wengru (1986). On Shuixizhuang see Guo Honglin (1989) and Liu Shangheng (1992).

52. Zha Xiazhong, "Wutishi xu" (preface to untitled poems), dated 1720, in Zha Weiren (n.d.); and Zha Pu (1722), *juan* 3, 15b, *juan* 7, 4b. A third brother, Zha Siting, suffered the wrath of the Yongzheng Emperor, who expropriated the household for Siting's membership in Lungkodo's clique. See *QSG, juan* 295, 10354; *QSLYZC*, 10/21/1726, 11/9/1726, 2/24/1727, and 6/25/1727. For a collective biography of the brothers see *QSG, juan* 271, 13366–13367.

53. The guest list is culled from the following sources: Shen Zhaoyun (1924), *juan shang*, 40b; *TJXXZ, juan* 1, 40a; Gao Ningwen (1982), *juan* 5, 21b; Li E (1884), *juan* 2, 15a–16b; and Hang Shijun (1888), *juan* 13, 15a. On Hang see *QSG, juan* 485, 13374; and see Hummel (1970, 1:276–277). He also claimed to be Weiren's relative by marriage. On Wan see *QSG, juan* 485, 13384; and see his collected poems (1756). Zhu Yizun, Zha Xiazhong, Hang Shijun, and Li E were all considered leading members of the Zhezhong (Central Zhejiang) school of poetry. See *QSG, juan* 485, 13386.

54. For a biography of Li E see *QSG, juan* 485, 13373; *QSL, juan* 71, 37b–38a; and Hummel (1970, 1:454–455).

55. Chen Yuanlong, "Shuixizhuang ji" (Memories of Shuixizhuang), in his *Ai'ritang shiji* (last preface dated 1736), *juan* 27, 3a–b. The relationship between Zha and Chen was described in Zha Weiren (1924 ed.), *juan zhong*, 4a. On Chen's distinguished career see *QSG, juan,* 289, 10263–10264; *BZJ, juan* 10, 277–278; and *QSL, juan* 14, 12b–14b.

56. On Chen Shiguan see *QSL, juan* 16, 146–149; *GCXZ, juan* 10, 275–277; and *BZJ, juan* 26, 166–167.

57. Zha Weiren (n.d.), *juan zhong*, 8b and 10b. Tianjin was elevated to a *zhilizhou* by a decree dated 11/4/1725. See *QSLYZC, juan* 36, 16b.

58. Zha Lubai (1941), *juan* 5, 17b–18b. Chen's essay was dated 1737 when he was an academician of the Grand Secretariat.

59. On the career of Chen Pengnian see *GCXZ, juan* 12, 327–332.

60. For his poetry in Tianjin see Yinglian (1783), *juan* 6, 3b, *juan* 8, 2a, 4b, 9a, 12a; and Li E (1884), *juan* 7, 5b.

61. Chen Yi (1750), *juan* 6, 4a.

62. Dai Yu'an (1986:15).

63. An increasingly common practice among merchants in late imperial China. See Long Denggao (1998).

64. For the civic works and a biography of Weiyi see Ji Yun (1812), *shang, juan* 16, 41b–43a. Ji, a trusted grand secretary for the Qianlong Emperor, knew at least two generations of the Zha family. He became a *jinshi* together with Weiyi's nephew Shanchang, and Weiyi's grandson Zhenyin attained the *jinshi* degree in 1784 under Ji.

65. Zha Li (1770), *juan* 32, 1a–1b. For his biography see *QSG, juan* 332, 10962–10963; *BZJ, juan* 85, 431–432; and Hummel (1970, 1:19–21).

66. Zha Weiren's eldest son, Shanchang (1729–1798), became a *jinshi* in 1754. A second son, Shanhe, was a successful salt merchant whose son Cheng became a *juren* in 1777. Zha Cheng's eldest son Naiqin became a *jinshi* in 1801. Zha Weiyi's grandson Bin was a *jinshi* of 1784; a grandson Yiqin a *juren* of 1843; and his great-great-grandson Yixin a *juren* in 1858.

67. On Chen, son of Yuanlong, see Chen Qiyuan (1989), *juan* 1, 11–12. On the marriage see Liu Shangheng (1990:54).

68. Chen Yi (1750), *juan* 10, 41a–42a. Zhu was highly regarded by Zhang Lin's nemesis, Li Guangdi. See *TJFZX, juan* 43, 6a–6b.

69. Zhaolian (1980), *juan* 2, 434, *juan* 3, 456.

70. *QSLJQC*, 2/24/1807. On Dai's distinguished career see *QSG, juan* 341, 11099–11100; *QSL, juan* 28, 2142–2152; and *GCXZ, juan* 21, 618–619.

71. *QYFZ, juan* 23, 39b; *QSLJQC*, 8/17/1809, 8/18/1809, and 8/29/1809. See also Jin Anqing (1984:43) and Chen Qiyuan (1989), *juan* 2, 27–28.

72. *QSLJQC*, decrees dated 9/12/1812, 9/19/1812, 10/3/1812, 10/26/1812; *QSG, juan* 356, 11318; and "Jiaqing shiqi'nian Changlu yanfa wubi'an," *LSDA* 4:20–35 (1989). See also Zhaolian (1980), *juan* 2, 418.

73. See *TJXXZ, juan* 21.1, 33a. On Fang's distinguished career see *QSG, juan* 290, 10270; *QSL, juan* 19, 24a–27b; Hummel (1970, 1:235); and Chen Kangqi (1983), *juan* 6, 135.

74. Chen Kai (1874:19b). For a biography of Hubai see Zhou Fan, "Zhang Xiaoyan xianshengchuan" (Biography of Zhang Xiaoyan), in Hua Guangnai

(1920), *juan* 4, 23b–24b. According to local folklore, Hubai continued his bureaucratic career as a judge in the netherworld. See Li Qingchen (1990), *juan* 3, 1a. His descendants continued to live in Tianjin, distinguishing the household with degree holders and virtuous women. See Xu Shiluan (1986:43–47 and 114–119).

75. Feng Xuezhang (1919).

76. Yan Zide (1985) and Xie Taofang (1997:322–329).

77. Yan Zide (1985:201).

78. Ibid., pp. 120, 174, 269, 338, 418.

79. Zhongguo xiquzhi bianji weiyuanhui (1990:5–7); Yao Xiyun (1981). For a list of scholar-literati signing a petition to outlaw such performances and official bans see *DGB* 12/8/1904, 12/13/1904, and 7/10/1905.

80. Yan Zide (1985:57–59).

81. Ibid., pp. 249–251.

82. Ibid., pp. 19, 75, 78, 106, 108.

83. See Yangcheng jiuke (1898), *juan* 5, 2a–b; and Wangyun jushi (1988). On the city god's annual inspection tour see Hua Naiwen (1986).

84. Li Ranxi (1986:348–349); Xin Chengzhang (1982:51). The Zhangs of "Haizhang wu" (see Chapter 5) underwrote the "Longting gongyi jingyin fagu"; Longting is the neighborhood in which their mansion stood. See Wangyun jushi (1988:47). For a scroll possibly depicting the event in 1884 see Zhongguo lishi bowuguan (1992).

85. Wangyun jushi (1988) and Duan Yuming (1992:297–314).

86. Song Di (1993:182–187).

87. Bakhtin (1968:73–75). The troupe was sponsored by a succession of salt merchants, including "Haizhang wu" and "Changyuan" Yangs. See Chu Zhifa (1990:94).

88. Zhongguo lishi bowuguan (1992:132).

89. Ibid., p. 123.

CHAPTER 5: SOCIAL SERVICES

1. Tsu Yuyue (1912); Rowe (1984:319; 1989:91); and Smith (1987). On the lack of civic spirit in Tianjin see Lieberthal (1980:181).

2. R. Bin Wong, "Confucian Agendas for Material and Ideological Control in Modern China," in Huters et al. (1997:311–312).

3. *TJXXZ, juan* 21.1, 1b, 14b.

4. On this distinctive characteristic of Chinese civil society see Ma Min (1995:289) and Wong in Huters et al. (1997:322).

5. Zheng Shoupeng (1980:436–438).

6. *QSLJQC*, 11/26/1801; the tabulation is based on various editions of the local gazetteer and the veritable records.

7. As candidly admitted in Xu Tianzui et al. (1927), *juan* 2, 20b. The bureaucratic procedure is described in Will (1990:79–126) and Li Xiangjun (1995:23–28).

8. The emperor uncovered the flood of 1761 in a routine audience with Tianjin's garrison commander; *XTJXZ, juan* 1, 2b; *TJXXZ, juan* 18, 23a.

9. Wei Xi, "Proposals for Disaster Relief" (Jiufangce), in He Changning (1903), *juan* 41, 4a. See also Ruan Yuan, "Distribution of Relief at Huzhou: A Poem Dedicated to Officials and Scholars" (Xingzhen Huzhou shi guanshi), ca. 1805, in Zhang Yingchang (1960, 2:543).

10. See, for example, *QSLTZC*, 8/29/1863.

11. *QSLJQC*, 8/16/1809, involving Baodi district. Even when tax deferment had been approved, it was not always executed by local officials. See, for example, *QSLTZC*, 10/31/1868, involving Zhili province.

12. "Baoshengsuo nuzhou chang yizhongbei" (Stele of the public cemetary, gruel kitchen for woman), dated 1877, Tianjin Municipal Museum. But the poem "Wailing in the Cold" ("Haohan xing") reported over two thousand casualties; see Mei Chengdong (1842), *juan* 4, 4b–5a, and *GXCDHL* I:562.

13. Zhang Boxing as cited in He Changning (1903), *juan* 41, 5b; Meng Chaohua et al. (1986:246).

14. Despite all the shortcomings of the relief effort. See He Hanwei (n.d.: 100–110).

15. *QSLJQC*, 12/4/1801.

16. *TJFZ*, *juan* 7, 12b.

17. *QSLTZC*, 5/13/1865; 12/6/1865.

18. A sample decree exhorting the wealthy and righteous of the realm to engage in such activities can be found in Zhongguo diyi lishi dang'anguan (1993, 1:74), entry dated 7/3/1724.

19. *QSLQLC*, 3/2/1736.

20. Memorial from Fuheng dated 12/27/1752 in Grand Secretariat archives *(Neige daku)* held at the Academia Sinica; *CLYFZJQ*, *juan* 7, 48b, 57b.

21. Jin Dayang (1980:88–91). So did the Lis of "Liangdian houjie" and Li Yunmei.

22. On the problems of the Feng household see Feng Xuezhang (1919) and Chapter 3. He also endowed a primary school named Yangzheng Xuetang and gruel kitchens.

23. For a description of soldiers assigned to firefighting in Kaifeng see Meng Yuanlao (1961:120) and Zheng Shoupeng (1980:393–416). On the relegation of firefighting responsibilities to private citizens see Shiba Yoshinobu, "Ningpo and Its Hinterland," in Skinner (1977:421–422).

24. Wang Shouxun (1938), *juan* 12, 2a; Lu Yitian (1984:304). For similar organizations elsewhere see Takashima Ko (1997).

25. Yangcheng jiuke (1898), *juan* 6, 5.

26. Lu Yitian (1984), *juan* 6, 304. For a general description of transport workers in Tianjin see *TJLSZL* 4:1–29 (1965); Lieberthal (1980:10–27); Geng Jie et al.(1985); and Hershatter (1986:115–139).

27. *TJFZX*, *juan* 7, 13a; *ZB*, 1/20/1896. See also Li Ranxi (1964:208) and Chen Liansheng (1984:37).

28. See Hao Jinrong (n.d.), *juan* 3, and Dai Yu'an (1986:101–102).

29. *ZB*, 3/1/1895. Tianjin, of course, is not unique. Similar generosity is recorded for Yangzhou's salt merchants. See Liu Miao (1982:16–24) and Zhang Haipeng et al. (1995:318–357).

30. For various estimates on the strength of the Taiping Northern Expeditionary Force see Michael and Chang (1966, 1:94, n. 55). The force approaching Tianjin is now estimated to have been around forty thousand.

31. Yao Xianzhi, *Manfang huibian* (Collected materials on the barbarians), as cited in Zhang Shouchang (1984:457).

32. Hao Fusen (n.d.), *juan* 5. For the organization of local militias elsewhere see Kuhn (1970).

33. See Hou Jing (n.d.), *juan* 1, 15a. Even the British consul was impressed by these fiery characters; see J. Morgan report to Beijing, dated 4/3/1871, in *FO* 647.19.

34. *TJFZ, juan* 43, 41b–43a; Ding Yunshu and Chen Shixun (1910). Ni, a commander who retired to resume his career as a salt merchant, donated twenty thousand strings; *TJXXZ, juan* 21.3, 25b.

35. Jin Dayang and Liu Yudong (1982:77) and Dai Yu'an (1986:17–18).

36. Xue Fucheng (1983), *juan* 2, 31.

37. *CL* 173.186, 291; Tianjinshi Zhengxie mishuchu (1974:9).

38. Wenqian's memorial to the throne dated 3/5/1874 in Ding Yunshu and Chen Shixun (1910), *juan* 2, 24a and 30a–b.

39. Ibid., *juan* 3, 1a–2b. Bei was a native of Tianjin who once served as a circuit intendant in Gansu. After this campaign, he was impeached for embezzlement and banished. Hua of the "Highsteps" was then serving as a head merchant. See "Tianjin yiwu shiji" (undated manuscript, Special Collections, Nankai University Library).

40. For everything except the beef supply. See Oliphant (1970, 1:330 and 428).

41. Ding Yunshu and Chen Shixun (1910), *juan* 4, 13b, 31b.

42. Ibid., *juan* 4, 26a. Such scrolls were usually reserved for imperial princes and grand secretaries. See Zhaolian (1980), *juan* 1, 376.

43. Ding Yunshu and Chen Shixun (1910), *juan* 4, 28a, 38b–39a.

44. *CL* 173.32, order issued by the governor-general of Zhili dated 12/24/1859.

45. Ibid., order from Senggerinchin dated 1/8/1860.

46. Ibid., report dated 3/1/1860.

47. See Wolseley (1972:87–319).

48. Thus Yoshizawa Seiichiro's argument that local militia under gentry control did not represent localism might not be entirely accurate. See Yoshizawa (1996:31–61).

49. *QSLXFC*, decrees issued 9/18/1860 and 9/30/1860; Ding Yunshu and Chen Shixun (1910), *juan* 5, 18a–b, *juan* 6, 2b–3b, 8a–10b.

50. Ding Yunshu and Chen Shixun (1910), *juan* 6, 27b.

51. Gao Ningwen (1982), *juan* 4, 28a–28b.

52. Qi Zhilu (1983:1–2); Mackinnon (1980:145); and Borthwick (1983:61).

53. Modeled after the Erudite Scholasticus exam *(boxue hongru)* and Erudite Literatus exam *(boxue hongci)*—special examinations conducted in 1679, 1733, and 1735 to entice eminent scholars into government service—the *jingji teke* was not unprecedented as a way to recruit talents, but the proposal was controversial. See *GXCDHL*, 12/16/1897, and Wang Yunsheng (1983).

54. *DGB*, 9/3/1911.

55. Qi Zhilu (1983:13).

56. Notable early graduates include Mei Yiqi, later president of Qinghua University, and Zhou Enlai whose work-study in France was financed by Yan Xiu.

57. *DGB*, 9/3/1911. On Lin, who began as a manager for Yan's salt monopoly, see Gao Ningwen, "Linjun xingxue beiji" (Stele in commemoration of Lin Moqing's promotion of education), and "Tianjin Lin xiansheng muzhiming" (Epitaph of Lin Zhaohan of Tianjin), in Wang Shouxun (1937), *siji* (4th coll.), *buyi* (suppl.), 4a–6a. For more about Wang and Li see the following chapters.

58. Zhang Bing is a grandson of Zhang Jinwen; Shiqing (1846–1922) is a member of the "Big Eight" Bian family. See *DGB*, 3/1/1903; Zhang Shaozu (1988: 84); and *Tianjin Bianshi zongzupu* (1930).

59. Lin worked as a manager for several salt merchants before turning to local education. Hua Zeyuan, whose father Shiming was Yan's classmate as *juren*, was a nephew of Hua Shiguan, Yan's brother-in-law. Yan's second daughter was married to Hua Zexun, Zeyuan's brother. On Bian see "Bian Gengyen xiansheng wanyen lu" (Essays in memory of Bian Yuchang) (1908); and *DGB*, 9/22/1908. His eldest son married a daughter of Feng Xuezhang; his nephew married Yan's eldest daughter.

60. By 1905 there were 3,804 students enrolled in Tianjin's schools. See *DGB*, 2/10–11/1905 and 4/16/1905. The province reported 36,344 students; see King (1911:56). Delegations from other provinces came to study Tianjin's system. See, for example, *DGB*, 5/2/1906; and Liu Yanchen and Wang Guinian (1984).

61. See Mackinnon (1980:57–61, 149–150); *YSKZY*, 2:670–672; *DGB*, 10/30/1906, 7/20/1905, 3/11/1910, 10/20/1906, 4/10/1911, 5/23/1919, and 3/25/1920.

62. Mackinnon (1980:51) argues that Zhili was relatively peaceful. A survey of sources suggests that disturbances as a result of financing the reforms were widespread and extended over a decade. See *DGB*, 8/28/1910; Zhongguo diyi lishi dang'anguan (1985, 1:49); Zhang Zhenhe and Ding Yuanying (1982); and cases of Zunhua, Qian'an, Yizhou, and Longyao in Prazniak (1999:97–125).

63. See, for example, *DGB*, 4/3/1909, 3/13/1909, 3/15/1909, 10/20/1906, 11/17/1906, 12/9/1906, 4/24/1910, 4/30/1910, and 3/3/1911.

64. Hu Shangyi (n.d.:app.).

65. Yan Xiu (n.d.), "Yanshi jiashu," letters dated 6/9/1908 and 6/17/1908.

66. Ibid., letters dated 2/15/1908 and 8/18/1908; Qi Zhilu (1983:11).

67. *DGB*, 8/11/1911.

68. This school was started in 1904 and merged with the Nankai Middle School in 1908. In 1911 some 2,000 taels of its operating budget was transferred to the Commercial Middle School (Zhongdeng Shangye Xuetang). See *CL* 173.466.

69. See *CL* 173.257, 260, 261, and 265.

70. *CL* 173.383, report of the head merchant to the commissioner dated 10/25/1908. More than 90,000 taels was raised each year.

71. Yan Xiu (n.d.), "Yanshi jiashu," letter dated 11/20/1906. Yan, taking a hint from Yuan Shikai, advised his close friend to divert the donation.

Chapter 6: Changing Times

1. For a convenient list and summary of these bankruptcies and crises see Negishi Tadashi (1911:1–5).

2. *DGB*, 1/27/1905.

3. Chan (1977:225 and 229); Du Li, "Lun Li Pingshu," in Fudan daxue lishixi et al. (1986:391).

4. Fewsmith (1983:617–640).

5. *DGB*, 6/2/1904; Zhang Taiyan, "Geming zhi daode" (Revolutionary morality), in Zhang Nan and Wang Yinzhi (1977, 2:516); Sonda Saburō (1975:43–55); Mackinnon (1980:163–179); Kurahashi Masanao (1984:45–66); Yu Heping (1993: 366–388); and Pearson (1997).

6. See *Shen Bao* (Shanghai Daily News), 5/11/1895; *DGB*, 8/27/1906; and *CL* 173.180, petition by the Beijing Syndicate dated 1/11/1904.

7. Detached from Changlu since 1693, the district was subjected to a bureaucratic tug-of-war among the salt divisions; *CL* 173.367 and *NW* 441.2723.

8. *QYFZ, juan* 132, 10b–15a; *CL* 173.479 and 173.489; Gan Houci (1910), *juan* 11, 12b–13a.

9. *Dongfang zazhi* (Eastern miscellany) 1(5) (1904):79–80; commerce *(shangwu)*, 1(11) (1904):131–132 and "Huiyi zhengwuchu dang" (Archive of the Council on Political Affairs), First National Archives, Beijing, 552.780.

10. See, for example, Song Zejiu, "Fenggao Tianjin zibenjia ji shangyejia" (Exhortations to Tianjin's capitalists and merchants), in *DGB*, 8/18/1904.

11. This company was established in 1906 by Li Zhentong with an initial capital of 6,000 taels and new machinery from Germany; see *DGB*, 7/20/1908, 7/25/1908, 7/28/1908, 8/1/1908. For Li's activities in local self-government see the next chapter.

12. Li Baoheng invested 2,000 yuan in the cigarette company, 1,000 taels in the insurance company, 1,000 taels in Da Qing Government Bank, and 550 yuan in Beijing's water company; see *TMA*, 128.3.2506. Wang Xianbin invested 500 yuan in the cigarette company and 1,750 taels in the insurance company; see *CL* 173.500, report on the expropriation of the Wang family. The "Philanthropist" Li household also contributed 600,000 of the 2-million-tael capital of the Tianjin-Pukou Surety Bank. See Jin Dayang (1980:78); and *TMA*, 128.2.1987.

13. On the Mu family see Mu Zhifang (1982) and Tianjinshi Zhengxie mishuchu (1974:6). The Mu business empire consisted of tea firms, pawnshops, salt monopolies, native banks, oil presses, and land. On the Tianjin electric light company see Gan Houci (1907), *juan* 20, 34a–36b.

14. The Yan household owned twenty shares of the company, and Yan Xiu provided a secondary personal guarantee for a 2,100-tael credit secured on shares of the Luanzhou Colliery and Beijing Electric Light Company. See Yan Xiu (1990:259).

15. *DGB*, 12/11/1909.

16. *DGB*, 11/1/1908. Wang Tongxian, no relative of Xianbin, owned the Chenglisheng salt firm and operated the monopolies of Huixian and Huojia districts (in Henan) and the three subprefectures of Zhangjiakou, Dushikou,

and Dolon. On the Yans' investment see "Yanshi jiashu," Yan Xiu's letter dated 12/13/1909.

17. Li Baoxian was the eldest son of Li Shiming (1849–1925), who was once a director of the company. Baoqian, who married Bian Shiqing's daughter, was the second son of Li Shiyu (1855–1917). See "Yan'gutang Lishi jiapu" (n.d.) and Zhou Zhijun (1981:22–23). On the Chee Hsin Cement Company see Feuerwerker et al. (1967:304–341).

18. His salt merchant father Liankui (1832–1881) operated under the corporate name of Xinchang. See "Yan'gutang Lishi jiapu" (n.d.).

19. The Luanzhou Colliery was founded in 1907 by Zhou Xuexi, who was Changlu commissioner from 1905 to 1906. The Lis invested 350,000 taels, while other salt merchants subscribed 150,000 taels. See Jin Dayang (1980:86).

20. See Boorman and Howard (1968, 2:319–321). Li also became one of the leading politicians of the Nationalist Party after his return to China. On the Yao family see Yao Xiyun (1989:204–242).

21. Subscription advertisement for the Oumei Doufu Gongsi (Tofu Company of Europe and America, the Chinese name for the Usine Caseo Sojaine at Colombes) in *DGB*, 9/24/1910. Wang subscribed 5,000 yuan; Li Baoheng invested 1,500. See also *CL* 173.500; *CL* 173.440; and *TMA* 128.3.2506. Yan Xiu also mobilized support from friends such as Sun Daosen, then circuit intendant in charge of industrial development. See Yan Xiu (n.d.), "Yan Fansun riji," diary entry dated 8/18/1910.

22. Yuan Shikai approved Wang's application with minor changes. See Tianjinshi dang'anguan (1990:254–260).

23. The Fangshan area is part of the Western Hills suburb of Beijing. See Shang Shoushan (1985:49–60) and Fang Xing (1981).

24. Wang's share was 340,000 taels; Li's was 320,000. For a shareholders list see *TMA* 128.2.2506.

25. Xu Jingxing (1978:124–161); Liu Minshan (1985:36–42).

26. *DGB*, 6/14/1903; Hu Guangming (1986:184).

27. *DGB*, 10/4/1902.

28. *DGB*, 10/4–5/1902, 10/11/1902, 10/24/1902; *YSKZY*, memorial dated 5/1/1903.

29. Mackinnon (1980:60); Yuan's memorial dated 5/1/1903 in *YSKZY* II: 780–781; Board of Revenue reply dated 5/12/1903 in Tianjinshi dang'anguan (1990:73–75).

30. *DGB*, 5/8/1903; *YSKZY*, memorial dated 6/15/1903. Wu, a native of Anhui, made his fortune as a comprador for the Tianjin branch of the Hongkong and Shanghai Bank Corporation. He was among Tianjin's earliest industrialists and a controversial member of its merchant community. See *DGB*, 1/15/1905 and 1/17/1905, for advertisements labeling Wu "a beast in human attire"; and Wu Huanzhi (1965). On Wang, a leading and unpopular member of Ningbo merchants in Tianjin, see Wang Zhizhou (1983) and *DGB*, 8/22/1908.

31. *DGB*, 3/18/1903, 10/10/1903, 10/11/1903, 10/20/1903; Gan Houci (1907), *juan* 21, 15b.

32. Gan Houci (1907), *juan* 21, 12b–13a; *DGB*, 3/20/1903 and 5/4/1903.

33. Gan Houci (1907), *juan* 21, 14b; Mackinnon (1980:166); and Ji Hua (1981:44). The formation of *shangwuju* in the major commercial centers in

China was first proposed in 1895 and briefly attempted during the Hundred Days Reform in 1898. See *GXCDHL* IV:3722–3723, 3803, 4095; Chan (1977:199–200); and Wang Pengyun, "Zou xingban shangwu shu" (Memorial on the promotion of commerce), in Chen Zongyi (1898), *juan* 29, 2a–b. The Tianjin *shangwuju* was formed in 1902; see *TJSHDAXB* I:1, n. 1.

34. Bian Yuguang (1844–1909), owner of Longshun, was a cotton cloth importer and a member of the "Big Eight" Bian family discussed previously. Ning Xingpu (1842–1928), also known as Ning Shifu, made his fortune exporting straw braids and hats. He also appeared frequently in salt-monopoly leases as the middleman or friend of the syndicate *(gangyou)*, as in *CL* 173.459, lease of the monopolies of Chenliu, Taikang, and Jixian dated 6/23/1911. Yao was the owner of the Deheng native bank.

35. Gan Houci (1907), *juan* 21, 15a–b. On the official character of the chambers of commerce during this period see Zhu Ying (1987).

36. *DGB*, 5/31/1903 and 6/4/1903.

37. See *TJSHDAXB* I:345–346, petition dated twelfth month of 1903.

38. Gan Houci (1907), *juan* 21, 15b; *DGB*, 8/1/1903, 9/19/1903, 10/4/1903; and *TJSHDAXB* I:31.

39. *DGB*, 12/30/1903.

40. *DGB*, 11/21/1905 and 12/3/1905.

41. *TJSHDAXB* I:30–31. This document, I believe, has been misdated "the second half of 1903" by the editors. It should be late 1904, as the proposal to establish chambers of commerce was approved on January 11, 1904 (see *GXCDHL* V:5122); the document referred to the directors' threat to resign as an event in the past year, that is, 1903.

42. This version differs from the appointment by merchants themselves described in Zhu Ying (1997:127). Hua, a *jinshi* of 1890, hailed from the "High-steps" Hua household. His sister married a member of the Shi family of Yanliuqing, and his son Zeyuan served as one of the three directors of Tianjin's educational promotion office. See Hua Changqing et al. (1909).

43. *DGB*, 5/28/1904 to 6/3/1904 and 10/14/1904.

44. See *TJSHDAXB* I:32–33, Zaizhen's letter to Yuan Shikai, and 33–35 and 43–53 for Yuan Shikai's comments on successive drafts and approval by the Ministry of Commerce. On Zaizhen's activities as minister of commerce see Kurahashi Masanao (1976) and Shen Zuwei (1983).

45. See, for example, petitions received by the chamber reported in *DGB*, 11/8/1904 and 12/18/1904.

46. The number of directors *(huidong)* and the trades represented were expanded from ten to twelve in 1905, fourteen in 1908, sixteen in 1909, and nineteen in 1910. See *DGB*, 3/10/1905; *TJSHDAXB* I:107–108; and Hu Guangming (1986:200–202).

47. *DGB*, 3/13/1905; *TJSHDAXB* I:44 and 54–57; and Chen Zhongping (1998:92–128).

48. See, for example, *TMA* 128.2.803 and 128.2.2188 and *DGB*, 12/25/1904, 5/31/1905, 6/5/1905.

49. *TJSHDAXB* I:305–315 and 315–325; *DGB*, 3/14/1908, 10/29/1909, 11/8/1909, 11/16/1909, 4/19/1910, 7/1/1910, 5/23/1911, 10/18/1911.

50. *TJSHDAXB* I:169–192.

51. The paper, originally named *Tianjinbao*, was renamed when Liu Meng-yang (1877–1943) took over as editor in late 1905. See *TJSHDAXB* I:154–162 and *DGB*, 9/19/1905. Liu, a native of Tianjin, subsequently became the editor of *Dagongbao* and an activist in local and national politics as vice-speaker of the Tianjin Provisional District Assembly. See Yuan Jinxi's preface to Liu Mengyang (1922).

52. *TMA* 128.2.3083; *DGB*, 10/13–14/1910. On the effects of this promotional tour see Yu Heping (1988).

53. On the fair see *TMA* 128.2.3024; Liu Jingshan (1987:18); and Ma Min (1985).

54. For a survey of proposals for monetary reform see Zhang Zhenkun (1979).

55. See Mackinnon (1980:59). Other sources suggest a profit of at least 1 million taels; see *CL* 173.285 and *Dongfang zazhi* 2(9) (1905): 195–197.

56. See *DGB*, 1/23/1904, 1/27/1904; 3/14/1906, 4/8/1906, 8/21/1906; 8/14/1906, 1/3/1907; and 4/13/1906, 12/29/1906 respectively.

57. *DGB*, 2/3/1904, 2/5/1904, 1/18/1908.

58. *DGB*, 2/15/1907, 12/30/1907, 3/15/1908, 3/22/1908, 3/26/1908, 9/16/1908.

59. See, for example, Shunzhi ziyiju (1910), *chenqing* (petitions), 1a; and Gan Houci (1910), *juan* 11, 22b–24a and 26b–27b.

60. *YSKZY*, memorial dated 8/8/1903.

61. See *CL* 173.343, petition by salt merchants for reduction and delay of interest and price increase payments and the controller-general's rejection dated 8/7/1904. See also *CL* 173.248, petition and comments dated 7/29/1905; and *CL* 173.207, petitions dated 7/19/1906 and 7/21/1906 by the salt merchants proposing that the exchange rate between copper cash and silver be fixed, using the average rate in the past six months.

62. *CL* 173.343, petition of Cang Yongning, official in charge of salt supply to Tianjin and Wuqing districts, to the commissioner dated 10/23/1907.

63. Indeed, Yuan Shikai commended Zhou Xuexi to the throne confidentially for his outstanding work in this regard. See *YSKZY*, memorial dated 7/3/1904.

64. *TJSHDAXB* I:426–427.

65. *TJSHDAXB* I:443–444, petition dated 12/27/1907.

66. *TJSHDAXB* I:456–457, letter from Chen Bi, minister of general accounts, to Yang Shixiang dated 3/12/1908; *GXCDHL*, memorial of Zhou Fu dated 7/19/1905; and *DGB*, 12/15/1907, 3/22/1908, 3/26/1908.

67. Gan Houci (1910), *juan* 9, 23a; *CL* 173.440.

68. *TJSHDAXB* I:133–134 and 447–448, minutes of a board meeting dated 1/12/1908; and 464–465, petition for the conversion to silver standard dated 4/13/1908.

69. *DGB*, 3/23/1908; Hu Guangming (1986:211); and King et al. (1988:201–202).

70. *TJSHDAXB* I:371–372, petition of the Chamber of Commerce to Yuan Shikai dated 12/10/1905 and Yuan's decision dated 12/12/1905.

71. *TJSHDAXB* I:350–353, notice issued 2/14/1908 and petition by forty-one merchants from Guangdong.

72. Imperial Maritime Customs Service (1909:57).

73. *FO* 228/1694, enclosure 64 of 12/8/1908.

74. See *FO* 228/1694, confidential memorandum to the British ambassador, Beijing, dated 12/8/1908; communication from Yang to the Foreign Ministry dated 3/22/1909 in *FM* 851, E-6-3; and *TMA* 128.3.1226, order from the circuit intendant of Tianjin Maritime Customs dated 12/24/1908; incoming and outgoing letters dated 2/1/1909, 2/21/1909, 3/4/1909. For a further analysis of this episode see Kwan (1998).

75. Meeting on 3/8/1909; brief filed in *FM* dated 3/22/1909.

76. *TMA* 128.2.30; 3.1226.

77. Ibid.; resolution of the first meeting of the Joint Commission in *TMA* 128.1.49 dated 5/22/1909.

78. *TMA* 128.2.1995; letters dated 4/1/1910 and 10/24/1910.

79. *FM* 851, E-6-3, Chen Kuilong's letter dated 2/7/1910.

80. *FM* 851, E-6-3, letter to Chen Kuilong dated 2/14/1910.

81. *FM* 851, E-6-3, memo from Finance Ministry to Foreign Ministry dated 11/5/1910.

82. Articles of organization for the bank reprinted in *DGB*, 10/16/1911 to 10/18/1911.

83. *TMA* 128.2.1995, Chen Kuilong's directive to the chamber dated 4/21/1911; Imperial Maritime Customs Service (1911:135).

84. *TJSHDAXB* I:378–380. The thirteen-point charter of the Public Assaying Bureau can be found in *DGB*, 10/3/1908.

85. Yuan Shikai's letter to Xu Shichang dated 6/29/1902; *YSKZY* II:681–686; and Jia Shiyi (1917, 1:434–444).

86. *DGB*, 5/10/1903; *YSKZY* II:781–783, memorial dated 5/10/1903.

87. Gan Houci (1910), *juan* 7, 19b–20b; *TMA* 128.3.886, order from the Stamp Duty Bureau dated 4/8/1908.

88. *Analects* XII:9.

89. Petition of Tianjin merchants dated 9/1/1910 in *TJSHDAXB* I.2:1706–1709.

90. *TMA* 128.3.886, petitions dated 4/11/1908, 4/16/1908, 6/12/1908, and instruction from Zhang Zhenfang to the Tianjin Chamber of Commerce dated 7/17/1910; *DGB*, 7/31/1910 to 9/27/1910; and Hu Guangming (1986:218).

## CHAPTER 7: SHIFTING POLITICS

1. Fogel and Zarrow (1997).

2. For a favorable view of the reforms see Reynolds (1993). A more critical perspective is advanced by Wei Qingyuan et al. (1993); Hou Yijie (1985; 1993); and Kishi Toshihiko (1996). On contemporary critics of the returned students see, for example, Gugong bowuyuan Ming-Qing dang'anbu (1979, 1:231 and 346). A review of recent scholarship can be found in Chen Xiangyang (1998).

3. Letter from Tao Xiang to Sheng Xuanhuai dated 5/17–29/1907 in Chen Xulu et al. (1979:54–55); and Wu Chunmei (1998:137).

4. Zaize's 1906 memorial to the throne in Gugong bowuyuan Ming-Qing dang'anbu (1979, 1:174–175); Wei Qingyuan et al. (1993:463).

5. Zhang Yilin (1947), *juan* 8, 38a.

6. Zaize's 1905 memorial to the throne. See Gugong bowuyuan Ming-Qing dang'anbu (1979, 1:111).

7. Letter from Tao Xiang to Sheng Xuanhuai dated 11/22/1906 in Chen Xulu et al. (1979:28–32); Wei Qingyuan et al. (1993:143–147).

8. The scandal is documented in *GXCDHL,* 5/7/1907, and *QSG, juan* 221, 9098. Yang became Wang Yisun's treasured concubine. Interview with Zhao Ju, August 10, 1994.

9. *DGB,* 6/2/1905. On the national boycott see Zhang Cunwu (1965); Zhu Ying and Liu Wangling (1984); and Field (1957).

10. *DGB,* 6/12/1905; He Zuo (1956:34); Mackinnon (1980:167); and *TMA* 128.2.2976, minutes of meeting dated 6/17/1905.

11. See Jiang Yuanhuan (1985:41).

12. *TMA* 128.2.2976, meeting dated 6/21/1905; *DGB,* 6/24/1905; Zhang Cunwu (1965:67); and Hu Guangming (1986:220).

13. *TMA* 128.2.2976, petition dated 6/27/1905 and Yuan Shikai's reply dated 7/3/1905. The emperor's edict was issued on 8/31/1905.

14. *TJXXZ, juan* 12, 9a–11b; *DGB,* 7/8/1906.

15. *CL* 173.345; *YSKZY,* memorial dated 8/28/1907; *DGB,* 3/27/1907 and 3/29/1907. On the bureau's activities see Tianjinfu zizhiju (1906; 1907) and Gan Houci (1907), *juan* 1.

16. For a membership list see Tianjinfu zizhiju (1906:27a).

17. See *DGB,* 9/18/1906 and 12/8/1906; Gan Houci (1907), *juan* 1, 23a–23b; and *YSKZY,* memorial summarizing the local self-government experiment dated 8/28/1907. For the list of ten representatives nominated by the chamber see *TMA* 128.2.2439, letter transmitted 11/16/1906.

18. *DGB,* 3/30/1907. On the theory and practice of local self-government see Philip Kuhn, "Local Self-Government Under the Republic: Problems of Control, Autonomy, and Mobilization," in Wakeman and Grant (1975:277–298). See also Teraki Tokuko (1962); Ding Yuguang (1993:9–22); and Ma Xiaoquan in Fogel and Zarrow (1997:183–211).

19. For successive editions of the provisional charter for self-government of Tianjin district see *DGB,* 9/3/1906, 3/30/1907 to 4/2/1907, and 1/29/1909 to 2/4/1909.

20. *DGB,* 4/21/1907, 5/4/1907, 5/13/1909, 8/3–4/1910. On 11/19/1906, Yuan Shikai ordered establishment of the district assembly and executive council within one month. See *TJSHDAXB* I:2288.

21. The composition of the 1907 assembly can be found in Kishi Toshihiko (1996:app. 1). Yang Xiceng from the Big Eight is one of the biggest Changlu merchants of the time. Liu Guangxi held the title of martial student. See *DGB,* 4/8/1909.

22. Kishi Toshihiko (1996:app. 1). His list of assemblymen for 1909 should be amended as follows: Sun Hongyi (see also Chapter 8) is the son of a salt merchant; Ning Cunshu is owner-manager of the Huaduan native bank; Li Zhentong is the founder of Huasheng Machine-Made Candle and Soap Company, Ltd. A list of the fifty-one members elected to the 1911 assembly can be found in *DGB,* 1/8–9/1911 and 6/2/1911.

23. *DGB,* 6/16/1907, 7/10/1907, 1/8–9/1911, 6/2/1911, 7/26/1911; *YSKZY,*

memorial dated 8/28/1907; and Gan Houci (1907), *juan* 1, 22a–22b. Li Baoxiang was the youngest son of Li Shiqi (1860–1899), youngest brother of Li Shiming. After his election to the Provincial Consultative Assembly, Li Shiming's chairmanship was assumed by Li Zihe. See "Yan'gutang Lishi jiapu" (n.d.) and *DGB*, 8/27/1909.

24. *DGB*, 3/13/1911, 8/21/1911, 9/28/1911; Wang Yunsheng (1983:103).

25. *DGB*, 3/8/1911 and 7/21/1911; *CL* 173.180.

26. *DGB*, 5/12/1909, 5/27/1909, 10/29/1909; *CL* 173.402. On the provincial consultative assemblies see Li Shoukong, "Gesheng ziyiju lianhehui yu Xinhai geming" (Federation of provincial consultative assemblies and the 1911 Revolution), in Wu Xiangxiang (1961); and Wei Qingyuan et al. (1993).

27. Sun was also elected to the provisional district assembly. See Sun Yushu (1986:42) and Lu Naixiang (1936). For more details of Sun's career see Fan Tiren (1981) and Dong Junrong (1986). These sources make no mention of his *juren* degree as listed by Zhang Pengyuan (1969:255).

28. Yan Xiu (1990:150).

29. For a list of the candidates see *DGB*, 3/23/1910 and 4/8/1910. Heading the list were Yang Xiceng of the "Big Eight" Changyuan Yang household (296,053 taels), Zhang Bing of "Hai Zhangwu" fame (186,426 taels), Li Shiyu of the "Philanthropist" Lis (138,413 taels), and other members of the Big Eight.

30. Yang's name did not appear on the list of assemblymen in Zhang Yufa (1971:427); but see *TMA* 128.2.2271, notice of Yang's election from Ning Fupeng to the chamber.

31. Shunzhi ziyiju (1910–1911), report of election results to the governor-general dated 1/23/1909. For a membership list see *DGB*, 12/2/1909; Zhang Yufa (1971:420–435 and 451, n. 11).

32. *DGB*, 7/27/1910, 11/1/1910, 12/30/1910.

33. Xiao Gongqin (1999:168–172). The report to the throne on the merits of constitutional monarchy was ghostwritten by Liang Qichao, the empress dowager's nemesis. See Dong Fangkui (1991:164–171).

34. Gugong bowuyuan Ming-Qing dang'anbu (1979, 1:173–176).

35. On Shanghai's self-government movement see Wu Guilong, "Qingmo Shanghai difang zhizi yundong shulun" (On Shanghai's local self-government movement in late Qing), in Zhongnan diqu Xinhai gemingshi yanjiu hui (1983); Goodman (1995:199–210).

36. Yuan Shikai's ruling dated 11/2/1905. See Tianjinshi dang'anguan (1990:187–190).

37. Gugong bowuyuan Ming-Qing dang'anbu (1979, 2:726–727).

38. See *DGB*, 12/26/1907, 4/13/1909, 5/17/1909, 9/17–18/1909, 3/8/1911.

39. *DGB*, 1/29/1909 to 2/1/1909, 4/16/1909, 5/23/1909, 6/21/1909, 7/3–6/1909, 8/12/1909, 9/7/1909, 12/25/1909, 12/31/1909; Hu Shangyi (n.d.).

40. *DGB*, 12/7/1907, 12/15/1907, 12/19/1907, notice to the district's bureau of disaster relief (Zhenfuju).

41. *DGB*, 17/11/1907, 1/20/1908, 5/29/1908, 6/24/1908, 5/23/1910, 6/2/1910, 8/7/1910, 10/7/1910, 11/3/1910, 12/5–8/1910, 3/31/1911, 4/28/1911, 11/17/1911.

42. See, for instance, resolutions to reduce surcharges by local officials in

*DGB*, 12/10/1910 and 4/5–10/1911. On the array of taxes and surcharges, reportedly the heaviest in Zhili, see *GXCDHL*, memorial by Wang Jinrong dated 12/21/1907.

43. *CL* 173.395, petition dated 6/27/1910. As a result of administrative reforms, the supervision of the salt monopolies had been detached from the Board of Revenue and transferred to a new office, the Controller-General of Salt Administration, in 1909.

44. *DGB*, 10/13/1910, 11/13/1910, 12/6/1910, 7/10/1910. This body is known as the Conference of the Governor-General's Yamen (Duchu huiyiting shenchake).

45. *DGB*, 4/14/1910.

46. Zhang Hailin (1998:136–156).

47. Zhili's electorate as a proportion of the total population led the country at 0.62 percent. See *DGB*, 8/5/1908.

48. Li Shoukong in Wu Xiangxiang (1961:321–373); Dong Junrong (1986: 40–43); and Sun Yushu (1986:40–46).

49. *Guofengbao* (National herald), 2/20/1910, in Zhang Nan and Wang Yinzhi (1977:592–596).

50. Li Shoukong in Wu Xiangxiang (1961:354–355).

51. Ibid., pp. 342–345; Zhang Yufa (1971:437).

52. Zhang Yufa (1971:486–490).

53. For the correspondence between Sun Hongyi and the Chamber of Commerce see *TMA* 128.1.28. On merchant participation in demonstrations see *DGB*, 2/21/1910, 5/28/1910, and 10/6/1910.

54. *DGB*, 4/10/1910, 3/7/1910, 3/9/1910; *TJSHDAXB* I:2320–2322; and *TMA* 128.2.2271.

55. On the concept of commercial warfare see, for example, Li Chen Shunyan (1972).

56. On this society see *TJSHDAXB* I:1899–1942.

57. *DGB*, 3/7/1910 and 5/11/1910; Hou Yijie (1993:272–273).

58. Sun Hongyi's speech reported in *Zhongwei ribao* (China and abroad daily), 2/16/1910, as cited in Li Shoukong in Wu Xiangxiang (1961:333). This argument was repeated by members of the National Consultative Assembly as reported in *DGB*, 4/16/1911, as well as educators and students in *DGB*, 4/9/1910, letter from the principal of Zunhua District Middle School.

59. *DGB*, 12/15/1910.

60. Li Shoukong in Wu Xiangxiang (1961:345); Qi Bingfeng (1966).

61. *DGB*, 11/20/1910, 11/24/1910, 12/1/1910; Jiang Yuanhuan (1985:42–43).

62. Wen Shilin, whose household dominated Yixingbu, a suburb of Tianjin, founded the Puyu Nüxue (Puyu Girl's School) with the support of Sun Hongyi. This school was active in fund-raising for self-government causes and reduction of the national debt. See Liu Qingyang (1955).

63. Yan Xiu (n.d.), "Yan Fansun riji," diary entry dated 1/8–9/1911; *DGB*, 1/10–11/1911; and Chen Kuilong (1983), *juan* 2, 53a–54b.

64. Li Dazhao, "Shibanian lai zhi huigu" (Looking back at the past eighteen years), *Zhili fazhuan shiba zhounian ji'nian teji* (Special anthology in commemoration of eighteen years of Zhili school on law and administration), *jiangyan*

(speeches), 5 (1923), as cited in Tianjin shehui kexueyuan lishi yanjiusuo (1987: 235). This school was financed by 55,000 taels from the annual contribution of 81,000 taels by the salt merchant He Fuxian in return for the privilege of operating the Koubei monopolies; see *CL* 173.383. Sun Hongyi reportedly financed Li's study at Waseda University in 1911; see Zhang Cixi (1970:3).

65. See, for example, reports in *DGB*, 6/10/1910 and 8/30/1910, on the district of Wuqing; 8/8/1910 and 11/27/1910 on the market town of Shengfang in Wen'an district; and a similar contest between gentry and merchants for leadership at the market town of Xinjin, Xulu district, as detailed in *DGB*, 1/1/1911.

66. For the speaker's political problems see *DGB*, 3/7/1911, 4/11/1911, 6/18/1911, 8/9/1911.

67. *DGB*, 10/17/1911. The district assembly criticized the arrangement, as well, as reported in *DGB*, 7/18/1910.

68. Shunzhi ziyiju (1910–1911), *chencheng* (petitions).

69. *CL* 173.372; *DGB*, 11/15/1910, 11/19–20/1910, 4/4/1911; and Shunzhi ziyiju (1910–1911), petition to the governor-general dated 1/30/1910.

70. *CL* 173.372, petition by the salt merchants to the commissioner dated 12/7/1910.

71. A study of the social composition of five provincial consultative assemblies concludes that 66.9 percent of the assemblymen were members of the upper gentry, defined as tribute students or above. See Zhang Pengyuan (1969) and see Hamaguchi Nobuko, "The Provincial Assembly and the Local Leaders in Zhili During the Late Qing Period," in Shingai kakumei kenkyūkai (1985:193–220).

## CHAPTER 8: THE CRASH

1. *DGB*, 7/19/1911 and 7/28/1911; *CL* 173.491; and *TMA* 128.3.2587, letter from the Chamber of Commerce to the commissioner. For a list of the salt merchants' properties see *CL* 173.459, 491, 493, 500, 517.

2. See Ji Hua (1984:128).

3. *DGB*, 6/19/1911.

4. Lin Chunye (1983:84); Hu Guangming (1994:101).

5. *TMA* 128.2.2068, undated translation of letter from the French consul to the Chamber of Commerce.

6. *CL* 173.117, petition of salt merchants, Li Hongzhang's reply dated 9/1/1901, and other unsuccessful petitions dated 3/23/1903, 9/7/1903, 10/24/1903.

7. *CL* 173.117, petition by Hua Xueqi dated 10/20/1901 and letter of authorization dated 3/7/1902. A member of the "Bei" Huas, he operated the household's salt firm Yuantaixing. Under Qing administrative procedure, the instruction slip is an informal notice or instruction on a sliver of white paper, often undated, from a superior office to subordinates covering a broad range of regular administrative chores. See Zhang Jianying (1882), *juan* 2, 4b.

8. *YSKZY*, memorial to the throne dated 11/18/1903.

9. See *CL* 173.178, order dated 6/4/1905 and petition of the head merchants dated 7/26/1905.

10. *CL* 173.178, petition by Wang Xianbin requesting a letter of authorization to be issued retroactively to the Russo-Asiatic Bank, dated 8/18/1909, and peti-

tion from the head merchants for a loan of 1 million taels from the Board of Revenue Bank dated eighth month of 1906.

11. See *CL* 173.117, 132, and 178.

12. See *CL* 173.402, Han Cao's objection dated 7/31/1909 to the receivership of his Xianghe monopoly. The commissioner ruled that the head merchants were acting within the law because Han was behind in his tax payments.

13. See *CL* 173.489, petition dated 10/3/1910; report of local officials dated 10/25/1911 in *CL* 173.486; and Yan Xiu (n.d.), "Yan Fansun riji," diary entries 10/13/1910, 10/25/1910, and 10/26/1910.

14. *CL* 173.178, petitions dated 2/12/1909 and 2/17/1909.

15. *CL* 173.178, letter dated 5/16/1910. To become eligible for diplomatic support in China, British banks routinely registered their loans with the Foreign Office. See Davis (1982:253).

16. *Xuezi yishuo* (Speculations on the study of government), *juan shang*, 21a, in *Huanhai zhinan* (1886). A superior need not comment or rule on the file.

17. *CL* 173.178, Zhang Zhenfang's report to Chen Kuilong dated 5/17/1910.

18. *Guofengbao* 2(9) (1911):3. The Imperial Maritime Customs trade report for the year took the same position, but for a different reason: "By his [Zhang's] proclamations, on which the loans were granted, he had made himself guarantor for the proper use of the loans."

19. *CL* 173.458, letters dated 3/30/1911 and 4/11/1911.

20. *CL* 173.458, instruction from Chen Kuilong to Zhang Zhenfang dated 4/1/1911; *CL* 173.462, report dated eleventh month of 1910; and *CL* 173.498, order from the commissioner to the head merchants dated 4/27/1911.

21. *CL* 173.459 and 500.

22. *CL* 173.498, Zhang Zhenfang's instruction to the head merchants dated 4/4/1911.

23. *TMA* 128.2.2068, proposal of salt merchants to the Chamber of Commerce dated 4/12/1911.

24. Ibid., proposal dated 4/18/1911.

25. *CL* 173.498, instruction from the commissioner to the head merchants dated 4/27/1911.

26. *DGB*, 6/7/1911.

27. *CL* 173.498, commissioner order dated 4/20/1911.

28. *TMA* 128.2.2068, Chamber of Commerce petition dated 5/2/1911 for an extension of the expropriation order.

29. Ibid., salt merchants' proposal dated 5/7/1911.

30. Ibid., report from Ning Xingpu dated 5/8/1911. Zhang Zhenfang concurred with the veto on 5/17/1911.

31. Beiyang junfa shiliao bianweihui (1992, 2:504), letter dated 10/16/1911.

32. Imperial Maritime Customs Service (1912:152).

33. *Xuantong zhengji* (1986), 12/31/1909, 2/25/1910, 4/13/1910, 5/19/1910; *QYFZ, juan* 5, 2a–11a. See also Watanabe Atsushi, "Shimmatsu ni okeru ensei no chūō shūkenka seisaku ni tsuite" (On the policy of the centralization of the Salt Administration in the late Qing period), in Nakajima Satoshi sensei koki kinen jigyōkai (1980, 1:657–680).

34. The nationalization program was proclaimed on 5/9/1911; the loan agreement was signed 5/20/1911. On the loan negotiations see King (1988: 439–450).

35. *Guofengbao* 2(11) (1911):3; *CL* 173.4912, notices sent by Zhang Zhenfang to Tianjin District Court dated 7/11/1911 and 8/11/1911, respectively. The draft civil and criminal procedural codes arrived too late to help the salt merchants. Clauses 133 and 134 of this draft, submitted in September 1911, would have made illegal the seizure of third-party property and taking into custody a defendant's family members.

36. *CL* 173.498, memorial submitted by Zhang on 6/2/1911; Yan Xiu (n.d.), "Yan Fansun riji," diary entry dated 6/3/1911.

37. *TMA* 128.2.2068, petitions from salt merchants dated 6/4/1911 and 6/5/1911; *DGB*, 6/13/1911 and 6/15/1911. See also Yan Xiu (n.d.), "Yan Fansun riji," diary entries dated 6/8–9/1911, for discussions among salt merchants on the surcharge.

38. At an annual interest rate of 7 percent for fourteen years. See *CL* 173.506.

39. Officially, thirty-six salt merchants had no loans outstanding although, in the case of Yan Xiu at least, such arrangements continued. See *CL* 173.456 and 173.473; see also Yan Xiu (n.d.), "Yan Fansun riji," diary entries dated 6/9/1911, 6/11/1911, and 6/16/1911.

40. A portion of the salt gabelle was assigned as collateral for the Boxer Indemnity, but Chinese officials prevented the foreign powers from assuming direct control over the collection and disbursement of the gabelle. See Wang Shuhuai (1974:111–114).

41. *CL* 173.461, Zhang's letters dated 6/20/1911 and 8/20/1911; *DGB*, 6/30/1911.

42. *DGB*, 6/18/1911 and 6/21–22/1911; *TMA* 128.2.2068, petition of forty-three salt merchants to the chamber requesting assistance to secure loans at a lower interest rate.

43. *TMA* 128.2.2068, series of three petitions, the last one dated 7/4/1911.

44. *DGB*, 6/14/1911 and 6/21/1911 respectively.

45. *CL* 173.459, petition by Ning Xingpu on behalf of the chamber dated 6/16/1911.

46. *TMA* 128.2.2068; *DGB*, 6/12/1911 and 6/16/1911.

47. *TMA* 128.2.2068, telegram dated 6/14/1911; *DGB*, 6/24/1911.

48. Most of these petitions are found in *CL* 173.459.

49. *TMA* 128.2.2068, petition of six public charities, joined by villagers in the northwestern sector of the district, dated 6/3/1911; *DGB*, 7/10/1911 and 7/21/1911; *CL* 173.459, petitions dated 7/24/1911 and 7/26/1911.

50. *DGB*, 8/3/1911.

51. *CL* 173.459, petition dated 7/18/1911.

52. *DGB*, 6/7/1911. Liu was editor of the *Dagongbao;* Wang was principal of Tianjin Public Middle School; Li was speaker of the Tianjin Municipal Assembly.

53. The meeting with foreign bankers took place on 6/6/1911; see *DGB*, 6/9/1911.

54. The petition, dated 6/10/1911, was reprinted in *DGB*, 6/20/1911. It was

also sent to the governor-general and the Ministry of Agriculture, Industry, and Commerce.

55. *DGB*, 6/10–11/1911; letter to native Tianjin officials serving in Beijing, dated 6/13/1911, in *DGB*, 6/21/1911.

56. *DGB*, 6/19/1911.

57. But see Yuan's commendation of his relative to the throne in *YSKZY* III:1314.

58. *CL* 173.459.

59. *DGB*, 6/8/1911, 6/10/1911, 6/13/1911; *CL* 173.459.

60. *DGB*, 6/23–24/1911, 6/26/1911, 6/28/1911, and 6/30/1911.

61. The Provincial Consultative Assembly might have been wrong. By requesting registration of their loans, the foreign banks had initiated the process.

62. *DGB*, 5/17/1911, 6/12–13/1911, 6/15/1911, 6/17/1911, 6/27/1911, and 7/1/1911.

63. *CL* 173.526, memorial dated 7/3/1911.

64. *DGB*, 8/14/1911 and 10/7/1911.

65. *DGB*, 7/14/1911.

66. *TMA* 128.2.2068, notice dated 6/12/1911.

67. *TMA* 128.3.2565, report of the Chamber of Commerce dated 8/17/1911; *CL* 173.491.

68. *DGB*, 10/5/1911; *CL* 173.503, report of Zhang Zhenfang to the governor-general dated 11/25/1911.

69. *Da Qing xinbian fadian* (1987), commercial law *(Shanglü)*, chap. 3, bankruptcy code, art. 43 and 45.

70. These issues were raised in a case brought by Ms. Chen (née Li) against Chen Binzhang who held the lease on Lincheng. See Zhili gaodeng shenpanting (1914, 2:130–132).

71. *DGB*, 7/28/1911; *CL* 173.457, petition by the Dexingcheng dated 7/22/1911.

72. One such arch was built in Wang Xianbin's honor in 1903; see *DGB*, 7/10/1911.

73. *DGB*, 12/31/1911. Leading salt merchants of the Lianghuai Division helped suppress an uprising at Yangzhou during the 1911 Revolution. See Zhou Zhichu (1988:47).

74. Lu Naixiang (1936:2) and Zhang Pengyuan (1969:197–198).

EPILOGUE

1. M. Zelin, "The Rise and the Fall of the Fu-rong Salt Yard Elite," in Esherick and Rankin (1990:84 and 105–106). See also Lin Jianyu, "Yanye zichan jieji yu Zigong difang yishihui" (Salt capitalists and Zigong local assemblies), in Peng Zeyi et al. (1991:394–410); and Chen Ran (1998).

2. For the case of Quanzhou see Wang Mingming (1999:368).

3. Suzhoushi dang'anguan (1982); Zhang Hailin (1999:197–203); Du Li, "Lun Li Pingshu," in Fudan daxue lishixi et al. (1986:391); Goodman (1995:201–207).

4. For the case of Canton see Michael Tsin, "Imagining 'Society' in China," in Fogel and Zarrow (1997:221–223).

5. Li Zehou (1996:29–30) and Xiao Gongqin (1999:318–319).

6. Duara (1988:87–117); Pearson (1997); Qiao Zhiqiang et al. (1997:857–880); Prazniak (1999).

7. *DGB*, 2/3/1912, 7/14/1912, 5/1/1913, 9/22/1913, 9/16/1914; letter from Yuan Shikai to Zhang Xun dated 1913 in Beiyang junfa shiliao bianweihui (1992, 1:435); Ding Yuguang (1993:145); Thaxton (1997).

8. For various schools in this debate over the necessity of the 1911 Revolution and how the reforms hastened the revolution, see Chen Xiangyang (1998:306–308).

9. The issue of whether merchant-gentry continued as a distinct social group is beyond the scope of this book. See Ma Min (1995:364–365).

# Glossary

*badajia* 八大家
*bangzi* 梆子
*bao'e renban* 包额认办
*baoxiao* 报效
*baoyue* 保约
*benming* 本名
Bian Yuguang 卞煜光
*bianyi zhangcheng* 便宜章程
*bili* 币利
Bohai 渤海
*caohetong* 草合同
*chang'an* 畅岸
Changlu 长芦
Changlu Baoshang Gongsi 长芦保商
　公司
Chen Kuilong 陈夔龙
Chengyi Kangxiang Guanshenghui
　诚议扛箱官圣会
*chengying* 承认
Chonghou 崇厚
Chouhuan Guozhaihui 筹还国债会
*chuanhu* 船户
*chuanluo* 串锣
*chuanpiao* 船票
*chuming de dongjia* 出名的东家
Dagukou 大沽口

Dai Quheng 戴衢亨
*daishang* 代商
*dajiafan* 大家饭
*dangjia* 当家
Daqinghe 大清河
Diguo Xianzheng Shijinhui 帝国宪政
　实进会
*ding* 丁
*dizhuyin* 滴珠银
Donghe 东河
*dongshihui* 董事会
Dou Rongguang 窦荣光
*fang* 房
Fang Bao 方苞
*faren jingli* 乏人经理
*fayan* 法谚
*fayu* 法语
*fenjia* 分家
*fenju bu xichan* 分居不析产
*fennian daizheng* 分年带徵
*fugang* 副纲
*fumuguan* 父母官
*fushou* 副手
*gandaying* 赶大营
*gang* 纲
*gangce* 纲册

197

*gangshou* 纲首
*gangyou* 纲友
*gaofei* 告费
Gaotaijie 高台阶
Gaoxian Tielu Gongsi 高线铁路公司
*gengming renban* 更名认办
Gongguju 公估局
*gongju* 公举
*gongmin shehui* 公民社会
*gongshi* 公事
*gongxin* 公信
*guandu shangxiao* 官督商销
*guanshang* 官商
*gudao* 贾道
Haihe 海河
*haihu* 海户
Haijinzhen 海津镇
*haizhangwu xiu paotai, xiaoshi yiduan*
海张五修炮台，小事一段
*hangcheng* 行秤
*huanghui* 皇会
*hunhunr* 混混儿
*jiajin* 加斤
Jiang Chenying 姜宸英
*jiaohang* 脚行
Jiaozhou 胶州
*jiaxian* 家仙
*jiazhang* 家长
*jichuan* 集船
Jiehe 界河
*jingji teke* 经济特科
Jinglisi 经历司
*jinshi* 进士
*kaocheng* 考成
Kudashi 库大使
*kunyun* 捆运
Kuo Zha 阔查
*li'an* 立案
Li Baoheng 李宝恒

Li Baoqian 李宝谦
Li Baoxian 李宝
Li Baoxiang 李宝详
Li Guangdi 李光地
Li Shanren 李善人
Li Shijian 李士鉴
Li Shiming 李士铭
Li Shiyu 李士钰
Li Shizeng 李石曾
Li Shizhen 李士
Li Shutong 李叔同
Li Xiu 李秀
Liangdian Houjie Li Shanren 粮店后
街李善人
Lianhuale 莲花落
*lijin* 厘金
Linqing 麟庆
Linqing Wanhufu 临清万户府
Lin Zexu 林则徐
Luanhe 滦河
*lufang* 炉房
Lugang Gongsuo 芦纲公所
*luhao* 卤耗
*luodao* 锣道
Meigui 梅桂（玫瑰）
Mei Wending 梅文鼎
*menmian laofei* 门面劳费
Mingzhu 明珠
*minshi* 民事
Mu Yunxiang 穆云湘
*neidachen* 内大臣
*neidian* 内店
Niguzhai 泥沽寨
Ning Fupeng 宁福彭
Ning Xingpu 宁星普
*ningxiang* 宁饷
*paiyan* 牌盐
*pi'an* 疲岸
*piaohao* 票号

*puhu* 铺户

*qianpu* 钱铺

Qingzhou Fensi 青州分司

Quanxuesuo 劝学所

Sanchakou 三岔口

*shangjie shanghuan* 商借商还

*shangshou* 赏收

*shangwuju* 商务局

*shangzhan* 商战

*shanhuo* 山货

*shenshang* 绅商

*shidiao* 时调

*shimin shehui* 市民社会

Shizheng Yihui 市政议会

*shouyan* 手眼

*shuicheng* 水程

*shuihui* 水会

Shuixizhuang 水西庄

*sijia huocheng* 死价活秤

*siyou* 私友

Songgotu 索额图

Song Zejiu 宋则久

Songzi Niangniang 送子娘娘

Sun Hongyi 孙洪伊

*taige* 抬阁

Taihangshan 太行山

*tanghao* 堂号

Tianfei 天妃

*tianjiang* 田酱（甜酱）

Tianjin Gongshang Yanjiuhui 天津工
    商研究会

Tianjin Shangwuju 天津商务局

Tianjin Shangwu Zonghui 天津商务
    总会

Tianjin Weichihui 天津维持会

Tianjin Xiancheng Dongshihui 天津
    县城董事会

Tianjin Xiancheng Yanjiuhui 天津县
    城研究会

Tianjin Xiancheng Yishihui 天津县城
    议事会

Tianjin Zizhi Yanjiusuo 天津自治研
    究所

Tianjinfu Zizhiju 天津府自治局

*timen* 体面

*tonggang dali* 通纲大例

*tongju gongcai* 同居共财

*tongnian* 同年

*tongrong* 通融

*tongxiang* 同乡

*tongyuan* 铜元

*tuyi* 土宜

*waidian* 外店

*wanfa* 玩法

Wang Guanbao 王观保

Wang Xianbin 王贤宾

Wang Yisun 王益孙

*weichuan* 卫船

*weizuizi* 卫咀子

*wenshan* 文善

*wojia* 窝价

*wushan* 武善

Wu Wen 吴雯

*wuxi bu cheng piao* 无息不成票

Xiangcihou Bianjia 乡祠后卞家

Xianxian 献县

*xianyin houke* 先引后课

Xianyouhui 宪友会

*xianzu* 现租

Xiaonanhe 小南河

Xihe 西河

Xin'an 信安

*xingzheng* 行政

*xishi* 细事

Xixiangji 西厢记

Xu Guangqi 徐光启

Xu Zhenming 徐贞明

*yanchuan hupiao* 盐船护票

*yanhutu* 盐糊涂

*yanhuayin* 盐花银

Yan Xiu 严修

*yanyunshi* 盐运使

*yanzheng* 盐政

*yangge* 秧歌

*yanglianyin* 养廉银

Yanliuqing 杨柳青

Yang Junyuan 杨俊元

Yang Shixiang 杨士骧

Yang Xiceng 杨希曾

Yangzhou 扬州

*yaopai* 腰牌

Yao Xueyuan 姚学源

*ya'zu* 押租

*yeshang* 业商

Yimuju 一亩居

*yin* 引

*yingyi* 应役

*yinzhuang* 银桩

*yiren shouchuang* 一人手创

Yongdinghe 永定河

*yuanzhuang yuanxie* 原装原卸

*yuding* 馀丁

Yu Ji 虞集

*yushangli* 裕商力

*yutie* 谕帖

*yuyin* 馀引

Yuyingtang 育婴堂

Zaize 载泽

Zaizhen 载振

Zha Li 查礼

Zha Sheng 查升

Zha Tianxing 查天行

Zha Weiren 查为仁

Zha Xiazhong 查夏重

*zhai'an* 在案

Zhang Boling 张伯苓

Zhang Hubai 张虎拜

Zhang Jinwen 张锦文

Zhang Lin 张霖

Zhang Xisi 张希思

Zhang Yingchen 张映辰

Zhang Zhenfang 张镇芳

*zhangfang* 账房

*zhangju* 账局

Zhao Zhishen 赵执信

*zhengke* 正课

*zhengti* 政体

*zhidan* 知单

Zhigu Piyansuo 直沽批验所

*zhiguafu* 职寡妇

Zhiguzhai 直沽寨

Zhili Baoshang Yinhang 直隶保商
    银行

Zhili Shangye Yanjiu Zongsuo 直隶商
    业研究总所

Zhili ziyiju 直隶咨议局

*zhishang* 职商

*zhishi* 知事

Zhou Shengchuan 周盛传

Zhou Xuexi 周学熙

*zhupi* 朱批

*zi minshi* 资民食

Ziyahe 子牙河

Ziyiju lianhehui 咨议局联合会

Zizhengyuan 资政院

Zizhi Qicheng Yanjiuhui 自治期成研
    究会

*zouxiao* 奏销

*zuanying* 钻营

*zu bu ya mai* 租不压卖

Zuo Guangdou 左光斗

*zushang* 租商

# Selected Bibliography

Adshead, S. A. M. 1970. *The Modernization of the Chinese Salt Administration, 1900–1920*. Cambridge, Mass.: Harvard University Press.
———. 1991. *Salt in Civilizations*. New York: St. Martin's Press.
Ahern, Emily M., and Hill Gates, eds. 1981. *Anthropology of Taiwanese Society*. Stanford: Stanford University Press.
Anon. 1986. *Tianjin shiji jishi wenjianlu* (A veritable record of things heard and seen in Tianjin). Reprinted Tianjin: Guji chubanshe.
Ao Chengnong. 1976. "Tianjinshi beijiao he Baodi xian fashen shiqi" (Discovery of stone tools in the northern suburbs of Tianjin city and Baodi district). *Kaogu* (Archaeology) 4.
Bakhtin, Mikhail. 1968. *Rabelais and His World*. Translated by Helene Iswolsky. Cambridge, Mass.: MIT Press.
Balazs, Etienne. 1964. *Chinese Civilization and Bureaucracy*. Translated by H. M. Wright. New Haven: Yale University Press.
Beiyang junfa shiliao bianweihui, comp. 1992. *Beiyang junfa shiliao: Yuan Shikai juan* (Historical materials on the northern warlords: Yuan Shikai). 2 vols. Tianjin: Guji chubanshe.
Bergère, Marie-Claire. 1989. *The Golden Age of the Chinese Bourgeoisie*. Translated by Janet Lloyd. Cambridge: Cambridge University Press.
Bernhardt, Kathryn. 1999. *Women and Property*. Stanford: Stanford University Press.
Bernhardt, Kathryn, and Philip C. C. Huang, eds. 1994. *Civil Law in Qing and Republican China*. Stanford: Stanford University Press.
Bernstein, Lewis. 1988. "A History of Tientsin in Early Modern Times, 1800–1910." Ph.D. dissertation, University of Kansas.
Bi Zhiyan. 1622. *Fujin shucao* (Memorials drafted by commissioner of Tianjin). Preface dated 1622.
Bodde, Derk, and Clarence Morris. 1967. *Law in Imperial China*. Cambridge, Mass.: Harvard University Press.

Boorman, Howard, and Richard C. Howard, comps. 1968. *Biographical Dictionary of Republican China*. 5 vols. New York: Columbia University Press.

Booth, William J. 1993. *Households: The Moral Architecture of the Economy*. Ithaca: Cornell University Press.

Borthwick, Sally. 1983. *Education and Social Change in China*. Stanford: Hoover Institution Press.

Bourdieu, Pierre, and Jean-Claude Passeron. 1990. *Reproduction in Education, Society, and Culture*. Translated by Richard Nice. London: Sage.

Brandt, Loren. 1987. "Review of Philip C. C. Huang's *The Peasant Economy and Social Change in North China*." *Economic Development and Cultural Change* 35(3): 674.

Brenner, Robert. 1992. *Merchant and Revolution*. Princeton: Princeton University Press.

Brook, Timothy. 1993. *Praying for Power*. Cambridge, Mass.: Council on East Asian Studies, Harvard University.

Brook, Timothy, and B. Michael Frolic, eds. 1997. *Civil Society and China*. Armonk, N.Y.: M. E. Sharpe.

Butcher, John, and Howard Dick, eds. 1993. *The Rise and Fall of Revenue Farming*. New York: St. Martin's Press.

Buxbaum, David, et al., eds. 1978. *Chinese Family Law and Social Change*. Seattle: University of Washington Press.

Calhoun, Craig, ed. 1992. *Habermas and the Public Sphere*. Cambridge, Mass.: MIT Press.

Chan, Wellington. 1977. *Merchants, Mandarins, and Modern Enterprise in Late Ch'ing China*. Cambridge, Mass.: Council on East Asian Studies, Harvard University.

Chen Chang Fu-mei and Ramon Myers. 1976–1978. "Customary Law and the Economic Growth of China During the Ch'ing Period." *Ch'ing-shih wen-ti* 3(5):1–32 and 3(10):4–48.

Chen Cheng-siang [Chen Zhengxiang]. 1984. *China: Essays on Geography*. Hong Kong: Sanlian shudian.

Chen Enrong. 1918. "Tianjin sangli shuolüe" (A brief treatise on funeral rituals in Tianjin). Mimeograph copy.

Chen Feng. 1988. *Qingdai yanzheng yu yanshui* (Salt administration and taxation during the Qing dynasty). Zhengzhou: Zhongzhou guji chubanshe.

Chen Hua. 1996. *Qingdai quyu shehui jingji yanjiu* (A study on the social and regional economy during the Qing period). Beijing: Renmin daxue chubanshe.

Chen Jingzhang, comp. 1992. *Zha Shenxing nianpu* (A chronological biography of Zha Xiazhong). Reprinted Beijing: Zhonghua shuju.

Chen Jinning. 1985. "Nanshufang" (The Southern Study). *Qingshi yanjiu tongxun* (Newsletter on Qing history) 2:26–30.

Chen Kai, comp. 1874. *Jinyi xuanjulu* (List of successful candidates of the civil service examination from Tianjin). Preface dated 1874.

———. 1877. *Jinyi xuke xuanjulu* (Supplemental list of successful candidates of the civil service examination from Tianjin). Preface dated 1877.

Chen Kangqi. 1983. *Langqian jiwen* (Things heard by a lowly secretary). 2 vols. Reprint of Guangxu ed. Beijing: Zhonghua shuju.

Chen Kewei. 1979. "Lun Xihan houqi de yiqi dadizhen yu Bohai xi'an dimou de bianqian" (Comments on a large earthquake during the Late Western Han dynasty and changes on the western coast of Bohai Gulf). *Kaogu* (Archaeology) 2:181–190.

Chen Kuilong. 1983. *Mengjiaoting zaji* (Miscellaneous notes from the Mengjiao pavilion). 1925 ed. Reprinted Beijing: Zhonghua shuju.

Chen Liansheng. 1984. "Tianjin zaonian de shuihui" (Firefighting societies in old Tianjin). *TJWSCK* 2:32–46.

Chen Qiyuan. 1989. *Yongxianzhai biji* (Miscellaneous notes from the Mediocre and Idle Studio). Reprinted Beijing: Zhonghua shuju.

Chen Ran. 1998. "Qingmo minchu Zigong yanye zichan jieji de fachan zhuangda ji qi dui shehui de yingxiang" (The growth of Zigong's salt industry-based bourgeoisie and its social effects in late Qing and Early Republic). *ZGSHJJSYJ* 2:46–56.

Chen Ran, Xie Qichou, and Qiu Mingda, eds. 1987. *Zhongguo yanyeshi luncong* (Essays on the salt industry of China). Beijing: Zhongguo shehui kexue chubanshe.

Chen Tieqing. 1985. "Tianjin Tianhougong" (The temple of the goddess of heaven in Tianjin). *TJWSCK* 4:19–56.

Chen Xiangyang. 1998. "Jiushi niandai Qingmo xinzheng yanjiu shuping" [Studies on late Qing reforms during the nineties] *JDSYJ* 1:297–315.

Chen Xulu et al., eds. 1979. *Xinhai gemeng qianhou* (Before and after the 1911 Revolution). Shanghai: Renmin chubanshe.

Chen Yi. 1750. *Chenxueshi wenji* (Writings of Undersecretary Chen).

Chen Yong. 1995. "Ming-Qing Tianjin chengshi jiegou de chubu kaocha" (Preliminary study of the urban structure of Tianjin during the Ming and Qing). *Chengshi shi yanjiu* (Urban history research) 10:25–63.

Chen Yuanlong. 1736. *Ai'ritang shiji* (Collected poems of Sun-Loving Hall). Last preface dated 1736.

Chen Zhongping. 1998. "Business and Politics: Chinese Chambers of Commerce in the Lower Yangtze Region, 1902–1912." Ph.D. dissertation, University of Hawai'i.

Chen Zongyi, comp. 1898. *Huangchao jingshiwen sanbian* (Collected writings on statecraft of our august dynasty, third compilation).

Chiang Tao-chang. 1983. "The Salt Trade in Ch'ing China." *Modern Asian Studies* 17(2):197–219.

Chow Kai-wing. 1994. *The Rise of Confucian Ritualism in Late Imperial China*. Stanford: Stanford University Press.

Chu Zhifa. 1990. "Chongshan gaoqiao" (Chongshan stilt troupe). *Tianjin dongjiao wenshi ziliao* (Historical materials on Tianjin's eastern suburb) 2: 93–97.

Chung, Stephanie P. Y. 1998. *Chinese Business Groups in Hong Kong and Political Change in South China, 1900–1925*. New York: St. Martin's Press.

Clegg, S. R., and S. G. Redding, eds. 1990. *Capitalism in Contrasting Cultures*. Berlin: W. de Gruyter.

Cohen, Jean L., and Andrew Arato. 1992. *Civil Society and Political Theory*. Cambridge, Mass.: MIT Press.

Cohen, Jerome, Edward Randle, and Chen Chang Fumei, eds. 1980. *Essays on China's Legal Tradition*. Princeton: Princeton University Press.

Cohen, Myron. 1976. *House Divided, House United*. New York: Columbia University Press.

Cohen, Paul A. 1984. *Discovering History in China*. New York: Columbia University Press.

Cohen, Paul A., and John E. Schrecker, eds. 1976. *Reform in Nineteenth-Century China*. Cambridge, Mass.: East Asian Research Center, Harvard University.

Council of the China Branch of the Royal Asiatic Society, comp. 1878. "Inland Communications in China." *Journal of the North China Branch, Royal Asiatic Society* 28:1–213.

*Da Ming lü.* 1989. Reprinted Nanjing: Guangning guji chubanshe.

*Da Qing huidian* (Compendium of Qing Codes). 1899 ed.

*Da Qing xinbian fadian* (New codes promulgated by the Qing dynasty). 1987. Reprinted Taipei: Wenhai chubanshe.

Dai Yu'an. 1986. *Gushui jiuwen* (Old stories heard around Tianjin). Tianjin: Guji chubanshe.

Davis, Clarence C. 1982. "Financing Imperialism: British and American Bankers as Vectors of Imperial Expansion in China, 1908–1920." *Business History Review* 56(2):236–264.

Ding Gang. 1996. *Jinshi Zhongguo jingji shenghuo yu zongzu jiaoyu* (Economic life and lineage education in late imperial China). Shanghai: Jiaoyu chubanshe.

Ding Yuguang. 1993. *Jindai Zhongguo difang zizhi yanjiu* (A study of local self-government in modern China). Canton: Guangzhou chubanshe.

Ding Yunshu and Chen Shixun, comps. 1910. *Zhanggong shangli junwu jilüe* (Record of Zhang Jinwen's support of military affairs). N.p. Cord-bound ed.

Dittmer, Lowell, and Samuel S. Kim, eds. 1993. *China's Quest for National Identity*. Ithaca: Cornell University Press.

Dong Fangkui. 1991. *Liang Qichao yu lixian zhengzhi* (Liang Qichao and the politics of constitutionalism). Wuchang: Huazhong shifan daxue chubanshe.

Dong Junrong. 1986. "Zichan jieji shangceng zhong yaoqiu jinbu de aiguozhe Sun Hongyi" (Sun Hongyi, a progressive patriot among upper-class capitalists). *TJSYJ* 1:40–43.

Duan Yuming. 1992. *Zhongguo shijing wenhua yu chuantong quyi* (Urban popular culture and traditional operatic arts in China). Changchun: Jilin jiaoyu chubanshe.

Duara, Prasenjit. 1988. *Culture, Power, and the State: Rural North China, 1900–1942*. Stanford: Stanford University Press.

Ebrey, Patricia, and James L. Watson, eds. 1986. *Kinship Organization in Late Imperial China, 1000–1940*. Berkeley: University of California Press.

Ehrenberg, John. 1999. *Civil Society*. New York: New York University Press.

Eisenstadt, Shmuel N., and Wolfgang Schluchter. 1998. "Introduction: Paths to Early Modernities—A Comparative View." *Daedalus* 127(3):1–18.

Esherick, Joseph. 1976. *Reform and Revolution in China*. Berkeley: University of California Press.

Esherick, Joseph, and Mary Rankin, eds. 1990. *Chinese Local Elites and Patterns of Dominance*. Berkeley: University of California Press.

Fan Bochuan. 1985. *Zhongguo lunchuanye hangyunye de xingqi* (The rise of China's shipping and transport industries). Chengdu: Renmin chubanshe.

Fan I-chun. 1992. "Long Distance Trade and Market Integration in the Ming-Ch'ing Period, 1400–1850." Ph.D. dissertation, Stanford University.

Fan Tiren. 1981. "Sun Hongyi yu Minzhi she" (Sun Hongyi and the People's Rule Society). *TJWSZL* 16:19–30.

Fang Bao. 1991. *Fang wangqi quanji* (Complete works of Fang Bao). Reprinted Beijing: Zhongguo shudian.

Fang Xing. 1981. "Qingdai Beijing diqu caimeiye zhong de ziben zhuyi mengya" (The coal mining industry in the Beijing area and incipient capitalism during the Qing period). *JJYJSJK* 2:186–212.

Fazheng xueshe, comp. 1962. *Minshu xiguan daquan* (Compendium of civil and customary law). 2 vols. Shanghai: Guangyi shuju, 1923. Reprinted Taipei: Wenxing chubanshe.

Feng Erkang. 1985. *Yongzheng zhuan* (A biography of the Yongzheng Emperor). Beijing: Renmin chubanshe.

Feng Jicai, ed. 1995. *Jiucheng yiyun* (Lingering charms of the old city). Tianjin: Yangliuqing huadian.

Feng Wenqian. N.d. Unpublished memoir. Private collection.

Feng Xuezhang. 1919. "Tianjin Feng Jieqing shi biannian jilu" (Chronological record of Feng Jieqing of Tianjin). Unpublished memoir. Preface dated 1919.

Feng Zikai and Song Yunbin. 1963. "Hongyi fashi" (Reverend Hongyi). *WSZLXJ* 34:100–115.

Ferguson, Adam. 1966. *An Essay on the History of Civil Society*. Edinburgh: Edinburgh University Press.

Feuer, Lewis S., ed. 1959. *Basic Writings on Politics and Philosophy: Karl Marx and Friedrich Engels*. Garden City: Anchor Books.

Feuerwerker, Albert, Rhoads Murphey, and Mary C. Wright, eds. 1967. *Approaches to Modern Chinese History*. Berkeley: University of California Press.

Fewsmith, Joseph. 1983. "From Guild to Interest Group: The Transformation of the Public and Private in Late Qing China." *Comparative Studies in History and Society* 25(4):617–640.

Field, Margaret. 1957. "The Chinese Boycott of 1905." *Papers on China, East Asian Research Center, Harvard University* 11:63–98.

Fogel, Joshua A., and Peter G. Zarrow, eds. 1997. *Imagining the People*. Armonk, N.Y.: M. E. Sharpe.

Fox-Genovese, Elizabeth, and Eugene Genovese. 1983. *Fruits of Merchant Capital*. New York: Oxford University Press.

Fu Zhufu. 1980. *Zhongguo jingjishi luncong* (Studies in Chinese economic history). 2 vols. Beijing: Sanlian shudian.

Fudan daxue lishixi et al., eds. 1986. *Jindai Zhongguo zichan jieji yanjiu xubian* (Studies on the bourgeosie in modern China: A sequel). Shanghai: Fudan daxue chubanshe.

Fuma Susumu. 1986. "Local Society and Actual Management of the Hall for Infant Relief in Qing Dynasty Songjiang." *Tōyōshi kenkyū* (Studies in Asian history) 44(3):55–90.

Gan Houci, comp. 1907. *Beiyang gongdu leizuan* (Documents by category of the commissioner of northern ports).

———. 1910. *Beiyang gongdu leizuan xubian* (Documents by category of the commissioner of northern ports, second compilation).

Gao Ningwen. 1982. *Zhiyu suibi* (Miscellaneous notes after the compilation of the local gazetteer). 1936 ed. Reprinted Tianjin: Guji shudian.

Gao Xiang et al. 1964. *Hejian fuzhi* (Gazetteer of Hejian prefecture). 1540 ed. Reprinted Shanghai: Guji chubanshe.

Gao Zhonglin et al. 1990. *Tianjin jindai jianzhu* (Architecture in modern Tianjin). Tianjin: Tianjin kexue jishu chubanshe.

Gellner, Ernest. 1994. *Conditions of Liberty.* London: Penguin.

Geng Jie et al. 1985. "Tianjin de banyun gongren" (Transport workers of Tianjin). *Tianjin gongyunshi ziliao* (Materials on the history of the labor movement in Tianjin) 6:1–35.

Ginzburg, Carlos. 1982. *The Cheese and the Worms.* New York: Penguin.

Glade, William P., ed. 1986. *State Shrinking: A Comparative Inquiry into Privatization.* Austin: University of Texas Press.

Goldsmith, Raymond W. 1987. *Premodern Financial Systems.* Cambridge: Cambridge University Press.

Goodman, Bryna. 1995. *Native Place, City, and Nation.* Berkeley: University of California Press.

Goodrich, L. Carrington, and Chaoying Fang, eds. 1976. *Dictionary of Ming Biography.* 2 vols. New York: Columbia University Press.

Gu Yanwu. 1990. *Tianxia junguo libingshu* (Guide to the empire). Reprinted Hong Kong: n.p.

*Guanzi* (Collected writings of Guan Zhong). 1920 ed.

Gugong bowuyuan Ming-Qing dang'anbu, comp. 1975. *Guanyu Jiangning zhizao Caojia dang'an shiliao* (Archival materials related to the Cao family of the imperial silk works in Jiangning). Beijing: Zhonghua shuju.

———. 1976. *Li Xu zouzhe* (Memorials of Li Xu). Beijing: Zhonghua shuju.

———. 1979. *Qingmo zhoubi lixian dang'an shiliao* (Historical materials on the preparation for constitutional monarchy in late Qing). 2 vols. Beijing: Zhonghua shuju.

Gugong wenxiangguan, comp. 1930–1943. *Wenxian congbian* (Archival materials). Beijing: Gugong wenxiangguan.

Guo Honglin. 1989. "Qingdai Qianlong chuqi Tianjin wenhua zhongxin—Shuixizhuang" (Shuixizhuang: Cultural center of Tianjin during the early Qianlong period). *Tianjin wenbo* (Studies on artifacts and museology in Tianjin) 3:40–42.

Guo Songyi. 1982. "Qingdai guonei de haiyun maoyi" (Domestic coastal trade of the Qing dynasty). *QSLC* 4:92–110.

Gutzlaff, Charles. 1968. *Journal of Three Voyages Along the Coast of China.* London: Westley & Davis, 1834. Reprinted Wilmington: Scholarly Resources.

Habermas, Jürgen. 1989. *The Structural Transformation of the Public Sphere.* Cambridge, Mass.: MIT Press.

Han Jiagu. 1979. "Tianjin diqu chenglu guocheng shitan" (Inquiry into the land formation process around the area of Tianjin). In *Zhongguo kaogu xuehui diyiqi nianhui lunwenji* (Proceedings of the first annual meeting of the Chinese Archaeological Society). Beijing: Kaogu chubanshe.

Hanagan, Michael, and Charles Tilly, eds. 1999. *Extending Citizenship, Reconfiguring States.* New York: Rowman & Littlefield.

Hang Shijun. 1888. *Daogutang wenji* (Collected writings from the Daogu Studio). N.p. Cord-bound ed.

Hao Fusen. n.d. "Jinmen wenjianlu" (Things seen and heard around Tianjin). N.p. Cord-bound ed.

Hao Jinrong. n.d. "Jinmen jishi shi" (Poems commemorating events in Tianjin). Undated manuscript held at the Tianjin Municipal Library.

He Baogang. 1997. *The Democratic Implications of Civil Society in China.* London: Macmillan.

He Changning, comp. 1903. *Huangchao jingshi wenbian* (Anthology of essays on statecraft). Reprint.

He Hanwei. n.d. *Guangxu chunian huabei de dahanzai* (The North China famine of 1876–1879). Hong Kong: Chinese University of Hong Kong Press.

He Yaofu. 1994. *Wanqing shishen yu jindai shehui bianqian* (The gentry of late Qing and modern social change). Guangzhou: Guangdong renmin chubanshe.

He Zuo, comp. 1956. "Yijiu lingwunian fanmei aigou yundong" (The anti-American patriotic movement of 1905). *Jindaishi ziliao* (Sources in modern Chinese history) 1.

Hegel, Georg Wilhelm Friedrich. 1967. *Hegel's Philosophy of Right.* Translated by T. M. Knox. Oxford: Oxford University Press.

Heidenheimer, Arnold. 1970. *Political Corruption.* New York: Holt, Rinehart & Winston.

Hershatter, Gail. 1986. *The Workers of Tianjin: 1900–1949.* Stanford: Stanford University Press.

Hitch, Margaret A. 1935. "The Port of Tientsin and Its Problems." *Geographical Review* 25(3):367–381.

Ho Ping-ti. 1954. "The Salt Merchants of Yang-chou: A Study of Commercial Capitalism in Eighteenth Century China." *Harvard Journal of Asiatic Studies* 17: 130–168.

Holub, Robert C. 1991. *Jürgen Habermas.* London: Routledge.

Hou Jing. n.d. *Xianyu yigao* (Scorched essays that survived). Tongzhi ed.

Hou Renzhi. 1945. *Tianjin zhi qiyuan* (The origin of Tianjin). Tianjin: Hautes Etudes Industrieles et Commerciales.

Hou Yijie. 1985. "Qingmo lixian yundongshi yanjiu shuping" (Review of the history of the constitutional movement in late Qing). *JDSYJ* 3:159–191.

———. 1993. *Ershi shijichu Zhongguo zhengzhi gaige fengchao* (Political reforms in early-twentieth-century China). Beijing: Renmin chubanshe.

Hu Guangming. 1986. "Lun zaoqi Tianjin shanghui de xingzhi yu zuoyong" (Nature and work of the Tianjin Chamber of Commerce in its early years). *JDSYJ* 4:182–223.

———. 1994. "Lun Qingmo shanghui dui Changlu yanwu fengchao de pingshi" (On the resolution of the Changlu crisis and the Tianjin Chamber of Commerce). *LSDA* 2:99–105.

Hu Shangyi. n.d. *Neishenglu* (A record of self-introspection). N.p.

Hua Changqing et al. 1909. *Huashi zongpu* (Genealogy of the Huas).

Hua Guangnai, ed. 1920. *Tianjin wenchao* (Collected writings from Tianjin).

Hua Naiwen. 1986. "Chenghuanghui lun" (On the city god's parade). *TJSYJ* 1: 70–73.

Huang, Philip C. C. 1991. "The Paradigmatic Crisis in Chinese Studies: Paradoxes in Social and Economic History." *MC* 17(3):299–341.

———. 1993. " 'Public Sphere'/'Civil Society' in China?: The Third Realm Between State and Society." *MC* 19(2):216–240.

———. 1996. *Civil Justice in China: Representation and Practice in the Qing*. Stanford: Stanford University Press.

Huang, Ray. 1974. *Taxation and Governmental Finance in Sixteenth Century Ming China*. Cambridge: Cambridge University Press.

———. 1989. "Shenmo shi ziben zhuyi?" (What is capitalism?). *Lishi* (Historical monthly) 13:108–109.

Huang Zongxi. 1955. *Mingyi daifanglu* (A plan for the prince). Beijing: Guji chubanshe.

*Huanhai zhinan* (Guides through the bureaucratic sea). 1886.

*Hubu zeli* (Regulations and precedents of the Board of Revenue). 1968. 1874 ed. Reprinted Taipei: Chengwen chubanshe.

Hummel, Arthur, ed. 1970. *Eminent Chinese of the Ch'ing Period*. 2 vols. Washington, D.C.: Government Printing Office.

Huntington, Samuel P. 1968. *Political Order in Changing Societies*. New Haven: Yale University Press.

Huters, Theodore, et al., eds. 1997. *Culture and State in Chinese History*. Stanford: Stanford University Press.

*I Ching*. 1963. Translated by James Legge. 1899 ed. Reprinted New York: Dover.

Imperial Maritime Customs Service. 1868. *Tientsin Trade Report for the Year 1867*. Shanghai: Imperial Maritime Customs Service.

———. 1909. *Trade Reports for the Year 1908: Tianjin*. Shanghai: Imperial Maritime Customs Service.

———. 1911. *Trade Reports for the Year 1911: Tianjin*. Shanghai: Imperial Maritime Customs Service.

———. 1912. *Trade Reports for the Year 1911: Tianjin*. Shanghai: Imperial Maritime Customs Service.

Ijūin Hikokichi. 1907. "Zai Tenshin teikoku sōryōjikan kankatsu kuikinai jijō" (Conditions within the sphere of jurisdiction of the Japanese Consul General in Tianjin). In *Shinkoku jijō* (Facts of Qing). 10 vols. Tokyo: Gaimushō Tsūshōkyoku.

James, Mervyn. 1974. *Family, Lineage, and Society*. Oxford: Clarendon Press.

Jernigan, Thomas R. 1905. *China in Law and in Commerce*. London: Macmillan.

Ji Hua. 1981. "Tianjin shanghui tanwang" (Reminiscences of the Tianjin Chamber of Commerce). *TJWSZL* 16:41–60.

———. 1984. "Changlu yanwu de liangda anjian" (Two major scandals of the Changlu Salt Division). *TJWSZL* 26:127–138.

Ji Yun. 1812. *Ji Wendagong yiji* (Posthumously collected works of Ji Yun).

Jia Shiyi. 1917. *Minguo caizhengshi* (Financial history of the republic). 2 vols. Shanghai: Shangwu yinshuguan.

Jiang Chenying. 1889. *Jiang xiansheng quanji* (Collected writings of Jiang Chenying).

Jiang Liangqi, comp. 1980. *Donghualu* (The Donghua records). Reprinted Beijing: Zhonghua shuju.

Jiang Shoupeng. 1996. *Ming-Qing beifang shichang yanjiu* (The North China market in the Ming and the Qing). Jilin: Dongbei shida chubanshe.

Jiang Yuanhuan. 1985. "Wusi yundong qian de Tianjin xuesheng yundong" (Student movements in Tianjin before the May Fourth Movement). *TJSYJ* 1: 41–50.

"Jiaqing shiqinian Changlu yanfa wubi'an" (The Changlu salt weight scandal of 1812). 1989. *LSDA* 4:20–35.

Jin Anqing. 1984. *Shuichuang chunyi* (Spring ramblings before the window of a boat). 1877 ed. Revised and reprinted Beijing: Zhonghua shuju.

Jin Dayang. 1980. "Tianjin Li Shanren" (Philanthropist Lis of Tianjin). *TJWSZL* 7:70–101.

Jin Dayang and Liu Yudong. 1982. "Tianjin Hai Zhangwu fajia shimo" (Rise and fall of Tianjin's Zhang family). *TJWSZL* 20:75–89.

Jincheng yinhang zongjinglichu Tianjin diaocha fenbu, comp. 1927. *Tianjin liangshiye gaikuang* (Overview of Tianjin's grain trade). Tianjin: Jincheng yinhang.

Johnson, David, Andrew J. Nathan, and Evelyn S. Rawski, eds. 1985. *Popular Culture in Late Imperial China*. Berkeley: University of California Press.

Kahn, Harold L. 1971. *Monarchy in the Emperor's Eyes*. Cambridge, Mass.: Harvard University Press.

———. 1985. "A Matter of Taste: The Monumental and Exotic in the Qianlong Reign." In Chou Ju-shi and Claudia Brown, eds., *The Elegant Brush*. Phoenix: Phoenix Art Museum.

"Kangxi nianjian guanyu yanwu de yushi zouzhang" (Memorials of censors related to salt matters during the reign of the Kangxi Emperor). 1985. *LSDA* 1: 15–21.

Katō Shigeshi. 1937. "Shindai no enpo ni tsuite" (On the Qing salt codes). *Shichō* (Historical trends) 7(1):1–13.

Ke Shaowen. n.d. "Hubu langzhong Ligong muzhiming" (Epitaph of Li, Bureau Chief at the Board of Revenue). Undated manuscript.

Keane, John. 1988. *Civil Society and the State*. London: Verso.

———. 1998. *Civil Society*. Stanford: Stanford University Press.

Kessler, Lawrence D. 1976. *Kang-hsi and the Consolidation of Ch'ing Rule, 1661–1684*. Chicago: University of Chicago Press.

Kevelson, Roberta, ed. 1994. *Codes and Customs*. New York: Peter Lang.

*Kikuchi Takaharu sensei tsuitō ronshū: Chūgoku kingendai ronshū* (Essays in memory of Professor Kikuchi Takaharu on modern and contemporary China). 1985. Tokyo: Kyuko shoin.

King, Frank, et al. 1988. *The Hongkong Bank in the Period of Imperialism and War, 1895–1918*. Cambridge: Cambridge University Press.

King, Harry E. 1911. *The Educational System of China as Recently Reconstructed*. Washington, D.C.: Government Printing Office.

Kishi Toshihiko. 1996. "Beiyang xinzheng tizhixia difang zizhi zhidu de xing-cheng" (The formation of local self-government under the political reforms of Yuan Shikai). Translated by Zhou Junqi. *Chengshishi yanjiu* (Urban history research) 11–12:124–153.

Koguchi Hikota. 1988. "Some Observations About the Settlement of Civil Disputes in the Qing Local Government." *Chūgoku-shakai to bunka* (Society and culture in China) 3:35–49.

Kōsaka Masanori. 1971. "Shindai no genan bōeki ni kansuru ichi kōsatsu" (A study of Qing coastal trade). *Bunka* (Culture) 35(1–2):28–55.

Kotenev, A. N. 1925. *Shanghai: Its Mixed Court and Council.* Shanghai: North China Daily News & Herald.

Kroker, Edward. 1959. "The Concept of Property in Chinese Customary Law." *Transactions of the Asiatic Society of Japan,* 3rd series, 7:123–146.

Kronman, Anthony, et al. 1979. *The Economics of Contract Law.* Boston: Little, Brown.

Kuhn, Philip A. 1970. *Rebellion and Its Enemies in Late Imperial China.* Cambridge, Mass.: Harvard University Press.

———. 1994. "Civil Society and Constitutional Development." In Léon Vandermeersch, ed., *La société civile face à l'État.* Paris: École française d'Extrême-Orient.

———. 1995. "Ideas Behind China's Modern State." *Harvard Journal of Asiatic Studies* 55(2):295–337.

Kurahashi Masanao. 1976. "Shinmatsu shōbu no jigyō sankou ni tsuite" (The business promotion policy of the Ministry of Commerce in the late Qing era). *Rekishigaku kenkyū* (Historical studies) 432:1–13.

———. 1984. "Qing mo shanghui he Zhongguo zichan jieji" (Chambers of commerce and the Chinese bourgeoisie in late Qing). *Zhongguo jindai jingjishi yanjiu ziliao* (Materials on the study of the modern Chinese economy) 2: 45–66.

Kwan Man Bun. 1997. "Customs and the Law: The Contracts of Changlu Salt Merchants." Paper presented at the Workshop on Contract and China's Economic Culture, Columbia University.

———. 1998. "The Foreign Import Crisis of 1907–1910 and the Tianjin Chamber of Commerce." Paper presented to the International Symposium on Chambers of Commerce and Modern China, Tianjin.

———. 1999. Jindai Tianjin yanshang yu shehui (Salt Merchants and Society in modern Tianjin). Tianjin: Renmin chubanshe.

———. 2000. "Order in Chaos: Tianjin's *Hunhunr* and Urban Identity in Modern China." *Journal of Urban History* 27. 1:73–89.

Lai Xinxia, ed. 1986. *Tianjin jindaishi* (A modern history of Tianjin). Tianjin: Nankai daxue chubanshe.

Laoxiang. 1984. "Jiefang qian Tianjin 'baishi' hangye jianwen" (Things seen and heard about the funeral business of Tianjin before 1949). *TJGSSLCK* 2: 74–94.

Levi, Margaret. 1988. *Of Rule and Revenue.* Berkeley: University of California Press.

Li Banghua. 1842. *Li Zongshugong ji* (Collected works of Li Banghua).

Li Boyuan. 1983. *Nanting biji* (Notes from the South Pavilion). 1919 ed. Reprinted Shanghai: Guji chubanshe.

Li Chen Shunyan. 1972. "Wanqing de chongshang chuyi yundong" (Mercantilism in late Qing). *Jindaishi yanjiusuo jikan* (Bulletin of the Institute of Modern History, Academia Sinica) 3:207–221.

Li Duan. 1983. "Zhuiyi xianfu Li Shutong shiji pianduan" (Fragmentary memory of my father Li Shutong's life). In Minmeng Tianjinshi weniyuanhui wenshi ziliao yanjiu xiaozu, ed., *Wenshi cankao ziliao huibian* (Collected reference materials on history and literature) 6:22–29.

Li E. 1884. *Fanxie shanfang quanji* (Complete works from the Fanxie studio).

Li Fu. 1983. "Jinbang badajia de bianqian" (History of the Big Eight merchants from Tianjin). *Urumuqi wenshi ziliao* 6:106–113.

Li Guangdi. n.d. *Rongcun yulu xuji* (Sequel to the collected sayings of Li Guangdi). Fushi cangyuan ed.

Li Guohao et al., eds. 1986. *Zhongguo kejishi tansuo* (Explorations in the history of science and technology in China). Shanghai: Shanghai guji chubanshe.

Li Huabin et al. 1986. *Tianjin gangshi* (History of the port of Tianjin). Beijing: Renmin Jiaotong chubanshe.

Li Keyi. 1989. "Qingdai yanshang yu biyin" (Salt merchants and imperial deposits and loans under the Qing). *ZGSHJJSYJ* 2:19–24.

Li Pengtu et al. 1964. "Changlu yanwu wushinian huigu" (Memories of fifty years in the Changlu salt business). *WSZLXJ* 44:124–155.

Li Qingchen (Zuichazi). 1990. *Zuicha zhiguai* (Record of strange events by a man intoxicated with tea). 1892 ed. Reprinted Tianjin: Tianjinshi Guji shudian.

Li Ranxi. 1964. "Jiu Tianjin de hunhunr" (The *hunhunr* of old Tianjin). *WSZLXJ* 47:187–209.

———. 1986. *Jinmen yanji* (Colorful stories of Tianjin). Wenhua ed. Reprinted Tianjin: Baihua wenyi chubanshe.

Li Tou. 1960. *Yangzhou huafanglu* (Record of the gaily decorated boats of Yangzhou). 1795 ed. Reprinted Beijing: Zhonghua shuju.

Li Wenzhi. 1983. "Lun Ming Qing shidai de zongzuzhi" (On the lineage system of the Ming and Qing dynasties). *JJYJSJK* 4:278–338.

Li Xiangjun. 1995. *Zhongguo fangzheng yanjiu* (Study on the administration of disaster relief under the Qing dynasty). Beijing: Zhongguo nongye chubanshe.

Li Yan. 1925. "Mei Wending nianpu" (Chronological biography of Mei Wending). *Tsinghua Journal* 2(2):609–634.

Li Zehou. 1996. *Zhongguo xiandai shishangshi lun* (Intellectual history of modern China). Taipei: Sanmin shuju.

Li Zhimin. 1988. *Zhongguo gudai minfa* (Civil law in ancient China). Beijing: Falü chubanshe.

Liang Jiamian. 1981. *Xu Guangqi nianpu* (Chronological biography of Xu Guangqi). Shanghai: Guji chubanshe.

Liang Qizhi [Angela K. Leung]. 1986. "Mingmo Qingchu minjian cishan huodong di xingqi—yi Jiang Zhe diqu weili" (The rise of unofficial philanthropy in late Ming and early Qing—examples from Jiangsu and Zhejiang). *Shih-huo*, n.s., 15(7–8):304–331.

———. 1997. *Cishan yu jiuji* (Charity and relief). Taipei: Lianjing chubanshe.

Liang Xijie and Meng Chaoxin. 1991. *Ming Qing zhengzhi zidu lunxu* (Treatise on the political system of Ming and Qing dynasties). Changchun: Jilin daxue chubanshe.

Liang Zhiping. 1996. *Qingdai xiguanfa* (Qing customary law). Beijing: Zhongguo zhengfa daxue chubanshe.

Lieberthal, Kenneth. 1980. *Revolution and Tradition in Tianjin*. Stanford: Stanford University Press.

Lin Chunye. 1983. "Qingmo Changlu leishang yangzhai fengchao" (The foreign loan crisis of Changlu bankrupt merchants in late Qing). *TJSHKX* 4: 82–86.

Lin Xi. 1997. *Tianjinren* [Tianjin-nite]. Hangzhou: Zhejiang renmin chubanshe.

Lin Yongkang. 1983. "Qingchu de Changlu yunshi yanzheng" (On the Changlu commissioner and salt during the early Qing). *Hebei xuekan* (Academic journal of Hebei) 3:84–88.

———. 1984. "Qianlongdi yu guanli dui yanshang e'wai panbo pouxi" (Analysis of extralegal extortions from salt merchants by the Qianlong Emperor and officials). *Shehui kexue jikan* (Anthology of articles on social sciences) 3:90–95.

———. 1986. "Qingdai Changlu yanshang yu neiwufu" (The salt merchants of Changlu and the Imperial Household Department during the Qing period). *GGBWYYK* 2:33–40.

Lin Zhenhan, comp. 1988. *Yanzhen cidian* (Dictionary of salt administration terms). Reprinted Zhengzhou: Zhongzhou guji chubanshe.

Liu Chang Bin. 1983. "Chinese Commercial Law in the Late Ch'ing (1842–1911): Jurisprudence and the Dispute Resolution Process in Taiwan." Ph.D. dissertation, University of Washington.

Liu Jingshan. 1987. *Liu Jingshan xiansheng fangwenlu* (Transcript of interviews with Liu Jingshan). Taipei: Academia Sinica.

Liu Kwang-ching, ed. 1990. *Orthodoxy in Late Imperial China*. Berkeley: University of California Press.

Liu Mengyang. 1922. *Zhi Ci zhengyao lucun* (Collected papers of my administration of Cizhou).

Liu Miao. 1982. "Qingdai Huizhou yanshang he Yangzhou chengshi jingji de fazhan" (Huizhou salt merchants and the development of Yangzhou's urban economy during the Qing period). Unpublished paper.

Liu Minshan. 1985. "Tianjin jindai zaoqi minzu gongye" (Early national bourgeois industrial enterprises in modern Tianjin). *TJSHKX* 3:36–42.

Liu Qingyang. 1955. "Tianjin guominjuan he Tongmenghui huodong de huiyi" (Memories of the citizens' donations and activities of the Tongmenghui in Tianjin). *Jindaishi ziliao* (Materials on modern history) 2:13–20.

Liu Qiugen. 1995. "Lun Qingdai qianqi gaolidai ziben de huodong xingshi" (Activities of usurious capital in early Qing) *ZGJJSYJ* 1:113–124.

Liu Shangheng. 1990. "Zha Weiren shiji biannian" (Chronology of Zha Weiren). *TJSZ* 1:48–54.

———. 1992. "Shuixizhuang xingfei kao" (Rise and fall of Shuixizhuang). *TJSZ* 1:28–32.

Liu Tao-tao and David Faure, eds. 1996. *Unity and Diversity: Local Culture and Identities in China*. Hong Kong: University of Hong Kong Press.

Liu Xiusheng. 1993. *Qing dai shangpin jingji yu shangye ziben* (Commodity economy and commercial capital in Qing China). Beijing: Zhongguo shangye chubanshe.

Liu Yanchen. 1943. *Jinmen zatan* (Ramblings about Tianjin). Tianjin: Sanyou chubanshe.

Liu Yanchen and Wang Guinian. 1984. "Tianjin jindai jiaoyu shiye fazhan gailüe" (A brief study of educational enterprises in modern Tianjin). *TJWSZL* 27:95–102.

Lo Shuwei et al. 1993. *Jindai Tianjin chengshi shi* (Modern Tianjin urban history). Beijing: Zhongguo shehui kexueyuan chubanshe.

Locke, John. 1965. *Two Treatises of Government*. New York: Mentor.

Long Denggao. 1998. "Cong kefan dao qiaoju" (From sojourner to settler). *ZGJJSYJ* 2:63–73.

Loux, Andrea C. 1992. "The Persistence of the Ancient Regime: Custom, Utility, and the Common Law in the Nineteenth Century." *Cornell Law Review* 79: 183–218.

Lu Naixiang. 1936. "Sungong hongyi xingzhuang" (Biography of Sun Hongyi). *Hebei yuekan* 10:1–5.

Lu Yitian. 1984. *Lenglu zashi* (Miscellaneous notes from the Cold Studio). 1856 ed. Reprinted Beijing: Zhonghua shuju.

Lu Yong. 1982. *Shuyuan zaji* (Miscellaneous records of the Bean Garden). 1810 ed. Reprinted Beijing: Zhonghua shuju.

Lufrano, Richard. 1997. *Honorable Merchants*. Honolulu: University of Hawai'i Press.

Ma Min. 1985. "Qingmo diyici Nanyang quanyehui shuping" (Appraisal of the first southern national fair to promote trade and industries in late Qing). *ZGSHJJSYJ* 4:73–78.

———. 1995. *Guanshang zhijian* (Between officials and merchants). Tianjin: Renmin chubanshe.

MacCormack, Geoffrey. 1996. *The Spirit of Traditional Chinese Law*. Athens: University of Georgia Press.

Mackinnon, Stephan. 1980. *Power and Politics in Late Imperial China*. Berkeley: University of California Press.

Mai Shudu. 1930. "Hebeisheng xiaomai zhi fanyun" (Wheat trade in Hebei province.) *Shehui kexue zazhi* (Quarterly review of social sciences) 1(1): 73–107.

Mandel, Ernest. 1968. *Marxist Economic Theory*. Translated by Brian Pearce. 2 vols. New York: Monthly Review Press.

Mann, Susan. 1987a. *Local Merchants and the Chinese Bureaucracy, 1750–1950*. Stanford: Stanford University Press.

———. 1987b. "Widows in the Kinship, Class, and Community Structures of Qing Dynasty China." *JAS* 46(1):37–56.

———. 1997. *Precious Records*. Stanford: Stanford University Press.

Mathias, Peter, and John A. Davis, eds. 1996. *Enterprise and Labour*. Oxford: Blackwell.

Matsura Akira. 1988a. "Mindai kōki no genkai kōun" (Coastal transport during late Ming). *Shakai keizai shigaku* 54(3):86–102.

———. 1988b. "Shindai Fukken no kaisengyo ni tsuite" (The Fujian coastal junk trade of the Qing period). *Tōyōshi kenkyū* 47(3):46–75.

Mei Chengdong, comp. 1842. *Jinmen shichao* (Anthology of poems from Tianjin).

Meng Chaohua et al. 1986. *Zhongguo minzheng shigao* (Draft history of civil administration in China). Harbin: Helongjian renmin chubanshe.

Meng Yuanlao. 1961. *Dongjing menghualu* (Reminiscences of the Eastern Capital). Reprinted Hong Kong: Shangwu yinshuguan.

Metzger, Thomas. 1973. *The Internal Organization of Ch'ing Bureaucracy*. Cambridge, Mass.: Harvard University Press.

Michael, Franz, and Chang Chungli. 1966. *The Taiping Rebellion: History and Documents*. 3 vols. Seattle: University of Washington Press.

Min Erchang, comp. 1987. *Beizhuanji bu* (Supplement to anthology of tombstone biographies). Reprinted Shanghai: Guji chubanshe.

Min Tu-ki. 1989. *National Polity and Local Power: The Transformation of Late Imperial China*. Edited by Philip A. Kuhn and Timothy Brook. Cambridge, Mass.: Council on East Asian Studies, Harvard University.

*Minglü jijie fuli* (Compendium of Ming codes with explanations and precedents). 1969. 1610 ed. Reprinted Taipei: Chengwen chubanshe.

Miyata Michiaki. 1986. "The Marketing Structure of the Chinese Coast in the Latter Half of the 19th Century." *Rekishi kenkyū* (Studies in history) 550:1–14.

Momose Hiromu. 1980. *Min Shin shakai keizaishi kenkyū* (Studies on the social and economic history of Ming and Qing). Tokyo: Kenbun.

Montesquieu, Charles Louis de Secondat. 1990. *The Spirit of the Laws*. Translated by Thomas Nugent. Chicago: Encyclopaedia Britannica.

Morris, R. J. 1998. "Civil Society and the Nature of Urbanism: Britain, 1750–1850." *Urban History* 25(3):289–301.

Mu Zhifang. 1982. "Tianjin Mujia he Zhengxingde chayedian" (The Mu family of Tianjin and Zhengxingde tea company). *TJWSZL* 20:68–74.

Mukerji, Chandra, and Michael Schudson, eds. 1991. *Rethinking Popular Culture*. Berkeley: University of California Press.

Multhauf, Robert P. 1978. *Neptune's Gift*. Baltimore: Johns Hopkins University Press.

Nakajima Satoshi sensei koki kinen jigyōkai, ed. 1980. *Nakajima Satoshi sensei koki kinen ronshū* (Studies on Asian history dedicated to Professor Nakajima Satoshi on his seventieth birthday). 2 vols. Tokyo: Kyuko shoin.

Negishi Tadashi. 1911. "Shina keizaikai no kiki" (Crises in the Chinese economy). *Tōa dōbunkai Shina chōsa hōkokusho* (Survey reports of China) 2(11):1–5.

Ng Chin-keong. 1983. *Trade and Society: The Amoy Network on the China Coast, 1683–1735*. Singapore: Singapore University Press.

Niida Noboru. 1962. *Chūgoku hōseishi kenkyū* (A study of Chinese legal history). 3 vols. Tokyo: Tokyo University Press.

Nishida Taichirō. 1974. *Chūgoku keihōshi kenkyū* (Studies on Chinese penal codes). Tokyo: Genpo.

Oliphant, Laurence. 1970. *Elgin's Mission to China and Japan*. 2 vols. Edinburgh: William Blackwood, 1859. Reprinted London: Oxford University Press.

Ono Kazuko, ed. 1983. *Min-Shin jidai no seiji to shakai* (Politics and society under the Ming and the Qing). Kyoto: Kyoto University Press.

Park, Nancy Elizabeth. 1993. "Corruption and Its Recompense: Bribes, Bureaucracy, and the Law in Late Imperial China." Ph.D. dissertation, Harvard University.

Pearson, Margaret. 1997. *China's New Business Elite.* Berkeley: University of California Press.

Peng Zeyi et al., eds. 1991. *Zhongguo yanyeshi guoji xueshu taolunhui lunwenji*
(Papers from the International Symposium on the History of the Chinese
Salt Industry). Chengdu: Sichuan renmin chubanshe.

Perkins, Dwight. 1969. *Agricultural Development in China, 1368–1968.* Chicago:
Aldine.

Ping Buqing. 1980. *Xiawei junxie* (Trivia collected beyond the rainbow). 2 vols.
1959 ed. Reprinted Shanghai: Guji chubanshe.

Posner, Richard A. 1977. *Economic Analysis of Law.* Boston: Little, Brown.

Postan, M. M., E. E. Rich, and Edward Miller, eds. 1963. *The Cambridge History of
Europe.* 4 vols. Cambridge: Cambridge University Press.

Prazniak, Roxann. 1999. *Of Camel Kings and Other Things.* Lanham, Md.: Rowman
& Littlefield.

Pu Songling. 1981. *Liaozhai zhiyi* (Strange tales from Make-Do Studio). 4 vols.
Qianlong rescript ed. Reprinted Jinan: Qilu shushe.

Qi Bingfeng. 1966. *Qingmo geming yu junxian lunzheng* (The controversy over revolution and constitutional monarchy in late Qing). Taipei: Academia Sinica.

Qi Meiqin. 1998. *Qingdai neiwufu* (The Qing Imperial Household Department).
Beijing: Zhongguo renmin daxue chubanshe.

Qi Zhilu. 1983. "Tianjin jindai zhuming jiaoyujia Yan Xiu" (Yan Xiu, noted edu-
cator in modern Tianjin). *TJWSZL* 25:1–45.

Qian Chenqun. 1751–1764. *Xiangshuzhai wenji* (Collection of essays from the
Fragrant Tree Studio).

Qian Yong. 1979. *Liyuan conghua* (Conversations from Liyuan). 2 vols. 1838 ed.
Reprinted Beijing: Zhonghua shuju.

"Qianlong nianjian Neiwufu guandang shiliaoxuan" (Selected materials on government pawnshops operated by the Imperial Household Department during the reign of Qianlong). 1985. *LSDA* 4:16–20.

Qiao Hong. 1960. "Ming-Qing erlai Tianjin shuihuan de fasheng ji qi yuanyin"
(Flooding of Tianjin and its causes during the Ming and Qing dynasties).
*Beiguo chunqiu* (Chronicle of the north) 3:86–91.

Qiao Zhiqiang et al. 1999. *Jindai Huabei nongcun shehui bianqian* (Rural social
change in modern North China). Beijing: Renmin chubanshe.

Rankin, Mary Backus. 1986. *Elite Activism and Political Transformation in China.*
Stanford: Stanford University Press.

———. 1992. "Some Observations on a Chinese Public Sphere." Paper prepared
for the Conference on Public Sphere/Civil Society in China, UCLA.

Ransom, Roger L. et al., eds. 1982. *Explorations in the New Economic History.* New
York: Academic Press.

Ren Penglian. 1871. *Da Qing lüli zengxiu tongzuan jicheng* (A revised and updated
compendium of Qing codes).

Reynolds, Douglas R. 1993. *China, 1898–1912: The Xinzheng Revolution and Japan.*
Cambridge: Council on East Asian Studies, Harvard University.

Riasanovsky, V. A. 1976. *Chinese Civil Law.* Tianjin, 1938. Reprinted Arlington: University Publications of America.

Roniger, Luis, and Ayşe Güneş-Ayata, eds. 1994. *Democracy, Clientelism, and Civil Society.* Boulder: Lynne Rienner.

Rowe, William T. 1984. *Hankow: Commerce and Society in a Chinese City, 1796–1889.* Stanford: Stanford University Press.

————. 1989. *Hankow: Conflict and Community in a Chinese City.* Stanford: Stanford University Press.

————. 1990. "The Public Sphere in Modern China." *MC* 16(3):309–329.

————. 1993. "The Problem of Civil Society in Late Imperial China." *MC* 19(2): 39–157.

Rozman, Gilbert. 1982. *Population and Marketing Settlements in Ch'ing China.* Cambridge: Cambridge University Press.

Saeki Tomi. 1956. *Shindai ensei no kenkyū* (A study of the Qing salt administration). Kyoto: Tōyōshi kenkyūkai.

————. 1970–1972. "Shindai Yōseichō ni okeru yōringin no kenkyū" (Study on "integrity-nourishing silver" during the Yongzheng period of the Qing dynasty). *Tōyōshi kenkyū* 29(1):30–60 (1970); 29(2/3):56–117 (1970); 30(4):55–92 (1972).

————. 1987. *Chūgoku enseishi no kenkyū* (Studies on the history of salt administration in China). Tokyo: Hōritsu Bunka.

Sakaguchi Takenosuke. 1903. *Hokushin chihū junkai fukumeisho* (Report of a tour of North China). Tokyo: Gaimushō tsūshō kyoku.

Salzmann, Ariel. 1991. "An Ancien Régime Revisited: Privatization and Political Economy in the Eighteenth-Century Ottoman Empire." *Politics and Society* 21 (4):393–423.

————. 1993. "Measures of Empire: Tax Farmers and the Ottoman Ancien Régime." Ph.D. dissertation, Columbia University.

Sasaki Masaya. 1954. "Ahen sensō izen no tsūka mondai" (Monetary problems before the Opium War). *Tōhōgaku* (Studies of the Orient) 8:94–117.

Schurmann, H. F. 1955. "Traditional Property Concepts in China." *Far Eastern Quarterly* 15(4):507–516.

Seligman, Adam. 1992. *The Idea of Civil Society.* New York: Free Press.

Shang Shoushan. 1985. "Touqing Gaoxian tielu yunshu gongshi shimo" (History of the Touli-Qinggang Cableway Transportation Company) *TJWSZL* 34:49–60.

Shen Defu. 1980. *Wanli yehuobian* (Collection of the wild in the reign of Wanli). 1827 ed. Reprinted Beijing: Zhonghua shuju.

Shen Hongchen et al. 1846. "Duxian, yanxian zougao" (Draft memorials of the governor general and the Changlu commissioner). Manuscript held in Special Collections, Nankai University Library.

Shen Jiaben. 1985. *Lidai xingfa kao* (Study of penal codes of successive dynasties). 4 vols. *Shen Jiyi xiansheng yishu* (Collected works of Shen Jiaben) ed. Reprinted Beijing: Zhonghua shuju.

Shen Zhaoyun. 1924. *Pengchuang fulu* (Supplementary essays from the studio with unkempt windows).

Shen Zuwei. 1983. "Qingmo Shangbu, Nonggongshangbu huodong shuping" (Appraisal of the activities of the Commerce Ministry in late Qing). *ZGSHJJSYJ* 2:100–110.

Shih, James. 1995. "Huizhounese wives and the rise of Huizhou merchants in late Imperial China." Unpublished paper.

Shimizu Taiji. 1928. "Minmatsu ni okeru Tenshin no kaikan" (Agricultural development of Tianjin in the late Ming dynasty). *Waseda daigaku bungaku shishō kenkyū* 7:113–157.

Shina chūtongun shireibu, comp. 1986. *Tenshinshi* (Almanac of Tianjin). Tokyo: Shireibo, 1909. Translated by Hou Zhentong. Tianjin: Tianjin difangzhi bianxiu weiyuanhui.

Shina chūtongun Shireibu Ōtsu shokutaku kōanhan, comp. 1937. *Hokushi kasen suiun chōsa hōkoku* (Report on river shipping in North China). N.p.: Ōtsu shokutakuhan.

Shingai kakumei kenkyūkai, ed. 1985. *Chūgoku kingendaishi ronshū* (Essays on modern and contemporary Chinese history). Tokyo: Kyuko shoin.

Shuili shuidian kexue yanjiuyuan, ed. 1981. *Qingdai Haihe Luanhe honglao dang'an shiliao* (Archival material on the flooding of the Hai and Luan rivers). Beijing: Zhonghua shuju.

"Shunzhi nianjian Changlu yanzheng tiben" (Memorials regarding the Changlu salt administration during the reign of the Shunzhi Emperor). 1988. *LSDA* 1: 9–16 and 2:12–18.

Shunzhi ziyiju, comp. 1910–1911. *Shunzhi ziyiju wendu leiyao chubian, erbian* (Documents of the Shuntian Zhili provincial consultative assembly by category, first and second compilation).

Sifa xingzhengbu, comp. 1969. *Zhongguo minshangshi xiguan diaochalu* (Survey of civil and commercial customs in China). 3 vols. Reprinted Taipei: Jinxue chubanshe.

Skinner, G. William, ed. 1977. *The City in Late Imperial China*. Stanford: Stanford University Press.

Skocpol, Theda, et al. 1985. *Bringing the State Back In*. Cambridge: Cambridge University Press.

Smith, Joanna F. Handlin. 1987. "Benevolent Societies: The Reshaping of Charity During the Late Ming and Early Ch'ing." *JAS* 46(2):309–334.

———. 1992. "Gardens in Ch'i Piao-chia's Social World: Wealth and Values in Late-Ming Kiangnan." *JAS* 51(1):55–81.

Sommer, Matthew H. 1996. "The Uses of Chastity: Sex, Law, and the Property of Widows in Qing China." *Late Imperial China* 17(2):77–130.

Sonda Saburō. 1975. "Shōkai no setsuritsu" (The establishment of chambers of commerce). *Reikishigaku kenkyū* 422:43–55.

Song Di. 1993. *Shehui fansan heyuan* (Society and its discord). Changchun: Jilin jiaoyu chubanshe.

Song Lian et al. 1976. *Yuanshi* (History of the Yuan dynasty). Reprinted Beijing: Zhonghua shuju.

Song Xiang et al. 1809. *Shandong yanfazhi* (Codes of the Shandong Division).

Strauss, Julia C. 1998. *Strong Institutions in Weak Polities*. New York: Oxford University Press.

Sumner, C. S. 1990. *Censure, Politics, and Criminal Justice*. Milton Keynes: Open University.

Sun Yushu. 1986. "Sun Hongyi shengping shiji" (A biography of Sun Hongyi).
  *TJWSZL* 37:40–71.
Suzhoushi dang'anguan, comp. 1982. "Suzhou shimin gongshe dang'an xuanbian" (Selected archival materials on citizens communes in Suzhou). In *Xinhai
  gemingshi congkan* (Studies on the 1911 Revolution) 4:53–197.
Takashima Ko. 1997. "Suiryūkai no tanjō" (Study on firefighting societies). *Tōyō-
  shi kenkyū* 56(2):45–84.
Tan Qixiang. 1981. "Xihan yiqian de Huanghe xiayou gudao" (The channel of
  the Yellow River in its lower reaches before the Western Han). *LSDL* 1:48–64.
————. 1986. "Haihe shuixi di xingcheng yu fazhan" (Formation and develop-
  ment of the Hai River system). *LSDL* 4:1–27.
Tang Lixing. 1993. *Shangren yu Zhongguo jinshi shehui* (Merchants and modern
  Chinese society). Hangzhou: Renmin chubanshe.
Tang Zhenchang. 1992. "Shimin yishi yu Shanghai" (Civil consciousness and
  Shanghai). *Twenty-First Century* 11:11–23.
Teraki Tokuko. 1962. "Shinmatsu Minkoku shonen no chihō jichi" (Local self-
  government in late Qing and early Republican China). *Ochanomizu shigaku*
  (Bulletin of Ochanomizu University) 5:14–30.
Thaxton, Ralph. 1997. *Salt of the Earth.* Berkeley: University of California Press.
Thompson, Roger. 1995. *China's Local Councils in the Age of Constitutional
  Reform, 1898–1911.* Cambridge, Mass.: Council on East Asian Studies, Har-
  vard University.
Tian Qiuye and Zhou Weiliang. 1979. *Zhonghua yanyeshi* (History of China's salt
  industry). Taipei: Shangwu yinshuguan.
Tian Wenjing. 1995. *Fuyu xuanhualu* (Administrative record of Henan province).
  Annotated ed. Zhengzhou: Zhongzhou guzhi chubanshe.
Tian Yukang. 1987. *Zhongguo fanchuan maoyi yu duiwai guanxishi lunji* (Essays
  on China's junk trade and foreign relations). Hangzhou: Zhejiang renmin
  chubanshe.
*Tianjin Bianshi zongzupu* (Genealogy of the Bian family). 1930. N.p.
Tianjin diwei wadi gaizao bangongshi (Office of Reclaiming Low-Lying Areas,
  Tianjin District), comp. 1958. *Tianjin zhunqu wadi gaizao jingyan* (Experience of
  reclaiming low-lying areas in Tianjin district). Beijing: Kexue puji chubanshe.
Tianjinfu zizhiju, comp. 1906. *Tianjinfu zizhiju wenjian luyao chubian* (Documents
  of the Tianjin prefectural self-government bureau, first compilation).
————. 1907. *Tianjinfu zizhiju wenjian luyao erbian* (Documents of the Tianjin prefectural self-government bureau, second compilation).
Tianjin shehui kexueyuan lishi yanjiusuo, Tianjin jianshi bianxiezu. 1987. *Tianjin jianshi* (Concise history of Tianjin). Tianjin: Renmin chubanshe.
Tianjinshi dang'anguan, ed. 1990. *Yuan Shikai Tianjin dang'an shiliao xuanbian* (Selected archival material of Yuan Shikai and Tianjin). Tianjin: Guji
  chubanshe.
Tianjinshi fangdichan chanquan shichang guanlichu, comp. 1995. *Tianjin lidai
  fangdichan qizheng* (Tianjin land deeds and titles from various periods). Tianjin: Renmin chubanshe.
Tianjinshi shanghui, comp. 1933. *Tianjinshi shanghui nianjian* (Almanac of the
  Tianjin Chamber of Commerce). Tianjin: Tianjinshi shanghui.

Tianjin shiyuan dilixi, comp. 1981. *Tianjin nongye dili* (Agricultural geography of Tianjin). Tianjin: Kexuejishu chubanshe.

Tianjinshi zhengxie mishuchu, comp. 1974. *Tianjin badajia ji qi houyi* (Tianjin's "Big Eight" families and their descendants). Tianjin: Tianjinshi Zhengxie.

Tianjinshi zhengxie wenshi ziliao yanjiuhui, ed. 1987. *Tianjin de yanghang yu maiban* (Tianjin's foreign importers and their compradors). Tianjin: Renmin chubanshe.

"Tianjinwei tunken tiaokuan" (Provisions on reclamation and colonization of the Tianjin guard station). 1624.

"Tianjinxian shuli diaocha baogaoshu" (Report on irrigation in Tianjin district). 1923. *Zhili shiye congkan* (Zhili industrial gazette) 1(4):1–3 and 1(5):1–3.

"Tianjin Yizhengtang Fengshi jiapu" (Genealogy of the Feng family). 1923. Mimeograph copy.

Tilly, Charles. 1975. *Formation of National States in Western Europe.* Princeton: Princeton University Press.

———. 1990. *Coercion, Capital, and European States, AD 990–1990.* Oxford: Basil Blackwell.

Tilly, Charles, et al., eds. 1994. *Cities and the Rise of States in Europe.* Boulder: Westview.

Torbert, Preston M. 1977. *The Ch'ing Imperial Household Department: A Study of Its Organization and Principal Functions.* Cambridge, Mass.: Council on East Asian Studies, Harvard University.

Tsu Yuyue. 1912. *The Spirit of Chinese Philanthropy.* New York: Columbia University Press.

Tu Wei-ming, ed. 1996. *Confucian Traditions in East Asian Modernity.* Cambridge, Mass.: Harvard University Press.

Tuo Tuo et al., comps. 1977. *Song shi* (Dynastic history of the Song). Reprinted Beijing: Zhonghua shuju.

Vandermeersch, Léon, ed. 1994. *La Société civile face à l'État.* Paris: École française d'Extrême-Orient.

Wakefield, David. 1998. *Fenjia: Household Division and Inheritance in Qing and Republican China.* Honolulu: University of Hawai'i Press.

Wakeman, Frederic. 1985. *The Great Enterprise.* 2 vols. Berkeley: University of California Press.

———. 1993. "The Civil Society and the Public Sphere Debate." *MC* 19(2):108–137.

———. 1998. "Boundaries of the Public Sphere in Ming and Qing China." *Daedalus* 127(3):167–189.

Wakeman, Frederic, and Carolyn Grant, eds. 1975. *Conflict and Control in Late Imperial China.* Berkeley: University of California Press.

Wan Guangtai. 1756. *Zhepo jushi shiji* (Collected poems of Wan Guangtai). Preface dated 1756.

Wan Xinping and Pu Wenqi. 1986. *Tianjin shihua* (History of Tianjin). Shanghai: Renmin chubanshe.

Wang Ding'an et al. 1905. *Lianghuai yanfazhi* (Codes of the Lianghuai Division). Reprint of 1893 ed.

Wang Fu. 1968. *Tang huiyao* (Compendium of Tang codes). Shanghai: Shijie shuju.

Wang Hongda. n.d. "Yangliuqing shiliao shuwen" (Historical materials on Yang-liuqing). Manuscript.

Wang Jingyu, comp. 1957. *Zhongguo jindai gongyeshi ziliao* (Source materials on industries in modern China). Pt. I. 2 vols. Beijing: Kexue chubanshe.

Wang Jiong et al. 1756. *Handan xianzhi* (Gazetteer of Handan district).

Wang Kerun. 1754. *Jifu jianwenlu* (Record of sights and sounds in the metropoli-tan area).

Wang Mingming. 1999. *Shiqu de fanrong* (Lost prosperity). Hangzhou: Zhejiang renmin chubanshe.

Wang Shaoguang. 1991. "Guangyu 'shimin shehui' de jidian shikao" (Reflec-tions on "civil society"). *Twenty-First Century* 8:102–114.

Wang Shirong. 1997a. *Zhongguo gudai panci yanjiu* (Study of judiciary rulings in ancient China). Beijing: Zhongguo zhengfa daxue chubanshe.

———. 1997b. *Zhongguo gudai panli yanjiu* (Study of judiciary precedents in ancient China). Beijing: Zhongguo zhengfa daxue chubanshe.

Wang Shouji. 1873. *Yanfa yilüe* (Brief discussions on the salt code).

Wang Shouxun. 1937. *Wang Ren'an ji* (Collected essays of Wang Ren'an).

———. 1938. *Tianjin zhengsu yuangeji* (Evolution of administration and customs of Tianjin).

Wang Shuhuai. 1974. *Gengzi peikuan* (The Boxer Indemnity). Taipei: Academia Sinica.

Wang Shuren et al. 1980. "Jiefangqian Hangu yanye shengchan ji jieji zhuang-kuang" (Salt production and class relationship in Hangu before 1949). *TJLSZL* 7:25–41.

Wang Wengru. 1986. "Tan Tianjin de Ming Qing yuanlin." (Gardens and retreats of Tianjin during the Ming and Qing). *TJSYJ* 1:13–21.

Wang Xingang et al. 1983. "Tianjinbang jingying Xidaying mouyi gaishu" (Gen-eral remarks on the business operations of the West Camp by Tianjin mer-chants). *TJWSZL* 24:171–188.

Wang Xitong. n.d. *Yizhai zishu* (Memoirs of Yizhai). 6 vols. N.p.

———. 1939. *Yizhai wenji.* (Collected essays of Yizhai).

Wang Youpu. 1924. *Jieshan ziding nianpu* (Chronicle of my life). Reprint of Qian-long ed.

Wang Yunsheng. 1983. "Yan Xiu yu xuezhi gaige" (Yan Xiu and educational reform). *WSZLXJ* 87:97–107.

Wang Zhizhou. 1983. "Wojia sandai maibanjishi" (Three generations of compra-dors in my family). *TJWSZL* 25:192–200.

Wang Zishou. 1965. "Tianjin diandangye sishinian de huiyi" (Memories of forty years in the pawnshop business of Tianjin). *WSZLXJ* 53:35–58.

Wangyun jushi. 1988. *Tianjin huanghui kaoji* (Study of the *huanghui*). 1936 ed. Reprinted Tianjin: Guji chubanshe.

Watson, James L., and Evelyn S. Rawski, eds. 1988. *Death Ritual in Late Imperial and Modern China.* Berkeley: University of California Press.

Webber, Carolyn, and Aaron Wildavsky. 1986. *A History of Taxation and Expendi-ture in the Western World.* New York: Simon & Schuster.

Weber, Max. 1951. *The Religion of China.* Translated by Hans H. Gerth. New York: Free Press.

————. 1958. *The City.* Translated by Don Martindale and Gertrud Neuwirth. New York: Free Press.

————. 1966. *Max Weber on Law in Economy and Society.* Translated by Edward Shils and Max Rheinstein. Cambridge, Mass.: Harvard University Press.

————. 1968. *Economy and Society.* Translated by Ephraim Fischoff et al.; edited by Guenther Roth and Claus Wittich. 3 vols. New York: Bedminster Press.

————. 1982. *General Economic History.* Translated by Frank H. Knight. New Brunswick: Transaction Books.

Wei Qingyuan. 1984. *Dangfang lunshi wenbian* (Essays on archives and history). Fuzhou: Fujian renmin chubanshe.

Wei Qingyuan and Wu Qiyan. 1981. "Qingdai zhuming huangshang Fanshi de xingshuai" (Rise and fall of the royal merchant house of Fan). *LSYJ* 3:127–144.

Wei Qingyuan, Gao Fang, and Liu Wenyuan. 1979. "Lun ziyiju" (The provincial consultative assemblies). *JDSYJ* 2:230–249.

————. 1993. *Qingmo xianzhengshi* (History of constitutional government in late Qing). Beijing: Zhongguo renmin daxue chubanshe.

*Wenxian congbian* (Selected historical documents from the Palace Museum). 1930–1943. Gugong wenxianguan ed.

Will, Pierre-Etienne. 1990. *Bureaucracy and Famine in Eighteenth-Century China.* Translated by Elborg Forster. Stanford: Stanford University Press.

Williams, Michael. 1988. "Merchant Banking Dynasties in the English Class Structure: Ownership, Solidarity, and Kinship in the City of London, 1850–1960." *British Journal of Sociology* 3:133–162.

Willmott, W. E., ed. 1972. *Economic Organization in Chinese Society.* Stanford: Stanford University Press.

Wolseley, G. J. 1972. *War with China in 1860.* London: Longman, 1862. Reprinted Wilmington: Scholarly Resources.

Wong, R. Bin. 1997. *China Transformed.* Ithaca: Cornell University Press.

Wright, Mary C. 1968. *China in Revolution.* New Haven: Yale University Press.

Wu Bangxing, ed. 1842. *Shuili yingtian tushuo* (Illustrations and discussions on irrigation and reclamation).

Wu Chunmei. 1998. *Yici shikong de jindaihua gaige* (An out-of-control modernizing reform). Hefei: Anhui daxue chubanshe.

Wu Huanzhi. 1965. "Guanyu wofu Wu Diaoqing shiji de huiyi" (Reminiscences of my father Wu Maoding). *WSZLXJ* 49:228–235.

Wu Jihua. 1961. *Mingdai haiyun ji yunhe de yanjiu* (Study of sea transport and the Grand Canal during the Ming dynasty). Taipei: Academia Sinica.

Wu Ou. 1931. *Tianjinshi nongye diaocha baogao* (Survey report of Tianjin's agriculture). Tianjin: Bureau of Social Affairs.

Wu, Silas. 1968. "Nanshufang zhi jianzhi ji qi qianqi zhi fazhan" (Establishment of the Southern Study and its early development). *Si yu yen* (Reflections and articulation) 5:6–12.

Wu Tan, comp. 1991. *Daqing lüli tongkai jiaozhu* (Annotated Qing Code). 1886 ed. Reprinted Beijing: Zhongguo zhengfa daxue.

Wu Wen. n.d. *Lianyangji* (Collected works of Wu Wen). Saoye shangfang ed.

Wu Xiangxiang. 1961. *Zhongguo xiandaishi congkan* (Anthology of modern Chinese history). 5 vols. Taipei: Zhengzhong shuju.

Wu Zhenyu. 1983. *Yangjizhai conglu* (Miscellaneous records of Yangji Studio). 1896 ed. Reprinted Beijing: Guji shudian.

Xi Shu et al. n.d. *Caochuan zhi* (Gazetteer of tribute-grain transport boats). Xuanlantang congshu ed.

Xiao Gongqin. 1999. *Weiji zhong de biange* (Reform amidst crisis). Shanghai: Sanlian shudian.

Xiao Guoliang. 1988. "Lun Qingdai yangang zhidu" (On the salt syndicate system of the Qing period). *LSYJ* 5:64–73.

Xie Taofang. 1997. *Zhongguo shimin wenxueshi* (History of urban literature in China). Chengdu: Sichuan renmin chubanshe.

Xin Chengzhang. 1982. "Tianjin badajia" (The Big Eight family of Tianjin). *TJWSZL* 20:39–54.

Xu Dingxin. 1983. "Jiu Zhongguo shanghui suyuan" (Origin of the chamber of commerce in old China). *ZGSHJJSYJ* 1:83–96.

——. 1986. "Zhongguo shanghui yanjiu pingshu" (Review of studies on chambers of commerce in China). *LSYJ* 6:81–93.

——. 1999. "Guanyu jindai Shanghai shanghui xingxui de jidian shikao" (Reflections on the rise and fall of the Shanghai Chamber of Commerce). *Shanghai shehui kexueyuan xueshu jikan* (Bulletin of the Shanghai Academy of Social Sciences) 1:11–18.

Xu Guangqi. 1979. *Nongzheng quanshu* (Comprehensive treatise on agriculture). 3 vols. Shanghai: Guji chubanshe.

——. 1984. *Xu Guangqi ji* (Collected works of Xu Guangqi). Edited by Wang Chongmin. 2 vols. Shanghai: Guji chubanshe.

Xu Jingxing. 1978. "Tianjin jindai gongye de zaoqi gaikuang" (Modern industries in Tianjin). *TJWSZL* 1:124–161.

Xu Shiluan. 1986. *Jingxiang bishu* (Notes in honor of Tianjin). Tianjin: Guji chubanshe.

Xu Song, comp. 1936. *Song huiyao jikao* (Collected government records of the Song dynasty). Beijing: Guoli Beiping tushuguan.

Xu Tianzui et al. 1927. *Xianzheng quanshu* (Manual on district magistracy). Shanghai: Shanghai zhengyi hezuoshe.

Xu Tongzi. 1935. "Heshuo shizu pulüe chugao xubian" (Brief introductions to genealogies of Hebei province). *Hebei yuekan* (Hebei monthly) 4:1–7.

*Xuantong zhengji* (Veritable record of the Emperor Xuantong). 1986. Reprinted Beijing: Zhonghua shuju.

Xue Fucheng. 1983. *Yong'an biji* (Miscellaneous notes from the Yong Studio). 1897 ed. Reprinted Nanjing: Renmin chubanshe.

Xue Zongzheng. 1982. "Qingdai qianqi de yanshang" (Salt merchants of early Qing). *QSLC* 4:49–64.

Yan Chongnian. 1989. *Yanbuji* (Essays on the craft of history from Beijing). Beijing: Yanshan chubanshe.

Yan Xiu. 1990. *Yan Xiu nianpu* (Chronological autobiography of Yan Xiu). Jinan: Qilu shushe.

——. n.d. "Yan Fansun riji" (Diary of Yan Xiu). Manuscript held in Special Collections, Tianjin Municipal Library.

——. n.d. "Yanshi jiashu" (Correspondences of the Yan household). Manuscript held in Special Collections, Tianjin Municipal Library.

Yan Zide. 1985. "Nichang xupu" (Sequel to the Bright-Colored Skirt compendium). Edited by Wang Tingshao. In *Ming-Qing minge shidiaoji* (Collection of folk songs and popular tunes of Ming and Qing). 2 vols. Shanghai: Guji chubanshe.

"Yan'gutang Lishi jiapu." n.d. (Genealogy of the Li family).

*Yan'gutang Lishi zupu* (Genealogy of the Li lineage). 1935. Tianjin: n.p.

Yanwuchu, comp. n.d. *Zhongguo yanzheng yange shi: Changlu* (History of the development of salt administration in China: Changlu). Beijing: Yanwuchu.

Yang C. K. 1967. *Religion in Chinese Society*. Berkeley: University of California Press.

Yang Duanliu. 1962. *Qingdai huobi jinrong shigao* (Draft history of money and finance during the Qing). Beijing: Sanlian shudian.

Yang Lien-sheng. 1987. *Zhongguo wenhua zhong bao, bu, bao zhi yiyi* (The meaning and significance of *bao, bu, bao* in Chinese culture). Hong Kong: Chinese University of Hong Kong Press.

Yang Shaozhou. 1989. "Jiefangqian Tianjin chi hongbaifanr de" (People who made a living out of marriages, birthday celebrations, and funerals in Tianjin before 1949). *TJWSZL* 46:234–244.

Yang Shounan. 1913. *Changlu yanzheng jiyao* (History of Changlu salt administration). Preface dated 1913.

Yang Wending et al. 1896. *Luanzhou zhi* (Gazetteer of Luan district).

Yang Zhen. 1996. "Suoertu yanjiu" (Study of Songgotu). *QSLC* 112–128.

Yang Zhongqi [Ji Jin]. 1915. "Zhili funü zhi zhiye" (Livelihood of women in Zhili). *Zhili shiye zazhi* (Industrial gazette of Zhili) 4(2) (February) and 4(3) (March).

Yangcheng jiuke, comp. 1898. *Jinmen jilüe* (Facts of Tianjin).

Yao Xiyun. 1981. "Tianjin shidiao de yanbian" (Transformation of Tianjin's "shidiao"). *TJWSZL* 14:160–169.

———. 1989. "Tianjin gulaodong Yaojia yishi" (Anecdotes of the Yao family east of the drum tower in Tianjin). *TJWSZL* 47:204–242.

Yao Ying. 1867. *Dongmingwen houji* (Supplemental essays of Dongming).

Ye Xiaoxin, ed. 1993. *Zhongguo minfashi* (History of Chinese civil law). Shanghai: Renmin chubanshe.

Ye Xiuyun. 1985. "Qingdai Changlu yanyunshisi ji qi suoshu jigou" (The Qing Changlu commissioner and his subordinate bureaucracy). *TJSYJ* 1:30–34.

*Yili* (Book of Rites). 1979. Reprinted Beijing: Zhonghua shuju.

Yinglian. 1783. *Mengtang shigao* (Collected poems from the Hall of Dreams).

"Yizhengtang Fengshi benzhi jiapu" (Genealogy of the Feng family). 1805. Manuscript.

Yoshizawa Seiichiro. 1996. "Tenshin danren kō" (On Tianjin's militia). *Tōyō gakuhō* 78(1):31–61.

Yu Henian. 1934. "Tianjin Shiyuanchuang kao" (The ancestral hall of the Zhang family in Tianjin). *Hebei yuekan* 2(7):1–4.

Yu Heping. 1988. "Lun Qingmo minchu Zhong Mei shanghui de hufang he hezuo" (Visits and cooperation between chambers of commerce in China and America in the late Qing and early Republican periods). *JDSYJ* 3: 110–118.

———. 1991. "Shanghui yu Zhongguo zichan jieji de ziweihua wenti" (Self-consciousness of the Chinese bourgeoisie and the chamber of commerce). *JDSYJ* 3:25–41.

———. 1993. *Shanghui yu Zhongguo zaoqi xiandaihua* (Chamber of commerce and early modernization in China). Shanghai: Renmin chubanshe.

Yu Yingshi. 1987a. *Zhongguo jinshi zongjiao lunli yu shangren jingshen* (Religious morals and the merchant spirit in medieval and modern China). Taipei: Luanjing chubanshe.

———. 1987b. *Shi yu Zhongguo wenhua* (*Shi* and Chinese culture). Shanghai: Renmin chubanshe.

———. 1994. "Cong Zhongguo guojia yu shehui guanxi kan Zhongguo minzhu-hua de qiantu" (The future of democratization in China as seen from state/society relations). *Shijie ribao* (World journal), January 1.

Yuan Cai. n.d. *Yuanshi jiaxun* (Household instruction of the Yuans). Congshu jicheng ed.

*Yuan dianzhang* (Precedents and statutes of the Yuan dynasty). 1990. Reprinted Beijing: Zhongguo shudian.

Yue Zhongjia. 1981. "Wo suo zhidao de Lugang gongsuo" (The Changlu salt merchants' guild that I know). *TJWSZL* 26:114–121.

Zelin, Madeleine. 1984. *The Magistrate's Taels*. Berkeley: University of California Press.

Zeng Yangfeng. 1915. "Lun baoxiao" (Reciprocal donations). *Yanzheng zazhi* (Journal of salt administration) 19(1):1–6.

———. 1936. *Zhongguo yanzhengshi* (History of salt administration in China). Shanghai: Shangwu yinshuguan.

Zha Li. 1770. *Tonggu shutang yigao* (Posthumously collected works of the Copper Drum Studio).

Zha Lubai, comp. 1941. *Wanping Zhashi zhipu* (Genealogy of the Zhas of Wanping).

Zha Pu. 1722. *Zha Pu shiji* (Collected poems of Zha Pu).

Zha Weiren. n.d. *Zhetang weidinggao.* (Unfinished anthology from the Cane Pond).

———. n.d. *Huaying'an ji* (Collection of poems from the hut under the shadows of flowers).

———. n.d. *Lianbo shihua* (Talking of poems). 1924 ed. Reprinted Beijing: Zhongguo shudian.

Zha Xiazhong. n.d. *Jingyetang shiji* (Collected poems of the Jingye Studio). Sibu congkan ed.

Zhang Chuanxi. 1995. *Zhongguo lidai qiyue huibian kaoxi* (Annotated contracts from Chinese history). 2 vols. Beijing: Beijing daxue chubanshe.

Zhang Cixi. 1970. *Li Dazhao xiansheng chuan* (Biography of Li Dazhao). Kyoto: Tomodachi.

Zhang Cunwu. 1965. *Guangxu sanshiyinian Zhong Mei gongyue fengchao* (The controversy surrounding the Sino-American labor treaty of 1905). Taipei: Academia Sinica.

Zhang Hailin. 1998. "Qingmo Jiangsu 'shangbian' qianlun" (Merchant-led disturbances in late-Qing Jiangsu province). *JDSYJ* 6:136–156.

———. 1999. *Suzhou zaoqi chengshi xiandaihua yanjiu* (A study of the early urban modernization of Suzhou). Nanjing: Nanjing daxue chubanshe.

Zhang Haipeng et al. 1995. *Huishang yanjiu* (Studies on Huizhou merchants). Hefei: Anhui renmin chubanshe.

Zhang Han. 1985. *Congchuang mengyu* (Dreamy ramblings before the Pine Window). 1897 ed. Reprinted Beijing: Zhonghua shuju.

Zhang Honglai. 1928. *Hunsangli zashuo* (Various aspects of marriage and funeral rites). Beijing: Wenhua chubanshe.

Zhang Hongyi. 1989. *Rujia jingji lunli* (Confucian economic ethics). Changsha: Hunan jiaoyu chubanshe.

Zhang Jianying. 1882. *Huanxiang yaoze* (Almanac for officials).

Zhang Jinfan, ed. 1990. *Zhongguo fazhishi yanjiu zongshu* (Studies on the history of China's legal system). Beijing: Zhongguo renmin gong'an daxue chubanshe.

———. 1992. *Qinglü yanjiu* (Studies on the Qing Code). Beijing: Falü chubanshe.

———. 1998. *Qingdai minfa zonglun* (History of Qing civil law). Beijing: Zhongguo zhengfa daxue chubanshe.

Zhang Jinfan et al. 1994. *Qingdai fazhishi* (History of the Qing legal system). Beijing: Zhongguo zhengfa daxue chubanshe.

———. 1998. *Qingdai fazhishi* (History of the Qing legal system). Beijing: Zhonghua shuju.

———. 1999. *Zhongguo minshi susong zhidushi* (A history of the civil litigation system in China). Chengdu: Bashu shushe.

Zhang Lü et al., comps. 1494. *Baoding zhi* (Gazetteer of Baoding district).

Zhang Nan and Wang Yinzhi, comps. 1977. *Xinhai geming qianshinian jian shilun xuanji* (Selection of current opinions in the decade before the 1911 Revolution). 3 vols. Beijing: Sanlian shudian.

Zhang Pengyuan. 1969. *Lixianpai yu Xinhai geming* (Constitutionalists and the 1911 Revolution). Taipei: Shangwu yinshuguan.

Zhang Shaozu. 1988. "Tianjin jindai jiaoyu de yange" (Evolution of modern education in Tianjin). *TJWSCK* 8:84–86.

Zhang Shouchang, comp. 1984. *Taipingjun beifa ziliao xuanbian* (Selected sources on the Taiping Northern Expedition). Jinan: Qilu shushe.

Zhang Tao. 1982. *Jinmen zaji* (Miscellaneous records of Tianjin). 1884 ed. Reprinted Tianjin: Guji chubanshe.

Zhang Xiaobo. 1995. "Merchant Associational Activism in Early Twentieth-Century China: The Tianjin Chamber of Commerce, 1904–1928." Ph.D. dissertation, Columbia University.

Zhang Yilin. 1947. *Xintaipingshi ji* (Collected works of the Peace of Mind Studio).

Zhang Yingchang, comp. 1960. *Qingshi duo* (Selected poems of the Qing dynasty). 2 vols. 1869 ed. Reprinted Beijing: Zhonghua shuju.

Zhang Yufa. 1971. *Qingji de lixian tuanti* (Constitutionalists of the Qing period). Taipei: Academia Sinica.

Zhang Zhenhe and Ding Yuanying. 1982. "Qingmo minbian nianbiao" (Chronology of popular uprisings in late Qing). *Jindaishi ziliao* (Materials in modern history) 3:108–181 and 4:77–121.

Zhang Zhenkun. 1979. "Qingmo shinianjian de bizhi wenti" (Problems of the currency system in the last decade of the Qing dynasty). *JDSYJ* 1:249–287.

Zhang Zhu. 1934. *Tui'enji* (Collected writings from the Withdrawal Studio). Sibu congkan zubian ed. Reprinted Shanghai: Shangwu yinshuguan.

Zhao Yi. 1982. *Yanbao zaji* (Miscellaneous notes from the exposed eaves). Reprinted Beijing: Zhonghua shuju.

Zhao Yuanli. 1934. *Cangzhai suibi* (Miscellaneous notes from the Cangzhai).
Zhao Zhishen. n.d. *Yishantang shiwenji* (Collection of poems and essays from Yishantang). Sibu biyao ed.
Zhaolian. 1980. *Xiaoting zalu* (Miscellaneous notes from Xiaoting). Expanded and reprinted ed. Beijing: Zhonghua shuju.
Zheng Kecheng. 1988. *Mingdai zhengzeng tanyuan* (Political conflicts of the Ming). Tianjin: Guji chubanshe.
Zheng Qin. 1988. *Qingdai shifa shenpan zhidu yanjiu* (Study of the Qing jurisprudence system). Changsha: Hunan jiaoyu chubanshe.
Zheng Shiwei et al. 1873. *Jinghai xianzhi* (Gazetteer of Jinghai district).
Zheng Shoupeng. 1980. *Songdai Kaifengfu yanjiu* (Study of Kaifeng during the Song period). Taipei: Guoli bianyiguan.
Zhili gaodeng shanpanting, comp. 1914. *Zhili gaodeng shangpanting pandu jiyao* (Selected rulings from the Zhili provincial superior court). 4 vols. Tianjin: n.p.
Zhongguo diyi lishi dang'anguan, comp. 1985. *Xinhai geming qianshinianjian minbian dang'an shiliao* (Historical materials on uprisings during the decade before the 1911 Revolution). 2 vols. Beijing: Zhonghua shuju.
———. 1993. *Yongzhengchao qijuzhu ce* (Daily records of the Emperor Yongzheng). 5 vols. Beijing: Zhonghua shuju.
———. 1996. *Kangxichao manwen zhupi zouzhe quanyi* (Translated memorials in Manchu with vermilion brush comments from the reign of the Kangxi Emperor). Beijing: Zhongguo shehui kexue chubanshe.
Zhongguo diyi lishi dang'anguan, ed. 1988. *Ming Qing dang'an yu lishi yanjiu* (Archival materials of the Ming and Qing periods and historical studies). 2 vols. Beijing: Zhonghua shuju.
Zhongguo diyi lishi dang'anguan et al., trans. 1990. *Manwen laodang* (Pre-1644 Manchu archives). 2 vols. Beijing: Zhonghua shuju.
Zhongguo haiyang fazhanshi lunwenji bianji weiyuanhui, ed. 1984–1988. *Zhongguo haiyang fazhanshi lunwenji* (Studies on the maritime development of China). 3 vols. Taipei: Academia Sinica.
Zhongguo lishi bowuguan, comp. 1992. *Tianjin Tianhougong xinghuitu* (Scenes from the Heavenly Consort's tour of Tianjin). Reprinted Hong Kong: Heping tushu gongsi.
Zhongguo xiquzhi bianji weiyuanhui, comp. 1990. *Zhongguo xiquzhi: Tianjin juan* (Gazetteer of Chinese opera: Tianjin). Beijing: Wenhua yishu chubanshe.
Zhonghua dilizhi bianjibu, comp. 1957. *Huabeiqu zirendili ziliao* (Geographical materials on North China). Beijing: Kexue chubanshe.
Zhongnan diqu Xinhai gemingshi yanjiu hui, ed. 1983. *Jinian Xinhai geming qishi zhounian qinglian xueshu taolunhui lunwenxuan* (Anthology of articles by young scholars from the conference to commemorate the seventieth anniversary of the 1911 Revolution). 2 vols. Beijing: Zhonghua shuju.
Zhou Fu. 1922. *Zhou Queshengong quanji* (Collected works of Zhou Fu). Preface dated 1922.
Zhou Guangyuan. 1995. "Beneath the Law: Chinese Local Legal Culture During the Qing dynasty." Ph.D. dissertation, UCLA.
Zhou Kai. 1840. *Neizisongzhai wenji* (Writings from the Self-Introspection Studio).

Zhou Shengchuan. 1902. *Zhou Wuchuanggong yishu* (Posthumously collected works of Zhou Shengchuan). Preface dated 1902.

Zhou Zhichu. 1988. "Wan Qing de Lianghuai yanshang" (Lianghuai salt merchants in late Qing). *Yanyeshi yanjiu* (Studies in the history of the salt industry) 3:46–50.

Zhou Zhijun. 1981. "Beifang shiyejia Zhou Xuexi" (Zhou Xuexi the industrialist of North China). *Gongshang shiliao* (Historical materials on industries and commerce) 2:16–39.

Zhu Jinpu. 1990. "Lun Kangxi shiqi de Nanshufang" (The Southern Study during the Kangxi period). *GGBWYYK* 2:27–38.

Zhu Kezhen. 1979. *Zhu kezhen wenji* (Collected writings of Zhu Kezhen). Beijing: Kexue chubanshe.

Zhu Shiqun. 1995. "Zhongguo shimin shehui yanjiu pingshu" (Studies on civil society in China). *Shehuixue yanjiu* (Studies in sociology) 6:41–45.

Zhu Xi. n.d. *Zhu wengong wenji* (Collected writings of Zhu Xi). Sibu congkan ed.

Zhu Ying. 1984. "Qingmo shanghui yanjiu pingshu" (Review of studies on chambers of commerce in late Qing). *Shixue yuekan* (Historical studies monthly) 2:112–117.

———. 1986. "Lixianpai jieji jichu xinlun" (A new hypothesis on the class nature of the constitutionalists). *Jianghan luntan* (Wuhan forum) 5:74–78.

———. 1987. "Qingmo shanghui guandu shangban de xingzhi yu tedian" (Official supervision and merchant operation nature of chambers of commerce in late Qing). *LSYJ* 6:137–149.

———. 1991a. *Xinhai geming shiqi xinshi shangren shetuan yanjiu* (New merchant organizations in late Qing). Beijing: Zhongguo renmin daxue chubanshe.

———. 1991b. "Qingmo xinxing shangren yu minjian shehui" (New merchants and civil society in late Qing). *Twenty-first century* 3:37–44.

———. 1996. *Wanqing jingjizhengce yu gaige cuoshi* (Late Qing economic policy and reforms). Wuchang: Huazhong shifan daxue chubanshe.

———. 1997. *Zhuanxing shiqi de shehui yu guojia* (Society and state in transition). Wuhan: Huazhong shifan daxue chubanshe.

———. 1998. "Jiawu chanhou Qingzhengfu jingji zhengci de bianhua yu shangren shehui di*wei* de tigao" (Changes in Qing economic policy and the rise of merchant status after the Opium War). *Guizhou shehui kexue* (Social sciences in Guizhou) 5:77–82.

Zhu Ying and Liu Wangling. 1984. "Qingmo shanghui yu dizhi meihuo yundong" (Chambers of commerce and the boycott of American goods in late Qing). *Huazhong shifan xueyuan yanjiusheng xuebao* (Bulletin of the Graduate School, Central China Normal College) 1:138–144.

Zhu Yizun. 1979. *Tangxiao ji* (Collection of laughter). Reprint of Kangxi ed. Shanghai: Guji chubanshe.

Zhu Yong. 1987. *Qingdai zongzufa yanjiu* (Study of Qing lineage law). Changsha: Hunan jiaoyu chubanshe.

Zuo Buqing. 1986. "Qingdai yanshang de shengshuai shulüe" (Brief treatise on the rise and fall of salt merchants during the Qing period). *GGBWYYK* 1: 49–58.

# Index

# About the Author

KWAN MAN BUN holds a Ph.D. in history from Stanford University. Before joining the department of history at the University of Cincinnati, where he is currently an associate professor, he taught for two years as a visiting lecturer in the department of history, Nankai University. He has published articles on Chinese economic, urban, legal, and business history, as well as an earlier version of *The Salt Merchants of Tianjin* in Chinese (Tianjin People's Press, 1999).

«Today two things seem to be modern: the analysis of life and the flight from life... One practices anatomy of the inner life of one's mind, or one dreams. Reflection or fantasy, mirror image of dream image... Modern is the dissection of a mood, a sigh, a scruple, and modern is the instinctive, almost sonambulestic surrender to every revelation of beatuy, to a harmony of colours, to a glittering metaphor, to a wondrous allegory.»

(Hugo von Hoffmansthal, 1893.)

# ADVERTENCIAS

El conjunto de este libro forma parte de varios años de lectura y reflexión sobre la obra de Valle-Inclán, y mis primeras incursiones sobre el tema de fin de siglo desde 1970. Páginas preliminares se han leído en conferencias (1985, 1986, 1987) y versiones primarias han ido apareciendo. En cuanto totalidad, responde a un estudio dialógico sobre «teorías de la modernidad» dividido en otras secciones (libros): Rubén Darío, Unamuno, y uno teórico sobre el «modernismo» y lo que llamo lo «imaginario social» como signo cultural de la modernidad, todos en vía de publicación. Asimismo una serie de trabajos sobre M. Bajtin y el pensamiento dialógico.

Quiero aprovechar para agradecer la generosidad de varias personas: Emma Susana Speratti Piñero, con quien durante años dialogué telefónicamente sobre Valle; Roberta Salper, que me dejó buena cantidad de textos publicados en periódicos; Jesús Rubio Jiménez, que me ha enviado fotocopias y material relacionado con el teatro finisecular; Eliane y Jean-Marie Lavaud, que me proporcionaron las publicaciones de la Universidad de Dijon. A todos, mi agradecimiento.

# LA PANTALLA TEORICA

Durante el curso de mi trabajo en literaturas hispánicas e historia de las ideas he comprobado la falta de una labor sistemática sobre cuestiones teóricas centradas en estas literaturas. Con frecuencia se acude a la práctica de la crítica para ilustrar principios generales, a despecho de las fértiles contribuciones que podrían derivarse de los nuevos caminos metodológicos que ofrecen la lingüística y la semiótica. El énfasis en el mensaje, la tendencia a considerar la literatura en términos de ideas políticas o de una estilística estrecha, ha sido una característica saliente de los estudios literarios hispánicos durante algún tiempo. Esto es particularmente notable en el caso de Valle-Inclán, no sólo en cuanto a la crítica decididamente ideológica de sus tendencias políticas biográficas —carlista, socialista—, sino también por lo que respecta al escrito formalismo con que a menudo se ha visto su obra: ambos son acercamientos externos, que por suerte van envejeciendo. Abundan los productos típicos de estas falacias metodológicas: los más difundidos son los que ven en sus textos una manifestación del pensamiento social y están peligrosamente cercanos a reducirlos a documentos históricos o material subsidiario para disciplinas afines.

Tenemos a nuestra disposición los recientes desarrollos en la lingüística, la crítica de la respuesta del lector *(reader-response)*, la estética de la comunicación y la semiótica, que merecen mayor atención, ya que abren nuevos caminos de análisis. Algunas de estas innovadoras propuestas postestructuralistas que sugieren claramente nuevas lecturas textuales son de especial interés para emprender una re-lectura de Valle. El tradicional concepto de «estilo» ha sido cuestionado y la relación entre «voces» en los textos —un concepto difundido en los escritos del círculo crítico fundado por Mikhail Bajtin a fines de la década de 1920-1930— propone precisamente nuevos modos de interpretación. Existe una profunda afinidad entre algunos conceptos de Bajtin y el proyecto sistemático de Valle, que abre sorprendentes posibilidades de análisis: *dialogía, carnavalización, enunciado, entonación, estilización, sátira, parodia.*

A estos conceptos quisiera añadir aquellos de *representación, espejo, mimesis, ideología y lo que llamo lo «imaginario social».* Todo ello está íntimamente ligado a los problemas de referencialidad y representación en los textos literarios. En nuestro caso en particular, las propuestas discursivas «modernas» de Valle-Inclán. Comencemos por lo central: hablamos en realidad de nuevas formaciones discursivas (en el sentido que Foucault le da a este término) para representar la «modernidad», lo «moderno», y de un nuevo sujeto social. Aludo, pues, a modelos referenciales que —en el caso específico de Valle— ilustran con mayor convicción la ideología (plural) y el sistema político dominante de intercambio que sustenta el modelo de representar la realidad. En palabras de Louis Marin sobre la ideología:

> L'idéologie [est] une philosophie moyenne des idées-représentation mais, aussi d'une représentation spéculaire et médiée des autres circuits d'échanges (Marin, 1975: 59).

Ideología, espejo, duplicación. No muy otra es la definición clásica de Althusser: la dialéctica entre la represión externa y la sujeción interna («ideología»). Esta se «representa» como un tipo de lenguaje y su realidad interna y, además, como una fuerza alternativa de revertir e invertir las estructuras de poder, los de explotación y los de la ley o leyes como «espejos» que se reflejan mutuamente, dialécticamente, en su realidad y su contrario. Es decir, para Althusser, la «ideología» es «la forma de "representación" de una relación imaginaria o imaginada entre el individuo y sus condiciones reales de existencia». En definitiva: la ideología como una estructura «narrativa» que articula la representación ideológica (1971: 162), noción que retoma Fredric Jameson en fecha más reciente. Comenzamos, pues, por recuperar el significado y la designación materialista de la metáfora del «espejo» en teoría del conocimiento.

Guiada por este motivo, he intentado concretar algunos de los enfoques críticos de manera muy ecléctica y, a partir de

**10**

una poética social, he formulado algunas propuestas para volver a examinar las obras de Valle-Inclán, como textos individuales y como obra de conjunto o «texto único». Si aceptamos que —sin tener en cuenta el género— sus obras (in)completas tienen una estructura total análoga a la de un «texto único», la cuestión de la unidad —debida a una diferente concepción del sentido y naturaleza de la textualidad— no debería ser más motivo de discusión académica. Artículos, cuentos, *Femeninas* o las *Sonatas,* o asimismo textos tempranos anteriores a 1913-1914, no son un proyecto de organismos separados: la obra de Valle se empobrecería terriblemente con ese corte. Toda su producción textual forma un sistema artístico de violaciones, desconexiones y transgresiones de reglas y normas muy específico. En particular, las convenciones y prohibiciones que gobiernan la selección de las palabras y la construcción de metáforas, la memoria del género (término de Bajtin), las posibilidades de tramas estrictamente definidas, clisés, modelos, convenciones para la reproducción del diálogo o del discurso dialectal. El esfuerzo del escritor para destruir un sistema de reglas familiares puede ser percibido como un rechazo de normas estructurales previas, basado en oposiciones o polémica y la búsqueda de un lenguaje deforme o creativamente desviado, que problematiza la relación del sujeto con la sociedad. El texto se convierte así en una forma articulada de una *representación* de lo *imaginario social* (concepto que propongo a partir de la definición de Althusser sobre «ideología» y la de Voloshinov/Bajtin de la conciencia como signo social) [1].

---

[1] Está claro que por «imaginario social» entiendo una forma de «representación» de la realidad, desde el punto de vista de una concepción del sujeto social semiótico y, como éste, refracta la ideología. Es decir, un grupo que se imagina solidario de sus propios valores y coherente con su proyecto colectivo, definición que adapto de manera «inversa» a partir de Baudrillard (1984: 79), en una deconstrucción de la relación que allí establece entre «lo imaginado» y «lo social», como imposibilidades. Por otra parte, adapto —en otro sentido— su idea del «espejo de la producción» (1983): es decir, lo invierto y tomo el texto (la producción literaria) como forma de hacer reconocer objetivamente las ideologías. Elaboro más detenidamente este concepto en *Rubén Darío, bajo el signo del cisne* (en prensa), en el capítulo «Lo imaginario social: el signo cultural del cisne». Véase también mi «The Social Imaginary: the Cultural Sign of Hispanic Modernism» (1987), *Critical Studies* 1: 1 (1989), 23-41. Ya escritas estas páginas, encuentro una noción de «imaginario social» en sentido análogo, pero no igual, en Beverley (1987), y desde luego la mía se asemeja más a la de Castoriadis (1985), desde la óptica de la filosofía política.

Me he ceñido a los experimentos técnicos con la estructura y la perspectiva que considero más importantes para delinear las siguientes posibilidades:

1. Valle-Inclán no elige un lenguaje delimitado —los lenguajes de la poesía, la prosa, el teatro, los lenguajes de los diversos géneros—, sino que supera esta limitación dentro de la corriente literaria conocida tradicionalmente como *Modernismo*. Son textos sin inscripción genérica y pertenece(n) simultáneamente a dos o más lenguajes o códigos que activan recursos metafóricos y metonímicos, que establecen un orden y lo violan. Esta estructura profunda de sentido se puede aprehender solamente por medio de un complejo acto de decodificación.

2. Pluralidad intencional de estilos y voces, sin unidad estilística; mezcla de lo cómico y lo serio; multiplicidad de tonos; mezcla de lo sublime y lo vulgar, lo que Bajtin llama la literatura «carnavalizada» de *relativité joyeuse*. Los textos están compuestos a partir de múltiples relaciones entretejidas: cartas, manuscritos, material histórico y sociológico, diálogos, parodia de géneros y estilos reconocidos como clásicos, caricatura y parodia de citas, paráfrasis, mezcla de prosa y verso, bilingüismo o poliglosia, falta de orden cronológico o forma lineal, ausencia de la oración que sintetiza la acción u oración sinóptica.

3. La decisión de demarcar lenguajes y códigos —tradición oral y popular (*aleluyas*, romances de cordel, proverbios, anuncios, titulares, artículos de periódicos)— permite una red compacta de subtextos sociales entretejida en la estructura como información referencial. Hay también un uso decidido de una red intertextual de material pictórico y musical en un sistema de inscripción intersemiótico, a tal extremo que a veces incorpora el acto de lenguaje en la escritura, obligando a sus lectores a «leer» o decodificar el signo inscrito: sirvan de ejemplo los signos pictográficos que inscribe como «voz» en *La pipa de kif:* leer se convierte en un arte.

Estos recursos técnicos estructurales o modos de «representación» de la realidad conducen inevitablemente a la destrucción de la épica y la tragedia, ya que el mundo está al revés. Se inicia con un universo de pactos y promesas (desde el pacto autobiográfico del marqués de Bradomín, a los pactos y juramentos señoriales de Montenegro) y desemboca en el mundo de pactos y promesas no cumplidas desde la Revolución de 1868 en adelante [2]. El espejo revela, por un lado, el rasgo misterioso e irónico de la duplicación seductora, y luego los pactos violados, los actos performativos en caricatura, e introduce entonces el despedazamiento carnavalesco.

Valle cala hondo en impropiedades, profanidades, excentricidades, risa, licencia para abolir jerarquías y degradar imágenes consagradas mediante la acentuación de lo grotesco y lo aparentemente trivial. Este juego está sometido a las reglas de una creativa destrucción y reconstrucción del lenguaje de los géneros clásicos, fundado sobre una tradición rica en el juego verbal, equivalente, por ejemplo, a la de James Joyce y Beckett.

Debido a sus notables implicaciones para el estudio de textos literarios, algunos procedimientos metodológicos recientes —los de Austin sobre actos performativos, la teoría crítica de la Escuela de Frankfurt, la deconstrucción, el concepto moderno de parodia y sátira, y en particular los derivados de las ideas de Bajtin/Voloshinov/Medvedev— pueden servir de base adecuada para examinar la obra de Valle-Inclán como un todo. Las citadas estrategias estructurales o rasgos constituyentes pueden ser estudiados de acuerdo a varias posibilidades, todas bajtinianas de origen y objeto, en el marco del texto como actividad social. En cuanto texto único —es decir, continuidad textual— propongo que la poética valleinclanesca está ligada a cuatro grandes categorías y métodos:

1. poética moderna o modernista: la carnavalización como «representación» de *lo imaginario social* en un juego especular de posiciones de sujeto (posición geométrica);
2. heteroglosia o incorporación de lenguajes y de lenguas;
3. liberación del poder o la autoridad de las palabras, subversión imprescindible para la libertad del lenguaje, que niega el monologismo y se opone al mito de un lenguaje único. Del lenguaje arcaico y rural pasa al «carnavalizado» citadino;

---

[2] Las nociones de «autobiografía y «memorias» son semejantes, pero no idénticas (May, 1979). En todo caso, en ambos discursos la estrategia es la de un yo que se contempla. En Valle, además, existe «a chronic tendency to treat himself as a character», observación de Victor Brombert (1968) sobre Stendhal. Volveremos sobre el género de memorias.

4. el recorrido de la estilización, la ironía y la parodia, entendidas desde un punto de vista contemporáneo [3].

La estructura invita a la alteridad que puebla todo significado;
el virtuosismo, el sentido de obra no acabada (abierta) siempre en borrador —nuevas versiones de personajes, situaciones,
temas— y la inscripción del habla (lo hablado, la oralidad),
permiten la superación de los lenguajes exclusivos, destronan-
do los géneros, en una crisis de la normatividad.

La concepción bajtiniana del enunciado como acto de naturaleza social más que individual (signo ideológico; 1928 en
1984; 1929 en 1983), así como su insistencia en la polifonía,
la heteroglosia y la poliglosia apuntan a establecer la interacción de una diversidad de lenguajes (extranjero, social, nacional). Estos conceptos son pertinentes para comprender la
dirección social de sus estrategias. En este sentido hemos de
señalar la importancia que cobra el tiempo. Los personajes
que pueblan el mundo valleinclanesco son profundamente históricos y revelan la marca definitiva del tiempo desde el
ángulo de refracción particular donde están impresas las tra-
zas de la época. La comprensión de Valle de estas fuerzas de
desarrollo histórico, tanto progresivas como reaccionarias,
está representada por tensiones que se materializan en extra-
ordinarias deformidades y perversiones.

A partir de este entramado de estrategias textuales y de
refractaciones y lenguajes, Valle apuntó a la destrucción de
todos los pre-conceptos falsos que habían distorsionado y se-
parado verdades históricas. Todas estas armoniosas estructuras
que he esbozado tan someramente dependen de las series rabe-
lesians introducidas con virtuosismo verbal. La obra de Valle,
su «texto único» —tanto prosa como poesía, tanto novela
como drama—, se inserta en la tradición de la literatura carnavalizada. El concepto contemporáneo de «texto único» a su
vez permite reconsiderar su producción textual a partir de
tres registros: la estructura dinámica, enriquecida por toda la
gama de textualidad que apunta Genette (1979, 1982), invita
a la alteridad que puebla todo significado; ningún texto o per-

_____

[3] Son pertinentes las observaciones de Hutcheon (1985) sobre la
parodia postmoderna, que retomo más adelante. Véase también a
Rose (1979), para quien la parodia moderna tiene una estructura auto-
referencial. Finlay (1988) ofrece interesantes hipótesis para distinguir
entre la ironía retórica, la alemana romántica y la moderna.

14

sonaje o situación es «cerrado», cada producción incorpora y asimila la anterior: personajes, situaciones, léxico, estrategias, discursos, unidades temáticas, cambios de título; la noción de un texto en «borrador», en suspenso siempre, para que no concluya.

La transtextualidad de su escritura tiene el aspecto de obedecer a esta regla de desdoblamiento, repeticiones y deslizamientos progresivos, en una superación de los lenguajes exclusivos, la destrucción de los géneros y crisis y ruptura de la normatividad. Su virtuosidad libresca y de estilo es una estrategia textual que apunta ante todo a destruir la jerarquía de valores establecida. Valle aspiraba a rebajar la autoridad y a elevar lo no oficial, lo marginal, a destruir la vieja y habitual pintura de un mundo que se había formado en el pasado y había sido sublimado en el culto religioso, la historia oficial y las prestigiosas categorías tradicionales y géneros de la literatura y otras formas de «representación» ideológicas. Intentó comprender y retratar falsedades y convenciones y ponerlas en descubierto, tal como eran. La extraordinaria fuerza de sus textos, su radicalismo —tanto estético como ideológico— se explica predominantemente por su enraigada carnavalización, por su conexión con realidades fundamentales. Apuntó a la destrucción de preconceptos falsos, verbal e ideológicamente, separando especularmente verdades históricas y mecanismos míticos o productores de mitos. La más importante fuente de carnavalización en Valle fue el lado no oficial del habla, de la historia, de las instituciones, de los individuos. Lo que pone en tela de juicio, deconstruye y desmitifica es una noción «oficial» del sujeto (lo español, la patria, la religión, la verdad), y representa la alteridad, lo otro, a veces lo heterogéneo[4]. Desmonta la realidad que el sujeto percibe y el lenguaje que media entre el sujeto y la realidad, a través de

---

[4] Valle desarrolla una «deconstrucción» en el sentido actual del término a partir de J. Derrida. Es decir: «For deconstruction irony is not a trope [...] but the systematic undoing [...] of understanding» (Harold Bloom, 1987: 4). Las semejanzas entre Valle y algunos «ideologemas» de la postmodernidad no debieran impedir que distingamos entre el proyecto político de modernidad de Valle con los textos culturales de las sociedades postindustriales. Jean-Marie Lavaud (1986, 1987) explica con claridad las deconstrucciones valleinclanescas con personajes y acontecimientos históricos, y E. Lavaud (1986) la deconstrucción del mito donjuanesco. Consúltense los interesantes números de *Hispanística XX*, 1986 y 1987. Salper (1988) ha llevado a cabo una excelente división de la obra valleinclanesca a partir de personajes recurrentes.

15

representaciones ideológicas de lo imaginario; narrativas que renarrativizan la realidad. Representa todo aquello aceptado como «oficial», y que al convertirse en clisé inamovible, ya estancado, no era creativo.

Partiremos, pues, de un análisis de la enunciación de una poética moderna y su práctica semiótica, para analizar luego los diversos proyectos de «representación» carnavalesca y especular de Valle, y cómo éstos se van articulando en su producción textual. Propongo analizar sus textos desde la perspectiva de un conjunto de *prácticas textuales,* un ejercicio de incredulidad en un todo orgánico dentro de un proceso de producción, que origina un proceso de recepción y de uso o de práctica, en el interior de su sistema de comunicación y de interacción (me apoyo en la definición de van Dijk sobre «Texte», 1984: 281). Desde este sistema semiótico se define la norma y la transgresión de la norma. Finalmente, situaré el proyecto moderno y el discurso cultural emancipatorio valle-inclanesco como un movimiento entre la ironía romántica, entendida ésta como una forma de relativizar los significados y los valores y la parodia y la sátira (incorporo la definición de Finlay, 1988). Estas estrategias le permiten desmontar los ejercicios de poder; Valle examina el «poder» —institucional, personal, de la tradición— en sutiles relaciones con experiencias y saberes y sus paradigmas de representación, a partir de una «pragmática» especular intensiva (término de Eco, 1988).

El «texto único» valleinclanesco es una puesta en escena de imágenes especulares para crear ilusiones de realidad; la metáfora de espejo le permite establecer el entramado de relaciones sociales en repeticiones, plagios, citas, parodias, reposiciones irónicas, juegos intertextuales. Todo lo incorpora, desde la musa popular al procedimiento serial para poner al receptor/auditor en crisis consigo mismo y con la tradición. Valle establece pactos con el receptor crítico a lo largo de un *continuum* (como diría Walter Benjamin) de interrogaciones y soluciones. La metáfora especular —«adecuación» para Bajtin, «totalidad» para Lukács, «homología» para Goldmann, «campo» para Pierre Bourdieu— está en el centro mismo de su composición y recomposición, innovación y repetición de «representaciones». Espejo que «refleja» y sistemáticamente des-refleja o distorsiona: achica, aleja, cuanto es «el bien, la verdad, la belleza», y magnifica la fealdad y la maldad. A veces una misma situación, un mismo personaje, pasan por espejos opuestos. Valle es a manera del demiurgo o demonio

16

del espejo «fantástico» del cuento de Hans Christian Andersen «The Snow Queen» (Blanca Nieves), que magnifica o achica algunos aspectos de la realidad, o distorsiona otros por completo [5]. Su juego especular es pragmático, en prótesis magnificante o reductora. Lo sagrado y lo profano adquieren realidad especular en la atmósfera de la ironía y la burla. Su proyecto moderno, además, dialoga con un nuevo público lector en interrogación crítica, proponiendo y legitimando un moderno «relato» o «gran narrativa» de la historia de España [6]. Sus espejos revelan los procedimiento de exclusión, los juegos de «poder», los tabús, los ritos de lo prohibido. Pone al descubierto lo que Foucault llama «el orden del discurso»:

> Tabou de l'objet, rituel de la circonstance, droit privilégié ou exclusif du sujet qui parle: ... ce sont les régions de la sexualité et celles de la politique! (1970: 11).

Su discurso cultural es una invitación para que, como Alicia, entremos en los espejos y vivamos esas imágenes virtuales como si fueran reales; porque son «reales».

---

[5] Consúltese el excelente artículo «Mirrors, Frames, and Demons: Reflections on the Sociology of Literature» (1988), de Priscilla Parkhurst Ferguson, Philippe Desan, Wendy Griswold, donde se alude —en otro contexto— al cuento de Andersen. Véase asimismo Eco (1988) y su análisis de los espejos.

[6] Ya que la bibliografía valleinclanesca es abundantísima, sólo remito a *aquellos* trabajos que están estrechamente vinculados a mi objetivo de presentar la obra de Valle como legitimadora de una nueva «narrativa». En pruebas este libro, han salido los siguientes artículos míos: «Práctica semiótica en Valle-Inclán», *NRFH XXXVI* (1988), 417-432; «Transgresiones e infracciones literarias y procesos intertextuales en Valle-Inclán». En Clara L. Barbeito, ed., *Valle-Inclán. Nueva valoración de su obra,* Barcelona: PPPU, 1988, 153-167.

17

Capítulo I

# LA POETICA MODERNA

«Si en la literatura de hoy existe algo nuevo
que pueda recibir con justicia el nombre de
modernismo, es ciertamente un vivo anhelo de
personalidad.»

(Valle-Inclán, 1902.)

«For the origin of historical culture, and of
its absolutely radical antagonism to the spirit
of a new time and a "modern consciousness"
must itself be known by a historical process.»

(Nietzsche, *The Use and Abuse of History*.)

## 1. LA MODERNIDAD/EL MODERNISMO

¿Estaría el fin de siglo hispánico —esa *belle époque*
europea— enamorado de sí mismo? Es decir, enamorado del
presente, en irónica frase de Nietzsche para definir lo que
se podría llamar *modernismo*. El aforismo de *La gaya ciencia*,
escrito entre 1881-1882, merece citarse por extenso:

A *los enamorados de lo presente*.—El cura que colgó
los hábitos y el presidiario cumplido quieren hacerse
un nuevo semblante; necesitan una cara sin pasado.
Pero ¿no habéis tropezado con hombres en cuyo rostro se refleja lo porvenir y que son lo bastante corte-
ses para con vosotros, los enamorados de la época
actual, para componerse un semblante sin porvenir?
(1984: 129).

¿Tendría conciencia de su evocación y necesidad cosmopolita de viajeros indefatigables de arrojo temerario? El análisis irónico surge de las reflexiones de otro moderno —Carlos Marx—, que en el *Manifesto comunista* (eds. 1872, 1888) escribe:

> con el mercado mundial aparece una literatura universal [con la] explotación del mercado mundial, la burguesía dio un carácter cosmopolita a la producción y al consumo de todos los países, se quitó a la industria su base nacional [...] Y esto se refiere tanto a la producción material, como a la producción intelectual. La producción intelectual de una nación se convierte en patrimonio común de todas. [...] La burguesía arrastra a la corriente de la civilización a todas las naciones, hasta a las más bárbaras (1965: 65).

Ambos testimonios de modernos —tan distintos— tienen rasgos en común; en particular la posición irónica del sujeto en su análisis de los indicios de un advenimiento de una época: el proceso de la modernidad y su discurso cultural.

De fecha mucho más reciente —en nuestra contemporaneidad—, la posición del sujeto es menos irónica, y apoya justamente la postura que Nietzsche burla. Citemos a Paul de Man:

> Modernity exists in the form of a desire to wipe out whatever came earlier, in the hope of reaching at last a point that could be called a true present, a point of origin that marks a new departure (1983: 143).

En parte, eso fue lo que se propusieron algunos modernistas desde finales del siglo XIX; no como un nuevo texto que nadie ha escrito, y que sólo se lee a sí mismo. La producción cultural de este período se caracteriza por la necesidad de crear un sentido de final, una forma de negatividad parcial; una lengua del *no* ante lo utilitario y mercantil. Sin duda que, matizada y recontextualizada, esta articulación de la realidad es el fundamento de los modernismos hispánicos, enraizado cada cual en proyectos emancipatorios afines dentro de una pluralidad cultural y política con objetivos semejantes: la legitimación de un proyecto colectivo, la creación de un «nuevo relato» o «narrativa», y un nuevo discurso cultural con su

20

nota constante de meditación sobre el poder absóluto. Este discurso cultural se constituye como integraciones históricas del pasado con anticipaciones correlativas al futuro de los pueblos, naciones o comunidades, que funcionan como ejes de integración social y de legitimación política. La práctica literaria mantiene un diálogo estrecho con las formaciones sociales que se inscriben textualmente, y el discurso emerge en línea de ruptura con el pasado como parte integrante del proceso de modernización y reflexiones críticas sobre la violencia y el poder. Esta liberación se justifica como un nuevo «asalto a la razón», y en su totalidad revela sus contradicciones más intensas hacia 1914, a raíz de la primera guerra mundial.

Desatiendo la definición habitual del modernismo (historia contada muchas veces), y me atengo a la noción que lo conecta con el discurso del proceso tecnológico de la modernidad o modernización. Entiendo este proceso en un sentido amplio; por tanto, la modernidad no es ni normativa, ni prescriptiva, ni «globalizadora» en su «representación» de los proyectos culturales (y sociopolíticos) de fin de siglo. En realidad, este concepto —moderno, modernismo, modernidad— es una categoría histórica y proyecto aún inacabado, con sus tonos distintos y diferencias decisivas sincrónicas y diacrónicas. A reserva de repetirme, sería inexacto identificar mi propuesta de un proceso moderno aún vigente con un puro ejercicio mental o nostalgia por el pasado. En conjunto, parto de un análisis discursivo para articular el proyecto valleinclanesco moderno y su continuado esfuerzo por «representar» dialógicamente las contradicciones y fracasos de la cultura española desde la coyuntura histórica de la década de 1890: las costumbres duraderas, las reputaciones fijas, el instinto del rebaño, los predicadores de moral, los ejercicios de cálculo, las mentiras institucionales. Son estas desconfianzas los indicios del advenimiento de una época, y los hombres nuevos precursores de un porvenir todavía no demostrado (que diría Nietzsche). Esta moral de la desconfianza, de sobreponerse al pasado y sus formas fijas, implica en Valle una actividad crítica basada en una práctica constante de la «estilización» a la parodia, y en el «extrañamiento» carnavalesco, forma de representación de la actualidad, del ahora. En esta práctica textual de casi medio siglo (1888-1936), Valle concretiza la «heroización irónica» del presente, que marca para Foucault la modernidad de Baudelaire (1984: 39-42), hasta afinar hacia 1913-1914 una «posición geométrica» en simultaneidades sociales, que le permite refractar la historia de España desde una posición de sujeto crítico. Su producción textual revela una interrogación crítica de las relaciones de poder, de violencia institucional, que va intensificando. El «texto único» valleinclanesco (a contracorriente siempre) representa un sumario selectivo de la modernidad desde sus primicias finiseculares. (Ejemplo análogo el de Unamuno, desde objetivos afines, pero con prácticas textuales distintas.)

Comencemos con un brevísimo recorrido de la modernidad como marco de referencia. En las literaturas occidentales, en general, se ha periodizado en tres generaciones: precursores, fundadores y creadores, con el quiebre fundamental de la primera guerra mundial (Wohl, 1986). Pero, tomado en conjunto, el proyecto moderno —que incorpora desde Baudelaire a Brecht, y las vanguardias sucesivas, representado por Ezra Pound, T. S. Eliot, Yeats, Thomas Mann, James Joyce, D. H. Lawrence, Mallarmé, Proust, Mayakovsky, Kafka, Musil, Wallace Stevens, Pirandello, entre los nombres reconocidos (Poggioli, 1962; Bradbury, McFarlane, 1978)— surge en Europa como resultado de una gran crisis histórica, que se puede fechar hacia mediados del siglo XIX, y, en lo que al mundo hispánico se refiere, se cristaliza, sobre todo en la coyuntura de 1898. Cabe pensar (y los textos finiseculares parecen sugerirlo) unas tentativas e ideología en común —incluso en sus divergencias—, en el proceso del modernismo (la periodización más difundida es entre 1890-1930, pero en el mundo hispánico, donde la crisis era más aguda debido a la coyuntura final de las guerras coloniales, la cronología podría ser distinta: 1880-1936). En su primera etapa, en el mundo finisecular europeo, se desarrolla como un intento deliberado de reacción y resistencia contra la tradición normativa, una ruptura con el pasado, desconfianza en el liberalismo, y la base moral de un futuro diferente.

Desde su inscripción inicial, este discurso cultural dialoga con el movimiento internacional obrero (la I Internacional), que se inicia en la década de 1860, y desde el principio incorpora buena parte de la conciencia intelectual europea (para comenzar los dirigentes, Marx, Engels, Bakunin), entregada a una filosofía del progreso y de justicia social. La vinculación entre intelectuales y movimiento obrero se abre paso en Francia con la Comuna (1871), y luego en la *belle époque* (1880-1900), cuando se produce una mayor concentración de «internacionalistas», en particular rusos (Kropotkin, Vera Zasulich).

22

Los experimentos del lenguaje de los simbolistas (entre otros grupos de radicales), en súbita explosión de intimidad, se alían a las causas revolucionarias: la *bombe esthétique* a que alude la famosa revista *Le Chat-Noir*. Este sello revolucionario se encuentra en el anti-burguesísimo *Mes prisons* (1893) de Verlaine, y en cafés y clubs nocturnos se oían hiperbólicos elogios de los atentados anarquistas ocurridos en Francia en 1892 (véase Zavala, 1977). No debemos hoy minimizar este contagio; el turbión de fin de siglo hermana Literatura y Revolución y entre malabarismos verbales, filigranas sensoriales y refinamientos aparece siempre las lecturas de Kropotkin, Malato, Bakunin, Max Stirner. Volveremos sobre ello.

La importancia del modernismo implica no sólo conquistas de expresión, sino un nuevo discurso cultural entre 1880-1900, que en el mundo hispánico irradió un centro magnético anti-imperialista y anti-militarista, y una voluntad estética profana e innovadora que originó soluciones diversas y apreciables. Ni la abstención política ni la indiferencia moral; estas posiciones de sujeto son la nota distintiva de grupos aparentemente en conflicto: noventaiochistas, simbolistas, decadentes, anarquistas literarios, bohemia revolucionaria (no la hedonista de Henri Murger); los «jóvenes», «gente nueva» de espíritu nuevo. Todos postulan el presente vivo y un futuro revolucionario siempre cambiante; el término *moderno* no tiene naturaleza; tiene historia, parafraseando a Dilthey. Esta acción conjunta finisecular —aún en sus diferencias— significa una postura afirmativa hacia la modernidad social y negativa ante la tradición anquilosada. Dentro de la poética histórica que propongo para situar el modernismo, en el mundo hispánico apenas es necesario recordar a sus precursores y fundadores en Cuba, Centroamérica y Suramérica, a raíz de la guerra de Cuba (1868-1878), fechas en que coinciden el radicalismo político y la nueva estética. Esta modernidad histórica se constituye en formas de producción y conceptos críticos en algunos núcleos peninsulares (de ellos los catalanes sin duda son «avanzados»).

Con cisnes, con mitos, princesas, voluptuosidad y jardines, las posiciones del sujeto (emisor, autor) nos ofrecen una imagen diferente del mundo, que renueva las experiencias; están socialmente orientadas con el propósito de legitimar su propio «relato» de emancipación política, intelectual y social. Esta re-narrativación emancipadora se afirma a su vez contra la «narrativa» de lo material y de la riqueza (el capitalismo, el imperialismo) y contra la exclusión (la represión cultural y social, la represión del movimiento obrero, por ejemplo). Las palabras darianas, muy adecuadas para designar el modernismo y sus tendencias en 1898 merecen recordarse: «Ese espíritu nuevo que hoy anima a un pequeño pero triunfante y soberbio grupo de escritores y poetas de la América española: el modernismo.» Durante su extensa y prolongada actividad crítica a la España del desastre no cesa de reiterar la nota distintiva y la filosofía del progreso de los poetas hispanoamericanos y las razones de esta voluntad de ser modernos:

> En América hemos tenido ese movimiento [el modernismo] antes que en España castellana, por razones clarísimas: desde luego por nuestro inmediato comercio material y espiritual con las distintas naciones del mundo, y principalmente porque existe en la nueva generación americana un inmenso deseo de progreso y un vivo entusiasmo, que constituye su potencialidad mayor, con lo cual poco a poco va triunfando de obstáculos tradicionales, murallas de indiferencia y océanos de mediocridad (*España contemporánea*, 1901; *OC* III: 300-7).

La definición de Darío es más bien sumaria y selectiva, y justo es tomar en cuenta este meritorio comienzo para evitar los tópicos de denominar a los «modernistas» finiseculares (sobre todo los americanos) como una especie de simbolistas «menores» o de «galicistas mentales». (Desde 1885-1886 el circunspecto Clarín ironizaba y minusvaloraba a los «naturalistas» de moda —que él llamaba «los grafómanos»— porque dividían sus capítulos en números romanos.) El modernismo surgió a contracorriente, y las palabras de Darío —a las que podríamos sumar otros testimonios contemporáneos (José Enrique Rodó, Horacio Quiroga, Amado Nervo, Jacinto Benavente, Santiago Rusiñol, Federico Urales)— revelan que en sus comienzos la noción de «moderno» afirma nuevas formaciones sociales y nuevos mecanismos directivos del mundo vital (incluso si remontamos la «modernidad» al siglo XVI, y su «querella entre antiguos y modernos»). No dice otra cosa este ideal que se impuso definitivamente desde las estéticas del Romanticismo hasta las posiciones de los modernos y las vanguardias de este siglo. De un modo restrictivo, Northrop Frye y Harold Bloom sostienen que el «modernismo» es en realidad un post-romanticismo camuflado, y Levin (1960) flexibiliza

24

el término para incluir toda «novedad». Hoy día es frecuente entre los nuevos-conservadores de la postmodernidad aludir al agotamiento de la modernidad cultural, en tesis menos que convincentes: la proclamación de lo postmoderno, que implica que el arte vanguardista (moderno) agotó su imaginación creadora y es improductivo.

Si bien la modernidad no se inicia como movimiento concertado en la década de 1880, durante este fin de siglo hispánico, asistimos a una amplia contaminación entre intelectuales de diferentes países, regiones y culturas para ajustarle cuentas a la moral «burguesa» en desarrollo de estrategias, de formas y de «representaciones». No tardan en reconocerse después de 1898. Las tendencias se concentran con la intención de abrir camino en nuevos territorios de la vida personal y social como órdenes inseparables. Interesa una nueva sensibilidad, que se concentra en el poder subversivo de la conciencia. Al cubano José Martí debemos en fecha tan temprana como 1882 un texto revelador que inscribe la nueva estética moderna: su prólogo al «Poema del Niágara», del venezolano José Pérez Bonalde, integra la naturaleza y el mundo interior, a una nueva percepción de la realidad y de la experiencia del yo (Zavala, 1987, 1988). El discurso poético afirma una concepción más democrática del mundo, mediante la formación de nuevos significados. Se legitima así la ruptura cultural y el clima de opinión de las nuevas sociedades modernas, que habían sustituido las coloniales formas de riqueza e intercambio de manera inversa: la definitiva mutación cualitativa en Hispanoamérica de sociedades no «coloniales». En España es decisiva esta modernidad en la concentración de la energía hacia condiciones más dignas, más conformes con un sentido más auténtico de la libertad (aún en sus contradicciones). En cuanto ruptura, en estas primicias finiseculares deriva del proceso de modernización y socialización; se trata, en definitiva, de una re-escritura de la historia y de un nuevo «relato» o «narración». De un extremo al otro este proyecto apunta a un reajuste de la historia. Obsérvese, sin embargo, que en la re-escritura de esta narrativa el soplo que se levanta desde América es voz de alerta contra los «yanquis», en postura desafiante. Darío, en su viaje a España de 1899, tiende el puente accesible para complementar las tendencias de la época. Ya en 1912, en su magnífico ensayo sobre Valle-Inclán, corrobora el espíritu de modernidad y lo aleja de escuelas y modas; éste fue

La demostración —en los primeros momentos, de nuestra lucha hispanoamericana por representarnos ante el mundo como concurrentes a una idea universal (Idea no Moda)— que comenzaba a llenar de una nueva ilusión, o realización de belleza, todo lo que entonces pensaba altamente en la tierra. En ello hay el anhelo de la novedad —y la antigüedad— que caracterizó a los Nuevos. Que mañana seremos Viejos (*A todo vuelo*, 1912; *OC* II: 787-795).

Si hemos de creerle, la historia del modernismo es más o menos coincidente en el mundo hispánico (teoría defendida por Onís y Juan Ramón originariamente), y resulta innecesario establecer diferencias tajantes (punto de polémica incluso hoy día [1]), pues por caminos distintos se llega a afirmaciones afines. Concebir el fin de siglo moderno como distancias es negarlo como puente en el pensamiento de la modernidad que desde entonces reafirma la estrecha relación entre el ser humano y la historia. Este problema de método que hoy por hoy se puede enriquecer a partir de la brecha abierta por Harry Levin

---

[1] Me parece evidente que incorporo el «modernismo» hispánico al proceso de modernización occidental. No establezco las distinciones —nada estables— de Bürger (1984) entre vanguardia y modernismo. Me parecen más pertinentes las observaciones de Poggioli (1962), que flexibiliza los términos y sugiere que la llamada «vanguardia» es un desarrollo del «modernismo» después de 1914, que legitima la postura moderna de ruptura cultural. En todo caso, lo que podemos comprobar es un clima de opinión. Lo que sea «modernidad» sigue siendo tema de discusión: para algunos desde Kant, sin descontar la famosa querella del siglo XVI. Hoy día es central en las teorías sobre el progreso: el contraste más notable está representado entre los postestructuralistas y la teoría crítica marxista. En lo que al mundo hispánico se refiere, y retomando la génesis del modernismo, me parecen pertinentes sobre todo las inteligentes observaciones de Paz (1962 en 1983), que no sólo incorpora los «clásicos» de la crítica sobre el modernismo, sino que además integra el proyecto al conjunto europeo, y subraya el radicalismo político de buena parte de los fundadores del modernismo. Véase también, aunque desde otra perspectiva, Jitrik (1978), y la compilación de Litvak (1975, y también 1975 b), en un importante libro, con el cual discrepo en muchos puntos. Finalmente, Cacho Viu (1984, 1987), imprescindible para el modernismo catalán. En otras líneas remito a la reciente valoración de Allegra (1982), Picón Garfield/Schulman (1984), el debate en *Insula* (junio 1987) y en especial el artículo de Schulman que encabeza su última compilación de trabajos sobre modernismo (1987), de lectura obligadas. Cf. también Zavala [1974, 1977, 1987, 1987a, 1987 b (en prensa)]. Remito asimismo a los artículos recogidos en *Eutopías* III: I (1987): *La crisis de la literatura como institución en el siglo XIX*, Wlad Godzich, N. Spadaccini, eds.

(y otros) hace más de un cuarto de siglo, y a través de las precisiones de Poggioli (1962) y Bürger (1984). El «modernismo» comienza como una fuerza subversiva y expresión de una resistencia revolucionaria cultural contra la experiencia alienante de las sociedades modernas burguesas y la división de trabajo que transforma el arte en mercancía. El arte se problematiza, y la forma termina por ser el contenido de los textos (Bürger, 1984: 27). En adelante, y he ahí la contradicción, ese arte de resistencia se convierte finalmente en mercancía, producción de mercado (Jameson, 1975, 1979). El precio fue la pérdida de la dimensión política del proyecto histórico de emancipación. Quizá más certero, en lo que al mundo hispánico se refiere, este proyecto se transforma en institución cultural, no necesariamente en «industria cultural» (tomo la frase de Adorno). El pensamiento crítico inicial termina por institucionalizar la nueva literatura (Zavala, 1987).

Lo decisivo es que esta re-narrativación histórica moderna incorpora problemas de diversa índole: sociales, políticos, de «representación», de auto-representación y una historia somática del cuerpo y su función en la historia. Los nuevos «saberes» (en el sentido que le confiere Foucault a este término) y las genealogías apuntan a tres categorías cognitivas: la técnica, la práctica y la emancipadora. La técnica, en cuanto significa nuevos métodos críticos de análisis; práctica en cuanto significa nuevos métodos (en el sentido de la filosofía pragmática), formas de emplear estos conocimientos; emancipadora en cuanto permite ver el desarrollo o no desarrollo de nuevos potenciales de emancipación, de resistencia y de rechazo, o de analizar la realidad conceptual de la opresión y la realidad material de la opresión, ambas realidades sociales (me apoyo en Habermas, 1974). El potencial emancipatorio reside en este nuevo arte que resiste asimilarse a las funciones ideológicas y a las esferas de valores de la tradición y se concentra en revelar las condiciones de vida, las relaciones sociales y sus relaciones con la producción intelectual, y las fuerzas culturales (sociales) de dominio: instituciones, mitologías, comportamiento, en el marco conceptual de una teoría del lenguaje implícita en los textos martianos (el portugués Eugenio de Castro no le va a la zaga). Sólo desde esta perspectiva puede percibirse la significación cabal de esta modernidad.

El discurso se concentra en la afirmación de un sujeto social responsable, autónomo y libre, contra una existencia social inmovilizada y sujeta a las leyes de representación del «lenguaje dominante». Esta nueva retórica (o retóricas) incorpora, además, la función que la tecnología (en sus diversas etapas históricas) comenzó a desempeñar, y como las tecnologías alteran las representaciones culturales, las epistemologías, las relaciones de producción e incluso las estructuras del deseo. Se cruzan así varias disciplinas que nos replantean las relaciones de poder desde los proyectos colectivos y narrativas emancipadoras. Se afirma —y Martí es de los avanzados en esta línea de ruptura— una relación dialógica con el pasado, contra teorías de lo que llamaré *imperialismo textual* e *imaginación totalitaria*. Lo que va quedando claro a lo largo de estas «narrativas» es la noción de proyectos históricos, destinos colectivos y un nuevo sujeto de la historia mediante representaciones emancipatorias de lo *imaginario social*.

Esta lógica de producción cultural nos remite a la definición del «modernismo» «moderno», en el uso dariano —con esta acepción— fechado hacia 1888 (Mejía Sánchez, 1950). El término es de origen francés, y ya se empleaba con este significado desde el siglo XVI —«modernista», defensor de una interpretación progresiva de la marcha de los tiempos, según la nota a una traducción de Vitrubio (en manuscrito nunca publicado entonces), debida a la mano del humanista Lázaro de Velasco:

> ¿Cómo llamar, en nuestra investigación, a los que en tan largo debate defienden la posición de los modernos? Los historiadores franceses se sirven en casos semejantes con toda facilidad del término «modernistas» (apud Maravall, 1966: 245).

(Resulta curioso que en su acepción seiscentesca cuanto en la decimonónica, el giro remite a las artes visuales o a la arquitectura. El mismo comentario puede decirse hoy día del «postmodernismo», que remite a la arquitectura, como antes «barroco» a las artes plásticas.)

La voz «modernista» se encuentra en Rousseau, aparece en inglés hacia 1737 y en español, otra vez, en la epístola LXXXII de las *Cartas marruecas* de Cadalso. En el siglo XIX lo «moderno» es expresión frecuente, fundamento de, por ejemplo, *El manifiesto comunista* de Karl Marx: abundan las referencias a «moderno yugo del capital», la historia «moderna», la burguesía «moderna», el arte «moderno», la producción «moderna», el mundo «moderno».

Bien claro lo vio un obrero de Sabadell en 1871, que en entusiasta soneto «A la Asociación Internacional de Trabajadores» une socialismo y modernidad:

Sin el *socialismo* en el mundo todo es muerto,
nada mejor que la *moderna sociedad*
que sin tiranos, ni privilegios, es lo cierto
que ha de conducirnos a mejor felicidad [...]

(apud Termes, 1977: 410)

Y Anselmo Lorenzo (el fundador del anarquismo en España) cita un texto de Bakunin de 1872 que bien merece reproducirse, por la relación que establece entre presente y porvenir:

nos vemos precisados a tener en cuenta el *presente*, la necesidad de acción que imponen los trabajadores de cada nacionalidad, los gobiernos y las leyes, pero sin perder de vista el porvenir (Termes, 344).

El parentesco con la cita inicial de Nietzsche es notable. Pero ninguno emplea modernismo, término que difunden en Francia los Goncourt (Greenburg apud Watson, 1984). Lo que permanece inalterado en estos registros es la naturaleza progresista del término. Ya en tiempos de Darío —y en la acepción finisecular—, Roggiano (1962) verifica el lejano origen francés del giro. En sus vueltas y revueltas de crisis en crisis y de continente en continente desde el siglo XVI (incluso antes), y en lo que al mundo contemporáneo se refiere, diferencia los modos de producción cultural modernos. Implica —creo— un modelo de representar la «imaginación» o la «fantasía ideológica» (expresión que adapto de Baudrillard, 1983) en su correlación con otros fenómenos: la emergencia o nacimiento de nuevas naciones y de estados autónomos modernos (en Hispanoamérica), y en España inscribe la liquidación del colonialismo imperial, y el legado pesimista de la Revolución de 1868 [2].

La voz, en su acepción de fin de siglo, significa en este contexto la formulación optimista de Estados más «modernos», con nuevas formaciones económicas y tecnológicas, y el desarrollo de nuevas nacionalidades con gobiernos autónomos de la política colonial. Moderno/modernismo desde entonces es

---

[2] El clásico de Rama (1970) desató una serie de trabajos ligando el modernismo con el mercado económico. Son importantes las aportaciones de Gullón (1964), Litvak (1979), Fernández Retamar (1979), Yurkievich (1976) y las recogidas por Schulman, ed. (1987). Es de sobra conocido que la bibliografía es abundantísima.

signo del proceso de modernización contemporáneo, en sus diversas fases, y lenguaje de la filosofía del progreso en su inevitable trayectoria negativa y positiva: la Revolución Mexicana (1910), la primera guerra mundial, la Revolución rusa. Ambas actitudes —lengua del *sí* y lengua del *no*—, por más opuestas que parezcan, poseen una nota en común: la libertad de levantarse contra lo normativo y prescriptivo. No han de experimentarse estos hitos históricos sólo como fenómenos políticos, sino que actúan a su vez como categorías que incorporan nuevas percepciones del tiempo y del espacio (velocidad, distancia, forma), aceleradas a partir de 1914 (bien visto por Kern, 1986). La metáfora de la «simultaneidad» (sobre la cual volveremos) es al lenguaje poético lo que son el teléfono, el telégrafo y el telémetro al lenguaje científico [3].

En suma, los móviles concretos del proceso de modernidad y su filosofía del progreso, es el encadenamiento de modelos teóricos ideológicos; un nuevo lenguaje de representación —en parte del pasado y en parte totalmente contemporáneo— en función de poderes y propiedades verbales de ensayar nuevas relaciones y conexiones. La referencia es aquí decisiva; implica una re-evaluación total del discurso cultural. Los cambios y signos de fuerzas productivas sustanciales fueron determinantes e indujeron a los individuos a asignarle nuevo sentido y valor a su comportamiento, a sus tareas, sus sentimientos, percepciones y esperanzas dentro de cada nueva nación. Esta referencia de un mundo liberado permite reconocer los resortes profundos de las actitudes mentales y revela cómo unas experiencias políticas —la guerra de Cuba, la guerra de Independencia (1895) y el año de 1898— se desplegaron en correlación con las distintas zonas de conocimiento, tipos de creatividad y formas de subjetividad en cada cultura hispánica específica. Fue una manera nueva de encontrarse en medio de la realidad y la tarea de interpretar este mundo por suspensión de la referencia descriptiva. No consistió ello en añadir al discurso ornamentos retóricos, sino re-evaluar todo el discurso cultural y todos sus componentes. El contacto entre diversas regiones y el ensanchamiento entre las zonas de intercambio condujo a su vez a un «cosmopolitismo» sustancial, a un internacionalismo. Ya para 1893 el catalán Santiago Rusiñol lo inscribe como nueva sensibilidad:

---

[3] Estudio las metáforas epistémicas sobre la simultaneidad y perspectiva en «Epistemic Metaphors of Time and Space: M. Bakhtin, K. Mannheim and the Modernists» (1989, en prensa).

tal es la forma estética de este arte espléndido y nebuloso, prosaico y grande, místico y sensualista, refinado y bárbaro, medieval y *modernista* al mismo tiempo (mi subrayado, apud Litvak, 1979: 100).

La analogía que establece Rusiñol es un nexo entre la antigua palabra y la nueva, el modernismo como un eslabón que cierra un círculo. La correspondencia entre estas realidades es verbal: el círculo que une las antinomias se concibe en la «imaginación». En gran medida la imaginación responde a una necesidad y llena una función: pone al descubierto las modalidades del ser. Es un medio de conocimiento de la realidad; es la toma de conciencia del nuevo espíritu. Poder irreal —la imaginación— asentado en la realidad misma. No es de extrañar que en 1897 el venezolano Emilio Coll identifique desde el *Mercure de France* este clima imaginario y esta potencia creadora del movimiento modernista con la insurrección de Cuba (Zavala, 1975; 1988 a). Esta se inscribe como *sociograma*, y en la dimensión verbal de significaciones nacientes, este modernismo induce a Darío a sacar a la luz lo «imaginario social» del signo del cisne (Zavala, 1987 b). Pero las palabras darianas comentando la génesis de *Cantos de vida y esperanza* merecen citarse:

> En «A Roosevelt» se preconizaba la solidaridad del alma hispanoamericana ante las posibles tentativas imperialistas de los hombres del Norte [...] (*Historia de mis libros, OC* I: 214-224).

En síntesis: la genealogía del modernismo se desarrolla a partir de signos y fuerzas distintos, no contradictorios. La consigna general de los precursores y fundadores finiseculares (a los cuales pertenece Valle-Inclán) es la liberación de las fuerzas productivas anti-institucionales, anti-colonialistas, anticlericales y profanas, y los contenidos de la producción cultural. En su inscripción histórica finisecular surge con una vocación de resistencia, como un discurso cultural que aspira a desenmascarar lo que ocultan la sociedad y la máscara «burguesa» liberal, objetivo que comparte con los socialistas y anarquistas. En nombre de una productividad auténtica explora otros lenguajes estéticos que rechazan la instrumentalidad y el conformismo. Programa de varios núcleos, revistas, proyectos: *Germinal* (luego *El País*), *Gente Nueva, La Revista*

*Nueva, La Revista Moderna, La Anarquía Literaria.* La historia se ha contado muchas veces; la extensa nómina incluye
escritores de diversos sectores y geografías: catedráticos uni-
versitarios y de instituto, publicistas, dramaturgos, bohemios,
*free lancers.* «Gente nueva» que, como Benavente o Azorín,
se declaran «anarquistas» o «anarquistas literarios», otros «socialistas». Las innovaciones verbales abundan: teatro re-teatra-
lizado, prosas poemáticas, novelas dialogadas (experimento de
Galdós), los experimentos de Valle, Unamuno. (En simultaneidad temporal sigue publicándose Galdós con éxito y tiene
una rotunda recepción *Las aventuras de Rougemont,* que co-
menzaron a publicarse en *Nuevo Mundo* en 1899.) La negación es creadora; la actitud crítica estalla en perpetua erup-
ción. La resignación ante la realidad inmutable es virtud de
estos jóvenes; desde 1895 Valle alterna prosas «exquisitas»
con crónicas sobre el movimiento político, el anarquismo, iconografías de políticos (Pablo Iglesias). Como Valle, otro «nihi-
lista», el bohemio Alejandro Sawa, desde las efímeras páginas
de periódicos y gacetillas, aboga por una nueva moral y una
historia crítica (en vocabulario actual). El «pensamiento moderno» —en frase de Sawa— es también, y sobre todo, anarquista (véanse los artículos que bajo ese título firmó Darío
en 1908, escritos por Sawa, Zavala, 1977).

La familiaridad del intelectual con los movimientos obreros emancipatorios y su proyecto cultural —que ya he mencionado— induce a referirse al artista como «proletario
intelectual», en neologismo difundido por Bakunin y los internacionalistas a partir de 1873 (Zavala, 1988), en un intento
de examinar la función del intelectual en la vida pública. El
«germinalista» de origen polaco-ruso, Ernesto Bark, empleará
con acierto el concepto contemporáneo, enlazándolo con la
bohemia (*Política social. El internacionalismo,* Madrid, 1900).
Max Weber retomará el giro «*intelligentsia* proletaria» en sus
reflexiones sobre la dependencia e independencia del intelectual décadas después. El problema sobre la función del intelectual (tan debatida por Marx y Bakunin) toma un giro
particular en 1898, con el caso Dreyfus, cuando Clemenceau
acuña el giro «intelectual» como clase intermedia entre la burguesía y el proletariado (Watson, 1984; Fox, 1976). Otros
giros se revelan por entonces: burgués/burguesía, cosecha
también de los internacionalistas.

Literatura, revolución o subversión: en estas tres palabras
se condensó la modernidad. Es también el reino de la subje-

tividad (socializada) que sirve de marco a un nuevo orden del espíritu y su representación ideológica cultural, como parte de una crisis general histórica que en cada zona geográfica toma rasgos particulares, y reúne diversos grupos que tienen objetivos comunes: bohemia revolucionaria, anarquistas literarios, anarquistas, socialistas, republicanos. En descrédito de este «frente común» la burguesía y sus instituciones movilizan los clisés y los términos agresivos y codificados: degenerado, decadente, revolucionario, extranjero (Bering, 1978). El objetivo anti-burgués (defendido por la Internacional desde 1864), consecuencia directa de una revisión de las formas burguesas de moralidad universal y la creación de nuevo sujeto social, agrupa los diversos grupos en una actitud reflexiva crítica. Aunque es fácil reconocer que en cada caso se trata de un ejercicio diferente, el programa (más o menos expresado) integra diversos sectores contestatarios; no debiera extrañar que el dirigente anarquista catalán, Federico Urales, proclame desde las páginas de *El Progreso* su posición de sujeto «modernista». En sus palabras:

> declaro que si por modernismo se entiende llevar a las tablas nuestras pasiones, nuestros infortunios y nuestros *problemas,* soy modernista. [...] No somos modernistas porque queremos. Lo somos porque el alma nuestra no se satisface con el manjar artístico que priva hoy. Nuestros gustos han de obedecer a una evolución del gusto, de ninguna a un capricho del escritor ni a una extravagancia del neurótico (2-I-1898).

Estos testimonios, que podrían multiplicarse en el modernismo, hallan expresión adecuada en los cambios introducidos por la revolución industrial y tecnológica y su nuevo *episteme* (conocimiento teórico). En su expresión lírica se transforma en una *sensation du nef* de la *beauté moderne* (que escribió Baudelaire); la forma de representación de otro mundo, mundo creado *en* y *por* el lenguaje (Bürguer, 1984). Este nuevo mundo de subjetividad se inscribe en la superficie temática de la literatura y en el trazo de las formas reactivadas e inventadas en el lenguaje, a menudo como «extrañamiento» de la realidad objetiva. La estrategia —de Baudelaire a Darío, Valle o Brecht— es la diversidad, la lengua del «no», el «desorden». La creación de otro mundo a partir de la imaginación supone la destrucción y «extrañamiento» de lo cotidiano, lo familiar:

33

mitos, paisajes, personajes. La especificidad de la producción imaginaria es su doble articulación cognitiva en la estructuración del pensamiento lógico: se le asigna al lenguaje un papel importante en el proceso de crecimiento, en la teoría del desarrollo. Lo que Vygotsky llamaría «lenguaje como encarnación de la historia cultural» (1962).

Señalo una vez más que las estrategias y los discursos culturales son polo de tensión tanto en Hispanoamérica cuanto en España (geografías a las cuales me limito, pues otros modernismos finiseculares no inscriben de manera tan activa el anti-imperialismo o anti-colonialismo). Estos toman cuerpo alrededor de la primera guerra mundial, que marca, en Valle, su «posición geométrica» (el «perspectivismo» orteguiano, el *objective correlative* de Eliot, el *ideogrammic method* de Pound, la *epiphany* de Joyce, la poesía crítica de Mallarmé, en su teoría anticomunicativa del lenguaje; la *supreme fiction* de Wallace Stevens). En el mundo finisecular hispánico existe una «unidad en la diversidad» que originó en su momento soluciones diversas y apreciables en el plano político y cultural.

Este discurso moderno —y en lo que a la producción textual valleinclanesca se refiere— induce al receptor/auditor a una cooperación activa, e interrogar los textos de forma crítica, para poner en juego un «extrañamiento» semántico y producir una experiencia especular en el dominio de lo imaginario. Se invita a colaborar en lo que llamo *lo imaginario social*, el espejo recíproco del objeto y su antítesis. El valor cognitivo de la imaginación especular radica en sacar a la luz estas operaciones y, mediante un proceso de «identificación», incorporar a su auditorio social en el acto de lenguaje. El público lector tenía sus motivos para irritarse con los «modernistas» o para quedar perplejo (como parece ilustrar la obra de Valle). Estas identificaciones se construyen en una historia de las semejanzas, las contigüidades, las correspondencias, dictadas por la situación histórica, que se inscriben en las superficies textuales con signos positivos y negativos: bueno/ malo, belleza/fealdad, escasez/opulencia, explotación/igualdad, ricos/pobres, burgués/proletario. Se introduce la sospecha al poner en entredicho los valores existentes; el discurso cultural se convierte en un ejercicio continuo de incredulidad. Se violan los códigos, las leyes habituales y los preceptos, y se miran los objetos (las naturalezas), de formas inesperadas, como ruptura de los sistemas, en reflexión crítica sobre el nuevo orden introducido. Se instala la desconfianza, la sospe-

34

cha, y el discurso fluye por oposiciones y negaciones en continua ruptura con el orden previsto y las formas de vida, en tensiones. Con frecuencia la posición del sujeto es irónica, por negaciones, que siembran la duda en el ánimo. Se ensayan nuevas formas discursivas con la convicción de quitar máscaras lógicas y morales, para indicar mejor y de modo inconfundible la hipocresía que encubre la grandilocuencia retórica y la norma que pesaba sobre la libertad, inmovilizada en formas fijas.

A pesar de estas proezas y del análisis crítico de la forma/ representación, ciertas formas del modernismo terminan por desembocar en producción de mercancía al reducirse finalmente en algunos casos a estilos personales y lenguaje privado. Se alimenta del sujeto individual y finalmente deviene en sí mismo su propio significado y la existencia autónoma del referente en la estructura social. Pero está claro que todas las perspectivas abiertas y toda la producción teórica de las formas de carnavalización —base de la poética de Valle-Inclán— en sus grados y variantes (desde el carnaval versallesco al carnaval de los oprimidos y al carnaval del cuerpo político) re-insertan el proyecto «modernista» en la base de «representación» social de la cual surgió como proyecto finisecular: la toma de conciencia de lo moderno en lo «imaginario», una «imaginación» irónica que subraya los abismos entre la realidad y lo «imaginario social».

Estas negaciones y reposiciones irónicas de la realidad son la lógica de los métodos del modernismo —del cual forma parte el discurso cultural valleinclanesco hasta 1936—, algo más que una escuela literaria «estetizante», «decadente» y alienada. (¿Llamaríamos alienado hoy día el discurso cultural de otros modernos: Ortega, Manuel Azaña, Pérez de Ayala, Eugenio d'Ors, Gregorio Marañón, Salvador de Madariaga?) Buena parte de la confusión histórica radica en que en su expresión finisecular se reconocen rasgos en común con otros «modernos» —los «simbolistas» y «decadentes» franceses (entre 1880-1900)—; en particular el agnosticismo, la obsesión por el erotismo y el inconsciente, el ocultismo, el perfil urbano (la gran «cosmópolis»). Sea cual fuere la denominación, entonces y ahora, desde diversas posiciones de sujeto, hay relaciones entre todos. En el caso particular de los hispánicos que nos ocupa se les atacó en su día de cosmopolitas «afrancesados», al situar a París como epicentro de la vida literaria. Estos tópicos no pueden ser hoy día considerados como punto de referencia absolutos, como los tuvieron en su momento: las afinidades y/o amistades personales entre unos y otros no debieran inducirnos a catalogaciones acríticas. Mallarmé no habla el mismo lenguaje de Huysmans, ni Darío el de Azorín o Baroja y ni siquiera Valle habla la misma «prosa» de D'Annunzio, pese a que compartan rasgos y lecturas. (En particular, el italiano carece de la relativización irónica de Valle.)

Atendiendo sólo a la «moral», el modernismo en sus variantes, se ha relacionado (desde entonces) con el espíritu de «decadencia» (término del alemán Max Nordau en su catálogo de «degenerados» —el *Entartung* de 1892). La denuncia contra los modernismos y esta subjetividad rebelde no finalizó con Nordau y con cuantos a final de siglo tenían una idea inadecuada de los modernos. En la década de 1930 la retoma Lucáks —por motivos diferentes a los de Nordau— y la refina e interrelaciona con el análisis de la alienación de Marx, y elabora su teoría de reificación a partir de los «decadentes» de la vanguardia y su «literatura de obras inacabadas», literatura de débiles, de ineptitud para vivir. La cuestión principal contra la vanguardia —que se remonta a los años después de la primera guerra mundial— era su incapacidad emancipatoria (la carencia del *Vernunft* hegeliano o un razón emancipatoria dinámica). La posibilidad histórica real del arte contemporáneo de vanguardia y su relación con una teoría crítica fue desafío para Brecht, Walter Benjamin, Ernest Bloch, T. Adorno, Lukács, que debatían en la década de 1930 las implicaciones emancipatorias de la «representación», del lenguaje, de las narrativas y la conciencia histórica. Para los representantes de la Escuela de Frankfurt y para Brecht, la obra de arte auténtica y de vanguardia se convierte virtualmente en el último residuo de la razón. Hoy por hoy, esta importante discusión cultural se ha rejuvenecido en la polémica entre el post-modernismo y el modernismo (en particular las diferencias entre Lyotard y Habermas).

No perdamos el hilo de nuestra modernidad. Originariamente surgió a contracorriente de las instituciones en el poder, como fundamento de una esperanza social. Esta práctica cultural y sus posiciones de sujeto, concretizadas a partir de la guerra hispanoamericana (1898), forman lo que Bourdieu (1984) llamaría un «campo literario» y su proyecto creador, con su espacio objetivo de relaciones que distribuye las estrategias y sus horizontes utópicos en unidad real de superación de lo antiguo y realización de lo nuevo en la escritura de una nueva «narración» histórica. Conviene recordar la definición de Bourdieu: «a field of forces acting on all those who enter this space and differently according to the position they occupy there, at the sme time as a field of struggle aiming to transform this field of forces» (1984: 5). En las oposiciones de este campo para la re-escritura de la historia intervienen los conservadores y los modernos; aquellos que defienden y reproducen las rutinas (el orden simbólico establecido y las instituciones que lo reproducen), y aquellos dispuestos a subvertir los modelos. Si valoramos adecuadamente el potencial, parece injustificado hoy día restarle coherencia y orientación política a este proyecto común, y su campo de regularidad (retomando el término de Bourdieu). No fue ésta una protesta impotente, sino una posibilidad emancipatoria de desciframiento del sujeto social, un discurso(s) sobre la «representación» donde el nuevo sistema viene a reflejarse en lo *imaginario social* de una subjetividad rebelde.

Las relaciones entre este discurso cultural y sus referentes en el proceso de la experiencia estética como instrumento crítico parte de un campo teórico, de un espacio de posibilidades de un sistema comunicativo complejo orientado hacia un tipo de experiencia redentora, aquello que Marx llamaba oponer «contraimágenes utópicas». Esta lógica de interrelación entre el «horizonte ideológico de expectativas», la estructura artística y su complejo sistema de actitudes discursivas correspondientes, apunta a nuevas formas de subordinación: en la era de la modernidad los productores de cultura de diversos campos sociales tienen como objetivo una nueva relación con los grupos dominantes. En particular, la autonomía y la independencia del medio social. Pero todavía estamos lejos de haber asimilado el sentido positivo de la empresa, y aún no hemos captado en su totalidad este proceso histórico de ruptura cultural y sociopolítica entre 1880 y 1930 y su variedad de direcciones. En su sentido amplio, esta transición hacia la modernidad y la idea de la belleza como una promesa de felicidad, de reconciliación con nuestra naturaleza interna y con la naturaleza externa (el hombre «interior» de Martí, la «síntesis» de Adorno), es un conjunto de tendencias interrelacionadas. La narrativa se inscribe con los «modernistas» americanos, los socialistas, los anarquistas, la generación llamada del 98 en su totalidad —que no se limita a los «reconocidos» o institucionalizados— incluso en su recodo conservador de 1905 ó 1910. Es una ética de la responsabilidad y de la sospecha de las «verdades» aceptadas, una crítica asentada en lo que Max Weber llamaría «desencantamiento del mundo» y «abrir nuevas alternativas históricas».

Conviene observar que a pesar de las aparentes diferencias, y quizá gracias a ellas, la concepción del discurso cultural específicamente moderno, su representación de lo *imaginario social* y su posibilidad emancipatoria, converge en un doble sistema de conexiones —sólo en apariencia contradictorias— para llevar a cabo un examen a fondo de las tradiciones, cánones y prácticas textuales, y crear un nuevo «subterráneo político». Las dos que menciono son complementarias: 1) las estrategias textuales se construyen a partir de los elementos subversivos de la lengua (dialogía, heteroglosia, poliglosia), el estilo, la inversión o desacato a la autoridad; se articulan mediante el espíritu de carnavalización (no «identificación», sino subversión de las ideologías dominantes); más que artificios estéticos, son un artificio social de selección; 2) la diversidad de estilos o lenguajes individuales forma un todo con un modelo posible político radical (no siempre revolucionario), y debe entenderse como construcción que aspira a ser auto-reflexiva y se rige por la percepción aguda de los espacios interiores, la naturaleza exterior e interior, a menudo como referencia irónica. (La recepción de lo que Paul Ricoeur denomina «filósofos de la sospecha» —Marx, Nietzsche, Freud—, así como Bakunin, y las filosofías de la incredulidad de Schopenhauer, Kierkegaard y luego Bergson y Husserl sirvieron de apoyo a estas reposiciones irónicas y los ejercicios de incredulidad a los cuales he aludido.) Estas estrategias de interioridad o auto-reflexión interna se potencian con el objeto de reapropiar un universo alienado y alienante; por tanto, la relación con el público se problematiza. El punto de partida es una puesta en perspectiva radical. Se confía en saberes exteriores al texto, en la capacidad contextual del receptor, de modo que preste atención a las estrategias, al contenido intertextual, al extrañamiento semántico: placeres reservados al lector crítico. (La relación semiótica entre lectura y escritura es distinta en Valle, Unamuno, Azorín, Borges, sobre todo.)

La generación precursora de esta subjetividad rebelde a la cual pertenece Valle-Inclán —la de los modernos— propone desde sus comienzos nuevos modelos de vida ante el desgaste de los que les fueron transmitidos. La irrealidad de su propia experiencia les llega de manera directa y maximalizada a través del espejo de la sociedad burguesa, después de la Revolución de 1868, y la parodia triunfal de las restauraciones, caciquismo, retórica, golpes militares, censura, leyes represivas, atentados. No son muchos los que se plantean como revisión histórica las actitudes gastadas, las actitudes mal interpretadas, el papel de los héroes junto con el auto-engaño; la obscenidad grotesca de las relaciones sociales.

Cuestión de formas también. Este discurso cultural se expresa mediante un virtuosismo verbal, nutrido de lecturas y «voces» del pasado, de aceptación o de polémica. En algunos («modernistas», bohemia revolucionaria, anarquistas) se libera también el cuerpo, sin metáfora, en la esfera del lenguaje (textos eróticos de Felipe Trigo, Eduardo Zamacois, Emilio Carrere, Ramiro de Maeztu, Vargas Vila, sin descontar la musa «arrabalera» popular que pasa al bolero caribe y al tango argentino; Zavala, 1988). Los anarquistas sobre todo difundieron el vitalismo sexual antiburgués (Litvak, 1981). En algunas transgresiones, el erotismo (Darío, Valle) se estructura alrededor de lo que hoy llamaríamos fuerza de liberación libidinal, seducción, placer, deseo, juego *(jouissance)*, en una estimulante profusión de estrategias de desublimación. (A propósito, se alude a veces a los «raptos dionisíacos» de Ortega.) Valle —si bien no es el único— privilegia la sexualidad y la enlaza con el lucro y la explotación, incluso a veces con la violencia, o bien con refinamientos transgresores —satanismo, necrofilia, pederastia, fetichismo, algolagnia— que agreden aquellos acorazados en su moral única (véanse las sugerentes páginas de Litvak, 1979).

La decanonización, la deslegitimación del pasado, la desmitificación valleinclanescas están asentadas en una teoría del sujeto *social* desmembrado por las fuerzas del poder —los gobernantes, el ejército, la monarquía, la iglesia—. Es justamente el discurso monológico y monoestilístico el que Valle fragmenta. Volveremos sobre ello.

Este proyecto moderno de re-narrativizar la historia, de crear un nuevo discurso cultural, opera por negaciones y afirmaciones de los discursos anteriores. A menudo, toma la forma de una empresa *individual* fundada en una energía de experimentos atrevidos en el horizonte de la cultura contra los valores residuales colectivos. El procedimiento puede producir tanto excelencia como trivialidades; pero en sus mejores expresiones pone en crisis al destinatario. El desafío engendra un doble código de transgresiones político y literario: 1) deconstrucción y desmitificación del Estado; 2) ideología anticolonial; 3) preocupación por los aspectos sociales (socialistas); 4) decanonización de las ideas recibidas; 5) reestructuración del concepto de moral; 6) ataque y asalto a la retórica; 7) cambios de posición del sujeto (desde el inicial «Yo soy aquel» dariano a la «posición geométrica» valleinclanesca, y al «perspectivismo» orteguiano). Cambios de posición del sujeto emisor, que en ciertas coordenadas incluso cambia de nombre: Martínez Ruiz/Azorín, o bien de ángulo de refractación. A través de estas coordenadas, algunos —en particular Valle, ejemplo que privilegio por razones evidentes— subvertirán y transgredirán la grama(tología), y crearán una (anti)estética fundamentada en los paradigmas siguientes: carnavalización, disolución de las «narrativas» o «relatos» aceptados (gobiernos militares, restauraciones, monarquías), desplazamientos de sentido, crítica de la mitología de la razón, heterodoxia (teológica, literaria y política), eclecticismo. Podríamos concluir diciendo que:

— la sorpresa y la novedad son estrategias para la estructuración de una estética radical, basada en las obras abiertas y la participación lectora;

— por tanto, la crisis del arte anterior se vale del procedimiento de las técnicas del *collage,* el *pastiche* (virtuosismo de Juan Ramón, dicho sea al pasar), el hábil empleo de la cultura popular o de aquellos aspectos de lo que hoy llamaríamos *mass media* (canciones, pancartas, literatura de cordel, folletín, anuncios, cine); la disolución de las fronteras entre la poesía, el drama, el lenguaje narrativo; el virtuosismo intertextual, el conocimiento enciclopédico;

— el procedimiento conduce a la falta de demarcación de las fronteras de los géneros tradicionales y la búsqueda de géneros «internos» *(sonite, druma, esperpento, nivola, novela poemática, greguerías);* Benedetto Croce llega a rechazar los géneros literarios (comentario que aprovechó Unamuno en 1910); la repetición y el diálogo con el pasado (dialogía) se construye a partir de: la cita, la parodia, la revisión irónica, el plagio, el autoplagio, el juego intertextual, la infinidad textual; la dialéctica entre la novedad y la repetición de los propios discursos; el texto único, abierto a cambios, variantes, invariantes, transformaciones, interrupciones, transmigraciones semánticas y sintácticas, transmigraciones genéricas (los poemas intercalados en obras de teatro o el verso libre empleado en la prosa: Valle, Unamuno, García Lorca, son maestros en estas estrategias);

— esta dialéctica moderna intenta colocar al destinatario en crisis consigo mismo por identificación o «extrañamiento» reveladores; establece un pacto con el lector crítico, que se desdobla, que se altera, que se vuelve interlocutor (en análisis de Bajtin sobre la dialogía, 1981).

El horizonte de este universo de transgresiones y disconexiones no es sólo de formas y apariencias, sino que obedece a la búsqueda privilegiada de los sentidos ocultos para ver y sentir el mundo (recuérdense los comentarios de Rusiñol), la inmanencia, las indeterminaciones profundas, conocidas por entonces con el nombre de sinestesia (base del modernismo, según Valle-Inclán y Darío; véase también Paz, 1983). En este dominio se libera la producción textual del sentido, el significante, el sujeto, el signo, y la reducción crítica del yo en formas y representaciones de la alteridad y la otredad, la radical heterogeneidad del yo, centrales en Unamuno, Machado, Pirandello y los famosos heterónimos de Fernando Pessoa y los alter-egos de Ganivet, Azorín y Gabriel Miró, Marcel Proust, y el Parodi (parodi-a) de Borges. Valle está bien acompañado. (Dicho sea al pasar, muchos de estos códigos se emplean hoy por hoy para describir el episteme de la post-modernidad como distinción cuantitativa y cualitativa). Estos códigos son a su vez un proceso de destrucción y de producción; le permiten a Valle «dramatizar» las profundas contradicciones de la sociedad hispánica, y «representar» el grotesco anacronismo de la escena política y el medio social, a través de las series «carnavalizadas». La heterodoxia (teológica y social), la falsa moral, el comportamiento «burgués», de rancios y estériles preceptos (objetivo también de Ortega), la destrucción de las «narrativas» históricas pretéritas (entre ellas la épica), serán el primer blanco valleinclanesco en un ejercicio constante de incredulidad. En sus desmitologizaciones primeras se centra en Eros y Thanatos; pero su Thanatos no se presenta como en la visión católica, armado de su guadaña; antes bien, surge bella, casi atrayente, sonriente o irónicamente seductora (parafraseo a Darío).

Hemos relacionado el proyecto emancipatorio de la modernidad y la «carnavalización»: empleo de los géneros paródicos en formas y estilos múltiples. La actualidad es el punto de partida —mitos, héroes— se re-actualizan aboliendo la distancia épica y las jerarquías. La risa carnavalesca —de farsas y esperpentos— acercan el pasado de manera directa y familiar. La voz, el discurso del otro, se mantiene a distancia: el discurso del otro (historia, héroes, mitos) se re-procesa desde el exterior, en proximidad inmediata, en un presente inacabado y abierto. En cuanto procedimiento es una actitud reflexiva y crítica *frente* y *sobre* el lenguaje. La sátira y la parodia son autocríticas, y el lenguaje revela el aniquilamiento de un viejo mundo y el nacimiento de uno nuevo. Ironía, sátira y parodia son en Valle intergéneros (en la acepción de Bajtin), para transformar el miedo en espectáculo —representación— crítico. Partamos de sus desmistificaciones primeras y del erotismo —Eros y Thanatos— como fuerzas de liberación libidinal negadas y suprimidas.

## 2. POETICA MODERNA Y PRACTICA SEMIOTICA

Las estrategias clave de la producción textual moderna que he bosquejado revelan trazos visibles de «carnavalización», de acuerdo con el concepto seminal de Bajtin. Dentro de esta práctica dinámica de estrategias y comunicación trataremos de aislar contextos de transgresiones diferentes y variadas. El sistema de Valle-Inclán muestra una fuerte tendencia a la creación de un mundo «al revés», en un ejercicio de incredulidad. Visto desde esta perspectiva, el *corpus* de su obra adquiere coherencia en el interior de un sistema de comunicación e interacción. La *cronotopía carnavalizante,* como la describe Bajtiun, o serie rabelesiana, puede ser reducida a siete categorías (Bajtin, 1981: 170; Todorov, 1981: 129): serie del cuerpo humano en sus aspectos anatómicos y fisiológicos, serie de la vestimenta humana, serie de la comida, seire de la bebida y embriaguez, serie del sexo (copulación), serie de la muerte, serie de la defecación (escatología, excrementos humanos). Cada una tiene su lógica y sus características dominantes; todas se entrecruzan, ya que normalmente más de una se encuentra en un texto o en una serie de textos.

La carnavalización literaria o cronotopo rabelesiano de Valle debe ser entendida en dos amplias secuencias: la de sus primeros escritos —cuentos, artículos, las *Sonatas,* las *Comedias bárbaras,* la trilogía de las guerras carlistas— articuladas sobre todo en las series del sexo y de la muerte (si bien no son las únicas), además en el interior de un universo de pactos, promesas y juramentos. Su espejo es *cóncavo,* y le permite ampliar, alargar y estilizar las figuras (como un pintor rena-

42

centista o como El Greco). El cuerpo humano y su voz va adquiriendo una variedad de formas y gestos diferentes: inicialmente aparece la estilización, luego la representación cínica (las farsas) que desembocan en alegorizaciones fantásticas y grotescas (los esperpentos, el *Ruedo*). El espejo supone una imagen *convexa* (y goyesca): los cuerpos aparecen desmembrados, despedazados y perfilan sus más crudos aspectos anatómicos. Las siete series bajtinianas se interpenetran: en la «carnavalización» permite una asunción jubilosa, una homología entre el cuerpo, lo imaginario, la estructura lingüística y la subversión social. (Viene al caso contrastarlas con las figuras grotescas y patéticas cervantinas en *La guarda cuidadosa* y *El juez de los divorcios*.)

La combinación de estas series —del sexo y de la muerte— abre el dominio de la experiencia visual: Valle integra recursos que se manifiestan claramente en la pintura. Tiene en común con los cuadros medievales, Durero y los prerrafaelistas un estricto sistema fijo de poses y gestos que le asigna a cada persona uno específico (léase *La lámpara maravillosa* a esta luz). A menudo son criaturas extenuadas, imágenes «bárbaras» virtuales; se integran en Bradomín con su revisión irónica, sus experiencias eróticas y su culto a la muerte. A nivel verbal se centra en los juramentos y las promesas, base lingüística del seductor, con la distancia irónica que le permiten las convenciones del pacto autobiográfico y los pactos de sangre [4]. Bradomín nos introduce en la «estrategia irónica» del seductor (adopto el término de Baudrillard, 1984, 95-112); el seductor espiritual, cuyo guión ha sido re-formulado por Kierkegaard: cálculo, encanto, refinamiento del lenguaje convencional, ingenio, *wit*. Sus artificios se apoyan en la ironía y la seducción diagonales, consciente de realizar obras de arte mediante operaciones del ingenio. Este seductor representa una «forma ascética de prueba espiritual, pero también pedagógica: una especie de escuela de la pasión, de mayéutica erótica e irónica a la vez» (como califica Baudrillard, 107, la estrategia del Johannes en el *Diario de un seductor*, de Kierkegaard).

---

[4] El universo de pactos y juramentos, actos de lenguaje performativos, está documentado en Austin (1962) y Searle (1977), con precisiones de Benveniste (1971) y los reparos de Derrida (1977). Véase asimismo a Shoshana Felman (1983). Estoy consciente de la distinción entre actos de lenguaje de la lingüística y los actos de lenguaje literarios, y de la polémica en torno a los actos performativos encabezada por los postestructuralistas, en particular Derrida y Paul de Man, véase la apretada síntesis de Norris (1983).

El lenguaje y los actos en los textos valleinclanescos corresponden a una revisión y desmitificación irónica de lo sagrado a través de la profanación sexual y los ritos de la muerte. «Adega» replantea este problema en cadena retórica con el profano mundo idílico de *Cenizas* (1899), *Jardín umbrío* (1903), *Flor de santidad* (1904), *Aromas de leyenda* (1907), *El yermo de las almas* (1908). No es necesario que se tengan en cuenta todas sus características, pero no carece de importancia que se apoyen principalmente en las series de lo sexual y de la muerte, y en los pactos de sangre (tema sobre el cual volveremos). En esta combinatoria los «héroes» señoriales —Bradomín y Montenegro— muestran la grandeza de lo viejo, del romanticismo novelesco, de los héroes clásicos; surgen de la misma atmósfera, pero sus profanaciones son semejantes, no idénticas. Estas representaciones especulares de la atmósfera señorial va desapareciendo, como se re-organizan los juramentos y promesas con Cara de Plata. Violentos oximorones sexuales crean nuevos significados dentro de cada texto, y Valle se aparta del lenguaje natural tanto como es posible. Acrece la complejidad de la estructura extra-textual en obras aparentemente simples, pero que no pueden ser descifradas adecuadamente sin complejas suposiciones y sin tener en cuenta toda una riqueza de conexiones cuturales más allá del texto. Lo que entendemos hoy como estructura profunda no puede ser codificado sin una elaboración intertextual del sentido muy complicada. Ejemplo palmario de estas estrategias enunciativas son la extensa descripción de la Niña Chole en *Sonata de estío* (catálogo de iconos sobre la mujer), la organización de la intrincada red intertextual de *El tablado de marionetas, Divinas palabras* y *La lámpara maravillosa*, que tematiza la doble semiosis lectura/escritura mediante citas, alusiones, elipsis, parodias, refractaciones irónicas del sujeto, que va cambiando de posición discursiva ante el lector crítico.

En estos textos, Valle re-ordena nuevas estructuras, nuevas representaciones especulares de la realidad, completamente consciente de que se aparta de los géneros convencionales. Sus lectores concretos, tanto el incauto cuanto el crítico, en general, estaban mal preparados para re-organizar las disonancias de estos textos, acostumbrados a que la mayor parte de la estructura fuera manifiesta; en otras palabras, la ilusión del *realismo*, la mimesis. Podríamos distinguir que las características obviamente dominantes en el sistema de convenciones aceptado eran: tramas evidentes, lenguaje más «natural», lenguaje demarcado para poesía y prosa, descripciones reconocibles, argumento lineal, escenario convincente. Es decir, los *loci communi* y la tipología de la prosa realista con sus reglas y estrategias fijas estructurales.

La «carnavalización» se enriquece y domina en *La pipa de kif* (1919), donde Valle nos ofrece la clave de las innovadoras y cambiantes jerarquías de sus códigos. Todas las series carnavalescas del cronotopo rabelesiano se incorporan en una funambulesca alucinatoria danza de sexo y muerte, en profanidades, excentricidades, parodias, risa, mutilaciones, borracheras, copulaciones violentas y *contra natura*. Valle denomina la «carnavalización» especular *farsa* y *esperpento*. Re-definida la estrategia y su objetivo, la producción textual cambia de signo. La conducta se vuelve mala-conducta, se desritualizan los gestos en posturas grotescas, despedazamientos del cuerpo, golpes (en las farsas), e imágenes especulares degradadas. La cara, la boca, la nariz, las zonas sensuales o erógenas se duplican en la radio de una lente de aumento o se ven reducidas a pequeñas o mínimas partes inconexas. Valle juega con las distancias; es a especie de imagen del telescopio invertido de la realidad cósmica (semejante a la imagen romántica). España se transforma en *ruedo*, una *corrida*, un *carnaval*, un *tablado*, habitado simultáneamente por liliputienses y gulliverianos, enanos y gigantes, monstruos carnavalescos. Las imágenes se parodian a sí mismas y los textos forman un sistema de espejos deformantes; espejos invertidos que alargan, acortan, desfiguran, agrandan, achican, engordan, adelgazan en diferentes direcciones y grados. El texto es la *arena* de duplicación paródica que caricaturiza, ridiculiza y deforma héroes, autoridades, ideologías, objetos.

Valle degrada las imágenes nobles y acentúa lo trivial y lo grotesco. Las convenciones artísticas y los textos clásicos tradicionales se parodian y exageran desproporcionadamente para reducir su prestigio, a la manera de la *parodia sacra* del Renacimiento y de la sátira carnavalizada de los siglos XVII y XVIII. La literatura carnavalizada permite resaltar ciertos objetos para dirigir la mirada del lector hacia el mundo que se desea «refractar» e implica al receptor(a) de una manera muy específica. Todo lector reconocerá estos rasgos dominantes de «carnavalización» en Valle; los cronotopos rabelesianos en sus entrecruzamientos —desde el principio, con el empleo casi puro de las series del erotismo y de la muerte, llamados tradicionalmente «decadencia»— son instrumentos especulares en-

45

caminados a destruir los sistemas ideológicamente cerrados por medio de una pluralidad de «voces» y de géneros. Los géneros entretejidos e intercalados refuerzan la heteroglosia y el dialogismo en una compacta red de estrategias textuales que colocan el enunciado en una relación particular con la realidad.

La carnavalización o libertad cómica se refuerza en alto grado mediante sus mismas cualidades intersemióticas. Valle incorpora múltiples códigos —música, palabras, gestos, objetos— en sus oposiciones e inversiones estructurales en un discurso contra las regularidades establecidas por las convenciones y la gramática. Su proyecto textual revela un proceso de *asimilación* de la voz («voces») de otro (otros), en una pluralidad de géneros y lenguajes. Deconstruye la cultura de los doctos y la de los legos, el lenguaje eclesiástico, la jerga política, mediante la incorporación de términos pictóricos, de arcaísmos, de neologismos, alteraciones de campos semánticos, de tropos, que asimila y transforma. El significado literario o el sentido se alcanzan por medio de elaboradas estrategias y operaciones. Re-apropia y re-articula una multiplicidad de *corpus* textuales, en un proceso de interacción especular. Explora y resemantiza estereotipos y clisés; el léxico de Valle está poblado de los enunciados de «otros», y en su escritura adquieren un nuevo significado en el contexto de otro campo semántico. Las estrategias semánticas desempeñan un papel muy importante desde sus primeros textos, en una doble voz u operación locutoria.

## 3. LA INTERTEXTUALIDAD. EL DIALOGISMO

Baroja recuerda a Valle afirmar que tomar un episodio de la Biblia y darle un aire nuevo «para él era un ideal». Concebía la lectura anterior —añade Baroja— como el «mejor sistema para producir obra literaria» (1949: 407). Podemos distinguir así que lectura y escritura son fases de un mismo y único proceso; la lectura de los propios textos y la lectura de los ajenos, en intercambio de signos, generan su producción textual en compacta red de envíos y simulaciones, como «ficción suprema».

Su actividad lectora se confirma a partir de la genética de los textos, su movimiento y sus instancias discursivas. No es sorprendente en estas circunstancias la persistencia de los

46

episodios sueltos, independientes, que luego integra; las adiciones y modificaciones y variantes estilísticas; las extrapolaciones de frases, personajes, situaciones de un discurso en otro; los intercambios genéricos; los intergéneros (ejemplo notable, *La lámpara*). Su escritura dista de ser un recinto cerrado; significativamente estas incrustaciones, reelaboraciones e interpolaciones hacen visible el aire libre, el diálogo o la polémica, el salir a la intemperie. Se levantan contra el enmohecido aparato en busca de la participación creadora en una sociedad inmovilizada por la letra (Speratti Piñero, 1968, estudia a fondo el entramado que suponen las variantes y cambios, y Salper, 1988, la elaboración de los personajes).

La presencia de subtextos sociales (modifico el término de Culler, 1981: 140) en la superficie de su obra responde a un proceso de lectura de sus propios textos y arroja luz en los de otros. Esta arquitectura textual, que a menudo reproduce sus propias fuentes de inspiración, abunda en textos de la literatura oral y satírica, los subtextos visuales o gráficos y los subtextos históricos: Zugasti, Carlos Rubio, crónicas, memorias, periódicos, así como las citas de autoridad de la tradición literaria que actúan en el anonimato (por ejemplo, la crónica de Aguirre, subtexto social de *Tirano Banderas,* como mostró Speratti Piñero [5]. O bien las referencias directas a Aretino, Casanova, Darío —esta dialogía sugiere una noción crítica de las técnicas y estrategias textuales. Estos subtextos sociales y culturales permiten construir un complejo entramado intertextual: uno apoya al otro. Todo es pretexto y alimento natural del proceso de lectura. Entre aventura y aventura se mueve esta intertextualidad cultural que revela una variedad de formas; no está reñida con la ironía ni la complacencia. De este mundo hecho de afirmaciones y negaciones (o voces de apoyo y de polémica) me limitaré a dos: los códigos culturales y los

---

[5] En *Palimpsestes* (1982), Genette sugiere que la intertextualidad es una forma de «transconxtualizar» o de «reciclar artístico», de tal manera que las relaciones textuales pueden ser también secretas. La «parodia» sería una de estas formas. Para Bajtin, en cambio, sería una forma de «dialoguismo» textual. La bibliografía en torno a la intertextualidad valleinclanesca es muy abundante; remito en especial a Speratti Piñero (1968), Zamora Vicente (1966, 1968), Zavala (1970a, 1970 b), Sinclair (1977), Schiavo (1980), Cattaneo (1987), Maier (1988). No son los únicos; ya Raimundo Lida había aludido hace años al placer que supone para el lector (crítico) este juego de envíos. Véanse los artículos recogidos en *Leer a Valle-Inclán en 1986, Hispanistica XX,* Université de Dijon, 1987.

códigos literarios, y el sujeto semiótico como emisor/receptor de los códigos ajenos y propios.

En cuanto emisor/receptor de otros textos, se advierte en la producción textual valleinclanesca una auténtica red de conexiones que absorbe y transforma: cruces intertextuales empleados como lenguaje autorizado y lo marginal que proviene de periódicos y canciones, en coro de voces dialógicas. Bien claro alude a este doble proceso semiótico como forma de verificación estética:

> En mis narraciones históricas la dificultad mayor consiste en incrustar documentos de época. Cuando el relato me da ocasión de colocar una frase, unos versos, una copla o un escrito de la época de la acción, me convenzo de que todo va bien. Esto suele ocurrir en toda obra literaria (apud Madrid, *Vida:* 109-111).

Los subtextos son de naturaleza metonímica, y toca al lector identificarlos. En otras ocasiones, el texto ajeno (voz ajena) es punto de partida, un diálogo para confirmar, aceptar o rechazar un punto de vista. Sirve de impulso o apoyo a su producción textual, y con frecuencia la voz ajena es polémica (la dialogía de la farsa y la parodia, y la ironía de la estilización). Todo este complejo de voces de apoyo focaliza nuestra atención en la «literariedad» de la escritura, y nos hace conscientes de los sistemas poéticos e históricos que apoyan su producción literaria y su profunda historicidad; el diálogo histórico con formas del pasado no «finalizadas» [6]. El proceso intertextual afirma el nuevo código en una tradición, y por tanto «universaliza» su sentido, o bien el subtexto se emplea en oposición, en polémica. Valle ensaya una operación de alta acrobacia para avivar la pasión descifratoria del lector(a). Sus símbolos visuales son ricos en significados y elementos contextuales. El folletín, los periódicos satíricos, el lenguaje

---

[6] Empleo aquí el término bajtiniano de «final» frente al postestructuralista de «obra abierta». El primero es un concepto históricamente determinado. Sobre estas distinciones, cfr. Zavala (1987 c). Este concepto bajtiniano de «final» está estrechamente vinculado a Marx; en sus palabras «ninguna formación social desaparece antes de que se desarrollen todas las fuerzas productivas que caben dentro de ella» (prol. *Contribución a la crítica de la economía política* (1859). Esta percepción histórica de «final», «finalizar» es también frecuente en la Escuela de Frankfurt, en particular Benjamin y Adorno. En definitiva, se une el discurso cultural a las formaciones sociales.

modernista estereotipado, el «castellanismo», la mitología, el teatro del Siglo de Oro, los héroes clásicos, el romancero, los romances populares son sólo algunas de las voces de apoyo en su polémica contra lo oficial; de ellas se vale para sus estrategias irónicas estilizadas, y su estrategia de la negatividad o el carnaval paródico de las farsas y esperpento.

No se trata, pues, de puro juego lúdico ni de un virtuosismo textual capcioso, ni de sólo tomarse en solfa las instituciones literarias, filosóficas y culturales, o juegos circulares de laberintos especulares sin historicidad ni referentes. La intertextualidad y el dialogismo desempeñan funciones muy especiales; la composición intertextual (de «voces» enmarcadas) no equivale a un mosaico de textos, o capas textuales o reminiscencias mediante los cuales las «voces» anteriores se funden. El concepto de intertextualidad definido a partir de las superficies textuales, se enriquece si empleamos el término bajtiniano de «voz» de otros (también «ajena») que en Valle-Inclán puede ser la propia voz, en la variedad de operaciones para interpolar frases, situaciones, descripciones, tomadas de textos anteriores. Su práctica intertextual es una dinámica en diferentes y variados contextos y direcciones. Las citas del pasado literario (encubiertas o en la superficie textual), signos y mensajes completos pueden ser encuadrados en otro sistema de signos como parte integral, pueden quedar como fragmentos o sufrir un cambio de función: lo importante es el encuadre.

Según Bajtin, la imaginación *dialógica* depende en alto grado de la poliglosia social y la orquestación de enunciados. Ambas constituyen lo que él llama *polifonía,* otra forma de aludir al dialogismo. La inserción de la diversidad de lenguajes que se orquestan en los textos valleinclanescos toman las formas de estilizaciones anónimas con distanciamientos, refracciones, reservas (Bajtin, 1981, cap. IV provee un cuadro). La *estilización,* entendida como «la representación literaria del estilo lingüístico de otro», destaca como estrategia principal. Las variaciones, la introducción de material lingüístico del pasado en temas contemporáneos, adquieren un virtuosismo de elaboración en la representación de los diversos dialectos y lenguas y dan un colorido dialógico a las estrategias y temas, particularmente antes de 1913-1914. Predominan las estilizaciones de la literatura renacentista, de las sagas· medievales, de las canciones de gesta, de la novela bizantina de aventuras —todas diferentes formas de los cronotopos de la novela (Bajtin, 1981)— y entran en acción en un léxico estilizado. Este diálogo de apoyo y polémica con lenguajes y tradiciones, con obras literarias de prestigio, toma también la forma de estilización paródica. La imagen del lenguaje activado por la estilización puede ser serena, artísticamente orientada, permitiendo así un máximo de esteticismo (pp. 360-364). En cambio, la *parodia* no estiliza la voz del otro de manera productiva, sino que la ataca destruyéndola. La estilización paródica no es una destrucción artificial y elemental del otro (escritor, época, género, tema), como sucede con la parodia retórica, sino una contigüidad de lenguajes:

> it must recreate the parodical language as an authentic whole, giving it its due as a language possessing its own internal logic and one capable of revealing its own world inextricably bound up with the parodied language (1981: 364).

Esta parodia cómica permite un reprocesamiento de casi todos los niveles del lenguaje literario corriente en la época, y en los textos de Valle se refracta desde diferentes perspectivas. En particular activa la dinámica textual de las *farsas* en sus innumerables posibilidades, y es un importante desvío de la misma estrategia de estilización empleada antes. Valle descentraliza, en cierto sentido, las intenciones culturales, semánticas y expresivas de un universo ideológico, en un disonante diálogo profundo de fuerzas sociales. Sus estilizaciones paródicas van de lo genérico a lo profesional y a otros lenguajes, dialectos y jergas, así como también al centro mismo del discurso autorial directo: didáctico-moral, sentimental, elegíaco, idílico. En cuanto parodia moderna «auto-reflexiva» (como califica Hutcheon, 1985, la parodia postmoderna), revela una versión «controlada» de reactivación del pasado en un contexto irónico. Opera por el mecanismo de inversión, y juego de «voces». Para captar el dinamismo de esta *imaginación dialógica* y esta poliglosia es necesario aclarar su estructura lingüística tan precisamente como sea posible.

## 4. ENTONACION Y ENUNCIACION

El «enunciado» (texto, palabra) adquiere significado con la «entonación»; ambos representan los cuantificadores y los índices de las relaciones de clase en el esquema de Bajtin

50

(1984: 296-297), ya que las distintas clases sociales (y géneros sexuales y edades, habría que añadir) emplean el mismo lenguaje. En toda palabra, en todo signo ideológico, están reflejadas las relaciones de clase; en consecuencia, el análisis de un texto literario supone descifrar *quién* habla, la «voz» de quién debe ser oída en el discurso (1928 en 1983: 123). Bajtin/Voloshinov establecen claramente que la entonación es un transmisor de relaciones sociales y es la expresión sonora de evaluación social, que se manifiesta a través de la selección y el orden de las palabras (sintaxis, puntuación, léxico). Representa el «tono» de voz interno y externo, e influye en la selección de palabras y su orden de composición en el enunciado concreto.

Pero la entonación permite también percibir la intertextualidad o las «voces» de otros. Los recursos más elementales se podrían resumir en los siguientes puntos: 1) signos gráficos de puntuación —mayúsculas, exclamación e interrogación, comillas, guiones—; 2) estructura de la oración: interrogativa, exclamativa, exhortativa, vocativa. Estos recursos presentan un interés particular para analizar la óptica (punto de vista) o forma de «focalizar» los problemas, realmente precisar el significado concreto de los enunciados. En realidad, son índices expresivos de la entonación y asimismo de cierto tipo de enunciados que caracteriza los textos literarios dialógicos.

Hemos señalado que los textos de Valle dependen en gran medida del dialogismo y la poliglosia. Para comprender mejor las relaciones de clase en sus textos, consideramos necesario analizar la entonación. Parto del concepto bajtiano que el enunciado es específicamente social, histórico, concreto y dialogizado y que refracta relaciones de clase. Me detendré en el análisis de varios ejemplos tomados de textos y épocas diferentes para mostrar los índices de entonación o las formas de composición que permiten organizar la heteroglosia y la poliglosia. Me centraré en tres estrategias:

1. Estilización paródica de lo genérico, lo profesional u otros estratos del «lenguaje común», tomados por el autor como «opinión pública», como aproximación verbal a la gente y a las cosas. Es decir, como *el punto de vista común* y el *valor generalmente aceptado*. Valle se distancia de ello, retrocede y lo objetiviza. El párrafo que abre «Aires nacionales» de *La corte de los milagros* será suficiente para ilustrarlo: se observará que los índices de entonación son guiones y/o signos de exclamación que representan la «voz» de otros.

51

# AIRES NACIONALES

## I

El reinado isabelino fue un albur de espadas: Espadas de sargentos y espadas de generales. Bazas fulleras de sotas y ases.

## II

El General Prim caracolea su caballo de naipes en todos los baratillos de estampas litográficas: Teatral Santiago Matamoros, atropella infieles tremolando la jaleada enseña de los Castillejos:
—¡Soldados, viva la Reina!

## III

Los héroes marciales de la revolución española no mudaron de grito hasta los últimos amenes. Sus laureadas calvas se fruncían de perplejidades con los tropos de la oratoria demagógica. Aquellos milites gloriosos alumbraban en secreto una devota candelilla por la Señora. Ante la retórica de los motines populares, los espadones de la ronca revolucionaria nunca excusaron sus filos para acuchillar descamisados. El Ejército Español jamás ha malogrado ocasión de mostrarse heroico con la turba descalza y pelona que corre tras la charanga.

## IV

—¡Pegar fuerte!
La rufa consigna bajaba de los alturas hasta la soldadesca, que relinchaba de gusto porque la orden nunca venía sin el regalo del rancho con chorizo, cafelito, copa y tagarnina. Los edictos militares, con sus bravatas cherinolas proclamadas al son de redoblados tambores, hacían malparir a las viejas. El palo, numen de generales y sargentos, simbolizaba la más oportuna política en las cámaras reales. La Señora, encendida de erisipela, se inflaba con bucheo de paloma:
—¡Pegar fuerte, a ver si se enmiendan! (*OE* I: 7-8).

2. El reprocesamiento cómico-paródico de casi todos los niveles de lenguaje literario es la clave que organiza la estrategia en las *farsas*. Estos ejemplos de *Los cuernos de don Friolera* son evidentes; el mismo procedimiento activa estos lenguajes en *La marquesa Rosalinda*. En la primera —texto bien conocido— la parodia permite atacar en un mismo punto dos lenguajes de la autoridad, el concepto del honor y el teatro del Siglo de Oro (Calderón):

> *Don Friolera.*—¡Pim! ¡Pam! ¡Pum!... ¡No me tiembla a mí la mano! Hecha justicia, me presento a mi Coronel. «Mi Coronel, ¿cómo se lava la honra?» Ya sé su respuesta. ¡Pim! ¡Pam! ¡Pum! ¡Listos! En el honor no puede haber nubes. Me presento voluntario a cumplir condena. ¡Mi Coronel, soy otro Teniente Capriles! Eran culpables, no soy un asesino. Si me corresponde pena de ser fusilado, pido gracia para mandar el fuego: ¡Muchachos, firme y a la cabeza! ¡Adiós, mis queridos compañeros! Tenéis esposas honradas y debéis estimarlas. ¡No consintáis nunca el adulterio en el Cuerpo de Carabineros! ¡Friolera! ¡Eran culpables! ¡Pagaron con su sangre! ¡No soy un asesino! (*OE* I: Escena VII: 1023).

El ataque polémico contra la institución literaria cobra relieve en la conocida caricatura paródica del epílogo:

> *Don Estrafalario.*—Toda la literatura es mala.
>
> *Don Manolito.*—No me opongo.
>
> *Don Estrafalario.*—¡Aún no hemos salido de los Libros de Caballerías!
>
> *Don Manolito.*—¿Cree usted que no ha servido de nada Don Quijote?
>
> *Don Estrafalario.*—Ni Don Quijote ni las guerras coloniales. ¿No le parece a usted ridícula esa literatura, jactanciosa como si hubiese pasado bajo los bigotes del Kaiser?
>
> *Don Manolito.*—Indudablemente, en la literatura aparecemos como unos bárbaros sanguinarios. Luego se nos trata, y se ve que somos unos borregos.
>
> *Don Estrafalario.*—¡Qué lejos de este vil romancero aquel paso ingenuo que hemos visto en la raya de Portugal! ¿Recuerda usted lo que entonces dije?

*Don Manolito.*—¡Me dijo usted tantas cosas!
*Don Estrafalario.*—¡Sólo pueden regenerarnos los muñecos del Compadre Fidel! (*OE* I: 1025).

3.   La heteroglosia, fundamental en los textos de Valle, puede ilustrarse con nitidez en la *Sonata de estío,* donde encontraremos estratos de diferentes lenguajes con diversas entonaciones sociales y raciales: el literario y preciosista de Bradomín, el sinuoso y seductor «americano» de la Niña Chole, el del negro, el de los indios. Las diferentes voces de los nobles, bandoleros, gitanos, nobleza de corte, clero, son el sustrato de todo el *Ruedo,* así como de las *farsas* y los esperpentos. La heteroglosia se convierte en una estrategia central en *Tirano Banderas* (1926) con sus contrastes entre el lenguaje de los indios mexicanos y el de los nobles y oficiales administrativos, en un español sincrético. Valle marca la heteroglosia por medio de signos de entonación: comillas, guiones para indicar diálogo directo e indirecto. El diálogo es también un elemento clave en *Jardín umbrío* (1903) y, por supuesto, en las *Comedias bárbaras* y los textos incluidos en *Retablo de la avaricia, la lujuria y la muerte* (1927), así como en los esperpentos. Este amplio uso de indicadores le permite crear la ilusión escénica: «Escribo de esta manera [en forma escénica] —dice— porque me gusta mucho, porque me parece la forma literaria mejor, más serena y más *impasible* de conducir la acción.»

Me limitaré a unas pocas citas de *Tirano Banderas,* texto altamente dependiente de la heteroglosia y la intertextualidad. Comencemos con el prólogo, cuando Filomeno Cuevas pasa lista:

—Manuel Romero.
—¡Presente!
—Acércate. No más que recomendarte precaución con ponerte briago. La primera campanada de las doce será la señal. Llevas sobre ti la responsabilidad de muchas vidas, y no te digo más. Dame la mano.
—Mi jefesito, en estas bolucas somos baqueanos

(*OE* II: 352).

En contraste con la entonación del mexicano de clase baja (el indio en este caso), Valle recurre a la transcripción fonética para reproducir los enunciados de un negro remero, mientras parodia simultáneamente a Espronceda:

> Y en las sombras del foque abría su lírico floripondio de ceceles el negro catedrático:

> Navega, velelo mío,
> sin temol.
> que ni enemigo navío,
> ni tolmenta, ni bonanza,
> a tolcel tu lumbo alcanza,
> ni a sujetal tu valor (p. 358).

Estas «voces» y clases sociales no son las únicas; la parodia a los *gachupines* de la delegación española reproducen a «dos voces» el grandilocuente discurso diplomático y político, la retórica oficial con sus fronteras bien definidas, «voces» que recogerá a su vez la narrativa sobre el dictador (Asturias, Carpentier, García Márquez, Roa Bastos, en especial). Don Celestino Galindo, saluda a Tirano Banderas en términos hiperbólicos que revela toda una visión histórica en reacentuaciones paródicas e irónicas:

> —La Colonia Española eleva sus homenajes al benemérito patricio, raro ejemplo de virtud y energía, que ha sabido restablecer el imperio del orden, imponiendo un castigo ejemplar a la demagogia revolucionaria. ¡La Colonia Española, siempre noble y generosa, tiene una oración y una lágrima para las víctimas de una ilusión funesta, de un virus perturbador! (p. 361).

Otra voz es la de Doña Lupita, la india vieja, que reproduce la obsecuencia de la sirvienta y la esclava, obsecuencia irónica:

> —¡Horita, mi jefe! [...]
> —¡Mándeme, no más, mi Generalito! [...] Viernes pasado compré un mecate pa me ajorcar, y un ángel se puso de por medio (p. 375).

Los diminutivos afectivos, las tergiversaciones idiomáticas, las distorsiones fonéticas (*j* por *h*) y otras irregularidades gramaticales distinguen su entonación y sus enunciados, mas el hecho que todos sus enunciados son oraciones exclamativas que indican su irónica actitud servil. Podrían multiplicarse los ejemplos tomados de este texto tan complejo en el que Valle experimenta innovaciones e intensifica la carnavalización, la dialogía, la heteroglosia, la poliglosia.

La orientación de la palabra en medio de enunciados y lenguajes de otros, aquí sólo esbozada, es central: hemos acentuado que la heteroglosia es una de las más importantes estrategias textuales de Valle, en cualquier forma que la incorpore. Por medio de ella, crea un discurso a dos voces de manera refractada. Su producción textual o «texto único» emerge como *actividad social* en una pluralidad de voces, pero esencialmente en una doble voz que expresa al mismo tiempo y simultáneamente dos intenciones diferentes: la parodia y su objeto. Ambos fertilizados en una conexión enraizada en la historia.

Capítulo II

# «EN EL FONDO DE UN ESPEJO DES-
VANECIDO»: CARNAVAL MODERNISTA

> «Como en el fondo de un espejo desvane-
> cido [...] Evocaba los nombres. Y aspiraba
> en ellos el aroma del jardín en otoño...»
>
> (*Los cruzados de la causa.*)

## 1. LO IMAGINARIO LIBIDINAL

Dentro de este universo de enunciados modernos no es por
azar que intentamos interrogarnos sobre la poética de Valle-
Inclán como totalidad en los últimos años. Su producción
textual invitaba a hacerlo. En repliegue damos toda una vuelta
a la rueda del tiempo, a la rueda de la historia literaria, que
compartamentaliza y fragmenta su producción en dos proyectos estéticos antagónicos: modernismo preciosista y esperpento. De ser así el discurso de Valle sería esquizofrénico, es
decir, de desencuentro alienado, fragmentado, mutilado; desplazamiento de sombras privadas de realidad y de centro. Uno
anularía al otro, pues no cabría la posibilidad de que el sujeto
emisor diera la vuelta a un mismo signo, situándose así en
contextos y entonaciones diversas. Creo que hemos intentado
hasta la fecha buscar una respuesta a una pregunta totalmente
equivocada. Sus textos apuntan a muy otra orientación, nada
esquizofrénica, si pensamos en personajes, imágenes, situaciones que se repiten y se recontextualizan, desde sus orígenes.
Sin embargo, pensado como totalidad, lo que destaca en Valle
es un objetivo anti-realista, anti-aristotélico (llámese a este
proyecto «modernismo», «farsa» o «esperpento»), cada vez
mejor asentado en un distanciamiento o desfamiliarización con

las convenciones. En el centro de su mirada se sitúa la convicción de que las evidencias son engañosas; revela que las palabras tienen hasta consecuencias físicas y que todas tienen su revés en la mueca licenciosa. Desde otro centro cobran peso distinto.

En cuanto texto único —es decir, continuidad textual— encontramos un todo articulado y definido a partir de *La medianoche. Visión estelar de un momento de guerra* (1916, 1917), cuando veremos el dominio de la imagen especular, su «concepción geométrica», que en términos modernos se denominaría «posición del sujeto». Quien ha llegado tan lejos como Valle en una voluntad artística anti-canónica desde sus orígenes, no puede retroceder. El cambio es de sentido de palabras prohibidas; las palabras contribuyen siempre a la creación de un ambiente de libertad: primero, desacralizándolas y «extrañándolas» en una atmósfera de elegancias nobiliarias y «decadencias»; segundo, dentro del esquematismo e innovación de las farsas y el carnaval trascendente. No se trata de un corte con la así llamada etapa «modernista», sino de una intensificación dialógica progresiva que se alimenta en un vaivén de tradición y novedad de múltiples tradiciones: *commedia dell'arte,* género chico, lo grotesco romántico, la cultura de la risa y de la plástica, Durero, Goya, Solana, Posada. (Todos relacionados con problemas de tiempo y perspectiva.) Si inicialmente los juramentos y las imprecaciones y desacralizaciones no tenían relación directa con la risa paródica, se van implantando en la esfera del lenguaje familiar y popular, sumergidas en el ambiente de farsa y lo carnavalesco total. Valle ubica —desde el principio— el lenguaje entre dos limitaciones (o libertades): el de las extravagancias exquisitas pero distanciadas primero, y luego el de la cultura de la risa paródica, extrañamiento revelador, donde las series carnavalizadas se manifiestan en forma especialmente intensa contra el discurso de la autoridad; es entonces un lenguaje propiamente carnavalesco.

Las *Sonatas* (el «modernismo») no son sólo una imagen visual de un mundo de exquisiteces, sino lo que Barthes (1957) llamaría «ambiente imaginario» que implica toda una forma de vida (estilo, ocio, chic). Forman parte de un discurso sobre la fascinación, el fetichismo, que al mismo tiempo se expone como revisión irónica y un análisis cínico. Estas «mitologías» (en frase de Barthes) actúan como lo «imaginario social»,

58

como un receptor imagina los mundos de las clases aristocráticas.

En las *Sonatas* y colecciones de cuentos anteriores todas las series rabelesianas se concentran en la sexualidad y la muerte, aunque no faltan otras (la vestimenta, el cuerpo, la comida, la bebida). Pero a través de estas dos series transgrede las normas y nos distancia del lenguaje religioso (equivalente, por ejemplo, a D'Annunzio o al Joyce del *Ulises*, si bien hay otros en la metaficción de la llamada post-modernidad). El lenguaje revela una completa impiedad, la irreverencia, la ironía (Litvak, 1979). Lo notable de este proceso es que se opera una inversión en relación con los símbolos en la polaridad Eros y muerte. El discurso se mantiene con el impulso destructor de sacar al exterior una relación muy equívoca, puesto que es a la vez el emblema de su presencia (mundo religioso) y el medio de su desaparición; es ciertamente un discurso dialógico, a «dos voces». Sirvan como norma los siguientes ejemplos: Bradomín recuerda a María Rosario con manos blancas y frías, diáfanas, como la hostia. Y dice:

> Al verla desmayada, la cogí en brazos y la llevé a su lecho, que era como un altar de lino albo y de risado encaje (*SP*, 1969: 25).

En el mismo texto comenta el Marqués:

> Yo me detuve porque esperaba verla huir, y no encontraba las delicadas palabras que convenían a su gracia eucarística de lirio blanco (p. 29).

Hasta aquí Valle.

El amor impío es el comienzo de la regla de otra ley. Toda la estrategia de su subversión tiende a apuntar frontalmente al poder y a oponerse a él, desde la posición de la evidencia absoluta. Pero Valle revela su propio secreto; baste recordar sus palabras en torno a las *Sonatas:* además de personaje nacional y eterno, Don Juan se caracteriza también por la «impiedad y el desacato a las leyes de los hombres». Y continúa: ha de desarrollar tres temas a través del mismo personaje; la falta de respeto a los muertos y a la religión, la satisfacción de sus pasiones saltando sobre el derecho de los demás, y la conquista de las mujeres (Zamora, 1966). Es decir: «demonio, mundo y carne, respectivamente» (apud Dougherty,

1983: 160). La intertextualidad —para Bajtin dialogismo textual— (lo que Genette, 1982, llamaría «trans-textualidad o relaciones evidentes o secretas entre los textos»), y la distancia irónica crítica con el tema donjuanesco revelan simultáneamente dos caminos: de apoyo y polémica. El marqués de Bradomín es un Don Juan, en efecto, pero «feo, católico y sentimental», cualidades en polémica con la tradición hispánica, más cercana al mundo de Shaw, por ejemplo. (Otra deconstrucción audaz la lleva a cabo Unamuno en *El hermano Juan*) [1].

Hemos aludido al universo performativo de pactos y juramentos que articula la escritura de Valle del ciclo gallego. Para comenzar, el pacto autobiográfico de las «memorias amables» que ya viejo escribe Bradomín en la emigración, a partir de un distanciamiento ya crítico. Memorias que reproducen un desafío esencial con el género de memorias donjuanescas [2]. Los textos de Bradomín se apoyan en actos performativos individuales (perlocucionarios), de promesas, juramentos de amor eterno, encaminados a ejercer el poder de la seducción. La fuerza de estos actos de lenguaje performativo está asentada en un juego sutil entre los performativos de juicio y los de comportamiento (ritual de conducta) y las promesas amorosas. La dimensión erótica y la lingüística se conjuran en el cuerpo, en una semántica corporal de incitaciones que adelantan y anticipan en incrementos de signos. Los actos de lenguaje (los performativos) del seductor sustraen «al discurso su sentido y lo apartan de su verdad», según Baudrillard (1984: 55), y su trampa consiste en «producir la ilusión (engaño) referencial de un enunciado que es por naturaleza auto-referencial» (Felman, 1983: 31). Se crea así la ilusión de un compromiso real o extra-lingüístico a partir de un enunciado que sólo se refiere a sí mismo. De ahí la incredulidad del Don Juan clásico; no cree porque induce a otros a creer mediante la práctica de la seducción (Rousset, 1978). Nuestro Bradomín representa una novedad enunciativa del seductor del mito, porque «cree», «no engaña».

---

[1] Eliane Lavaud ve con claridad, pero en muy otro sentido, que Valle deconstruye el mito donjuanesco, en «Las *Sonatas:* un ejemplo de deconstrucción», *Hispanística XX,* 49-72.

[2] Estoy consciente de la diferencia entre las nociones de autobiografía y memorias, en particular de las distintas relaciones del narrador con su narratario y el héroe: en las memorias no hay identidad entre narrador y narratario; véase Lejeune (1975, 1976). Salper (1988) ofrece interesantes distinciones.

Sin embargo, como el seductor «obedece ruegos», solicita juramentos de aborrecimiento, promete amores eternos; la promesa es el espacio del «yo». Bradomín no da lecciones ni emite juicios sobre el bien y el mal, ni prescribe castigos desde una jerarquía social o moral superior. Se limita a ofrecerle al lector el poder supremo del deseo, al margen de los poderes y las autoridades institucionales. Inscribe el deseo y la seducción como irreverentes; la seducción se presenta a la luz de los «celos», sin fanfarronería, deconstrucción de las representaciones tradicionales de Don Juan. A Bradomín le interesa sobre todo la irreverencia, la estrategia espiritual: María Rosario *(SP)* estaba destinada a un convento, la incestuosa Niña Chole liba al amor «en siete copiosos sacrificios» ofrecidos a los dioses «como triunfo de la vida» (p. 62). Concha es una moribunda, «flor enferma»; pero la deconstrucción mayor es que el Marqués era «un místico galante, como San Juan de la Cruz» (*SP:* 25), estrategia que lo acerca al modelo de seductor espiritual irónico, como el Johannes de Kierkegaard. Cuando otros desesperan, Bradomín sonríe; el orgullo es su mayor virtud y su divisa, «Despreciar a los demás y no amarse a sí mismo» (*SE:* 76).

El universo de *Las comedias bárbaras* (1905, 1908, 1923) y la trilogía de *La guerra carlista* (1908-1909) se compone también de juramentos, promesas y juramentados. A medida que se acerca a la era isabelina, la corte, la Septembrina, los textos descubren la época de los pactos y las promesas rotas [3]. Su discurso se orienta —entre las exqjuisiteces y las deformaciones posteriores— en el trasfondo de las luchas endémicas entre las agencias del poder «feudal». El carlismo de los mayorazgos y representa una especie de árbitro, un poder capaz de finalizar una guerra, la violencia y el saqueo. Los poderes que «representa» en su texto único —entre variantes y variabilidades— son el del ejército con su poder de muerte, la iglesia como poder de lo social y lo personal, la policía y la justicia como poderes punitivos, y el poder superestructural del estado en relación con otros nexos de poder que inciden sobre el

---

[3] El libro de Shoshana Felman (1983) sobre los actos performativos literarios de Don Juan es de rigor. Braudillard, por su parte, relaciona seducción y poder; seductivo aire de familia, pero que debemos situar en su contexto sociohistórico, al margen de sus teorías sobre el «simulacro». Asimismo es importante recordar que los actos de lenguaje performativos se deben situar dentro de la dimensión pragmática de la comunicación.

cuerpo, la sexualidad, la familia, la consanguinidad, el conocimiento, la tecnología (incorporo y adapto ideas de Felman, 1985: 106-111).

La genealogía familiar, así como los espacios, son fundamentales para revelarle al lector las «mitologías» y la forma de vida comunitaria, así como el «ejercicio del poder». Cada espacio social tiene una función diferente, ya que cada espacio equivale al ámbito de relaciones sociales y es parte de la forma en que se ejerce el poder (bien visto por Foucault, 1979; 1984: 152-153).

El espejo «desvanecido» de los espacios cerrados de Bradomín revela el envés irónico del donjuanismo, la heroicidad grandiosa del pasado y las promesas y pactos de los grandes señores y el aroma de las flores marchitas, con su vejez señorial y melancólica. En textos posteriores el espejo se invierte, y refleja los pactos no cumplidos, las des-seducciones engañosas, como veremos.

Para recrear este mundo de las promesas y los juramentos, Valle se vale de la estrategia de la seducción, y de los espejos que estilizan los lugares y los personajes por donde en otro tiempo pasó la vida amable de la galantería y del amor. En ambas situaciones, Valle recrea estos mundos a través de un lenguaje a «dos voces» que apunta una forma de vida: merece recordar aquí a Wittgenstein, «To imagine a language means to imagine a form of life» (*Philosophical Investigations*, 1953: 55).

Todas estas estrategias de distanciamiento irónico formulan la hipótesis de una burla, de una irrealidad fundamental del mundo, de un violento desafío que se filtra y juega de una forma a otra en la anamorfosis y en la metamorfosis: las palabras así filtradas son irónicas. Valle «desfamiliariza» (*ostranenie*) lo convencional y lo normativo. En un mundo social que controla la enunciación, sus textos nos ponen en contacto con un discurso *ilícito*. Y nuestro nuevo Don Juan, además, juega a las alternancias épicas como clisé, y al clisé como épica (semejante pero no igual al modernista norteamericano Wyndham Lewis).

Un punto de aclaración: hoy sabemos que los enunciados no tienen significado fuera de una situación comunicativa específica. Así, pues, un mismo campo semántico, incluso una misma palabra, pueden significar cosas diferentes, incluso opuestas (Bajtin, 1985; Voloshinov / Bajtin, 1977). Ambos enunciados se combinan dialógicamente, no se cancelan; son voces textuales irónicas. Tal es el caso del léxico religioso en Valle; visto desde este ángulo, la correlación entre léxico religioso y desacralización estalla en conexiones en las *Sonatas*. *Hostia, altar, eucaristía, lirio blanco, encaje*, están en encadenamiento recíproco como vértigo de seducciones, de libaciones (Aretino); apuntan al oscuro objeto del deseo. Eros, el unificador, instala un aprofunda mutación en la cultura e invita a los miembros de la colectividad (sus lectores) a descifrar el acontecimiento y reconocer lo desconocido. No sólo afecta así el mismo discurso religioso, sino el conjunto de actividades de la cultura, en reversiones e inversiones. Lo ceremonial ritual se desmiente, y el orden de la liturgia libera la seducción; recordémoslo en su funcionamiento puro en el ruego de Bradomín:

> ¡Azótame, Concha! ¡Azótame como a un divino Nazareno! ¡Azótame hasta morir! (*SO*).

Intenciones semejantes han de encontrarse en *Epitalamio. Historia de amores* (1897), *Corte de amor. Florilegio de honestas y nobles damas* (1903), *Flor de santidad. Historia milenaria* (1904), *Aromas de leyenda* (1907), *El yermo de las almas* (1909), *Historias perversas* (1907), *Aguila de blasón: comedia bárbara* (1907). Las series todas convergen mediante el juego combinado de refinamientos eróticos y de culto a la muerte —Eros y Thanatos—; también la evocación de sentimientos elementales, época y paisaje ajeno a toda ley de anacoretas, almas en pena, endemoniados, mendigos, villanos humildes, hidalgos altivos y audaces. Sin más, recuérdense las «abluciones al amor» de Bradomín y la Niña Chole con el trasfondo mexicano de altar, campanas, cantos monjiles. O bien, en *Sonata de primavera* (1904), cuando Bradomín establece una analogía entre San Agustín y el libertino Casanova (doble heterodoxia), y lo edificante de las *Memorias* del último, catecismo para aprender las seducciones del cuerpo. Dicho sea al pasar, la alusión representa una lectura deconstructiva de las *Confesiones* de San Agustín, figura central de la ética cristiana, bandera de batalla de la moral contrarreformista (Mateo Alemán, por ejemplo). En otros textos abundan las sonrisas sensuales de Dalilas, Giocondas, «mujeres fatales» o estilizaciones renacentistas, las intertextualidades con modelos transgresores italianos, con el modernismo, entre tantos otros, sirve de apoyo para la voluptuosidad y la profanación.

Es importante subrayar que las series carnavalizadas de la ropa, la comida, la bebida, el cuerpo, nos llegan en esta fase de producción textual bajo el signo de contraste entre Dios y Satán: Beatriz es «de blancura eucarística» *(SO)*, mientras desde el fondo del palacio, el silencio palpitaba «como las olas del muerciélago Lucifer» (véase Litvak, 1979). O bien el oximoron de *Sonata de primavera,* texto en que Bradomín inicia su juego seductor en la cámara mortuoria de monseñor Gaetani. En la de *Otoño* narra los amores de una agonizante. Valle focaliza el cuerpo femenino a partir de la tradición clásica, en estilizaciones y partes «púdicas». Su óptica fetichista de «ideal» de relaciones amorosas cuyo origen se remonta al amor cortés: la mirada del narrador se regodea en los ojos (suplicantes, llorosos, guarnecidos de lágrimas); en las manos y los dedos (pálidas, ideales, transparentes a la luz, transparentes como las de una santa). Toda una iconografía se despliega y se profana. En contraste, las del capellán del cuento *Beatriz,* «atenazadas y flacas». Este reduccionismo del cuerpo y su semántica nos llega continuo y graduado y cortado y discontinuo. La mujer es objeto de reverencia, y su cuerpo aparece como un sistema de partes en movimiento o estático; cada juntura o intersticio es capaz de despertar emociones diversas, históricamente determinadas. La mirada está codificada en una tabla de invariantes y variantes siempre las mismas; gramática aceptada, organizada en torno a un modelo dual único: buena/mala, púdica/impúdica. La Venus púdica del Renacimiento en la iconografía, inmortalizada en «La Fornarina» de Rafael. Palabra e imagen se corresponden, y cobran especificidad. A partir de esta tradición, Valle estiliza los actos y el cuerpo femenino —«inanimada, santa, blanca», «cuerpo de mujer galante»—, o bien «actitud de cariátide», «lascivo encanto, como si se hallase medio desnuda, en nido de sedas y encajes»). La vestimenta ofrece refinamientos transgresores (túnica blanca y monacal de Concha en sus citas nocturnas); en cambio, don Juan Manuel en *Femeninas* infunde miedo: «pero un miedo sugestivo y fascinador», cuando no tiene «el poder sugestivo de lo tenebroso».

Todo este universo de refractación de voces le permite la «estilización» irónica (ironía romántica) en sus referencias a la tradición. En la *Sonata de invierno* (1905) —se recordará— el narrador afirma: «Yo no aspiro a enseñar, sino a divertir [...] Para mí, haber aprendido a sonreír es la mayor conquista de la Humanidad.» Pocos ejemplos bastan de un amplísimo inventario: la Niña Chole es, como aquellas mujeres «ardientes y morenas, símbolos de la pasión, que dijo un pobre poeta de estos tiempos» *(SE)*, o bien, traía «aquella sonrisa que un poeta de hoy hubiera llamado estrofa alada de nieves y rosas» *(SE);* en otro momento comenta «era una réplica calderoniana». El procedimiento de humorismo en las *Sonatas* está ampliamente registrado por la crítica; la estrategia irónica se produce en el choque entre el «yo» del Marqués viejo que recuerda su juventud. La superficie textual de las «memorias amables» lo constituye la coincidencia y la coexistencia de la duplicación de «yos». La escritura emerge como espejo, que refleja el espacio del «yo» actual y el del pasado, las duplicaciones engañosas, la ironía de la duplicación y reduplicación de seducciones. Es un «yo» que se mira, y varía sus puntos de vista, al situarse en perspectivas distintas. Este doble registro se expresa en un relativismo moral en dobles registros; el personaje que se vira vive simultáneamente dos momentos distintos de su vida. En palabras del narrador:

> ¡El destino tiene burlas crueles! Cuando a mí me sonríe, lo hace siempre como entonces, con ‘la mueca macabra de esos enanos patizambos que en la luz de la luna hacen cabriolas sobre las chimeneas de los viejos castillos (*SO*, 1969: 122).

La ironía estilizada permite este doble espejo de *yos* que se miran, de personas gramaticales que observan sus propios gestos, de lenguajes performativos y denotativos. La estilización y su parodia se concentran y se diseminan de texto en texto en este gran *texto único*. Los dos mundos conviven, las series se interpenetran, siempre en dobles registros que no se anulan. Conviven la belleza y la fealdad, lo excelso y lo terrestre, los refinamientos y la grosería. Así, por ejemplo, la descripción del cura de San Gundanar en «El rey de la máscara» (1892), cuento temprano, se alimenta de la serie anatómica: «magro y astuto de perfil monástico y ojos enfoscados y parduzcos como de alimaña montés»; o bien los mendigos y endemoniados del peregrinaje a Santa Baya Cristalmide tan temprano como *Flor de santidad* (1904) tienen «cabezas deformes y manos de palmípedos», mientras las endemoniadas sueltan blasfemias y espumas por la boca, con sus corpiños rasgados. Otros peregrinos tienen manos velludas, y bocas sin dientes. Todo este universo emplea la totalidad de las series carnavalizadas, pero la diferencia con otros textos posteriores radican en la intención: no se *parodian* los gestos ni los mundos, no se «representa» un carnaval de oprimidos. En definitiva, la fragmentación del cuerpo no tiene intención de parodiar la bufonería de la historia. Recordemos, dentro de estas series, al personaje Electus, o Ciego de Gondomar, viejo grosero, con boca semejante a sandía abierta; el parentesco con la carnavalización salta a la vista; lo que falta es la risa desmitificadora. Compárese este mismo mundo con *Divinas palabras* (1920); de Galicia toma lo heroico, los clisés de la epopeya —el mundo de linajes, de santos, de almas en pena, de duendes y de ladrones— y lo contrapone a lo anti-heroico, en una especie de oximoron social.

Estamos ahora en mejor posición para medir la función de estos contrastes; Valle recoge elementos dispersos, diseminados por la cultura, y los reintroduce en un marco que permite que estos poderosos elementos anti-narrativos se re-narrativicen dentro de una producción de estilo centrífugo. Las oposiciones binarias de la sociedad se revelan en su genuina contradicción dialéctica, como la oposición hegeliana Siervo/Señor, el microcosmos de la superficie textual es un espejo reductor que revela las fuerzas negativas en dos dimensiones estáticas, en una objetivación de la vida social. La prosa «modernista» de Valle re-estructura violentamente convenciones literarias arcaicas —la epopeya, el romance, la hagiografía, las confesiones, las memorias, la narración medieval, el nacimiento de la prosa y el cuento, Chaucer, Boccaccio, las imágenes de Giotto—. Los textos están plagados de estereotipos, de paradigmas, clisés, de tradiciones culturales del pasado, de formas muertas. El lenguaje es teatral o dramático, siempre «artificial», como corresponde a una exégesis, a un comentario sobre los paradigmas originales.

Toda esta etapa se articula por medio de la «memoria de géneros», de estereotipos, de la vida cotidiana trivial que Valle reintroduce, re-inventa, en representación más alegórica que mimética, como si estuviera re-escribiendo un gran libreto operático, re-interpretándolo en nuevas situaciones, poses, restaurándole vitalidad a las páginas amarillentas del pasado. Valle «interpreta», nos descodifica este gran palimpsesto histórico, e interviene directamente para explicar los gestos, las poses de sus personajes, sus dialectos, tan cargados ya de tradición, que han perdido por entonces su propia posibilidad de comunicar. La complejidad «representativa» de estos textos

—tan aparentemente sencillos— radica justamente en que son a la vez texto y su comentario, escritura y exégesis, producción y recepción, siempre en doble semiosis, y el autor, el demiurgo que está por encima de sus personajes. Toca al lector la tarea de decodificación mediante complicadísimos mecanismos y operaciones que desmonten esa narrativa «alegórica», que a su vez debe ser reconstruida a partir de trozos, de fragmentos de información, recreados mediante el proceso de extrañamiento o el extrañamiento revelador *(verfremdungseffekt)* brechtiano. El lector debe descifrar múltiples niveles: lingüísticos, alegóricos, icónicos ciertamente al margen de cualquier representación «realista». Una vez logrado este proceso de desciframiento, la narrativa alegórica nos permite descodificar los signos; es una especie de espiral, de circularidad semiótica.

La trilogía de *La guerra carlista* (1908-1909) es —desde esta perspectiva— singular. Conviven el viejo linajudo Juan Manuel de Montenegro, su sobrino Bradomín, «viejo dandy», ciegos, voluntarios carlistas, contrabandistas, cabecillas, monjas, sacristanes. El narrador mira en *Los cruzados de la causa* (1908) «como en el fondo de un espejo desvanecido», con ojos vueltos al pasado (*OE* II, p. 111), como si la materia y el argumento pertenecieran al novelón y al folletín románticos. En contraste, léase la comedia bárbara del mismo año *Romance de lobos* (1908), otra vertiente del mismo tema y con idénticos personajes; predominan aquí las blasfemias, los erotismos descontrolados, las bajas pasiones. Montenegro llega a ser la alegoría de un Cristo, rodeado de su cohorte de mendigos y traicionado por los caínes. Con Montenegro y su prole se derrumba el viejo tronco. La alegoría narrativa viene a través del pastiche inter-semiótico y lingüístico; una imagen religiosa, de los pasos de Semana Santa, en una lengua arcaizante, casi medieval, para revitalizar el estereotipo político-religioso. La descripción alegórica pasa a un *close-up* o *blow-up* (como en fotografía o cine) de nuestra percepción:

> El Caballero interpone su figura, resplandeciente de nobleza: Los ojos llenos de furias y demencias, y en el rostro la altivez de un rey y la palidez de un Cristo (*OE* II: 679).

Un detalle interesante: además del espejo recíproco que estiliza y/o deforma la misma imagen, también se resemantiza

67

el lenguaje. Valle juega a la alternancia de imágenes y de vocablos. Si ya antes hemos hecho hincapié en el lenguaje sacro desacralizado, el giro se va volviendo más transgresor y cargado de la mueca licenciosa. Me centraré ahora en el vocablo *cabrón,* por representar obviamente la anti-norma. En *Las comedias bárbaras* se emplea como alusión al demonio, o al macho de la cabra (significados neutros del diccionario), y en *Romance de lobos* y *Cara de Plata* (1923) pasa a significar el insulto cargado de connotaciones sociales, la blasfemia, que luego desmonta por la burla y la parodia´ en *Los cuernos.* Se recordará el pasaje: Don Friolera es un carcamal viejo, aburrido de su mujer. Pero se ve obligado a vengar su honor porque: «en el cuerpo de Carabineros no hay maridos cabrones».

Lo que presenciamos de texto en texto es el anverso y el reverso de un mismo mundo; una suerte de inversión constante, de representación, de comentario. El principio subyacente en esta inversión (*renversement,* por emplear el término de Foucault) es el intercambio de significados. En el texto narrativo (al igual que en los experimentos anteriores), *eros* viene cargado de valoraciones artísticas y estéticas; en el texto dramático pasa a significar la fuerza primaria, el desenfreno que conduce al latrocinio y a la muerte, como doce años después en las equívocas *Divinas palabras.* Y no es texto privilegiado.

En resumen: los primeros artículos periodísticos, los cuentos recogidos en *Femeninas,* las *Sonatas, Flor de santidad, Jardín umbrío,* acentúan la sexualidad, el satanismo; actitudes que enorgullecen al marqués de Bradomín, y luego a Juan Manuel de Montenegro en el ciclo bárbaro de tema carlista. Puebla su mundo con la representación alegórica de clérigos, mendigos, escribanos, putas, alcahuetas, hidalgos, endemoniadas, brujas, en un universo de enamoramientos, seducciones, sacrilegios, amores perversos, incestos, adulterios, prácticas sexuales minoritarias. Crea unidades narrativas en gran expansión espacial y temporal, de espirales lingüísticas, icónicas, ritmos sintácticos, dobles articulaciones del lenguaje hablado y escrito, fonética y gramática. Revitaliza giros, imágenes, personajes, situaciones; palabras sobrecodificadas, temas y motivos sobrecodificados del arsenal literario y cultural, en un virtuosismo intertextual de inversiones y reversiones, en curvaturas imaginativas que obliga al lector a un complejísimo proceso de decodificación y desciframiento. Articula sus escrituras en toda la gama de «voces» de los «architextos» estudiados por Genette (1979), esas amplias categorías discursivas, de modos de enunciación, de composiciones genéricas de la metaficción más contemporánea [4]. Su discurso le revela al lector la maravilla de un mundo dialogizado, plural, lleno de legibilidades y de *hipotextos,* siempre transformados. Los ecos de frases, de fragmentos, de léxico aparecen como alusiones vagas o interferencias, en una compleja red de *transtextualidades,* en relaciones que aceptan y niegan, unen y separan al lector con textos anteriores, en permutaciones semánticas de un lenguaje en espiral. La tríada tradicional de los géneros discursivos —la lírica, la épica, el drama— se deconstruye, desaparece, se borra, se libera, se volatiliza.

Este mundo dialógico de intercambios verbales asciende a un pasado infinito y nos revela que los significados pasados no son estables, porque no están concluidos, agotados ni terminados: no existe nada muerto. Los trae del *horizonte ideológico* para dialogar con ellos, en afluencias y entrecruzamientos. La suya es una literatura literaturizada, compuesta de imágenes y palabras, no de grandes acciones. Su «texto único» se revela como un espectáculo de la transfiguración; los sujetos y las situaciones pierden su aura y su autenticidad. Valle se vale del clisé de la épica, lo desempolva, y en *blow-up* nos trae la imagen del pasado a nuestra percepción, la re-programa como amplios *collages* culturales llenos de lugares comunes, de exotismos pretéritos, de detalles minuciosos, decorados medievales. La acción (para poblar el mundo de esta gramática especial de palabras y gestos) es afuera, al aire libre; espacio-paradigma de la épica, y contrario a las cerradas habitaciones burguesas de Galdós y Clarín, por ejemplo. Pero este mundo externo de acciones es sólo textual, pues Valle nos muestra la imagen, y nos ofrece el comentario, la lectura. Es propiamente un recurso *dialógico,* de intercambio de «voces», pero «voces que no se excluyen, sino que coexisten en contigüidad sin cancelarse. Incorpora las voces del pasado en polémica, apoyo, refutación, como información suplementaria, que se pueden percibir de manera directa en un mismo contexto, en un amplio circuito comunicativo de espirales y círculos sin fusión.

Si en esta etapa orquesta las profanaciones e impiedades culturales y religiosas a partir de una distancia crítica irónica,

---

[4] También Unamuno revela esta dimensión textual metaliteraria; los teóricos postestructuralistas citan más a Borges en este sentido. Hutcheon (1980, 1985, 1987) ve como signo de modernidad este metacomentario.

la «posición del sujeto» («posición geométrica») se sitúa desde una perspectiva de sátira y parodia en las farsas populares «entre lo trágico y lo grotesco». Los protagonistas ingresan en un proceso intensivo de degradación paródica, de juegos especulares. De la carnavalización estilizada (Saturnalia clásica) en sus gradaciones irónicas nos sitúa en la farsa paródica y la sátira. No debemos sentir la sospecha que las farsas ofrecen soluciones divertidas, ni son reducibles a la escatología y la obscenidad, a lo bajo corpóreo y al despedazamiento carnavalesco en una lengua popular transgresora. Observan reglas fundamentales y están cargadas de datos importantes; proponen una multiplicidad; son la intuición de esa multiplicidad en su regulación de las instancias. Las farsas (luego los esperpentos) están en choque con la cultura oficial, que se le hace aborrecible a Valle y le provocan una reacción de burla o desdén, de engaño y de risa contra lo académico, lo castellanizante, la tradición, lo cerrado y satisfecho en multiplicidad de tonos y de voces. Tal imbricación se le hace intolerable. Al llegar a este encuentro acentúa el rasgo de profanación y transgresión, y sus relaciones con el pasado histórico serán más críticas y polémicas.

La objetivación y densidad paródica con géneros y lenguaje se renueva: todo conduce a la destrucción épica de la historia oficial de España. Valle absorbe en unidad interna los géneros y temas de prestigio —los mitos clásicos, el teatro del Siglo de Oro, el Romanticismo, el fin de siglo—, así como los menores, para representar y re-vertir las imágenes, donde destrona por el humor y la risa los valores desgastados, los valores inmutables e intocables. Por medio de la parodia, deconstruye otros textos y otros discursos; permite la «representación» cómica y ridícula de normas y convenciones institucionalizadas.

Valle juega al *reverso* siempre, a las estrategias fatales de la intercambiabilidad, a la inversión del sujeto. Un desafío especial, en este pensamiento «circular» (dialógico) moderno, es la denegación crítica de Bradomín después de 1920; bajo el espejo ridículo e impotente del esperpento, el personaje pierde su belleza, su autenticidad y su funcionalidad. Pasa a ser entonces un «cínico farsante», «un viejo verde». La clave de esta denegación crítica del Don Juan está en la abolición de su aura tradicional, su autoridad y su capacidad de ilusión y seducción. El sujeto familiar se convierte en monstruosamente extraño, en un doble movimiento de desfamiliarización, por una deposición histórica, de parodia y de sátira. No es el único modelo cultural; también Otelo, Homero, Bradomín. En sus propias palabras:

> La vida [...] es siempre la misma, fatalmente. Lo que cambia son los personajes. [...] Antes, el Destino car gaba sobre los hombros —altivez y dolor— [...] Hoy, ese Destino es el mismo: la misma su fatalidad, la misma su grandeza, el mismo su dolor. Pero los hombres que los sostienen han cambiado. [...] De ahí nace el contraste, la desproporción, lo ridículo (apud Dougherty, 1983: 192, 1930).

## 2. «SOY EL HISTORIADOR DE UN MUNDO QUE ACABO CONMIGO»

> «He asistido al cambio de una sociedad de castas [...] y lo que vi no lo verá nadie. Soy el historiador de un mundo que acabó conmigo.»
>
> (Valle-Inclán, 1924.)

Nos aproximamos aquí a un territorio donde convergen estética e ideología; el marqués de Bradomín anuncia el paso unificador entre el mundo de aristócratas y el pueblo. La obra de teatro (1907) permite la re-articulación de ambas esferas sociales. Si la España finisecular y de principios del siglo XX autoriza a constatar el desarrollo de nuevas prácticas sociales y teorías económicas —el capitalismo en ciertas zonas, los problemas regionales, el problema agrario, la última guerra carlista, el movimiento social y las organizaciones obreras, la pauperación del minifundio gallego y el latifundio andaluz, el fracaso político—, todo este universo contextual, a su vez, se revela en el signo lingüístico. Valle opera por un «imaginario social utópico» en estas estilizaciones, una especie de redefinida convención literaria cara al modernismo de los jardines galantes, el mundo «pastoril» y elegíaco, casi un *locus amoenus* clásico, donde el ocio, la recreación, las «locuras heroicas», el apartamiento secreto de los amantes, el oasis erótico, dominan el espacio narrativo. Predomina lo «imaginario nostálgico» al mismo tiempo que una deconstrucción de lo «imaginario real», donde las enajenaciones de la moralidad, la ley y el estado centralizante no existen, se anulan. Valle no «representa» propiamente dicho una edad de oro, sino un distanciamiento del contexto histórico-social. Su lenguaje «modernista» se levanta como desviación y depuración de la tradición representativa, ya inadecuada.

Los textos, en su articulación de las series rabelesianas (sexo, muerte, vestimenta, cuerpo, comida, bebida y embriaguez), reúnen el amor místico y el amor profano (integrado como un todo gnóstico de tiempo cíclico y visión totalizadora, irreversible en *La pipa de kif*, como veremos). Conviene recordar sus observaciones sobre unos lienzos de Julio Romero de Torres en 1912 por su diálogo con sus propios textos:

> [los lienzos] tienen un encanto arcaico y moderno, que es la condición esencial de toda obra que aspire a ser bella, para triunfar del tiempo. Porque eso que solemos decir arcaico, no es otra cosa que la condición de eternidad por cuya virtud las obras del arte antguo han llegado a nosotros (*Nuevo Mundo*, apud Dougherty: 60) [5].

Huye, sí, de la «actualidad momentánea», y progresivamente insiste cada vez más en la «noción eterna del centro», en abarcar el conjunto y no los detalles mudables; en hacer algo eterno de la actualidad, en una visión totalizadora.

En estas producciones textuales, Valle no «representa» la clase dominante española (no lo son ya los señores «feudales» ni los señoríos, ni las «castas»), tampoco la dimensión de esplendor de imperio guerrero, o gobierno imperial o riqueza. Mira en el «fondo de un espejo desvanecido», como en litografías antiguas, una dimensión de *comunidad* ya seudo-real, de «un mundo que acabó conmigo», en sus palabras (1924, apud Dougherty, 147). Como el hidalgo quijotesco, el héroe de sus *Sonatas* es «galante, feo, sentimental» (en términos cervantinos, católico, cortés, desprendido o liberal), y los pazos y palacios de Bradomín o Montenegro (clan feudal), son los espacios donde se representa este «imaginario social utópico», ya desvanecido. Pero su *locus amoenus* —Galicia, Italia, Méxi-

---

5 Virginia Garlitz ha enlazado la relación de Valle con la Exposición de 1908 y los artistas del Nuevo Café de Levante; véase «La evolución de *La lámpara maravillosa*», *Hispanística XX*, 194-195. Prepara un libro sobre *La lámpara*. Matilla (1972) vio con sagacidad el expresionismo dramático de las *Comedias bárbaras*, en libro no suficientemente valorado en la crítica hispánica.

co— se articula en una dirección: aquella de una dimensión representativa estética e imaginaria, ya no realizable como forma de vida concreta, como no son realizables la epopeya ni la elocuencia en ruinas. De ahí los procedimientos de «estilización» e «ironía», en particular las «voces» en polémica (la tradición, la religión institucionalizada), y al mismo tiempo recurre al empleo del «horror», aspecto que tanto lo aproxima a ciertas metaficciones contemporáneas (analizadas por Kristeva, 1980). Valle «representa» los poderes del horror, de la abyección, de lo impropio en gradaciones (muertes, cadáveres, canibalismo), aquello que la crítica califica de «decadentismo».

Mediante estas profanidades —refinadas o «bárbaras»— perturba el orden, el sistema centralista (véase Allegra, 1986). En este universo ni la ley, ni el Estado, ni la Iglesia imponen límites; Valle redobla mediante actos, gestos y lenguaje la fragilidad de la ley, del lenguaje autoritario, en desconexiones, negaciones, transgresiones, denegaciones. El arma es el «humor», la «risa»; la risa es vehículo para superar la abyección (Kristeva, 1980: 15). Risa refinada, que en gradaciones y duplicaciones se va transformando en parodia, gesto, mueca: el ejercicio continuo de incredulidad. La premisa es la misma, pero la abyección, el horror, la corrupción, la saturnalia serán en adelante los gobernantes, los sistemas, que matan en nombre de la vida, de aquellos que viven al servicio de la muerte: Religión, Estado, Moral, Derecho. La risa, la «estilización», el humor, la ironía, la parodia se elaboran dialógicamente, y se integran como alteridad amenazadora e integradora. De la abyección mundana pasamos a la abyección socio-política y a refractar especularmente por la risa distanciada la infamia de los gobernantes.

Valle se inicia con un proyecto, no para ser recuperado, sino como desvanecida ruina cultural (y, por tanto, socio-histórica), ya objeto de contemplación, a partir de una poética que revela, simultáneamente, la disgregación ideológica y un nuevo proyecto cultural. Entre la sublimación cultural y el desastre emerge el proyecto «moderno» de Valle, en relación de disidencia y práctica subversiva. Resulta importante recordar que el «modernismo» de Valle nunca se hizo indispensable, ni fue «institucionalizado», y que todavía en la era franquista se censuraron sus procacidades. Hasta fecha muy reciente, tal vez Antonio Machado fuera uno de los escasísimos lectores de *Femeninas*, y que Azorín anota que *Epitalamio* (1897) causó indignación por inmoral. En este sentido la distinción de Brecht entre «*being* popular» y «*becoming* popular» (1979) permite captar las zonas de su discurso.

Bien: «lo moderno» se suele inscribir en el cultivo de una forma rebuscada; la dificultad del lector(a) con el virtuosismo formal, intertextual, anti-normativo, anti-convencional, aristo-cratizante y clasista: el famoso «a la minoría siempre» de Juan Ramón. En el fondo, preciso es reconocer que el de Valle es un discurso anti-mercantilista, anti-consumo, contra una literatura «mercantil» de éxito comercial y gran actividad empresarial: el folletín, la literatura rosa, la novela regiona-lista, la naturalista, el teatro burgués; todo lo rancio y de pre-ceptos estériles. Cultiva la dificultad como estrategia para «desfamiliarizar» o incomodar al lector y enajenar el texto para evitar su incorporación en la industria cultural (visto por Adorno, en el caso de la vanguardia europea); incluso desde la crónica periodística en su realidad de «proletario intelec-tual», rechazó los discursos tradicionales.

Podríamos caer en la fácil tentación de identificar a Valle con una literatura cuyo proyecto social sería convertirse en instrumento de legitimación del conservadurismo, o de esca-pismo histórico, o un discurso sin bases políticas o sociales concretas (absolutamente improbable, dado que todo signo es ideológico). Su deliberado uso de una escritura rebuscada, «aristocratizante», dista de ser un «ejercicio del poder» (en frase de W. Benjamin sobre la tragedia barroca), y se acerca más bien a un discurso de las minorías (no minoritario), que re-territorializa una práctica discursiva de la periferia, contra el culturalismo castellanizante y su ideología hegemónica. Su heteroglosia y dialogía (en sus estilizaciones) son justamente lo inverso de un discurso «especular», que se devuelve su pro-pia imagen, un discurso sin «otro», que crea el espejismo de su identidad. Si hay algo visible como permutación de signos —su bilingüismo y heteroglosia— es lo «otro», el «otro» dis-curso, contra el monoestilismo y la monología del discurso literario y político institucionalizado. Valle «representa» la posibilidad de la subversión del sujeto, a través de otras prác-ticas del significante. Su «texto único» significa la construc-ción de una producción literaria desde la *periferia,* de la hete-rogeneidad, en un quiebre anti-mnemónico y anti-mimesis. Ese corte que se debatió en la década de 1930 como los programas contrapuestos del «realismo» y del «modernismo». La defensa de Brecht no podría ser más acertada:

No se le puede prohibir a la literatura el empleo de las nuevas técnicas adquiridas por el hombre contemporáneo, tales como la capacidad de registros simultáneos, la abstracción atrevida o la combinación rápida. [Mi traducción: Literature cannot be forbidden to employ skills newly acquired by contemporary man, such as the capacity for simultaneous registration, bold abstraction, or swift combination] (1979: 75).

Las «memorias amables» de Bradomín, y el ciclo de Montenegro, así como cuentos y textos anteriores, evidencian además otra intención: crear una literatura francamente «popular» (cf. Hormigón, 1972); pero valga distinguir —como Brecht— entre lo «popular» y lo «popularizado» o «populachero». Recuérdese que para el escritor alemán, popular significa cuanto es comprensible para las masas, adoptando, enriqueciendo sus formas de expresión, incorporando su punto de vista al mismo tiempo que se lo corrige o confirma; representar al sector más progresista del «pueblo» de manera que pueda asumir su liderazgo; por tanto, una literatura que sea comprensible a otros sectores sociales, que se relacione con sus tradiciones y las desarrolle y que le comunique a aquel sector del pueblo que aspira al liderazgo, los logros de aquel sector que dirige la nación en ese momento (p. 81). Valle cumple algunos de estos compromisos, en su «representación» de una Galicia «feudal» y carlista, apegada a tradiciones, pero al mismo tiempo «lo otro» del liberalismo centralizador. Quizá la más clara distinción se establezca en la diferencia entre las «locuras heroicas» del carlismo y la «sanción ética» o «furor ético» que caracteriza la historia de España desde Isabel la Católica, según sus palabras en 1930 (Dougherty, 209). La misma distinción geográfica se observa a través del lenguaje: los idiomas no salen de las calles y los bulevares de las ciudades, dice: «En las ciudades sólo nacen el argot de los canallas y las germanías [...] Las ciudades corrompen a los idiomas y sólo el campo y la luz los conservan, los renuevan y los depuran» (Dougherty, 1925: 135). No es de extrañar que las farsas y esperpentos sean «citadinos», de la actualidad contemporánea, y en argot y germanía.

Las «memorias amables» de Bradomín, a su vez, mantienen su distancia irónica con el pasado, y mediante la intertextualidad parodia las filosofías pesimistas, los tópicos de regeneracionistas y noventaiochistas, y toda aquella visión apocalíptica finisecular que lamenta el final del imperio. Este espejo estilizado e irónico se «representa» en múltiples detalles de figuraciones textuales y proyectos gestuales, juegos combinatorios de significantes y significados. Valle busca lo asocial, las estilizaciones irónicas, el ritualismo gallego, al mismo tiempo que se toma en solfa la «seriedad» y «solemnidad» de la literatura normativa. Valga como magnífico ejemplo aquel transgresor fin del mundo, cuando se corona a Safo y a Ganimedes. Eros y Thanatos cumplen una función de «representación» ideológica en lo imaginario libidinal, y el cuerpo (individual y político), si fragmentado (el fetichismo de los códigos y convenciones tradicionales desde el amor cortés), no forma parte aún de un gran carnaval de los oprimidos, de una somática y semántica social.

El cine —y sus técnicas— recién introducidas en 1905 le permitirán replantearse otras formas de significados y significantes, entre ellos el cuerpo: sus muecas y sus gestos. Basta una confusión del signo y del cuerpo, una reducción, y el rasgo del humor es más cruel, se niega entonces toda la retórica idealizada de la seducción y la perfección del pasado.

En cuanto práctica sexual, la estrategia valleinclanesca se caracteriza por el intento de desfamiliarizar el lenguaje, los personajes, empleando todos los registros anti-convencionales y anti-normativos, desde el más riguroso «preciosismo» al lenguaje descarado y arrabalero. En cuanto prácticas semióticas, ambos lenguajes comparten, en la estructura profunda, más semejanzas que diferencias. La diferencia es ilusoria, puesto que en ninguna de las aparentemente distintas prácticas textuales el enunciado corresponde al discurso que sucede en la realidad, o lenguaje «natural». Ambos son los engranajes de unas estructuras comunicativas de participación lectora, determinadas por un contexto socio-político que pone en tela de juicio el sistema de valores del lector/receptor en el espacio textual.

Capítulo III

# LA POSICION GEOMETRICA: IRONIA
# Y PARODIA

«Reservamos nuestras burlas para aquello
que nos es semejante.»

(*Los cuernos.*)

## 1. IRONIA Y PARODIA

El giro que toman estas series —sexualidad y muerte—
y la carnavalización a partir de 1910 ó 1914, más o menos,
aunque aparecen también diseminadas en la superficie textual
antes, es un cambio de signo; la ironía objetiva se instala y del
espejo cóncavo que alarga y estiliza las figuras, con un tinte
de «espejo desvanecido», recurre al convexo, reductivo y de-
gradador. El espejo (y volveremos sobre ello), por distinción
de los límites, abre a la escena lo imaginario y su representación en una multiplicación de cuerpos y sus imágenes, en
redundancias e hipertrofias. Valle pasa las imágenes por una
onda de irrisión, de reversiones de sátira y de parodia; a través de ambos recursos explota activamente el modo de desaparición de los lenguajes institucionalizados literarios y políticos.
En el movimiento entre la ironía y la parodia, con las farsas
hace una puesta en escena del «asesinato simbólico» de las
clases políticas (frase que adapto de Baudrillard, 1983, invir-
tiendo su sentido).

Parece necesaria una distinción entre sátira y parodia, a
partir de las sugerentes observaciones de Bajtin (1981: 51-83)
y de Hutcheon (1985), que nos permitirán distinguir el objetivo de las farsas y de los esperpentos. La sátira crea héroes
cómicos, i. e. Hércules, Odiseo; es decir, rebaja la grandeza

77

a través de la comicidad. La parodia, en cambio, crea imágenes, no realidades; el objeto de la parodia (lo parodiado) no pertenece en sí a los géneros que parodia, sino más bien son mundos inter-genéricos o extra-genéricos. Son fragmentos de una totalidad unificada, plurigenéricos, pluriestilizados, despiadadamente críticos y burlescos, y reflejan en toda su amplitud la heteroglosia y las múltiples voces de una cultura dada. La heteroglosia lo envuelve todo, como un espejo que cambia las formas, las alarma, las achica, las recorta, las deforma. Así cualquier palabra, especialmente la del discurso dominante, se refleja como un enunciado más o menos confinado o cercado, lenguaje de coto cerrado, donde la palabra pierde su polisemia. O, dicho de otra forma, retiene un solo significado: el que le impone el discurso del poder. El enunciado confinado es el típico y característico de una época; caduco, desgastado, envejecido, muerto y está listo, por así decirlo, para ser transformado y renovado (Bajtin, 1980: 68-83).

El discurso paródico —y continúo con las pertinentes observaciones de Bajtin— revela simultáneamente dos estilos, dos lenguas que se yuxtaponen, dos puntos de vista lingüísticos, dos enunciados. En definitiva, cada enunciado está confinado como entre signos de puntuación, entre comillas, que le permiten al lector u oyente percibir ambos enunciados como contigüedad. Por otra parte, la parodia supone «dos voces» (transconceptualización para Genette, 1982, y Hutcheon, 1985), que cerca las «representaciones» de otros objetos artísticos y pone al descubierto sus convenciones y estrategias. La parodia sería «intra-mural» y la sátira «extra-mural», con objetivo social.

Si bien ambas series se interpenetran, en las farsas, Valle se mueve entre la alegoría representativa, a la ironía representadora; provoca así una alteración del mismo objeto hasta sus consecuencias extremas, se distorsiona en una reversión activa al ser cuestionado, solicitado. En vuelta de tuerca la sexualidad y la muerte se parodian, se invierten, se reversabilizan. Matones, prostitutas, embaucadores, cuatreros, seres que reptan en desviaciones sexuales de coitos en burdeles y actos *contra natura* (incestos, violaciones ahora en el fango). La muerte y la sexualidad se hacen hipostáticas en un movimiento de deflexión y reflexión especular. Cambian los espacios; de los elegantes pazos, palacios o lujuriosos ambientes vamos descendiendo a los sórdidos de las ciudades (en particular el Madrid «absurdo, brillante y hambriento» de *Luces*). El resorte es desfamiliarizar —el extrañamiento revelador—, bien sea por medio de exquisiteces irreverentes o mediante el lenguaje chabacano y grosero. Las imágenes se perciben en una especie de inversión del carnaval erótico versallesco al espejo cóncavo del carnaval trascendente o histórico.

Como detalle secundario interesa recordar ahora que el principio de *ostranenie* (extrañamiento) de los formalistas al que hemos aludido antes se elaboró en 1914, como eslabón con el futurismo ruso (Steiner, 1984: 48-53). La idea de Shlovski era señalar que el arte es un objeto funcional, cuyo propósito es transformar la percepción del receptor y guiarla de lo práctico a lo artístico, extrayéndolo así de las asociaciones cotidianas. La deformación no radica en el lenguaje, sino en los hechos y en el proceso de representación verbal. En Valle el efecto se agudiza y adquiere otras proporciones desde la perspectiva de la «representación» de las «mitologías» a su inscripción decidida como efecto ideológico. El espejo que nos ofrece no es un simulacro, sino una proyección verídica del mundo arriba y abajo, en un espectáculo de farsa y carnaval, como los espejos de Solana que reflejan el pasado proyectándose en el presente. Sólo el continuo ejercicio del desconcierto, en una suerte de mutua negación de discursos, de alteraciones y violaciones de lenguajes en orientaciones cada vez más procaces, en una distancia de la tiranía de la realidad impuesta y un antagonismo que permite el juego. Las nociones precisas se desafían; amor y muerte pueden intercambiar sus acepciones más sublimes y más vulgares: *La pipa de kif* se entiende a la luz de esta poética dual donde reconstruye y destruye las formas rituales de amor y muerte; se las libera.

Unos detalles nos permitirán recontextualizar la pragmática especular de Valle. A final de siglo representantes diversos de un universo gráfico y teatral incorporan todo un lenguaje que se levanta contra la norma, que pone de relieve los conflictos entre la palabra constativa y la performativa, en juegos especulares. Estos textos (con los cuales en particular dialoga Valle, como veremos) revelan la función de disimulo y enmascaramiento de los lenguajes de la autoridad, en derroches de significantes y confluencia de inversiones. En particular, importa recuperar la crítica del teatro burgués; espacios privilegiados del universo contestatario y anti-burgués de anarquistas y socialistas. Esta crítica se inclina, sobre todo, hacia el ejercicio del espejo y sus alternativas como degradación de todo saber anterior, de toda autoridad, como negación final de los referentes y con una redefinición de la cultura (Zavala, 1988). Abundan, pues; referencias al «espejo», el «espejo de la sociedad»: espejo que debe reflejar costumbres y moral. Este es el espejo, que, en definitiva, debe quebrarse para revelar las «identidades» impuestas por los discursos dominantes. Los anarquistas y socialistas lamentan la corrupción, las canciones indecorosas, las escenas de taberna, la guasa, la broma. La crítica va dirigida contra un teatro anti-especular, que revela, no la realidad, sino su simulacro, y contra los «representantes» literarios de la burguesía que revelan «ficciones». La posición del sujeto es central en estas «representaciones especulares»; Valle intensifica entonces la creación de un discurso a-genérico, de libertad, «representado» por el cuerpo.

Las series se entretejen —el cuerpo, la bebida, la comida, la ropa, el sexo, la muerte—, en contradanza desafiante. La deflección y reflexión especular tienen su regla fundamental: «La posición geométrica del narrador», revelación de *La medianoche* (1916, en 1917). El mundo se convierte cada vez más en gesto; las referencias sirven para precisar, teatralmente —por así decirlo—, el gesto que se parodia, en inversión de valores, en el interior del lenguaje. La dialogía es progresivamente más polémica, de lenguajes disonantes, en contigüidad sin fusión. Valle deconstruye y carga el lenguaje y los gestos de un potencial mayor de extrañeza. Trampa por trampa, imagen por imagen, se violentan; los heroicos guerrilleros se transforman en chulos callejeros; los elegantes nobles en señoritos afeminados o jaquetones; las grandes gestas en rencillas, las grandes pasiones en coitos vulgares; los grandes himnos patrióticos en solfa de opereta. Algo de la desmitificación de las tradiciones se percibe en la serie narrativa de *La guerra carlista*, donde Valle ironiza sobre la necesidad de Montenegro de mantenerlas vivas a través de Cara de Plata, que se complace en tratar a punta de látigo a los administradores de las tierras, y en la obra de teatro *El Marqués de Bradomín* (1907).

Podríamos multiplicar los ejemplos, pero algunas conclusiones, siquiera provisorias, son pertinentes. Dije al principio que las series carnavalizadas revelan la resistencia de Valle a ajustarse a los cánones y reglas del arte vigente, y un rechazo a los moldes oficiales impuestos por las instituciones en el poder. Son el fermento de un nuevo arte que se opone a los órdenes jerárquicos y aristocráticos, regidos por la norma. Las series encuentran su intensidad máxima dentro de este universo lingüístico espacial, que se alimenta de la corriente populuar, de los antiguos dialectos, refranes, proverbios, lecturas de modelos clásicos italianos, del ocultismo, de tradiciones gallegas o celtas, entre tantas «voces» de apoyo que Valle reivindica y transcodifica. La contradanza de las series carnavalizadas le permiten la ruptura, el juego dual, la estrategia para liberar su amplia y profunda polémica con lo oficial, con las formas convencionales —como la urbanidad o los moldes cortesanos—, con el dogmatismo, la autoridad y las prescripciones estériles. Todo este desacato se armoniza en su poética, decididamente hostil a toda formalidad limitada, e incluso a toda perfección definitiva. Aspectos éstos que lo acercan a algunos importantes sistemas de codificación y estrategias de la metaficción reciente, de la contemporaneidad más moderna (Zavala, 1988 a) [1].

Este anverso y reverso, de gesto y mueca, de cuerpos estilizados y fragmentados, de personajes que aparecen, desaparecen y reaparecen, se apoya en la re-escritura constante, en la noción de un discurso en movimiento, de una producción que se re-produce siempre, en una especie de universo circular, en grados de duplicaciones, donde los códigos se transcodifican vertiginosamente. El texto se dispone como una doble semiosis de escritura y lectura, en una red de envíos y re-envíos, de un sujeto semiótico social que cambia de óptica, de posición, de focalizaciones, enmarcando, desenmarcando y re-enmarcando un mismo mundo. Volveremos sobre esta circularidad ligada al problema del tiempo.

Si los ejemplos que he mencionado parten del sistema carnavalizado, el conjunto de códigos determinó un sistema de imágenes y su concepción artística anti-canónica, anti-ortodoxa, anti-institucional. Las desacralizaciones librescas y las deformaciones de algunos personajes están casi siempre relacionadas con la Iglesia o con los ritos (endemoniados, penitentes, curas). Un paso más, y el blanco es la corte, el gobierno, la política. La inversión se dirige siempre contra la inmutabilidad ficticia del mundo; contra el lenguaje dogmático. Es decir, propongo que la mezcla de estilos, la no demarcación de los géneros históricos y literarios conduce a la no subordinación, uno de los importantes rasgos de la «modernidad». Valle retoma una misma historia, un mismo argumento, desde múltiples ángulos y diversos nexos intertextuales, de figuras siempre cambiantes que interrogan la legitimidad. Las

---

[1] Cito siempre por la edición de *Obras Escogidas* (1971), 2 vols.

escenas, los tipos humanos, los temas, se intercambian, se re-codifican, se re-semantizan, en amplios espirales. El teatro se «reteatraliza» (en frase de Pérez de Ayala, apud Rubio, 1988: 33).

Ante el espectáculo de la historia oficial, nos subraya el desorden, lo que Nietzsche llamaría «la parodia y bufonería de la historia», el moralismo dogmático de la política, y especialmente de aquella ordenada por una naturaleza providencial y trascendente que busca como ejemplos o esquemas los símbolos del pasado. Valle desmonta el totalitarismo y toma el único camino que queda libre: estamos en el elemento de la libertad en nuevas inflexiones. Esta libertad representa la desviación de la norma, de su lenguaje y sus familias de frases y de símbolos y sus presentaciones y representaciones legítimas. Con pensamiento crítico, Valle busca pasajes, hilos conductores entre las esferas de lo personal y lo colectivo desde la revolución desmultiplicada de 1868. Quizá sus diversas y heterogéneas producciones textuales se pregunten (y nos pregunten) qué hacer con los fragmentos de esa revolución. Busca la cadena de acontecimientos desastrosos desde las Cortes de Cádiz —e incluso desde tiempos más remotos— de destrucción y construcción y nueva destrucción, bajo la regencia de reyes y militares cambiantes, en su mayoría poco afortunados. Lo que se pregunta —y nos pregunta— es qué les hizo entonces, qué hizo esperar a todos que precisamente esa revolución septembrina rompería la cadena de desgracias; que precisamente Prim traería una suerte de edad de oro. Se pregunta —creo— por qué se hacen prepotentes los deseos que se fundan en errores. Y aquí —justamente en esta pregunta— radican su «modernidad» y contemporaneidad.

Se comprende ahora —confío— desde qué perspectiva se ha propuesto Valle como método general los desplazamientos enunciativos, en calidad de destinatario y de emisor. La palabra (el lenguaje) desmiente la posición del discurso; semejante violencia constituye un punto de partida. Valle violenta la idea del referente (imagen, palabra). La referencia común a una instancia reconocida por los dos interlocutores. Lo engañoso y lo cierto van juntos, no como contrarios en un sistema sino como un cuerpo (objeto) que posee un anverso y un reverso que asoman a la superficie. La figura y su gesto, el cargo y su representación se desplazan, como red de discontinuidades. La suya es una confusión sembrada en el orden de la significación de disfraces y máscaras: un dios Pan viejo, un reina achorizada, un príncipe vestido de bufón, un violador que se hace pasar por la reencarnación de Cristo, una honra en la cual ya nadie cree, un latín eclesiástico que se vuelve contra sí. La serpiente se muerde la cola. Valle cruza, bajo el signo lingüístico, dos direcciones de sentido: el objeto (referente) y su parodia.

La desviación va en aumento con los años. Imagen, forma, signo, se sublevan, fragmentan, comprimen y desfiguran. Cunden las inversiones del afuera y del adentro, de lo anterior y lo posterior, de la verdad y la mentira, en alteración especular en el seno mismo del discurso. Podemos establecer fácilmente la presencia de *dos* lenguajes, de *dos* escenas, de *dos* imágenes, funcionando como espejos recíprocos, en simultaneidad de enunciados.

Un encadenamiento seductor invita a intercambiar los signos y sus lenguajes; Valle fuerza el lenguaje para hacer jugar lo irreal con su propia realidad, la apariencia con la imagen en regla irónica para que el lector o auditor no le conceda un sentido único a lo que no lo tiene. Para salvar la ilusión de este sentido, redistribuye los signos en intensidades, por regiones geográficas, clases sociales, sexos, épocas históricas. No estamos con la producción textual que aliena, sino con la que comunica; la que revela con transparencia inexorable la obscenidad institucional.

En gradaciones, idénticas profanaciones van tomando formas de parodia, de derrocamiento bufonesco, con las groserías blasfematorias. Me limito a unas pocas. Cualquier lector podrá reconocer las palabras de Cristo en el siguiente diálogo entre Pachequín y Doña Loreta en *Los cuernos:*

> *Doña Loreta.*—¡Tú me perderás!
> *Pachequín.*—¡Si me amas, sígueme!

Entre la profanación de Bradomín, a que aludimos antes, y ésta intervienen la burla y la risa. O bien, contrástense las nuevas inflexiones que adquieren los incestos en las *Sonatas,* con el insinuado entre Pedro Gailo y Simoniña en *Divinas palabras.*

El sustrato que lo nutre es el mismo. Reúne lo heterogéneo en delirios de fuerza anti-dogmática y anti-autoritaria. Valle entrona entonces la risa popular, este mundo infinito de formas y manifestaciones, con sus deformidades, imprecaciones, juramentos, y sus degradaciones de lo noble, de la tradición, de los conceptos del honor y de la honra. Quisiera reforzar específicamente en este contexto mi propuesta de un *texto único* alimentado de la carnavalización, no sólo a partir de las siete series canónicas, sino por su objetivo: la poética de Valle se rige por un principio *regenerador* (central para Bajtin) y *renovador,* que excluye el temor y aspira a erradicar el miedo. Miedo contra lo estático, lo inerme, lo inmutable; Valle aspira a vencer poniendo en juego funcional la desmitificación, la desacralización y la burla/parodia/risa. Pasa su producción textual por el espejo de la posición geométrica del narrador, como la famosa rima del candil de Bécquer: de lejos una estrella, más cerca una luz, y al frente un vulgar y miserable candil.

El grado de estilización y/o de parodia se altera y transmite a través del contenido de la desfamiliarización o extrañamiento *(ostranenie),* mediante imágenes semejantes al extrañamiento revelador o *verfremdung* de Brecht. El objetivo es desmitificar, bien sean relaciones sígnicas estilizadas de las *Sonatas* (y los códigos anteriores), o las líneas paródicas de la mofa y la burla, interpretables a partir sobre todo de 1919. Los paradigmas se dispersan y se encuentran, se atraen y se repelen, dentro de un registro de explosiones de heteroglosia, enunciados que se contradicen, se apoyan y polemizan. Todas las partes forman esferas concéntricas, que juegan siempre a su contrario, a la alternancia. Puesto que la sociedad —sea la española o cualquier otra— no es estática, Valle invita a subvertir las instituciones que esclavizan, a revertir las imágenes, para que veamos su opuesto, la contra-realidad que libera.

## 2. SIMULTANEIDAD: «CERRAR EL CIRCULO»

Cité antes, a propósito de la deflexión y reflexión especular, la «Breve noticia» que sirve de prólogo a *La media noche,* texto justamente elogiado. Conviene recordar la importantísima regla fundamental sobre la posición geométrica del narrador. Quisiera complementar ahora mi referencia anterior, subrayando que la posición geométrica se percibe como *limitación;* la posición geométrica del narrador (la posición del sujeto) «está limitada por». Pero Valle se preocupa por advertirnos que aquel que pudiese estar a la vez en diversos lugares, como los teósofos dicen de algunos fakires, y las gentes novelescas de Cagliostro, tendrían de la guerra una visión, una emoción y una concepción en todo distinta de la que puede tener el mísero testigo, sujeto a las leyes geométricas de la materia corporal y mental. Intuición taumatúrgica, la llama; intuición que es

> comprensión que parece fuera del espacio y del tiempo, no es, sin embargo, ajena a la literatura y aún puede asegurarse que es la engendradora de los viejos poemas primitivos, vasos religiosos donde dispersas voces y dispersos relatos se han juntado, al cabo de los siglos, en un relato máximo, cifra de todos, en una visión suprema, cuasi infinita, de infinitos ojos que cierran el círculo (*OE* II: 781).

Si me he detenido a reproducir este extenso pasaje se debe a que apunta de manera insoslayable a la concepción de un texto único y de posiciones de sujeto que lo incluye todo, que cierra el *círculo* de «voces», imágenes y signos, visión no personal, sino colectiva. En lo que a la escritura se refiere, lo acerca a Mallarmé, en su concepción de un «libro» suma de todos, y a las fórmulas que propone en el prólogo al *Golpe de dados* (*Un coup de dés*, 1914), sobre el empleo de sangrías de imprenta y los espacios en blanco. Estas subdivisiones intiman una visión *simultánea* y totalizadora de la página. En Valle, el texto es la zona de encuentro de voces dispersas, vistas desde todos los puntos, *focalizadas* socialmente; es decir, de manera colectiva, en *simultaneidad* [3]. Si bien no emplea este concepto, éste se inserta como *incipit* del texto. Para Valle el círculo se cierra con el acopio de «voces»; lo que en palabras de Bajtin equivale a la arquitectura dialógica que celebra la alteridad, proceso comunicativo complejo y variado. Esta categoría —diálogo— está relacionada con el principio de simultaneidad; es decir, no *igual a*, sino *simultáneamente con*, en contigüidad, no fusión (véase Clark, Holquist, 1984:

---

[2] Es de observarse que estos paradigmas forman parte de lo que E. Waugh (1984) establece como serie taxonómica de la narrativa postmoderna.

[3] Abundan los trabajos sobre el teatro; véase en especial Lyon (1983) y Osuna (1982) sobre las acotaciones, y el esclarecedor de Carlos Serrano (1987). Me parecen además imprescindibles las precisiones de Rubio Jiménez (1988) sobre el teatro de Ramón Pérez de Ayala, que permite contextualizar a Valle.

101-2). En cuanto principio regulador, es el trasfondo de las categorías bajtinianas de *polifonía, diversidad social* y *heteroglosia*. La intuición taumatúrgica de Valle —creo— se puede leer en este trasfondo epistemológico de palabra, significado, lenguas, dialectos, lenguajes. Para Bajtin «síntesis trascendente» (ibídem, 38), para Valle «cerrar el círculo». Algo de esto intuyó Speratti-Piñero (1968), que alude al proceso de simultaneidad en *Tirano Banderas,* pero en muy otra dirección. En realidad el propósito de presentar «simultáneamente» imágenes, forma parte de sus experimentos con el tiempo (bien visto por Salper, 1988). Semejante a la cámara cinematográfica, inscribe los textos como cuadros sucesivos en narraciones organizadas teatralmente. Permite —en definitiva— la visión totalizadora.

No es casualidad que la metáfora y la concepción de la «simultaneidad» se concretizara a partir de su experiencia como testigo ocular el frente bélico en la primera guerra mundial. De alguna manera está relacionada con nuevas tecnologías: el cine y las líneas telefónicas que, en 1914, le dieron la oportunidad a los poderes europeos de regular sus intervenciones (Kern, 1986). La metáfora panóptica apoya la percepción de un vasto presente simultáneo. A tal punto que Apollinaire concibió un poema a transmitirse por medio del teléfono («Les fenêtres»). En este clima de opinión, Ortega concibe su «perspectivismo» como un punto de vista sobre el universo. En contraste —y desde una postura más cercana a Valle y sus círculos—, Joyce define la *epifanía* como una visión momentánea o percepción extratemporal. La experiencia bélica le permite a Valle en 1914 re-afirmar sus experimentos anteriores.

Si retomamos el diálogo con Mallarmé, para proseguir la relación entre lo especular y la simultaneidad, hay un «espejo» en *Un golpe de dados* porque significado y significante se reflejan mutuamente, lo que Lyotard (1979: 369) llama «sobrerreflexión». El espejo invierte y deforma la imagen, y produce el proceso definible como carnavalización, un efecto de prótesis que amplía la adquisición de estas imágenes, de estos lenguajes, a partir de un centro que es la suma de sus prácticas discursivas. Una concepción especular alucinatoria donde la conciencia de sí, la toma de conciencia del lector/auditor obliga a traducir los datos sensoriales y a descodificar las reglas de los complejos verbales apropiados para verse como «otro», desfamiliarizarse, en función de lo social.

86

Esta forma anómala, alucinatoria, es el proyecto que establece Valle desde 1902 en «Modernismo», que incorpora como prólogo a *Corte de amor* (1914) y la era argentina funambulesca que anuncia en *La pipa de kif*. Propongo que ambos lenguajes *coexisten,* no se anulan. El juego especular de la serie carnavalizada le sirve siempre de apoyo para atacar los dogmas fundamentales y los sacramentos, la ortodoxia aristotélico-católica y retórica, y transgredir y profanar los límites impuestos por la ideología oficial, el lenguaje normativo de los géneros aristotélicos y el de la religión perceptiva. Valle explora la *stasis* impuesta por la *autoridad,* y le «suelta el cuerpo», en gestos, farsas, guiñoles, muñecos: en uno u otro caso, su licencia es siempre una meditación dialógica sobre la libertad.

Si, como afirma Bajtin, cada época tiene sus normas de propiedad y lenguaje oficial aceptado, y su vocabulario y las expresiones que permiten hablar libremente, de llamar las cosas por su nombre, sin cortapisas mentales ni eufemismos, todos tenemos amplias esferas de enunciaciones aún no hechas públicas e inexistentes desde el punto de vista del lenguaje literario escrito (1968: 188, 421). Valle-Inclán convierte su texto único en la zona de encuentro de este universo de enunciados.

Y el *círculo se cierra* con el lenguaje que no se debe decir, por la gente que lo dice. La esfera del radio entre lo permitido y lo no permitido (lo decente y lo indecente) se acerca en dos amplios subtextos: el carnaval, la cultura de la risa (institución social) y el realismo grotesco, expresión o tradición literaria (sobre estas categorías, Clark, Holquist, 1984: 299). El mundo funambulesco de inversiones alucinatorias —con su intertextualidad profunda con románticos modernistas y simbolistas— es un mundo patas arriba en relaciones sígnicas de referentes o mundo al revés, caro a la imaginería popular de antigua estirpe, y frecuente en las aleluyas del siglo XIX. Establece un universo de carnaval, interpretable como consecuente de opereta; en relación lógica de implicación la reina es achorizada, los generales de baraja, los gobernantes desgobernados. La imagen se produce causalmente con la realidad. En sus palabras: «Busco, más que el fabular novelesco, la sátira encubierta en ficciones casi de teatro» (*A B C,* 7-XII-1928, apud Dougherty, 170-171).

Dije *círculo,* simultaneidad y contigüidad de enunciados, es decir, el lenguaje que se parodia y la parodia del lenguaje —o el reflejo mutuo de significado y significante de Mallarmé— y no es ocioso juego de palabras. El lenguaje oficial —literario, político, religioso, de clases sociales, de sexos, de regiones, entre tantos otros— se ubica así entre dos realidades sociales: el discurso oficial que se parodia recuperado por el lenguaje de los personajes de farsa, cuya *entonación* comunica al oyente/lector el grado de parodia. Los referentes no están ausentes; son dos presencias en la radio de percepción del intérprete.

Esta forma de libertad valleinclanesca es posible sólo por la «voz» o «voces» que se perciben por medio de la entonación cuya función ya hemos indicado. Este es el mecanismo social por excelencia, que transfigura la norma en anti-norma, la retórica en anti-retórica, el discurso serio y trágico en risa. Esta inversión es *simultánea*, coexiste en tiempo y espacio, como lo uno y lo otro, como el cuerpo y su sombra, en absoluta distancia o extrañamiento, pero no en disociación. Valga de un riquísimo repertorio, la mención de algunos poemas de *La pipa*, así como las tempranas farsas (que analizaremos con detalle). La entonación sirve de apoyo a la alteración especular, como en la farsa *La cabeza del dragón* (1909 en 1926). La acotación marca las «voces» de la parodia y lo parodiado (del significado y el significante en Mallarmé):

> El pavón, siempre con la cola abierta en abanico de fabuloso iris, está sobre la escalinata de mármol que decoran las rosas. Y al pie, la góndola de plata con su palio de marfil. Y los cisnes duales en la prora bogando, musicales en su lirada curva (*OE* II: 1016).

Debemos detenernos aquí para recordar la serie dariana de «Los Cisnes», y la metáfora sobre el signo de interrogación del cuello del ave. En ambos casos son metáforas socialmente connotadas (Zavala, 1987).

La parodia del lenguaje modernista (o falta de decoro de la retórica tradicional) sirve de apoyo a la *Farsa y licencia de la Reina castiza;* la distancia irónica proviene del narrador o acotador. El rey sale correteando y «La vágula libélula de la sonrisa bulle/sobre su boca belfa, pintada de carmín». No es difícil reconocer la «Sonatina». En red de asociaciones y deconstrucciones, el pintarrajeado rey, como la princesa dariana, busca novio.

Veamos otros casos de farsas paródicas. En *La farsa italiana de la enamorada del Rey* (1920) se percibe un tono noven-

taiochista (frecuente en *La pipa*) contra la literatura castellanizante en los versos que describen la decoración. Dado el
contexto, se parodia la falsedad del tópico:

> sobre la cruz de dos caminos llanos
> y amarillentos, una ventana clásica,
> corsarios, labradores, estudiantes
> sestean por las cuadras y pajares [...]
> El patio de la venta es humanista
> y picaresco, con sabor de aulas [...]
> tiene un vaho de letras del Quijote.
> El cielo azul, las bardas amarillas,
> y el hablar refranero: Las Castillas (*OE* II: 197).

Léase a paródica luz «castellanizante» el monólogo de Maese
Lotario «Sólo ama realidades la gente española» (p. 231).

En esta misma farsa el desciframiento del lector crítico
descubre un retintín de regusto calderoniano; el teológico «Ah
de la vida» se transforma en «Ah de la casa», que emite el
Escudero. Los saltos son proverbiales en este texto: Altisidoro
lee en alta voz unos versos plagados de lugares comunes modernistas, de *El Quijote,* entre otros decodificables. Vista a
otra luz (la satírica-paródica, se entiende), muy otro es el
referente de *princesa de los cuentos, azules pensamientos,
rosas.* Esta farsa tiene como subtexto cultural polémico el castellanismo estereotipado y el Cid Campeador (aquello de
«¡Santiago y cierra España!»). La canción de amor trae «los
azufres de Francia», según el rey Carlos III —objeto de sátira
despiadada—, acto de lenguaje denotativo que remite muy
directamente al lenguaje conservador y tradicional a partir del
cordón sanitario por la Revolución francesa.

En las farsas, el lenguaje «modernista» está socialmente
connotado, en su objetivo desmitificador. La parodia se concentra en héroes literarios y de la tradición. En *La cabeza del
dragón* los subtextos satirizados son personajes quijotescos, el
*Orlando furioso,* la mitología y la música wagneriana (entre
tantos, véase Rubio, 1987). Buen cristal rebajador convierte al
dios Pan en un Duende que lleva aún las cicatrices de los
cuernos. En un campo de voces polémicas más amplio, el
vasto subtexto cultural proviene de los cuentos infantiles, de
los cuentos de hadas y de las estampas y litografías infantiles
(cigüeñas, duendes), así como de algunos cuentos darianos
(Rubio, 1987). Todos estos subtextos le permiten a Valle re-

codificar y desmitificar los cuentos de hadas, su contenido erótico (dimensión que conocemos ahora gracias a Bettelheim, 1977), y apuntar en una dirección política.

*La marquesa Rosalinda* (1912), farsa sentimental y grotesca, revela en la superficie textual una voz polémica con el lenguaje modernista en un amplio subtexto literario de lugar común. Los personajes se parodian a sí mismos (en aguda observación de Montesinos, 1966), y las corrientes poéticas antiguas y modernas. El léxico y los metros poéticos son motivo de sátira dialógica: Lohengrin, el cisne de Leda, las marquesas, princesas, las fuentes, cuando no alude directamente a Voltaire, Banville, Goya. En realidad, no queda títere con cabeza en el arcano cultural y literario, desde la mitología greco-latina:

> Seamos a un tiempo comediantes
> de reyes, de cisnes y de nidos (*OE* I: 828).

Y en boca de Arlequín, un magnífico «travestido» del arte moderno (término de Bajtin, 1978), saltan en procesión los subtextos románticos, parnasianos, simbolistas, modernistas. He aquí como termina la primera jornada:

> [...] Ahora medita
> Arlequín, como los cisnes y las flores,
> e interroga a la blanca margarita,
> que sabe el porvenir de los amores (830).

Otro subtexto dariano evidente es la acotación sobre la «alegre risa» de Amaranta: «Como una amapola/ríe, ríe/ríe. ¡Oh linda garganta/que anuncia los días de la Carmañola» (840). Esta figura de farsa canta el calendario festivo popular de la época del terror de la Revolución francesa, himno de batalla de las gestas populares a partir de entonces. La marquesa Eulalia dariana, en cambio, juega con el trillado tópico del carnaval versallesco.

La simultaneidad a que hemos aludido no sólo se revela mediante el lenguaje (en sus referencias e interferencias), también es polo de interés en los espacios, las acotaciones, las apostillas; los personajes coexisten en dos realidades. En el castillo de fantasía conviven el príncipe disfrazado de bufón, el duende «que canta un ritmo sin edad, como las fuentes, los pájaros, como el sapo y la rana». En el universo textual de

Valle todo es un vasto *como,* a diferencia del *más que,* o la búsqueda de la hipérbole absoluta de Góngora, por ejemplo. Los elementos heterogéneos —como en la realidad cotidiana— conviven; coexisten en un mismo espacio y tiempo el duende, el sapo, las cigüeñas que escuchan con una pata al aire y su actitud «anuncia a los admiradores de Ricardo Wagner». En el mundo —real o ficticio— se albergan príncipes y bufones, princesas y maritornes, como se albergan ricos y pobres, gobernantes y gobernados, espadones y obreros, bohemios y académicos, todo en *totalidad simultánea,* no como barcos que se cruzan en la noche.

Como estrategia textual para descubrir esta simultaneidad de voces, Valle emplea una amplia red intersemiótica, que incorpora desde los elementos tradicionales hasta la transición secuencial del cine, de focalización fragmentaria. En «Preludio» a *La marquesa Rosalinda* (1912) hace coexistir lo diverso:

> Olor de rosa y de manzana
> tendrán mis versos a la vez,
> como una farsa cortesana
> de Versalles o Aranjuez (*OE* I: 14).

En el mundo valleinclanesco todo *recuerda a, es como,* se presenta *a la vez.* Los mundos, las voces, están en dialogía, no en oposición binaria esto/lo otro, sino en situación de ambos/y. Valle sobrepasa los oximorones ofreciendo lo uno y lo otro, o lo uno y lo diverso simultáneamente. En definitiva, lo trágico es a la vez grotesco, la realidad es engaño, todo en coexistencias. Los estilos, como las voces, se yuxtaponen en intensidades: *Tirano,* los esperpentos, *El ruedo,* como antes las farsas, se alimentarán de voces oficiales y no oficiales, del orden y de la revolución, del centro y de la periferia. Lenguajes siempre en contigüidad, que destruyen el mito de un lenguaje único, de una verdad única, de una sola realidad.

Esta deconstrucción está asentada en dos supuestos: primero, no da por sentado que haya un solo lenguaje único posible; segundo, destruye el mito del monologismo ideológico, que se basa en la noción que el lenguaje es homogéneo, y está libre del juego de diferencias entre los varios discursos y dialctos que constituyen la lengua nacional (véase Voloshinov/Bajtin, 1973). En su totalidad, este mundo es un rechazo de lo homogéneo. Lo que nos revela Valle es cuántas realidades había en España además de la oficial, que se consideraba única, y quién determinaba la frontera entre lo visible y lo invisible.

Volvamos sobre el concepto de *simultaneidad* bajtiniano y su relación con el principio de circularidad valleinclanesco, aunque sólo sea para sugerir —muy provisoriamente— algunas analogías. Aludimos a *La medianoche* y, de manera oblicua, a *La lámpara* [4], donde elabora su teoría del círculo: los círculos concéntricos, las simetrías especulares en estrecha relación con el tiempo, el espacio y la visión estética. Todo este sentido de simultaneidad se transforma con el tiempo en la base de *Tirano Banderas*, novela estructurada sobre la simultaneidad temporal del relato, en doble dimensión siempre de dinamismo y *stasis* (¿la simultaneidad del *Golpe de dados?*). Pero la estructura simétrica no es novedad en 1926 (véase Speratti-Piñero, 1968; Díaz Migoyo, 1985); la había ensayado en *Sonata de estío*. Luego reconoce, en 1913, que allí intentó resolver en lo posible el espacio y el tiempo, hacer que lo acaecido en diversos puntos geográficos pasara en un solo día (1913 en Dougherty, 49-50). La técnica —y sigo ahora a Salper (1988)— se manifiesta también en 1907, con *Aguila de blasón*, para crear la ilusión de continuidad, enfocar distintos tiempos y situaciones desde numerosas perspectivas, ensanchando así las dimensiones espaciales. Continúa el experimento en *La medianoche*, aunque malogrado —como él mismo reconociera— y finalmente alcanza su auténtico logro en *Tirano*. En cuanto estrategia semiótica, originó soluciones diversas y procedimientos afines.

El caso es que esta búsqueda está a su vez estrechamente vinculada a sus experimentos (y de otros «modernos», tal Mallarmé) con la forma y con el lenguaje. En 1907, Valle afirma que busca armonizar lo «lírico y lo grotesco» y resolver cómo engarzar las palabras «aún alternando a veces el significado de los términos» (1907, en Dougherty, 100). Parecería que alude a las farsas. Años después aclarará el principio rector de su poética: «habría que hacer algo en un modo popular, y con un sentido eterno de la actualidad» (Dougher-

---

[4] *La lámpara* comienza a atraer el interés que se merece; véase en particular Allegra (1982 a) y Garlitz (1986), Cattaneo (1987), Maier (1988). Me parecen evidentes las analogías con la poética de Mallarmé, si bien en Valle cobran un sentido más «socializado».

[5] No entro en discusiones sobre el rechazo bajtiniano de la parodia moderna, que se explica históricamente. Aprovecho sus sugerencias en torno a la parodia como discurso con doble orientación, así como las apreciaciones de Hutcheon (1985) en este sentido.

ty: 15). Este sentido eterno y presente simultáneos adquiere —como es sabido— su más nítida exposición en *La lámpara* en un lenguaje metafórico que se nutre de la teosofía y las filosofías orientales (alimento también de Mallarmé). Sin embargo, expone el doble cerco del término emparejando el tiempo y el espacio como indisociables:

> la conciencia quebranta el círculo de las vidas para deducir la recta del Tiempo. Consideramos las horas y las vidas como yuxtaposición de instantes, como eslabones de una cadena, cuando son círculos concéntricos al modo que los engendra la piedra en la laguna (*OE* I: 580).

Los textos, el lenguaje, emergen como grandes círculos donde una palabra remite a otra, un texto a otro, la lengua al habla, el abajo al arriba, una voz a otra, una imagen a su contra-imagen, cada vez con mayor nitidez. Estos espejos recíprocos reflejan —simultáneamente— el anverso y el reverso, la realidad y la contra-realidad en refractaciones especulares de alteridades. Como totalidad, revelan diversos intentos de escribir el mismo texto, en respuesta nunca fragmentaria a las mismas preguntas esenciales.

En definitiva: el círculo valleinclanesco y la «síntesis trascendente» de Bajtin significan un sistema de cambios intercambiables de percepción de la realidad, de lo enunciado, y no enunciado. Todo ello depende de la posición geométrica para arquitecturar la realidad en su alteridad simultánea. El círculo dista de ser *repetición,* representa más bien la metáfora de la profunda categoría sobre los planos espaciales y temporales de los cuales Valle-Inclán se vale para organizar el mundo empírico y la alteridad siempre renovada del lenguaje y la comunicación.

El texto único de Valle se mueve de lo irónico, a la mofa a la burla a la parodia en cambios e intercambios, en síntesis de los diversos géneros y sub-géneros de la tradición carnavalesca. Toma y retoma de diversos puntos de la tradición literaria clásica hasta la popular y visual —la tradición celestinesca, el sainete, el entremés, el teatro de títeres. «Todo el saber es un recuerdo» —escribe en *La lámpara* (I: 570)—, y este recuerdo, también memoria del género, le llega como eslabones de una cadena que se disemina en formas varias y diversas de las mismas imágenes.

La producción de Valle se nos presenta, desde esta posición geométrica, en duplicidad de planos; el narrador se vuelve crítico y disminuye cada vez más la autoridad de la posición valorativa de los otros y aprovecha todas las posibilidades de la heterogeneidad de los géneros discursivos (orales y escritos), los cambios históricos en los estilos, la alteración de los sujetos discursivos o alternancia de hablantes, en reacentuación paródicas e irónicas, en combinaciones absolutamente libres de palabras ajenas y propias, llenas de entonaciones y de expresividad. Su texto único nos abre a un producción literaria de multiplicidad de tonos, donde tanto lo serio cuanto lo noble pierden su carácter exclusivo y único [6].

---

[6] Readapto y amplío un primer esbozo de este capítulo, «Poética de la carnavalización en Valle-Inclán», en *Formas carnavalescas en el arte y la literatura*, Javier Huerta Calvo, ed. Barcelona: Serbal, 1989.

Capítulo IV

# LA MUSA FUNAMBULESCA

> Por la divina primavera
> me ha venido la ventolera
> . de hacer versos funambulescos
> (un purista diría grotescos).

*(Aleluya.)*

## 1. AMOR MISTICO/AMOR PROFANO

El carnaval político estalla en la concentrada heteroglosia
y los ritmos paródicos de la poesía de Valle-Inclán, de tan
mala recepción entonces y ahora. *Claves líricas* (*Aromas de
leyenda. La pipa de kif. El pasajero*, 1907, 1919, 1920) le
descubren al lector los juegos y estrategias como totalidad. La
poesía «programa» descubre dos partes nítidamente articuladas: lo uno y lo otro, o el mundo y su contrario, la doctrina
mística y la erótica. El punto de partida es un viraje hacia
ambas caras de una sociedad desde el lenguaje; el milagro del
lenguaje poético o vulgar, tema desarrollado en *La lámpara
maravillosa*, en la sección «El milagro musical» (Cattaneo,
1979) [1].

A partir de una lectura dialógica yuxtalineal quisiera someter
a discusión la articulación entre ambos textos poéticos (tomo
como unidad *Aromas* y *El pasajero*, en adelante *Claves líricas*), estructuradas sobre una concepción dual del mundo y
sobre la estratificación del lenguaje (o lenguajes) literario
coetáneo. En conjunto, en cuanto práctica textual, revelan la
función social de la experiencia lírica a través de un doble
sistema de conexiones y selecciones: 1) el filtro social media-

---

[1] Una primera versión ligeramente distinta de este capítulo la constituye «La poética de Valle-Inclán: la entonación como práctica textual», en *Quimera, cántico, busca y rebusca de Valle-Inclán*, ed. Juan
A. Hormigón, Madrid: Ministerio de Cultura, 1989, 233-246.

tizado por los espacios internos; 2) la producción literaria como proyecto cultural transmitido a través de estrategias textuales que se insertan en la serie carnavalizada. Más bien articulan de manera definitiva el viraje al «carnaval político». Actos de lenguaje ambos sistemas, con valor performativo (como vimos antes), que atraviesan los textos en una amplia gama de mediaciones y relativizaciones entre texto y sociedad.

Los poemas de *Claves líricas*, como Anillo de Giges, traen a la superficie, las formas internas y externas de un discurso en proceso, anti-institucional siempre, cuyo propósito es institucionar la nueva literatura o textualidad (la farsa y el esperpento). El doble sistema que sugiero —interioridad y carnaval— organiza la estructura espacial en nuevos universos sociales. Al reunir estos textos, Valle nos invita a trazar líneas de comunicación con el pasado a través de una doble vertiente esotérica/mística y la curvatura populachera. En los poemas se programan la intensificación, el doble sistema inicial ahora en su combinatoria definida. El género poético le permite articular los diversos lenguajes en sus dobles sistemas y combinatorias, siempre dentro de una revolución literaria y formal, cuyo objetivo es desmontar, deconstruir valores en el interior de una veta crítica radical. Mediante el poder evocador de nuevos códigos —el místico/esotérico y el carnavalizado—, Valle incorpora en su lírica horizontes marcadamente anti-institucionales desde el *exterior* de sistemas de valores de la tradición, la cultura y las normas y convenciones aceptadas.

Partimos, pues, de esta premisa de diálogo intertextual con sus propios textos, dialogía de apoyo y polémica con su propia voz. Será posible analizar el mundo valleinclanesco a partir de ahora considerando sus estrategias y una armazón constructiva dialógica que hace estallar la pluralidad de estilos: el sublime y el vulgar, el clisé y la novedad, lo exótico, lo excéntrico, la desviación, de forma semejante a otros poetas finiseculares, y pienso muy especialmente en Darío (según he demostrado en páginas dedicadas al fin de siglo 1987 y 1987 b [en prensa]). En ambos discursos —*Claves líricas* y *La pipa*—, Valle experimenta con el lenguaje, la estructura, en dicción coloquial y/o de exquisiteces verbales, en disonancia expresiva con el lenguaje literario y las instituciones.

### Claves líricas: los espacios internos

Comenzaremos por *Aromas de leyenda* (1907, 14 poemas) y *El pasajero* (1920, que incluye composiciones anteriores),

96

núcleo de 33 poemas que integra bajo el subtítulo integrador de *Claves líricas* [2]. Esta escritura dialoga con toda la producción gallega, los cuentos primeros, las *Sonatas*. La crítica ha dado por sentido el «modernismo» escapista de estos textos en contraste con el «compromiso» directo de *La pipa*. No sin razón el primer núcleo se ha situado en la etapa galleguista, a partir de las alusiones a jardines, paisajes, pobladores. En conjunto, ambos textos presentan la búsqueda del enigma a través de una reforma verbal arcaizante (al igual que los textos en prosa ya mencionados). Ante todo, se centra en la movilidad de las imágenes, reflejos todas de la contemplación del arte (en diálogo con *La lámpara*). Estas imágenes son las tensiones de la espiritualidad, en un esfuerzo sostenido por superar las fronteras de la percepción sensible y del entendimiento; una búsqueda de la circularidad simultánea. El poeta se regodea en la significación mística de las palabras, como los monjes medievales (sobre todo *El pasajero*). Valga como ejemplo del pasado aquel Raban Maur, monje benedictino (silgo XIX) que compuso un opúsculo sobre la naturaleza de las cosas, la propiedad de las palabras y su significación mística (apud Duby, 1983: 104). Esta tradición estética/mística encuentra su máxima expresión en San Agustín, luego en el adorno y el alarde del esoterismo del *trobar clus,* vertido en un lenguaje que sólo los iniciados pueden descifrar.

Las *Claves* de Valle se nos presentan como una especie de reescritura del *Roman de la Rose* (y sus espejos deformantes) que ya Guillaume de Lorris había conducido por alegorías hasta la lúcida gratificación del amor, en ese incandescente progreso ascensional del amor por la Rosa (véase el estudio de Batany, 1973). Las nuevas claves valleinclanescas son de la misma familia espiritual de este arte litúrgico y especular que celebra los esplendores de la sensibilidad creadora, de la naturaleza, en un nuevo ciclón de unión entre *natura naturans*

---

[2] Cito por *Opera Omnia,* vol. 9, 1930. Una advertencia: un cotejo de los textos (ed. *El pasajero,* 1920, y *Claves líricas,* 1943) mostraría un gran número de variantes, cambios y supresiones sustanciales con las versiones publicadas en *Los Lunes de El Imparcial.* A saber: cambios de títulos, eliminación de estrofas y versos completos, léxico, organización estrófica. Por ejemplo, «Rosa de Bronce» se titula en el periódico «Rosa del Rebelde». Se observará también que, a partir de 1918, coexisten poemas de *El pasajero* con otros que incorporara en *La pipa.* He de agradecerle a Roberta Salper el haberme facilitado fotocopias de lo publicado en *Los Lunes.* Consúltese el indispensable cotejo de Serrano Alonso (1987).

y *natura naturata*. Todo este mundo de alegorías e imágenes se expresa en un bilingüismo consciente (como Rosalía de Castro antes), encaminado a mostrar las tensiones sociales, además de juegos intersemióticos que unen el signo pictográfico al signo fonético.

Valle puebla este «idílico» mundo arcaizante con peregrinos, leprosos, ermitaños de los retablos medievales, apoyándose en una red de intertextos litúrgicos y del «modernismo» arcaizante, estrategia del Rubén de «Cosas del Cid» o de «Los motivos del lobo», de Mallarmé en *Vathek*, de Lytton Bulwer, entre tantos otros. *Claves* se articula a partir de un virtuosismo métrico, léxico y rítmico en diálogo con las artes medievales de ascetismos y formas perfectas. Los poemas se nos muestran como extensos juegos de palabras, de signos fonéticos y pictográficos, cuyas resonancias y acordes descansan sobre las relaciones alegóricas y simbólicas. El discurso progresa por alusiones, reflejos, saltos; las *claves* son clave de un misterio nunca definitivamente explicado, susceptible de descifrarse siempre al igual que una partitura musical que no se descifra de una sola vez, sino que es capaz de ejecuciones siempre renovadas (cf. Courbin, 1977: 19, sobre el mundo medieval). Son espacios cerrados, antípodas del torneo, de las justas.

El pasajero (¿en diálogo con el peregrino de las *Soledades* de Góngora?), es un peregrino-espectador que nos revela el *ying* y el *yang* de su interioridad; lo uno y lo otro. Es también, como en Góngora, el lector; nos muestra que leer es interpretar, y los signos fonéticos y pictográficos comunican, no se pierden en el placer del texto. A modo de paréntesis, justo es señalar los cambios de título del libro; en *Los Lunes de El Imparcial* (3-IV-1918), donde publica algunos poemas, parece haber sido *Talismán metafórico*, en otra ocasión se anuncia como *Poemas de las rosas* [3]. El sentido metafórico/simbólico del conjunto poemas se nos ofrece como clave en «Rosas del Rebelde» («Rosa de bronce» en *Claves*), que en su versión de 1920 está dividido en cuatro secciones: *El pasajero, Laureles, Tentaciones, Talismán*. El pasajero/caminante siente todas las tentaciones del mundo y goza las rosas (rosa hiperbólica, matinal, vespertina, mística, métrica, pánida, de melancolía, de

---

[3] Según Emma S. Speratti Piñero (1974: 163), se iba a llamar *Poemas de las rosas*. A estas flores se le atribuían ciertas propiedades y tienen valor simbólico. Véase la relación con *La lámpara* (Cattaneo, 1979). También remiten al *Roman de la rose* y su juego especular-deformante.

Oriente). La rosa es movimiento, anverso y reverso, misticismo y liturgia, pero en ella está también la *gula, voluptas,* la carne con vida dispuesta a los placeres (la Psiquis dariana). El pasajero es el sujeto de la tensión entre la realidad y el «enigma» que ronda la voz lírica; véase a la luz de esta tensión «La rosa del reloj» (107) y «Rosa de Oriente» (105).

En la superficie textual se proyecta el mundo de los caminos, en un paisaje móvil, de ermitaños, de predicadores nómadas, de los santos patrones y las fiestas del cristianismo, a manera de gran retablo del mundo. En el mismo punto brota la textura carnavalizada subyacente de la literatura popular, de atavío de fiesta cortesana, que apenas encubre la lubricidad y el estremecimiento culpable de la fiesta erótica, dentro del cristianismo ascético y estoico. La *rosa voluptas* del pecado es, como la de Darío, la flor sexual, que al entreabrirse conmueve carne y espíritu.

No es este pasajero valleinclanesco (tampoco el peregrino de Góngora) el arquetipo paulino, sino un producto social: en su solar, Galicia, observa un mundo que entra en agonía, sin que exista nada nuevo para reemplazarlo. La tensión entre la apariencia y la realidad se concentra en una lucha entre el «adentro» y el «afuera»; son éstos los espacios internos de una experiencia lírica finisecular que significó en su momento el rechazo de la institución literaria y de las convenciones morales y religiosas. Estos espacios internos conllevan una función social transgresora contra el horizonte social de expectativas de la colectividad española. No es un «yo» escapista, sino un «yo» en su más profunda socialización. Las palabras de José Martí sobre la musa moderna nos servirán de guía: «[no] cabe más lírica que la que saca cada uno de sí propio, como si fuera su propio ser el asunto único» (pról. a J. Pérez Bonalde, 1882). En comunidad con los modernistas americanos, Valle pone de relieve las tensiones internas como afirmación contra la «burguesía literaria», en frase de Darío, aquellos que comercian con el arte (Zavala, 1987). ¿No será este pasajero, como el peregrino de Góngora o el caballero andante cervantino, uno que comparte la tarea de representar una caduca realidad social o histórica, y se propone reconstruir el lenguaje partiendo del lenguaje? (sobre Góngora, Molho, 1976; Gómez Moriana, 1985, para Cervantes).

Comencemos con algunas advertencias sobre el léxico de *Claves:* Valle hace coexistir lo sagrado y lo profano, la carne y el espíritu, la religión y la superstición, el rito y la heterodoxia, en este mundo de polaridades, casi transido del maniqueísmo cátaro. En este mundo social se descubre el predominio de una serie de oposiciones combinatorias; en realidad, el mundo es ambivalencia: placer de vivir y angustia de morir, en una huida. Si fijamos los campos semánticos que recubren cada una de las palabras del vocabulario social, la rosa —carnal o sexual— se describe a veces con un léxico cargado de resonancias peyorativas, tal la onomatopeya «gló-gló-gló» de seres que reptan en la «Rosa del pecado» (111), cercana ya a los desarticulados y animalizados conjuros de *La pipa*. (En línea de afinidad, Luis Palés Matos empleará este lenguaje desfamiliar o «a-poético» en *Tún tún de pasa y grifería*, 1933.) El lenguaje roza los mundos posibles, las selecciones de léxico son un filtro social: el yo lírico baja al pecado (*fango, estercolero*) o asciende a los esotéricos enigmas cabalísticos (*arcano, signo, ciencia, gaya, cirios, karma*) o se regodea con el sobrecodificado léxico modernista (*abril, lirio, espejo, estrella*). El gran virtuosismo verbal e intertextual e interdiscursivo de Valle se enriquece con un repertorio conocido y en las repetidas asociaciones semánticas de aves simbólicas y mitológicas, de ritos. La rosa, en definitiva, está ligada a la inspiración poética, a la sexualidad del texto, en diálogo fructífero con Darío (véase Zavala, 1983 y 1987 b).

Este primer filtro social de *Claves* designado por el sujeto interno recrea la pluralidad de estilos y de voces, pues Valle organiza el lenguaje para liberarlo del marco jerárquico; profana por medio de liturgias y ritos del pasado, que re-actualiza. En esta subversión desarticula las prácticas discursivas rituales. Tomo un ejemplo de esta vastísima red de asociaciones: su diálogo con el andariego transgresor, el Arcipreste (y ya he mencionado fugazmente el *Roman de la rose* y las *Soledades*). Cualquier lector medianamente informado puede reconocer el subtexto del *Libro de buen amor* en la Clav. XIII «Asterisco», soneto que en *Los lunes* (3-VI-1918) se titula «La gata», en consonancia con la transgresión de *La pipa*. El título cambia, no el contenido:

> ¡Qué linda es la dueña! ¡Qué airoso gracejo!
> ¡Cómo se divierte, sola, ante el espejo! (115).

Pero simultáneamente y en el mismo punto, el arcipreste medieval se vincula por métrica, léxico y tono con los versos darianos «Ya viene el cortejo». Valle opera desplazamientos en el plano textual e incluye espacios correlativos a diferentes prácticas de discurso literario. En esta palabra a dos «voces» se textualizan el mundo que se representa y el mundo representado (remito a Bajtin, 1980). La superficie textual es' un encuentro de disonancias, o *regio dissimilitudinis;* mediante alusiones, evocaciones (abiertas o veladas), Valle se apropia de otros discursos, especialmente del lenguaje imputativo de su tiempo, que desritualiza. La suya es dialogía polémica con la ambivalencia del carnaval.

En los libros que comento —a *Aromas* y a *El pasajero* me refiero— el mundo arcaico feudal de clérigos y mendigos convive y opera dentro de las series carnavalizadas de la sexualidad y la muerte, si bien como universo hierático y fijo, en diálogo con la pintura medieval: el espejo es designador rígido, luego alucinatorio. La voz lírica se regocija en la pintura del mundo a-urbano, a-citadino y erige en su centro la estatua de la inspiración, de la palabra/logos, de la Rosa, como imagen de las virtudes a practicar. Todo se vuelca en claves sociales cifradas, que disponen los elementos de una nueva iconografía. Son versos emblemáticos cuyas figuras alegóricas contradicen el arte urbano y burgués que rechaza los emblemas de un universo de fábula y magia. Las *claves* presentan la minuciosa descripción de criaturas desconocidas; son claves sociales, objetos extraños, la suma de unas experiencias en signos elementales, en una red de intersticios en la que se puede insinuar, perder, el «pasajero». El espejo o *speculum mundus,* también *speculum in aegnimate,* alarga, estiliza; se espiritualiza el instinto sexual y la transferencia hacia las señales de devoción y de piedad. La imagen en clave es sobre todo un llamado de atención; advierte la presencia de fuerzas hostiles que tienden trampas, que obstruyen el camino. Fuerzas todas con nombre de *Rosa;* grados de impureza y pureza carnal, en metamorfosis de rostros y cualidades de signos dispersos, en falsa armonía, reagrupados en una desacralizada superficie de oposiciones. Los signos son monjes, peregrinos, ermitaños ascético-místicos de un bosque cortés que se distribuyen en el espacio textual con aparecidos, demonios o ángeles, portadores todos del mensaje estético/político.

Al yuxtaponer dialógicamente estos textos y los de *La pipa* propongo que ambos son discursos políticos, cuya intención es invitar a reforzar las relaciones sociales. Si todo lenguaje es comunicación social y en cuanto tal revela las estratificaciones lingüísticas y el significado de cada palabra en sus condiciones

101

sociales e históricas específicas, ambos discursos textuales ponen de manifiesto un proyecto de sociedad. Valle concibe la poesía lírica como productora de ideologías mediante el refinamiento de la construcción literaria. Si mi lectura yuxtalineal es aceptable, *Claves* se inserta como re-escritura, en una estilización del pasado (en el sentido de Bajtin, 1980: 68), no como una parodia, como veremos. La sátira o la parodia comienzan propiamente con las sarcásticas risas de la duda.

En ambos casos —estilización o parodia— el emisor es el mismo; este emisor manipula ambos lenguajes, el de la enunciación simbólica y el inclinado hacia la lengua hablada. Dos registros en los que las mismas palabras no significan las mismas cosas. Las palabras conservan su polisemia y cambian imperceptiblemente de significación. Esta dispersión de sentido nos obliga a la *discretio,* a distinguir las diferencias. En cuanto sistema, la clave, la rosa, es un signo, el argumento de una teología/teogonía. Si le interesa aquí la norma es porque ésta hace tangible aspectos que Valle quiere reprimir y combatir y convierte así en infinitas las transgresiones. En los textos se despliega un sistema de valores; en el proceso de selecciones de este discurso, ejerce su presión cada uno de los modelos antagonistas: la norma y la transgresión de la norma. Y todo está en clave en nuestra lectura yuxtalineal: la(s) primera(s) del misterio y en *La pipa,* la de su explicación, la esfinge revela su secreto. Dialoga a su vez con su poética del «modernismo», donde alude a preceptos «alucinatorios».

Volvamos ahora sobre esa cara de la moneda: *La pipa de kif* (1919), libro justamente considerado como programa estético, donde alude a sustancias alucinógenas, que alteran los órganos sensoriales. Estas le permiten interpretar las sensaciones. Capta así una cultura enteramente oral y gestual de bajos fondos, como técnico «especular» que se propone fijarla. Semejante marco inicial obliga al «yo» lírico a «contar» lo que ha visto por sí mismo, oído y recogido de «informadores». Si los procedimientos ocultos especulares de *Claves* deforman de una manera estilizada, llega ahora el momento de volver la vista a «historias verdaderas», a reconstruir percepciones. En estos dieciocho poemas lo imaginario no se aparta tanto de lo simbólico ni de lo real, o al menos nos re-interpretan la imagen que la norma y la tradición —con su monopolio desorbitado sobre la escritura— hacían con ella. Los textos permiten además un cristal alucinatorio de comparación en el gran desfile de la sociedad post-septembrina con aspecto de carnaval, que Valle transforma en espectáculo para representar su mascarada. Todos son piezas en un tablero, pero los que juegan son los dirigentes, que mueven al peón y a la dama y al alfil. Las estrategias textuales se complican en el incesante, comercio de que son objeto los protagonistas/antagonistas. En su totalidad —cerrando el círculo a partir de una posición geométrica— el texto es una especie de teatrillo pedagógico, de farsilla en verso, donde las palabras rituales se desritualizan, como en los entremeses o en el teatro breve de los siglos XVI y XVII. Esta «prótesis especular» (sobre este término, Eco 1988) se entronca de manera definitiva con las farsas. Fuera de esta imagen especular, la imagen es un engaño perceptivo. Reconcilia y rehabilita así la carne o lo corporal; la sexualidad sacralizada en la superficie de los textos anteriores (y no me limito a la poesía) se revela en lo propiamente carnal de su fondo. Cada texto de *Claves,* en cuanto producción textual, está regido por una moral distinta; en *La pipa* domina la procacidad, el desenfado, el desvío de la norma se inscribe plenamente en las estructuras de otra esfera social.

El área de la licencia se despliega en el centro mismo del «ruedo ibérico», que en *La pipa* se llama, sencilla y llanamente, «Romántica Casa de Fieras del Buen Retiro», en «Bestiario» (Clav. V, 179). Metáfora política carnavalizada que Valle consideraba «original y típica», al publicar el poema como avance en *Los Lunes* (1-IX-1919). Su representación de la realidad confronta lo popular con los dominios del poder y de la política; lo popular se presenta a la luz de una cultura que se define por su contrario, por lo que no es (la sacralización de lo culto, científico, racional, noble). Valle desenmascara las prácticas culturales que separan y rechazan con arrogancia aquello que se llama «popular», por reacción a esas designaciones cualitativas o a los juicios valorizantes. El poeta baja a los abismos para darles voz; provoca su presencia amenazadora, caprichosa, sediciosa, furiosa —teatral, se podría decir—, puesto que es simultáneamente la representación de lo «real» y su disimulación. Dos voces y dos presencias.

*La pipa* alucinatoria nos descubre con lucidez la fase de la relajación de la moral forjada por un sistema de rapiña, de independencia agresiva de los jaquetones de actos valerosos (jaques, circo, presos, coimas), de actos de fuerza. ¿No es la *clave* una sociedad que de día en día se hacía más brutal? (la del caciquismo, la de los espadones, la del proletariado *lumpen*). En definitiva, la sociedad represiva y moralizante regida por los turnos, los tricornios, que mutila y persigue con cuartelazos y golpes. Valle representa al «bestiario» alucinante, agente de la discontinuidad cultural y social, que silencia las disidencias: la Iglesia y el Estado, responsables de la semiología del silencio. Esta sociedad se representa como una especie de feria itinerante, de circo y mascarada, de exhibición descarada de hombres y mujeres —arriba y abajo— que gallean por corrales y cotos. Los personajes de este carnaval son excelentes competidores de torneos, de mímica y gestos. En suma: de farsa.

El lector descubre en estos textos —la pluralidad de *Claves*— dos coyunturas maestras de un discurso poético: en los dos extremos de la cadena social se realiza la voluntad de la transgresión contra el desgaste de los resortes íntimos de las viejas instituciones. Valle desmitifica los referentes, desfamiliariza al emisor y encamina la lengua literaria, el lenguaje propiamente dicho, al centro de la parodia, que revela la combinatoria y funcionalidad del juego político especular. Parece desafiar a la vez el poder, las exhortaciones de la iglesia y la moral social; en definitiva, el poder cristalizado y el rigor de sus principios. La estilización, desfamiliarizadora, se inscribe ahora en la parodia: el extrañamiento revelador.


## 2. SERIE CARNAVALIZADA

Empecé por relacionar la parodia y la heteroglosia; en los dos primeros libros de poesía, en cuanto práctica textual, la heteroglosia condiciona y gobierna las operaciones del sentido. En *La pipa* se apoya en una heteroglosia explosiva, de lenguajes de época, lenguajes literarios, de clase social, de profesiones, de oficios que contrasta, con frecuencia, la urbe y el campo. Pasamos de la estilización (donde no falta, como vimos, la ironía romántica) de la Galicia rural y del «preciosismo» esotérico, al caló de los bajos fondos andaluces y madrileños, en sus gesticulantes voces.

Comencemos por lo obvio: la relación de *La pipa*, en cuanto poética social, con las farsas, en particular *La marquesa Rosalinda* (1913), texto donde establece conexiones entre los planos triviales y reflexivos de la intertextualidad. El preludio de la farsa advierte:

Enlazaré las rosas frescas
con que se viste el vaudeville
y las rimas funambulescas
a la manera de Banville (*OE* I: 797).

Parece asegurarse el diálogo con las *Odes funambulesques* de
Théodore de Banville (Schiavo, 1971), subtexto de apoyo también de *La pipa*. Reúne en esta estrategia alucinatoria un gri-
morio de los nuevos lenguajes literarios y amplía sus horizontes ideológicos a partir de una magistral orquestación de
enunciados. Un año después de estos poemas aparece *Farsa
y licencia de la Reina castiza* (1920), mosaico del mundo carnavalizado, de un mundo al revés. En virtud de esta cadena
retórico-política presenta aquí la vanidad trágica de disonancias, libertades, procacidades, en oximorones agudos, desplazamientos de lo cotidiano. Una vez elegido como signo, en el
ámbito de su representación, todo sonido y toda imagen son
significativas en el dominio imaginario.

El lenguaje paródico que se desarrolla como voluntad creadora en *La pipa* se puede aislar en dos núcleos sutiles entre
sátira y parodia. Además de la heteroglosia paródica, cuyos
rasgos he señalado (pero no demasiado), el *ars poetica* de
Valle se caracterizará con mayor intensidad por el amplio uso
de las lenguas nacionales de las diversas regiones peninsulares
y ultramarinas, inmersas dentro de los «lenguajes» que coexisten dentro de una misma cultura y una comunidad hablante
específica. Este plurilingüismo y heteroglosia sirven de marco
y encuadran las series carnavalizadas de *La pipa,* que se am-
plían hasta cubrir la amplia gama del cuerpo y su anatomía
y fisiología. La ropa, la comida, la bebida y la borrachera, la
sexualidad (copulaciones), la muerte, la defecación o crapología, todas estas series están orientadas contra las «mitologías»
políticas. Cada una tiene su lógica y su intención y su propósito en esta vasta red de estrategias textuales encaminadas a la
profanación desmitificadora. Valle se recrea con mayor nitidez
en la transgresión de la norma, en las imágenes especulares
cóncavas y convexas, en los desplazamientos de la vida habitual, en una orquestación de lenguas, jergas. El lenguaje de
los bajos fondos y las gesticulantes actuaciones de los personajes de circo, feria, carnaval, se unen a la degradación de las
imágenes de autoridad, y a la desmembración del cuerpo con
propósito crítico. Es ciertamente una poética social «crítica»,
contra la bufonería política de la historia. La risa de la parodia

destrona los mitos y se inicia su objetivo de «asesinato simbólico» de la autoridad. La intertextualidad, por otra parte, es
arma polémica contra las lenguas literarias caducas, polémica
que había encontrado cauce abierto en las farsas. Conviene
señalar ahora algunos ejemplos de esta articulada y compleja
programación de transgresiones e infracciones en *La pipa*.

a) *Heteroglosia paródica*

Bastarán unos pocos ejemplos para ilustrar las comple-
jidades de la vasta red paródica. Sirva de inicio la Clav. I, es
decir, el poema que le da el título al libro. Conviene aclarar
que, *fuera* del contexto o de las prácticas textuales de *La pipa*,
el poema sería de riguroso corte modernista, como supone la
crítica (M. Borelli, 1965; Durán, 1974). Sin embargo, dentro
del marco paródico del texto, apunta otro contenido ideológico: la parodia del «modernismo», entendido como receta
envejecida, ensayada también en *La cabeza del dragón*, y desde otra posición geométrica, en *Luces de bohemia*. En este
poema el proyecto del sujeto enunciador es crear tensiones en
el lector y una situación conflictiva entre los enunciados. En
contigüidad (no fusión), como espejo refractario, coexisten dos
lenguas literarias y culturales, aquella de la poesía moderna,
o «modernista», y su parodia, parodia que se capta no a través del vocabulario o de la sintaxis, sino por medio de la
*entonación*. El poeta inventa una voz con una especie de
vitalidad coral llena de entonaciones socialmente orientadas,
encaminadas a re-evaluar el léxico en la situación concreta
del texto. Entresaco algunas: *azul cristal, risa délfica, ritmo
órfico, místicas luces, sonrisa socrática, grito azul, vágula ci-
mera, niña Primavera, Princesa Corazón de Abril* (con mayúsculas las últimas), *rosa, cabellos de oro, cuento oriental, azul,
Aurora, rosado tul, divino canto, voz azul*. Todo lector de
poesía ha de reconocer este vocabulario, que semeja una receta
o un *hand-book* de léxico poético; o más bien, de un supuesto
repertorio poético, palabras con *pedigree* se podría decir (y
valga la metáfora). Léxico modernista, sin duda, pero ahora
en otro campo semántico con distinta entonación, destaca la
distancia que separa el estilo de su estilización paródica y su
desplazamiento hacia nuevos significados. Ya estamos familia-
rizados con esta estrategia que va dependiendo, en mayor
grado, de la «posición geométrica». Sugiero que la clave *social*
para captar los elementos redistributivos en el espacio textual

aparece en el cierre del poema, donde la voz narradora o el «yo» lírico opera un cambio de sentido o significado mediante la entonación, derrumbando así el preciosista mundo anterior. La posición geométrica (como en la ironía romántica) produce la parodia:

> Si tú me abandonas, gracia del hachic
> Me embozo en la capa y apago la luz.
> Ya puede tentarme la Reina del Chic:
> No dejo la capa y le hago la † (160).

Propongo que este cambio de registro y de «posición geométrica» destruye el discurso literario en la construcción textual misma. Un detalle más: la orientación social del texto, la clave social, por así decirlo, lleva a la voz poética a crear una estrategia textual que incorpora al lector(a) en el horizonte ideológico y la situación concreta del diálogo, pues la palabra final es un signo: el de la cruz. Se borran así las fronteras entre la oralidad y la escritura, decisión que significa, creo, un llamado de atención al lenguaje como acto performativo. La enunciación se propone como acto esencialmente social en el proceso semiótico entre lectura/escritura. En narratología este verso se denomina «oración clave» (Fowler, 1977).

Otro paso es la Clav. II «¡Aleluya!»; si en el otro texto comentado Valle ha incorporado un signo, el proceso intertextual e intersemiótico lo conduce ahora a una interjección polisémica, pues *aleluya* pertenece tanto a un campo semántico-cultural religioso cuanto al intersemiótico de imagen política popular. En el poema que comento, en su función de sacerdote laico y bufo, el «yo lírico» lanza su ¡aleluya! a los feligreses (lectores), a las personas respetables de la Academia y a los viejos retóricos que imponen la norma. En definitiva, los textos restauran la polisemia contra el discurso monológico.

Veamos otra construcción paródica, esta vez una polémica orientada contra las manidas imágenes del paisajismo noventaiochista en Clav. XII «El preso»:

> Camino polvoriento del herrén amarillo
> Declinando la tarde. En la loma, un castillo (223).

Nos equivocaríamos con identificar el vocabulario y atmósferas parodiados sólo con el machadiano (*camino polvoriento, tarde poniente, perfiles inciertos, moza castellana*). Sospecho

107

que en realidad el registro o trompetilla lingüística bufa va contra el castellanismo o lo castellanizante en cuanto trivialidad difundida del mito totalizador y del discurso autorizado. Esta parodia es semejante al registro anti-modernista, por rancio y estéril, y se hace frecuente a partir de esta década (después de la muerte de Darío). Una vez más, el cierre poético del texto marca la entonación:

> Y saluda una voz netamente española:
> —He d'ir a Medinica cuando te den piola (225).

No es, por cierto, recurso novedoso en su poética; estas dos «voces» en tensión son modalidad productiva de la intertextualidad polémica, sustancia de sus textos (sobre este tipo de intertextualidad, Zumthor, 1976). El registro de la trivialidad castellanista —santo y seña finisecular— aparece ya definitivamente en conjunción de discursos textuales en *El pasajero*. Un soneto publicado en *Los Lunes de El Imparcial* (3-VI-1918) bajo el título de «Ciudad de Castilla» («Rosa del caminante» en *Claves*), se apoya, para revertirlo, en el código alusivo al paisajismo castellanizante del 98: *álamos, fuentes, ríos,* designadores rígidos de un mundo «estilizado». La parodia y repulsa del castellanismo cobran bulto en 1919 (año de publicación de *La pipa*); en sus propias palabras: «Castilla está muerta, porque Castilla mive mirando atrás, y mirando atrás no se tiene una visión del momento» [4]. Es decir, el pasado no permite una posición de sujeto totalizadora, sólo nostálgica; escapa la posición geométrica.

Si mi lectura de *La pipa de kif* es aceptable, el lenguaje o la «voz» que Valle incorpora como «lo otro» especular alucinatorio en este texto sería la germanía, lo chulo, el teatro bufo, el aleluya, el romancero macabro y escabroso de crímenes y atropellos. Lo «popular» está en contigüidad con el casticismo y lo académico de la retórica oficial, que no se limita al lenguaje, sino que abarca las acciones. Léase a esta luz la Clav. XVII, «La tienda del herbolario» (249), cuya estrategia textual de «alucinaciones» está afincada en un vasto cuerpo de interrelaciones sociales entre los hablantes. En el horizonte extra-verbal —espacial, semántico y de valores— parodia no sólo la lengua literaria, sino que polemiza contra un lenguaje castella-

---

[4] Comentario recogido en el volumen *La pintura vasca, 1909-1919,* Madrid: V. Hernández, 1919, y en Serrano Alonso, 1987: 264.

nizante, unos mitos, una historia oficial, en un vaivén entre «lo uno y lo otro». Me limitaré a dos casos: Pizarro es héroe desde una ladera geográfica y verdugo desde la otra. En «simultaneidad», la posición geométrica orienta el signo ideológico:

(Tuvo en las Indias las mismas manos,
Allá son reyes y acá marranos) (253).

O bien, y en diálogo con el poema-programa «Nos vemos», la contigüidad de las dos «voces» del giro *melancolía:*

Melancolía del Indio. Pena
De los que arrastran una cadena (255).

Palabras son acciones (actos de lenguaje) para Valle, aun cuando se recree, aparentemente, en el mundo de la transgresión y la infracción de la musa bohemia. Sirva de ejemplo privilegiado su viaje por los paraísos artificiales (hashish, marihuana, coca, kif, opio), el espejo alucinatorio de los sentidos, donde alude de manera oblicua a las conocidas frases de Marx sobre el opio del pueblo. Este «paraíso» es humo o adormidera inquisitorial en España:

Yerba del Viejo de la Montaña
El Santo Oficio te halló en España (258).

El «Finis» del poema es también una invitación al lector a incorporarse al signo, a decodificar su sentido profundo de «obra abierta», pues termina con el signo de *etcétera.* Pero merecen subrayarse unas palabras de cautela: la transgresión religiosa de Valle es contra los excesos de la iglesia, contra la rígida moral normativa, nunca contra los dogmas. Se inscribe así en un anti-clericalismo de antiguas raíces en su vertiente anti-inquisitorial.

b) *Carnavalización*

Como signo de desarrollo contigüo o paralelo en esta explosión paródica/polémica, parecería evidente que las series bajtinianas son clave social para representar la otra cara de España. Es decir, en los textos poéticos, con ojo técnico, Valle presenta una especie de *close-up* de los personajes, situaciones y lenguajes que determinan los mitos nacionales; son sus ico-

109

nografías, sus «raros». Valle selecciona en *La pipa* una lengua literaria y una posición de sujeto con el objetivo de desmontar los mitos nacionales, a través de los diversos personajes que transmiten los rasgos pertinentes de la Iglesia, el Estado, el castellanismo, el romancero oficial, la conquista, los héroes nacionales. Su punta de lanza va contra todo lenguaje(s) y retórica(s) que intenta un monopolio desorbitado sobre los horizontes ideológicos. El chulo, el jaque, el criminal, el matón, la cacique/beata pueblerina desfilan en sus poemas, así como los mitos nacionales y las manifestaciones históricas en que éstos se expresan. A partir de la morfología de las series carnavalizadas en su estructura dinámica veremos el sistema de constantes semióticas en que éstas se manifiestan a través de transformaciones sucesivas en el texto valleinclanesco. En sus prácticas discursivas redistribuye las series en ejes de selección y las intensifica; cada serie adquiere un sesgo cada vez más crítico en los poemas:

1. *El cuerpo y su anatomía y fisiología:* Valle se regodea en la desmembración, la fragmentación (semejante, pero no igual a Quevedo). A partir de ahora la representación del referente no reproduce el cuerpo completo; vuelve síntomas las anomalías del cuerpo y pone en escena el belfo, la garra, el ojo hostil, la jeta, los ojos pintados, la pintada tarasca, el curdela narigudo, el hocico, la oreja, el moño, los rizos, el pie, el cogote, la jeta cetrina, el habla rijosa, las piernas.

2. *La ropa:* La descripción está estrechamente relacionada con la caricatura y la lujuria: la liga rosada, la enagua, el pañolón, la falda, la rosa del pelo, los peines, los anillos, la saya rota, las fajas, las calcetas.

3. *La comida:* Serie ligada a los espacios interiores en las tabernas y los mesones. Nunca las comidas pantagruélicas de la serie rabelesiana. Más bien funciona como referente social mediante alusiones a ciertos alimentos de las clases populares: azafrán, pimentón.

4. *La bebida:* Normalmente, como en textos anteriores, está enlazada también a los sórdidos espacios interiores, tabernas y personajes de bajos fondos (tabernas, de contrabando, cuarteles con vahos de mostos, rinas, navajas, sordas libaciones. En resumen:

Silla que se desbarata,
Mesa que se escachifolla,
Jaleo, risa, bravata
Y bambolla («El circo de la lona», 199).

5. *La sexualidad:* En vuelta de tuerca pierde sus elegancias y sacrilegios satánicos de donjuanes blasfemos y voluntaristas, de hidalgos valientes con pasiones perversas y minoritarias. La sexualidad se inscribe con mayor intensidad en la prostitución, el vicio, el lodazal, los personajes que reptan insolentes. Revela un mundo de relaciones sexuales envilecido y descarado entre amancebados, bandoleros y criminales. Lejos estamos ya de los amores incestuosos y de los refinamientos sexuales de Bradomín e, incluso, de los Montenegro; en el espacio textual se inscribe la desacralización de la nobleza —tan importante en los esperpentos— para apuntar a los gobernantes desgobernados.

Un breve inciso para reforzar mi lectura de las intensidades que cobran las series a partir de *La pipa*. En el poema «Fin de carnaval», publicado primero en *Los Lunes* (3-III-1919), la estrofa alusiva a los desmanes sociales de la aristocracia (por metonimia, el Marqués-militar sodomita), ofrece una importantísima variante. La versión periodística que comento carece de referencia sexual explícita, debido a la censura o auto-censura características del periodismo, o bien responde a imperativos de la genética textual.

El texto del periódico dice:

Y bajo el foco de Wolta
Hace el portugués
Un soldado de la escolta
¡Talla de seis pies!

En cambio, en *La pipa* la estrofa lee:

Y bajo el foco de Volta
Da cita el Marqués
A un soldado de la Escolta,
¡Talla de seis pies! (172).

La variación intensifica, sin lugar a dudas, un proceso selectivo orientado hacia un horizonte ideológico polémico, de «asesinato simbólico» de las clases dirigentes. En otra vuelta de tuerca, farsas y esperpentos inscriben la sexualidad y lo bajo corpóreo, la crapología y la borrachera a las clases dominantes. ·

Dentro de esta serie sexual relacionada con lo bajo corpóreo cabe situar la desmembración del cuerpo (lo que D. H. Lawrence llamaba «words below the navel»); la furia que engendra lujuria se establece aquí mediante una hábil selección léxica: pai-pai, la pierna, pechona, el anca, anca de yegua real (una prostituta de burdel), zancaja, senos encorsetados, olor de senos, pechona y redonda. Estas descripciones selectivas muestran sus variaciones en *La reina castiza* (1920, 1922), en una combinación simbiótica, si bien en grados mediadores diversos.

6. *La muerte:* La práctica textual orienta el código contra la muerte por honra o por hazañas heroicas, y se crea una tensión intertextual entre la tradición cultural y su duplicación textual concreta. Valle desacraliza el misterio, y la muerte viene ahora ligada a locuras homicidas: garrote vil por matricidio. Otro desplazamiento discursivo lo conduce a la parodia de la muerte por honra en *La reina castiza,* en conjunción de discursos contra el teatro clásico, duplicador y reproductor de esa ideología.

7. *Lo bajo escatológico* (excrementos, crapología): *Apenas* visible en la superficie textual. La serie está enlazada por alusión e implicitación con ciertos espacios: el arroyo, el burdel, el circo, el carnaval, la taberna, los mesones, los corrales. Esta serie no parece formar parte sustancial del horizonte de expectativas de sus lectores concretos, a diferencia del siglo XVII, por ejemplo (la picaresca, la poesía satírica).

La redistribución de estas series a partir de *La pipa,* poética social que se levanta como índice de las intensificaciones, sirve para darle forma a un mundo hiperbólico, de exageraciones, de crímenes, crónicas macabras, atropellos, articulado contra la aparente austeridad y el rigor de las instituciones, contra el discurso ritual. Varios de los poemas aluden de forma directa al mundo social que parodian: el gobierno, la iglesia, la nobleza (entiéndase monarquía). Unos elementos contextuales nos servirán de apoyo. Los poemas fueron escritos durante el reinado de Alfonso XIII, que marca la Semana Trágica (1909), ejecuciones, asesinatos, manifiestos militares (los junteros), huelgas, atentados, coaliciones entre catalanes, republicanos y socialistas contra los partidos tradicionales. En suma: los gobiernos de Eduardo Dato, el conde de Romanones y Antonio Maura, dentro de la gran crisis de 1917. En definitiva, el trasfondo de los esperpentos y del *Ruedo Ibérico*, en esa historia política entre 1898-1923 dramáticamente subrayada por las crisis de 1909 y 1917. El subtexto social, interdiscursivo e intertextual de *La pipa* apunta a la rutina encorsetada del ceremonial de la corte, el desgaste de los políticos incoloros y desacreditados, de las figuras de comparsa, del comadreo e intrigas tras bastidores y, naturalmente, la reaparición del Ejército en la política y la manifestación aguda de la primera guerra mundial. Inscribe el desgobierno que le da a España el aspecto de carnavalada y de retórica inoperante, de verbalismos ante una crisis económica, los enriquecimientos escandalosos y los choques entre «aliadófilos» y «germanófilos».

Valle lanza su flecha contra esa «España esencial» —en frase de Maura— y contra aquélla de pacotilla y junteros que proclamaban la renovación del país, exaltando el mito nacional. Se recordarán aquellos elogios que se publicaron en *El Sol* (1916): «las cenizas de Daoíz y Velarde deben removerse en sus espulcros y la cruz de Constantino, el signo de la nueva fe, brilla en el firmamento de la patria» (apud Carr, 1979: 485). De manera oblicua parodia Valle esta «cruz» en el texto que le da el nombre a *La pipa*.

Si mi lectura es aceptable, sugiero que los poemas clave son «Bestiario» (Clav. V), «El circo de la lona» (Clav. VI), «La Infanzona de Medinica» (Clav. IX) y «La tienda del herbolario» (Clav. XIII). No parece necesario insistir en la transgresión y desmitificación que revelan estos poemas: el bestiario es un zoológico social, mediante el cual personifica los mitos castellanizantes: el león que bosteza, el oso que se despereza en un ambiente de la primera guerra mundial. Es un bestiario de símbolos desmitificados, en el espacio abierto de un parque, antaño romántico:

> ¡Olvidada Casa de Fieras,
> Con los ojos de la niñez
> Tus quimeras
> Vuelvo a gozar en la vejez!
> Muere la tarde.—Un rojo grito
> Sobre la fronda vesperal.—
> Y abre el círculo de su mito
> El Gran Bestiario Zodiacal (187).

España es, según esta imagen paródico/polémica, carpa de feria, gesto, retórica. El *Circo* es el antecedente del *Ruedo,* con su chusma, rameras, saltimbanquis, payasos, animales amaestrados y humanizados (vieja tradición en la serie literaria de vertiente crítica). Este circo de lona, hoy es

¡Gran parasol remendado
Que abres al vuelo gigante
Como el escudo dorado
Del Atlante! (192).

No hemos de necesitar excesivo ingenio crítico para asociar la lona y España (imagen visual tal vez de la piel de toro). Otro detalle adicional: «La Pepona» (muñeca de trapo, según Durán, 1974), bien podría encubrir también el nombre paródico de algún político, procedimiento frecuente en el periodismo satírico decimonónico desde al menos *El Zurriago*. ¿José Canalejas quizá? La Pepona —imagen de muñeca, político, realidad social— es un ahora y siempre:

La Pepona al mono
Grita, sube el tono,
Por mayor encono
Le habla en catalán.
Y bajo la silla
El otro se humilla,
Que esto fue en Castilla
Tiempos que aún están (196).

Las alusiones, nada veladas, a la política oficial, saltan a la vista. El trasfondo es, sin duda, la Lliga Catalana y sus desastrosas consecuencias socio-económicas. En este micro-tablado de marionetas el mono, a su vez,

Puja de anarquista
Y es el gran fumista,
Exhibicionista
Internacional (197).

Pone en escena a un animal hablante que evoca la presencia del fuego: *humo*/fumo alucinatorio. No hemos de recurrir a malabarismos mentales para reconocer la referencia al desarrollo del anarquismo (sobre todo aquél de la propaganda por el hecho) que se desató en aquellos años. La relación sígnica se representa mediante palabras e imágenes. La relación que

114

las vincula se podría aclarar a través de un análisis a fondo de la prensa satírica, de aleluyas, estampas, memorias, documentos, material visual. Estos antecedentes darían fructíferos resultados para identificar la alusión intertextual e interdiscursiva de estos poemas, y su objetivo de representación de la bufonería política.

«La Infanzona de Medinica» reúne una serie de rasgos negativos sobre la aristocracia pueblerina y su relación con la Iglesia que es preciso señalar. D. Estefaldina es agorera, ignorante, supersticiosa, beata, final de una estirpe de grandes nombres. Ahora, en cambio, es su reverso:

> Oprime en las rentas a sus aparceros
> Los vastos salones convierte en graneros,
> Da buenas palabras al que llora pan (211).

Para finalizar, un recuento nada exhaustivo. «La tienda del herbolario» nos descubre una polémica pluridimensional contra un sistema de valores, apoyado en un texto marxista difundido: «la religión es el opio del pueblo». La yerba que adormece, la encontró el Santo Oficio, y ya se puede soñar en este diccionario y geografía de estupefacientes y paraísos artificiales. El contenido social de «opio del pueblo» se yuxtapone en dialogía a los paraísos baudelerianos y a los maravillosos efectos alucinatorios de los órganos sensoriales.

El itinerario paródico/polémico de Valle es el hilo conductor de los textos de *Claves líricas,* que por gradaciones e intensidades nos conduce al mundo del marginado en Galicia. Su «gaita gallega» (como la llama en *La pipa*) observa el tablado desde el exterior del sistema, su posición geométrica transforma la ironía romántica en parodia moderna.

Comencé por sugerir que *Claves líricas* y *La pipa* representan un todo articulado, un complejo de estrategias textuales y prácticas discursivas guiadas por objetivos semejantes: la profanación desmitificadora. Parten de una óptica especular diferenciadora —el mundo gallego en *Claves*— para subrayar la diversidad y divergencia del mundo peninsular, cuya política y gobernantes no renuncian a una unidad ilusoria: la «España esencial». Es decir, una, grande, siempre católica. En libre invención, por medio de la astrología de las palabras, Valle concentra su polémica contra esta tradición. Los espacios internos forman parte del complejo sistema comunicativo que dota la experiencia lírica de una función social en el *episteme* mo-

115

derno. *Claves* y *La pipa* son portadores de un proyecto cultural y portavoces de un compromiso; en este doble espacio que sugiero —espacios internos y carnavalización—, Valle hace amplio uso de convenciones y normas en nuevos campos y diversos universos sociales. Genera discursos potenciales al re-interpretar, polemizar y re-escribir el pasado, re-inscibiéndolo en el presente («Que esto fue en Castilla/tiempos que aún están»). La actitud polémica/paródica contra las expresiones del discurso ideológico —filosófico, religioso, moral, histórico, político, literario— se intensifica, y va explorando la ambigüedad, la dualidad del lenguaje re-procesándolo y enmarcándolo en una vertiente de «voz» cómico/paródica, en juego especular. Las voces parodiadas son en realidad todos los niveles del lenguaje literario oral y escrito de su época.

Estos textos poéticos son una invitación al lector para explorar la coexistencia de la multiplicidad de discursos, que no son solamente distintos, sino contradictorios. Una invitación a tomar conciencia de que los sistemas ideológicos ligados a estas enunciaciones se contradecían, y que de ninguna forma se podía vivir sin polemizar con ellos. La práctica textual dialógica es semejante en los tres libros de poemas; Valle parte de la estilización o lenguaje literario de otros, y desemboca en la estilización paródica, encaminada a destruir el lenguaje representado y su sistema de valores[5].

A la luz de la relación semiótica entre texto y lector cabe puntualizar que el rasgo más importante del sistema comunicativo es un enunciado (o mensaje) re-presentado desde un punto de vista particular (ideología), encaminado a ser re-interpretado y re-colocado en el espacio y el tiempo. En «simultaneidad» y a partir de una «posición geométrica» (posición del sujeto), en estos textos Valle hace contiguo lo que normalmente no se asocia, destruyendo así en cierta medida lo familiar, creando nuevas normas al destruir las antiguas. Los poemas proponen una poética social que lleva a sus últimas consecuencias al desfamiliarizar el lenguaje poético y al reducir a lo grotesco el lenguaje del poder. En adelante instala la risa desmitificadora, esa fuerza especial con capacidad de desmontar «el objeto de la falsa cáscara verbal e ideológica que lo cubre» (Bajtin, 1981: 237).

---

[5] Bajtin (1980: 362-365) establece esas importantes distinciones sobre la estilización paródica, como vimos.

Capítulo V

# EL CARNAVAL POLITICO:
# EL ESPERPENTO

La palabra se intuye
por el gesto...

(*Las galas.*)

## 1. «EL GENERO CHICO MULTIPLICADO
POR CUATRO»

La sátira de las farsas, decididamente después de «la musa
funambulesca» («prótesis» con funciones alucinatorias), que
anunciaba en *La pipa* se transforma en los *esperpentos*. El
giro es la lógica re-sematización de un léxico decimonónico,
pues el vocablo se registra con significado afín en el folleti-
nista Wenceslao Ayguals de Izco y en Galdós (Zavala, 1972).
Como neologismo de sentido también aparece en México
(1871), donde significa «culebrón» o «comedia mala». La
nueva acepción política de este vocablo —así como el de *farsa,
fantoche, pelele, bululú*— nos comprueba hoy la riqueza de
los universos semánticos de Valle, los madrileñismos de su
habla achulada y su re-articulación social a partir de *Luces
de bohemia: Esperpento* (1920, 1924). En los próximos años
le preceden *Farsa y licencia de la Reina castiza* (1920, 1922),
*Los cuernos de don Friolera* (1921, 1925), *Las galas del di-
funto* (1926) y *La hija del capitán* (1927). Toda una nueva
concepción libidinal y somática del cuerpo se articula a partir
de entonces, en variadas inversiones y direcciones y despedazamientos carnavalescos, así como un nuevo modelo de energía psíquica y una renovada y re-acentuada dinámica ideológica, que si bien textualizada antes, estalla ahora en un sistema

117

«narrativo» ideológico que desmembra la maquinaria externa del cuerpo.

Comencemos por lo obvio: que estos espantajos cómicos liberan del miedo (observación de Bajtin sobre la literatura carnavalizada). Valle intenta liberar a su auditorio social de la tradición asfixiante, pero no deja de haber diferencias entre las «farsas esperpénticas» y los «esperpentos». Cabe distinguir en un mismo objetivo y proyecto dos vías, como veremos. Esta atmósfera de libertad nos propone, no una imagen de la «realidad» (mimesis), sino una alternativa, otra «representación» de lo que he llamado lo *imaginario social* en degradaciones y despedazamientos carnavalescos del poder, de la autoridad (o autoridades), en anversos y reversos.

Valle convierte en terreno movedizo la represión directa (la policía, el ejército, las prisiones, la corte de justicia), a una subjeción interna («ideología») en los esperpentos, sobre todo *Luces*. En este texto las categorías especulares de Althusser cobran forma; éstas se pueden resumir de la forma siguiente: «there are no subjects except by and for their subjection [...] our idea of Society and the Law depend uppon each other and reflect each other» (1971: 182). El texto único de Valle se mueve en estas dos direcciones ideológicas de la represión externa y la sujeción interna («ideología»). Esta —y sigo a Althusser— se «representa» como un tipo de «lenguaje» esperpéntico y su realidad interna y como una fuerza alternativa de revertir e invertir las estructuras de poder. Valle muestra los «lenguajes» del poder, los de explotación y los de la ley (leyes) como «espejos» que se reflejan mutuamente. Opone al discurso ideológico del poder otro discurso alternativo empleado por algunos grupos y clases sociales contra la sociedad opresiva. Crea todo un lenguaje político en juegos especulares de ideologías externas e internalizadas.

*Luces* apunta una batalla campal entre un concepción «moderna»/modernista del arte —Max Estrella— y su reducción en la época de «la industria cultural» (en la frase de Adorno) a caricatura institucionalizada, el «loco vidente»: otras figuras y profesiones caricaturizados son también el amigo periodista, el académico, el ministro, los amigos de Max. Todos ya excedentes de un mundo —el de la bohemia «anarquista» finisecular— ya consumido y consumado; es el «modernismo» institucionalizado el que usurpa el poder (como el Primer Magistrado de Carpentier). Ahora es pose estéril, ya sin capacidad de seducción, después de las violentas alteraciones sociales a partir

118

de la década de 1910, la primera guerra mundial impérialista y la Revolución rusa, entre tantos otros elementos contextuales. Se recordará que El Preso está consciente del aire de pasado de Max: «Su hablar es como de otros tiempos», le dice. No es extraño que aparezcan aquí «fantasmas» del pasado —Darío, Bradomín, el Ministro, incapaces ya de actos performativos, de palabra de seducción, son propiamente «ausencias» (en el sentido de Benveniste, 1971)— en una noche ciertamente llena de augurios, que nos permite poner este texto en diálogo con el *Ulises* de Joyce, en aquellos dos capítulos prodigiosos donde Bloom y Stephen hacen un recorrido desde Mabbot street, hablando sobre música, literatura, Irlanda, Dublín, París, amistad, mujeres, prostitución, la iglesia, el celibato, la nación irlandesa, el pasado en una atmósfera alucinatoria y fantasmagórica.

Ya se sabe que el complejo texto de Joyce se cimenta en la alegoría del regreso de Odiseo y su encuentro con Circe; no menos alucinante el paseo del «Homero» bohemio por las calles madrileñas y su encuentro con otras Circes, también en una atmósfera de pesadilla, sueño, magia. En la oscuridad de la calle cuanto ha ocurrido durante el día reaparece a otra luz; todo objeto se anima y adquiere vida propia, amenazante y enigmática, en intercambios entre la «realidad» y su «representación». Ambas situaciones (la de Joyce y la de Valle) comparten rasgos significativos, mediante la estrategia del «expresionismo», re-articulación «moderna» de la visión carnavalesca del mundo, en sus explosiones del sujeto social y del lenguaje.

Volvamos sobre otros rasgos de la visión carnavalesca que enlazan a Valle con esta tradición, partiendo de las observaciones de M. Bajtin sobre la *subsistencia* de este estilo (1968, 1970, 1978, 1983). Valle saca excelente partido de su reforma verbal llevándola adelante, y enriquece cada vez más su discurso con acarreo de las obscenidades y lo bajo corpóreo, lo bajo escatológico y los ritos lascivos, re-acentuados a partir de *La pipa de kif* (como vimos). Pero además re-articula la dimensión política, apoyándose en una «contemporaneidad» sustancial, fácilmente deconocible dentro del horizonte de expectativas de su público (lector/a) concreto. En cuanto tradición, las características de la visión carnavalesca en su orientación política de extrañamiento revelador descubren una nueva actitud respecto a la realidad; el pasado se actualiza, se moderniza exageradamente. Intencionalmente todo es presente y alude al presente, dentro de una atmósfera de libre invención y actitud crítica o polémica con la tradición, que subraya la pluralidad de estilos y voces. El autor carnavalesco renuncia a la unidad estilística de la epopeya, la tragedia, la retórica, la lírica, y mezcla lo sublime y lo vulgar, lo serio y lo cómico. El proceso reacentuado es Valle exige una relación distinta con el material literario; en esta doble voz, al lado de la palabra que *representa* (el significador) está la palabra *representada* (lo significado), el referente siempre es otro, y es la base de la «parodia».

En este universo «carnavalizado» merece la pena que volvamos a distinguir los dos tipos de «representación» del esperpento: la «farsa» esperpéntica y los esperpentos «trágicos». En estos últimos —*Luces de bohemia* y *Divinas palabras*— los personajes trágicos aparecen como residuos del pasado, y la sociedad los percibe como «pose», «máscara», «carnaval modernista», «farsa». Son figuras o clases sociales de ocaso, fantasmas trágicos, desubicados, especies de «fósiles vivientes» en una sociedad distinta (adapto el término de Mircea Eliade).

El complejo entramado intertextual de *Luces de bohemia* se disemina en varias direcciones y establece una relación clásica entre «locura» y «verdad» de manera metonímica; como tropo literario y como representación del lenguaje. El virtuosismo dialógico del texto se enriquece a la luz de un amplio diálogo cultural que abarca buena parte del discurso sobre la locura, reactivado por los románticos. De Nietzsche cabe recordar su lapidaria frase: «To belief in truth is precisely madness» (*Das philosophen buch*), y de Nerval aquellas páginas proféticas donde afirma que la locura final será probablemente aquella de creerse poeta (apud Felman, 1985). La «locura» de Max —«¡Soy el primer poeta de España! ¡El primero! ¡El primero! ¡Y ayuno!»— adquiere una función irónica que indica la lucidez valleinclanesca de inversión, de recontextualizar situaciones a través de la «palabra».

Los actos performativos son a manera de zona de fuerzas para reconvertir la realidad a través de una retórica desmitificadora como contra-balance de la retórica oficial de la ley, la fuerza, el estupor burocrático, el comercio representado a partir de los personajes de la pequeña burguesía: libreros, tenderos, taberneros que defienden la santidad de la propiedad privada [1]. El lenguaje especular de estos textos tiene el propó-

---

[1] Véanse las agudas precisiones de S. Felman (1958), sobre Balzac (105-106), y su «contrabalance» de la sociedad francesa.

sito de deconstruir y desmitificar el formidable engaño de la historia de España. El diálogo se inscribe como una verdad total, que libera a los interlocutores de las convenciones y de las normas de la buena educación (semejante al manifiesto surrealista de Breton, *apud* Felman, 1985: 107). Max está consciente de sus limitaciones, de su situación de marginado, de haber perdido la posibilidad de actos de lenguaje performativos: «Latino, ya no puedo gritar».

Distinta es en cuanto esperpento *Divinas palabras*, «tragicomedia de aldea», acción trágica sin dignidad que se podría analizar a partir de las teorías de Frantz Fanon *(Los condenados de la tierra)* y del *Anti-Dühring* de Engels en torno a la violencia: la explotación, la violencia y la deshumanización se revelan en la desnudez de aquellos hambrientos expoliados y de fatalismos suicidas. En esta «tragicomedia de aldea» la atmósfera de religión, de magia y de fuerzas sobrenaturales provocan al miedo; el miedo que produce el lenguaje. Nada positivo surge, pero el espejo no es deformante, corresponde más bien a una visión *crítica* (en el sentido actual del término a partir de la Escuela de Frankfurt) [2]; Valle desmonta la ignorancia y la situación social que alimenta la lujuria, la crueldad, la hipocresía, la cobardía, el crimen. El lenguaje zoológico se centra en el hidrocéfalo idiota —Laureano—, lucrativa herencia para unos cuantos pobres diablos. La lujuria natural es la prenda de Mari-Gaila y de Séptimo, y la cobardía de Pedro-Gailo —que, como Lázaro, vuelve la mejilla a la promiscuidad de su mujer— se refracta en un espejo deforme del drama del honor, y a su vez se desata su lujuria de borracho contra su hija Simoniña. El texto es una zona de contrastes de los cuerpos y sus gestos: el hermoso y desafiante desnudo de Mari-Gaila «llena de ritmos clásicos» y los «brazos negros, largos, flacos» del sacristán, «negro y zancudo». En la aldea todos son culpables de crueldad contra el hidrocéfalo obeso, de enorme cabeza greñuda y vientre inflado. La obesidad del cuerpo que se engulle a sí mismo.

La «carnavalización» de estos dos textos tiene objetivo y perspectiva crítica-paródica de la sociedad y ofrecen la posibilidad de una cesura (aunque sea momentánea) con sus estructuras, leyes y verdades dogmáticas que determinan el punto o lugar que cada ser humano ocupa en el cuerpo social. Según Bajtin:

---

[2] Desde la perspectiva de la *teoría crítica,* «the literary artist turns into our ally where the is the spokesman for the *collective* of *outcasts* [...] of all those who bear the burden of society» (Lowenthal, 1987: 7).

> The basis of laughter which gives form to carnival rituals frees them completely from all religious and ecclesiastic dogmatism, from all mysticism and piety (1968: 7).

La risa del carnaval no sólo libera al actante de estos discursos monológicos y autoritarios, pero no es espectáculo para ser observado; exige la participación colectiva:

> Carnival is not a spectacle seen by the people; they live in it, and exeryone participates because its very idea embraces all the people. While carnival lasts, there is no other life outside it. During carnival time, life is subject only to its laws, that is, the laws of its own freedom. It has a universal spirit; it is a special condition of the entire world, of the world's revival and renewal, in which all take part. Such is the essence of carnival vividly felt by all participants (p. 7).

El parentesco entre la literatura carnavalizada y los esperpentos se puede establecer si tomamos en cuenta la conocidísima definición del esperpento que aparece en *Luces*. Se observará que el sujeto semiótico enunciador es el bohemio ciego, trágico excedente del pasado. Su definición es una *estrategia de negación*, un ataque cuyo objetivo es alterar el comercio institucional del arte (carácter esencial de la vanguardia para Bürger, 1984). Su orientación social procede de la observación que el arte institucionalizado y el discurso ideológico oficial están encaminados a destruir y expropiar los «lenguajes» individuales para neutralizarlos y dominarlos (monología *versus* heteroglosia). El esperpento se «representa» como un tipo particular de lenguaje, aquel que los grupos sociales dominados re-apropian, re-territorializan. Invita a la alteridad que puebla todo significado, para que uno y otro se pongan en contigüidad. En definitiva, representa la lengua usurpada, abusada y expropiada, a la cual se le re-confiere su poder performativo como medio para expresar las necesidades materiales y concretas de las experiencias de los individuos y grupos marginados. Esperpentos y farsas privilegian el habla, la voz hablada; en realidad se inscriben los enunciados del intercambio verbal real.

122

El lenguaje «deformado» y «deformante» de la estética del esperpento se levanta como contra-balance de las autoridades y los poderes que imponen un lenguaje único y hegemónico. El esperpento tiene dos funciones, dos lenguajes y un idéntico objetivo: la estrategia de la negación contra las leyes y las normas impuestas. «Los héroes clásicos reflejados en los espejos cóncavos [...] El sentido trágico de la vida española sólo puede darse con una estética sistemáticamente deformada», para corresponder a la realidad (mimesis anti-mimética), ya que España es «una deformación grotesca de la civilización europea». Sujeta a matemática perfecta (la estrategia de la negación), la deformación desaparece: «Mi estética actual es transformar con matemática de espejo cóncavo las normas clásicas» (Esc. 12).

Esta visión carnavalesca o carnavalización literaria que Valle re-incorpora a través de su matemática perfecta se compone a su vez de varios rasgos, que proviene desde sus orígenes en la sátira menipea, que Bajtin ve como «esencia del género» y no estratificación de cánones (1970: 151-186). En la producción textual de Valle se re-organizan y re-asimilan algunos al combinarlos con la fantasmagoria, el «simbolismo» y un «naturalismo» de bajos fondos —escatológico, grosero— (Loureiro, 1988, se centra en lo grotesco). Subraya los escándalos, las extravagancias, que ponen en tela de juicio la unidad trágica o épica del mundo y abren una brecha en lo inamovible, la norma, lo respetable, a través de la profanación desmitificadora. Valle saca excelente partido de los violentos contrastes —oximorones—, las transformaciones bruscas, los géneros intercalados (voces de apoyo y polémica), llevándolos adelante paródicamente, con humor o risa. Todo conduce e induce a la destrucción de un mundo estratificado y, por tanto, artificial.

Humor, risa, en efecto, pero el humor del esperpento y de la farsa esperpéntica dista del superficial y trivial (cercano al kitsch) de otros contemporáneos, Gómez de la Serna, por ejemplo, o los autores del género chico. En este sentido se acerca al concepto más actual de parodia, la parodia contemporánea, mediante la cual el autor(a) «does nos claim to speak from a position outside the parodied» (Hutcheon, 1985). Se aparta de la imitación que ridiculiza —el ingenio dieciochesco, la sátira tradicional—, y es más bien una «repetition with critical distance that allows ironic signaling of difference at the very heart of similarity» (Hutcheon, 1987).

La carnavalización literaria valleinclanesca re-orienta la imaginación (cuya función social ya hemos indicado) e invita a transformar la ficción en «realidad», al recrear un mundo al revés. Valle se regodea en señalar las convenciones arbitrarias, las excentricidades, las alianzas imposibles entre las esferas sociales, mediante insinuaciones de naturaleza teatral y melodramáticas, y las profanaciones que inducen a la risa (más destructiva que el «humor» o la «ironía» estilizada). Las jerarquías —piedad, religión, etiqueta—, es decir, cuanto dicta la desigualdad social o los privilegios de clases, se abolen y se reemplazan con una actitud libre y familiar, en una re-organización de las relaciones humanas, que se oponen al mundo socio-jerárquico de la vida corriente. Conducta, gestos y lenguaje se liberan del marco jerárquico (edad, cargos, títulos, fortuna, sexos), y se convierten en excéntricos, en desplazamientos y despedazamientos de la vida habitual. Cuanto la jerarquización o códigos oficiales separa, dispersa o desconecta, entra en contacto: lo sagrado y lo profano, lo sublime y lo insignificante, lo alto y lo bajo, lo aristocrático y lo plebeyo. La profanidad y la transgresión son la norma; se instala el sacrilegio de lo genésico, del cuerpo. Se parodian, además, los textos y las palabras sagradas (heterodoxia religiosa y retórica), se destrona directamente el mundo de la tradición. La risa no significa pura negación del objeto/sujeto parodiado; las imágenes se parodian mutuamente, forman un sistema de espejos deformantes que las alargan, las recortan, las desfiguran en direcciones y grados diversos, en modulaciones mayores.

Si sus primeros textos se orquestan a través de los ritos lascivos, las luchas «bárbaras», producto de la ignorancia y la opresión, con las farsas y esperpentos las profanaciones y desmitificaciones apuntan más directamente los sistemas sociales en la corte, en la urbe, aquel espacio de «argot y germanía». El lenguaje aristocratizante y arcaico se re-convierte en un contra-lenguaje del literario y cultural al uso al servicio de las concepciones dogmáticas del mundo. Este contra-lenguaje, riquísimo en inflexiones sociales, permite descubrir los abusos que encubren las justificaciones «legales» y «morales» ante sus víctimas. La «abyección» proviene de las clases dominantes, que persiguen por igual y con celo al bohemio y al obrero anarquista y le imponen un código tradicional al pobre Friolera, moderno Otelo atrapado por unos lenguajes y normas alienantes, que también transforman en marginado al ex combatiente de Cuba, Juanito Ventolera. Valle opera bajo el resorte de lo que hoy llamaríamos la aporía social de la «deconstrucción» [3]. Habré de mover sólo alguno de los resortes. '

El proceso intensivo de degradación, la escatología, la obscenidad, se «representa» con mayor agudeza a través de la semántica del cuerpo. Las farsas primeras, luego los esperpentos, se alimentan —como es sabido— de los géneros menores: género chico, romances de cordel, el folletín, el periodismo satírico, las aleluyas, la literatura oral. El procedimiento no es nuevo, siempre ha existido una vena cómica y paródica en la literatura; baste recordar el género de la sátira desde la Edad Media. Aún más recientemente, la sátira del siglo XVII, el teatro dieciochesco, el Romántico y, posteriormente, bastante más cercano a Valle-Inclán, las parodias del teatro realista (tema sobre el cual volveré en otra ocasión). A modo de ejemplo señalaré algunos títulos significativos: *Feúcha; parodia de la comedia del insigne Pérez Galdós, Mariúcha*, de Antonio Casero y Barranco (1903); *Electroterapia; humorada ...en verso. Parodia del drama en cinco actos Electra*, de Gabriel Merino y Pichilo (1901); *La de San Quintín; juguete cómico*, de José Estremera (1880); *La de vámonos; humorada cómico-lírica*, de Felipe Pérez González (1894); *¡Alerta! pseudo-parodia político musical del famoso drama de ...Electra*, de Federico R. Escacena (1901). Tampoco faltan las parodias de Echegaray: *¡Barbiana! ...parodia de Mariana*, de Diego Jiménes Prieto (1896); *El final de un lío...sainete. Parodia del prólogo de un drama de D. José de Echegaray*, de Baldomero Alvarez (1892).

Dentro de este ambiente de humorada, juguete cómico, parodia político musical, conviene recordar otros títulos significativos, que se re-inscriben en el esperpento. Además de los conocidos, gracias al excelente bajorrelieve de Zamora Vicente (1968), en algún otro se percibe el diálogo de voces, frases o espacios: *Los carvajales*, de Manuel Martínez Barrionuevo (1885), *El pan de la emigración*, de R. Leopoldo Palomino de Guzmán (1874), y *El martes de carnaval*, de Juan Redondo (1891), además de la zarzuela de Antonio Fernández Lepina, *La corte de los milagros* (1909). No faltan las inscripcio-

---

[3] Por aporía de la deconstrucción debe entenderse un lenguaje autorreflexivo, los «blinds spots of paradox» a que alude de Man (1979). Lentricchia (1983) ofrece una excelente definición. Me parece preciso subrayar que la aporía valleinclanesca es *social*, ya que el lenguaje está socialmente orientado.

nes intersemióticas de navajas, títulos de aleluyas, entre tantas otras incorporaciones de subtextos sociales.

No se le pasan por alto a Darío en su viaje a España en 1899 otros sectores de innovación y afirma que lo mejor de la España finisecular son los caricaturistas de los periódicos, en particular Ortega y Sancha (Zavala, 1970, 1972). Sus comentarios sobre este último son reveladores y se pueden enlazar con los subtextos sociales del esperpento. Sancha —según Darío— deforma la realidad y sus deformaciones «recuerdan las imágenes de los espejos cóncavos o convexos; es un dibujo de abotagamiento o elefantiasis: monicacos macrocéfalos e hidrópicas marionetas» (apud Zavala, 1970). No es el único subtexto social pictórico valleinclanesco que se apoya en la caricatura política, antes había incluido a Goya, Posada, Solana, Durero. El esperpento y las farsas incorporan todo lenguaje que se levante contra la norma, que ponga de relieve los conflictos entre la palabra constativa y la performativa, en juegos especulares. Valle dialoga con todo subtexto que le permita revelar la función de disimulo y enmascaramiento de los lenguajes de la autoridad, en derroche de significantes y confluencia de inversiones. Dialoga e incorpora el desparpajo, y se apoya en cuantos deconstruyen la supuesta «sobriedad», el honor y la «verdad» de los mitos nacionales. Re-dirige sus inversiones.

El diálogo de Valle con estas «voces» populares es a la vez de apoyo y de polémica. Se acerca y se aleja, se parece y se distingue de todo un universo gráfico y teatral finisecular: en especial la crítica del teatro burgués de anarquistas y socialistas, el teatro en libertad y el teatro artístico de Benavente (se recordará que aquél actuó en una de sus obras). Valle, que ha pormenorizado en incontables ocasiones su ascensión al esperpento, soslaya estos espacios privilegiados, que él conduce a los límites del discurso y hace proliferar y potencializarse. Este universo contestatario y antiburgués se inclina preferentemente hacia el ejercicio del espejo y sus alternativas como degradación de todo saber anterior, de toda autoridad, y como negación final de los referentes (Zavala, 1988). Veamos algunos textos en diálogo con los «espejos deformantes» de Valle.

En 1894, el anarquista Salvador Canals publica la crónica «El teatro anarquista: la cara y el espejo», y califica de melodrama una obra que gozó de cierto éxito. *El pan del pobre,* de Francos y Llana. En su violenta repulsa, juega con las nociones espejo/cara, realidad/teatro, y finaliza que mientras la realidad madrileña sea de abusos de los señoritos, nadie puede protestar: «La realidad es lo que hay que cambiar, y entonces cambiarán sus reflejos» (apud Rubio, 1982: 156). La noción del teatro como «espejo» de la sociedad, y como vehículo de ideas regeneradoras, es temprana, aparece en crónica firmada con las iniciales V. S. en *El Socialista*, 1887. En ella se somete el teatro burgués a una durísima crítica, porque éste refleja —escribe el autor— la imagen de crisis y descomposición interna: la corrupción, las posturas lascivas, lo más hediondo de la sociedad, las canciones indecorosas, las escenas de taberna y de café, el eclipse de lo serio y el triunfo de lo grotesco, la sustitución del actor por el payaso, la guasa, la broma, «todo eso gusta al público que aplaude estúpidamente su propia caricatura» (apud Rubio, 126).

De círculos socialistas surge en 1900 otra crítica que se puede poner en diálogo y polémica con el teatro de Valle. Un anónimo autor levanta su contra-palabra en «Los obreros y el arte», en desafío ante el «teatro por horas», de estupideces pornográficas, atento «sólo a facilitar la digestión de los satisfechos o a provocar las carcajadas de la multitud famélica e ignorante» (Rubio, 157). La inercia del teatro burgués es blanco de la renovación propuesta por Benavente, con su teatro artístico, de muñecos y *Figulinas*. Estos moldes anti-burgueses se redoblan y aumentan su potencial en el esperpento valleinclanesco, mediante una inversión, que no facilita la digestión de los satisfechos, ni está encauzada a provocar la carcajada de los ignorantes. Se orienta más bien a la creación de un discurso de libertad para destronar el miedo, en su insubordinación contra las reglas establecidas y en conspiración contra el poder. Su escritura esperpéntica postula el espectáculo, la teatralidad performativa.

La crítica de la realidad burguesa de anarquistas y socialistas y su visión de un teatro especular-mimético se inscribe como voz en el esperpento deformante de Valle, que «representa» la realidad en juego de sistemas y de dos paradigmas, el de la realidad/espejo, y el del disfraz/realidad en movimientos ondulatorios. Sus personajes ponen de manifiesto simultáneamente dos versiones de sus estados y clases, de sus nombres (como veremos), en el bifurcado carácter de la farsa, en contigüidad de las dos voces y las dos realidades que el espejo deformante «representa» en sus antagonismos, con impulsión motora.

Esta red intertextual e intersemiótica de lo que hoy llama-

127

ríamos *mass media* (pinturas, signos, espectáculos, cine, estampillas, afiches, gráficos, litografías) le sirve una vez más de armadura contra la cultura oficial estancada. Valle «representa» especularmente los antivalores de una moral pública y una responsabilidad colectiva, que se le hace aborrecible y su objetivo es provocar una reacción de burla o desdén y de risa contra lo académico, lo castellanizante, la tradición, lo cerrado y satisfecho, en multiplicidad de tonos y de voces. Tal imbricación de relaciones sociales falsas y artificiales se le hace intolerable en la promiscuidad moral de todas sus formas, y revela entonces el espectáculo violento del cambio en una inversión que implica a sus espectadores(as) y lectores(as) a dar vuelta a las imágenes. Revela el funcionamiento real en los abismos de lo social (*mise en abîme* de la aporía de la deconstrucción) [4]; al llegar a este encuentro el rasgo de profanación y transgresión se acentúa, y sus relaciones con el pasado histórico y el presente serán más críticas y polémicas.

La objetivación y densidad paródica con géneros y lenguajes se renueva; representa el espectáculo de todo aquello por lo cual se había pagado tan caro a partir de la Revolución de 1868, y las razones y motivos por los cuales sus defensores la habían dejado caer en la indiferencia y se aceptaba su producto como una fatalidad. Valle busca la pulsión burlona en su destrucción épica de la historia oficial de España. Absorbe en unidad interna los géneros y los temas de prestigio y les da vuelta; destrona por el humor, la risa y la «tragedia grotesca» los valores desgastados, los valores inmutables e intocables. En su pulsión burlona nos libera del miedo y desenmascara la simulación a través de la ley de la reversibilidad [5].

Desde el punto de vista discursivo, Valle muestra el choque entre la palabra autoritaria y la palabra de convicción interna, choque que Bajtin propone como base de las posibilidades polisémicas y dialogizantes del discurso novelístico (1978: 111-112). La pluralidad de lenguas, la heteroglosia, se elaboran mediante el empleo de arcaísmos, germanía, dialectos

---

[4] Para de Man el *mise en abîme* significa: «self-cancellation and self-constitution». Es decir, «thematic category is torn apart by the aporia that constitutes it, thus making the categories effective to the precise extent that they eliminate the value system in which their classification is grounded», apud Lentriccchia (1980: 179); véase asimismo Hutcheon (1985), Norris (1985).

[5] Baudrillard (1984) hace pertinentes observaciones sobre los poderes de la seducción. Adapto e «invierto» algunas de sus ideas en un marco socializado.

sociales, modos de ser de grupo, jergas profesionales, lenguajes de generaciones y edades, lenguaje de corrientes ideológicas, políticas, literarias, lenguaje de círculos, cenáculos, logias masónicas; todo ello en un complejísimo mosaico que se levanta contra la palabra estratificada y autoritaria. Valle mantiene una connivencia crítica/irónica con el poder, la ley, el orden, y despierta los géneros orales bajos (conjuros, concejas, recetas, dichos populares, proverbios, canciones, chistes), en duplicidad fundamental, en estrategia que pretende un desafío para filtrar una teoría sociológica del campesinado, del mundo rural gallego, de la urbe. En este último espacio social, el empleo del lenguaje de la «plaza pública» y de los golfos citadinos explora de manera prodigiosa las posibilidades de coexistencia y contraste entre la lengua culta y la popular; dos semánticas y dos somáticas libidinales.

Conviene recordar que Valle percibe el poder en la década de 1920 como una monstruosidad a gritos y representa sus imágenes siempre al borde del ridículo, en sus rasgos más grotescos. Con ironía objetiva, filtra las palabras, los espíritus y los cuerpos y los confunde, acopla imágenes con su contraimagen idéntica grotesca. El rostro, en particular la exageración de la nariz y la boca, desempeñan un papel principal. La cabeza, las orejas y la nariz se animalizan; los ojos se presentan en sus protuberancias. Del cuerpo destaca lo que sobresale, cuanto quiere romper los confines; especial atención al vientre y a las partes que remiten a los órganos genitales. El realismo grotesco se convierte en instrumento único para «representar» la farsa, lo grotesco de los gobernantes que revuelcan su ponzoña por el tablado. La historia de España se desritualiza, y corresponde a la cantada por romanceros y copleros; la nueva Clío es musa popular y arrabalera, que lleva chinela de orillo. Sirva, a modo de ejemplo, el significativo extenso pasaje de *Viva mi dueño*:

A la Historia de España, en sus grandes horas, nunca le ha faltado acompañamiento de romances, y la epopeya de los amenes isabelinos hay que buscarla en las coplas que se cantaron entonces por el Ruedo Ibérico. Tomaba Apolo su laurel a la puerta de las tabernas, como en la guerra con los franceses, cuando la musa populachera de donados y sopistas, tunos y rapabar-

129

bas, era el mejor guerrillero contra Bonaparte. Todo España, en aquellos isabelinos amenes, gargarizaba para un Dos de Mayo (1961: 1242).

Sus reconstrucciones son excavaciones en el subsuelo histórico. Como el lenguaje, la literatura y la historia están amuralladas de tradición, cercadas y erizadas de casticismo. Valle reconquista una herencia popular, lo que le lleva a intentar muchos injertos y cruzamientos. El descubrimiento no fue casual; corresponde a una poética social, a una visión de mundo, una manera de sentirlo, conocerlo y analizarlo en sus consecuencias extremas. Con su musa arremangada, reveló un mundo sepultado de objetos y sujetos engañosos, un presente entregado a la simulación y al engaño. A partir de su posición de sujeto de análisis («la posición geométrica»), reversabilizó su objeto, logró una inversión del saber, desafiando las normas, los lugares comunes, lo aceptado, la indiferencia, la estrategia de las apariencias que dominaba en su profunda inmoralidad [6]. Toda esta escritura convoca un receptor(a): Valle al lector(a) y auditor(a) crítico.

## 2. «LA MUSA MODERNA SALTA LUCIENDO LA PIERNA»

*Incipit parodia.*

(Nietzsche.)

Cuesta trabajo imaginar el juego de espejos invertidos que fragmenta el cuerpo social. Detrás de esa pantalla paródica y de la desmembración del cuerpo y lo bajo corpóreo hay un modelo de «representación», una semántica política, que toma una onda de irrisión y reversión, de explotación paródica en *Farsa y licencia de la Reina castiza* (1922), que con desenvoltura define «befa de muñecos». Podríamos decir que es una puesta en escena del propio objeto que presenta su propio modo de desaparición: el cuerpo que se fragmenta, se destru-

---

[6] Buero Vallejo (1966) y Ruibal (1969) aluden a las relaciones de Valle con los espectadores. Para Buero la tercera postura («mirar desde arriba») impera. Consúltese también Greenfield (1972) y las apreciaciones críticas recientes de Carlos Serrano (1987), y el artículo citado de Rubio (1988) sobre las ideas teatrales de Pérez de Ayala.

ye, se quiebra, se auto-parodia. El lenguaje que se auto-anula, que se des-referencializa, que estalla en significantes; estas estrategias hacen que el espectador/lector pierda toda ilusión. El espejo anti-ilusión, desilusiona, en su proyección verídica de la Corte. El espectáculo despierta la ironía del espectador(a), que en lo *imaginario social* ejecuta la subversión de la clase política. En su ironía feroz, Valle descompone los «muñecos» que se engañan a sí mismos, en una disimulación radical; el espejo deformante es el de la objetividad. Demuestra la escena política en su dramatización artificial, en su jerarquía engañosa. Desde el principio predomina lo hiperbólico, la exageración: la terminación *ón* del superlativo da la tónica. La sátira y lo bajo corpóreo, en un lenguaje barriobajero, son ahora la norma. El conocido apostillón inicia el rito desmitificador: la corte isabelina es befa y farsa, caricatura de periódicos satíricos, mueca, burla. Y para cantarla, su musa moderna «enarca la pierna, / se cimbra, se ondula, / se comba, se achula». Lo bajo corpóreo hiperbolizado y exagerado, le permite degradar los símbolos del poder, sobre todo la Corte. La animalización —procedimiento tradicional desde la cultura clásica y re-actualizado durante el siglo XVIII por los fabulistas, Torres Villarroel y el padre Isla— apunta direcciones muy específicas. Todo un zoológico fantástico reaparece (fijado ya como signo negativo desde *La pipa*); lo que importa son las «representaciones», a *quiénes* y *cómo* se les confiere esta degradación.

Se levanta ahora la supremacía del sujeto, cada vez más objeto en sus ceremonias y malignidades. Se podría llamar «la estrategia irónica» y el «genio maligno de lo social» (adopto, en muy otro sentido, estos términos de Baudrillard, 1985), en su mercancía absoluta. Las obesidades, lo obsceno de los tejidos adiposos hipertrofiados y proliferantes son la norma. El cuerpo crece o se disminuye en simulación e imagen de los sistemas; la redundancia genética es la de todo un sistema. El cuerpo pierde su forma y su regla, el lenguaje gestual lo lleva a los límites de lo obsceno visible. El cuerpo encarna la morfología y la semántica de la sociedad desestructurada y deforme, des-seduccionada de lo fascinante. El cuerpo corresponde al mundo exterior, a las contradicciones históricas que encuentran su imagen en el espejo de lo deforme, en la deficiencia mental o física (como el hidrocéfalo de *Divinas palabras*). Las imágenes han perdido ya su credibilidad en formas hipertrofiadas, anómalas y monstruosas. Las obesidades de

131

cuantos todo lo engullen y la flaccidez de cuantos han engullido su propio cuerpo: ratas, pajarracos, murciélagos, zancudos.

Abundan como antes los referentes de las «cabezas de lechuza», «los ojos de pajarraco», la apariencia «ratonil», el «perfil de lechuza»; la Reina se «representa como «yegua en celo», cuando no muestra su «pechuga hiperbólico acordeón», o «hace guiñadas», mientras muestra las «fofas mantecas» tras la muselina blanca. La pobre Isabel II, enamorada incontinente, lleva también «sus narices de Borbón, encendidas como un mamey». No le va mejor al Rey, queda reducido a un irrisorio eunuco, y su boca belfa va «pintada de carmín». Ministros, ejército se deforman: el ministro de *Luces de bohemia* «asoma en mangas de camisa» y los quevedos son «dos ojos absurdos» que le bailan sobre la panza. Mientras Agustín Miranda, el «Pachá Búm-Búm» de *La hija del Capitán* es «saturnal y panzudo, veterano de tiros y juergas», o bien Vinoso y risueño, con la bragueta desabrochada». Por su parte, Torre Mellada semeja un pelucón perfumado, así como otros miembros de la nobleza.

*Martes de Carnaval* ofrece extraordinarios contrastes visuales: la vieja del prostíbulo en *Las galas* es «obesa, grandota, con muchos peines y rizos: Un erisipel le repela las cejas» (*OE* I: 969). Juanito Ventolera, en cambio, es «alto, flaco, macilento, los ojos de fiebre, la mente terciada, el gorro en la oreja, la trasquila en la sien. El tinglado de cruces y medallas daba sus brillos buhoneros» (970). Doña Tadea, la beata chismosa, «se santigua con la cruz del rosario» y «clava sus ojos de pajarraco»; es «pequeña, cetrina, ratonil». Doña Loreta, el «ángel de mi hogar» (evidente parodia de las representaciones de la mujer burguesa), a ojos de Friolera es una fondona tarasca, mientras Don Lauro Rovirosa se describe con un «ojo volante».

Merece que destaquemos dos puntos: en un mismo texto Valle hiperboliza para degradar, o minimizar: su cristal es cóncavo y convexo. Amplifica imágenes, como cristal de aumento, o las reduce, las achica; con el mismo instrumento acerca o aleja los objetos. Su mira es simultáneamente telescopio o microscopio, como el ojo de la cámara de cine. Su mundo está poblado de gigantes y enanos. En segundo lugar, las imágenes «representadas», que forman parte de todo un programa político a través de un aparato libidinal, las emite un tercero, el «acotador», que se inserta como personaje hablante o actante en la obra. El procedimiento viene del teatro de marionetas; herencia que Valle deconstruye y disuelve, pero que le permite este paradigma de libertad .para «representar» lo *imaginario social:* corte, estado, se «representan» en su multiplicación de identidades, que ofrecen al espectador el espejo de su contrario. Nos proponen las imágenes negativas, simultáneamente la «representación» de lo que *no* son la corte, el estado. Reina, Rey, académicos, militares, eclesiásticos, son «personajes», en espacios infinitos de teatro dentro del teatro, personas y personajes, en sus gestos, sus tonos. Se transforman en signos icónicos en el escenario, cuerpos y gestos metonímicos que apuntan simultáneamente a señas de identidad y su parodia. En términos de configuración y uso del cuerpo, éste «representa» la realidad, en su esencia ideológica.

Es digno de observarse que glotonería y sexualidad, como en la tradición rabelesiana, van unidos: fondona, crasa y de conocidos devaneos eróticos, Isabel II se lo come todo por deglución: hombres y país (pueblo, estado). Su apetito es voraz. En cambio, el Rey consorte, pequeñín, untado de carmín, juguetón como perrito faldero, opera una deglución a la inversa. Si nos detuviéramos a analizar académicos, políticos, nobles, las referencias a lo bajo corpóreo predominan. Sirvan algunos ejemplos en este amplio programa estético: en *La corte* la Reina es «chungona y jamona, regia y plebeya», y el Rey «menudo y rosado». El marqués de Torre Mellada, un «vejete rubiales, pintado y perfumado con melindres de monja boba», o bien «tiene típica morisqueta de fantoche», en *Viva mi dueño* hace «buches de paloma real». El barón de Benicarlés de *Tirano Banderas* (1926), allí ministro plenipotenciario de su Majestad Católica, tiene «carnosos párpados», o bien «le hacían rollas las manos y el papo», gusta además de cenáculos decadentes, «la fiesta de amor sin mujeres». Como los reyes, la glotonería y la sexualidad en desenfreno se dan en un mismo orbe en esa corte que se definía como católica, de moral rigurosa y actitud sobria, en la retórica política y religiosa al uso.

En contraste, el dictador Tirano Banderas tiene «paso de rata fisgona», «olisca de rata fisgona», cuando no semeja una «calavera humorística». El Coronelito Domiciano de la Gándara, presenta el «vientre rotundo y risueño de dios tibetano». Se les define en término de antagonismo con la apariencia convencional de sus títulos y cargos: en las farsas y en los esperpentos la fealdad, la deformidad, la degradación, proviene no de las marionetas, sino de los personajes/personas que trastrocan sus gestos, los invierten, los tergiversan. Los espejos no nos proponen una alternativa de lo social, sino su imagen real; la realidad anatómica del cuerpo es la «representada».

Recuérdese la Comisión de Damas en *La hija del Capitán* y la matrona gorda, Doña Simplicia: «La tarasca infla la pechuga buchona, resplandeciente de cruces y bandas, recoge el cordón de los lentes, tremola el fascículo de su discurso» (*OE* I: 1093). Su discurso es hiperbólico y grandilocuente: el alcohólico Miranda, Pachá Búm-Búm, es «Príncipe de la Milicia», las mujeres «ángeles de los hogares», en diálogo con los ditirambos de la burocracia colonial en *Tirano*. En ambos casos se siente la «voz» parodiada de la retórica político-teológica imperial, y además la parodia de la prensa destinada a la lectura de las mujeres, en su imagen tradicional de la *foemina impotens,* doblemente feliz en labios de una «feminista».

En otro extremo de este *voyeurismo* continuo sobre la obscenidad y el «espejo» en su proyección verídica del mundo, Juanito Ventolera en *Las galas,* el soldado desengañado, es un Don Juan jacarandoso y chulapo, «algarero y farsante». Pero también se rebela contra las galas, el ejército, la fanfarria nacional, poniéndose fuera de la ley «como otro Ravachol», al mismo tiempo que despoja a un muerto y mediante chulería vulgar conquista sus damas. El «héroe militar» es en sí la imagen virtual del espejo convexo:

> El desconcierto de la gambeta y el visaje que le sacude la cara, revierten la vida en una sensación de espejo convexo. La palabra se intuye por el gesto, al golpe de los pies por los ángulos de la zapateta. Es un instante donde todas las cosas se proyectan colmadas de mudez. Se explican plenamente con una angustiosa evidencia visual (*OE* I: 973).

El sujeto se reversabiliza en estos textos, y se empuja a sus reductos, se metamorfosea en una inversión del saber y se inscribe de forma visual y legible en la esfera del lenguaje. Valle libera las formas reales, las despoja de sus máscaras, y las muestra rebasando sus límites, en su realidad virtual/real. La pragmática del espejo convexo radica en el poder de proporcionarle a los referentes —reyes, corte, académicos, militares, tiranos, amor, muerte, autoridad, vida, poder— su modo de representación anatómica grotesca real. No es teatro de gritos el suyo, sino «de estados de conciencia», afirma en 1923 (apud Dougherty, 102-5). La imagen especular tiene su origen en lo *imaginario social.*

Guiñol o carpa de circo, los espejos valleinclanescos operan como «canales» (adopto el término de Eco, 1988: 18-20), y tienen funciones magnificantes o reductoras; los referentes del poder ostentan vientres exagerados, las carnes, fofas y adiposas de la glotonería, la enfermedad o el vicio. Mujeres en corsé, como la coronela de *Los cuernos,* otras con falda bajera; se sugiere la protuberancia de pechos, nalgas, vientres. Convexidades y orificios remiten a sudores, grasas, copulaciones; la deglución de otros cuerpos. O, por el contrario, la delgadez extrema y el olisquear de ratas, en un zoológico y bestiario de alimañas rapaces.

Tampoco queda la Iglesia bien parada; si ya el Cura de Lantañón era calvo, seco y con tonsura, como Farruguiño y el Capellán, las beatas (tal la de *Los cuernos*) son secas y fisgonas. Sus gestos y cuerpos corresponden a la definición metonímica de la religión que ya había ofrecido don Juan Manuel, al regresar a su casa, en *Romance de lobos:*

> La religión es seca como una vieja... ¡Como las canillas de una vieja! Tiene cara de beata y cuerpo de galgo... (*OE* I: 618).

La imagen especular va adquiriendo otras proporciones; en *El ruedo ibérico* y en las farsas, Sor Patrocinio y el Padre Claret se representan envueltos en una atmósfera de mentira, ignorancia, si bien en «olor de santidad» siempre. El lenguaje paródico revela siempre su lado oculto, la otra cara, el otro referente: *musicales quejas, celestes mensajes, exudaba fragancias de rosas y nardos, rostro seráfico* (léase a la luz de dobles referentes *Viva mi dueño*). En todo caso ambos representan la superstición, el poder adquirido por la ignorancia, el «opio del pueblo» al que alude en *La pipa:* «la figura de la monja tenía un acento de pavor milagrero y dramático» (*Corte, OE* I: 232). A través de estas imágenes, Valle sugiere el terror cósmico, el miedo a lo desconocido, lo infinito poderoso; es una especie de esfera cuyo centro está en todas partes del Reino y su circunferencia en ninguna. Un camaleón con dos caras —la de monja boba y la de consejera de reyes—. El misterio, el miedo, el terror los circundan, los protegen; todo ello es lo contrario de la risa desmitificadora.

El ejército, los militares, saltan como figuras de estampa litográfica, fuentes de escándalo y extravagancias, o bien son ridículas figurillas, empequeñecidas, recortadas. Prim caracolea «su caballo de naipes», y su gallarda figura cabalga sobre «un bélico corcel de tíovivo», con «albures de cuartel y arrogancias de matante» (Corte, OE: I, 211; Baza, 1961: 181). En otras ocasiones llega untado de cosméticos y «botas de charol con falsos tacones, que le aumentaban la estatura» (Baza, 161). El héroe es en realidad «un pobre histrión con acento de actriz bufa»; la parodia va contra el héroe trágico de la historia y sus palabras sagradas. Prim, y los otros militares, son figuras de actualidad en esta doble voz: su imagen y su contra-imagen. Su objetivo es demostrar «la moneda fullera» [7].

Esta degradación de la palabra autorizada, de las imágenes o símbolos de las instituciones en el poder, de los hechos y héroes históricos, forma parte de un mundo de guiñol, de feria, de cartel, de corrida, farsa, can-can, en una pluralidad de estilos y voces. Valle recorta, alarga, hincha, polemiza con el material literario anterior. Religión y tradición son formas muertas, inservibles, que mutilan o asfixian. Los géneros intercalados le permiten subrayar su destronamiento; los varios niveles o formas de intertextualidad son amplios palimpsestos deformados y deformantes en direcciones diversas. Lo respetado y lo respetable, lo social y lo cultural le sirven de subtextos en su labor de profanación desmitificadora. En sus propias palabras: «El arte es bello porque suma en las formas actuales evocaciones antiguas, y sacude la cadena de siglos (La lámpara maravillosa). Veamos algunos ejemplos de la amplitud de esta amalgama de «voces».

De la conjunción de subtextos que sirven de apoyo conviene recordar los estereotipos y arquetipos del folletín; transpo-

---

[7] En contraste, compárese la imagen grotesca y paródica de Prim con la de Cara de Plata siempre a caballo, unas veces para evitar encontrarse con deudores, otras para pasearse caracoleando por el pueblo. Por cierto, Jameson (1981) alude a la «reificación de la humanidad» (concepto de Lukács), que impone la igualdad a todos los seres humanos. Naturalmente que estoy consciente que la carnavalización varía históricamente, como ya he sugerido, y además de si los personajes «representados» son o no históricos. El mecanismo depende mucho de la diferencia entre sátira o parodia para despojar a los personajes históricos de todo rastro de dignidad.

siciones metonímicas que el lector identificaría con cierta facilidad, por su larga tradición. Me centraré en algunos de los arquetipos más evidentes, y luego estableceré el diálogo con un subtexto paródico más importante: el romancero y el romance popular o «vulgar».

Es lugar común que Valle presenta en la etapa de las farsas y del esperpento los rasgos negativos de la nobleza, el clero, los ministros. Las voces de apoyo provienen de múltiples tradiciones: la literatura anti-nobiliaria y anti-clerical de la sátira medieval, humanista, erasmista y quevedesca. Los curas son venales y avarientos, la aristocracia ociosa y despilfarradora, los ministros retóricos. Pero, además de las voces de autoridad de la literatura culta, aprovecha también la sátira romántica del folletín y la novela popular decimonónica, además del periodismo satírico burlesco (que a su vez fue voz de apoyo en la literatura democrática). Muchas de las figuras grotescas carnavalizadas de Valle dialogan con Ayguals de Izco; los antagonistas son como el fray Patricio de *María, la hija del jornalero* (1845-6): «bajo de estatura y estúpidamente gordo [...] lujurioso como un mico». En estos códigos narrativos los personajes se presentan en su función de signo y símbolo: protagonistas y antagonistas reciben representaciones distintas. Al igual que los folletinistas, Valle revela cierta tendencia a la denominación simbólica, que se concentra en los personajes de la aristocracia, los militares y en los tipos populares. Ayguals crea la imagen reductora de una marquesa de Turbias Aguas y Ramón Cabrera, el cabecilla carlista, se reduce al Tigre del Maestrazgo; Ramón Navarrete elabora un grotesco barón de la Celada (*Madrid y nuestro siglo*, 1845-1846). Los ejemplos abundan en esta extensa tradición que presenta el choque entre antagonistas y protagonistas estereotipados. Valle reelabora los estereotipos y arquetipos, los re-codifica en una nueva producción de sentido y desmitificación social.

Es digno de observarse también que las ficciones valleinclanescas están centradas en torno a un calendario festivo (como *El Buscón*, véase Cros, 1980), en un vasto campo intertextual o subtexto cultural. Así, por ejemplo, *Tirano Banderas* remite directamente a la libertad de carnaval del 2 de noviembre, Día de los muertos, calendario emocional que en México brinda la oportunidad para la burla y la sátira al gobierno. Es un símbolo polisémico —artes gráficas y calendario festivo—; de ahí que Tirano sea «calavera humorística», y que las

137

tres narraciones que integran *El ruedo* traigan resonancias de carnaval (como *La pipa de kif*). Asimismo *Cara de Plata* (1923) coincide con la feria de Viana, *Divinas palabras* se sitúa en el espacio de ferias; mientras el final de *La hija del Capitán* (1927) despliega el espectáculo público y música marcial que consagra el recién establecido gobierno del general Miranda.

Otros subtextos son francamente polémicos y apoyan la dialogía paródica: Valle ofrece imágenes especulares paródicas del lenguaje monológico oficial. Los ejemplos son innumerables: el fragmento de Espronceda que adapta a la pronunciación defectuosa del piloto negro en *Tirano;* la alteración de conocidos versos románticos para acentuar la sátira. Darío le brinda en el mismo texto, en parodia, la ocasión para caracterizar emociones falsas: «fanfarrias de históricos nombres sonoros» en polémica con «nombres sonoros y raros enigmas» *(Prosas profanas).* O bien «Las águilas jóvenes» están en polémica con «Salutación del águila». En la misma superficie textual, el ministro del Uruguay se mofa del de Ecuador, aludiendo al verso «sentimental, sensible, sensitivo», en diálogo con el «yo soy aquel» dariano. Preciso es señalar que esta retórica de la tradición poética más difundida (Espronceda, Darío, otros modernistas) sirve de apoyo al universo esperpéntico de esta novela, pero que son los seres grotescos que reptan (ministros, oficiales) los sujetos semióticos cuya entonación carnavaliza y parodia, en estas referencias librescas. Excepción sea hecha del piloto negro y la transcripción fonética de «La canción del pirata», complejo nudo dialógico de literatura y escritura, y de sincretismo metonímico.

El lugar común literario, la «opinión pública» difundida, la «voz del pueblo» (en frase de Feijoo), emergen como amplios subtextos polémicos. El clisé cultural, social y literario, es el soporte de buena parte de la producción textual valle-inclanesca. Los ciegos mienten, los gitanos roban y mienten, los lúbricos son reyes moros o musulmanes, los celosos son berberiscos y otelos: el Rey es «celoso como un berberisco», o alguien es «celoso como un Otelo». Otro personaje no dice mentiras «como un puritano»; los soldados son fanfarrones (tradición que se remonta a Cervantes, Alemán, Quevedo). En el lugar común literario —el modernista, se entiende— hay parques, jardines, princesas, marquesas, arlequines, duendes, príncipes, cisnes, mirtos, laureles, rosas, pavos reales. Los nombres de los personajes, en farsa o en serio, son también

lugares comunes de la literatura carnavalizada: el Rey Mico-
micón (dos veces mico), el General Fierabrás, Maritornes, Rosalinda, Colombina, Arlequín, el reino de Tartarín. Pero re-
codificados en el contexto del carnaval político de la musa
«funambulesca, carnavalesca», el Duende es en realidad un
Pan desgastado (Pan sin cuernos de chivo, Pan sin Eros).
Aquí la mitología, allá el modernismo o la literatura «castellanizante» de receta, o los personajes de guiñol y de teatro de
títeres, o los lugares comunes del teatro del Siglo de Oro (la
honra calderoniana), todo apunta a la deconstrucción y desmitificación. Los travestidos culturales y sociales parecen
indicar que los mitos oficiales son ilusiones y apariencia. Sólo
a través del signo distanciado se logrará la desmitificación
social: el signo distanciado (la «posición geométrica»), la
distancia que separa al objeto de su percepción. En boca de
Don Estrafalario:

> Si nuestro teatro tuviese el temblor de las fiestas de
> toro, sería magnífico. Si hubiese sabido transportar
> esa violencia estética, sería un teatro heroico como
> la *Ilíada*. A falta de eso, tiene toda la antipatía de los
> códigos, desde la Constitución a la Gramática (*OE* I:
> 1003).

*Los cuernos* está asentado en un firme proceso de voces
de apoyo y de polémica: los dramas de honor de la tradición
literaria, Shakespeare, los dramones románticos sobre el honor, los dramones coetáneos de Echegaray, Arniches, Leopoldo
Cano, Eugenio Sellés y los romances populares de la temática
de los crímenes de honor. El romance de ciego le sirve de
punta de lanza para degradar el espíritu conquistador y teológico, puesto que el romancero alienta esta ficción (o representación de la conquista y la colonización). El romancero
emerge como un subtexto cultural polémico; una voz polémica.
En sus palabras:

> ya no somos una raza de conquistadores y teólogos,
> y en el romance alienta siempre esa ficción. Ya no es
> nuestro el camino de las Indias ni son españoles los
> Papas, y en el romance perdura la hipérbole barroca,
> imitado del viejo latín cuando era soberano del mun-
> do (apud Gómez de la Serna, 1944: 138).

El rechazo de Valle se debe situar en el contexto de una polémica anti-imperialista contra la idea centralista y colonial de los defensores del gran imperio setecentesco. El romancero opera para Valle en una especie de *imaginario social* imperialista, lejano ya en el tiempo después de la guerra hispanoamericana y, como se sabe, bandera de lucha del tradicionalista y conservadurismo peninsular durante la guerra civil y el estado franquista. A Valle no se le escapan las ideologías conservadoras del romancero, ni la barbarie y violencia de la epopeya.

Muy otra es la dirección de su lectura del romancero vulgar, que le sirve de subtexto de apoyo. El romance de cordel, que abarca los aspectos truculentos de la sociedad, en inversiones de la norma, opera como voz «popular» de apoyo. Se recordará que buena parte de este romancero (de gran vitalidad hasta finales del siglo XIX, y subtexto de apoyo para Pío Baroja, por ejemplo) abunda en tópicos y temas escatológicos y transgresores: incestos, asesinatos, parricidios, violaciones, abortos, bandidos convertidos en héroes, las fechorías de adarga y lanza. El pliego de cordel, como el cartelón y las aleluyas, proceden de un mismo tronco (Caro Baroja, 1969: 409-427): son la otra cara, permiten un cristal doble donde se yuxtaponen los dos niveles culturales (arriba/abajo), que funden todas las realidades en una. Estas se interpenetran, mediante un lenguaje chocarrero de plaza de abastos, de carnaval, de feria, de fiesta popular. Sus inversiones de risa festiva funden en cara/cruz la sociedad; el romance vulgar es «lo otro» de la lengua culta y de la literatura institucionalizada; se inspira en los niveles de realidad contrarios a lo aceptado, a la norma codificada. No por otro motivo son blanco de las iras de los ilustrados (Jovellanos, Meléndez Valdés, Campomanes); ofrecen la crónica histórica «oral», son propiamente fuente del folklore popular, en sentido semejante a algunos almanaques procaces y divertidos [8]. Se inspiran en la chismografía palaciega, como la prensa amarilla actual, y desmontan, rebajan —como en espejo cóncavo— los héroes; en vuelta de tuerca, héroes y heroínas son a-típicos, provienen de los sectores marginados. Su aire de familia con la sátira periodística, el género chico y otros discursos menores, salta a la vista. El pliego y su progenie están en complicidad con el lector crítico;

---

[8] Torres Villarroel e Isla son autores enraizados en la tradición oral y en la carnavalización (Zavala, 1987 a).

los valores se invierten en mundo al revés, donde dispersas voces y relatos se juntan en otra posición geométrica.

Dentro de este universo de sátira y parodia en su entronque con el romancero popular, la farsa *La enamorada del Rey* (1920) es texto privilegiado. Dialoga con el *Quijote* y la locura, a través de Mari-Justina, que ha enloquecido —según su abuela ventera —por haber oído «los romancillos que vende el ciego». Sorbidos los sesos, la joven le da vuelta a la realidad y se «representa» al rey joven y hermoso: por arte de birlibirloque, la «representación» de la nieta de. la ventera se hace realidad, pues el rey (fantoche viejo) cae presa de la ficción. María-Justina, por su parte, ve desplomarse las imágenes creadas por la literatura de evasión representada en los romances, el rey salta al retablo, y declara a Maese Lotario consejero real. «Justicia poética» o «diálogo de representaciones»: el texto invierte ambas realidades, en juego recíproco entre la realidad y su imagen[9]. Como representación de lo *imaginario social,* toca al destinatario(a) recodificar la lectura a la inversa, y trasponer y re-contextualizar la farsa. En boca del rey:

> Quiero trocar por normas de poesía
> los chabacanos ritos leguleyos,
> sólo es buena a reinar la fantasía,
> y está mi reino en manos de plebeyos (*OE* II: 981).

Del lenguaje constativo pasa a una invitación a los actos performativos y a invertir los actos performativos («ritos leguleyos») de las promesas rotas de un mundo carente de dignidad.

El lugar común social y cultural, la cultura popular, son sistemas que se interpenetran: ambos destronan la cultura oficial, las instituciones autoritarias. El carnaval valoriza el poder efímero de lo falso; como en el rito carnavalesco analizado por Bajtin (1968, 1978), las injurias y los golpes destronan al monarca en superimposiciones textuales, fuente inagotable de ambigüedades significativas. La coherencia procede de un sistema de imágenes y temas folklóricos y populares que se insertan en la perspectiva carnavalesca: un reflejo especular del sistema social, percibido como sistema de inver-

---

[9] Según Sobejano (1968), en Zahareas (ed. 159-171), la obra representa la inserción de Valle al ideal quijotesco noventaiochista. Greenfield (1972: 195-197) apoya esta interpretación.

sión y transgresión. Los mecanismos y procedimientos que permiten esa distancia irónica —aquí sólo esbozados— re-instauran un discurso auténtico del amplio discurso usurpado. El lenguaje, como el espejo, engaña o desengaña; las interpolaciones, glosas, voces, lugares comunes, permiten precisar dentro de qué perspectiva se sitúa una visión de mundo. Lo que Valle-Inclán pone en tela de juicio o valora es la adecuación o inadecuación de cierto tipo de discurso. El discurso no engaña; sólo engaña si actitudes, palabras y ademanes desdicen lo que son los actantes, en una perspectiva de inversión.

Capítulo VI

# LOS ESPANTAJOS COMICOS Y LA LIBERACION DEL MIEDO

*Serio ludere*
*Similis hilaris*

## 1. ACTIVIDAD SOMATICA

Las farsas y los esperpentos valleinclanescos tienen un propósito: liberar al público y al lector del miedo, del rigor de la tradición asfixiante, invitando a sus interlocutores a imaginarse solidarios, con los valores invertidos y con el proyecto colectivo traicionado desde la Revolución de 1868. Valle persigue su objetivo a partir del uso constructivo de los actos de lenguaje; choques y deconstrucciones entre actos performativos y actos constativos, en la dimensión pragmática del discurso. Su «texto único» se articula en la cadena hablada en unidades de actos de lenguaje, en el marco pragmático de la comunicación. La función esencial del acto de habla o acto de lenguaje puede constituir en un hacer gestual significante, capaz de ser inscrito en el paradigma de otros gestos sonoros comparables (van Dijk, 1976, Mayoral ed., 1987). Dentro de este orden de comunicación, la parodia le permite «hacer público» el lenguaje; en cierto sentido podríamos decir que Valle pasa del acto de habla privado (individual) de sus primeros textos —cuyas promesas y pactos confirmaban la continuidad individual y las «ideologías» personales (Bradomín, Montenegro)—, al acto performativo público, pacto entre gobernantes y gobernados, locutores e interlocutores en la arena política [1]. La producción de los pactos implica que la

---

[1] Pratt (1977, y sobre todo 1986) establece la diferencia entre actos performativos privados y públicos.

palabra se libera de su lugar de inscripción marcando y observando los espacios expresivos.

Este universo de genealogía pluridimensional de pactos puede captarse a lo vivo en las *Comedias bárbaras,* que nos ponen en presencia de los problemas de los bienes individuales (de manera más directa que las *Sonatas* y los pactos y juramentos del seductor) y los pactos comunales. El lenguaje va en dirección de una experiencia que no es verbal, sino perceptiva: los despedazamientos del cuerpo, los sacrilegios a la muerte y las operaciones profanatorias violentas. El enunciado formal que permite vislumbrar los sustentos del discurso son las promesas de eternidad de don Juan Manuel. Nos hallamos en presencia de dos formas de ser del enunciado: el hacer gestual performativo y el pacto o contrato de veridicción del Mayorazgo. Aun si tomamos en cuenta que están escritas en fechas muy distintas —*Cara de Plata* es casi una parodia esperpéntica—, razón no le falta a Matilla (1972) en plantearlas como una sola obra dramática. Designan y fusionan muchas instancias enunciativas e históricas; ejemplifican, en cierto sentido, la «simultaneidad» histórica y geográfica de performativos, pues los problemas no sólo abarcan a Galicia, sino que pueden ser aplicables a toda España: la desintegración de los mayorazgos y la emergencia de la clase media (en particular *Cara de Plata*). A nivel visual, se inspiran en Durero y su concepción de los espacios.

Los performativos gestuales y semánticos de *Aguila de blasón* y *Romance de lobos* (1907) dan soporte a los pactos de verificación de los herederos del mayorazgo y sus luchas por adquirir bienes: el hacer gestual se inscribe en la lógica de la violencia y la muerte. *Romance de lobos* es centro de maravillosas deformidades gestuales y dialogismo: un vértigo de pasiones introduce en el drama histórico la disputa de los hijos-lobos por los bienes familiares frente al cadáver amortajado de la madre. Los sentimientos elementales, la época y el paisaje son ajenos a toda ley y reinan la fuerza bruta y la barbarie. El lenguaje florido y sentencioso de unos se mezcla con el habla baja y rufianesca. Los textos forman parte de esa *revisión irónica* del performativo individual del pasado y sus actos gestuales. El mayorazgo, Don Juan Manuel, piensa para sí pactos performativos ante la tumba de su esposa, al jurarle: «vendré pronto y para siempre a tu lado», mientras le promete a sus hijos que de no cumplirse su última voluntad «he de alzarme de la sepultura si no fuese cumplida». En este mundo de mayorazgos y de campesinos ignorantes, incluso el satanismo y lo demoníaco significan formas de *jurar con, pactar con* («conjuro»), acto de lenguaje performativo que recorre toda una cadena de situaciones y contextos desde el principio de la producción textual valleinclanesca. Los «conjuros» se van convirtiendo en pactos reversabilizados y parodiados —la tardía *Cara de Plata, El embrujado* (1913), *Divinas palabras*—, son verdaderas oposiciones que repercuten en la somática corporal. Una vez situado el lector crítico, capta el choque de intereses de una sociedad pre-moderna, pre-tecnológica organizada a partir del latifundio, de la política municipal, el pauperismo, la lucha entre la nobleza y la Iglesia, el terror teológico y herético. El texto es tierra virgen de intereses y sentimientos. *Cara de Plata* se inicia con un problema legal sobre acceso a un puente; los campesinos dan testimonio falso en connivencia con el abad de Latañón, que, convencido de que Satanás ha encarnado en los Montenegro, se decide conjurar al Diablo para humillar a sus enemigos en el puente. La batalla de arrogancia entre Cara de Plata y el cura tiene su origen en la aplicación de la ley. Entre conjuro y conjura, Fuse Negro representa el envés del gran absurdo en el juego de fraudes y sacrilegios mutuos.

Volvamos a la somática/semántica, que también forma parte del universo especular y sus referentes: aquí los «espejos devanecidos». Si partimos del hecho de que «meaning belongs to a word in its position between speakers» (Voloshinov/Bajtin, 1977: 102), y que la parodia moderna es un discurso *double-directed*, auto-reflexivo y especular (Hutcheon, 1985), ésta se revela también como instrumento crítico (Rose, 1979). El lector está ante un espejo que pone en crisis la frontera de los referentes, el relato, la ficción, el encuadre. Si retomamos la definición de «ideología» propuesta por Althusser —«la forma de "representación" de una relación imaginaria o imaginada entre el individuo y sus condiciones reales de existencia» y como estructura «narrativa»—, el espejo virtual valleinclanesco revela el choque entre actos performativos y constativos y la deconstrucción de unos y otros a nivel público colectivo [2]. En términos genéricos, se podría hablar del cho-

---

[2] La definición más precisa de los actos performativos aparece en Austin, *Philosophical Papers* (1976: 233-252); a ella remito. Tomo en

que entre la ironía, la sátira y la parodia; en los primeros textos predominan los actos de lenguaje privados y en las farsas y esperpentos, los públicos. La experiencia especular recorre la imagen ilusoria y el espejo convexo: la pragmática del espejo representador se vale del enunciado y la posición del sujeto enunciador.

La actividad somática/pragmática de los actos de lenguaje valleinclanescos se sitúa en una actividad corporal y un *uso* del lenguaje gestual muy específico que permite enmarcar el enunciado en cambios de entonación (al cual ya hemos aludido); un elemento tonal expresivo de los comportamientos. Este cambio de entonación (por tanto, de locutor en su función activa) es central en el proceso dialogizador. Si mi propuesta es aceptable, revela formas de «representar» el sujeto semiótico, el *yo*. A simple vista parece que debemos partir de los enunciados de la posición del sujeto emisor; Pratt (1986) parece permitir resolver el principio del problema. Según ella, los actos de lenguaje privados, los pactos y las promesas, son sintomáticos del «commitment to a unified subject» (1986: 62) [3]. La exactitud e interacción en estos actos «is determined by the intentions these individuals form towards each other, and the quality of interaction depends on personal qualities, like rationality, sincerity, self-consistency, of the individuals involved» (p. 62). Si seguimos su argumento, los actos de lenguaje están anclados en un sujeto unitario y esencial, mientras los hablantes se comunican a través de una posición social («a socially constituted position», 63). En cambio, los textos están construidos para múltiples y diversos emisores(as): «literary works are public speech acts» (p. 61). Ahora bien, si estas premisas son válidas para el problema que nos ocupa, nos dicen que los actos de lenguaje valleinclanescos en su construcción interna apuntan ambos objetivos (lo privado y lo público) [4].

Volvamos sobre la actividad somática, y los pactos performativos individuales en el enunciado particular de sus primeros textos —que ya hemos analizado desde el punto de vista

cuenta los reparos de Domínguez Caparrós (1987), que advierte que los actos de lenguaje en literatura son un *uso* del lenguaje común en circunstancias especiales. Empleo estos conceptos para plantear problemas específicos de la teoría literaria.

[3] Lo cual ha llevado a Derrida (1977) a deconstruir la teoría de Austin y Searle; véase Norris (1983: 30-33).

[4] Dejo de lado el hecho de que en cuanto pacto de escritura, se dirige a una multiplicidad de lectores(as), ya que el pacto literario es acto de lenguaje público.

de ironía estilizada—, enlazándolos a algunas de las series carnavalizadas y a un tipo definido de «carnavalización» moderna. Se recordará que el lenguaje somático/pragmático de algunas producciones está situado en un *locus amoenus* elegíaco, especie de *beatus ille* idílico, y la fragmentación del cuerpo femenino de las damas galantes corresponde a la tradición de la canción de amor y la lírica de Occidente. La memoria del género (otra vez en términos de Bajtin), o el «continuum mémoriel» (concepto de Zumthor, 1976, 320) se inscribe en la superficie textual como saber: el sujeto semiótico representador mantiene la clásica focalización masculina (ciertamente fetichista), sobre el cuerpo: la bella mano, il bel piede, il bel naso, i belli occhi, regiones del cuerpo que le llegan a Valle de manera directa e indirecta desde los orígenes de la lírica provenzal. Cuerpos(s) focalizado(s) por Bradomín, a su vez —como vimos— deconstrucción en inversión irónica de la leyenda del Don Juan, como Juanito Ventolera es su «representación» paródica. Ambos enunciados se apoya en el mismo subtexto donjuanesco con distinta «entonación»: en el contexto socioeconómico señorial representado por Bradomín y sobre todo por Montenegro objetiviza los pactos y juramentos individuales.

Los actos performativos relevan formas de mantener un género de vida, el *locus amoenus* de los mundos galantes, las guerras de religión y los desenfrenos y lubricidades elementales de los mayorazgos que ostentan el poder. La producción textual tematiza el poder; dichos son hechos en el contexto de una situación social privilegiada donde el individuo (rey, noble, clan feudal) desempeñaba un papel privilegiado en la conjunción de poder y saber para mantener las promesas contraídas con sus interlocutores —amantes, hijos, familia, campesinos del «feudo». Para estos receptores(as) las promesas individuales de los «poderosos» —de dar vida, hacienda y honra o quitarlas— eran acciones cumplidas en el mundo social. Valle selecciona los sujetos parlantes mediante la ritualización de los discursos: Montenegro tiene «la nobleza de un príncipe que recibe los dones de sus siervos» (*Aguila*, 79), y ojos de sus criados y de los mendigos y leprosos es «el padre de los pobres», el «espejo de los ricos», «Castillo fuerte», «Toro de valentía» (54). Al mismo tiempo se ríe de la justicia, que para él sólo sirve para ayudar a niños, mujeres y ancianos.

Un hilo conductor útil lo constituyen las relaciones consanguíneas en este *locus anoenus,* elemento importante en la constitución del poder y su tematización. Esta sociedad campesina es una donde los sistemas de alianza, la forma política y la jerarquización entre siervos y señores y la herencia que legitimiza el poder y la sucesión, predominan. En rigor, Valle constituye este discurso y «representa» una sociedad donde el hambre, las epidemias, las enfermedades, la muerte y la violencia son lugares comunes, actos cotidianos y evidentes. Hay que añadir los siguientes requisitos: en estas relaciones de lucha y de poder, la «sangre» era fuerza legitimadora de mayorazgos y señoríos, y elemento importante en los mecanismos del poder de una sociedad basada en los sistemas de alianza, abolengos y linajes (adapto de Foucault, 1984, 1985). El privilegio del abolengo provenía de su papel instrumental (poder derramar la sangre), de su funcionamiento en el orden de los signos (poseer determinada sangre, ser de la misma sangre, arriesgar la sangre), y también de su precariedad (fácil de difundir, sujeta a agitarse, demasiado pronta para mezclarse, rápidamente susceptible de corromperse (1984: 178).

Cabría evocar en este encuadre una analogía entre el carlismo y Galicia con la época romana y las tribus germánicas, y su política enderezada a conservar las castas. Aún después de inoperantes, los mayorazgos continuaban una reactivación de su poder y luchaban por sus títulos, propiedades y formas de vida. Pese a que resultaban ya incompatibles con el sistema económico y social del liberalismo (como las tribus germánicas en el nuevo sistema romano), y eran incapaces de destruir el nuevo sistema político, los Montenegro (y los carlistas) aspiraban a hacerse de un espacio. Son «sobrevivientes ideológicos» (en frase de Althusser sobre las tribus germánicas, 1971: 147); aunque su base económica había desaparecido después de las guerras y las desamortizaciones, la superestructura ideológica continuaba en vigor.

En la sociedad decimonónica campesina gallega que Valle «representa» especularmente, el poder proviene de la consanguinidad, los agentes a su servicio y todo el aparato de estado y de dominación de clase: el honor de la guerra, de la fuerza, del saber, del hacerse obedecer, de triunfar sobre la muerte, del poder de defender la sangre con armas bélicas. Frente a este poder y saber, los agentes represivos están a su disposición —verdugos, justicia, medicina—; estos agentes son responsables de la marginación de la comunidad, la prisión, la delincuencia, el suplicio. El poder habla a través de la sangre; ésta es «realidad con *función simbólica*» en estas sociedades

148

(Foucault, 1984). De ahí la importancia del sexo y sus agentes: llamarse Bradomín, ser de la estirpe de Montenegro, ser criado, molinero, barragana, pobre, alcahuete, bufón, prostituta, leproso, enfermo, mendicante del mayorazgo confiere poderes. Procrear, darle hijos, servirle al «despótico», de «nobleza de príncipe» que «recibe los dones de sus siervos» significa, a su vez, un tipo de poder: el de arrimarse al buen árbol. He ahí la fuerza de los personajes, y la revisión irónica de las acotaciones que re-orientan algunos de sus actos performativos. El primogénito Don Pedrito viola a Liberata y «Bajo la vid centenaria revive el encanto de las epopeyas primitivas que cantan la sangre, la violación y la fuerza» (*Aguila,* 97). El Mayorazgo, a su vez, firma documentos con una mano descarnada, donde «las venas azules parecen dibujar trágicos caminos de exaltación, de violencia y de locura» (148). O bien «bebe con largura, y muestra aquel apetito animoso, rústico y fuerte de los viejos héroes en los banquetes de la vieja Ilíada» (332).

La ironía inversora, además de la establecida por el acotador en las *Comedias bárbaras,* está representada en Don Galán, el bufón de muecas grotescas, o risa pícara, o careta de cartón, con su «carnavalesca cortesía». El personaje funciona a manera de espejo inversor irónico (no paródico); el hombre de placer es a ojos de Don Juan Manuel «una voz de mi conciencia». Y así explica su función:

> Don Galán con sus burlas y sus insolencias edifica mi alma, como Don Manuelito edifica la tuya con sus sermones (*Aguila,* 155).

Uno y otro dicen «las verdades amargas». La identidad histórica entre la servidumbre bufonesca, el libertinaje y el poder de los mayorazgos y la inversión irónica se aclara en una acotación:

> La imagen del bufón aparece en el fondo de un espejo, y el Caballero la contempla en aquella lejanía nebulosa y verdeante como en la quimera de un sueño. Lentamente el cristal de sus ojos se empaña como en nebuloso cristal del espejo (*Aguila,* 286-87).

Las intervenciones de Don Galán (cuyo nombre es una inversión irónica) se desarrollan en la inminencia irreversible de las cosas, el lenguaje revierte la realidad y los objetos. Valga como ejemplo el siguiente diálogo que antecede a la parodia de *Los cuernos:*

> *El Caballero.*—¡Don Galán, qué hacemos con unos hijos que conspiran para robarnos?
> *Don Galán.*—Repartirles la hacienda para que nos dejen morir en santa paz.
> *El Caballero.*—¿Y después?
> *Don Galán.*—¡Jujú!... Después pediremos limosna (*Aguila,* 69).

En este espejo irónico que refleja el pasado se vive en el engaño, la violencia y el crimen. En el mundo que nos recrea Valle, en el espejo del pasado, la violencia debe estar dirigida; bien claro lo vio Cara de Plata, que se redime en cuanto miembro del linaje para «hacer honor» a su nombre:

> Le digo a usted la verdad. Xavier Bradomín me ha convencido de que los hombres como yo sólo tenemos ese camino en la vida. El día en que no podamos alzar partidas por un rey, tendremos que alzarlos por nosotros y robar en los montes. Ese será el final de mis hermanos (*Aguila,* 225).

En su «representación» de lo *imaginario social,* Valle revela a un grupo solidario con sus propios valores y coherente con un proyecto colectivo, ya terminado históricamente en la refractación del narrador. A tal punto, que la prole de Montenegro traiciona este proyecto, violando juramentos y promesas y comportamientos de clase. El «espejo desvanecido» es el de las promesas individuales. Las *Memorias* del viejo Bradomín operan desde un género institucionalizado —el pacto autobiográfico— donde los yos se observan en dobladuras y se superponen en contigüidades (no fusiones) en el tiempo [5]. Bradomín, que organiza sus *Memorias* en su vejez, no es idéntico al individuo al que inscribe como signo en los textos (aparece en doce, según Salper, 1988), en inversiones de edad y desplazamientos discursivos. Está más cercano al Bradomín que aparece como «fantasma irrisorio» (tiene ya casi un siglo) en la noche madrileña que oscurece y apaga para siempre las

---

[5] Véanse las reglas que propone Bruss (1974) para el acto autobiográfico, que re-contextualizo a partir del concepto de *memorias.*

«luces de bohemia». Resta por decir que en su amplia decons-trucción y *mise en abîme,* el «memorioso» Bradomín es al mismo tiempo «desmemoriado», e inscribe textualmente su reformulación y nuevo punto de vista y a menudo descree sus propias afirmaciones. Encarna «un recordar para saber» —en frase de *La lámpara maravillosa*— que observa con ironía (la así llamada «Romantic irony») que relativiza todo significado y todo valor.

El acto de lenguaje literario de Bradomín revela el poder y la autoridad en un mundo específico, durante la era fernan-dina y 1834, que marca las convulsiones y rupturas entre la España liberal y la carlista, entre el centro y la periferia en su economía dual. Epoca ésta de emergencia de la modernidad, donde se inscriben los desvíos, los distintos comportamientos y los pactos individuales vigentes hasta la Revolución de 1868 y la Restauración.

La función del espejo desvanecido es duplicar estos pactos y juramentos individuales, mientras que en las farsas y es-perpentos no sólo duplica, sino que invierte. Los actos de lenguaje performativos son auto-referenciales (por tanto, indi-viduales) en estos textos, comprometen un *yo* y un *tú;* prometen amores, pasiones eternas (odio/amor), despedidas, placeres sensuales, causas políticas, protección, liberalidad, honestidad, hidalguía. Significan especies de cláusulas «ope-rativas», aquellas que, en palabras de Austin, «actually per-form the legal act which is the purpose of the instrument to perform» (p. 236). Y en un contexto *(setting)* específico, en el cual el *yo* y el *tú* pueden aceptar y llevar a cabo el pacto; pacto comunitario que finaliza con la muerte de Montenegro y el advenimiento de la raza de caínes y lobos. En la comedia bárbara *Romance de lobos,* al morir el hijo vinculero, la voz de los hijos lo augura: «¡Malditos estamos! ¡Y metidos en un pleito para veinte años!» (*OE* I: 679). Los performativos lite-rarios son ahora «infelices» (*infelicitous,* para Austin), porque los pactantes no son ya totalmente responsables de sus accio-nes. Un paso más, y las promesas se rompen, engañan, pierden su fuerza de seducción y su poder; del gesto «versallesco» o de la gesta antigua, se reduce los cuerpos a pedazos y se instala la distancia geométrica del juego de espejos deformantes.

Unas palabras sobre la somática libidinal en estos textos: las *Comedias bárbaras* en su totalidad revelan las formas loca-les de sometimiento y focalizan la degeneración moral del mayorazgo a través del apetito sensual y la codicia, los pactos diabólicos y el poder real de los juramentos de sangre. Esta maquinaria se articula por los códigos fundamentales que rigen su lenguaje y sus esquemas perceptivos, mediante despedazamientos del cuerpo, muertes violentas, coitos sacrílegos, seducciones satánicas, violaciones, el demonio lúbrico. En nombre de esta jerarquía de prácticas, el primogénito, don Pedrito, en *Aguilas de blasón,* viola a la molinera y le suelta los mastines, que le desgarran las vestiduras. En el otro extremo los otros vástagos —el hermoso Cara de Plata y el novicio desalmado Farruquiño— profanan una tumba y roban un cadáver para vender el esqueleto por una onza de oro, apremiados por la falta de dinero (Jornada IV, Esc. VI). Tras varios intentos de desprender la carne de los huesos, el último hierve los huesos (el diálogo con el tío-verdugo de Pablos del *Buscón* sirve de voz de apoyo). Entre tanto, Cara de Plata y la Pichona se van al lecho, Farruquiño se vale infructuosamente de las tijeras para desprender la piel del esqueleto: «se oye el golpe de las tenazas sobre las costillas de la momia y los suspiros de la manceba y el rosmar del gato», según la acotación. De «farsa carnavalesca» define el acotador la escena entre don Juan Manuel y la nueva barrigona (la molinera violada) en un comportamiento que revela los bajos instintos y saber/poder del vinculero. Para esconder a su amante de la mirada de su mujer (revisión irónica del amor cortés), la manda meterse bajo la mesa, y luego la hace salir en cuatro patas, chistándola como a un perro.

El léxico en esta producción textual, centrado en el poder y los performativos de los mayorazgos como «realidad en su función simbólica» está cargado de violencia: degüellos, cortar manos, cabezas, lengua. De una figura a otra lo conspicuo es el poder del cuerpo, la fuerza bruta, el gesto desdeñoso o servicial, la mirada maliciosa o engañosa, o bien los juramentos, las imprecaciones, las maldiciones, las amenazas.

*Romance de lobos* textualiza la fragmentación del cuerpo de la madre muerta («la cabeza lívida rueda en el hoyo de la almohada» o «se le caen las quijadas»). Por su parte, el Mayorazgo abre la sepultura a su regreso a la casa hidalga, jurando enloquecido amor eterno. La alusión a despedazamientos corporales es más evidente durante la pelea a muerte entre don Mauro y Oliveros (el hijo ilegítimo). Don Mauro agarra sus presas para destrozarlas; el diálogo entre el padre de Oliveros y los hermanos Montenegro antes de la lucha destaca la fragmentación violenta del cuerpo:

> Don Rosendo.—¡Lo malo será que te arranque la lengua!
>
> Oliveros.—La defienden los dientes. [...]
>
> Don Rosendo.—Defensa de mujer.
>
> Oliveros.—Y de lobo.
>
> Don Mauro.—¡No te los haga yo dejar clavados en la tierra!
>
> Oliveros.—¡Mucho hablar es!...
>
> Don Gonzalito.—Si los quieres bien, no los saques al aire.
>
> Oliveros.—¡Mírenlos! (OE I: 651).

Diálogo semejante se encontrará en la Jornada tercera entre Fuso Negro, La Mujer del Morcego y Don Juan Manuel:

> El Caballero.—Si yo hubiera naufragado aquella noche vosotros también habríais segado mi cabeza, aun cuando llevase una corona. Se la venderíais a mis hijos y os la pagarían bien.
>
> La Mujer del Morcego.—¡No diga tal, señor!
>
> Fuso Negro.—Se la presentaríamos en una fuente de plata cuando estuviesen sentados a la mesa.
>
> El Caballero.—Y se la comerían como un rico manjar.
>
> Fuso Negro.—Don Pedrito diría: «¡Yo quiero la lengua!» Don Gonzalito diría: «¡Yo quiero los ojos!» ¡Y cómo le habían de chascar bajo los dientes! (OE I: 665).

En *Divinas palabras,* tan cerca y tan distinta, la fragmentación y los despedazamientos se concentran en el hidrocéfalo, cuando, muerto ya, los canes aúllan, el sapo croa, y los cerdos intentan devorar el cadáver del idiota (la escena dialoga con el principio de *Tirano Banderas*). El idiota se representa en exageraciones grotescas: «La enorme cabeza, lívida, greñuda, viscosa, rodaba en el hoyo como una cabeza cortada». La somática corporal adquiere otro sesgo en las farsas y esperpentos, unida al engaño histórico que sigue manteniendo las promesas rotas, y las conversaciones arbitrarias sobre las que se apoyan los actos performativos en la esfera sociohistórica. Los performativos son aquí convenciones, y el enunciado una mera ficción social. En adelante, los actos de lenguaje conllevan mayor dispositivo de intensidades y producen más energía diferencial. Valle ordena los textos con mayor rigor y complejidad. Los performativos se cargan de «teatralidad» y se *inscriben* textualmente en un encuentro más estrecho lo hablado y el gesto. Valle privilegia el habla del cuerpo.

## 2. SEMANTICA/SOMATICA

> «Hay un gesto que es el mío, uno solo [...] sobre la inmovilidad de la muerte recobrará su imperio el gesto único...»
>
> (*La lámpara maravillosa.*)

El hacer gestual se instala, inscrito en el paradigma de otros actos de lenguaje performativos: el acto de gobernar, el acto de escribir, el acto de hablar. Invertidos, se convierten en pactos rotos, performativos «infelices» a nivel público/político. La parodia transgrede todas las normas y los pactos; se auto-reflexiona sobre ellos en cadenas discursivas. Lo que se presenta es la dimensión pública/política de las promesas: gobernar mal, escribir pegados a tradiciones y clisés, hablar con grandilocuencia y retórica vacía. En definitiva, prometer para no cumplir, hablar para mentir, escribir para repetir. Lo gestual pragmático se inscribe: muñecos, estafermos, marionetas son el instrumento crítico para presentar las inversiones. Se activa el pasado desde una distancia irónica; todo performativo literario se filtra en dos «voces», en dos «gestos», a veces, incluso en producción de apodos: Alberto Saco/el Jándalo, La Encamada/Floriana, Cara de Plata/don Miguelito, Max Estrella/Mala Estrella, Sinibaldo Pérez/Chuletas, Rosa Galana/La Galana, Pedro Gailo/El Latino. Los sagrados gestos de la autoridad civil y religiosa, de las ceremonias, del poder se convocan en gestos profanos y degradados, ceremonias sacrílegas que invierten los términos [6]. Léase a esta luz *Martes de carnaval* en sus descuartizamientos, muertes grotescas y sacrílegas, y compárese con los sacrilegios en *Divinas palabras,* y el entierro grotesco y sacrílego de Max Estrella. Contrástense esos «gestos» y «voces» «chillones» y desenca-

---

[6] Fernández Cifuentes (1986) hace inteligentes observaciones en torno a Valle, al compararlo con los muñecos de Lorca y situarlos en la literatura carnavalizada. Sumner Greenfield (1972) alude con justeza a un «teatro problemático».

jados con los sacrilegios de las *Sonatas*, las copulaciones frente a cadáveres y con cadáveres, en el mundo de gestos y ritos exquisitos o «bárbaros». En las farsas y esperpentos la muerte pierde su carácter trágico y ritual, como en el asesinato por honra de la bolichera La Mona en *Los cuernos*, cuando el Bulubú le dice a El Fantoche que «si la camisa de la bolichera huele a aceite», «olisqueé a qué huele el pispajo», le «abra con la bayoneta en la pelleja un agujero». A lo que responde El Fantoche: «¡Me comeré en albondiguillas el tasajo de esta bribona y haré de su sangre morcillas». Muerta ya,

> El Bululú.—Al pie de la muerta, suene usted, mi teniente, un duro, por ver si despierta. ¿Mi teniente, cómo responde?
> El Fantoche.—¿Cómo responde? Con una higa, y el duro esconde bajo la liga (*OE* I: 1001).

De igual dimensión de parodia sacrílega y grotesca, la muerte de Floriana en *La rosa de papel;* entre batallas de cotillanas y el borracho Julepe, se engala a la difunta, con saya nueva, y una rosa de papel «para adornar el lívido nudo de las manos yertas». Jule le trae una «corona de pensamientos y follaje de latón con brillo de lutos» menestral y petulante «de un sentimentalismo alemán». Y la acotación no podría ser más demoledora:

> Simeón deposita la corona a los pies de la difunta [...] La difunta, en el féretro de esterillas doradas, tiene una desolación de figura de cera, un acento popular y dramático. La pañoleta floreada ceñida al busto, las cejas atirantadas por el peinado, las manos con la rosa de papel saliendo de los vuelillos blancos, el terrible charol de las botas, promueven un desacorde cruel y patético, acaso una inaccesible categoría estética (*OE* I: 714).

Al final, Julepe cae presa del demonio lúbrico con la muerta, pide a gritos que la embalsamen, exige entonces amores al cadáver pintarrajeado, mientras cae una velilla, enciende la habitación y arden los cuerpos. *Finis.*

El dispositivo transgresor está presente en *La cabeza del Bautista* (1924), recodificación en anverso y deconstrucción crítica multidirigida: el texto bíblico, la obra de Oscar Wilde

(*Salomé*, 1893), el libreto de Richard Strauss (1896), las ilustraciones de Aubrey Beardsley [7]. Si el texto de Wilde representa un extraordinario acierto mimético, ciertamente Valle deconstruye la atmósfera trágica y lo convierte en «melodrama para marionetas». El asesinato cometido por el viejo Otelo, Don Iri, de Alberto Saco, el Jándalo, en brazos de La Pepona termina en un sacrílego rito necrófilo.

Estos ritos sacrílegos y el regusto por la necrofilia son piezas vitales en movimientos teóricos; lo que cambia es la «voz», el «gesto», el uso del acto de lenguaje, la perspectiva, los actantes. «El grito chillón» de las marionetas y muñecos se instala como deformación grotesca del habla elegante, del «hablar de otros tiempos» de Max, o las voces acariciadoras y susurrantes, y las sonrisas amables y prudentes de damas devotas, abates galantes, o la engolada voz de gran señor de los Montenegro, o el habla visigótica de Oliveros, o las bárbaras imprecaciones de Montenegro y los hijos-lobos. La «voz» y el «gesto» del cuerpo político se revelan en los esperpentos en las máscaras del vicio, las cien máscaras de ficción y las facciones materializadas de gestos que eliminan el sistema de valores en auto-cancelaciones contiguas, en ambivalencias burlonas y sarcásticas.

El cuerpo se convierte en enunciado y sus gestos en entonación, lenguaje estrechamente vinculado con el cronotopo de carnaval, y forma parte de una pragmática de la comunicación. Valle revela la fisiología del cuerpo social, y como ésta se transparenta por el dispositivo de la entonación —que revela *quién* ejerce el poder— en sus diversas expresiones internas y externas. Son interacciones verbales semióticas: el mimo, el lenguaje gestual, los gestos condicionados [8]. En las farsas y esperpentos (textos dramáticos y/o en prosa), el tropo del cuerpo adquiere contenido político, y refracta los problemas filosóficos de representación del sujeto semiótico: la duplicación virtual que funciona como una duplicación del cuerpo objeto y el cuerpo sujeto, que se desdobla: el yo-para-

---

[7] El texto de Wilde, escrito originariamente en francés, se presentó en París en 1896, y no se levantó la orden de censura en Inglaterra hasta 1931. Lisa Davis (1973) ha estudiado la recepción de Oscar Wilde en España y la polémica en torno a esta obra.

[8] Voloshinov/Bajtin en *Marxisme* (39) dan buena cuenta de esta pragmática gestual. Gonzalo Sobejano (1988) ha visto con perspicacia el grito exultante de Valle y la distribución esticomática de las frases; este cambio de enfoque de un mismo parlamento es justamente la dialogización paródica.

mí, y el yo-para-otro. El gesto corporal produce un enunciado en una especie de lengua natural en un tipo específico de situación comunicativa.

Ahora bien, si estas conclusiones son válidas, nos dicen que son actos de lenguaje literario públicos, dentro de una noción pragmática sobre el cuerpo (auto-conciencia, regeneración, comunicación), y una pragmática del espejo. El cuerpo y sus actos de lenguaje son el tropo estructurador en una inversión regeneradora de los referentes. El cuerpo y sus gestos performativos en su existencia física emergen como una producción imaginaria-política y el momento en que ésta se hace discrepante. El despedazamiento, la fragmentación de los poderosos —a la cual ya hemos aludido— revelan la «otredad» virtual de las imágenes monoestilísticas y el lenguaje monológico. Se levantan contra un discurso especular narcisista, que se devuelve su propia imagen y que sólo piensa su propia imagen; es decir, el lenguaje de actos performativos engañosos, de promesas rotas. Se levanta contra una imagen unívoca del cuerpo político —los reyes gobiernan, las instituciones tienen razón, la Iglesia dictamina para que acatemos, las relaciones sociales son «rosadas» y desprovistas de luchas y facciones, el lenguaje literario tradicional debe ser aceptado, el sujeto está integrado al cuerpo político.

El sujeto fragmentado, roto, despedazado, desarticulado, es, sobre todo, el de cuanto producen actos de lenguaje públicos, que traicionan en su actos de lenguaje privados. Toda una teoría del Estado centralista y monológico se pone en «gramática parda». En lo *imaginario social* las libertas/licencia del lenguaje (censurado por la retórica aristotélica), actualiza las instancias sociales de una humanidad redimida, aunque sólo sea transitoria. Las farsas y esperpentos operan como una especie de acelerador histórico, y representa la lucha de clases. Son una invitación a salir de la impotencia, a estremecerse en ese choque creador, a subvertir el poder y el orden y desafiar las jerarquías. Valle privilegia el cuerpo y sus gestos, para fecundar el discurso de los engañados y liberar por la risa ambivalente, «utópica», un nuevo pacto.

# CONCLUSION

Modos de representación todos: modos de representación especular. Lo imaginario, lo simbólico, son signos que apuntan a nuestro problema. Una experiencia especular que tiene su origen en la imaginación —en *lo imaginario social*— y que se va convirtiendo en diversas formas y juegos especulares. Las imágenes valleinclanescas salen y entran por los espejos en virajes entre el yo especular y el yo social. Toda una fenomenología y epistemología parte de los espejos: planos, antiguos, borrosos, desvanecidos, alucinatorios, curvos, cóncavos, convexos. Las imágenes así reflejadas pueden ser del tamaño del objeto, se pueden acercar, alejar, invertir, agrandar, achicar. Aparecen imágenes reales e imágenes virtuales; estas últimas incitan al lector crítico a percibirse dentro del mismo radio, en la misma pantalla, como un renovado retablo de Maese Pedro que nos invita a saltar al tablado.

Toda una pragmática de los espejos —el espejo como acto performativo— sirve de modelo referencial para representar la modernidad, «lo moderno». Hablamos en realidad de nuevas formaciones discursivas, de un nuevo sujeto social con su particular posición geométrica, decidido a representar la realidad y sus ideologías, en duplicaciones especulares. Las preguntas que se plantea el sujeto emisor concreto (el «yo» lírico, el narratario, el acotador, el demiurgo) es elaborar el potencial artístico y político de la praxis de la imaginación. Problema muy moderno, muy siglo XXI.

Valle-Inclán (y otros modernos) instan al receptor/lector a interrogar los textos de forma crítica; no el lector ingenuo, sino aquel que en «lo imaginario» puede captar las duplicaciones, el espejo recíproco del objeto y su antítesis. El espejo o la mimesis especular —mimesis en el sentido de Adorno; es decir, «formas de representación» ficticia no reales o referenciales, el «acercamiento lejano»— equivale a otra forma de con-

159

cebir «lo imaginario», lo «ilusorio», espejos todos que reflejan las condiciones materiales de la existencia. El valor cognitivo de la «imaginación» especular radica en sacar a la luz estas operaciones y, mediante un proceso de «identificación» o «extrañamiento revelador», incorporar a su auditorio social en el acto de lenguaje. «Identificaciones» en una historia de las semejanzas, las contigüidades, las correspondencias (los referentes), dictadas por la situación histórica, que se inscriben en las superficies textuales como oposiciones con signos negativos y positivos. La función semántica y la sintáctica permiten que un vocabulario (patria, país, familia, religión, arte, amor) se produzcan y distribuyan las significaciones con una función de identidad o «reconocimiento» o de «otredad» y distorsión. En esas condiciones de quiasmos y cesuras, Valle invita a reflexionar sobre las relaciones de semejanzas o de equivalencia que se fundamentan en las palabras, las clasificaciones y los cambios de sentido. Recojamos aquí unas palabras de Foucault en *El discurso del poder*: «la historia del orden de las cosas sería la historia de lo Mismo —de aquello que, para una cultura, es a la vez disperso y aparente y debe, por ello, distinguirse mediante señales y recogerse en identidades» (1985: 62).

El discurso cultural/especular de Valle se incorpora a lo que Paul Ricoeur llama «escuela de la sospecha»: aquellos que examinan críticamente la verdad o falsedad de unas determinadas proposiciones y desenmascaran ilusiones y autoengaños. Es decir, cuantos nos inducen a sospechar de aquello que se nos ofrece como verdadero. Entre otras sospechas, la de las mitologías; si entendemos por «mitologías» representaciones ideológicas. En palabras de Marx:

> Todas las mitologías domeñan, dominan, moldean las fuerzas de la naturaleza en la imaginación y por la imaginación: desaparecen, pues, cuando estas fuerzas son dominadas realmente (Intr. *Economía política*, 1854).

Se observará que Marx alude muy directamente a problemas de «representación», «imaginación» y sujeto representador. Las oposiciones (u oximorones) a las cuales he aludido revelan construcciones enunciativas de la lucha de clases. La metáfora del espejo permite establecer nexos entre ideología, representación e identificación. El espejo (cóncavo y convexo para Valle) ayuda al sujeto a reconocerse, pero a su vez el sujeto debe romper el espejo que le presenta una realidad prefabricada, y moverse hacia la verdadera realidad social.

La producción valleinclanesca, desde diversas «posiciones geométricas», se inclina hacia el ejercicio del espejo y sus alternativas como degradación de todo saber anterior, de toda autoridad. Como negación final de los referentes y con una redefinición de la cultura. Lo que deseo señalar es que, desde diversos supuestos y en contigüidades (no yuxtaposiciones ni exclusiones), su arte nuevo, «moderno», es un discurso que aspira a representar la realidad en juego de sistemas y de dos paradigmas: el de la realidad/espejo y el del disfraz/realidad, en movimiento ondulatorio. Contraposiciones, oximorones que pongan de manifiesto, simultáneamente, dos versiones de sus estados y clases, en el bifurcado carácter de la realidad social, en contigüidad de las dos «voces» y de las dos «realidades» que el espejo (deformante o no) representa en su antagonismo, con impulsión motora. El reflejo y su inversión permiten que por un proceso de «identificación» y su contrario, y en lo *imaginario social,* se logre «representar» el «asesinato simbólico» de los opresores y de las clases explotadoras. El espejo —en su juego recíproco— es parte de la «narrativa» emancipadora.

En la lectura concreta más exacta del proyecto moderno de Valle interviene toda una teoría de la imaginación y su función social. Su producción asimila el pasado, asimilación selectiva, que aspira a dirigir la «memoria colectiva» hacia los emblemas y las «ideologías» que esclavizan. Su proyecto creador (lo que Pierre Bourdieu llama «campo intelectual») fue el de crear «contra-imágenes utópicas». Situar el valor en las posibilidades emancipatorias de las formas culturales, crear una memoria colectiva, un «subterráneo político» (en frase de Voloshinov/Bajtin, 1977, que retoma Jameson como «inconsciente», 1981), en su auditorio social concreto. Un «subterráneo político» que permitiera introducir narrativas de emancipación. Su discurso cultural (bien acompañado de otros modernos, y de anarquistas y socialistas) se orienta hacia la formación de nuevos saberes (históricos, sociales, culturales), en polémica contra el sedimento del pasado. Se construye el yacimiento de «nuevas memorias» a partir de la inscripción de la crisis social. Son discursos que aspiran a designar algo distinto: nuevas «imágenes» o «representaciones» de un mundo mejor, «iconografías» de alegría y de optimismo. Y, ¿por qué no?, de utopía emancipatoria; en su designación más positiva.

161

# REFERENCIAS

Allegra, Giovanni. 1982. *Il regno interiore*. Milano: Jaco Books.

—. 1982a. Trad., com. intr. *La lampada maravigliosa (esercizi spirituali)*. Lanciano: R. Carabba.

—. 1986. «Decadentismo, milenarismo y "barbarie" en Valle-Inclán». En: *El reino interior,* tr. ampliada. Madrid: Encuentro Ediciones, 266-327.

Althusser, Louis. 1969. *For Marx,* tr. B. Brewester. London: New Left Books.

—. 1971. *Lenin and Philosophy and Other Essays*. NY: Monthly Review Press.

Austin, J. L. 1962. *How to do Things with Words*. Harvard Univ.

—. 1976. *Philosophical Papers*. Oxford Univ. Press.

Bakhtin, Mikhail. 1968. *Rabelais and his World,* tr. H. Isowolsky: Cambridge, MIT Press.

—. 1970. *La poètique de Dostoievski*. Paris: Seuil.

—. 1977 (V. N. Voloshinov). *Le marxisme et la philosophie du Langage*. Paris: Minuit.

—. 1978. *Esthétique et théorie du roman*. Paris: Gallimard.

—. 1981. *The Dialogic Imagination,* ed. M. Holquist, C.

Emerson, M. Holquist. Austin: Univ. of Texas Press.

—. 1983. «The Construction of the Utterance». En: *Bakhtin School Papers. Russian Poetics in Translation,* vol. 10, Oxford.

—. 1984. *Problems of Dostoevsky's Poetics,* ed. tr. Caryl Emerson, intr. Wayne C. Booth. Manchester Univ. Press: Univ. of MIN.

—. 1985. *Estética de la creación verbal.* México: Siglo XXI.

Baroja, Pío. 1949. *Memorias. Obras completas,* vol. VII, Madrid: Biblioteca Nueva.

Barthes, Roland. 1957. *Mythologies.* Paris: Seuil.

Baudrillard, Jean. 1983. *El espejo de la producción.* México: Gedisa.

—. 1984. *De la seducción.* Madrid: Cátedra.

—. 1985. *Las estrategias fatales.* Barcelona: Anagrama.

—. 1987. *Cultura y simulacro.* Barcelona: Kairós.

Batany, J. 1973. *Approches du Roman de la Rose.* Paris: Seuil.

Benveniste, Emile. 1971. *Problemas de lingüística general,* volúmenes I, II. México: Siglo XXI.

Bering, Dietz. 1978. *Die Intellektuellen.* Stuttgart.

Bettelheim, Bruno. 1977. *The Uses of Echantment. The Meaning and Importance of Fairy Tales.* NY: Vintage Books.

Beverley, John. 1987. *Del Lazarillo al sandismo: Estudios sobre la función ideológica de la literatura española e hispanoamericana.* Prisma Institute.

Bloom, Harold, et al. 1987. *De-construction & Criticism.* NY: The Continuum Publ. Co.

Borelli, Mari. 1961. *Sulla poesia di Valle-Inclan.* Palatine: Torino.

Bourdieu, Pierre. 1984. «La Champ littéraire. Préalables critiques et principes de méthode». *Lendemains,* 9:36: 5-20.

Bradbury, Malcolm, James McFarlane eds. 1978. *Modernism. 1890-1930.* Londres: Peuguin Books.

Brecht, Bertolt. 1979. «Popularity and Realism». En: *Aesthetics and Politics. Debates between E. Bloch, G. Lukács, B. Brecht, Walter Banjamin, T. Adorno.* Trans. editor Ronald Taylor. London: NLB.

Brombert, Victor. 1968. *Stendhal: Fiction and the Themes of Freedom.* NY: Random House.

Bruss, Elizabeth, W. 1974. «L'autobiographie considerée comme acte littéraire». *Poétique,* 17: 14-26.

—. 1976. *Autobiographical Acts: The Changing Situation of a Literary Genre.* Johns Hopkins Univ. Press.

Buero Vallejo, Antonio. 1966. «De rodillas, en pie, en el aire». *Revista de Occidente,* 44-45:132-145.

Bürger, Peter. 1984. *Theory of the Avant-Garde,* tr. Michael Shaw. Manchester Univ. Press: Univ. Of MIN. Press.

Cacho Viu, Vicente. 1984. *Els modernistes i el nacionalisme cultural. Antología.* Barcelona: eds. la Magrana.

—. 1987. «Modernismo catalán y nacionalismo cultural». *Eutopías* III:I: 135-154.

Cardona, Rodolfo, A. N. Zahareas. 1970. *Visión del esperpento. Teoría y práctica de los esperpentos de Valle-Inclán.* Madrid: Castalia.

Caro Baroja, Julio. 1969. *Ensayo sobre la literatura de cordel.* Madrid: Revista de Occidente.

Carr, Raymond. 1979. *Spain. 1808-1939.* London: Oxford Univ. Press.

Castoriadis, C. 1985. *L'institution imaginaire de la société.* Paris: Seuil.

Cattaneo, Mariateresa. 1979. «Il viandante nel labirinto. Varianti e invarianti in Valle-Inclán». *Studi Ispanici,* IV: 105-129.

—. 1987. «Desviación de un trazado autobiográfico: *La lámpara maravillosa*». En: John P. Gabriele, ed. *Genio y virtuosismo de Valle-Inclán.* Madrid: Orígenes, 115-124.

Clark, Katerina, M. Holquist. 1984. *Mikahil Bakhtin.* Harvard Univ. Press.

Courbin, H. 1977. *L'imagination créatrice dans le soufisme d'Ibn Arabi.* Paris.

Cros, Edmund. 1980. *Ideología y genética textual. El caso del "Buscón".* Madrid: Cupsa.

Culler, Jonathan. 1975. *Structuralist Poetics*. Cornell Univ. Press.

Darío, Rubén. 1950-53. *Obras completas*, 5 vols. Madrid: Aguado.

Derrida, Jacques. 1977. «Limited inc. abc». *Glyph, II:* 162-254.

Díaz Migoyo, Gonzalo. 1985. *Guía de Tirano Banderas*. Madrid: Fundamentos.

Domínguez Caparrós, José. 1987. «Literatura y actos de lenguaje». En: José Antonio Mayoral, ed. *Pragmática de la comunicación literaria*. Madrid: Arcos/Libros.

Dougherty, Dru. 1983. *Un Valle-Inclán olvidado: entrevistas y conferencias*. Madrid: Fundamentos.

Duby, Georges. 1983. *Tiempo de catedrales. El arte y la sociedad, 980-1420*. Barcelona: Argot.

Durán, Manuel. 1974. «Valle-Inclán en 1913-1918: El gran viraje». En *De Valle-Inclán a León Felipe*. México: Finisterre.

Dijk, Teun van. 1984. «Texte». En *Dictionnaire des Littératures de langue Française*, eds. J. P. de Beaumarchais, Daniel Couty, Alain Reyl. Tome III, p-z. Paris: Bourdas.

— ed. 1976. «Pragmatics and Poetics», *Pragmatics of Language and Literature*. Amsterdam: North-Holland Publ.

Eco, Umberto. 1988. *De los espejos y otros ensayos*. Barcelona: Lumen.

Felman, Shoshana. 1983. *The Literary Speech Act. Don Juan with L. Austin, or Seduction in Two* (1980). Cornell Univ. Press.

—. 1985. *Writing and Madness (Literature/Philosophy/Psychoanalysis)*. Cornell Univ. Press.

Fernández Cifuentes, Luis. 1986. *García Lorca en el teatro: La norma y la diferencia*. Univ. de Zaragoza.

Fernández Montesinos, José. 1966. «Modernismo, esperpentismo o las dos evasiones», *Revista de Occidente*, 44-45:

(Homenaje a Valle-Inclán) 146-165 (también en Zahareas, ed.).

Fichter, William. 1952. *Publicaciones periodísticas de D. Ramón del Valle-Inclán anteriores a 1895.* México: El Colegio de México.

Finlay, Maraike. 1988. *The Romantic Irony of Semiotics.* Berlin/NY/Amsterdam: Mouton de Gruyter.

Fernández Retamar, Roberto. 1979. *Calibán y otros ensayos.* Cuba: Casa de las Américas.

Foucault, Michel. 1970. *L'ordre du discours.* Paris: Gallimard.

—. 1984. *Foucault Reader, ed. Paul Rabinow.* NY: Pantheon.

—. 1985. *El discurso del poder.* Buenos Aires: Folios Eds.

Fowler, Roger. 1977. *Linguistics and the Novel.* London: Methuen.

Fox, Inman E. 1976. «El año de 1898 y el origen de los "intelectuales"». En *La crisis del intelectual de 1898.* Madrid: Cuadernos para el Diálogo, 9-16.

Garlitz, Virginia. 1986. «La evolución de *La lámpara maravillosa*». En *Leer a Valle-Inclán en 1986. Hispanistica XX,* 193-196.

Genette, Gérard. 1979. *Introduction à l'architexte.* Paris: Seuil.

—. 1982. *Palimpsestes.* Paris: Seuil.

Gómez de la Serna, Ramón. 1944. *Don Ramón del Valle-Inclán.* Buenos Aires: Espasa-Calpe (Austral 472).

Gómez-Moriana, Antonio. 1985. *Le subversión du discours rituel.* E. du Préambule: Quebec.

Greenfield, Sumner. 1972. *Valle-Inclán. Anatomía de un teatro problemático.* Madrid: Fundamentos.

Gullón, Ricardo. 1964. *Direcciones del modernismo.* Madrid: Gredos.

Habermas, Jürgen. 1974. *Theory and Practice.* Trad. John Viertel. Londres.

Herrero, Javier. 1980. «Fin de siglo y el modernismo. La virgen y la hetaira». *Revista Iberoamericana*, 110-111: 30-50.

*Hispanística XX.* 1986. *Leer a Valle-Inclán en 1986.* Université Dijon.

*Hispanística II.* 1987. *Média et représentation dans le monde hispanique au XXe siècle.* Université Dijon.

Hormigón, Juan Antonio. *Ramón del Valle-Inclán. La política, la cultura, el realismo del pueblo.* Madrid.

Hutcheon, Linda. 1980. *Narcissitic Narrative: The Metafictional Pardox.* Ontario: Wilfrid Laurier Univ. Press (1984, Methuen).

—. 1985. *Postmodern Parody.* London: Methuen.

—. 1987. «Beginning to Theorize Postmodernism». *Textual Practice* 1:1:10-31.

*Insula.* 1987. «El estado de la cuestión. Modernismo y modernidad».

Jameson, Fredric. 1975/6. «The Ideology of the Text». *Salmagundi*, 31-32: 204-246.

—. 1979. *Fables of Aggression. Wyndham Lewis, the Modernist as Fascist.* Univ. of Cal. Press.

—.-1981. *The Political Unconscious. Narrative as a Socially Symbolic Art.* Cornell Univ. Press.

Jitrik, Noé. 1978. *Las contradicciones del modernismo: productividad poética y situación sociológica.* México: El Colegio de México.

Kern, Stephen. 1986. *The Culture of Time and Space: 1880-1918.* Londres:

Kristeva, Julia. 1980. *Desire in Lauguage. A Semiotic Approach to Literature and Art.* Columbia Univ. Press.

—. 1980a. *Pouvoirs de l'horreur.* Paris: Seuil.

Lavaud, Eliane. 1986. «Las *Sonatas:* un ejemplo de deconstrucción», *Hispanística XX,* 4:49-72.

Lavaud, Jean-Marie. 1986. «El Marqués de Bradomín: Coloquios románticos. Análisis de una modalidad de creación». *Hispanística XX,* 4:125-148.

—. 1987. «Déconstruction du personnage, présénce de l'histoire dans *La cabeza del dragón* et *La hija del capitán*. *Hispanística XX*, 5:63-79.

Lejeune, Philippe. 1975. *Le pacte autobiographique*. Paris: Seuil.

Lentricchia, Frank. 1980. *After the New Criticism*. London: Methuen.

—. 1983. *Criticism and Social Change*. Chicago Univ. Press.

Levin, Harry. 1960. «What was Modernism». *Massachusetts' Review*, 1:609-630.

Litvak, Lily ed. 1975. *El modernismo*. Madrid: Taurus.

—. 1975a. *A Dream of Arcadia. Anti-Industrialism in Spanish Literature*, 1895-1905. University of Texas Press.

—. 1979. *Erotismo fin de siglo*. Barcelona: Antonio Bosch.

—. 1981. *Musa libertaria*. Barcelona: Antoni Bosch.

Loureiro, Angel. 1988. «A vueltas con el esperpento». En: Angel Loureiro, coord. *Estelas, laberintos, nuevas sendas. Unamuno. Valle-Inclán. García Lorca. La Guerra Civil*. Barcelona: Anthropos, 205-233.

Lowenthal, Leo. 1987. «Sociology of Literature in Retrospect». *Critical Inquiry*, 14:1: 1-15.

Lyon, John. 1983. *The Theater of Valle-Inclán*, Cambridge Univ.

Lyotard, Jean F. 1979. *Discurso, figura*. Barcelona: Gili.

Madrid, Francisco. 1944. *La vida altiva de Valle-Inclán*.

Man, Paul de. 1983. *Blindness and Insight. Essays on the Rhetoric of Contemporary Criticism*. Univ. of Min. Press.

Maravall, José Antonio. 1966. *Antiguos y modernos*. Madrid: Sociedad de Estudios y Publicaciones.

Marin, Louis. 1975. *La critique du discours: sur la "Logique de 'Port-Royal' et les Pensées" de Pascal*. Paris: Minuit.

Marx, Carlos, Federico Engels. 1965. *Sobre la literatura y el arte*. Cuba: Editora Política.

Matilla, Alfredo. 1972. *Las "Comedias bárbaras": historicismo y expresionismo dramático*. Madrid: Anaya.

May, Georges. 1979. *L'Autobiographie*. Paris: Seuil.

Maier, Carlo S. 1988. «Literary Re-Creation, the Creation of Deadership, and Valle-Inclán's *La lámpara maravillosa*. *Hispania*, 71: 217-226.

Mejía Sánchez, Ernesto. 1951. prol. *Los primeros cuentos de Rubén Darío*. México: FCE.

Molho, Maurice. 1977. *Semántica y poética (Góngora, Quevedo)*. Barcelona: Crítica.

Nietzsche, Federico. 1984. *La gaya ciencia*. Mallorca: José J. Olañeta.

Norris, Christopher. 1983. *The Deconstructive Turn*. London: Methuen.

—. 1985. *Contest of Faculties. Philosophy and Theory after Deconstruction*. London: Methuen.

Osuna, Rafael. 1952. «Un guión cinematográfico d eValle-Inclán: *Luces de bohemia*». *Bulletin of Hispanic Studies*, 59:120-128.

Parkhurts Ferguson, Patricia. P. Desan, W. Griswold. 1988. «Mirrors, Frames, and Demons: Reflections on the Sociology of Literature». *Critical Inquiry*, 14:3:421-430.

Paz, Octavio. 1983. «El caracol y la sirena» (1962). En: *Los signos en rotación y otros ensayos*. Madrid: Alianza, 90-104.

Picón Garfield, Evelyn, Ivan A. Schulman. 1984. *"Las entrañas del vacío". Ensayos sobre la modernidad hispanoamericana*. México: Cuadernos Americanos.

Poggioli, Renato. 1962. *Theory of the Avant-Garde*. Londres.

Pratt, Mary Louise. 1977. *Towards a Speech Act Theory of Literary Discourse*. Indiana Univ. Press.

—. 1986. «Ideology and Speech-Act Theory». *Poetics Today*, 7:1 59-72.

Rama, Angel. 1970. *Rubén Darío y el modernismo: circunstancia socioeconómica de un arte americano.* Venezuela: Univ. Central de Caracas.

Roggiano, Alfredo A. 1987. «Modernismo: origen de la palabra y evolución de un concepto» (1962). En Schulman ed. 1987, 39-50.

Rose, Margaret. 1979. *Parody/Metafiction.* London: Croom Helm.

Rousset, Jean. 1978. *Le mythe de don Juan.* Paris: Colin.

Rubio Jiménez, Jesús: 1982. *Ideología y teatro en España 1890-1900.* Univ. de Zaragoza.

—. 1987. «*La cabeza del dragón:* el final del sueño modernista». *Hispanística XX,* 5: 37-52.

—. 1988. «Ramón Pérez de Ayala y el teatro. Entre Momo y Talía». *España Contemporánea,* 1:1:27-53.

Ruibal, José. 1969. «Escribir contra el público». *A B C,* 12 de marzo de 1969.

Salper, Roberta. 1988. *Valle-Inclán y su mundo: Ideología y forma narrativa.* Amsterdam: Rodopi.

Schiavo, Leda. 1971. «Tradición literaria y nuevo sentido en *La marquesa Rosalinda. Filología,* 15:2:291-297.

—. 1980. *Historia y novela en Valle-Inclán. Para leer "El ruedo ibérico".* Madrid: Castalia.

—. 1988. «La "barbarie" de las *Comedias bárbaras».* En: Loureiro, coord., 191-204.

Schulman, Ivan A. ed. 1987. *Nuevos asedios al modernismo.* Madrid: Taurus.

—. 1987. «Modernismo/modernidad: Metamorfosis de un concepto». En Schulman ed., 11-38.

Searle, John R. 1977. «Reiterating the differences». *Glyph* 1: 198-208.

Serrano, Carlos. 1987. «Valle-Inclán et les "Dramaturgies non-aristoteliciennes": Les termes d'un débat», *Hispanística XX,* 5: 53-61.

Sinclair, Allison. 1977. *Valle-Inclan's Ruedo Ibérico. A Popular View of Revolution.* Londres: Támesis.

Sobejano, Gonzalo. 1988. «Culminación dramática de Valle-Inclán: el diálogo a gritos». En Angel G. Loureiro, coord., 111-136.

Speratti-Piñero, Emma S. 1968. *De "Sonata de otoño" al esperpento (Aspectos del arte de Valle-Inclán).* Londres: Támesis.

—. 1974. *El ocultismo en Valle-Inclán.* Londres: Támesis.

Steiner, Peter. 1984. *Russian Formalism: A Metapoetics.* Cornell Univ. Press.

Termes, Josep. 1977. *Anarquismo y sindicalismo en España. La Primera Internacional (1864-1881).* Barcelona: Crítica.

Todorov, Tzvetan. 1981. *Mikhail Bakhtine. Le principe dialogique.* Paris: Seuil.

Valle-Inclán, Ramón del. 1922. *Aguilas de blasón. Comedia bárbara dividida en cinco jornadas. Opera Omnia,* vol. 14. Madrid.

—. 1930. *Claves líricas. Versos. Opera Omnia,* vol. 9. Madrid.

—. 1961. *Viva mi dueño.* Madrid: Espasa.

—. 1969. *Sonatas.* Est. prol. Allen W. Phillips. México: Porrúa.

—. 1971. *Obras escogidas.* Madrid: Aguilar, 2 vols.

Vygotsky, Lev. 1962. *Thought and Language.* MIT Press.

Watson, Stephen. 1984. «Criticism and the Closure of "Modernism"». *Substance,* XIII:1: 15-30.

Waugh, Patricia. 1984. *Metafiction: the Theory and Practice of Self-Conscious Fiction.* London: Methuen.

Wittgenstein, Ludwig. 1955. *Philosophical Investigations.* London:

Wohl, Robert. 1986. «The Generation of 1914 and Modernism». En: Monique Chafdor, R. Quiñones, A. Wachtel, eds. *Modernism: Challange and Perspectives*. Univ. of Illinois Press.

Yurkievich, Saul. 1976. *Celebración del modernismo*. Barcelona: Tusquets.

Zahareas, Antony N. ed. 1968. *Ramón del Valle-Inclán: An Appraisal of his Life and Works*. NY: Las Américas.

Zamora Vicente, Alonso. 1966. *Las "Sonatas" de Valle-Inclán*. Madrid: Espasa.

—. 1969. *La realidad esperpéntica (Aproximación a "Luces de bohemia")*. Madrid: Gredos.

Zavala, Iris M. 1970a. «Notas sobre la caricatura política y el esperpento». *Asomante*, XXI:28-34.

—. 1970b. «Historia y literatura en el Ruedo Ibérico». En: *La revolución de 1868. Historia, pensamiento y literatura*. Clara E. Lida, I. M. Zavala, eds. NY: Las Américas.

—. 1972. «Del esperpento». *Homenaje a Joaquín Casalduero*. Madrid: Gredos, 493-496.

—. 1974. *Fin de siglo: Modernismo, 98, bohemia*. Madrid: Cuadernos para el Diálogo.

—. 1975. «1898. Modernismo and Latin American Revolution». *Revista Chicano-Riqueña*, 3:4:43-48.

—. 1977. Ed. intr. Alejandro Sawa. *Iluminaciones en la sombra*. Madrid: Alhambra.

—. 1983. «El movimiento del texto: genética de "los Cisnes I" de Rubén Darío». *Serta Philologica F. Lázaro Carreter*. Madrid: Cátedra, 615-632.

—. 1987. «Lírica y fin de siglo: Rubén Darío bajo el signo del cisne». *Eutopías. La crisis de la literatura como institución en el siglo XIX*, III:I, 179-196.

—. 1987a. *Lectores y lecturas del discurso narrativo dieciochesco*. Amsterdam: Rodopi, 1987.

—. 1987b. *Rubén Darío bajo el signo del cisne*. Ed. La Torre: Puerto Rico (en prensa).

173

—. 1987c. «Dialogía, voces, enunciado: Bajtin y su círculo». En: Graciela Reues, ed. *Teoría y crítica literaria en la actualidad*. Madrid: Cátedra, 1989.

—. 1988. «Espejo, reflejos. Anarquismo y literatura». *Las tradiciones culturales del anarquismo español*. Coloquio Internacional. Amsterdam, 1-4 de junio de 1988 (en prensa).

—. 1988a. «On the (Mis)uses of the Post-Modern: Hispanic Modernism Revisited». En: T. d'Haen, E. Bertens eds. *Postmodern. Fiction International*. Amsterdam: Rodopi. 83-113.

Zumthor, Paul. 1976. «Le carrefour des rhétoriqueurs. Intertextualité et rhétorique». *Poétique*. 7: 317-337.

# INDICE